DUBLIN CASTLE

From Fortress to Palace

To our spouses/partners:

Con Brogan, Una Ryan and Eileen Whyte

Frontispiece Aerial view of Dublin Castle in 2010; from north-west.

DUBLIN CASTLE

From Fortress to Palace

VOLUME 2

The Viking-age Archaeology

By

Ann Lynch, Conleth Manning and Ken Wiggins

Incorporating results of excavations carried out by

Marcus Ó hEochaidhe

With specialist contributions by

Laura W. Adlington, Lorna Anguilano, Anne Carey, Aislinn Collins, Brenda Collins, Cecily Cropper, Nikolah Gilligan, Steve Mandal, Margaret McCarthy, Clare McCutcheon, Cormac McSparron, Aonghus Moloney, Caitríona Moore, Fionnbarr Moore, John Nicholl, Louise Nugent, Ellen OCarroll, Barra O'Donnabhain, Aidan O'Sullivan, Ian Riddler, Paul Rondelez, Ulrich Schmölcke, Órla Scully, Siobhán Scully, Paul Stevens, Nicola Trzaska-Nartowski, Penelope Walton Rogers, Elizabeth Wincott Heckett and Joanna Wren.

NATIONAL MONUMENTS SERVICE

DUBLIN CASTLE
From Fortress to Palace

General Editors
Ann Lynch and Conleth Manning

VOLUME 1 (Published 2022)
Vikings to Victorians: a history of Dublin Castle to 1850
by Seán Duffy, John Montague, Kevin Mulligan
and Michael O'Neill

VOLUME 2
The Viking-Age Archaeology
by Ann Lynch, Conleth Manning and Ken Wiggins

VOLUME 3 (Parts 1 and 2)
The Medieval and Post-Medieval Archaeology
by Ann Lynch, Conleth Manning and Ken Wiggins

Published by the National Monuments Service, Dublin,
on behalf of the Government of Ireland

Le ceannach díreach ó
FOILSEACHÁIN RIALTAIS,
BÓTHAR BHAILE UÍ BHEOLÁIN, BAILE ÁTHA CLIATH 8.
D08 XA06
(Teil: +353 46 942 3100 nó Riomhphost: publications@opw.ie)
Nó trí aon díoltóir leabhar.

To be purchased from
GOVERNMENT PUBLICATIONS,
MOUNTSHANNON ROAD, DUBLIN 8.
D08 XA06
(Tel: +353 46 942 3100 or Email: publications@opw.ie)
Or through any bookseller.

ISBN: 978-1-4468-8096-8

Designed by Caitlin Quinn and Claire Rubira,
Vermillion Design Consultants

Copy-edited by Elizabeth Mayes and Ken Wiggins

Printed by Print Media Services

Print Project Manager: Marie Harpur

An Roinn Tithíochta,
Rialtais Áitiúil agus Oidhreachta
Department of Housing,
Local Government and Heritage

OPW
Oifig na
nOibreacha Poiblí
Office of Public Works

Contents

Authors and Contributors ix

Acknowledgements x

Foreword xii

Chapter 1: Introduction 1

Chapter 2: Historical and archaeological background 9

2.1 A summary of the history of pre-Norman Dublin 10
2.2 Archaeological background 13

Chapter 3: The Excavations 19

3.1 The Cork Tower area: house plots of the tenth/early eleventh centuries 20
3.2 The Powder Tower area, Cutting 1: the eastern town defences 45
3.3 The Powder Tower area, Cutting 2: urban layers and a possible street 63
3.4 The Bermingham Tower area: tenth-century gully and ditch 79
3.5 The Cross Block area: house plots of the tenth and eleventh centuries 87

Chapter 4: The Finds 103

4.1 Introduction 104
4.2 Antler and bone 106
4.2.1 Objects and waste of antler, bone and ivory
Ian Riddler and Nicola Trzaska-Nartowski 106
4.2.2 The bear tooth
Ulrich Schmölcke 147
4.2.3 The ogham inscription on comb E748:54
Fionnbarr Moore and Ken Wiggins 148
4.3 Metal artefacts 151
Órla Scully and Louise Nugent
4.4 Stone 168
4.4.1 Artefacts
Anne Carey 168
4.4.2 Petrographical analysis
Stephen Mandal 173
4.5 Flint lithics 177
Siobhán Scully
4.6 Jet and jet-like artefacts 180
Paul Stevens
4.7 Wood 184
4.7.1 Wooden artefacts
Aidan O'Sullivan and Caitríona Moore 184
4.7.2 Structural wood
Aonghus Moloney and Ellen OCarroll 194
4.8 Leather 200
John Nicholl
4.9 Pottery 204
Clare McCutcheon
4.10 Ceramic roof tiles 208
Joanna Wren
4.11 Amber artefacts 211
Cecily Cropper
4.12 Glass 215
4.12.1 Artefacts
Cecily Cropper 215
4.12.2 Microscopical analysis of window glass and crucible fragment
Laura W. Adlington 221
4.13 Textiles and animal fibre 224
4.13.1 Textiles
Elizabeth Wincott Heckett and Aislinn Collins 224
4.13.2 Dye analysis
Penelope Walton Rogers 227

4.14 Metalworking 228
4.14.1 Metalworking remains
Paul Rondelez 228
4.14.2 Microscopical analysis of metallurgical debris
Lorna Anguilano 234

Chapter 5: Human remains
Barra O'Donnabhain 237

Chapter 6: Faunal remains
Margaret McCarthy 243

Chapter 7: Plant and insect remains
Brenda Collins and Nikolah Gilligan 257

Chapter 8: Radiocarbon dates
Cormac McSparron 283

Chapter 9: Discussion and conclusions 295

Appendix
List of finds by category 311

Bibliography 317

Authors and Contributors

Laura W. Adlington Wayne, Pennsylvania, USA.

Lorna Anguilano Brunel University, London, UK.

Anne Carey Archaeologist, National Monuments Service, Dublin.

Aislinn Collins Cork.

Brenda Collins Dublin.

Cecily Cropper Melksham, Wiltshire, UK.

Nikolah Gilligan Drogheda, Co. Louth.

Ann Lynch former Senior Archaeologist, National Monuments Service, Dublin.

Steve Mandal Irish Heritage School Ltd, Co. Offaly.

Conleth Manning former Senior Archaeologist, National Monuments Service, Dublin.

Margaret McCarthy Rostellan, Midleton, Co. Cork.

Clare McCutcheon Bandon, Co. Cork.

Cormac McSparron Queen's University Belfast.

Aonghus Moloney former archaeologist with the Irish Archaeological Wetland Unit, University College Dublin.

Caitríona Moore Archaeology and Built Heritage Ltd.

Fionnbarr Moore Senior Archaeologist, National Monuments Service, Dublin.

John Nicholl Leixlip, Co. Kildare

Louise Nugent Dublin.

Ellen OCarroll Glenageary, Co. Dublin.

Barra O'Donnabhain Department of Archaeology, University College Cork.

Marcus Ó hEochaidhe† former Assistant Inspector of National Monuments, Dublin.

Aidan O'Sullivan Professor of Archaeology, UCD School of Archaeology, University College Dublin.

Ian Riddler Stratton, Cornwall, UK.

Paul Rondelez Macroom, Co. Cork.

Ulrich Schmölcke Centre for Baltic and Scandinavian Archaeology (ZBSA), Schleswig, Germany.

Órla Scully Tramore, Co. Waterford.

Siobhán Scully Finds Specialist, IAC Ltd, Kilcoole, Co. Wicklow.

Paul Stevens Kilkenny.

Nicola Trzaska-Nartowski Stratton, Cornwall, UK.

Penelope Walton Rogers The Anglo-Saxon Laboratory, York, UK.

Ken Wiggins Bray, Co. Wicklow.

Elizabeth Wincott Heckett Cobh, Co. Cork.

Joanna Wren The Milepost, Slieverue, Co. Waterford.

Acknowledgements

The authors wish to acknowledge the assistance of all who helped in bringing the Dublin Castle project to fruition and in particular those who contributed to this volume on the Viking-age archaeology. Foremost are the many individuals that worked on the excavations (a full list will appear in Volume 3) including the supervisors who were closely involved in the 'Viking' areas: Claire Cotter, Mary O'Donnell, Ruairí Ó Baoill and Brenda Collins. Muiris de Buitléir (NMS) established the master survey grid for the site. The on-site finds processing was ably managed by Úna McConville and Mary McMahon and Úna continued in this role during much of the post-excavation period. Excavating in close proximity to fragile / partially demolished historic buildings required stringent safety measures implemented on the advice of Arup engineers and we acknowledge the input of Ralph McGuckin in this regard. Clerk of Works P.J. Dolan and his team from the OPW Trim depot serviced the equipment needs of the excavations and helped keep the show on the road. The archaeological excavations were carried out in close co-operation with the OPW project architects Klaus Unger and David Slattery and on-site logistics were ably (and cheerfully) managed by Dublin Castle staff especially Tom Doyle and Barry Flynn. McInerney building contractors facilitated access to parts of the Cork Tower area during construction which allowed further excavation of Viking-age deposits.

The excavations concluded in January 1987 when a programme of post-excavation analysis commenced. Given the hiatus between the premature conclusion of this work and publication, all specialist reports were revisited and updated. The contribution of the many specialists to telling the story of the Viking-age levels at Dublin Castle is gratefully acknowledged.

All artefact drawings in Section 4 are by Sadhbh Moddel except Fig. 4.3: 2a/b, 3, 6, 8; Fig. 4.4: 6a/b, 8, 9; Fig. 4.5: 2, 10; Fig. 4.12: 7-9; Fig. 4.23: 3; Fig. 4.24; 1-9, 4, 5 and Fig. 4.25: 1-4 which are by Patricia Johnson. Fig. 4.17:1-6 and Fig. 4.18: 1, 2, 4, 6-9 are by Aidan O'Sullivan. Patricia Johnson also undertook the scanning and layout of all artefact drawings in preparation for publication. Martin Halpin digitised the many site drawings and prepared the final figures in Chapter 3 for publication while Conor McHale produced Figs 1.1-3 and 2.1-2. Bob Corrigan (OPW) produced the original site drawings of the 1961-2 excavation which have stood the test of time. The assistance provided by Dr Siobhán Power, Beatriz Mozo and Patrick Morrissey of Geological Survey Ireland in regard to Fig. 4.13 is greatly appreciated. Our thanks also to Matthew Ryan for his original artwork in Fig. 9.1.

Unless otherwise stated, the copyright of all photographic images remains with the Photographic Archive, National Monuments Service, Government of Ireland. The published photographs were taken by site directors Ann Lynch (Pls 3.1, 3.4, 3.5, 3.8, 3.16, 3.36-40) and Conleth Manning (Pls 3.2, 3.6, 3.7, 3.9-15, 3.19-27, 3.29-34) and National Monuments Service photographers Jim Bambury (Pls 3.41-3.50, 4.15), Con Brogan (Pls 1.1, 3.17, 3.18, 3.28, 3.35, 4.3) and John Lalor (Pls 4.1, 4.2, 4.4-4.14, 4.16-4.35, 5.1-5.3). Our thanks also to Tony Roche and Lynn McDonnell of the NMS Photographic Archive for their assistance in sourcing and preparing images for publication.

We acknowledge the assistance of our colleague Edward Bourke in facilitating access to the NMS archive especially during the difficult pandemic times and our colleagues in the National Museum of Ireland who provided assistance as required. We thank the late Jack (J.B.) Maguire for encouragement and sharing his knowledge of the 1961-2 excavation. Ken Wiggins thanks Dolores Kearney for discussing the wooden loom piece and Professor Michael Barnes for commenting on the surface markings of the stone lamp. The helpful comments of the peer reviewer are gratefully acknowledged. Our colleague Pat Wallace shared his immense knowledge of Viking-age Dublin, and we thank him for his encouragement and for contributing the Foreword to this volume. The design and layout of this volume were in the capable hands of Vermillion Design and we wish to thank Claire Rubira in particular for her patience and attention to detail.

The archaeological programme at Dublin Castle has been fully financed and supported by the National Monuments Service. We wish to thank the successive Chief Archaeologists, Peter Danaher, David Sweetman, Brian Duffy and, most recently, Michael MacDonagh for their unstinting support.

Foreword

Publication of the Dublin Castle excavations is welcome for a number of reasons, not least the intrinsic contribution these discoveries make to the overall understanding of Viking-age Dublin. The Vikings are central to the historical narrative of our capital city and our cultural identity and this volume is the first comprehensive report on the results of any Dublin Viking-age excavation.

It is important to place these Dublin Castle excavations within the context of archaeological excavations carried out across the city. The two excavation campaigns described in this series were carried out by Dr Ann Lynch at the Bermingham Tower/Cork Tower and the Children's Court sites and by Conleth Manning in the Powder Tower and Genealogical Office areas between 1985 and 1987. A third was undertaken by the late Marcus Ó hEochaidhe in 1961-62 under the Cross Block. That pioneering Dublin excavation preceded by a year Breandán Ó Ríordáin's extensive National Museum of Ireland excavations at High Street, Winetavern Street and Christchurch Place (1963-76). The National Museum's final excavations in Dublin were at Wood Quay and Fishamble Street between 1974 and 1981.

The placing of the castle discoveries in this volume within the broader context of other excavations in Dublin by the National Museum of Ireland and more recent development-led excavations offers an approach towards completeness. The bringing together of all the excavated sites within the castle complex in a schematic chronological plan and knitting together the archaeological evidence affords a wonderful insight into this corner of Viking-era Dublin.

The distances in the modern castle complex may be the same as those of a millennium ago but our experience of them is completely different from that of the citizens of Viking-era Dublin. Narrow streets, low buildings and the attendant congestion meant a lot more activities and urban habitation would have been crammed into what is now an accessible, open and hard-surfaced area. Although well separated from one another and too small in respective areas to allow open area excavation, the various excavations in the castle complex have nevertheless furthered our understanding of the character and layout of the Hiberno-Norse town.

The archaeological evidence from the castle excavations, although limited in scope, is impressive in terms of tenth and eleventh-century features. While later eleventh and early twelve-century remains are poorly preserved across the various sites, the linking together by the authors here of flood and defensive embankments with elements of the town's dwelling and street infrastructure is a major achievement.

Before these excavations, there had been little investigation of the south-east corner of the Hiberno-Norse settlement, including in the posited area of the king's residence and associated features such as the royal mint. The limited scale of the excavations did not allow exposure of any presumably embanked area to protect the royal family, nor produce evidence for the site of a court, associated buildings and a mint. Indeed, the absence of any coins, dies and blanks as found in other excavations across Dublin, which would be expected in the area of a mint, suggests that the moneyer, weight master and lead workers perhaps operated nearer the non-ferrous metalworkers, thought to be centred west of the castle near the later cathedral area around Christchurch Place.

The excavations have added important information to what is already known on dwellings, streets, yard and property boundaries, pits and the disposal of rubbish as well as on the town's defences. They have confirmed the dominance of the main Dublin house type (my Type 1) as identified in the excavations at Fishamble Street. Recognition of stone facing at the foot of the embankment found within what became the later Powder Tower underlines the likelihood of a unified approach to defensive embanking along at least a considerable stretch of the town defences. This had to have been undertaken by a strong central authority (the royal family) and argues for the existence of such a defensive structure around the whole town.

The quality of the different groups of artefacts from the castle excavations is at times illuminating and their specialist treatment here is to be commended. A bow saw and clamp, and notable artefacts relating to textile manufacture such as the probable mortised loom piece (unique in an Irish context), intact ripple and glass linen smoother provide fresh insights into the industry of Viking-era Dublin and complements evidence from other relevant excavations across the city. The discovery of an unperforated amber bead suggests that finishing amber jewellery may have been a domestic hobby given that there was then a succession of amber workers' workshops at Fishamble Street.

The two composite antler combs inscribed in different languages and different scripts have to rank among the greatest discoveries in the whole archaeology of Dublin. Whether the comb with ogham script was owned or inscribed by ANE (modern Irish Áine = Anne) cannot be known, though it is clear that ANE was a Gaelic speaker and is further evidence of the multi-linguistic nature of eleventh-century Dublin, with three languages and various scripts. The other comb, with the name of Unnr or Uni carved in runic characters may have been made in the Scandinavian homelands. Taken together these inscriptions are witnesses to the multilingual culture of Hiberno-Norse Dublin, not least to a literate indigenous presence in the town. Although it is uncertain whether the runic inscription was done in Dublin or whether the person mentioned lived in the town, the comb in question is an example of international exchange and trade in the contemporary Viking world.

The Gaelic inscription highlights the human backdrop to the world in which the combs were made, used and valued. Apart from having to be considered in the cultural and linguistic melting pot that was the eleventh-century town, the inscription on the locally made comb raises possibilities of ownership, gift giving and even hints at the possibility of an emotional subtext, considerations which raise these finds above normal parameters and place them among the most important objects ever found in Dublin.

That the discoveries from the Dublin Castle excavations can generate such reflection on the character of the Viking- age town is a tribute to the excavators and the commitment of the National Monuments Service and all involved in bringing these findings to publication, meeting the obligation to publish knowledge of state-funded archaeological discoveries.

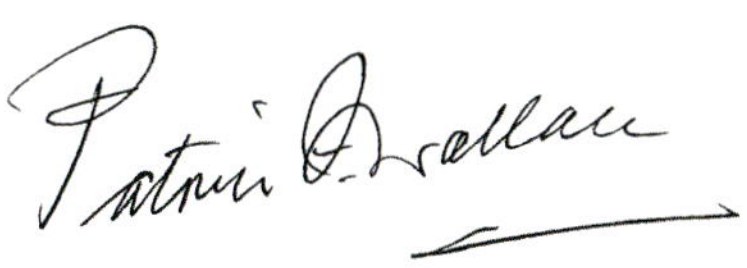

Pat Wallace
Excavator of Wood Quay and Fishamble St

Chapter 1
Introduction

Pl. 1.1 Aerial view of Dublin Castle during building works in 1988; from north-west. Facade of St. Werburgh's church at bottom right (Ronnie Norton Photography).

Chapter 1
Introduction

Background

Dublin Castle was the centre of English and later British military power and government in Ireland until January 1922, when it was handed over to the Irish Provisional Government. The large stone castle that was constructed at Dublin on foot of a royal mandate issued by King John in 1204 was one of the largest and strongest castles built in Ireland. In plan it was roughly rectangular with large circular corner towers and a twin-towered gatehouse in the middle of its north side (Fig. 1.1). The castle was built in the south-east corner of the medieval walled town with the River Poddle flowing along its south and east sides and a wide and deep moat on its west and north sides. Following a fire in 1684, plans were drawn up to replace the medieval castle with an imposing quadrangle of buildings and by the middle of the eighteenth century this transformation had been completed. In 1775 the Bermingham Tower at the south-west corner was rebuilt with thinner walls leaving just the south-east corner tower, the Record Tower, as the only recognisable element of the medieval castle to survive (Frontispiece).

The south side of the quadrangle contains the state apartments where the chief governor or viceroy of Ireland held court for social and ceremonial occasions (Fig. 1.1). Since 1922 the state apartments have continued to be used for ceremonial events, in particular St Patrick's Hall which is used for the inauguration of the Presidents of Ireland and for receiving and entertaining foreign heads of state. The centrepiece of the northern range of the Upper Castle Yard is the former Genealogical Office, crowned by the Bedford Tower and flanked by two massive arched gateways. On the north side of the Lower Castle Yard stands the Treasury Building, dating from 1714, while on the south side, extending eastwards from the Record Tower, is the neo-Gothic Chapel Royal, completed in 1814. In the early 1960s the Cross Block separating the Upper Yard from the Lower Yard was demolished and rebuilt followed by the rebuilding of the eastern half of the state apartments. In the 1980s a decision was taken to carry out a major programme of rebuilding and new construction within the castle complex. These works were deemed necessary because of the poor structural condition of the many buildings on the north side of the Upper Yard and the need for modern conference facilities for Ireland's upcoming Presidency of the European Union in 1990.

Limited archaeological excavations were carried out when the Cross Block was being rebuilt. These excavations, directed by Marcus Ó hEochaidhe of the National Monuments Branch, Office of Public Works (OPW), over a three-month period in 1961/62, recorded for the first time the depth of survival of archaeological remains on the site and highlighted the continuity of settlement from the pre-Norman or Viking-age period (Fig. 1.1: 1961/62 excavations; Fig. 1.3: no. 5). These were the first archaeological excavations to be undertaken in urban medieval Dublin and, while an account of the results is included here, the main subject of these volumes is the large programme of excavations that took place between 1985 and 1987 in conjunction with the above-mentioned major construction project. Dublin Castle is in state ownership, managed by the Office of Public Works, and the archaeological excavations were directed by Ann Lynch and Conleth Manning of the National Monuments

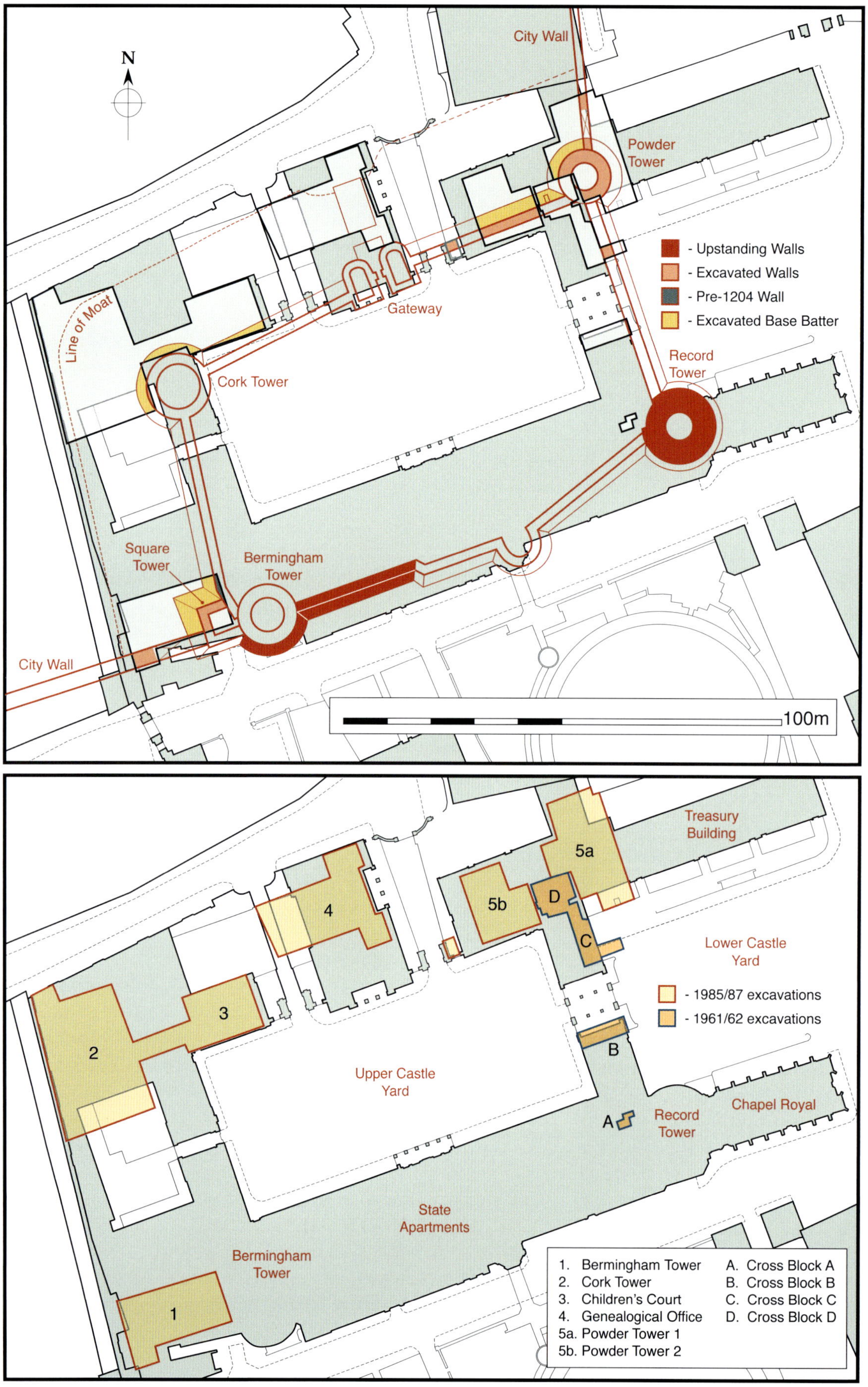

Fig. 1.1 Plan of present-day castle with outline of medieval castle superimposed (top); plan of present-day castle showing excavated areas (bottom).

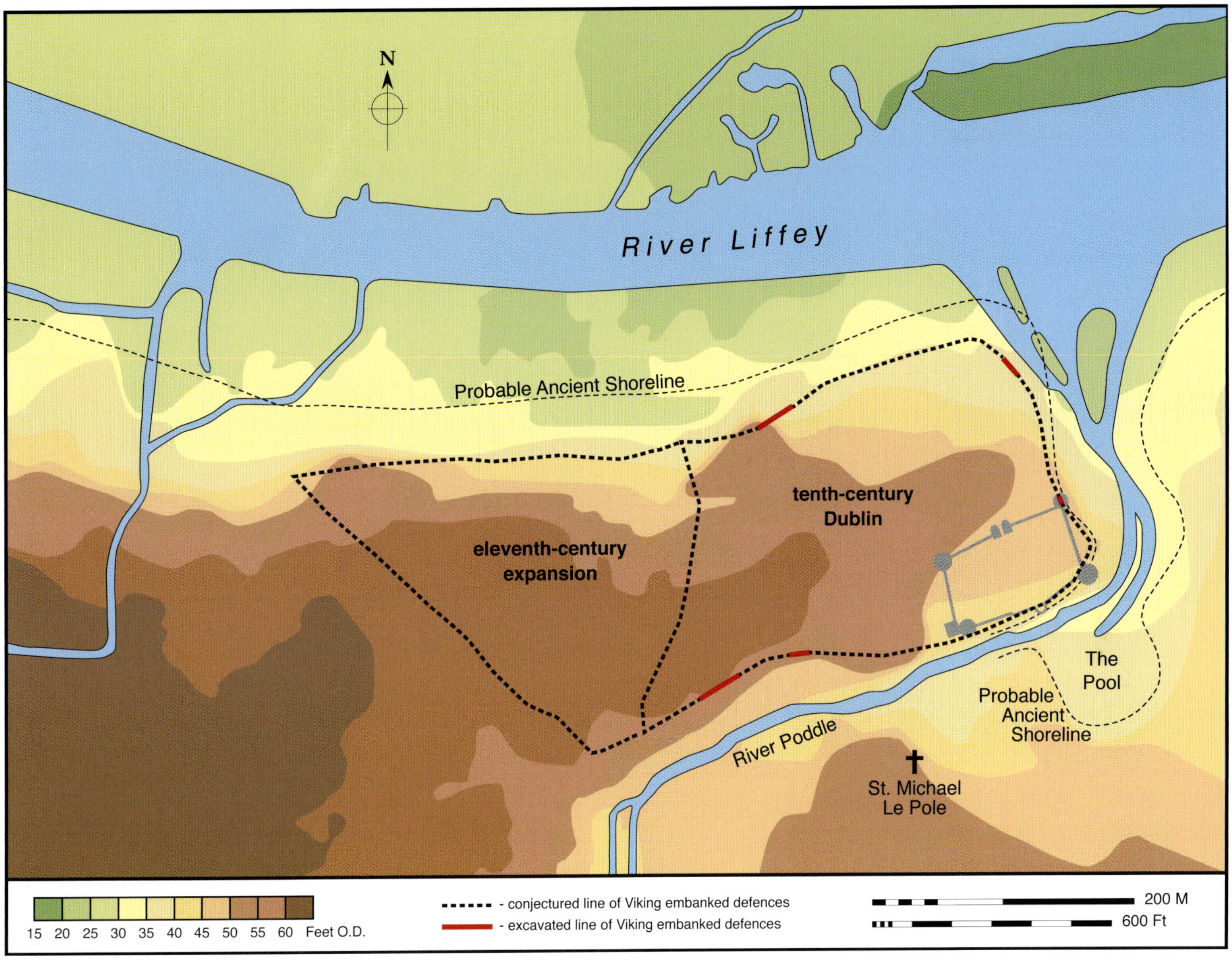

Fig. 1.2 Topographic map (after Wallace 2016) showing approximate extent of the Viking-age settlement (after Halpin 2005) and the plan of the medieval castle superimposed. The Rivers Liffey and Poddle are as shown on Speed's map of 1610.

Service (NMS), then part of the OPW. The location and extent of the excavations were dictated by the proposed developments and, since most of the structural failures had occurred along the north side of the castle where the backs of the Georgian buildings had been constructed on moat deposits, this is where archaeological investigation was concentrated (Fig. 1.1: nos 3–5a/b). Also, a new conference centre in the north-west corner of the castle complex and new kitchens in the south-west corner necessitated extensive excavation of the castle moat in these areas (Fig. 1.1: nos 1 and 2).

The digging of foundation trenches in the thirteenth century for the curtain walls and corner towers of the castle and the digging of the massive moat on the north and west sides removed all earlier deposits within their footprint. However, Viking-age remains survived outside the edge of the moat in the north-west corner of the modern castle precinct (Fig. 1.3: no. 1), encapsulated within the foundation walls of the Powder Tower (Fig. 1.3: no. 2), cut into the subsoil within the square tower formerly attached to the Bermingham Tower (Fig. 1.3: no. 4) and in a narrow strip between the north curtain wall and the façade of an eighteenth-century building (Block 8) of the quadrangle, between the Powder Tower and the castle gateway (Fig. 1.3: no. 3).

A programme of post-excavation work was put in train immediately following the completion of excavations in January 1987. Summary stratigraphic reports were prepared for each excavation area, specialist reports were completed for most categories of artefacts, finds drawings were prepared, environmental analyses were carried out and the faunal remains were examined (Lynch and Manning 1990). Full publication of the results, however, did not follow due to the ongoing work commitments of the directors of excavation,

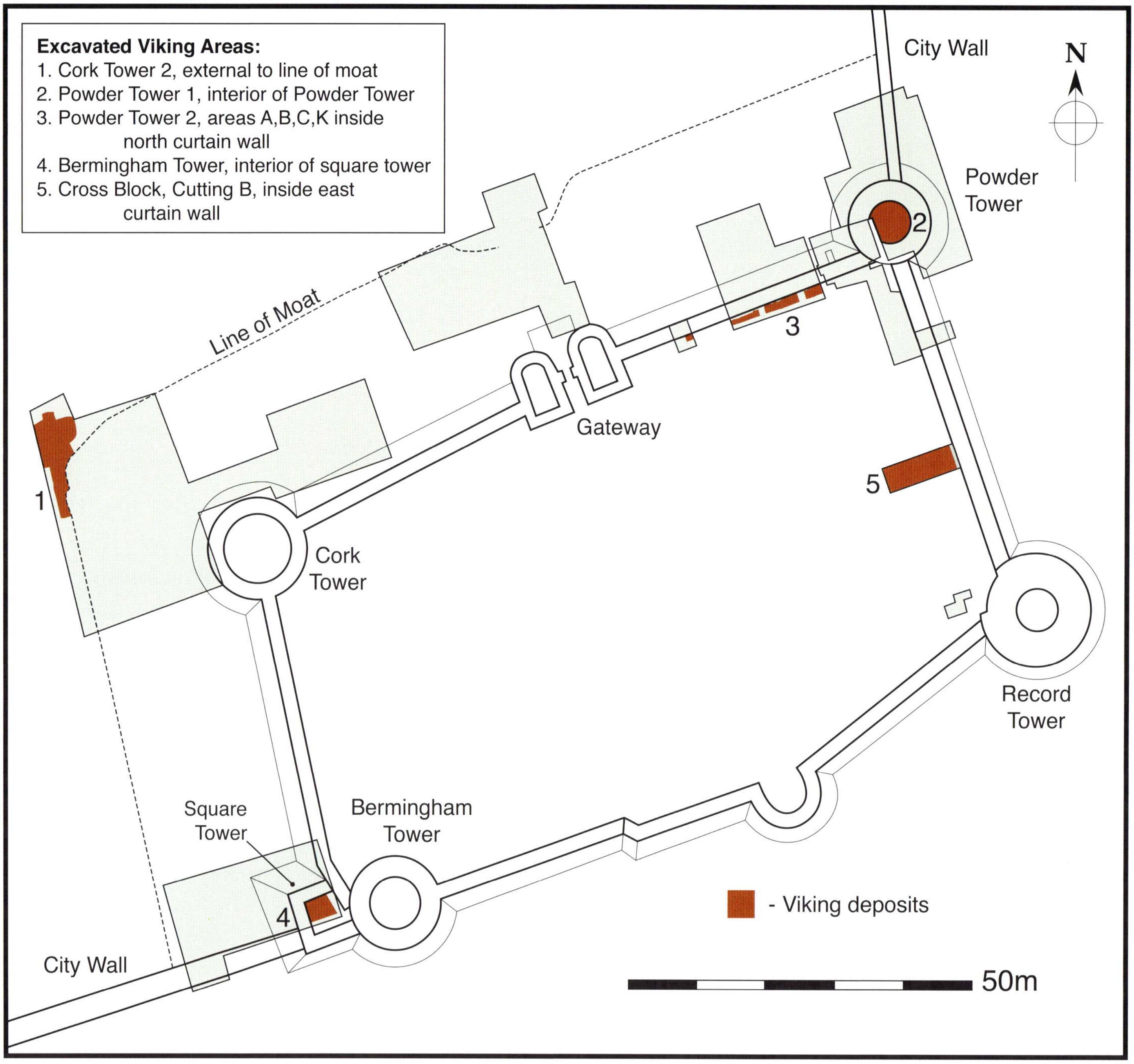

Fig. 1.3 Location of Viking-age deposits excavated.

although a summary was published in 2001 (Lynch and Manning 2001). The Dublin Castle publication project was reactivated in 2014 when, in collaboration with the OPW, a detailed history of the castle site was commissioned by the National Monuments Service. This important study (Duffy *et al.* 2022) is the first volume in the series and provides historical context for the archaeological reports to follow. A review of the excavated material and the post-excavation analyses carried out in the 1980s and 1990s was completed towards the end of 2015 and a programme for publication was drawn up. Ken Wiggins was contracted by the National Monuments Service to co-ordinate this work in September 2016 in conjunction with the directors of the excavations, Ann Lynch and Conleth Manning. The results of the 1985–7 excavations and those of 1961–2 are to be published in two volumes: the current volume covering the Viking-age or pre-castle period and a further volume in two parts dealing with the medieval and post-medieval archaeology.

The Local Topography

The embanked and later walled town of Dublin was founded on a low ridge at the confluence of the River Liffey and its tributary, the River Poddle, both being tidal at this point (Fig. 1.2). The underlying bedrock is part of the Lucan Formation known as Calp limestone that consists of layers of fine-grained Carboniferous limestone interleaved with layers of black shale (Marchant and Sevastopulo 1980). The overlying soils are grey-brown podzolics derived from calcareous glacial till. An important fording point on the River Liffey, Áth Cliath (the ford of the hurdles), may have been situated just to the west of the Poddle/Liffey confluence and is the name by which Dublin is known to this day in the Irish language (Manning 2022). The ridge, rising to *c.* 17m (55 feet) OD was sharply defined by the River Poddle that skirts its south side before swinging north-east and joining the Liffey. On the south side of the ridge the Poddle expanded into a tidal pool called Duiblinn or Duibh linn (meaning black pool in Irish). An ecclesiastical settlement named Duiblinn is mentioned in Irish sources and was probably located to the west of the pool. This was the name adopted by the Scandinavians for their settlement and also became the name for the town in English. The original ninth-century Viking settlement is likely to have been located around this tidal pool but there has been much debate on when the focus of settlement moved from the pool to the ridge, where in due course the town was established.

The 1985-7 Excavations

Archaeological excavations commenced in April 1985 and continued until January 1987. As noted above, the areas excavated were determined by the proposed building works. The archaeological investigations were factored into the building programme and where possible took place in a scheduled timeslot between the demolition and construction phases. The buildings along most of the north side of the Upper Castle Yard were demolished apart from their front façades and were rebuilt using piled foundations. The nineteenth-century Block 10, which extended into the Lower Yard abutting the Treasury Building, was fully demolished and rebuilt. The west block of the Upper Castle Yard was retained and conserved. A new conference hall was built in the north-west corner of the castle precinct and a new kitchen block at the south-west corner. Ann Lynch initiated work with excavations in the areas of the Bermingham Tower, the Cork Tower and the Children's Court (Fig. 1.1: nos 1–3) while Conleth Manning continued the project with excavations at the former Genealogical Office and in the area of the Powder Tower (Blocks 8, 9 and 10) (Fig. 1.1: nos 4 and 5a/b).

Given the restricted areas available for excavation and the proximity of retained façades, the size, location and stepped profiles of the cuttings were determined by safety considerations as advised by Arup engineers. Wherever possible, large areas were opened but as excavations proceeded into the castle moat (maximum original depth *c.* 10m), safety precautions resulted in much reduced areas being accessible for investigation. The pre-castle or Viking-age archaeology had survived at the Cork Tower, in the Powder Tower cuttings and to a lesser extent at the Bermingham Tower (Fig. 1.3: nos 1–4). Detailed stratigraphic reports for these excavations have been lodged in the National Monuments Service Archive and more nuanced accounts are now presented here. The original feature numbers have been retained throughout to ensure consistency with the primary excavation archive.

The 1961–2 Excavations

An account of Cutting B in the Cross Block excavation is also included here because of the importance of the Viking-age evidence uncovered there (Fig. 1.1: Cross Block B; Fig. 1.3: no. 5). This excavation was never completed to subsoil and the only source available to the authors was an unpublished preliminary report (Ó hEochaidhe 1962) together with the artefacts and a number of photographs. The lack of a site diary or feature/layer descriptions means that the level and standard of information available on this excavation is very different from that available for the later excavations. However, the archaeology uncovered was rich and included a fine collection of artefacts, which are all included in Chapter 4 below. The account of Cross Block Cutting B has been written using the preliminary report as the main source and reassessing the findings in the light of subsequent excavations in Dublin. This excavation is significant as not only the first archaeological excavation to be carried out at the castle but also the first within the centre of Dublin. It was followed later in 1962 by the first of the great series of excavations carried out in the centre of Dublin by the National Museum of Ireland, which highlighted the international importance of the well-preserved archaeology of Viking-age Dublin.

Conventions And Terminology

Dublin Castle is a site of enormous importance within what is known worldwide as 'Viking Dublin'. The Vikings were seaborne raiders and adventurers turned conquerors and rulers, whose influence in Ireland was strongest in the earlier Viking Age of the eighth to tenth centuries. Nonetheless their legacy continued as a dominant influence in Dublin at least until the Anglo-Norman invasion of 1169-70 and its aftermath. We therefore take the 'long view' on the Viking Age and use the term to cover the period between their foundation of Dublin in the 840s to the later twelfth century. In practical terms, this means all pre-castle deposits have been included in this classification. Given the mixed ethnicity and hybrid material culture of the inhabitants of Dublin, the term 'Hiberno-Scandinavian' is also used here especially in relation to the eleventh and twelfth centuries. Deciding on a succinct descriptive terminology for the period covered by this volume is a difficult issue and we acknowledge that there has been some vigorous academic debate on the subject (e.g. Wallace 2016, xii, xiii; Clarke 2020).

Unless otherwise stated, all calibrated radiocarbon ages are quoted in the text at 2 sigma (95.4%) probability. The terminology used when describing the Viking-age structures follows that used by Wallace (1992). It should also be noted that the chronological phases described in Chapter 3 below are individual to each of the different excavation areas and do not imply a general site chronology.

Chapter 2
Historical and archaeological background

Chapter 2.1
A summary of the history of pre-Norman Dublin[1]

The earliest historical evidence for settlement at Dublin is an early ecclesiastical site called Duiblinn that is mentioned in the *Annals of Ulster* under the year 790, when its abbot Siadal died (Mac Airt and Mac Niocaill 1983). The exact location of this church site is uncertain except that it is likely to have been close to the broad tidal pool in the Poddle river, a tributary of the River Liffey. This pool gave its name to Dublin, a name derived from Duiblinn (in Irish *duibh linn*, meaning black pool), a site now occupied by the garden immediately south of Dublin Castle. Suggestions that the enclosure of this ecclesiastical site is reflected in the curving streets to the south-east of the pool have not been supported by archaeological excavation. A more likely location is that to the west of the pool around the church sites of St Michael le Pole and St Brigit where occupation and burials dating from the pre-Viking period have been found (Fig. 1.2).

It had long been accepted that the earliest Scandinavian settlement in or around Dublin was the *longphort* (ship-camp) at Duiblinn, which is mentioned in the annals in 841 (Mac Airt and Mac Niocaill 1983). However, Scandinavians were active in the area since the late 790s and their camp may have been at Duiblinn, even if only seasonally, since that time. The first recorded Viking raid on an Irish church was that on Rechru (probably Lambay Island) in 795 (Fig. 2.1). In 798 Vikings raided St Patrick's Island off Skerries, Co. Dublin and the fact that in the same year they took a tribute of cattle would strongly suggest that they had a land base by this time in the Dublin area. Archaeological evidence indicates Viking settlement and burial around the pool of Dublin in the decades before the 840s (see Chapter 2.2 below) and there are references to Viking raids in the area in the same period at places like Howth, Lusk, Swords and Clondalkin.

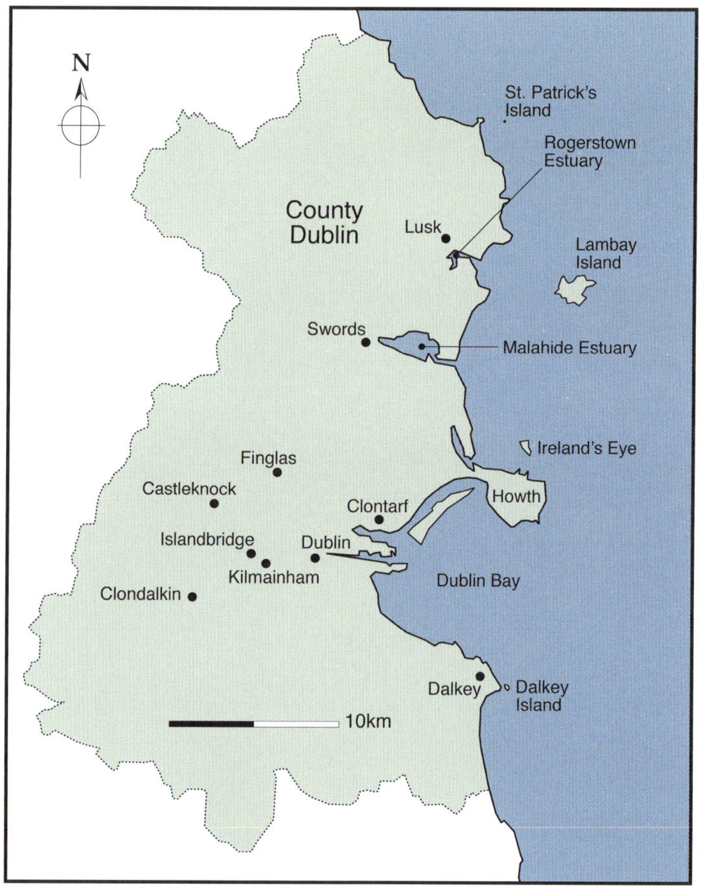

Fig. 2.1 Map of County Dublin showing locations mentioned in text.

1 This is a summary of the relevant section of Seán Duffy's text on the medieval history of Dublin Castle in volume 1 of this series (Duffy *et al.* 2022). Full references can be found there.

While Duiblinn undoubtedly refers to the pool in the tidal reaches of the Poddle south of the later castle and is the origin of the names used for Dublin in Scandinavian languages and English, Áth Cliath or Baile Átha Cliath is the name long used, and indeed still used, in the Irish language for Dublin. Áth Cliath means the ford of the hurdles and it was clearly an important and strategic ford on the Liffey. There is some uncertainty as to its exact location. It has generally been accepted that it was on or close to the site of the first medieval bridge at Dublin but there is also a possibility that it was further west at Islandbridge (Fig. 2.1). Initially Áth Cliath and Duiblinn were separate places, and the annals record that the Vikings first took Áth Cliath in 837, which, if it referred to Islandbridge, might help to explain the cemetery of Viking burials there (Harrison and Ó Floinn 2014).

The *longphort* of Duiblinn was attacked by the kings of Tara and Lagore in 849 and laid waste. This is the last time the settlement at Dublin is referred to in the Irish annals as Duiblinn; thereafter it is always referred to as Áth Cliath. This may indicate a change of location from the area around the south side of the pool to the ridge to the north, the site of the later medieval walled town and castle. The earliest dates from the Exchange Street Upper/Essex Street West excavations, on the slopes of the ridge between the castle and the Liffey, lend support to the suggestion that Scandinavian settlement was established on the ridge between the Liffey and the Poddle in the latter half of the ninth century (see Chapter 2.2 below). From this time there was probably continuous or almost continuous occupation of this ridge by Scandinavians and their descendants up to the taking of Dublin by the Anglo-Normans in 1170.

In the early 850s there was a struggle over control of Dublin between two groups of Scandinavians referred to in the Irish annals as the *Dubgenti* ('Dark Heathens') and the *Fingaill* ('Fair Foreigners'). The Dubgenti won out and supplied the kings/leaders of Dublin for generations to come. A strong Scandinavian leader, Amlaíb, whose activities ranged throughout Ireland and across the Irish Sea in the 850s and 860s, was based in Dublin, showing that Dublin was already becoming the most important Scandinavian settlement in Ireland. In 871 there is a reference to Amlaíb and his kinsman Ímar coming to Dublin with a fleet of 200 ships (Mac Airt and Mac Niocaill 1983).

In 902 the kings of Brega and Leinster attacked Áth Cliath (Dublin) and drove the 'heathens' from it. It was probably only the Scandinavian leaders and soldiers who were driven out while the merchants and tradesmen remained under temporary Irish control until Sitriuc, grandson of Ímar, recaptured it in 917. This was followed in 919 by a battle between the Irish and the Scandinavians at Islandbridge in which the Irish were defeated and the king of Tara, Niall Glúndub, was killed. The following year the new king of Tara, Donnchad Donn, defeated the Scandinavians, with the result that Sitriuc abandoned Dublin. His kinsman Gofraid retook Dublin in 921 and ruled it for the following thirteen years. After Gofraid died, Dublin was burned in 936 by Donnchad Donn. Gofraid was succeeded by his son Amlaíb and Dublin was besieged by Donnchad Donn and his northern allies in 938 and the lands around it, which were controlled by the Hiberno-Scandinavians, were plundered by them.

There was a major attack on Dublin in 944 by the kings of Brega and Leinster:

> The destruction brought upon it was this, i.e. its houses, partitions, ships and all other structures, were burned; its women, boys and common folk were carried into bondage, its men and warrior-folk were killed. (*Annals of the Four Masters* 942 [=944]; O'Donovan 1851)

What is clear from this account is that by this stage Dublin is described like a town with houses and property divisions (partitions), women and children. An account in the *Chronicum Scotorum* under 943[=944] refers to the 'taking of the *dún*' of Dublin (Hennessy 1866). *Dún* in this instance appears to indicate a fortified town.

After the king of Tara, Máel Sechnaill mac Domnaill, defeated the king of Dublin, Amlaíb Cúarán, at the battle of Tara in 980 he besieged the '*dún*' of Dublin for three days and nights before the town submitted. Even more indicative of strong defences around the town was the aftermath of the battle of Dublin in 989 when the victorious Máel Sechnaill besieged the town for twenty nights before the inhabitants surrendered because they had no fresh water. They were then forced to accede to his demand of an ounce of gold yearly out of every plot in the town.

By the 990s the Scandinavian kings of Dublin had intermarried with the Irish dynasties, notably with the Uí Fáeláin dynasty of Leinster leading to an alliance between Máel Mórda of Leinster and his nephew Sitriuc Silkenbeard of Dublin. Máel Mórda frequently based himself in Dublin in the late 990s. The ambitious Munster king Brian Bóraime defeated the united army of Máel Mórda and Sitriuc at the major battle of Glenn Máma in 999, after which Brian spent a week in Dublin, carried off gold, silver and captives and burned the *dún*. Sitriuc had to recognise Brian as his overlord but a few years later was conspiring again with his Leinster allies against Brian so that he and his son Murchad besieged Dublin from September to Christmas 1013 without success. This led to the famous battle of Clontarf the following year, where the Munstermen and other Irish allies were successful against the armies of Leinster, Dublin and their Scandinavian allies but Brian himself, king of Ireland since 1002, was killed.

After the death of Brian Bóraime, Máel Sechnaill mac Domnaill resumed the high-kingship and in 1015 with his Irish allies marched on Dublin and burned the *dún* and its suburbs. In 1052, the king of Leinster, Diarmait mac Máele na mBó of Uí Chennselaig in South Leinster, captured Dublin and made himself its king. From the mid-eleventh century different Irish provincial kings vied with each other to gain control of Dublin almost as an essential prerequisite to be in contention for the high-kingship of Ireland. This was the end of independent Scandinavian power in Dublin because all subsequent Viking-descended local rulers were clients of Irish kings. At times there appears to have been a hierarchy of three kings with power over Dublin: 1) the high king or aspirant to the high-kingship; 2) the son of the high king or a provincial king who owed allegiance to the high king and was sometimes based in Dublin and 3) a Hiberno-Scandinavian king of Dublin. The kings of Leinster regarded Dublin, being within Leinster, as part of their birthright and this led to many struggles over Dublin. After Diarmait mac Máele na mBó gained control of Dublin he placed his son Murchad there as king. Murchad died in Dublin in 1070 and was buried there.

Murchad was replaced by his cousin Donnchad but he was deposed by the Munster king Tairdelbach ua Briain in 1072, who appointed the Hiberno-Scandinavian Gofraid in his place. In 1075 Tairdelbach installed his own son Muirchertach as king of Dublin. When Tairdelbach died in 1086, Muirchertach lost control of Dublin to the Leinster king, Donnchad, but regained control on Donnchad's death in 1089 only to lose it again to the Hiberno-Scandinavian Gofraid Méranach. Muirchertach recaptured Dublin in 1094, expelled Gofraid and continued to control Dublin for the following twenty years. It is probable that the defences of Dublin were upgraded to a stone wall during this period of relative stability under Muirchertach Ua Briain (Wallace 2016, 139–40).

When Muirchertach fell victim to illness in 1114 he installed his son Domnall Gerrlámhach as king of Dublin. Domnall defeated the king of Leinster at Dublin in 1115. In 1118 the new aspirant for the high-kingship, Tairdelbach Ua Conchobair of Connacht, marched on Dublin, expelled Domnall and the Munstermen and assumed the overlordship of Dublin with Énna, son of Donnchad of Uí Chennselaig, ruling Dublin and Leinster under him.

A letter of this period (*c.* 1121) refers to the burgesses of Dublin, indicating that by this time Dublin had been legally established as a town. Énna's deputy in Dublin appears to have been Torfind mac Turcaill. Members of this family continued to serve as Hiberno-Scandinavian kings of Dublin up to the time of the Anglo-Norman invasion though always under the overlordship of Irish kings.

When Énna died in 1126 Tairdelbach Ua Conchobair installed his own son Conchobar as king but the Dubliners rebelled against him and drove him out the following year. When Diarmait Mac Murchada became king of Leinster in 1134 he was also already in control of Dublin. Between 1141 and 1156 the kingship of Dublin changed hands frequently, showing how sought after it was as a prize. In 1154 Muirchertach Mac Lochlainn from the far north marched on Dublin and won overlordship of it with Diarmait Mac Murchada ruling it on the ground for him along with the Mac Turcaill family. The annalists recorded Diarmait Mac Murchada as enjoying great power over Dublin for four years from 1162.

After Muirchertach Mac Lochlainn died in 1166 the new high king Ruaidrí Ua Conchobair marched on Dublin and the inhabitants submitted to him. Diarmait Mac Murchada was banished overseas, where he enlisted the help of Henry II of England to regain his kingdom. In 1169 an Anglo-Norman army landed near Wexford and soon regained much of Leinster for Diarmait. In 1170, now led by the latter's son-in-law Strongbow, they captured and burned Dublin and massacred many of its inhabitants. Henry II came to Ireland in 1171 and claiming Dublin, Wexford and Waterford as his own, gave Dublin to his men of Bristol.

During the later phase of the history of pre-Norman Dublin it appears certain that there must have been a stronghold within the *dún* or fortified town of Dublin from which Irish kings could control the walled town. There may even have been a second stronghold or at least kingly residence where the Hiberno-Scandinavian Meic Turcaill resided. One or other or both are likely to have been on at least part of the site of Dublin Castle and may even have been an early form of castle, whether of timber or stone or a mixture of both, though there are no specific references to such a stronghold in the pre-Norman period. However, there are references to a castle in Dublin soon after 1170 and it is possible that the Anglo-Normans used an older fortress or its site.

Chapter 2.2
Archaeological background

Introduction

The non-artefactual archaeological record for Viking-age Dublin can be divided into three main categories – burials, habitation/settlement evidence and embanked defences – and will be described below under those headings. The first archaeological excavation of Viking-age deposits in the centre of Dublin took place at the Cross Block of Dublin Castle in 1961–2 (see Chapter 3.5), but, long before then, the chance discovery of Viking furnished graves in the course of quarrying and other activities, stretching as far back as the late eighteenth century, were dramatic physical evidence for the part played by the Vikings in the origins and growth of Dublin. The Cross Block excavation at Dublin Castle opened a small but highly revealing window on the nature of urban life in Viking-age Dublin. The excavated features included remains of successive post-and-wattle houses, built one over the other and the remains of a timber-built pathway. Excavations subsequently carried out by the National Museum of Ireland (NMI) within the historic core of Dublin, from 1962 until 1981, built on the promise shown in the initial limited investigation at Dublin Castle, revealing large areas of well-preserved habitation evidence for the Viking-age town. Further evidence for early settlement came to light when large-scale excavations were carried out at Dublin Castle in 1985–7.

Numerous excavations have taken place in the urban historic core of Dublin since archaeological work was completed at Dublin Castle in early 1987, particularly during the construction 'boom' years of the 1990s and the first half of the following decade. These excavations continue to expand the archaeological record and broaden our knowledge of burial practices, habitation and all aspects of everyday life as well as the urban defences of Viking-age Dublin. A summary of current knowledge is presented here to allow the excavated evidence at Dublin Castle to be discussed in context.

Burials

The Irish Viking Graves Project initiated in 1999 under the auspices of the NMI culminated in 2014 in the publication of a reappraisal and reclassification of all the evidence for Viking graves and grave goods in Ireland (Harrison and Ó Floinn 2014). The study affirmed that there are 107 known furnished Viking graves in Ireland. A great many of these (53) are from the Kilmainham-Islandbridge complex in Dublin (Fig. 2.1) which is regarded as the most important Viking cemetery outside Scandinavia (*ibid.*, 223–8). Furnished Viking-age burials from Kilmainham were found between *c.* 1785 and *c.* 1864, discovered by workmen during railway construction and other land improvement works. Most of the discoveries from Islandbridge were made between 1860 and 1869. The construction of the War Memorial Park at Islandbridge led to the discovery of additional Viking graves in 1933–4 (known as the Inchicore graves). The Inchicore burials have particular significance in that three discovered in 1934 were the first to be excavated by professional archaeologists Adolf Mahr and Seán P. Ó Riordáin of the NMI. The furnished burial rite was practised by Vikings in Ireland from *c.* AD 830–930 and Harrison and Ó Floinn concluded that 'there is evidence for some 401 distinct grave-goods' (*ibid.*, 73). Furnished Viking graves contained a range of Insular objects as well as those of Scandinavian origin, including weapons such as swords, spearheads and axe heads, shield bosses and shield fittings, brooches, beads, ringed pins, stick pins and many other artefact types.

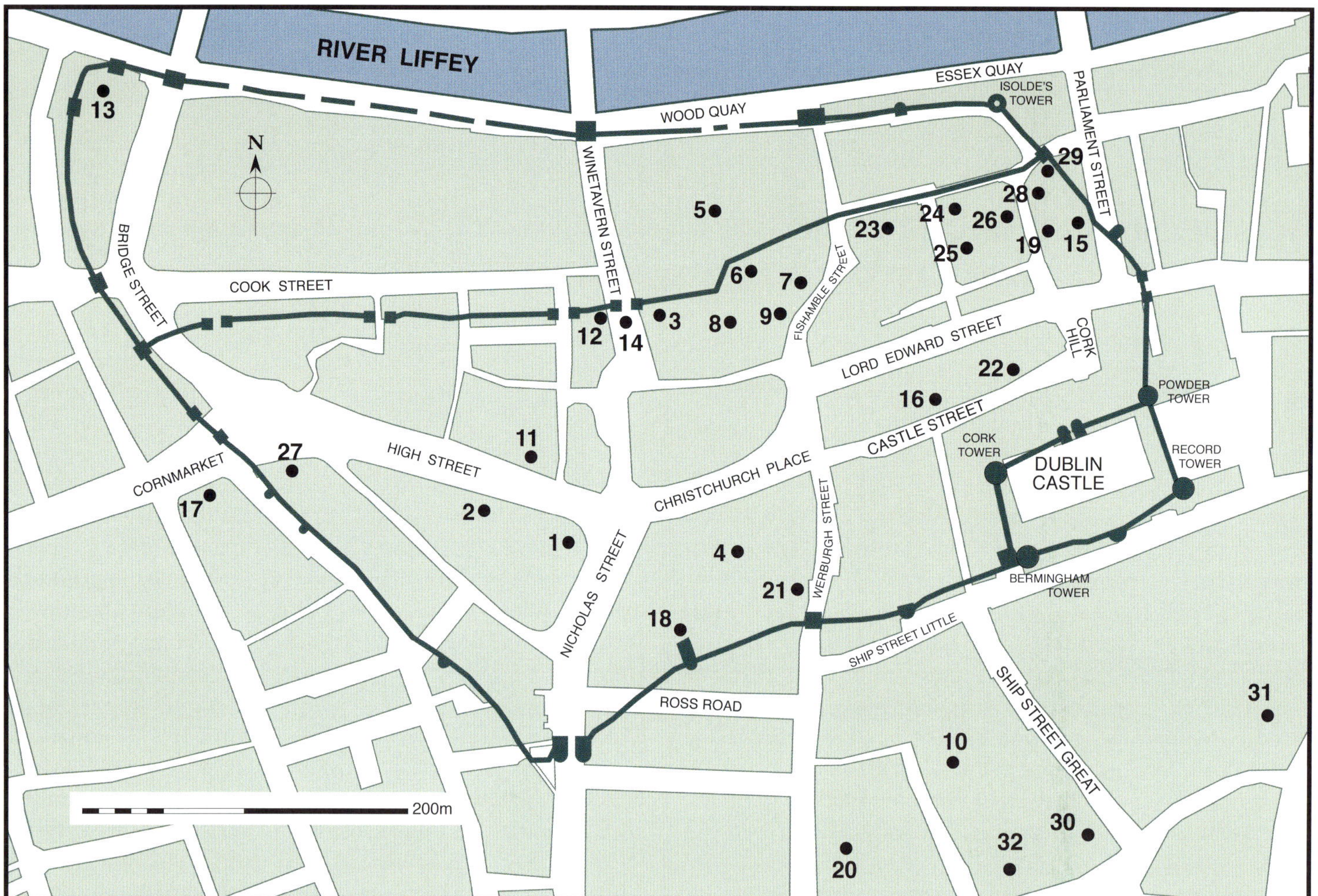

Museum excavations (1962–81)
1 - High Street I (1962–3: E43)
2 - High Street II (1967–72: E71)
3 - Winetavern Street (1969–72: E81)
4 - Christchurch Place (1972–76: E122)
5 - Wood Quay (1974–76: E132)
6 - Fishamble Street I (1976: E141) and (1975–6: E148)
7 - Fishamble Street II (1978–80: E172
8 - John's Lane (1978–79: E173)
9 - Fishamble Street III (1980–1: E190)

Excavations 1981–2005
10 - St. Michael Le Pole/Ship Street Great (1981: E217)
11 - High Street (1989: E476)
12 - Winetavern Street (1989: E485)
13 - Bridge Street (1989: E510)
14 - Winetavern Street (Site I) (1990: E543)
15 - Parliament Street (Site D) (1991: E635)
16 - Castle Street I (1992–3: 92E77)
17 - Cornmarket/Lamb Alley (1992: 92E109)
18 - Ross Road/Christchurch Place (1993: 93E10)
19 - Exchange Street Upper/Parliament Street (Site A) (1993–4: 93E143)
20 - Bride Street (1993: 93E153)
21 - Werburgh Street (1994: 94E25)
22 - Castle Street II (1994: 94E177)
23 - Temple Bar West: Site A (Fishamble Street) (1996–98: 96E245)
24 - Temple Bar West: Site B (Essex Street West) (1996–98: 96E245)
25 - Temple Bar West: Site C (Copper Alley) (1996–98: 96E245)
26 - Temple Bar West: Site D (Exchange Street Upper) (1996–98: 96E245)
27 - Back Lane/Lamb Alley (1996–7: 96E300)
28 - Exchange Street Upper (Site B) (1997–98: 96E40 and 98E198)
29 - Essex Gate (Site C) (1997: 96E40)
30 - Ship Street Great (2002: 01E772)
31 - South Great George's Street (2003: 99E414)
32 - Golden Lane (2005: 04E1030)

Fig. 2.2 Map of the medieval walled town of Dublin showing location of Viking-age excavated sites referenced in the text.

A small number of furnished Viking graves have been found on modern archaeological excavations, located close to where the enclosed tenth-century town of Dublin was established: one at Ship Street Great in 2002 (Fig. 2.2: no. 30; Simpson 2005, 32–4), four at South Great George's Street in 2003 (Fig. 2.2: no. 31; *ibid.*, 34–48), and two at Golden Lane in 2005 (Fig. 2.2: no. 32; O'Donovan 2008), all of which are discussed at length in Harrison and Ó Floinn (2014). Further to the north-west, a single female burial was excavated in 2004 at Church Street, Finglas (Fig. 2.1;

Kavanagh 2007; Harrison and Ó Floinn 2014, 533–7). Only one modern archaeological excavation outside Dublin has revealed a furnished Viking grave, that at Woodstown, Co. Waterford excavated in 2004 (Russell 2014, 80; Harrison 2014a; and Harrison and Ó Floinn 2014, 663–8). In 2008 a small rescue excavation of a single male grave was carried out the War Memorial Park, Islandbridge, following a report to the NMI of the discovery of a Viking sword and spearhead (Sikora *et al.* 2011; Harrison and Ó Floinn 2014, 500–03). Recent developments in the sequencing of ancient DNA have allowed the genetic ancestry of these burials to be analysed. As expected, the notion of Viking identity is a complex one and while the majority of the Irish Viking genomes harboured high levels of Norwegian-like ancestry, the burial from Ship Street Great showed very little Scandinavian ancestry and he belonged to a lineage most common in north-west Ireland (A. Margaryan *et al.*, 2020).

Habitation

Prior to the excavations at the Cross Block of Dublin Castle in 1961–2, the archaeological potential of the area around Christ Church Cathedral had been demonstrated by Thomas Matthew Ray, Assistant Registrar of Deeds, who attended the digging of service trenches between 1856 and 1862, amassing a collection of over 700 artefacts in the process, many of which were of Viking-age date. Ray kept a diary in which details of where each object was found were recorded, his enthusiasm for preserving and learning from objects linked to Dublin's past foreshadowing by a hundred years the archaeological excavations that were to transform our understanding of the Viking contribution to Dublin's urban origins (Wallace and Ó Floinn 1988; Breen 1980).

Several months after the identification of Viking-age deposits at Dublin Castle, the NMI commenced the excavation of a site at the junction of nearby High Street and Nicholas Street under the direction of Breandán Ó Ríordáin (High Street I; Fig. 2.2: no. 1). The site produced an abundance of tenth- to twelfth-century material, including the remains of post-and-wattle houses similar to those found at Dublin Castle, as well as much evidence for comb making, leatherworking and metalworking. The finds assemblage was significant and included a gilt bronze disc-brooch decorated in the tenth-century Borre style (Ó Ríordáin 1976). This was the first of a series of NMI-funded excavations that continued up to 1981. Between 1967 and 1972 Ó Ríordáin excavated another site further west along the south side of High Street (High Street II; Fig. 2.2: no. 2). This produced the remains of post-and-wattle houses fronting onto High Street and an extension to the site produced large amounts of leather and was interpreted as a leatherworking quarter. There was much evidence relating to comb making and the finds included highly ornate bone trial pieces in the eleventh-century Ringerike style (Ó Ríordáin 1970).

In 1969 Ó Ríordáin went on to excavate at Winetavern Street (Fig. 2.2: no. 3; Ó Ríordáin 1971), on the north side of Christ Church Cathedral and, when that was completed in 1972, he commenced an excavation at Christchurch Place, to the east of Nicholas Street, which was completed in 1976 (Ó Ríordáin 1981; Fig. 2.2: no. 4). Foundation remains of 26 buildings were excavated at Christchurch Place (Murray 1983). The NMI's campaign of excavations in Dublin's historic core culminated in its work at Wood Quay in advance of the construction of a new civic offices complex. Excavations at Winetavern Street were also related to this proposed development. The south-east portion of the site, along the west side of Fishamble Street (Fishamble Street I–III and linking at its southern end with a small site at John's Lane), remains to the present day the most renowned of all the Viking habitation sites excavated in Dublin (Fig. 2.2: nos 6–9). In 1974 Patrick Wallace of the National Museum was appointed as director of excavations at Wood Quay, a role he retained until the excavations came to an end in 1981. In all, fourteen plots were excavated along Fishamble Street, with up to thirteen successive layers of houses. Foundation remains of over 120 buildings were recorded, constituting 'Europe's best preserved and most extensive corpus of tenth and eleventh century building evidence from any site west of the Elbe' (Wallace 2016, 22; fig. 2.1). The overall depth of stratified remains was *c.* 3m, with a timespan of *c.* AD 920 to 1100.

In the years since excavations at Dublin Castle were completed in 1987, several other sites in the city centre have been investigated, shedding further light on the nature of settlement in the Viking-age town. Further work was undertaken at High Street in 1989 (Fig. 2.2: no. 11; Murtagh 1990) and excavations took place between 1992 and 1994 at two different sites on Castle Street (Fig. 2.2: nos 16 and 22) which revealed a substantial ditch, post-and-wattle buildings, timber-lined pits and three coin hoards (Byrne 2015; Clarke *et al.* 2018, 88). One of the most significant sites was at Exchange Street Upper/Parliament Street, excavated in 1993/1994 (Fig. 2.2: no. 19). Radiocarbon determinations for two house structures (Structures A and B) suggested that habitation in the Viking town could be pushed back to the ninth century, earlier than was believed to be the case in regard to the NMI excavations of 1962–81, which dated the origins of the settlement to the early tenth century (Gowen with Scally 1996). Excavations at Essex Street West/Exchange Street Upper between 1996 and 1998 produced evidence in support of Scally's contention that this area of Dublin was occupied by the Vikings from the mid-to late ninth century (Fig. 2.2: nos 23–26; Simpson 1999). Radiocarbon determinations for a Phase 1 post-and-wattle house (Structure I) excavated at Site D (Exchange Street Upper) dated it to 'between the late seventh and late ninth centuries, with the balance of probability placing it

Chapter 3.1
The Cork Tower area: house plots of the tenth/early eleventh centuries

Introduction

The most extensive area of Viking-age deposits uncovered during the 1985–7 excavations was in the north-west corner of the modern castle precinct, where a new conference hall and ancillary buildings were to be constructed. This is referred to as the Cork Tower area (excavation E296) after the adjacent north-west corner tower of the medieval castle. Initially, two large cuttings, Cork Tower cuttings 1 and 2 (CT1, CT2), were excavated and Viking-age deposits were recorded outside the edge of the thirteenth-century moat in CT2 (Viking Area (VA) 1). Two small test trenches, one that extended westward to the boundary wall (T1) and another to the north (T2), were also excavated but safety concerns did not allow for investigations to extend any closer to the surrounding boundary walls (Fig. 3.1; Pl. 3.1). During the construction phase, however, when archaeological monitoring indicated that significant Viking-age layers immediately north of CT2 were to be mechanically removed, a decision was taken to redeploy part of the team then working on the Powder Tower excavation to this area (Viking Area (VA) 2). A better understanding of the stability of the boundary wall to the north allowed previous engineering safety restrictions to be relaxed somewhat and permitted excavation to be conducted closer to it in this area. This excavation was undertaken under major time constraints and with the agreement and cooperation of the building contractor, who was already involved in construction on the site. The time constraints and salvage nature of the excavation meant that some evidence (e.g. animal bones) was not retrieved (Pls 3.2, 3.3). The results of both phases of excavation are presented together here.

Pl. 3.1 View of Cork Tower Cutting 2 (Viking Area 1); castle boundary wall in background and edge of moat in foreground; from south.

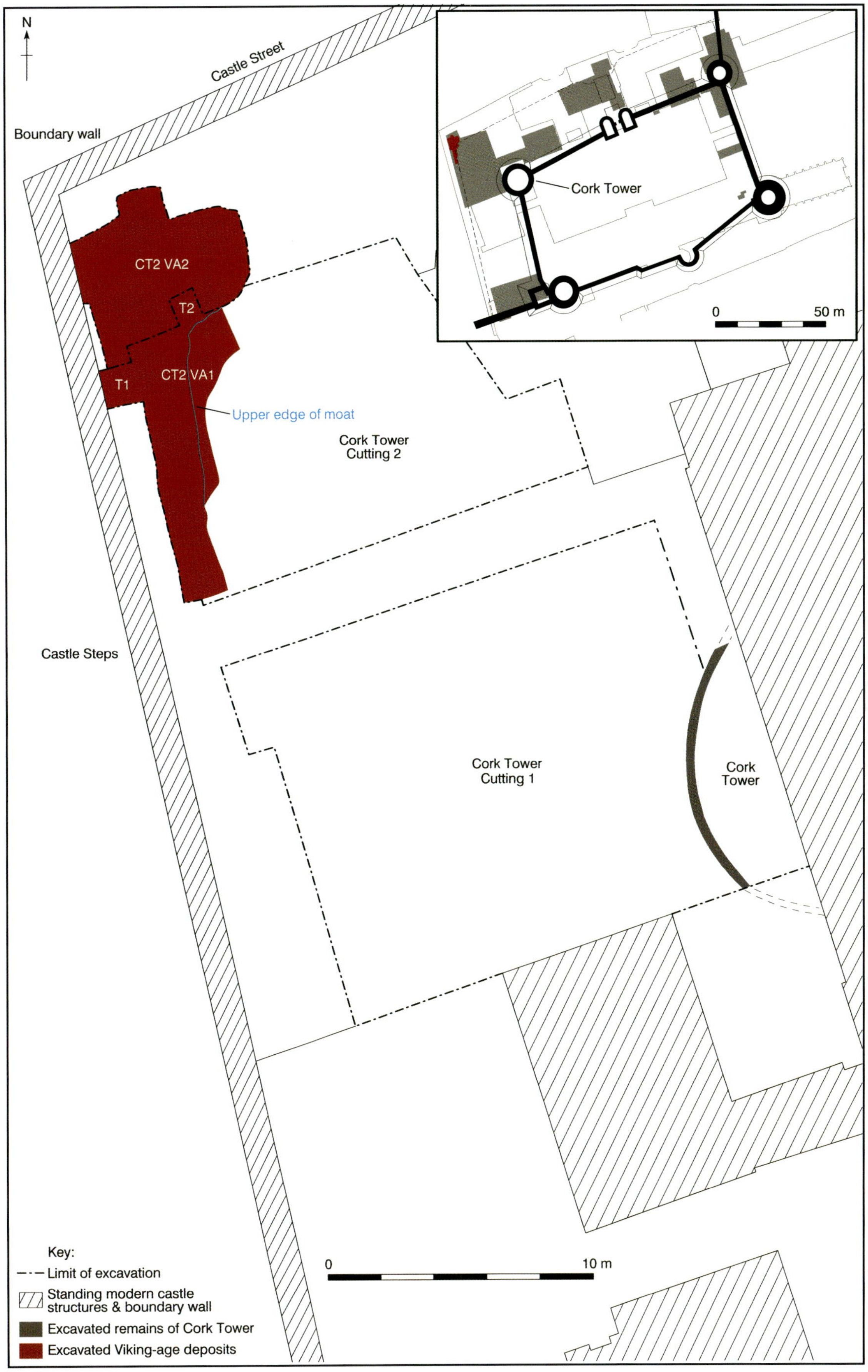

Fig. 3.1 Cork Tower cuttings and location of excavated Viking-age deposits.

Pl. 3.2 Salvage excavation in Cork Tower Cutting 2 (Viking Area 2) during building construction; from south.

Pl. 3.3 General view of Cork Tower Cutting 2 (Viking Area 2) during building construction with excavation in progress in north-west corner. The moat of the medieval castle is in the centre of the photograph and the excavated base of the Cork Tower is visible at bottom right; from south-east.

The Viking-age deposits were exposed in an irregular wedge-shaped area measuring *c.* 16m north/south by max. *c.* 6.5m east/west within the angle formed by the early nineteenth-century castle boundary wall, with Castle Street lying to the north and the Castle Steps laneway to the west. The clay-cut edge of the moat defined the eastern limits of the deposits while the boundary wall imposed safety restrictions on the west and north sides, with excavation extending as far as the western wall in only two limited areas (Fig. 3.1). Before its enclosure within the modern castle precinct in c.1806, this area was heavily populated by artisan dwellings fronting onto Cole Alley, which linked Ship Street with Castle Street just to the west of the boundary wall. Although demolished close to ground level, the remains of these eighteenth-century houses together with associated drainage works were uncovered underneath the modern concrete yard and were discovered to lie directly on top of the surviving Viking-age deposits (Figs 3.10, 3.11). The digging of the castle moat in the thirteenth century obliterated the

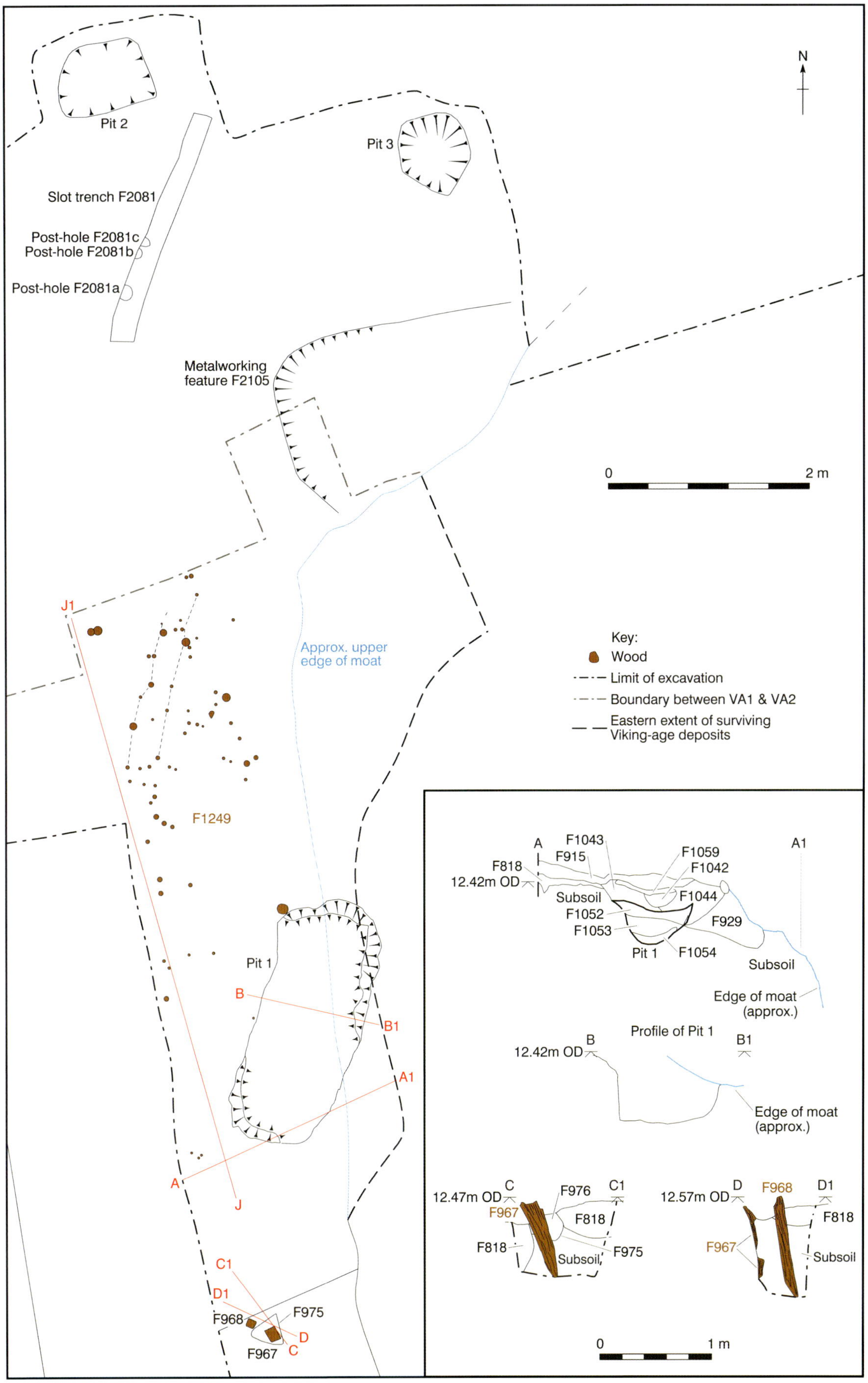

Fig. 3.2 Cork Tower, Cutting 2; Phase 1 features.

underlying Viking-age deposits where it extended into the underlying subsoil. However, along its upper sloping edge there was considerable mixing of deposits where Viking material was still *in situ* under moat fill layers and the interface between the two contexts was often difficult to discern. This had resulted in a small number of pottery sherds from moat-fill layers being attributed to Viking-age contexts during excavation and, while noted below, these sherds will be published as part of the medieval/post-medieval finds assemblage of Dublin Castle (Lynch *et al.*, forthcoming b).

The Viking-age stratigraphy in this area indicated six phases of activity. The earliest occupation (Phase 1) comprises ephemeral structural evidence in the form of random stakes, the remains of three pits and metalworking debris. In Phase 2 the area was sub-divided into two plots and associated structural wood was recovered. The construction and occupation of a Type 1 Viking house (House 1) belongs to Phase 3. In Phase 4, House 1 was abandoned and large pits were dug. The construction, occupation and destruction of House 2 belongs to Phase 5 and its replacement by House 3 belongs to Phase 6. It should be noted that these phases of activity relate only to this particular area of the castle excavations.

Pl. 3.4 Post-excavation view of cesspit (Pit 1, F1041); south-east corner truncated by test trench; from south-west.

Phase 1

PITS

The earliest feature exposed was the remains of a large cesspit (F1041) cut into subsoil, the surface of which was at 12.42m OD (Pit 1, Fig. 3.2; Pl. 3.4). The upper levels of this pit on its eastern side were cut by the sloping edge of the castle moat but its full plan was exposed at a lower level where it was revealed as roughly rectangular with rounded corners and measuring 2.4m (north-south) by 1.04m (east-west) and up to 0.6m deep. The primary fill (F1054) was organic brown/black silty clay, up to 100mm deep in which faecal material containing hazelnuts, the seeds of blackberries/raspberries, barley, fat-hen, common orache, cultivated flax and stones of blackthorn /sloe was identified (see Chapter 7). Overlying this deposit there was a layer up to 0.15m deep of grey silty clay (F1053) with small stones, occasional flecks of charcoal and fragments of decayed wood and this in turn was covered by a pungent grey/green silty clay (F1052), up to 90mm deep. The remains of Pit 1 were stratified under shallow deposits of silty clays with small to medium stones, some sandy lenses and occasional flecks of charcoal (Fig. 3.2, A–A1).

Two other pits may be assigned to Phase 1. A sub-rectangular pit (F2075) was uncovered at the northern end of the site, close to the boundary wall (Pit 2, Figs 3.2, 3.16). It measured 0.94m (east-west) by 0.68m and was 0.29m deep. The fill (F2094) was soft black organic clay containing seeds of blackberry/raspberry, common orache and fat-hen, suggesting its use as a cesspit. Another roughly circular pit (F2082) was uncovered *c.* 3m to the east (Pit 3, Fig. 3.2). It measured 0.46m by 0.36m and was at least 1m deep. It was not bottomed out as it extended below the local water table. The fill (F2089) was crumbly brown/grey sandy silt with frequent small stones. No finds were recovered from these two pits.

STAKES/STAKE-HOLES

Just over 50 stakes/stake-holes (F1249/F2088) were recorded in the subsoil, some of which probably belong to Phase 1 activity but the levels from which they were inserted could not be discerned with any degree of certainty. Neither was any pattern of distribution noted, although a possible double north-south alignment over a 2.2m length is tentatively suggested (Fig. 3.2). Decayed wood survived in many of the stake-holes and one stake was recorded only in section (Fig. 3.10).

TIMBER POSTS

The remains of a large timber post (F967) were found *in situ* at the southern end of the Viking-age deposits. Rectangular in section (0.15m by 90mm) and 0.70m long, the post had been set within a post-pit (F975) but its pointed end was driven into the subsoil (F1017) well below the base of the post-pit. The post-pit was cut into redeposited subsoil (F818) and was filled with a dark grey silty clay with flecks of black clay (F976) (Fig. 3.2, C–C1, D–D1). Immediately to the north-west and at the same stratigraphic level, a second timber post (F968) was also uncovered. This post was square in section (90mm) and 0.90m long with a pointed end. It also had been driven through redeposited subsoil (F818) into the subsoil below but did not have a post-pit (Fig. 3.2). Several layers of redeposited subsoil were recorded resting on undisturbed subsoil in this area, ranging from the yellow silty sand (F818) to orange/brown sandy clay (F1233) and yellow silty sand flecked with charcoal (F929). Deposit F818 was subject to disturbance and produced a number of finds intrusive to Phase 1. These included part of a decorated antler comb (E296:31158), burnt to a white colour, but tentatively identified as being Viking in origin and probably of late tenth/early eleventh century in date (see Chapter 4.2.1); the discovery of eleven sherds of thirteenth/fourteenth-century pottery from the same layer can be attributed to contamination of the context by later fill material on the edge of the moat.

METALWORKING FEATURE AND METALWORKING DEBRIS

Traces of a hearth (F2098) comprising burnt orange clay and ash overlying a thin layer of charcoal were recorded in section as resting on subsoil at the extreme north-west corner of the area excavated, close to the castle boundary wall (Figs 3.15, 3.16). Part of an oval-shaped depression (F2105) cut into subsoil was recorded nearby. The surviving remains of this feature measured 2.4m east-west by 1.6m and was up to 0.3m deep (Figs 3.2, 3.14). It would originally have been roughly oval in outline but its southern edge had been truncated by the digging of the castle moat and its eastern edge was outside the limit of excavation. The fill (F2078) comprised a grey gravelly ash with small stones, burnt bone, wood fragments and shell. This deposit also contained a large amount of ironworking residue including eight complete smithing hearth cakes and multiple vitrified clay tuyère fragments. On the basis of the metalworking debris contained in fill F2078, depression F2105 is interpreted as the remains of a metalworking feature.

LINEAR FEATURE

A linear slot-trench (F2081) was recorded just south of Pit 2 at the northern end of the area (Fig. 3.2). This feature, aligned north-east/south-west, was 2.38m long by 0.24m wide and averaged 70mm in depth with three post-holes cut into its base. The first (F2081a), 0.40m from the southern end of the trench had a diameter of *c.* 0.14m; the second post-hole (F2081b) was oval-shaped, measuring *c.* 0.1m by 60mm, and the third (F2081c), also oval-shaped, measured 0.1m by 80mm.

GENERAL STRATIGRAPHY AND MATERIAL CULTURE

A number of different deposits or layers were associated with Phase 1 occupation. Those recorded in the southern half of the area comprised a mixture of stiff brown and grey clays with inclusions of wattle fragments, ash and some animal bone. A radiocarbon date of cal AD 770–966 (95.4% probability) was obtained from a sample of animal bone (pig pelvis) recovered from one of these deposits (F1228; Fig. 3.10) (see Chapter 8).

Similar clays were recorded at the northern end of the area with inclusions of charcoal, ash, burnt bone, shell, wood fragments and small stones. A thick layer of charcoal and ashy clay with burnt bone and shell (F2071) was stratified on subsoil. It contained a fragmented amber ring (E296:48564), a hone with traces of red dye (E296:48563) and an iron nail (E296:48565). Two fragments of human skull (not available for analysis) were recovered from deposit F2073, also stratified on subsoil (Figs 3.15, 3.16). This layer also contained an iron loop-headed ringed pin (E296:48568), an iron belt buckle (E296:48567), a piece of sawn goat horn core (E296:48566) and a small amount of possible tuyère-related metalworking residue (see Chapter 4.14.1). An iron knife (E296:48574) was recovered from a lens of dark organic material (F2080) resting on subsoil.

Two artefacts were found on the surface of the subsoil, a wooden nail (E296:48593) and a perforated antler tine (E296:48569).

Phase 2

This phase of activity includes the first indication of the division of the area into two different property plots, Plot 1 to the south of a pathway and Plot 2 to the north.

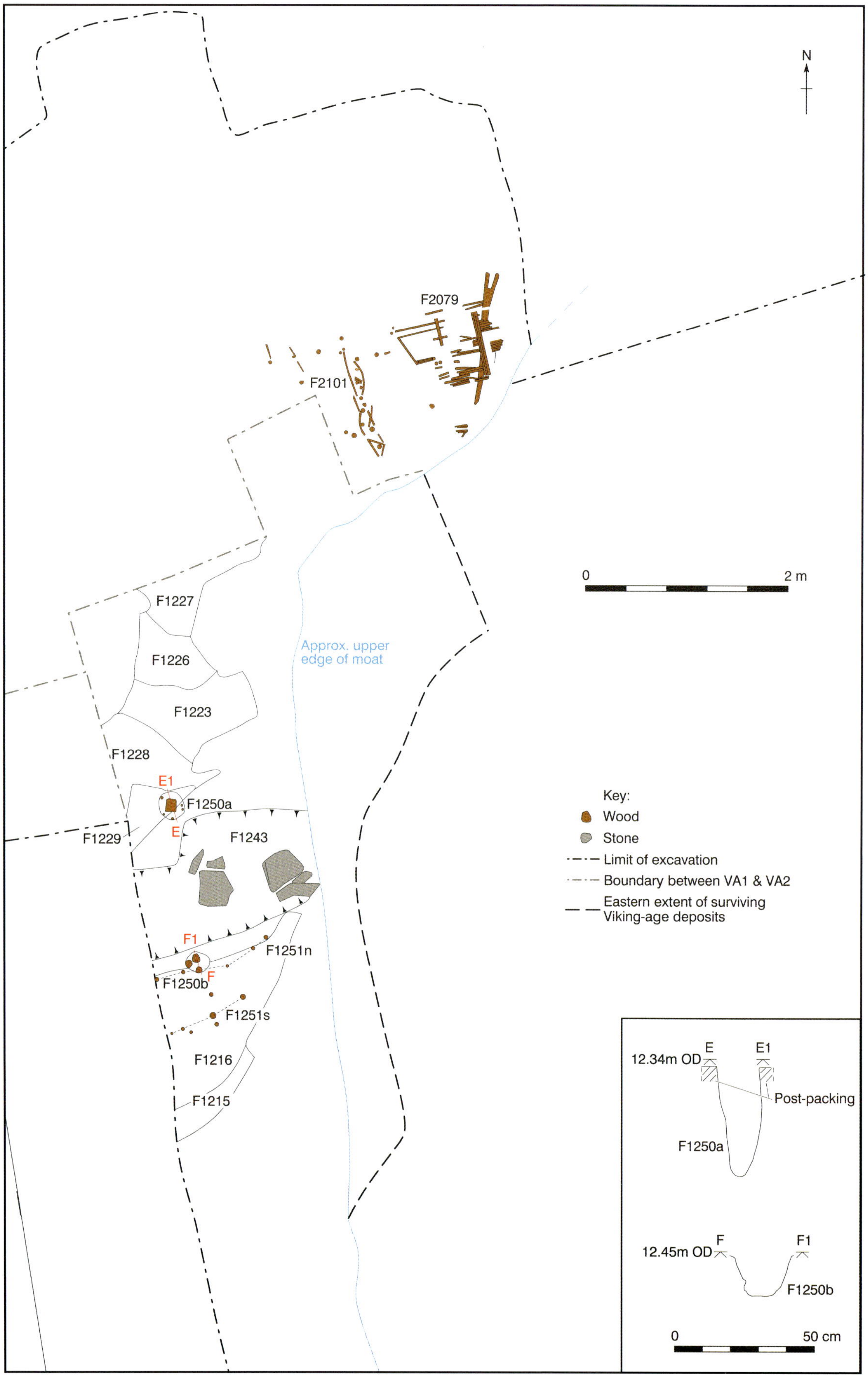

Fig. 3.3 Cork Tower, Cutting2; Phase 2 features.

PATHWAY

A shallow depression (F1243) *c.* 1.26m wide and 0.1m deep was aligned east-west across the southern part of the site (Fig. 3.3). The bottom of this depression was partly paved with large flagstones while the remainder was roughly cobbled with smaller stones, suggesting use as a pathway (Pl. 3.5). Subsoil from the digging of this feature was redeposited along its south side (F1216) and contained a piece of worked flint (E296:48469) and two bone fragments, possibly a pin (E296:49423) and a needle (E296:48462).

Two parallel lines of stakes (F1251) 0.5m apart and aligned east-west had been set into the redeposited subsoil (F1216) on the south side of the pathway while two large post-holes (F1250a/b) were set on either side of it (Fig. 3.3). The stakes in the northern alignment (F1251n) were badly charred while those of the southern alignment (F1251s) were not charred and survived to a greater height. The post-hole (F1250a) on the north side of the pathway measured 0.2m by 0.17m by 0.4m deep and was filled with a brown-grey silty clay with pieces of decayed wood. The post had been set within a post-pit (diameter 0.3m) around the edges of which a number of small stakes had been set. The post-hole on the south side (F1250b) measured 0.2m in diameter by 0.13m deep with three stake-holes in its base. These timber posts may have supported a small gate linked to a light timber fence on the south side of the pathway.

The east-west pathway and associated posts and stakes are the first indications of a sub-division of this area into two different plots.

PLOT 1

The area south of the pathway is referred to as Plot 1. Here the redeposited subsoil (F1216) containing the lines of stakes was covered by a mid/dark brown and grey clay (F1215) with wattle, ash and some animal bone. This in turn was covered by a layer of dark brown organic material (F1212) with frequent wood fragments and slightly charred 'grassy' material, up to 0.6m deep. At the same stratigraphic level, a deposit (F1070) comprising spreads of white, grey and yellow ash with frequent charcoal produced a small piece of slag and a possible tuyère fragment (Fig. 3.11). The surface of this deposit was characterised by a series of small depressions or hollows (F1083–1086).

Deposit F1212 marked the end of Phase 2 activity and the ash/charcoal layer (F1070) overlay the walkway and extended into the southern edge of Plot 2.

PLOT 2

Plot 2, the area to the north of the pathway, was covered with clay deposits similar to those in Plot 1 (Figs 3.3, 3.10, 3.11). A layer of silty clay (F1223/1217) with small stones and partially charred wattle contained a crucible fragment associated with glass working (E296:S1029) and an antler

Pl. 3.5 Paving slabs of Phase 2 pathway (F1243); upcast clay (F1216) to left of ranging rod.

Pl. 3.6 The remains of Phase 2 wattle panel (F2079); from north.

pin (E296:48461). A radiocarbon date of cal AD 896–1024 (95.4% probability) was obtained from a sample of animal bone (sheep/goat radius) recovered from this layer. At a similar stratigraphic level, a stony grey clay (F1227) produced animal bone (pig radius) from which a radiocarbon date of cal AD 895–1022 was obtained (95.4% probability). Stratified above this level was a small spread of charcoal-flecked grey stony clay (F1081) that contained several pieces of metalworking debris including a smithing hearth cake and tuyère fragments.

Fragments of a wattle panel (F2079) survived in the north-east corner of Plot 2 (Fig. 3.3; Pl. 3.6). The interwoven wattle strands varied in length from just 60mm to 0.6m and averaged 20mm in diameter while the posts averaged 40mm in diameter. The eastern end of the panel incorporated a long, forked timber aligned north-south and measuring 1.3m long by 0.1m wide. The panel was stratified above the Phase 1

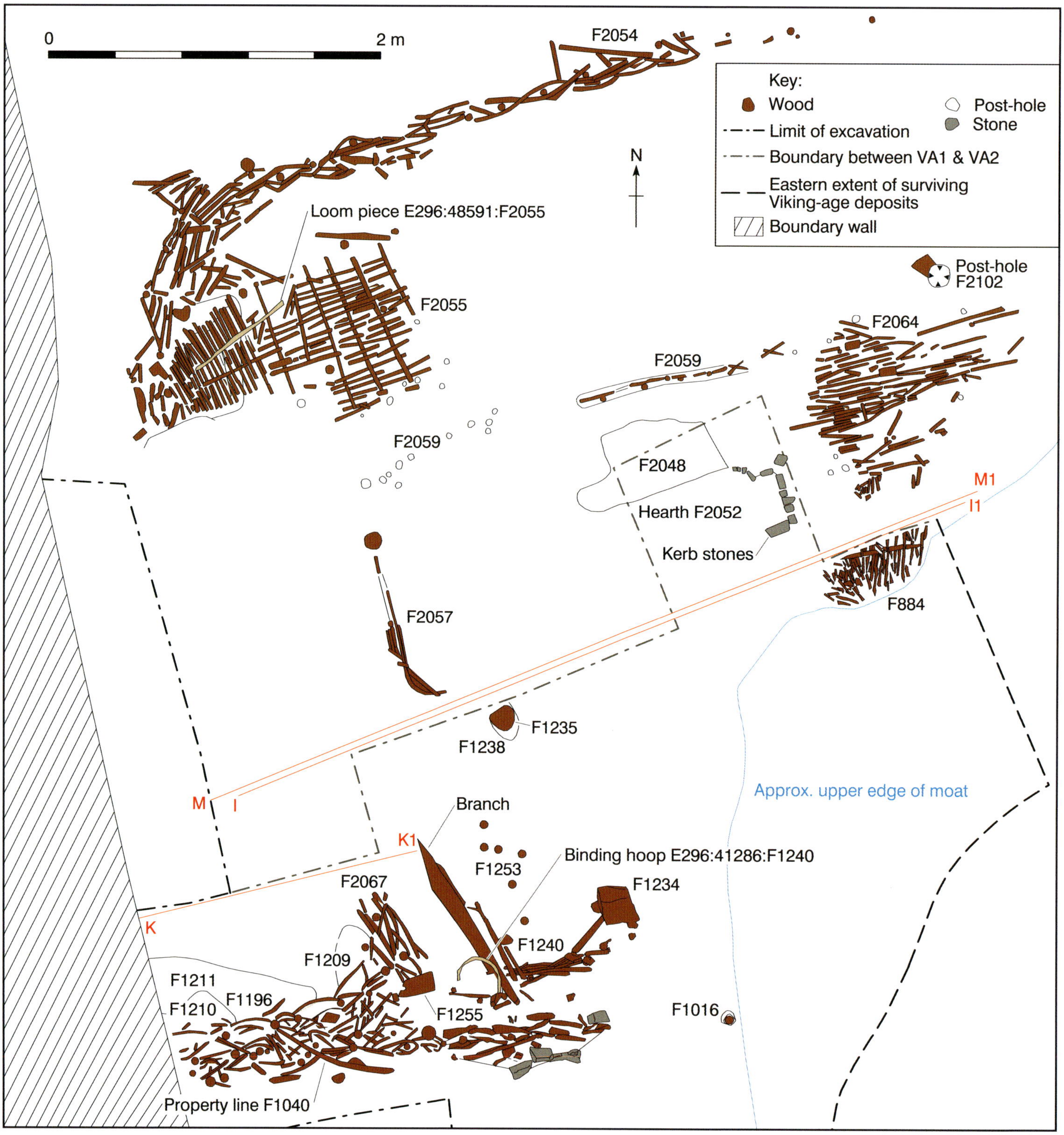

Fig. 3.4 Cork Tower, Cutting 2; Phase 3 features including remains of House 1.

depression (F2105) that contained metalworking debris and under a thick black organic silty clay (F2063/F1222) with frequent hazelnuts and wood fragments and occasional pieces of burnt bone and small stone (Fig. 3.14). A fragment of a jet finger ring (E296:48487) was recovered from deposit F2063/F1222 in addition to a human skull (not available for analysis). An area of burning (F2066) and associated ash spread (F2065) in the vicinity of the wattle panel produced a fragmented amber ring (E296:48560), a fragment of tuyère (E296:48561) and a bone pin (E296:48559).

Pl. 3.7 House 1 (Phase 3); the timber-lined pit (Pit 4a, Phase 4a) has obliterated most of the western end wall. The curving edge of the medieval moat is visible at top left; from north.

The remains of a post-and-wattle wall (F2101) survived *in situ* just to the west of the wattle panel (Fig. 3.3). The wall was aligned north-south with a surviving length of *c.* 1.28m. It incorporated numerous wattle strands and around twelve uprights averaging 40mm in diameter.

Phase 3

In this phase the incipient property division in Phase 2 that created Plot 1 to the south and Plot 2 to the north is further developed. The first definite evidence for a house structure in this area belongs to this phase.

PROPERTY BOUNDARY

The remains of a post-and-wattle fence (F1040) were exposed just to the north of the pathway belonging to Phase 2 (Figs 3.4, 3.11). It extended east-west over a distance of *c.* 2.5m and survived to heights of up to 0.2m. It was truncated at the west end by the nineteenth-century castle boundary wall and became less well-defined towards its eastern end where the large stake (F1016) close to the edge of the moat appears to be the final surviving element (Fig. 3.4). The fence averaged 0.2–0.3m in width with the posts set randomly either in the middle or at the sides.

A length of single post-and-wattle fencing (F1196) had been constructed on the north side of the western end of the property boundary and was secured to it by woven strands of wattle (Fig. 3.4). The posts of this short stretch of fence were set *c.* 2m apart and at its eastern end it was tied into the south-west corner of House 1 (see below), presumably to provide additional support by securing the corner to the property boundary. Two upright posts of this fence had been driven through a deposit of dark grey/brown silty clay (F1197) up to 50mm deep that contained a waste flake of amber (E296:48417). A deposit of brown slightly charred organic clay with frequent small fibrous strands (F1209) filled the gap between fence (F1196) and the wattle wall of House 1.

PLOT 1

The area south of the property boundary (Plot 1) was covered with deposits of silty clays the predominant one of which was a thick brown organic clay (F1068) with numerous pieces of wattle and straw, twigs and some animal bone (Fig. 3.11). It also contained a small amount of metalworking debris (slag and vitrified ceramic tuyère fragments) and a piece of leather (E296:40259). Just to the south of property boundary F1040, and partially underlying it, was a deposit of medium brown clay (F1201/1202) with frequent wattle fragments, straw and charcoal flecks. This layer was truncated to the west by the castle boundary wall and a radiocarbon date of cal AD 719–885 (95.4% probability) was obtained from a cow horn core recovered from this deposit but following Bayesian analysis, this date is considered to be the result of residual deposition (see Chapter 8).

PLOT 2

HOUSE 1

House 1, the earliest of the three houses recorded in this area, was the most coherent and complete in terms of ground plan and lay immediately north of the property boundary in Plot 2. The surviving elements included the north-west and south-west corners, part of the north wall, internal divisions, the remains of a central hearth and wattle mats. The north-east corner was outside the area excavated while the south-east corner had been destroyed by the digging of the thirteenth-century castle moat. No evidence of the doorway had survived because of disturbance by a Phase 4a pit (Pit 4a) and the house was orientated with its long axis roughly east-west (Fig. 3.4; Pl. 3.7).

The house walls were of single-line post-and-wattle construction. Little of the south wall (F1240) survived and its remains were a maximum of 0.1m high. A large branch-like length of wood about 1.4m long and 0.14m wide had been laid diagonally across the south-west corner of the house, at the base of the wall and partially overlying it was a small wooden binding hoop (E296:41286) that was incorporated into the structure of the wall (Fig. 3.4; Pl. 3.8). The decayed remains of a large square timber post (F1234) lay just inside and was tied into the eastern limit of the surviving extent of wall. It measured 0.2m by 0.2m in section although much of it had been removed by the digging of a later cesspit (Pit 6) belonging to Phase 4c (see below). The post appeared to have been sitting directly on the contemporary ground surface and may have acted as a roof support. A limited length of the west wall (F2067) survived. The remains comprised a 0.5m-long strip of fragmented wattle strands incorporating two uprights 40mm in diameter and set 0.2m apart.

The rounded north-west corner of House 1 survived along with a 4.2m-long stretch of the north wall (F2054) (Fig. 3.4; Pl. 3.8). The remains of five posts of the north-west corner survived. They averaged 40mm in diameter and were between 0.20m and 0.4m apart. Sixteen posts of the north wall remained *in situ* and averaged 60mm in diameter and were between 0.14m and 0.4m apart. The wattle strands woven around the posts were 20mm in diameter and varied in length from 60mm to 0.56m.

No evidence of a doorway had survived in the west end wall due to extensive disturbance caused by Pit 4a (F2096) belonging to Phase 4a. In general, Viking Type 1 houses (as defined by Wallace 1992) had a doorway at both ends but the east end of House 1 lay outside the area of excavation and had also been impacted severely by the digging of the castle moat.

INTERNAL FEATURES

House 1 retained traces of several of the internal features usually associated with Type 1 houses: post-and-wattle partitions, a central hearth and wattle screens or mats (Fig. 3.4).

The house had at least two internal divisions. A post-and-wattle partition (F2059) aligned east-west (i.e. parallel to the long axis of the house) separated the north aisle or bench/bed area from the central area where the hearth was located. It comprised, at its east end, a number of small posts set in a thin, horizontal wooden frame and to the west a line of small post-holes and fragmentary wattle, giving an overall extant length of *c.* 2.75m. There were seventeen posts in the partition, averaging up to 40mm in diameter and set at varying distances apart, other than those on the bed/bench frame that were at 0.1m intervals. The frame was 1.2m long by up to 80mm wide. The few strands of wattle found in association with this feature ranged in length from 0.1m to 0.5m and they were 20mm in diameter.

The second internal partition (F2057) was aligned north-south (i.e. perpendicular to the sides of the structure) approximately midway between the hearth and the probable location of the doorway in the west end wall. This post-and-wattle wall survived up to 0.98m in length and had a pronounced curve on its south end. A large post (diameter 0.1m) at its north end may have helped stabilise the structure the function of which is unclear, but which possibly served as a windbreak, shielding the hearth from a doorway in the west wall.

The remains of two wattle mats survived within House 1, the better preserved of which (F2055) was located in the north-west corner (Pls 3.7, 3.9). This survived in the form of a roughly rectangular panel, 1.5m long (east-west) by 0.9m and consisted of strands of wattle interwoven at right angles with most of the long pieces aligned north-south. The wattle pieces varied in length from 60mm to 0.8m and were 20mm in diameter. The fabric of the mat closest to the curving north-west corner of the house was particularly well made and quite well preserved. A number of finds were associated with this wattle mat including a decorated leather strap end (E296:48578), a small wooden loom piece (E296:48591) found resting on the surface of the mat (Fig. 3.4) and metalworking residue comprising a fragment of crucible (E296:48545) and a fragment of vitrified ceramic tuyère material. An irregular formation of eight small post-holes was uncovered along the south-east edge of the mat. A deposit of matted organic material (F2053) comprising twigs, leaves and moss lay on the wattle mat and contained a fragment of woollen cloth (E296:48595). Beetles identified in this deposit include those that would have been introduced from outside and were associated with animal excrement and rotting organic plant material and also include a species that could be related to birds nesting in the roof or fowl being kept in the house (see Chapter 7).

The second wattle mat (F2064) was not as well preserved and was truncated on its south side by the castle moat. It measured 1.2m east-west by 1m and the fragmentary wattle strands were largely aligned east-west. The length of the strands varied from 40mm to 0.54m and they were 20mm in diameter. A number of small post-holes was uncovered

Pl. 3.8 Fragmentary remains of south wall (F1240) of House 1 (Phase 3) incorporating binding hoop (E296:41286:F1240). Remains of post-and-wattle property boundary (F1040) visible just to the right; from west.

around the surviving edges of the mat. These were typically *c.* 40mm in diameter but with a single large exception (F2102). A fragment of tuyère (E296:48558) and an amber ring fragment (E296:48557) were found in the remains of the wattle mat.

The remains of a rectangular hearth (F2052) associated with House 1 consisted of twelve kerbstones of varying sizes partially enclosing a deposit of burnt clay and ash, while an adjacent deposit of ash (F2048) *c.* 60mm deep probably represents rakings from the fire (Fig. 3.4; Pl. 3.10). Only the eastern kerb was complete and measured 0.32m in length while just 0.28m survived along the north side and 0.2m survived on its south side.

The remains of six stakes (F1253) were uncovered close to the south-west corner of the house. A large wooden post (F1235, 0.15m diameter) set in a post-pit (F1238) just to the north of these stakes may have functioned as a roof support.

Pl. 3.9 North-west corner of House 1 (Phase 3), with wattle mat (F2055). Timber-lined pit (Pit 4a) belonging to Phase 4 is at top right; from north.

OCCUPATION DEPOSITS

Much of the interior of House 1 had been disturbed by later pits but some evidence of occupation did survive in the south-west corner. A deposit of highly organic material (F1252) comprised mostly of straw and pieces of wattle was uncovered mainly against the inside of the house wall and may be the remnants of bedding material (Fig. 3.10). This organic layer lay on top of a fawn sod-like layer (F1067) with evidence of charring from which a piece of leather (E296:45944) was recovered. A layer of fine black, gritty ash (F2060) appeared to represent the floor level of the house at the time of construction as the partitions F2059 and F2057 had been cut into it and the hearth lay on top of it. An unfinished bone pin-beater (E296:48551) and a wooden bucket stave with an iron attachment (E296:48552) were recovered from this layer.

Two further deposits were associated with the occupation of House 1 (Figs 3.15, 3.16). An organic brown clay with evidence of charring (F2061) lay on the ash layer (F2060) and contained many wood fragments, bone and hazelnuts and artefacts including a curved iron bar and pointed iron tool (E296:48553, E296:48554) and a piece of stitched leather (E296:48579). Evidence of food remains recovered from this deposit includes seeds of blackberry/raspberry, wheat, common orache, fat hen and knotgrass (see Chapter 7). Overlying this layer was a grey/brown organic layer (F2047/F2069) containing textile fibres (E296:50008), wood fragments (E296:48536), an antler tine (E296:48535), an iron nail (E296:48538) and a set of iron tweezers (E296:48539). Eight fragments of human bone derived from at least two individuals, including a child of about ten years of age, were recovered from this organic layer (see Chapter 5).

Pl. 3.10 Remains of hearth with kerbstones (F2052), within House 1 (Phase 3); from north.

Phase 4

This phase of activity relates to the digging of a series of pits following the abandonment of House 1. It is divided into three sub-phases (4a, 4b, 4c) for ease of discussion.

Phase 4A

PROPERTY BOUNDARY

The Phase 3 post-and-wattle property boundary (F1040) was covered by a thick sod-like deposit (F1200) comprising dark brown organic clay with occasional charcoal and moderate woody fragments. This in turn was overlain by a similar organic clay (F1193, Fig. 3.5) with twig-like inclusions. A radiocarbon date of cal AD 777–975 (95.4% probability) was obtained from a pig tibia recovered from deposit F1193 but, following Bayesian analysis, is considered to be the result of residual deposition (see Chapter 8).

While the remains of House 1 walls and the boundary fence (F1040, F1196) were covered by organic clays, some posts belonging to the property boundary projected above the covering clays and appear to have been reused in Phase 4a. A new line of stakes (F1195a–k) was laid down just to the north of the pre-existing boundary and survived over a distance of 1.4m (Fig. 3.5). The stakes appear to have been arranged in pairs but at irregular intervals. No wattle strands had survived but a weaving line of charcoal and ash (F1186) uncovered between and above these stakes is consistent with the remains of a burnt wattle wall. Fragments of partially burnt wattle were attached to a stake (F1194) which in turn was attached to some of the projecting posts belonging to the earlier property boundary.

PLOT 1

The area south of the property boundary contained no obvious structures. It was covered by a thick (max. 0.17m) layer of dark grey silty clay (F1039) containing a lot of charcoal and pockets of bone and shell which was stratified under a layer of dark beige silty clay (F1005) with flecks of charcoal and which was 70mm deep.

PLOT 2

The main feature in Plot 2 was the remains of a large, partially collapsed timber-lined pit (Pit 4a, F1245/F2096) filled with a series of organic deposits (Figs 3.5, 3.10, 3.15; Pls 3.7, 3.9, 3.11). This pit had been cut from roughly the same level as the property boundary (F1195) but appeared to be slightly later than its burning. The pit cut through the west end of underlying House 1 and extended into Phase 2 levels. The pit was recut in Phase 4b and this resulted in the removal of much of the fill belonging to Phase 4a. Only the east side and part of the north side of the pit were exposed and it had been truncated by the castle boundary wall on the west while Pit 4b had destroyed much of its south side.

Pit 4a had been lined on its east side with long timbers (F2042, Timbers 1-3) held in place by at least three large vertical posts (F1074, F2099, F2100). Timber 1 was 2.4m long, 0.17m wide and 0.1m thick and had a groove cut into it that measured 80mm long, 10mm wide and 10mm deep. This groove may have been intended to secure a vertical element (which did not survive) and was the only surviving evidence of joinery in the lining of the pit. Timbers 2 and 3 were both 2.6m long. The surviving timbers on its north side (F2042, Timbers 5-7) were shorter, with Timber 5, measuring 1.12m in length, being the most substantial. The only surviving evidence for the south side was a vertical corner post (F1074) and a small number of collapsed timbers (Fig. 3.5). A vertical post (F2099) *c.* 0.2m in diameter was also found *in situ* at the north-east corner and a post-pit (F2085) also 0.2m in diameter marks the position of a further vertical timber on the north edge of the pit. A further post (F2100) was uncovered at the south end of Timber 4, *c.* 50mm east of the edge of the pit. This post *c.* 0.2m in diameter, straddled the edge of a stone-lined pit (F2086), oval in plan (0.44m long by 0.32m and 0.61m deep) filled with a pungent organic clay with some burnt bone and mussel shells.

Pit 4a had a maximum surviving depth of 0.45m and the fill comprised four main deposits: F2058, F2056, F2062 and F2050 (Fig. 3.15). The remains of wattle matting (F2076) measuring 0.65m by 0.4m lined the base of the pit (Figs 3.5, 3.15; Pl. 3.12). A range of artefacts was found associated with this wattle matting including an iron bolt (E296:48571) and iron nail (E296:48572), part of a turned wooden plate (E296:48594) and a piece of tuyère (E296:48570). The surviving fabric of the wattle mat was associated with a deposit of pungent dark brown sandy clay (F2077) containing shell, bone, wood fragments and skull fragments of a 'robust' young adult male (see Chapter 5). The deposits resting on the wattle matting included a reddish-brown organic clay (F2058) with frequent wood shavings, some up to 70mm long, which contained a bone needle (E296:48550) and a small amount of metalworking residue. Another deposit of black gritty clay (F2056) with burnt wood, charcoal, ash and frequent hazelnuts contained two pieces of flint (E296:48549), a fragment of tuyère (E296:48547), a small amount of metalworking residue and an iron and antler gaming piece (E296:48546). A third deposit (F2062) was a pungent brown silty clay with patches of charcoal, fragments of wood, shell and some medium to large stones which also contained part of a wooden barrel head or base (E296:48592) and part of a decorated composite antler comb (E296:48556). A significant amount of cultivated flax seed was identified in the fills of this pit. Overlying these basal deposits was a mix of ash with brown clay containing shell, charcoal, bone and occasional large stones (F2050) from which a square-headed nail (E296:48543) was recovered (Fig. 3.15).

Small traces of what were later identified as fills of Pit 4a were recorded in the northern section face of the 1985 excavation before the full extent of the feature was exposed during the later salvage excavation. These deposits within the southern edge of the pit comprised silty clays with inclusions of charcoal, wood fragments, ash, burnt bone, burnt shell and small amounts of animal bone (F1224, F1208, F1206, F1205; Figs 3.10, 3.11). Artefacts recovered include a wooden bucket base (E296:48454), an unidentified wooden object (E296:48446) and a sherd of thirteenth/fourteenth-century pottery (E296:42295) which must be intrusive to its context (F1224).

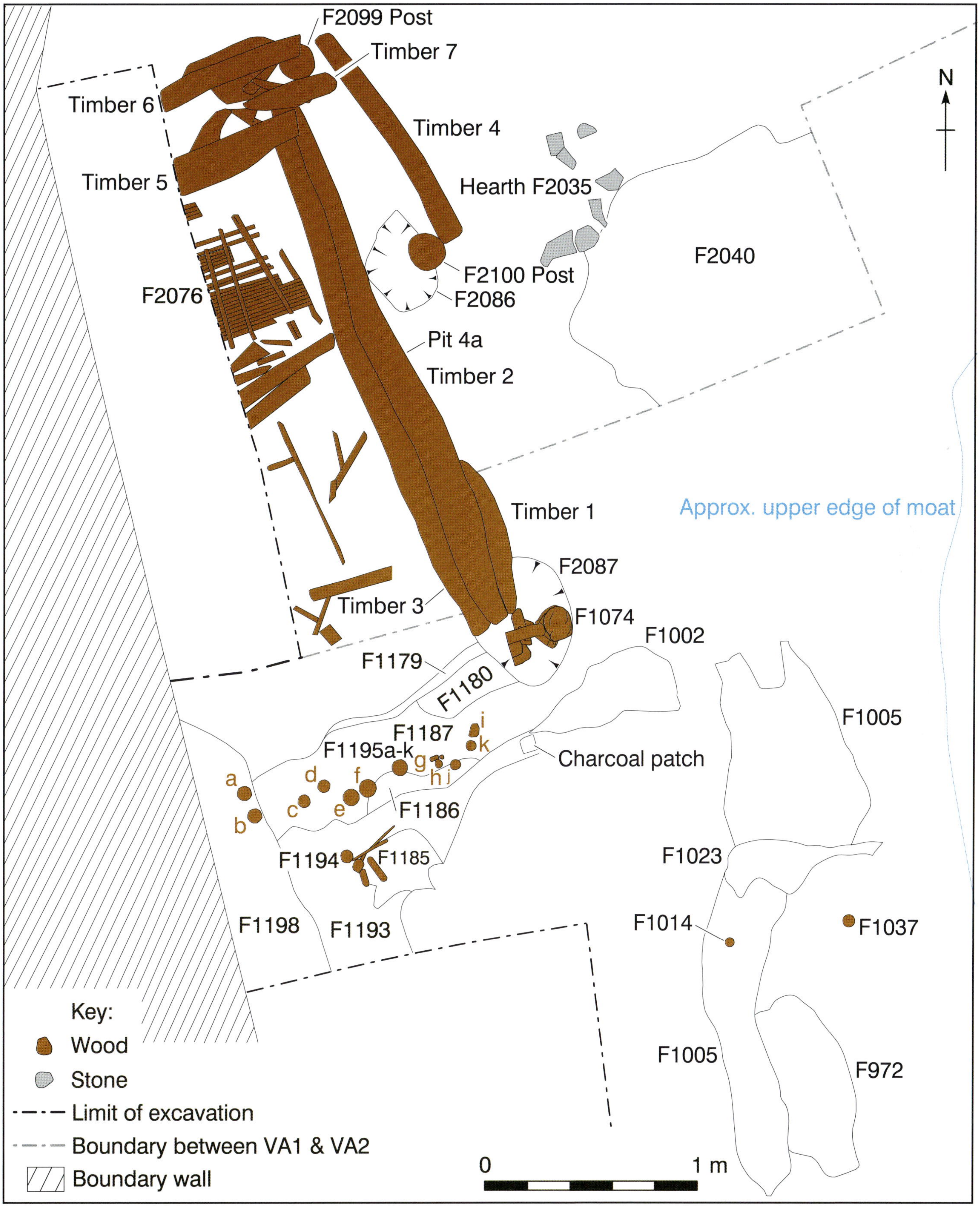

Fig. 3.5 Cork Tower, Cutting 2; Phase 4a features.

GENERAL STRATIGRAPHY

The remains of a hearth (F2035) *c.* 1.1m east of Pit 4a appear to be contemporary with it (Fig. 3.5). The hearth comprised seven partially displaced kerb stones, suggesting overall dimensions of *c.* 0.6m by *c.* 0.5m. The hearth remains contained a wooden peg or rod with bark attached (E296:48587). A deposit of brown organic clay (F2040) with frequent bone and shell was contemporary with the hearth.

The remainder of Plot 2 was covered by a thick layer of organic deposits (F2045, F2046, F2051, F1023, F1005, F1039) containing charcoal, ash, wood fragments, wood shavings, straw, moss and bone fragments. A range of artefacts was recovered from these clays: two leather strips (E296:48577), a piece of textile (E296:48600), two bone pins (E296:48528, 48530), two bone needles (E296:48529, 48532), a goose ulna that was polished and used as an implement (E296:48531), a hone stone (E296:48533), a wooden pin (E296:48589), a copper alloy boss (E296:48540), an iron loop-headed ringed pin (E296:50005), a thin strip of gilded bronze (E296:48544), an incomplete antler axe blade cover (E296:36958) and a decorated antler comb (E296:33418). A sherd of thirteenth/fourteenth-century pottery (E296:33484) was recovered from F1023 and can be attributed to the adjacent moat-fill layers.

Phase 4B

PROPERTY BOUNDARY

The property boundary appears to have gone out of use in this sub-phase and the area was covered by a thick brown sod-type layer (F779) with charcoal inclusions and evidence of burning. This layer partially covered the top of Pit 4a and was overlain by moat material (F746), which must account for the eight sherds of medieval pottery recovered from it. A glass mount/gaming piece (E296:28479) and a fragment of a human frontal bone from an older child or adolescent were also recovered from F779.

PIT 4B

Timber-lined Pit 4a was recut to provide a roughly oval-shaped pit (F1244/F2092, Pit 4b) that was truncated by the castle boundary wall to the west. This pit measured *c.* 3.2m (north-south) by at least 2.4m wide and was *c.* 0.5m deep (Figs 3.6, 3.10–3.12, 3.14, 3.15).

The pit was filled with deposits of silty clay with varying amounts of organic material including wattle fragments, twigs, straw, charcoal and fragments of wood and bone. Seeds of barley, common orache and fat hen were also identified in these deposits, indicating the presence of cess material and a flea species often associated with dry material of animal origin such as skins, hooves, feathers, bones, etc. was also recorded (see Chapter 7). Two sherds of French green-glazed pottery (E296:48448, E296:48449) were recovered from deposit F1199 at the bottom of the pit (Fig. 3.12). Two sherds of late medieval pottery (E296:36050, E296:31197) were also recovered from deposit F775 within the pit, together with an antler gaming piece (E296:31757) and a small amount of metalworking residue. This pit was in turn cut by a post-Viking-age pit, which could explain some contamination of its deposits. The top of Pit 4b was covered with six or seven flat stones (F2025) to stabilise the ground prior to the construction of House 2 in Phase 5 (see below).

PIT 5

To the south of Pit 4b, in what was Plot 1 in earlier phases, the truncated remains of Pit 5 (F1248) were recorded (Fig. 3.6). This flat-bottomed pit survived to a maximum depth of 0.4m and the remains of four wooden posts were alined along its northern edge (F944, F946, F980, F984). These posts averaged 120mm in diameter and 0.37m in length. The fill of Pit 5 was a silty brown clay (F999) with flecks of iron

Pl. 3.11 Timber-lined Pit 4a (Phase 4a); from east.

Pl. 3.12 Wattle lining (F2076) on base of Pit 4a.

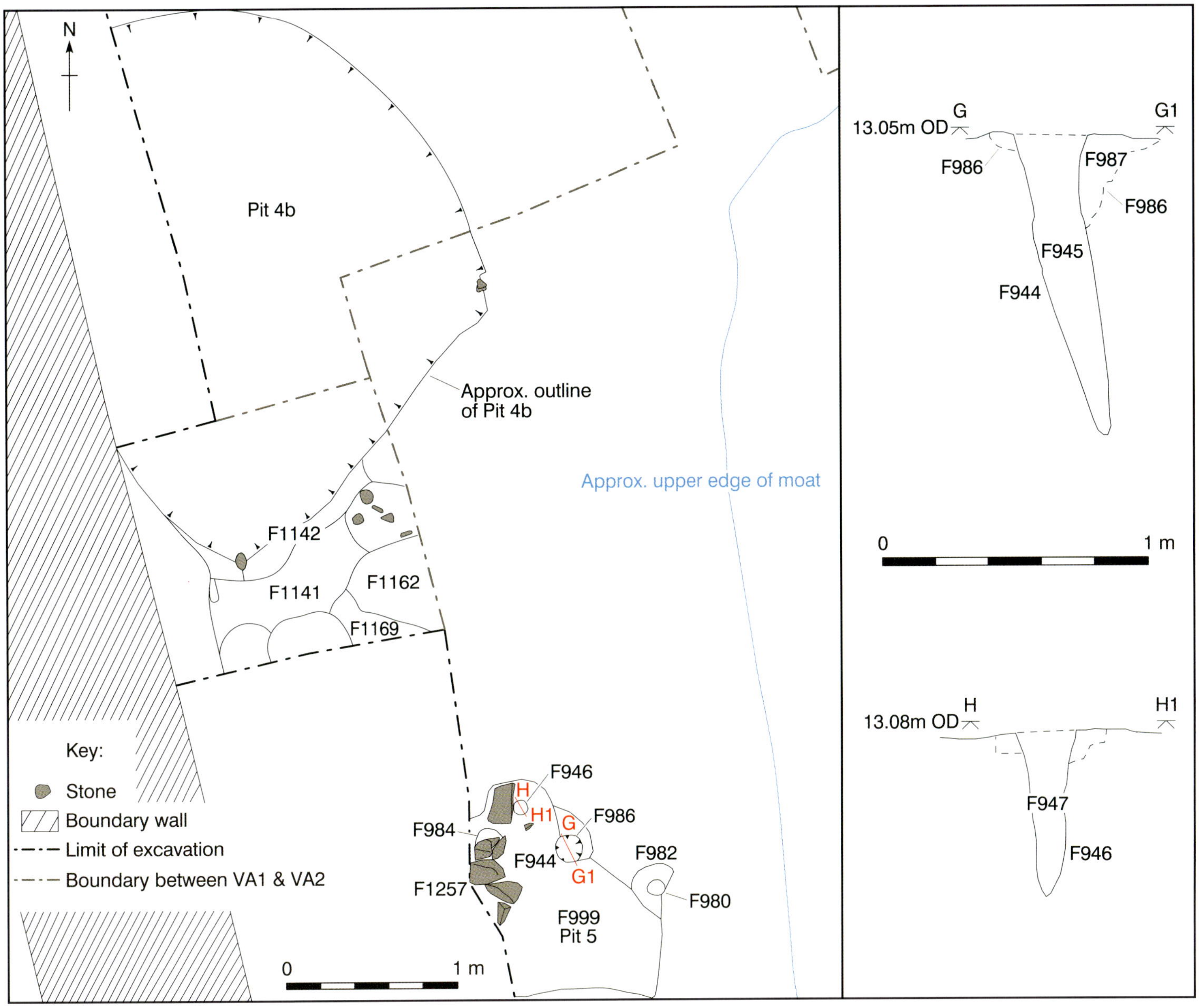

Fig. 3.6 Cork Tower, Cutting 2; Phase 4b features.

staining, frequent charcoal and small/moderate stones. A radiocarbon date of cal AD 778–994 (95.4% probability) was obtained from a sample of animal bone (a pig metacarpus) recovered from the fill F999 of this pit but, following Bayesian analysis, is considered to be the result of residual deposition (see Chapter 8).

General stratigraphy

A deposit of blue/grey silty clay with frequent charcoal flecks (F1254) was stratified on layer F779 mentioned above as partly overlying Pit 4a. Deposit F1254, which sloped from west to east, was partly contaminated with redeposited moat material (F746) but also contained a fragmentary antler comb with a runic inscription (E296:50058), which probably dates from the mid/late tenth century (see Chapter 4.2.1). A range of deposits assigned to Phase 4b included several 'sod-like' layers comprising dark brown compact clays with charcoal staining, small stones and fibrous organic inclusions.

Phase 4C

Few contexts can be assigned with certainty to this sub-phase other than Pit 6 and its associated ground surface (F1183) and Pit 7 (Figs 3.7, 3.13, 3.14).

Pit 6

Pit 6 (F1246) was uncovered *c.* 0.4m to the east of Pit 4a where its eastern edge had been cut by the castle moat and a test-pit had truncated its northern edge (Fig. 3.7). This

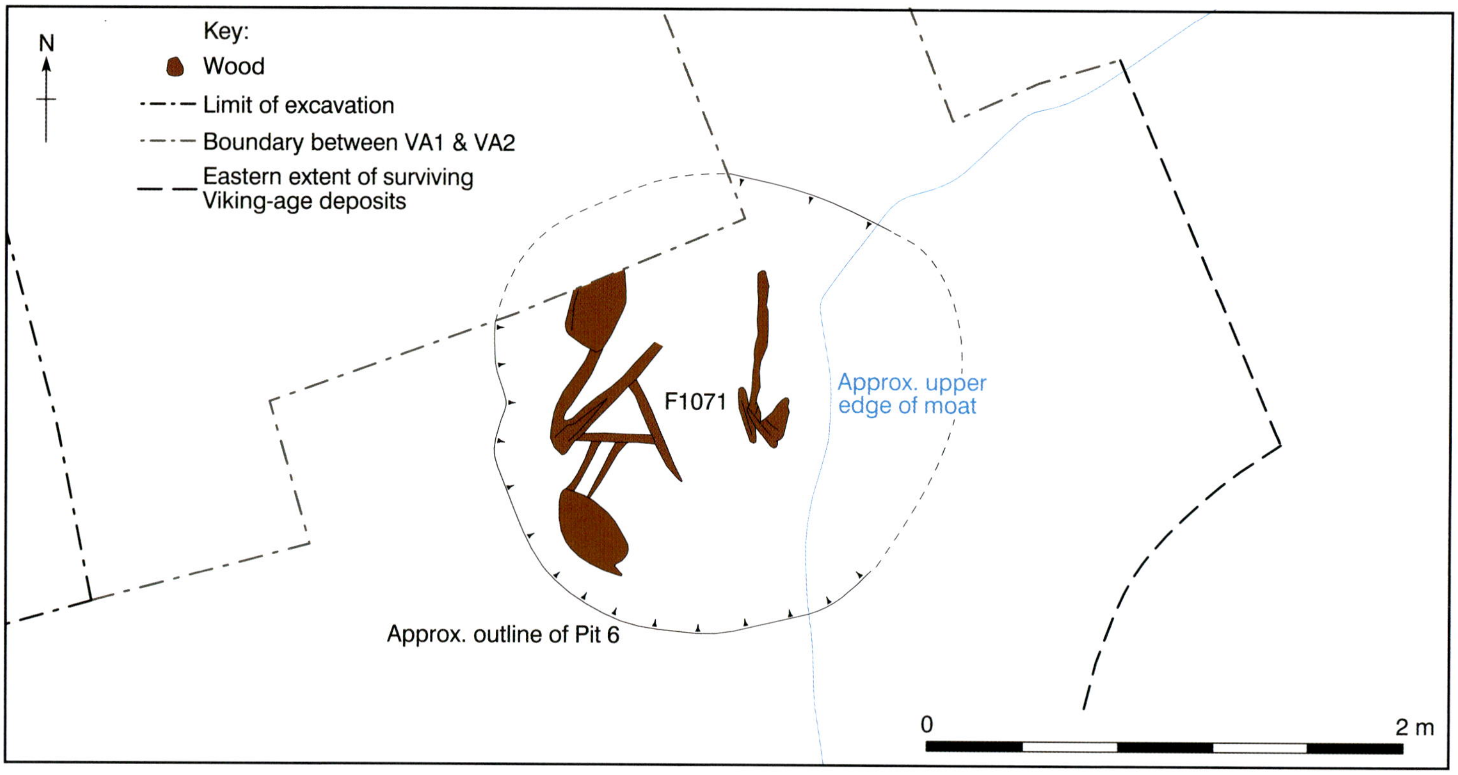

Fig. 3.7 Cork Tower, Cutting 2; Phase 4c features

flat-bottomed pit would have been almost circular in plan (*c.* 2m diameter) and was 0.6m deep. The lowest fill within the pit (F1091) comprised a pungent brown/green organic deposit with wattle fragments, grass, straw, bone fragments and frequent blackthorn/sloe stones. A piece of leather (E296:48470) was recovered from this deposit. Overlying the basal fill was a brown silty clay (F1071) with decayed plant material, fish bones, shells and occasional charcoal flecks together with numerous pieces of decayed wood, wattle and branches. Analysis of these two fills revealed moss and faecal concretions including seeds of blackberry/raspberry, bilberry, common orache, fat hen, rowan, apple pips and stones of blackthorn/sloe. The identification of two species of fleas confirms the presence of cess material and animal waste (see Chapter 7). The upper level of the pit fill comprised thin alternating bands of silty grey clay and soft decayed wood (F1045) from which a bone spindle whorl (E296:36068) was recovered. This layer was partially stratified beneath the sloping moat-fill layers (F988, F996).

PIT 7

The remains of Pit 7 (F2090) were identified in section M–M1 that cut into the west side of Pit 6 (Fig. 3.14). It was up to 0.5m deep and was filled with mottled grey clay with flecks of charcoal, small stones, bone and ash (F2104).

Phase 5

This phase is represented by the construction of House 2 overlying the pits belonging to Phases 4a–c and House 1 (Phase 3).

PROPERTY BOUNDARY

No evidence was recovered for the property boundary dividing Plot 1 and Plot 2 (i.e. to the south of House 2) but traces of a property boundary (F2041) did survive immediately to the north of House 2 which must have demarcated the northern limit of Plot 2 (Fig. 3.8; Pl. 3.13). This consisted of a line of post-and-wattle *c.* 1.5m long containing fifteen or more posts (up to 80mm in diameter) and occasional long pieces of wattle. This plot boundary was integrated with the north wall of House 2.

HOUSE 2

The excavated evidence for House 2 comprised part of its west wall (F2006) including the doorway and part of the north wall (F2030). The surviving remains of the north wall consisted of a single line of post-and-wattle extending east-west over 2.48m (Fig. 3.8; Pl. 3.13). Almost thirty posts had survived, ranging from 40mm to 90mm in diameter, and the wattle was very fragmentary. This wall appears to have been incorporated into the north wall of House 3 belonging to

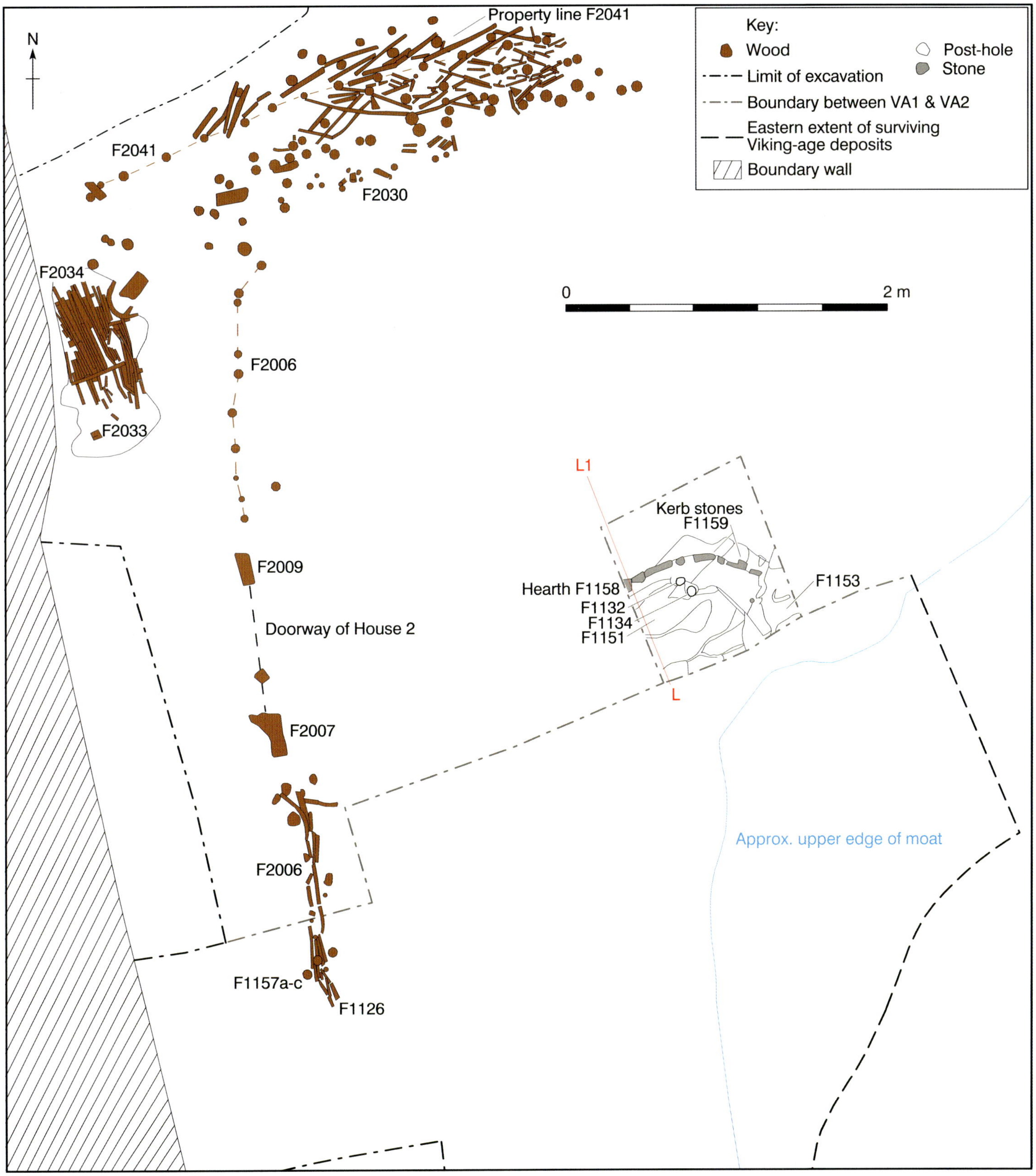

Fig. 3.8 Cork Tower, Cutting 2; Phase 5 features including remains of House 2.

Phase 6 (see below). The west wall (F2006/F1126) was traced for *c.* 4.6m and between the doorway and the north-west corner of the house, the line of the wall was represented by just ten burnt posts. To the south of the doorway evidence of a burnt post-and-wattle wall survived but no definite corner was recognised.

An entrance to House 2 was located roughly mid-way in the west wall and was defined by two doorjambs (F2007, F2009) spaced 0.78m apart but with no *in situ* threshold bar (Fig. 3.8). The northern jamb was rectangular in section (0.18m by 70mm and 0.4m long) while the southern one was 0.26m by 0.18m and 0.56m long and both were charred. The socket of the southern jamb had been cut into the fill (F2092) of Pit 4b (see above).

INTERNAL FEATURES

The excavated remains of House 2 straddled both areas of excavation (the early excavation and later salvage excavation) and this, together with disturbances caused by the digging of the castle moat and overlying eighteenth-century structures, has rendered it difficult to definitively identify associated features and deposits at this level. The remains of a hearth (F1159) stratified above thin deposits of charcoal and clays containing ash, charred wattle, mussel shells and animal bone may be associated with the use of House 2 (Figs 3.8, 3.10, 3.13; Pl. 3.14). Just the north-eastern quadrant of the hearth had survived, defined by an arc of eight kerb stones. The lowest fill (F1165/F1166) of the hearth, up to *c.* 80mm deep, was a mixture of brown sand and burnt clay with frequent charcoal. It sloped from north to south and midway across the hearth it had slumped by 80mm due to collapse of the underlying fill of Pit 6 (see above Phase 4c) (Fig. 3.13). The upper layer within the hearth (F1151) comprised burnt clay and sand. Overlying the hearth was a mixed layer of clay, ash, charcoal and sand (F1150) into which two stake-holes (F1132, F1134) had been cut (Fig. 3.8).

No other structural features had survived within the excavated remains of House 2 but a range of clay deposits with inclusions of charcoal, shell, bone, ash, gravel, wood and wattle fragments were associated with use of the house. A number of artefacts were recovered from these deposits: an iron spearhead (E296:48516), two bone pins (E296:48515, 48520), a worked bone object (E296:48514), a square-headed iron nail (E296:48510), a wooden peg (E296:48599), a fragment of a composite antler comb (E296:48511), a wooden pin (E296:48597), an unidentified wooden object (E296:48586), a piece of twisted gold wire (E296:48520), a lignite bracelet (E296:48525), a hone (E296:48517), a bone needle (E296:48523), an iron barrel padlock key (E296:48518), a fragment of an amber bead (E296:48522), a rectangular amber pendant (E296:48526), a wooden stave (E296:48588) and a glass bead fragment (E296:48527). Two fragments of human bone and the broken crown of a human tooth were also recovered from these deposits (see Chapter 5). Beetles identified from these floor deposits would have been introduced from outside and were associated with animal excrement and rotting organic plant material. Mites and fly puparia were identified in possible bedding material comprising ferns and mosses (see Chapter 7).

EXTERNAL FEATURES

The remains of a wattle panel (F2034) were found outside the north-west corner of House 2 (Fig. 3.8; Pl. 3.15). This panel measured 0.8m by 0.5m and a piece of leather (E296:48576) was found associated with it. Overlying the wattle remains were two deposits (F2032, F2033) of clay with charcoal flecks, wood fragments, straw and leaves. Other deposits contemporary with House 2 extended outside the west wall including a cluster of stones (F2025) that covered the fill of Pit 4b (Phase 4b) and from which a fragment of a wooden

Pl. 3.13 North wall (F2030) of House 2 (Phase 5) with posts of property boundary (F2041) visible just above the ranging rod; from north.

Pl. 3.14 Remains of hearth (F1158) within House 2 (Phase 5) with arc of kerbstones; from south. Eighteenth-century drain and associated disturbance on right.

disc (E296:48585) was recovered and layers of ash, charcoal and burnt clay (F1117, F1170, F2026) that may have derived from the burning of the west wall of the house.

Phase 6

This final surviving phase of Viking-age activity is represented by the remains of House 3, which replaced House 2, and its associated deposits. There was no evidence for a property boundary at this level.

HOUSE 3

Limited remains of the north and west walls of House 3 survived in the area excavated (Fig. 3.9). The north wall extended for *c*. 1.5m from the north-west corner and comprised a single row of posts and wattle (F2012) that had been interwoven with the underlying north wall of House 2 (Pl 3.16). The posts ranged from 40mm to 80mm in diameter and were spaced *c*. 0.2m apart. The surviving wattle strands were between 60mm and 0.44m long. An iron knife (E296:50004) was found in association with the north wall. The west wall (F2001), including a doorway could be traced for *c*. 4.3m. The timber jambs of the doorway and a threshold bar had survived *in situ*. The northern jamb (F2004) was a rectangular post measuring 0.16m by 0.1m and was 0.49m long while the southern jamb (F2002) was more irregular in shape measuring 0.36m by 0.1m by 0.62m long (Fig. 3.9). Both jambs had been set into sockets cut into the underlying Pit 4b. The threshold bar (at 13.29m OD) was a single piece of wood 1.02m long by 60mm wide that abutted the southern jamb but stopped 0.14m short of the northern jamb. Two smaller pieces of wood lay beside the threshold bar. Only ephemeral traces of the wall survived extending from the doorway to the north-west corner of the house. These comprised a number of stakes and fragments of wattle. The area to the south of the doorway had been badly disturbed but some stakes and wattle could be traced for *c*. 0.8m. A number of artefacts were found in association with this section of the west wall: an unfinished amber proto-bead (E296:48505), an iron nail (E296:48506), three pieces of leather (E296:48575), a woollen textile fragment (E296:48598), three bone needles (E296:48500, 48501, 48502), a bone awl (E296:48503) and a bone blade (E296:48504).

INTERNAL FEATURES

Due to extensive disturbance there were few surviving internal features in House 3. There was no definite hearth, but an ash spread (F2010) was recorded in an area roughly corresponding with the hearth in underlying House 2. This ash spread contained two antler comb fragments (E296:48507, 48508). A number of stakes (F2018) to the north-east of the doorway may be contemporary with the use of House 3 and the remains of a wooden plank (F2019) were found between them and the doorway.

A series of deposits were recorded in section I-I1 that belonged to Phase 6 and had survived the extensive disturbance caused by eighteenth-century activities (Fig. 3.10). These deposits would have accumulated within House 3, the earliest of which was a lens of burnt clay (F826) over which thin layers of clay with varying amounts of charcoal, ash, stones and shell had been deposited (F821–F825) (Figs 3.10, 3.13). Many of these deposits are likely to have been associated with a hearth. Two sherds of pottery, a glazed Ham Green base sherd (E296:48110) and an unglazed Dublin cooking ware sherd (E296:48110) were recovered from the uppermost layer (F821) belonging to Phase 6. These, together with the pottery recovered from overlying deposit F820, must be attributed to the truncation of these features by the adjacent eighteenth-century drain and wall trench (Fig. 3.10). Three stake-holes (F1114, F1122, F1124) were recorded cut into F820 (Fig. 3.9).

Pl. 3.15 Wattle panel (F2034) outside north-west corner of House 2 (Phase 5).

Pl. 3.16 Remains of post-and-wattle north wall (F2012) of House 3 (Phase 6); from north-west

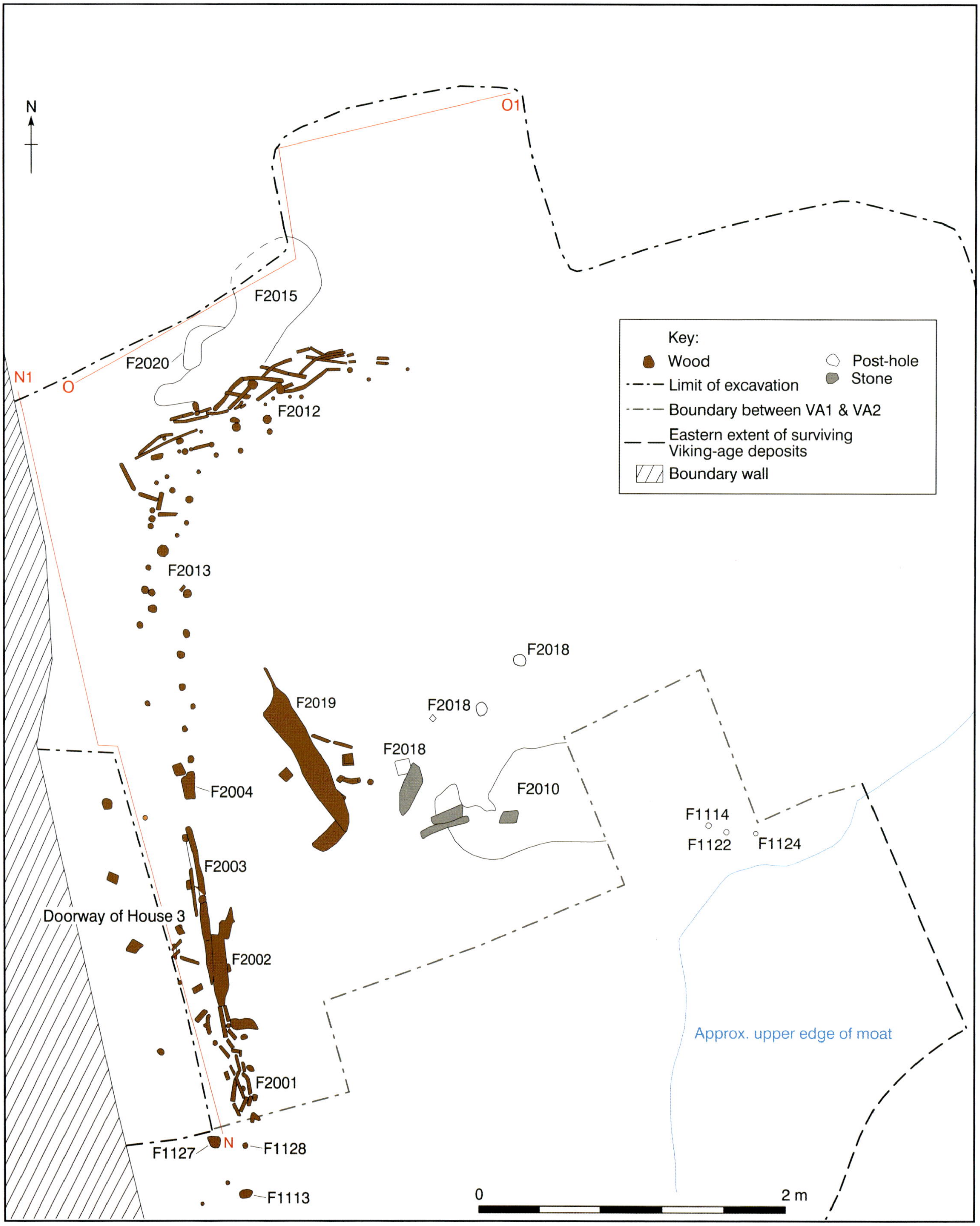

Fig. 3.9 Cork Tower, Cutting 2; Phase 6 features including remains of House 3.

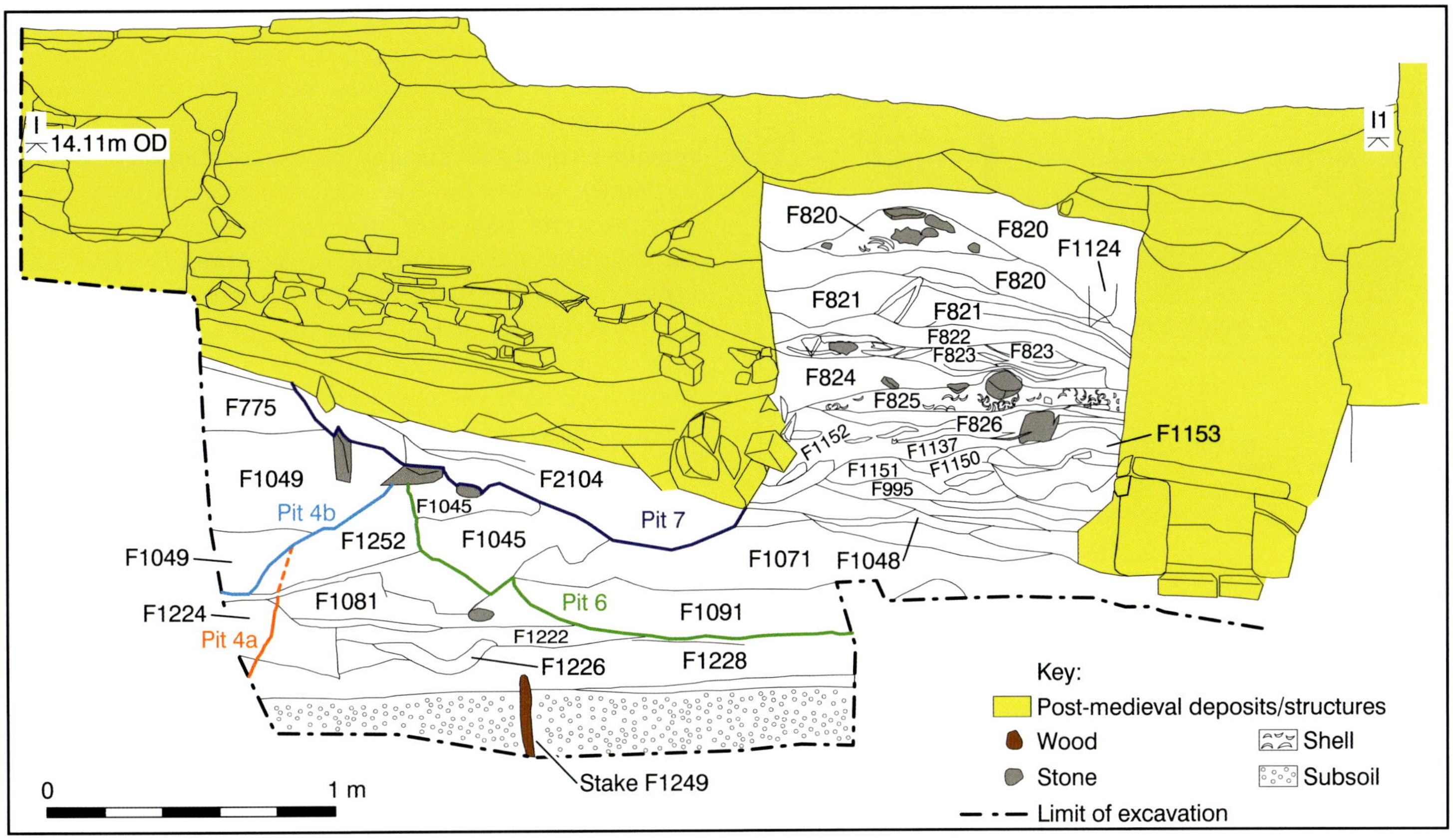

Fig. 3.10 Cork Tower, Cutting 2; south-facing section I-I1 (for location see Fig. 3.4).

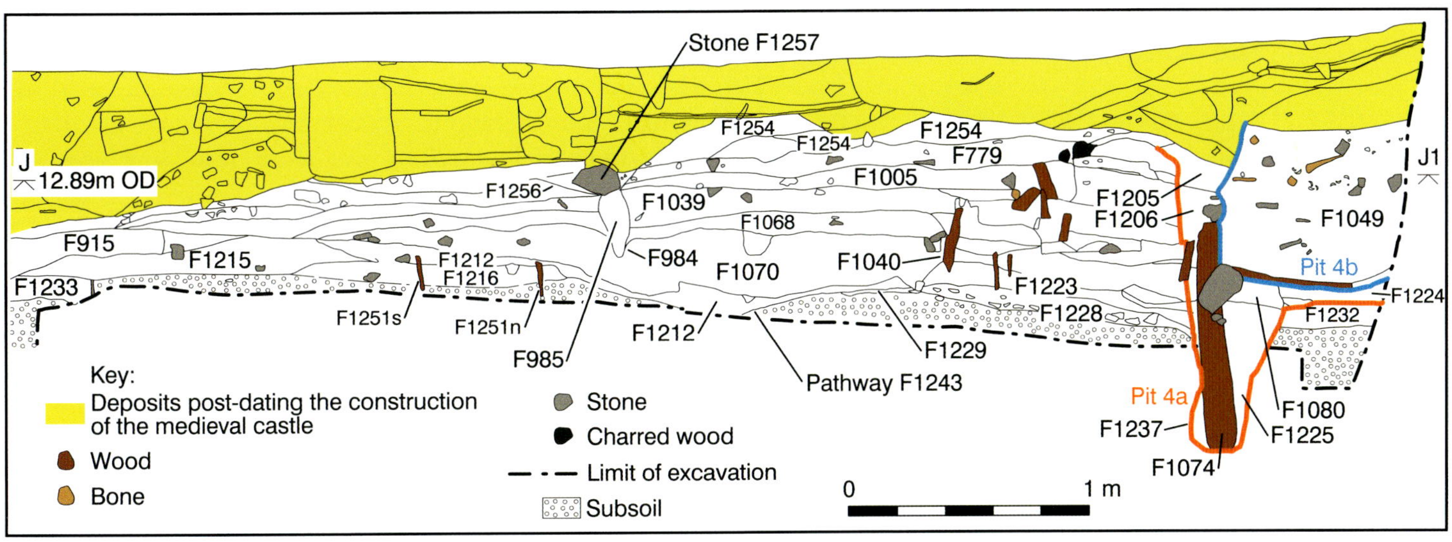

Fig. 3.11 Cork Tower, Cutting 2; east-facing section J-J1 (for location see Fig. 3.2).

EXTERNAL FEATURES

Some features external to the plan of House 3 were possibly contemporary with Phase 6. A deposit of charcoal and ash (F2015), from which a piece of worked wood (E296:48596) and an iron nail (E296:49509) were recovered, lay against the north wall of the house (Fig. 3.9). At the northern edge of the area excavated, a soft brown organic clay with a large amount of shell (F2021) contained the remains of an antler saw (E296:48513), part of an antler comb (E296:48512) and a wooden object (E296:48583) (Fig. 3.16). A deposit of brown silty clay with an abundance of hazelnuts (F2008) lay to the west of the doorway of House 3 and contained a fragment of a turned wooden plate (E296:48581).

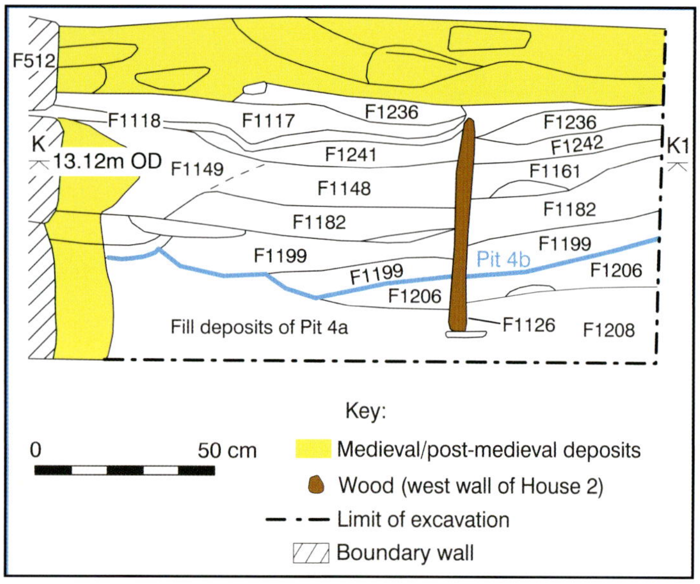

Fig. 3.12 Cork Tower, Cutting 2; south-facing section K-K1 (for location see Fig. 3.4).

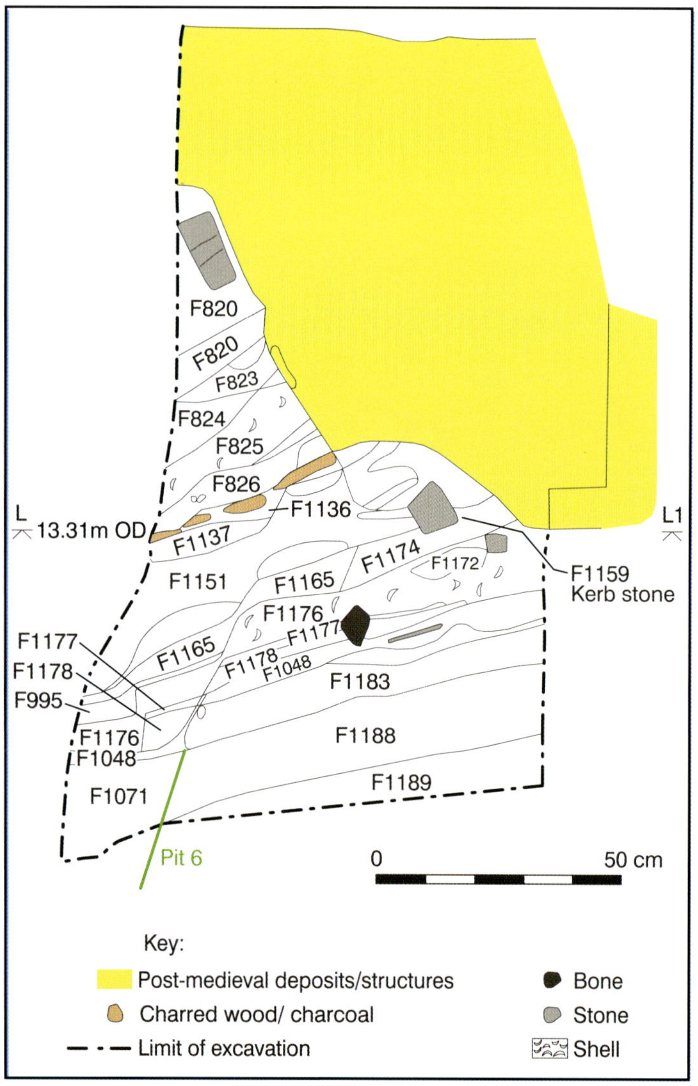

Fig. 3.13 Cork Tower, Cutting 2; east-facing section L-L1 (for location see Fig. 3.8).

INTERPRETATION

Although limited in area and cut away on the east by the thirteenth-century castle moat and on the west and north by nineteenth-century walls, these Viking-age deposits provide a significant insight into the development of early settlement in Dublin. The stratified remains of domestic structures and associated artefacts represent a sequence of six phases of activity ranging in date from the late ninth century to the late tenth/early eleventh centuries.

The earliest evidence of activity comprises features cut into the subsoil, which in this area is at *c.* 12.2m OD and would have been the upper south-east facing slope of the ridge. Given the ongoing debate about the location and extent of the ninth-century Viking *longphort* (ship camp) and subsequent expansion of the Viking settlement of Dublin, this evidence for early Viking-age domestic settlement is of particular significance (see Chapter 9 for full discussion). The nature of the Phase 1 evidence, dated to AD 770–968, suggests activity associated with nearby domestic habitation, probably in backyards where cess material and refuse were dumped. The presence of metalworking residue including smithing hearth cakes and tuyère fragments indicates iron smithing was carried out in the immediate environs.

The next phase of activity (Phase 2), dating roughly to the early tenth century, includes the construction of a surfaced pathway running east-west, which is the first indication of the creation of separate plots. Timber posts and stakes associated with the pathway further reinforce the suggestion of a boundary. To the north-east of the pathway, close to the edge of the castle moat, fragmentary structural remains may belong to a workshop or shelter associated with industrial activities including iron smithing and possibly glass working.

The first definite property boundary appears in Phase 3, when a post-and-wattle fence was constructed running east-west just to the north of the earlier pathway. This divided the area into Plot 1 to the south and Plot 2 to the north. No structural remains were recorded in Plot 1 but the silty clay deposits contained a small amount of metalworking debris, pieces of wattle, straw, twigs and animal bone.

House 1, the first house to be constructed in Plot 2, fits the classification of Type 1 Viking-age houses in Dublin as defined by Wallace (1992). This is the most common house form in the Viking archaeological record in Ireland and has been described as the 'Dublin house *par excellence* throughout the tenth and eleventh centuries and possibly a type that endured at least until the coming of the Anglo-Normans in the second half of the twelfth century' (*ibid.*, 1, 9). The Type 1 house was typically rectangular in plan with post-and-wattle walls, rounded corners and usually a doorway in each end. The thatched roofs were supported on

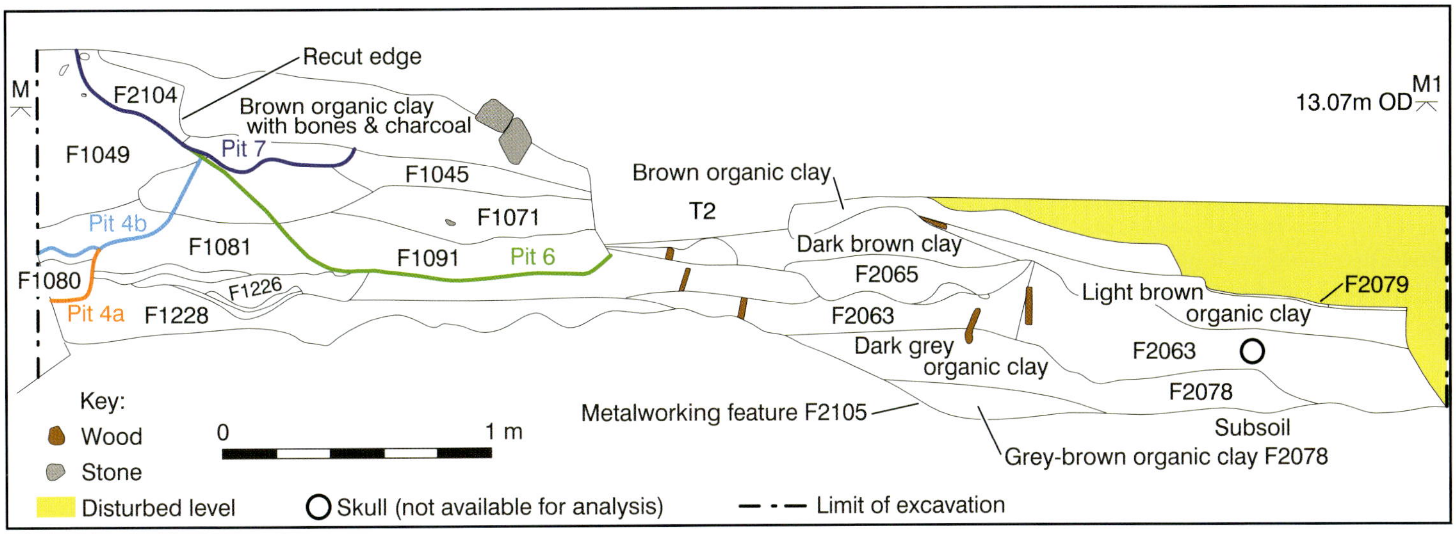

Fig. 3.14 Cork Tower, Cutting 2; south-facing section M-M1 (for location see Fig. 3.4).

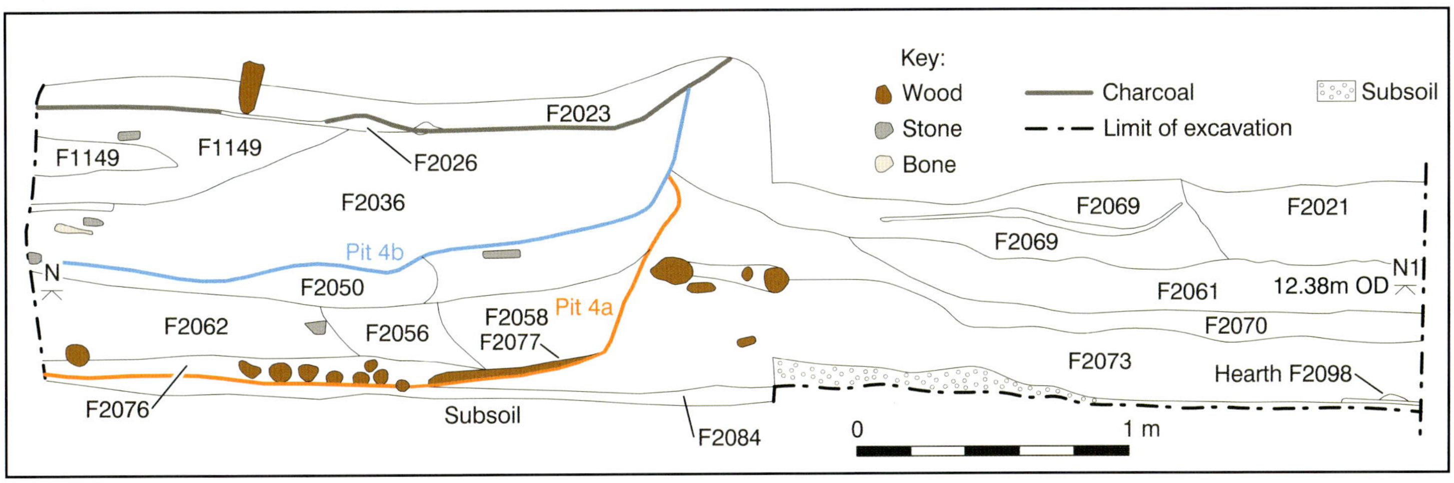

Fig. 3.15 Cork Tower, Cutting 2; east-facing section N-N1 (for location see Fig. 3.9).

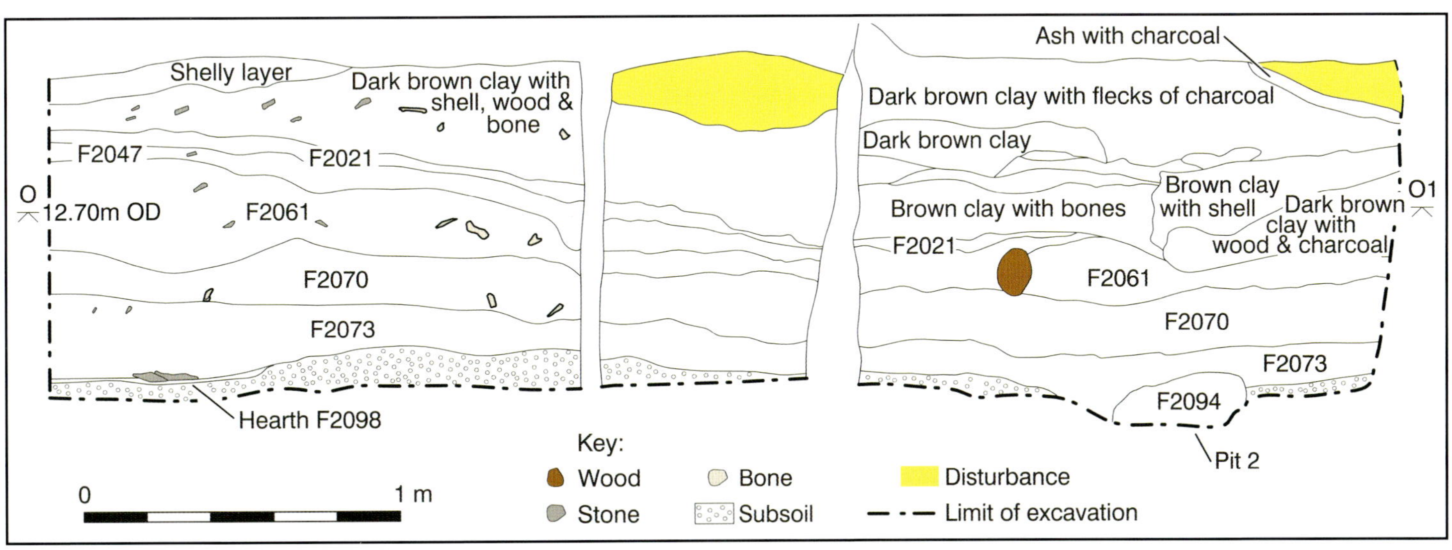

Fig. 3.16 Cork Tower, Cutting 2; south-facing section O-O1 (for location see Fig. 3.9).

stout internal posts. The floor space was divided into three longitudinal strips – a central walkway flanked on either side by a narrower raised bedding/seating area which was often separated from compartmented corners. The central hearth was often stone-kerbed or paved (*ibid.*). Although badly disturbed, sufficient survived of House 1 to determine its width as *c.* 5m and, assuming the stone-lined hearth was centrally placed, its length can be estimated as *c.* 6.4m, giving a floor area of approximately 32m^2. This places House 1 in the small to medium category of Type 1 houses as recorded in nearby Fishamble Street (Wallace 1992, Part 1, 11). The north-west corner of the house was best preserved, where a wattle mat had survived in what would have been a corner compartment. A small wooden loom piece and a fragment of woollen cloth were found on this wattle mat, suggesting weaving activities within the compartment; a fragment of a crucible and a tuyere were also found in association with the mat. Traces of two internal partitions had survived, one of which extended east-west and defined the edge of the seating/bedding 'aisle' while the short north-south partition located between the doorway in the west end and the central hearth possibly acted as a draught excluder. The internal floor surface appeared to have been covered with a fine layer of black gritty ash at the time of construction.

Following the demolition/abandonment of House 1, the associated property boundary was also largely covered over, although a few of its posts that projected above the covering clays were incorporated into a more ephemeral wattle fence that burnt down and was not replaced. This area again seems to have reverted to use for the disposal of refuse and cess material belonging to nearby habitation. A large timber-lined pit (Pit 4a) was constructed (and later recut – Pit 4b) and filled with what appears to be mostly domestic refuse with just a small amount of metalworking residue. Three smaller pits were subsequently cut and filled with similar deposits, with one (Pit 6) containing faecal material. A spindle whorl, two bone needles and a bone pin indicate work with textiles, while a small number of tuyère fragments and metalworking residue point to a continuation of industrial activity in the area. The clay deposits associated with this phase of activity (Phase 4a–c) had well-preserved organic inclusions including wood shavings, ash, charcoal, nuts, shell, grass, moss, straw and animal bone, suggesting a damp muddy environment in the immediate environs. Two radiocarbon dates were obtained from animal bone recovered from these pits but Bayesian analysis indicated these bones must be the result of residual deposition. Stratigraphically, a mid/late tenth-century date can be suggested for this hiatus in house building.

House building recommenced in Phase 5 with the construction of House 2 overlying the pits but almost exactly on the footprint of House 1 (Phase 3), suggesting a continuity of planning and building layout in this area. No evidence of a property boundary between Plots 1 and 2 survived but a post-and-wattle fence was incorporated within the north wall of House 2, suggesting a boundary between Plot 2 and another plot to the north. The fragmentary remains of House 2 included a doorway in the west end and the remains of a stone-kerbed hearth may be associated with the use of the house. The burnt and charred posts and wattle indicate that House 2 was destroyed by fire.

House 3 (Phase 6) was built to replace House 2 and this represents the final phase of Viking-age activity for which evidence survived in this area. There was little time lapse between these final two phases as the post-and-wattle north wall of House 3 incorporated elements that survived *in situ* of the north wall of House 2. Extensive disturbance caused by medieval and post-medieval activity meant that little survived of House 3 other than its north-west corner and the doorway in the west end wall.

Chapter 3.2
The Powder Tower area, Cutting 1: the eastern town defences

Introduction

Cutting 1 in the Powder Tower Area (Excavation E324) encompassed much of the surviving base of the Powder Tower, the circular north-east corner tower of the medieval castle, as well as part of the castle moat and the city wall north of the tower. The area with pre-castle deposits was confined to a circular area within the Powder Tower (Fig. 3.17; Pls 3.17, 3.18). When the Powder Tower was built in the early thirteenth century, the foundation trench for its massive circular wall was cut down to bedrock, leaving this circular area of earlier deposits, up to 5.95m in diameter, encapsulated within the base of the tower. The lowest floor in the tower was above these deposits so that they were left *in situ*. In the eighteenth century, when the tower was demolished, its base was left in place to a height of 5.85m, which was well above the top of the 3.75m-high pre-castle deposits. These deposits consisted of the build-up layers of a succession of enclosing defensive banks of the Hiberno-Scandinavian town, which ran in a north-south direction at this point.

Once the upper level of these early deposits was uncovered (F160) and appeared to be the upper surface of a north-south bank, a wide east-west trench was initially excavated across them (Fig. 3.27; Pl. 3.23). When what appeared to be the lowest bank, the stone-faced bank (F427), was uncovered, a narrow east-west slot trench was excavated across it (Fig. 3.18; Pl. 3.21), but the remainder of this bank was left *in situ*.

Phase 1

PHASE 1A CLAY BANK AND PHASE 1B STONE-FACED CLAY BANK

The bedrock beneath the castle is of a type known in Ireland as Calp limestone (Marchant and Sevastopulo 1980). It consists of layers of fine-grained Carboniferous limestone interleaved with layers of black shale. In this area the surface of the bedrock stepped down from a maximum of 4.8m OD on the west side to 2.9m OD to the east. It is possible that this was the natural stepped-bedrock slope of the edge of the Poddle estuary around the ninth/tenth century AD (Figs 3.20, 3.21, 3.28).

The stone-faced clay bank (F427; Figs 3.18, 3.19, 3.28; Pls 3.18–3.21) which incorporated the Phase 1a clay bank sat directly on the bedrock. It was aligned north-south and only its external east-facing slope survived in this confined area within the tower. Its maximum surviving height was 2.76m on the west side and it is not known how much higher it may have been. The eastern edge of the bank was roughly in the middle of the area excavated, leaving an area up to 3m wide that would have been external to it. This area is below high tide level and therefore would have been open to the ebb and flow of water in the Poddle estuary. The stone facing of the bank, where best preserved on the south side, consisted of over twenty irregular courses. The facing (F514) of the northern half of the surviving bank had slumped forward in antiquity and had at the time been roughly repaired (Fig. 3.18; Pls 3.19, 3.20).

Pl. 3.17 Base of the Powder Tower during excavation with the Record Tower visible in background; from north.

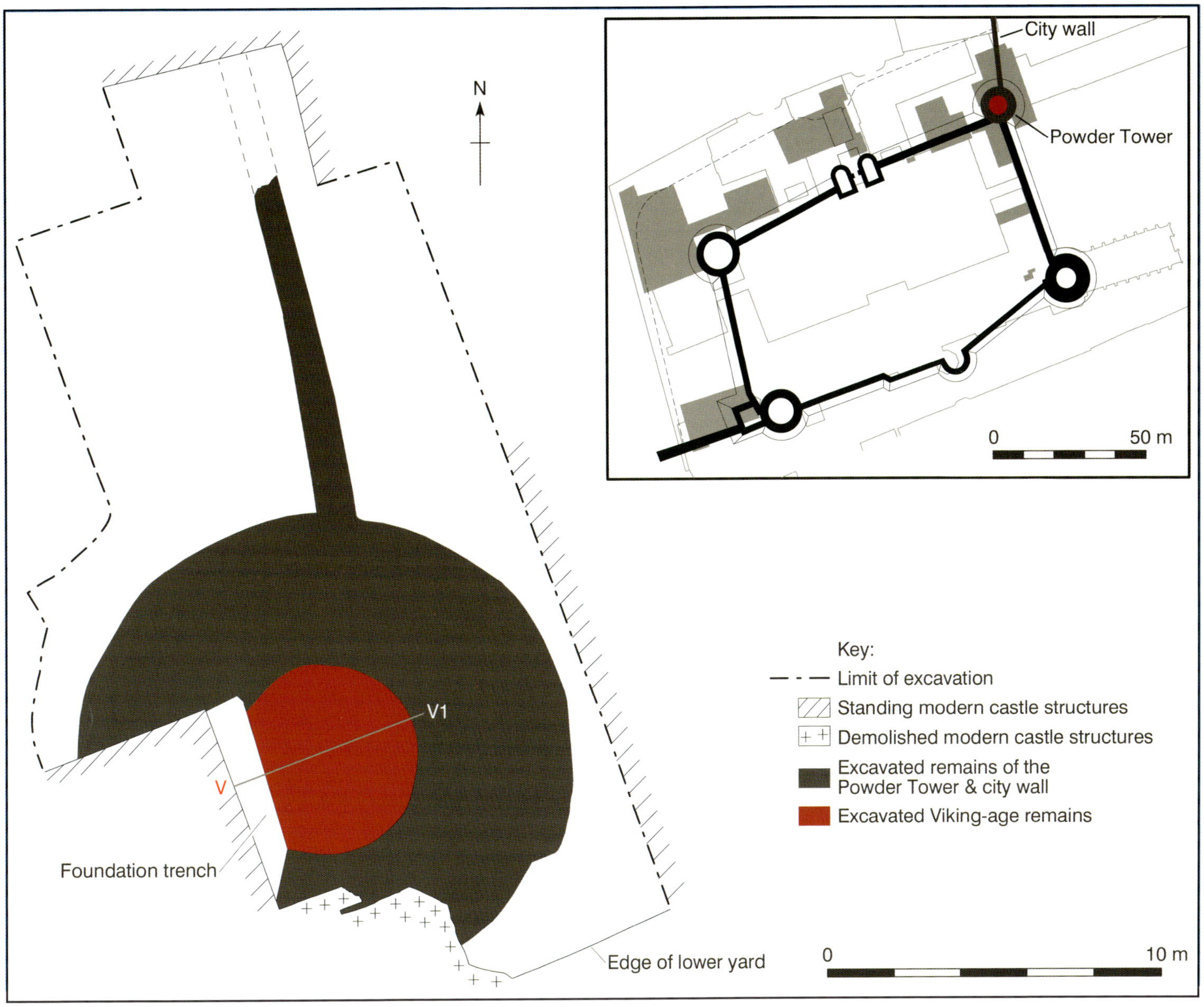

Fig. 3.17 Powder Tower, Cutting 1; location of Viking-age deposits.

Pl. 3.18 Remains of stone-faced bank (Phase 1b) revealed within base of the Powder Tower. Cross Block foundation at top left; from south-east.

At the time of the excavation, it was anticipated that this bank would be preserved for viewing by visitors to the castle and consequently only a narrow slot trench (F537) was cut into it, at a point just to the north of the well-preserved southern half. The clay layers that make up the bank were recorded in this trench (Figs 3.20, 3.21). The two basal layers were light-grey-green silty clays – F567, the primary layer, which had flecks of orange clay and lay on the bedrock, and F562, which contained some stones and also lay partly on bedrock. Above F562 was a thin layer of charcoal (F566). It is likely that these basal clay layers represent the earliest (Phase 1a) bank, with the overlying charcoal layer possibly representing a destructive burning. There is no evidence that it had a stone facing. This Phase 1a bank survived to a maximum height of 0.95m.

Pl. 3.19 Phase 1b stone-faced bank fully exposed within base of Powder Tower; from east.

Pl. 3.20 Phase 1b stone-faced bank during excavation; from north.

The Phase 1b bank consisted of further layers of clay deposited on top of the Phase 1a bank but in this case having an external stone facing to protect it from the tidal waters of the Poddle. The earliest of these (F561), a compact dark brown clay, was directly above the charcoal layer (F566). Two layers were stratified above F561, both being dark grey-brown organic clay with charcoal, bone and shell (F556 and F557) (Figs 3.20, 3.21). Above F556 was a grey sandy silt with shell and bone (F563). Above this was a thin layer (F560), a mottled grey clay with some small stones below a thick layer of a grey silty clay with stones, charcoal, bone and shell (F559). The uppermost surviving layer of the bank was F558, a mottled orange-brown clayey silt with stones, charcoal and shell. An organic deposit of grey-brown clayey silt with some wood fragments was noted between the lower stones of the facing of the bank.

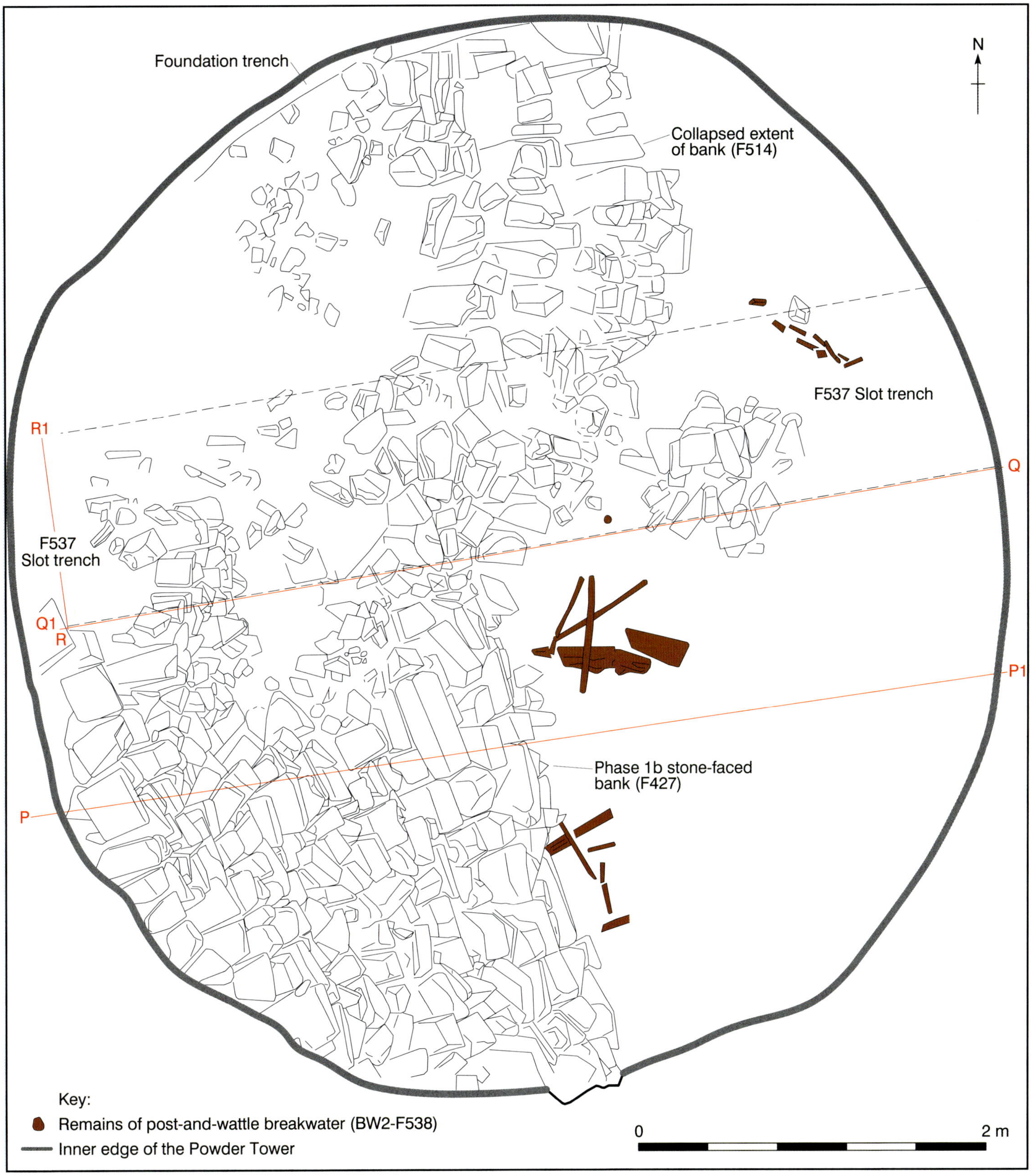

Fig. 3.18 Powder Tower, Cutting 1; Phase 1b stone-faced bank and remains of Phase 1a breakwater BW2.

Fig. 3.19 Powder Tower, Cutting 1; Profile (P-P1) of Phase 1b stone-faced bank (for location see Fig. 3.18).

WATTLE BREAKWATERS AND FORESHORE BUILD-UP

Remains of wattle fencing were recorded outside the bank and running roughly parallel with it. These are interpreted as breakwaters (BW 1–7) to protect the bank from the tidal waters of the Poddle and to assist in the build-up of mud here at the base of the bank. The earliest layers here were left *in situ* apart from those excavated in the slot trench (Fig. 3.20). The slot trench was given a context number (F537) because during its excavation a number of artefacts were recovered which cannot be assigned to a particular layer. These were a sherd of Portuguese red ware pottery dating from the thirteenth century (E324:13397), a fragment of amber (E324:13395), a bone pin fragment (E324:13394) and a crucible fragment (E324:13396).

BREAKWATER 1 (BW1)

The earliest deposit here was F539 (also recorded as F542), organic brown clay with inclusions of wood, shell, bone and charcoal. Above this was F548, a brown-yellow stony clay with patches of yellow clay, large stones, shell, bone, charcoal and wood. It also contained a driven wooden stake, 0.54m long and 50mm wide, the only encountered evidence for the earliest breakwater (BW1; Figs. 3.20, 3.28). This breakwater was contemporary with the Phase 1a bank. A brown organic gritty material with charcoal and shell (F552) appeared to have built up against BW 1, while covering both was a brown organic clay with bone, shell, wood and wattle fragments (F551).

Layers at this low level were discontinuous across the area excavated. A number of other layers predated F551 and these included F530, which produced a fragmentary bone comb (E324:13390), a rectangular antler plate, possibly part of a bow saw (E324:13391), a gaming piece of walrus skull bone (E324: 13392), a spindle whorl fragment (E324: 13393) and an amber chip (E324: 13389).

BREAKWATER 2 (BW2)

Above F551 were deposits F550 and F546. Deposit F550 was a loose grey gritty clay with wood, shell and charcoal. The remains of a small stake 0.18m long and 40mm wide (Fig. 3.20) marked the eastern limit of this deposit and was part of a second breakwater (BW 2). It appears that such midden material was dumped behind the breakwaters to help protect the bank from the tidal flow. Layer F546 was a gritty brown organic clay with shell, bone and wood, which partly overlay F550 and extended eastwards from it. It contained a lens of

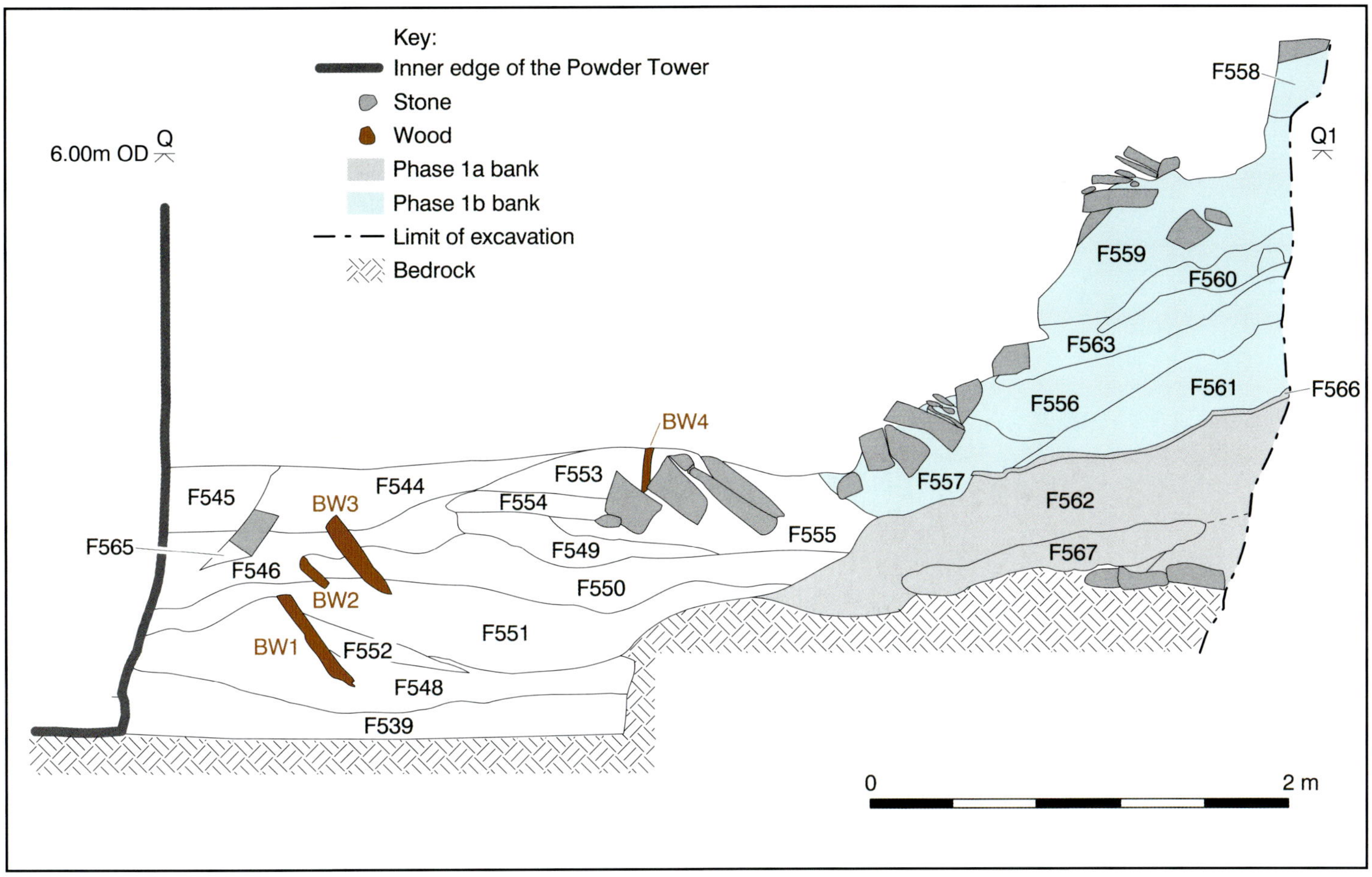

Fig. 3.20 Powder Tower, Cutting 1; north-facing section (Q-Q1) of slot trench (for location see Fig. 3.18).

grey gritty clay (F565). To the south of the slot trench, close to the base of the bank, a brown gritty clay with bone, stone and unworked flint (F535) was stratified above F550. A row of large stones (F536) close to the bank marked its eastern edge. These were left *in situ*. F535 produced a club-headed copper-alloy stick pin (E324: 13398) and a flint scraper (E324: 13399). This breakwater, which was only partially excavated, was possibly contemporary with the Phase 1a bank.

BREAKWATER 3 (BW3)

The evidence for BW3 (F547) consisted of a single stake recorded in section. The stake was 0.44m long and 90mm wide (Fig. 3.20). The bottom end was pointed. The stake was driven through deposit F551 (described above); the section suggests it was driven through deposit F550, and it must also have been driven through deposit F546 (described above). BW3 was probably the earliest breakwater feature contemporary with the Phase 1b stone-faced bank. Deposits most likely contemporary with BW3 include F553, grey-brown clay with charcoal, bone and shell, and deposit F554 (stratified below deposit F553), dark brown gritty clay (Figs 3.20, 3.28).

BREAKWATER 4 (BW4)

The most complete of the post-and-wattle breakwater features (BW4) was established on the surface of deposit F511, a brown organic gritty clay (Figs 3.20, 3.22, 3.28; Pl. 3.22). This breakwater (F509) consisted of ten posts, roughly 0.2m–0.25m apart, with interwoven wattle, extending for a distance of 2.8m on a north-east/south-west axis (Fig. 3.22). The longest section of the feature was established 0.7–0.8m from the bottom course of the stone-faced bank (Pl. 3.22). At the southern end the line changed direction, continuing westward for another 0.8m, after which it changed again, heading southward, parallel to and tight against the bottom edge of the bank. The main (2.8m long) section of the breakwater had collapsed slightly to the east. Between eight and ten separate strands of wattle weave were noted between the uprights. The wattle pieces varied greatly in length from 60mm to 0.54m and they were generally 20mm in diameter. The posts in this section of the breakwater varied in length from 80mm to 0.66m and they were 40mm in diameter. The posts appeared to get increasingly larger as they approached the first turn in the alignment, which altered the direction

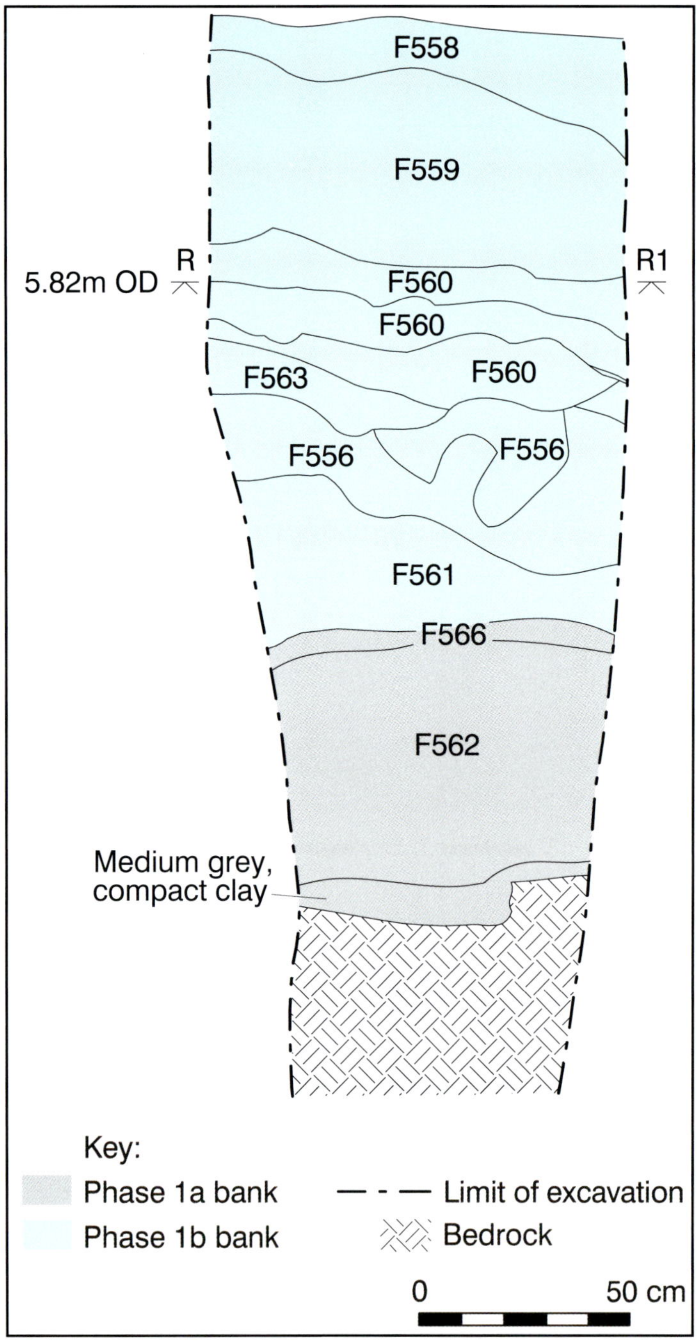

Fig. 3.21 Powder Tower, Cutting 1; east-facing section (R-R1) of slot trench (for location see Fig. 3.18).

Pl. 3.21 Slot trench (F537) excavated through stone-faced bank; accumulation of dark Phase 1a deposits visible against base of bank; from east.

of the breakwater towards the bank. The largest post was located at the turn; it was 0.84m long by 60mm in diameter and had a pointed end (Pl. 3.22).

The second section of the breakwater (0.8m long), perpendicular to the stone-faced bank, consisted of three posts, with eight to ten strands of wattle around them. The wattle pieces were of variable length, the largest 0.62m long; they were 20mm in diameter. The wattle of this section clearly overlapped with that of the longer section, demonstrating that the feature was of uniform construction (Fig. 3.22). The two easternmost posts were partly covered by a number of stones, which may have tumbled from the bank. The posts were 0.6m and 0.65m long and 40mm in diameter.

The third, southernmost, section of the breakwater was the least well preserved. The wattle strands were less complete, the most substantial piece 0.34m long. All pieces were 20mm in diameter. The wattle appeared to overlap with the middle section of the breakwater, confirming continuity of build. The most substantial upright of this section had an exposed length of 0.26m and was 40mm in diameter; it had collapsed slightly to the north (Fig. 3.22). A radiocarbon date of cal AD 904–1025 was obtained from an ash wood sample from BW4 (UBA-35663; see Chapter 8).

One of the posts of BW4 was discovered in the F537 slot trench (Fig. 3.20). It was driven through deposits F553 and F554 (described above).

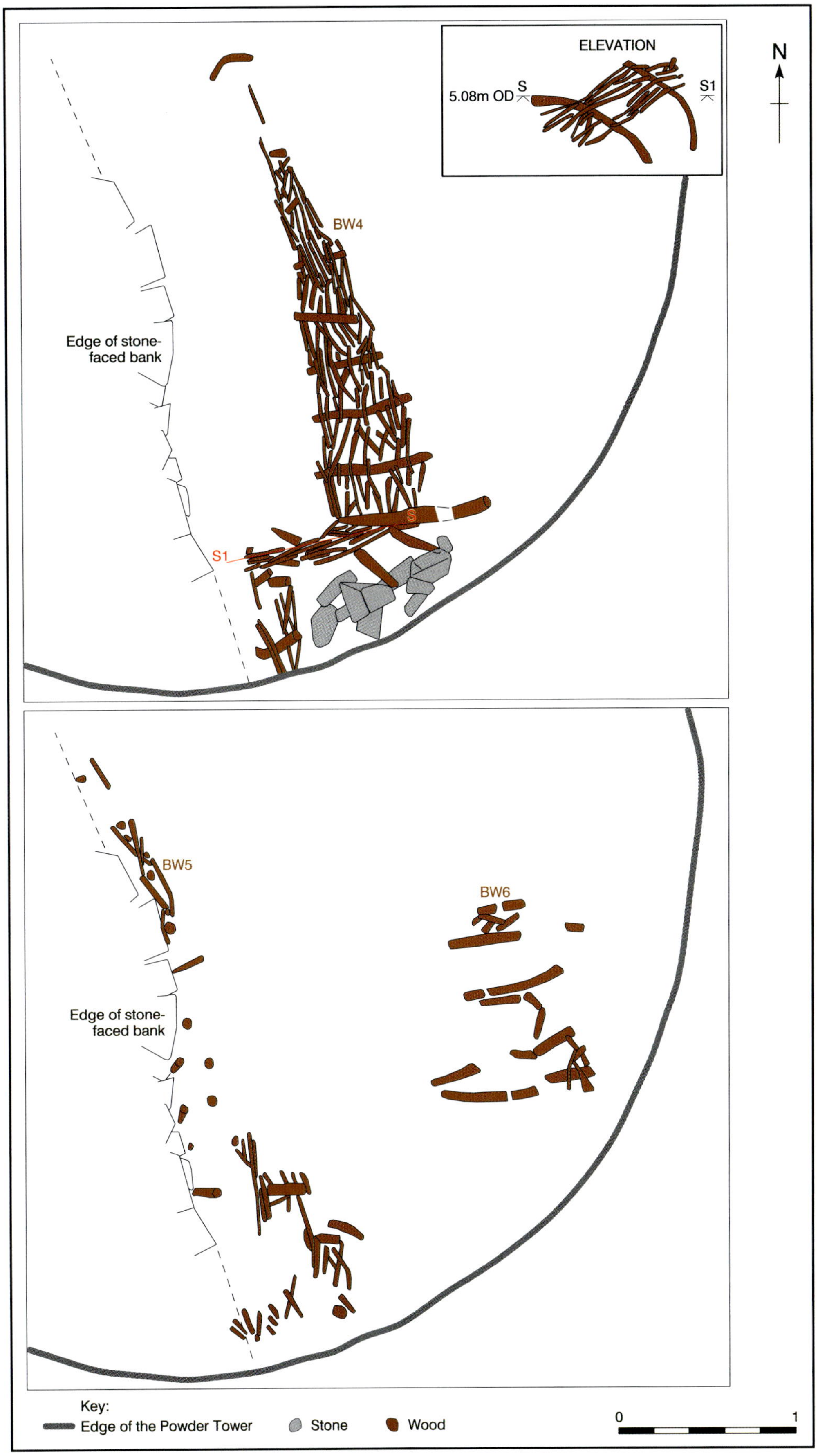

Fig. 3.22 Powder Tower, Cutting 1; (top) Phase 1b breakwater BW4, with (inset) elevation S-S1; (bottom) Phase 1b breakwaters BW5 and BW6.

Pl. 3.22 Detail of Phase 1b breakwater (BW4, F509) close to the base of Phase 1b bank visible at bottom; from west.

BREAKWATER 5 (BW5)

Another breakwater feature (BW5) was uncovered in a brown gritty deposit (F507) stratified on layer F511, about 1m west of BW4, closely set against stone-faced bank F427. This structure (F508) consisted of the remains of twelve posts (some of which had collapsed eastwards) and interwoven wattle (Figs 3.22, 3.28). It extended on a north-north-west/south-south-east axis for a distance of *c.* 3.3m close to the base of the stone-faced bank. The posts were between 0.24m and 0.3m apart and 40mm in diameter. The survival of the wattle was patchy. The existing strands were of varying length, up to a maximum of 0.6m and the pieces were 20mm in diameter. In the best-preserved section, at the southern end, the wattle weave survived between eight to ten strands deep.

BREAKWATER 6 (BW6)

Much of this area, apart from the stone-faced bank, which it abutted, was covered by layer F501 (also recorded as F516) (Fig. 3.28). It was directly stratified on deposit F506, grey gritty clay, and also stratified on deposits F511 and F507; deposit F506 contained an iron buckle pin (E324:13388), as well as a single fragment of human skull. Deposit F501 was rich organic brown clay with fragments of wood, bone, shell and charcoal flecks; it contained an antler tine end (E324:13387). Deposit F501 was the latest layer in which a breakwater for the stone-faced bank was discovered.

The remains of breakwater 6 (F515–BW6) consisted of the remains of six collapsed (to the east) posts and scanty remains of wattle lengths (Figs 3.22, 3.28). It was *c.* 1m long, aligned north-south. The uprights were between 0.1m and 0.3m apart, varied in length from 0.26m to 0.6m and were 40mm in diameter. The most substantial piece of wattle was 0.2m long and 20mm in diameter.

Two deposits, F503 and F504, are possible evidence for another breakwater at the level of layer F501 and abutting the edge of the stone bank (F427). F503 was a small deposit of degraded wood and iron staining. Deposit F504 was a badly preserved timber found within layer F501.

Phase 2

CLAY AND TIMBER BANK

In Phase 2 a low timber-reinforced bank was constructed against the edge of the stone-faced bank, using the deep accumulation of deposits that had amassed around the series of Phase 1b breakwaters as a base (Fig. 3.28; Pl. 3.23).

The deposits that constituted the Phase 2 clay bank were laid down on layer F501, the uppermost layer outside the Phase 1b bank. Larger deposits alternated with smaller ones. Deposit F497 was stratified on layer F501; it extended over most of the site and abutted the stone-faced bank (F427).

Pl. 3.23 Phase 2 clay and timber bank during excavation in central east-west cutting; poorly preserved east-west timbers are visible under the ranging rod; from east.

It was gritty grey silty clay, with some fragments of wood (recorded as F499). Two of the wood pieces were the remains of posts 40mm in diameter.

Three layers were stratified above F501: a purplish organic material (F500), a rich grey silty material (F502) and a mottled grey-brown silty sandy clay with occasional shells, bones and pieces of charcoal (F505), while two layers were stratified above F497: a grey-brown silty organic clay with shell and some wood fragments (F498) and a pungent organic mottled grey clay with charcoal and occasional shell (F492). The latter contained an unfinished bone pin (E324: 12998).

A mottled organic clay (F491) was stratified on deposits F492 and F498; it contained a fragment of an amber pendant (E324:13000) as well as some wattle fragments (F496). The wattle remains comprised a dozen or more interwoven strands over a distance of *c.* 1.44m, on a north-south axis. The longest wattle strand was 0.35m; the pieces were all 20mm in diameter. There were no uprights associated with the wattle remains, which suggests that the material was not part of an *in-situ* structure connected to the bank, but more likely a discarded section of a wattle screen deposited randomly in the core of the bank as it was being constructed (Fig. 3.23).

A deposit of brown organic clay (F470, also recorded as F484) was stratified on layer F491. The F470 deposit contained lenses of grey silty clay (F493) and produced a fragment of a jet/jet-like bangle (E324:12989).

TIMBER FRAMEWORKS

The excavation of the Phase 2 bank uncovered the remains of three levels of timber frameworks: FW1a (F495), FW1b (F494) and FW2 (F406).

FRAMEWORK 1A (FW1A)

The remains of a timber framework associated with the above deposits of the clay bank were discovered where deposits F470 and F492 interfaced (F495–FW1a), and at a slightly higher level in deposit F470 (F494–FW1b).

FW1a (F495) was a mixture of large (oak?) timbers in the north-east of the bank, and smaller more fragmented wood remains lying to the south-east (Fig. 3.23). The largest timber (aligned east-west) was 1.2m long and 0.12m wide; it sloped gently west-east, from 5.79m OD at the west end to 5.37m OD at the east end (timber a). A smaller timber lay parallel to it, 0.25m to the north. It was 0.54m long and 0.12m wide; this timber also sloped west-east (5.68m OD to 5.42m OD) (timber b). A third east-west timber lay 0.14m east of the largest timber; this was 0.8m long and 0.14m wide; it lay more or less flat on the bank – the west end (5.16m OD) was 20mm lower than the east end (timber c). Extending to the south of this for a distance of 0.6m was a trail of degraded wood up to 0.14m wide (timber d).

The remains in general were consistent with an interlaced gridwork of timber. A number of the FW1a (F495) wood pieces were registered as finds. The pieces retained for study were thirteen portions of rods (E324:10823) and eleven irregular fragments (E324:10822). A radiocarbon date of cal AD 984–1149 (UBA-35662; see Chapter 8) was obtained from a hazel wood sample from the F495 wood assemblage, suggesting a probable mid-eleventh-century date for the construction of the bank.

The more fragmentary wood pieces (roughly 30 pieces in total) in the south-east area of the bank, comprised six to seven lines of fragmented timbers aligned east-west across the middle of the bank. The lines were roughly parallel but spaced at varying intervals. The most substantial piece of wood (timber e) was 0.34m; it lay flat at 5.62m OD. They were generally 40mm wide, though a few were up to 80mm wide (Fig. 3.23).

FRAMEWORK 1B (FW1B)

The evidence for FW1b (F494) was uncovered in deposit F470 in the north-east area of the clay bank and consisted of 22 pieces of wood of varying shape and size, closely grouped together and covering an area measuring roughly 2.55m (north-south) by 1.9m (Fig. 3.24). The most substantial piece of wood was 0.48m long and 0.21m wide. The wood pieces were irregular and poorly preserved and the sense of an ordered arrangement, which is clear from the regular formation of the FW1a remains, is absent from the plan of the surviving remains. Some of the pieces are aligned north-south, others are on an east-west axis, and a few are overlapping.

A number of deposits made up the upper level of the clay bank. Deposit F474, stratified on deposit F470, was grey silty clay containing bone and shell; it contained a wooden disc (E324:13402). Deposit F475, sterile yellow silty clay, was stratified on deposit F474. Two deposits (F480 and F483) were stratified on deposit F470 in the north-east area of the clay bank. They were both yellow-brown shelly deposits. To the south-west, deposit F469 was stratified on deposit F470. It was grey silty clay with some bone, shell and charcoal.

All the above deposits were in turn stratified under layer F410, which covered the whole of the Phase 2 bank. The layer was gritty grey clay with some charcoal, bone and shell; it contained part of a decorated bone comb (E324:12980). A deposit (F482) of pungent yellow organic material was stratified on deposit F410.

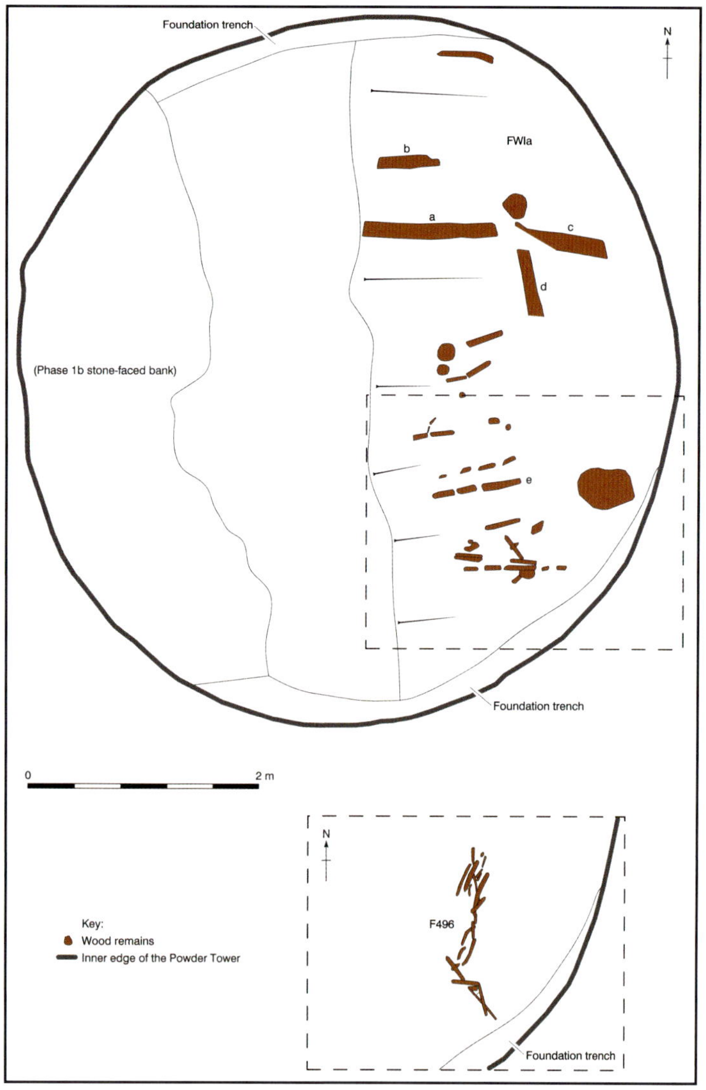

Fig. 3.23 Powder Tower, Cutting 1; framework timbers FW1a of Phase 2 bank with (inset below) wattle F496 stratified below FW1a.

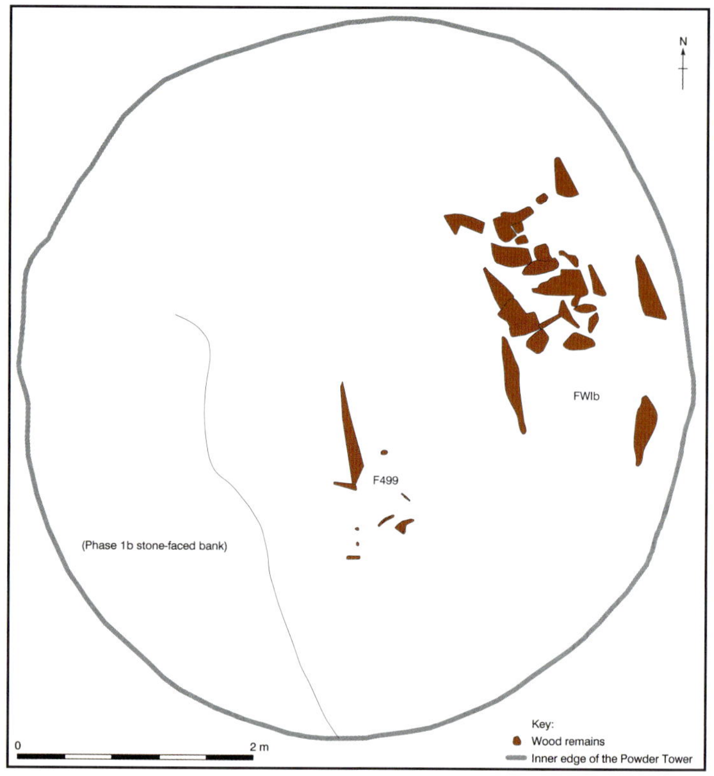

Fig. 3.24 Powder Tower, Cutting 1; framework timbers FW1b and fragmented wood F499 of Phase 2 bank.

FRAMEWORK 2 (FW2)

A deposit (F401) of mottled grey organic clay with some charcoal and bone was stratified on layer F410 and contained the following artefacts: the shaft of a bone needle or pin (E324: 12984), an antler tine end (E324:12985), pieces of flint (E324:12986 and E324:12981), and an iron nail head (E324:12983). Within F401 were two distinct lenses: a rough square, 0.5m across, consisting of decomposed iron (F476) and containing a tuyère fragment, and a grey-black clay with frequent shell (F464) containing a roof tile fragment (E324:13006). The wooden elements of FW2 (F406) were set into deposit F401. These comprised the uppermost elements of a timber framework in the Phase 2 clay bank (Fig. 3.25). The north-south elements of FW2 consisted of timber a, 1.02m long and 0.14m wide, at the top of the bank on the south side and a second decayed timber, 1.9m long and 0.2m wide, running parallel some 1.15m to the east (timber e). Further east was another larger outline of decayed wood (timber f). At right angles to these were three east-west timbers: the southernmost, 2.2m long and up to 0.14m wide (timber b), a second timber (timber c), lying 0.5m to the north, was 1.94m long and up to 0.16m wide, and a third short timber (timber d), lying 0.84m to the north, was 0.7m long and 0.12m wide. This framework sloped downwards to the east by about 0.3m and the manner in which FW2e overlay FW2c and underlay FW2b suggests that it was an interwoven timber framework (Fig. 3.25).

The most northerly east-west timber (Fig. 3.25, timber g) was 1.5m north of timber c and 0.66m north-west of timber d; it was 0.54m long and up to 0.14m wide; it had a slight west-east slope, from 6.09m to 5.99m OD. Fragmentary pieces of wood along the top of the bank suggest that the timbers originally extended along the full length of the bank. A small wooden dowel, 40mm in diameter, found 0.12m south of timber g at the northern end of the formation, was the only evidence for the pegs that would have held the timber framework in place. There were other small fragments of wood found along the bank at the same level. Although they did not link up with the main timbers, they were probably part of the framework.

A number of deposits of the clay bank were stratified on deposit F401. Deposit F400 was a rusty brown shelly deposit in the middle of the bank. Deposit F409, in the south-east part of the bank, was red-brown organic clay with frequent

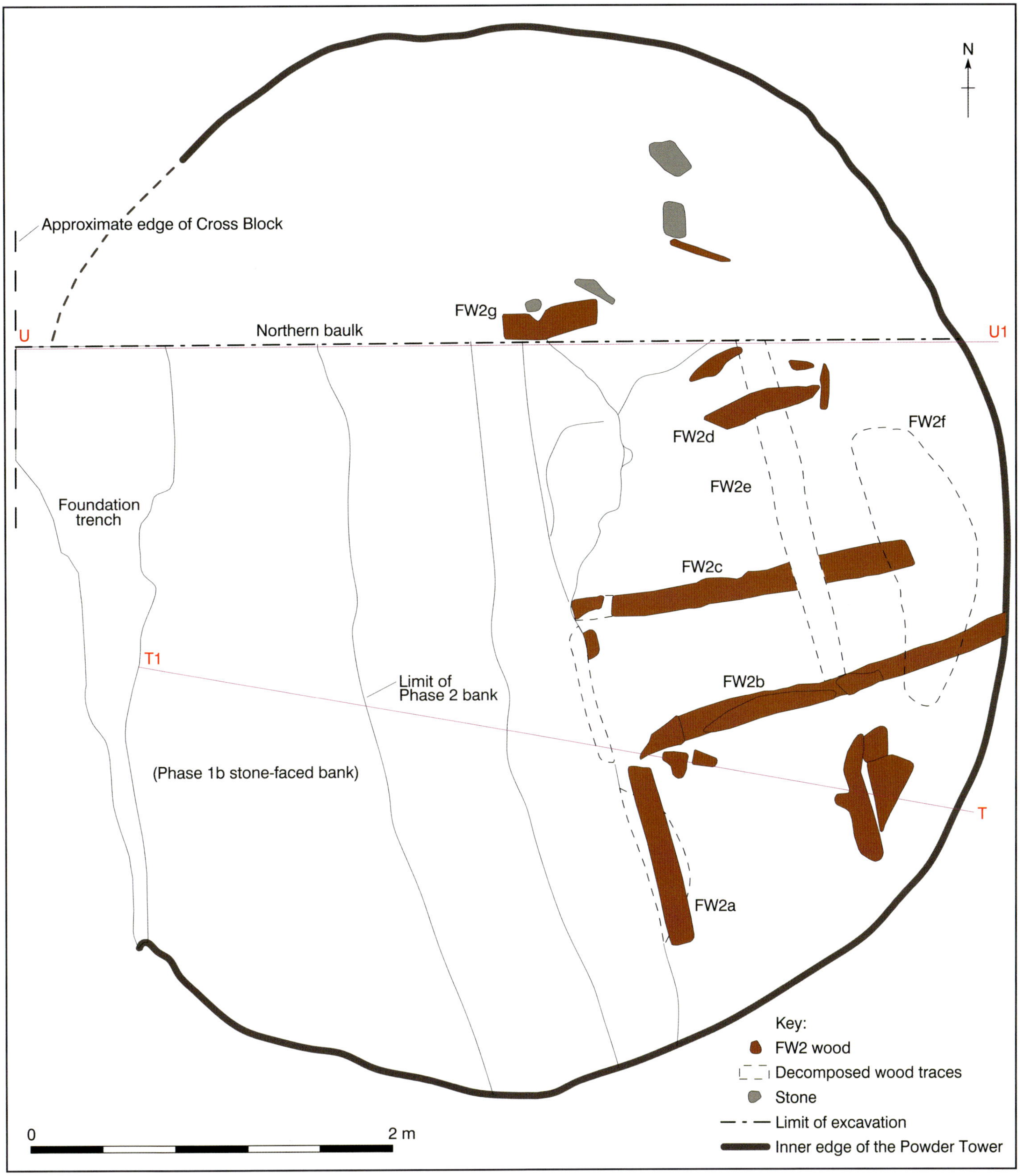

Fig. 3.25 Powder Tower, Cutting 1; framework timbers FW2 of Phase 2 bank.

wood, shell and bone. Deposit F413 was brown shelly clay at the bottom of the bank. Deposit F466 was yellow-grey clay, resembling redeposited subsoil, located in the north-eastern extent of the clay bank.

The above deposits were all stratified below deposit F197 (also recorded as F458). This was the latest deposit of the Phase 2 clay bank (Figs 3.26, 3.27). It was mottled gritty grey clay with bone, shell and charcoal. The part of the deposit numbered F458 contained a roof tile fragment (E324:12931).

The surviving evidence confirms that much use was made of timberwork in the construction of the Phase 2 bank, although this material was not well preserved. Because the eastern (i.e. riverside) face of the bank was obliterated by the building of the Powder Tower, it is not possible to say whether the bank was faced with a timber revetment. However, it is likely that the horizontal timberwork embedded in the bank was secured on the east side to a vertical timber retaining wall. In the absence of physical evidence for the river frontage of the Phase 2 bank such an interpretation is a matter of conjecture. The longer timber elements on the bank, aligned roughly east-west, were sloping to the east (towards the river). This sloping is consistent with the gradual deterioration of such a revetment of the bank over time with the revetment being pushed over to the east by the pressure of the clay behind it leading to a slumping of the eastern part of the bank.

Phase 3

POST-BANK LEVELLING

There was a further series of layers above the Phase 2 bank. These layers covered both the surviving top of the Phase 1b stone-faced bank and the Phase 2 bank that had been built against it (Pls 3.25, 3.26).

The lower Phase 3 deposits comprised material tipped directly over the exposed upper extent of the Phase 1b stone-faced bank (F427) and, further east, on the surface of the Phase 2 timber-reinforced bank. The deposits covering the Phase 1b stone-faced bank included F434, F417 and F429 (Fig. 3.27). Deposit F434 was reddish-brown clay/estuarine mud; it was cut by two stake-holes. Deposit F417 consisted of crushed shells in light grey-brown silty clay with some iron staining and was up to 150mm deep (Pl. 3.24). The deposit contained some pieces of tile and a sherd of unglazed French medieval pottery (E324: 12817). Deposit F429 was brown shelly material.

Another deposit (F422) was partially stratified on the Phase 1b stone-faced bank and in part on Phase 2 deposit F500. This was a green-brown gritty clay resembling redeposited subsoil, with some charcoal flecks, shell and bone. A sherd of pottery was recovered from deposit F422 (E324: 12988) and has been identified as a Dublin-type ware body sherd, dating from the thirteenth century. A deposit (F423, including lenses of charcoal F428) was stratified on deposit F422. It was green/grey-brown clay with some lenses of redeposited subsoil, bone, shell and charcoal flecks as well as stones; it also contained a lens (F428) of charcoal. Deposit F175 was stratified on the edge of the Phase 1b bank, overlying deposits F434 and F417 (Figs 3.27, 3.28). It was gritty grey clay with frequent shell, charcoal, bone and stone.

Another steeply sloped Phase 3 deposit (F198) was stratified on deposits F175, F417 and F429 (Figs. 3.26, 3.27, 3.28). It was greenish clay mixed with redeposited subsoil; it contained two pieces of curved roof tile (E324:12086–8). Deposit F455 (yellow redeposited natural clay) was stratified on deposit F429 and below deposit F452.

Deposit F196 (Figs 3.26, 3.27, 3.28), also steeply sloped, was stratified on deposits F198 and F183. It was mottled orange-grey clay. Deposit F176 (Figs 3.26, 3.27, 3.28), another steeply sloping deposit, was stratified on deposit F196. It was grey clay, quite gritty, with frequent shell, charcoal, bone and stone; up to 0.4m deep. Deposit F196 was also stratified on deposit F185 (green-grey clay). Deposit F196 was abutted by deposit F173 (grey organic clay similar to deposit F198).

Other lower Phase 3 deposits directly covered the surface (F197) of the Phase 2 clay and timber bank. These include deposits F199, F473, F463 and F459 (abutting deposit F429) (Figs 3.26, 3.28). Deposit F199 was brown shelly clay. Deposit F473 was grey-black silty clay deposit with frequent stone, burnt bone and shell; it contained a worked antler tine (E324:13005). A stake-hole was cut through the deposit. Deposit F463 was mottled light brown clay, and deposit F459 light brown clay. Deposit F191 (mottled grey clay) was stratified on deposit F199 (Figs 3.26, 3.28); it contained a perforated bone pin fragment (E324: 13228).

Deposit F183 was in part stratified on the surface of the Phase 2 clay bank (Figs 3.26, 3.27, 3.28). It was mottled

Pl. 3.24 Phase 3 shelly deposits (F417, F429) during excavation; from north-east.

brown-grey clay; it contained a perforated pig metapodia (E324:12857). A deposit (F452) was stratified between F429 and F183 (Fig. 3.27). It was grey-brown organic material with some clay content, bone and shell; it contained a Class 8 stud-headed copper alloy stick pin (E324:7352).

The lower deposits comprising the body of the Phase 3 level were sealed by layer F174 (Figs 3.26, 3.27, 3.28). It was red-brown organic clay with flecks of charcoal, bone and moderate shell; it contained a large hone (E324:11889) and a sherd of glazed medieval pottery (E324: 11985). Deposits F182 (Fig. 3.27) and F178 (Fig. 3.26; also recorded as F184) were stratified on deposit F174. Deposit F182 was greenish-grey clay; it contained three sherds of pottery – an unglazed south-east Wiltshire body sherd of twelfth-century date (E324: 13224) and two sherds of French medieval pottery (E324: 13225 and 13226). The first of these sherds (E324:13225) is a Saintonge green-glazed body sherd, dating from the thirteenth to the mid-fourteenth century. The second French sherd (E324:13226) is an unglazed rim sherd of Seine Valley white ware, dating from the eleventh century. Deposit F178 (Figs 3.26, 3.28) was thin orange-red organic material; it was in part stratified on deposit F180 (grey-brown organic material). Deposit F177 (Figs 3.26, 3.28), sloping south-north, was stratified on deposit F178. It was grey shell material with charcoal and bone and contained a sherd of glazed French pottery (E324: 11895). The sherd is a body sherd with applied thumbed strip of Seine Valley highly decorated ware, dating from the thirteenth century.

Deposit F174 was abutted by deposit F449 (brown shelly material with charcoal and bone). Deposit F448 (dark shelly material with frequent charcoal flecks and fish bones), abutting F182, was stratified on F449. Deposit F447 was stratified on F448; it was sandy brown clay with much charcoal and fish bone and contained a sherd of glazed French pottery (E324: 12855). The sherd is a green-glazed body sherd with applied strip of Seine Valley highly decorated ware, dating from the thirteenth century. Deposit F445 (a thin red layer similar to deposit F178) was stratified on deposit F447. Deposit F444 (Fig. 3.27) was stratified on deposit F445; it was brown/grey shell deposit with some charcoal and bone.

The entire body of the Phase 3 material was sealed by layer F160 (Figs 3.26, 3.27, 3.28; Pls 3. 25, 3.26). This layer (mottled brown clay with charcoal) was the latest context pre-dating the construction of the Powder Tower. Layer F160, the western extent of which sloped west to east, covered almost the whole of the interior area of the tower, measuring *c.* 5.55m (north-south) by 4.85m (Pl. 3.26). The edge of the layer was truncated around much of its circumference by the cut (F479) for the foundations of the tower, except along the western extent where it was cut by the trench (F57) for the foundations of the eighteenth-century Cross Block (Fig. 3.28; Pl.3.26); the middle of the layer was truncated by the insertion of a section of mortared red brick and stone foundation pad (F9). A spread of mortar (F166) and another of sand (F97) stratified on layer F160 were more than likely associated with the construction of the Powder Tower in the early thirteenth century.

Pl. 3.25 Phase 3 post-bank layers (F183, F174, F178, F160) visible in section; from north.

Pl. 3.26 Post-medieval brick and stone foundation (F9) cutting layer F160, on the surface of Phase 3 layers; from south-east.

Layer F160 contained two antler tines (E324:12683 and E324:12685) and five sherds of medieval pottery. The pottery included examples of Seine Valley white and highly decorated wares, Leinster cooking ware and Portuguese red ware. A rim sherd (E324:13406) of Seine Valley white ware, heavily stamped with a cross motif, is dated to the eleventh/twelfth century. A rim sherd (E324:12682) and body sherd (E324:12681) of Seine Valley highly decorated ware date from

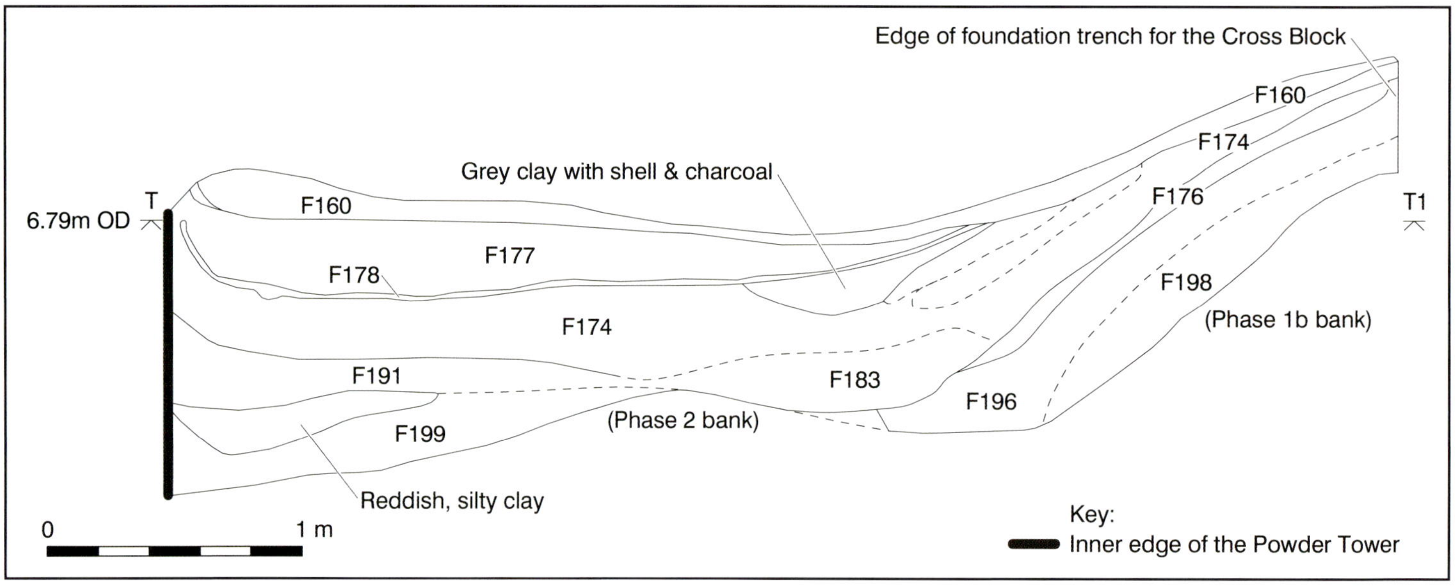

Fig. 3.26 Powder Tower, Cutting 1; north-facing section (T-T1) of Phase 3 levelling deposits (for location see Fig. 3.25).

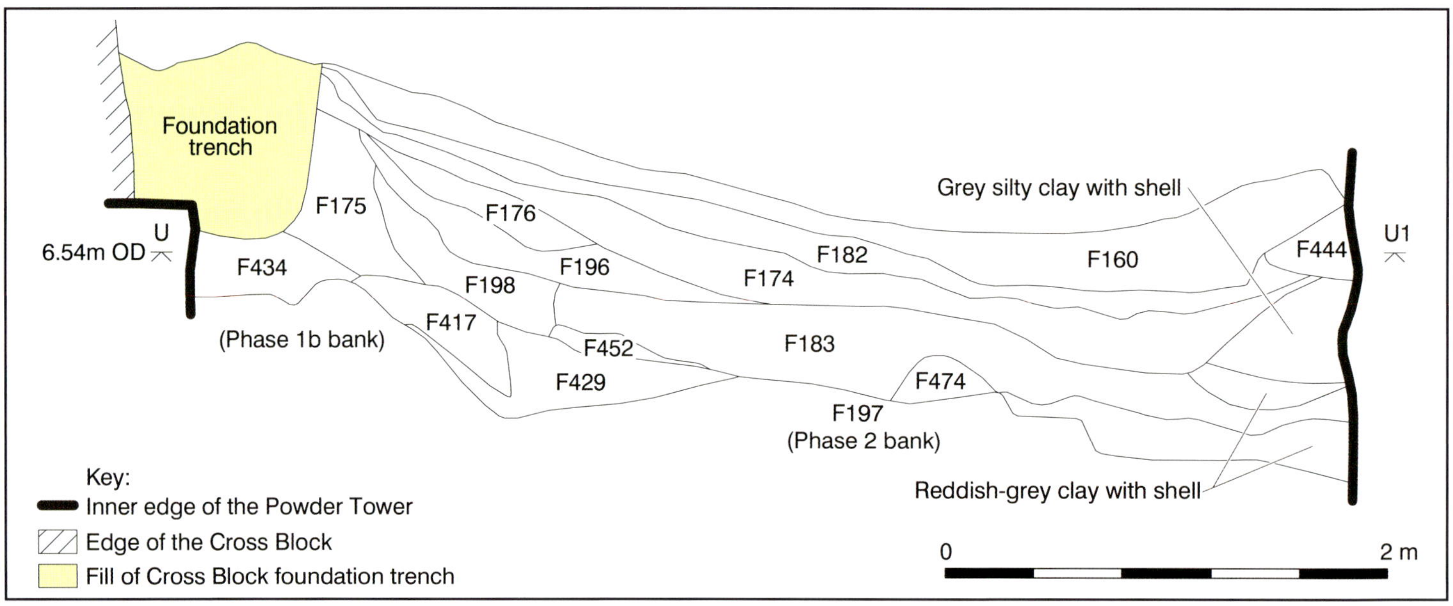

Fig. 3.27 Powder Tower, Cutting 1; south-facing section (U-U1) of Phase 3 levelling deposits (for location see Fig. 3.25).

the thirteenth century. A rim sherd (E324:12675/7–9) of Leinster cooking ware has a date range of late twelfth century to the mid-fourteenth century. A body sherd (E324:12680) of Portuguese red ware is dated to the thirteenth century. These sherds of pottery, consistent with the early thirteenth century, could have become trampled into the layer right up to the time when construction of the tower was getting underway, possibly as late as the late 1220s.

Layer F160 also contained human bones, consisting of up to 75 fragments of human skull and two loose teeth, comprising the largest assemblage of human remains from any Viking-age context at the castle. The assemblage represented a minimum of three individuals – two adults and a non-adult. The skull fragments of one of the adults, a male, exhibited at least three blade wounds causing death, and consistent with attempted decapitation (see Chapter 5).

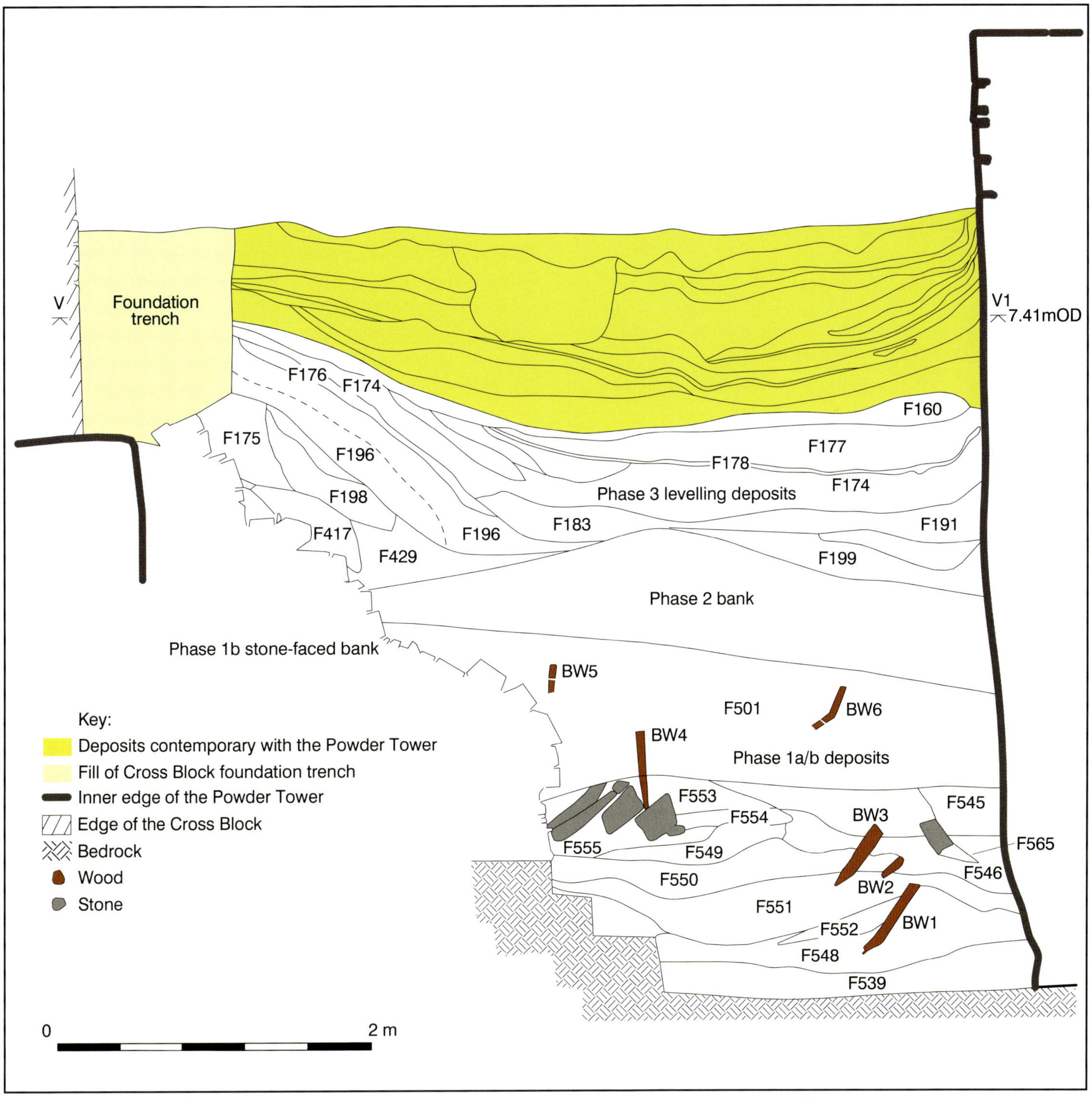

Fig. 3.28 Powder Tower, Cutting 1; composite south-facing section (V-V1) of Phases 1-3 deposits incorporating profiles P-P1, U-U1 and Q-Q1 (reversed) (for location see Fig. 3.17).

Interpretation

The limited size of this area, within the confines of the circular walls of the Powder Tower, makes interpretation of the features found difficult. What is clear is that these features were all part of, or related to, defensive banks or the wall of about 1100 on the east side of the Hiberno-Scandinavian town flanking the estuary of the Poddle. These defences were on roughly the same line as the later, thirteenth-century east curtain wall of the castle and east wall of the city.

The stone-faced clay bank (F427) was interpreted on site as the earliest bank at this location though it should be stressed that only one narrow trench was excavated into it. A reassessment of the section drawing (Fig. 3.20) suggests that there may have been an earlier clay bank incorporated within the stone-faced bank represented by layers F567 and F562, with a thin charcoal layer (F566) on its surface possibly indicating destructive burning. Layers F567 and F562 were laid directly on shelving bedrock, which was probably exposed on the shore of the Poddle estuary. This possible earliest bank in the sequence here is referred to as Phase 1a, while the stone-faced bank is called Phase 1b. The Phase 1a bank, as it survived, looks insignificant and non-defensive. It may always have been low and intended more as a flood barrier or may originally have been taller and suffered serious erosion from tidal high water in the estuary. At least two (BW1–2) if not three of the wattle breakwaters appear to be contemporary with it and are evidence of attempts to protect it from high water. These breakwaters appear to have had layers of soil and midden material dumped behind them to help protect and buttress the bank. Difficulties with protecting this bank from erosion may have led to the Phase 1b bank having a stone facing. This appears to have been a much more substantial bank than that of Phase 1a, even allowing that the latter could have been eroded, but the highest west part of it was cut away by the building of the Powder Tower. It was presumably surmounted by a strong wooden palisade (Fig. 9.1). The stone-faced bank also suffered erosion and slumping and required further wattle breakwaters (BW3–7) to protect it from high water. Most of the north part of the surviving portion had slumped outwards and had been repaired in a perfunctory manner. Radiocarbon dating indicates that the stone-faced bank (Phase 1b) was built in the tenth century with a date range centring on the middle of the century. The Phase 1a bank could possibly be early tenth century.

A problem with interpreting the evidence for the Phase 2 bank is that the outer or eastern edge of it was cut away by the building of the Powder Tower. Surviving timbers within it show that it was timber framed/laced and these timbers are likely to have been secured to an upright timber wall on the outer eastern face of the bank, forming a defensive barrier washed by high water in the Poddle estuary. Radiocarbon dating indicates that this bank was built in the eleventh century. Considering that the stone-faced bank, even in its incomplete state, rises higher that the Phase 2 bank, an alternative interpretation would be that the Phase 2 bank was merely a secondary protective bulwark in front of the stone-faced bank.

The layers of Phase 3 are also difficult to interpret. If it was bank material, it includes neither the inner nor the outer face and there was no evidence of timber lacing within it. The finds from these layers date mainly from the twelfth to early thirteenth century, possibly right up to the time the Powder Tower was built. There is good evidence from other excavations that by about 1100 a stone wall was built around Dublin (Wallace 2016, 138–42; Simpson 2000, 38–41). As no trace of it was found in this small area, its line must be either to the east or west. If to the west, it would have had the advantage of height and could have been built on well-settled material of the stone-faced bank. The layers of Phase 3 could have been built up by dumping over the wall and their make-up is consistent with this. If the wall was to the east, it would have been lower and lapped by high water. In that case the Phase 3 layers could be the result of dumping behind the wall to help build up the ground level.

The early-thirteenth-century east curtain wall of the castle, which formed the east end of Cutting B in the Cross Block (see Chapter 3.5 below), was the first defensive feature to impinge on or cut across the Viking-age habitation deposits excavated in that cutting. The line of the Viking-age defensive banks and wall, therefore, must at this point, over 30m south of the Powder Tower, have been further to the east possibly following an easterly curving protrusion of the shore of the Poddle estuary.

Chapter 3.3
The Powder Tower area, Cutting 2: urban layers and a possible street

Introduction

Cutting 2 in the Powder Tower area was located under the building at the east end of the north side of the Upper Castle Yard (Block 8), i.e. between the Justice Gate and the north-east corner of the quadrangle (Figs 1.1, 1.3). As part of the development, this building was demolished, apart from its south-facing façade which fronts onto the Upper Yard. Excavation below basement floor level soon revealed that remains of the north curtain wall (19.9m long) of the medieval castle survived here, running east-west at a slight angle to the building (Fig. 3.29; Pls 3.27, 3.28). The curtain wall was founded on boulder clay thus removing all pre-castle layers within its footprint apart from a few features that were cut into the subsoil and were visible where parts of the curtain wall had been completely quarried away by eighteenth-century builders. All surviving remains of the medieval curtain wall were left *in situ* during the excavation. The digging of the deep wide moat of the castle outside the curtain wall to the north removed all pre-castle deposits in this area. Therefore, the only area where pre-castle layers could survive in Cutting 2 was in the long narrow east-west strip between the medieval curtain wall and the retained south wall of Block 8. This strip was divided into three by two north-south internal walls, which were also founded on subsoil. The resulting three narrow rectangular areas of pre-castle deposits (Areas A, B and C) were each boxed in by later walls. A fourth area of pre-castle layers (Area K) was excavated in an extension of the cutting at the south-west corner, outside the west wall of Block 8 and immediately south of the curtain wall of the medieval castle (Fig. 3.29). The curtain wall survived to a higher level here and was used as part of the foundation of the Justice Gate. As a result, the deepest pre-castle deposits in Cutting 2 survived here, though the area available for excavation was very small. Pre-castle features, cut into the subsoil and available for

Pl. 3.27 Remains of the north curtain wall of the medieval castle in Powder Tower Cutting 2; from east. The Viking-age deposits in Areas A, B and C survived between the upstanding eighteenth-century façade wall of Block 8 on the left and the curtain wall.

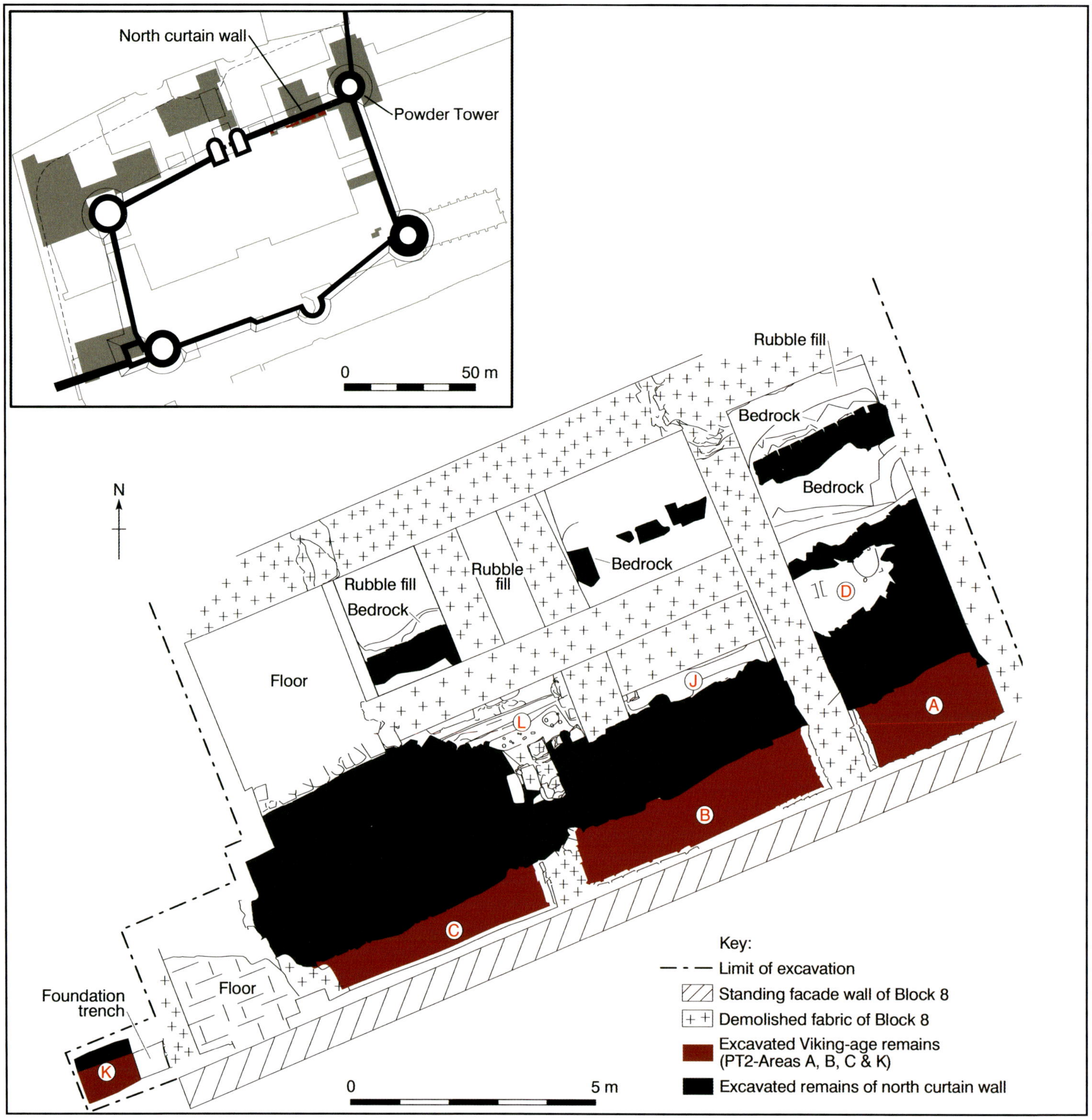

Fig. 3.29 Powder Tower, Cutting 2; location of Viking-age deposits.

excavation where the curtain wall was quarried away in the eighteenth century, were excavated in Areas D, J and L.

What needs to be emphasised about the pre-castle deposits in Cutting 2, almost all of which belong to the Viking-age period, is that the cutting of many wall foundations through them to at least subsoil level caused them to dry out, with consequent decay of wood and other organic remains. Area A, in the south-east corner, measured 2.9m by 1.4m and contained up to 1m of stratified deposits. Area B, immediately to the west, measured 4.95m by 1.2m and had a maximum depth of 0.45m of stratified pre-castle deposits. The middle part of this area had been disturbed

Pl. 3.28 General view of Powder Tower Cutting 2; from west. Remains of north curtain wall of medieval castle visible on right, roughly parallel with the façade of the eighteenth-century Block 8. Pre-castle deposits survived in the narrow gap between the curtain wall and later façade.

by a post-medieval feature some 1.25m by 1.25m (F257/F292) that was dug to subsoil and partly truncated a pit (F286). It may have been an unrecorded test pit from the 1960/70s. Area C, to the west of Area B, measured 4.6m by 0.75m and had a maximum depth of 0.5m of stratified pre-castle deposits. Area K measured 1.76m east-west by 0.76m north south and pre-castle deposits here survived to a depth of 2.45m.

The features and layers across these different areas are described below under the phase to which they belong. Only Areas A and K had evidence for phases beyond Phase 3, with Phases 4 to 8 represented in Area A and Phases 4 to 18 in Area K.

Phase 1

An intermittent surface of pebbles or cobbles was common to all four areas investigated along the inner edge of the north curtain wall. In the middle two areas (Areas B and C) the cobbles were found directly on the surface of the subsoil, although in Area C they were confined to a band in the centre of the area. In the areas at the east and west limits of the excavation (Areas A and K) the cobbles were pressed into the surface of a layer of redeposited subsoil stratified on the subsoil. A few stake-holes were recorded in the subsoil below the cobbles in Area K.

AREA A

In this area no features were cut directly into the subsoil (F225), a compact light brown stony clay. Layer F349, orange-brown clay, was similar to the subsoil and stratified on it, but included specks of charcoal and was mixed with patches of soft grey clay. The surface of this layer sloped west-east from *c.* 8.4m to *c.* 8.2m OD and was covered with intermittent patches of pebbles (F344) similar to those found in Area K. Several stake-holes comprising two alignments (Alignments 1 and 2) and a large post-hole (F345) were cut into layer F349 (Figs 3.30, 3.31; Pl. 3.29).

ALIGNMENT 1

The first alignment comprised six stake-holes (F375a, b and e–h) aligned north-west/south-east (Fig. 3.30). It was 1.4m long and was cut off to the north by the curtain wall of the castle and to the south by the facade of Block 8. The stake-holes were at 0.18m intervals; they were 70 to 90mm in diameter and between 0.12m and 0.26m deep. An oval cut (F375c), 0.18m by 0.11m and 80mm deep, lay next to stake-hole F375b, and a small cut 30mm in diameter by 30mm deep (F375d) lay to the north of stake-hole F375e.

There were six stake-holes in two groups of three on the west side of Alignment 1. Three stake-holes were in the north-west corner of the area. Stake-hole F375k was 70mm in diameter and 0.11m deep; stake-hole F375j was 60mm in diameter and 10mm deep and stake-hole F375I was 50mm in diameter and 70mm deep (Fig. 3.30). Three stake-holes were also in the south-west corner of the area: stake-hole (F375l) was 70mm in diameter and 0.31m deep; stake-holes F375m and F375n were 90mm in diameter by 0.28m and were 0.13m deep.

ALIGNMENT 2

A group of six stake-holes (F375o–t) at 0.16m intervals formed a curving line running roughly east-west in the eastern half of the area and this alignment would have converged with Alignment 1 at a point roughly below the line of the inner edge of the curtain wall. The alignment was 1.6m long but was cut to the north by the curtain wall and most likely continued beyond the limit of excavation to the east. The stake-holes were roughly 60mm in diameter, with depths ranging between 90mm and 0.28m. A stray stake-hole (F375u) lying just a short distance to the south of the series was 60mm in diameter by 0.12m deep (Fig. 3.30).

A larger post-pit feature (F345) was on the western side of Alignment 1, next to the edge of stake-hole F375k. It was sub-circular in plan, 0.35m (east-west) by 0.3m and 0.24m deep (Fig. 3.30). The fill (F346) was brown clayey silt with occasional bone fragments.

AREA B

The subsoil in Area B (sloping west-east from *c.* 9.2m to *c.* 8.6m OD) was noticeably higher than in Area A and consisted of a compact light brown stony clay (F225). The surface was studded with closely spaced pebbles or cobblestones (F368), similar to but more numerous than the patchy pebbles noted on the subsoil in Area A (Pl. 3.30). The straight-sided modern disturbance (F257/F292) had removed this layer of pebbles. Two features were cut into the subsoil, a stake-hole (F390) and a pit (F286) (Figs 3.32, 3.33).

Pl. 3.29 Stake-holes of Alignments 1 and 2 visible in redeposited subsoil (F349) in Area A.

The pit (F286) was oval in plan, aligned east-west and was truncated to the north by the curtain wall (F200). The pit was 1.7m long (east-west) by 0.8m; it was up to 0.56m deep. A stake-hole (F391) was cut into the base of the pit at the eastern end; it was 0.1m in diameter and 0.22m deep. The basal deposit within the pit (F299) was reddish-brown clay with charcoal specks. There were slight traces of wood on the floor of the pit, which suggested that the feature may have had a wattle or timber lining, but preservation was very poor. Deposit F293 was stratified on deposit F299; it was clay with some bone, charcoal and fragmented shell and also containing a cut bone cylinder (E324:13031). Deposit F366, rusty light brown clay, was also stratified on deposit F299. A concentration of stones (F288) was stratified on deposit F293. Another fill deposit (F367) was grey-brown clay lying against the western end of the pit, one side of which was studded with pebbles in the same way as the surface of the surrounding subsoil. This suggests that part of the edge had broken away and fallen into the pit after fill F299 was deposited. The upper fill of the pit (F287) was brown clay with charcoal and shell.

An isolated stake-hole (F390) was cut into the subsoil 1.95m east of pit F286. It was sub-circular, 0.15m (east-west) by 0.11m and 0.11m deep (Fig. 3.32). The bases of three tiny wooden stakes were found upright in the subsoil to the south-west of pit F286.

A burnt spread (F255) up to 60mm deep was stratified on the subsoil. Four other deposits were also stratified on the subsoil. Deposit F228 was dark brown clay with frequent bone, charcoal specks, fragmented shell and fragments of wood (Fig. 3.33). It contained an antler tine (E324:7812) and an antler wedge (E324:1023). Deposit F294 was smooth grey-brown clay with moderate bone and charcoal specks, up to 0.12m deep. Deposit F296 was dark grey clay with charcoal specks, shell, small stones and occasional bone; it contained a fragment of a jet-like finger ring (E324:3715). Deposit F295 was a thin brown clay deposit stratified on the subsoil. A radiocarbon date of cal AD 895–1030 (95.4% probability) was obtained from an animal bone sample (sheep/goat vertebra) from deposit F296.

AREA C

The subsoil level was at roughly 9.26m OD at the western end of the area and at *c.* 9.37m OD at the eastern end, but a broad strip in the middle of the area, roughly 2.2m wide (east-west), studded with cobblestones (F392), was noticeably lower, with levels typically between about 9.12 and 9.17m OD (Figs 3.34, 3.35). A number of features were cut into the surface of the subsoil at this level of activity. At the eastern limit of the area these comprise an alignment of stake-holes (F376a–g) and a post-hole (F336) with an associated linear cut (F377), and a formation of three stake-holes (F378a–c). A post-hole (F306) and a pit (F340) were uncovered at the western end of the area.

A cut (F377) in subsoil at the eastern end of the area was related to the establishment of a probable post-and-wattle wall on a north-west/south-east axis, represented in the subsoil by stake-hole formation F376a–g and post-hole F336. The orientation of the F377 cut was north-west/south-east adjacent to the stake-holes; at the north-west limit of the stake-hole formation the orientation changed to north-south (Fig. 3.34). The F377 cut appeared to continue northward where it was truncated by the curtain wall; to the south it appeared to terminate at the edge of a large sub-circular stone, beyond which the ground was truncated by the façade of Block 8. The surviving extent of the feature had an excavated length of 0.82m; it was 0.25m deep. Post-hole F336 was not fully excavated since the north-west extent of its edge was truncated by the curtain wall. The post-hole was sub-circular, 0.3m (north-south) by 0.3m and 0.3m deep. The lower fill (F338) was waterlogged brown silty sand; the upper fill (F337) was green-brown clayey silt.

Post-hole F336 lay at the north-western end of a linear formation of stake-holes (F376a–g). The seven stake-holes were spread over a distance of 0.68m (north-west/south-east), commencing just south of post-hole F336, and continuing close to the Block 8 wall (Fig. 3.34). The stake-holes were not arranged in a single line but appeared to be organised into three pairs (a/e, b/f and c/g, with d on its own, but with the series obliterated at this point by the later wall) creating a double line extending south-east of the post-hole. Four of the stake-holes (b, d, f, g) were circular, roughly 60mm in diameter and with depths ranging from 60mm (F376g) up to 0.22mm (F376b). The other three (a, c, e) were oval; F376a clearly would have accommodated two stakes and this may have been the case with the c and e stake-holes as well. The oval examples were roughly 100mm by 60mm, with depths of between 0.23m and 0.26m.

Three stake-holes (F378a–c) in the subsoil were spread out on an east-north-east/west-south-west axis over a distance of 0.68m to the west of post-hole F336 (Fig. 3.34). The stake-holes had diameters of between 60 and 80mm and depths of 40mm (F378a), 0.2m (F378b) and 0.1m (F378c).

There were two features cut into the subsoil at the western end of the area – pit F340 and post-hole F306. Only part of the eastern extent of pit F340 was excavated, since the feature was truncated to the north-west by the inner edge of the curtain wall, to the west by stone and brick floor F396 and to the south by the façade of Block 8, F201. The feature had an excavated length (north-south) of *c.* 0.65m by *c.* 0.59m and was 0.4m deep (Fig. 3.34). The fill (F341) was waterlogged green-brown sandy silt with frequent bone. Post-hole F306 was *c.* 0.24m east of the pit. The northern extent was truncated by the inner edge of the curtain wall. The feature was roughly 0.21m in diameter and *c.* 0.15m deep. The fill was soft dark grey clay with some stones (F305).

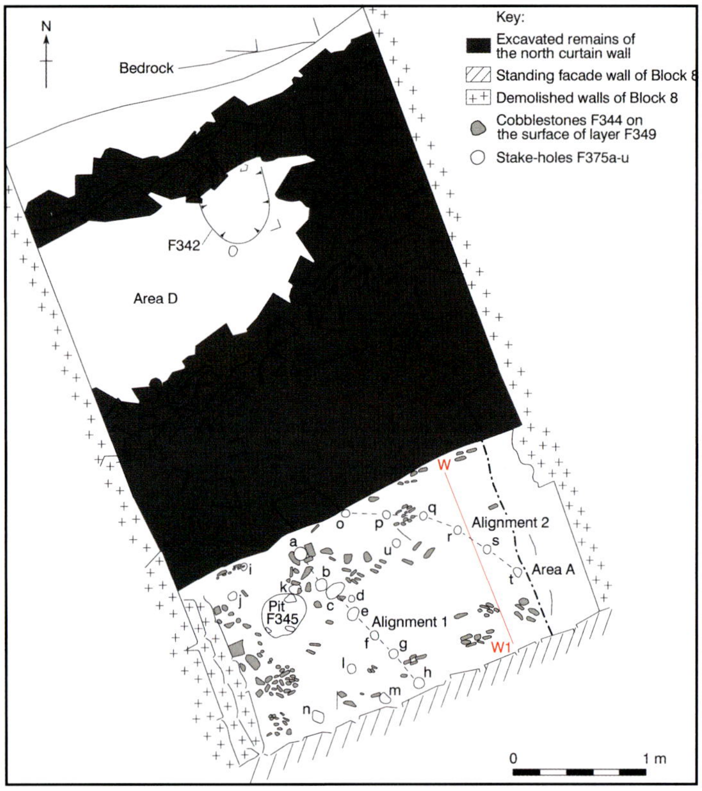

Fig. 3.30 Powder Tower, Cutting 2; Phase 1 features in Areas A and D.

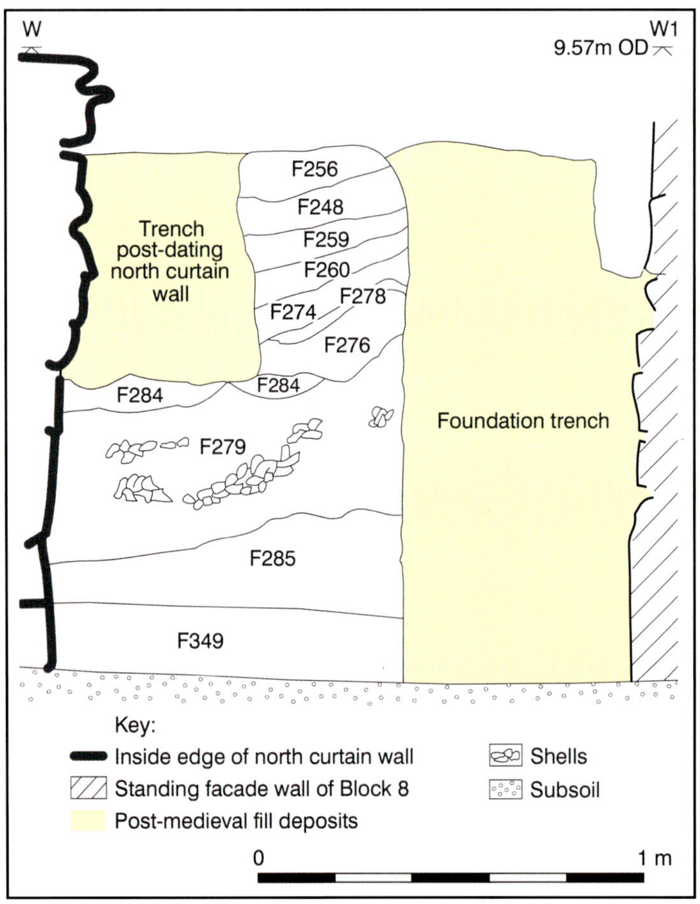

Fig. 3.31 Powder Tower, Cutting 2; west-facing section (W-W1) of Area A (for location see Fig. 3.30).

The cobblestone surface (F392) comprised an area at subsoil level densely packed with small to medium-sized stones (Fig. 3.34). The feature was approximately 2.2m wide (east-west), located *c.* 1m east of pit F340 and extending eastward to close to the edge of stake-hole formation F376a–g and large post-hole F336. The typical level on the cobblestones (*c.* 9.16m OD) was around 0.21m lower than the surface of subsoil exposed at the eastern end of Area C, on the eastern side of linear cut F377 (9.37m OD).

The main Phase 1 deposit was a waterlogged green-brown sandy silt with frequent bone (F335) that contained an unfinished antler comb tooth segment (E324:8808), an antler tine (E324:8807) and a sawn antler wedge (E324:8809). The deposit was revealed at the eastern end of the area, stratified on the subsoil, and abutting cut F377 through the subsoil. The narrow area of paving stones (F379) revealed at this end of the area, and associated with Phase 2 activity on the site, was stratified on deposit F335.

AREA D

The remains of a circular pit (F342) were found in a patch of subsoil exposed where the stonework of the north curtain wall had been removed, 2.2m north of Area A. The northern half of the feature was destroyed by the construction of the curtain wall. The surviving southern extent of the pit was 0.52m (east-west) by 0.46m and 0.23m deep (Fig. 3.30). The fill (F343) was grey-brown silty clay with frequent animal bones. At the base of the cut was a circular patch of charcoal and gravel, 0.2m in diameter and 20mm deep.

AREA K

The subsoil in Area K was between 9.83m and 10m OD. Phase 1 evidence comprised five dispersed stake-holes (F382a–e) cut into the subsoil (Fig. 3.36, Pl. 3.32).

AREA L

Several stake-holes and a patch of oxidised clay were revealed on the subsoil in a narrow strip exposed beneath the curtain wall, roughly 2.15m north of the west end of Area B and *c.* 2.3m north of the east end of Area C. Evidence for a large pit-like feature (F371) was recorded in section below the base of the curtain wall. The surface of the subsoil as revealed in Area L lay around 9.15m OD.

A grouping of stake-holes (F384a –j), possibly evidence for a double line of uprights on an east-north-east/south-south-west axis, was distributed over an area measuring around 0.72m (east-west) by 0.2m (Fig. 3.32; Pl. 3.31). The formation comprised two single stake-holes (F384a, h) and four stake-hole pairs (F384b/c, d/e, f/g, i/j). The features were organised into an alignment consisting of (from west to east) F384a, b/c, d/e, f/g. Offset slightly to the north of this were stake-hole F384h and, 0.26m to the east, stake-hole pair F384i/j. The stake-holes were typically 40mm

Pl. 3.30 Cobblestones (F368) on subsoil in Area B, cut by later pit (F286), curtain wall at top; from south-east.

Pl. 3.31 Stake-hole formation (F384a-j) in subsoil in Area L. Pit (F371) visible in section at bottom right.

in diameter, apart from single stake-hole F384a (70mm), which was also the deepest example (0.26m). The depth range otherwise was between 0.15m and 0.25m. Most of the stake-holes contained no fill; one or two were filled with mortar only.

A sub-circular patch of oxidised clay on the subsoil (F385) was *c.* 026m east of the F384 alignment (Fig. 3.32). It was roughly 0.32m (east-west) by 0.26m. Three stake-holes (F386a–c) were cut into the subsoil around the edges of the burnt patch. Stake-hole F386c was 40mm in diameter and 0.35m deep. The other two were larger, both 60mm in diameter, with depths of 0.38m (F386a) and 0.43m (F386b).

A much larger feature (F371) was preserved in the north-facing section created in the thirteenth century when the subsoil was cut during the digging of the moat and construction of the battered lower part of the north curtain wall which formed the inner face of the moat. The southern extent of the feature was sealed by the base of the curtain wall. The northern half was destroyed by the digging of the moat. As seen in section, the pit-like cut of F371 was *c.* 0.6m wide (east-west) and *c.* 0.7m deep (Fig. 3.32). The lower fill (F387) was redeposited subsoil, above which was a deposit (F388) of soft, organic grey-brown clay. The fill deposits had become compressed over time by the weight of the overlying base of the curtain wall, and as they dried out and contracted the masonry of the wall gradually subsided into the body of the cut.

Phase 2

AREA A

Deposit F285 was stratified on Phase 1 layer F349 (Fig. 3.31). It was crumbly dark brown-grey silty clay with inclusions of shell fragments, wood shavings, bone and occasional stones. It contained an antler connecting plate from an antler comb

Pl. 3.32 Stake-holes (F382a-e) in subsoil in Area K.

case (E324:1024), examples of which have been dated to the tenth century, an antler tine (E324:8791) and an antler wedge (E324:1025). This layer lay under deposit F279, a medium brown silty clay with moderate charcoal patches, mussel shell and bone. It contained an amber bead (E324:3989), a bone pin beater (E324:919), a bone needle case (E324:6097), and a large, pointed bone blade (E324:6098). Deposit F279 produced metalworking evidence in the form of two partial smithing hearth cakes and four fragments of likely tuyere. The combined depth of deposits F285 and F279 was *c.* 0.6m. The Phase 2 evidence in Area A was completed with layer F284, stratified on deposit F279. It was creamy light brown silty clay with occasional charcoal flecks, a very fine well-structured clay that came out in blocks, but also containing frequent large stones. As deposit F284 and the underlying level F279 were being excavated, it was evident that elements of the two alternated and were mixed together to a certain extent, suggesting both were laid down at the same time.

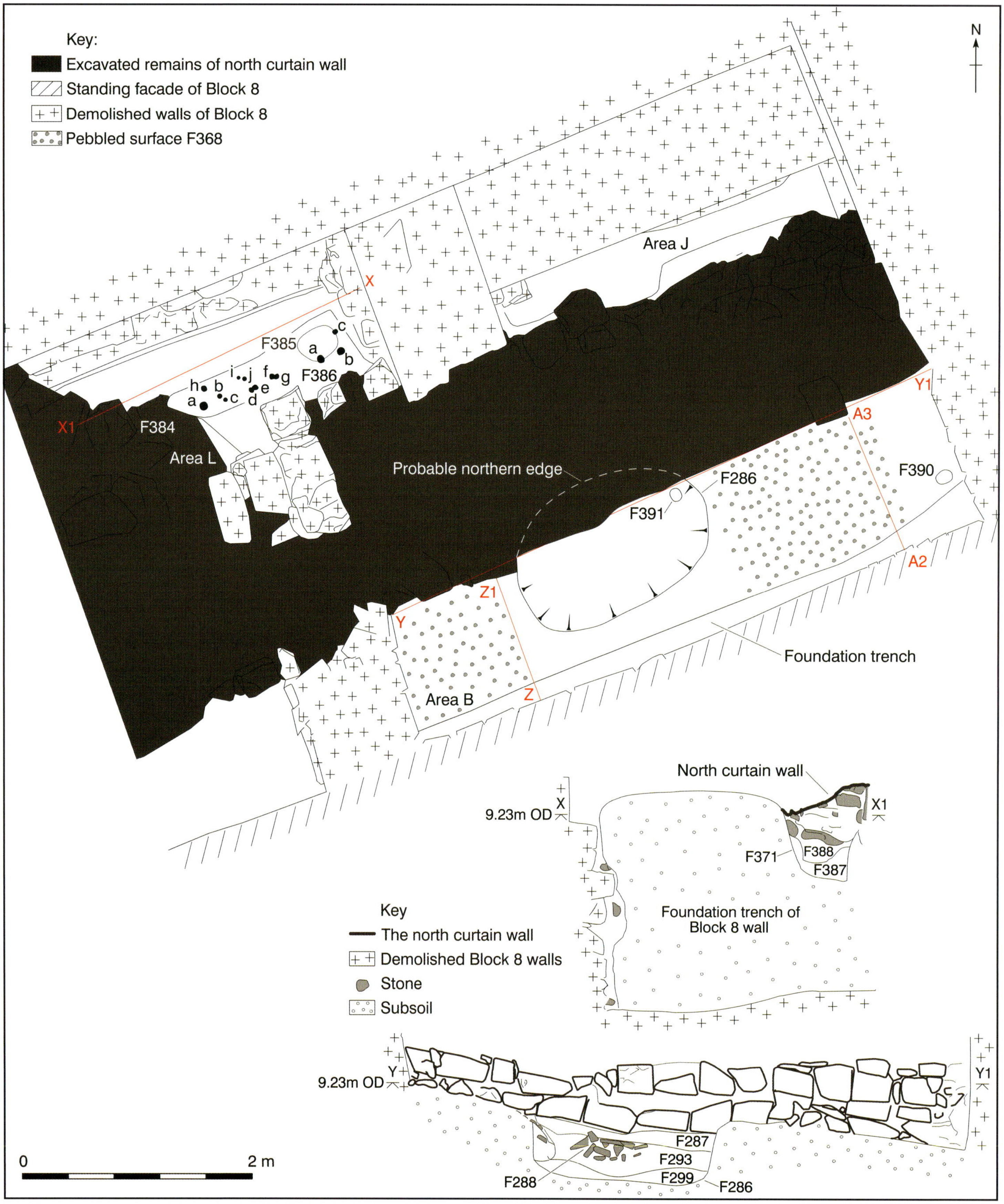

Fig. 3.32 Powder Tower, Cutting 2; Phase 1 features in Areas B and L and sections X-X1 and Y-Y1.

AREA B

Deposit F252 was stratified on Phase 1 deposit F228. It was compact green-grey stony clay with some charcoal, stone, shell and bone, up to 0.12m deep (Fig. 3.33). Deposit F283, also stratified on deposit F228, was stiff dark grey-brown clay with charcoal spots, bone, shell and stone; it contained an antler tine (E324:13030) and a notched antler wedge (E324:8792). Deposit F229 was also stratified on deposit F228. It was smooth mid brown clay with charcoal specks, occasional stone, bone, fragmented wood, some shell and a small piece of slag. Deposit F230, stratified on deposit F229, was the latest surviving Viking-age deposit in Area B. It was brown clayey silt with frequent charcoal specks, some burnt and unburnt bone.

AREA C

The main evidence for Phase 2 in Area C comprised two paved surfaces, a narrow, paved area (F379) on a north-west/south-east axis at the eastern end of the area, and similar but much wider paving (F380) at the western end of the area, the two features separated by a broad strip that was covered with cobblestones (F392) in Phase 1 but contained organic clay deposits F300 and F301 in Phase 2. At the eastern end of the area paved stone formation F379 partially intruded on the Phase 1 alignment of stake-holes (F376a–g) but did not conceal post-hole F336 or linear subsoil cut F377 (Fig. 3.38). One of the Phase1 stake-holes (F376e) lay below the corner of one of the large slabs of the F379 paving; stake-hole F376d lay below one of the smaller stones. The paving was truncated to the north and south by the north curtain wall and the façade of Block 8. The paving (F379) comprised six large flat stone slabs and a number of smaller stones, with an excavated length of *c.* 0.84m (east-west) by *c.* 0.9m (Fig. 3.38; Pl. 3.33). The largest of the stones was 0.36m (north-south) by 0.2m and 0.1m thick. The stones had an average surface level of 9.38m OD and had been placed over Phase 1 deposit F335 (see above). The level of subsoil directly east of Phase 1 linear cut F377 (9.37m OD) corresponds closely with the level on the paved surface of F379. So, although it is the case that two of the stake-holes of the F378 alignment were covered by paving slabs, it is still possible, particularly since post-hole F336 was not covered by a paving stone, that a boundary line, established in Phase 1 against a linear cut in the subsoil, was maintained in Phase 2, with stone paving F379 in turn placed next to it.

At the other end of the area, roughly 1.5m west of the F379 stones, a more substantial body of paving stones (F380) was discovered. The west end of Area C was impacted to a considerable extent by disturbance related to the construction of Block 8 in the eighteenth century. A deposit of grey-brown clay (F303) excavated here was found to contain some very large stones with mortar attached, and this material was interpreted as backfill related to the building of the foundations of the façade of Block 8. However, other large stones (F380) emerged directly below the line of disturbance, and it was evident that these were *in situ* and formed part of the pre-castle stratigraphy of the site. The paved area (F380) had excavated dimensions of *c.* 1.86m (east-west) by *c.* 0.66m (Fig. 3.38). The largest stone was roughly triangular, measuring 0.42m (east-west) by 0.35m and 0.15m thick. It is clear that the surface continued originally to the south and west under Block 8 wall F201 and floor F396 and to the north under the inner edge of the curtain wall F200. The typical surface level on the F380 paving stones was 9.41m OD.

While the two areas of paving could be seen as two separate parallel pathways, it makes more sense, in view of the underlying roadway, to assume that they are part of a single paved surface and that the paving in the middle portion of the road was either robbed or if made of timber,

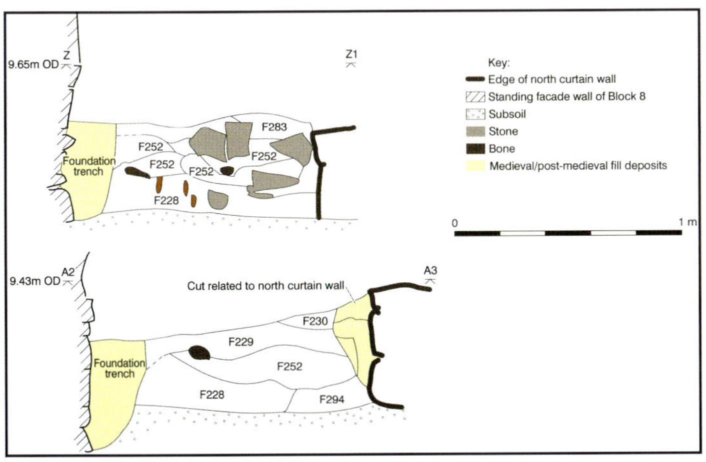

Fig. 3.33 Powder Tower, Cutting 2; east-facing sections (Z-Z1 and A2-A3) of Area B (for location see Fig. 3.32).

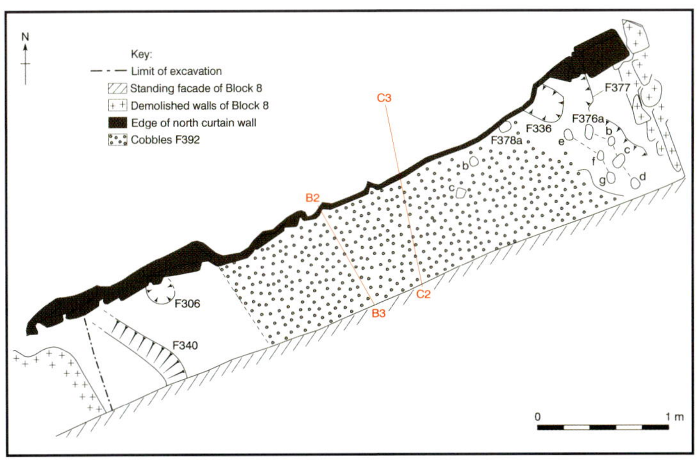

Fig. 3.34 Powder Tower, Cutting 2; Phase 1 features in Area C.

had rotted away. The paving stones extending to the west could be part of a plot entrance perpendicular to the paved road.

Deposit F301 was stratified on the Phase 1 cobblestones covering the surface of the subsoil in the middle part of Area C (Fig. 3.35). It was dark grey clayey silt with frequent animal bones, 0.1m deep. A radiocarbon determination of cal AD 779–1032 (95.4% probability) was obtained from an antler sample from layer F301. Deposit F300, gritty sandy clay up to 0.2m deep with occasional shell and bone fragments, was stratified on both deposit F301 and cobblestones F392 (Fig. 3.35). The surface of the layer, at around 9.38m OD, was roughly equivalent to the surface of the two paved areas (F379 and F380) on either side of it.

AREA K

Layer F363 was stratified on the subsoil. It was yellow-grey silty sand (redeposited subsoil), with inclusions of charcoal, bone and occasional shell and was up to 0.14m deep (Figs 3.36, 3.37). The surface of layer F363 (lying around 10.07 to 10.11m OD) was covered with patchy cobbles/pebbles (F383) in a manner similar to cobbles F344 in Area A, F368 in Area B and F392 in the middle part of Area C. A single stake-hole (F381) was cut into the surface of the layer.

Phase 3

AREA A

A deposit of dark grey-brown sandy clay (F276) with moderate charcoal patches, shell, pebbles and fragmented bone was stratified on Phase 2 layer F284 (Fig. 3.31). This deposit had a gritty, ashy texture and contained a bone pin (E324:918) of a type datable to the mid-tenth century, tuyère fragments and iron-smithing hearth cakes. Deposit F276 was cut by a pit-like feature (F281), the full extent of which is unknown due to truncation by later features (trench F242 dug along the inside edge of the curtain wall, and trench F246 for the foundation of Block 8 wall F201). The feature was *c.* 0.78m (east-west) by an excavated 0.32m, and 0.14m deep. The lower fill was a black charcoal and ash spread, up to 20mm deep (F282), that contained a small quantity of vitrified ceramic material, possibly tuyère fragments, animal bone and burnt wood chippings. A square, flat stone (110mm by 100mm and 30mm thick) lay on this fill. The upper fill was a brown clayey silt with some patches of charcoal and mussel shells and occasional stone (*c.* 40mm in diameter) and burnt wood (F277) that contained a glass stud or inset (E324:916), a perforated hone (E324:915), a smithing hearth cake and a vitrified ceramic fragment. An animal bone sample (a sheep/goat metacarpus) from the lower fill of the pit returned a date of cal AD 885–1013 (95.4% probability, constrained from AD 922 to 995 by Bayesian modelling; see Chapter 8).

Deposits F278 and F275 were both stratified on fill F277 of pit F281 and on deposit F276. Deposit F278 was pale yellow sandy silt with some charcoal patches, ash and stone (Fig. 3.31). Deposit F275 was compact gritty yellowish-brown sandy silt with some charcoal, pebbles and shell fragments and occasional bone.

The discovery of iron slag and tuyères in deposit F276, as well as in both fill deposits of pit F281, cut into the surface of deposit F276, along with the ashy nature of deposits F276 and F278, suggests that Phase 3 in Area A was associated with ironworking activity.

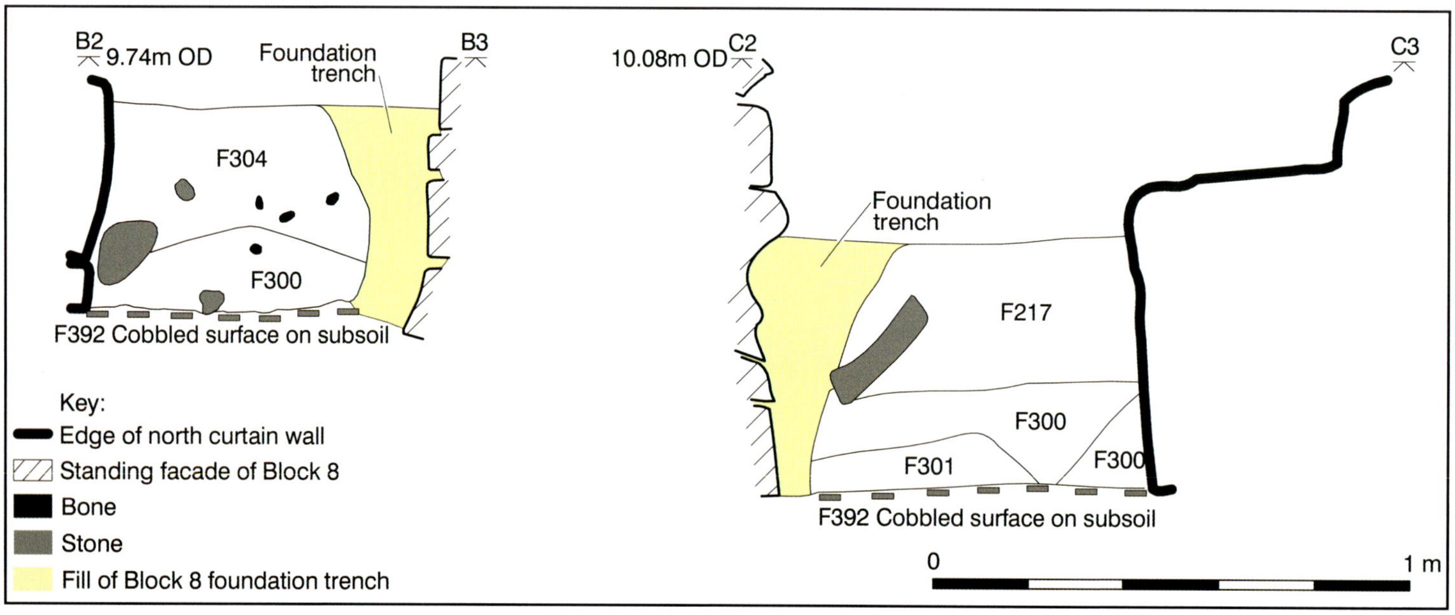

Fig. 3.35 Powder Tower, Cutting 2; west-facing (B2-B3) and east-facing (C2-C3) sections of Area C (for location see Fig. 3.34).

Pl. 3.33 Phase 2 paving stones (F379) in Area C.

AREA C

The Phase 3 evidence in Area C comprises the final phase of Viking-age activity to survive in the archaeological record for this area of the site. The evidence was very limited but indicated a break in continuity with the pre-existing settlement pattern, with both Phase 2 paved areas (F379 and F380) covered by relatively deep deposits, bringing about a complete change to the layout and nature of habitation in the locality, although due to the restricted scope of the excavation it is not possible to determine the exact nature of this change.

Two post-holes were cut into the surface of deposit F300. Post-hole F331 was 0.2m in diameter and 0.14m deep; the fill was brown clayey silt with wood fragments. Post-hole F332, located 0.15m to the south-east of post-hole F331 and truncated to the south by the edge of wall F201, was 0.18m (east-west) by 0.14m and 0.22m deep; the fill was soft silty brown sand with fragmented wood, possibly the remains of a slender post.

Deposit F304 (Fig. 3.35) was stratified on deposit F300 in the middle of the area. It was green-brown silty clay with frequent small stones and shell, many animal bones and some charcoal spots; the deposit was up to 0.3m deep and contained an antler wedge (E324:8810). Deposit F217 (Fig. 3.35), stratigraphically corresponding with deposit F304, was greenish sandy clay, very rich in shell fragments and bone, with small stones and charcoal spots; the deposit contained an antler comb, which can be dated broadly to the period *c.* 950 to *c.* 1150 (E324:3789), the end piece of an antler comb (E324:6100) and an antler tine (E324:13029).

At the eastern end of the area, two deposits were stratified on the paving stones (F379). Deposit F333 was a thin spread of grey clay with fragmented wood and deposit F334 was dark brown clay with fragmented wood, shell and charcoal. The Phase 3 deposits were the latest surviving Viking-age remains in Area C and were discovered following the removal of disturbed fill dating from the eighteenth century.

AREA K

Deposit F362, stratified on layer F363, was light brown silty clay with stones, bone and charcoal (Fig. 3.37).

Evidence for Later Phases

The assignment of the remaining layers in Areas A and K to phases is largely speculative and is based on changes in the stratigraphy that may reflect changing activities.

AREA A (PHASES 4 TO 8)

Evidence for a possible additional five phases of activity (Phases 4 to 8) in Area A is represented in section by a series of superimposed clay layers post-dating the metalworking activity of Phase 3. Because the later foundation trenches (F242 and F246) were so wide, pre-castle deposits at this level survived only in a 0.4m-wide strip.

Phase 4 comprises a yellow silty clay with shells (clam and mussel), patches of charcoal and pebbles (F274) stratified on Phase 3 deposits F275 and F278 (Fig. 3.31). Deposit F273 was stratified on deposit F274. It was deep brown-grey silty clay with frequent charcoal and ash, some bone, shell and pebbles and was 0.2m by 0.4m and up to 50mm deep.

Phase 5 is represented by layer F260, stratified on Phase 4 deposits F273 and F274 (Fig. 3.31). It was compact light grey-buff silty clay with fine flecks of charcoal, but otherwise sterile. At the Phase 6 level, deposit F259 was stratified on layer F260. It was smooth dark brown sandy clay with frequent charcoal flecks and shell fragments, including whole clam shells, occasional fragments of bone and pieces of unworked flint.

Deposit F248 (Phase 7), stratified on Phase 6 deposit F259, was similar to layer F260 (Phase 5), consisting of patchy green to light brown-buff silty clay with frequent stones (averaging *c.* 50mm across), fragmented shell and charcoal flecks. The Phase 8 deposit (F256) was the latest pre-castle deposit excavated in Area A, stratified on Phase 7 deposit F248 and under a compact layer (F244) dating from the post-medieval period. It was dark brown silty clay with occasional bone fragments, shell and small pebbles (Fig. 3.31).

AREA K (PHASES 4 TO 18)

The stratification recorded in Area K goes well beyond the evidence for the earliest three phases, as outlined above (Fig. 3.37; Pl. 3.34). Phase 4 is represented by two deposits of clay stratified on deposit F362 (Phase 3): a dark brown silty clay with lighter brown clay lenses, frequent charcoal specks, some bone, occasional fragments of shell and pebbles (F350) and a crumbly mid brown humic clay with frequent shell fragments, some bone and stones (F361). A date of cal AD 888–1014 (95.4% probability; constrained from AD 939 to 1015 by Bayesian modelling, see Chapter 8) was obtained from an animal bone sample (sheep/goat metacarpus) from layer F361.

Pl. 3.34 Remains of Phase 17 clay floor (F310/F312) in Area K, eighteenth-century wall at left.

Phase 5 comprises deposit F360, dark brown silty clay with frequent bone and stones, some shell fragments and charcoal flecks, stratified on Phase 4 deposit F361. The sequence continues into Phase 6 with layer F359, stratified on Phase 5 deposit F360. It was dark brown clay, virtually sterile apart from occasional bone and when excavated it came away in blocks. Deposit F358 was stratified on layer F359. It was dark brown clayey sand with frequent charcoal flecks, small to medium stones and occasional shell fragments and bone. Phases 1–6 of the Area K stratified sequence may represent the continuity of habitation on the site throughout the course of the tenth century.

Phase 7 consists of layer F357, sterile light brown-tan clay; occasional charcoal flecks, stratified on Phase 6 deposit F358. Deposit F356, stratified on layer F357, was mid brown silty clay with occasional shell and bone. Phase 8 layer F355, sterile light grey clay, was stratified on Phase 7 deposit F356. Deposit F354, dark brown silty clay with occasional pebbles, was stratified on layer F355 (Fig. 3.37).

Deposit F327 (Phase 9) was stratified on Phase 8 deposits F354 and F355; it was dark brown clay with frequent fragmented shell and pebbles and some patches of charcoal. Deposit F327 contained a piece of leather (E324:8794) and fragments of curved ceramic roof tile (E324:8795/96/99 and E324:8797/98) were also found in this context. Such tiles can potentially date from the early eleventh century. Deposit F330, stratified on deposit F327, was gritty grey silty sand with moderate flecks of charcoal and fragmented shell. Deposit F353, also stratified on deposit F327, was gritty dark grey sandy silt with occasional charcoal. Deposit F352 was stratified on deposit F353; it was dark brown-black silty sand with occasional charcoal; up to 20mm deep. There was a seam of charcoal (F352a) 5mm deep along the base of deposit F352.

In Phase 10 the digging of a substantial pit (F374) truncated several earlier deposits, including Phase 8 deposits F355 and F354, and Phase 9 deposits F327, F330, F353 and F352; the base also cut Phase 7 deposit F356 (Fig. 3.37). Only the north-eastern quadrant of the pit was excavated as the outline of the feature continued beyond the limits of the excavation area to the west and south. The excavated extent of the pit

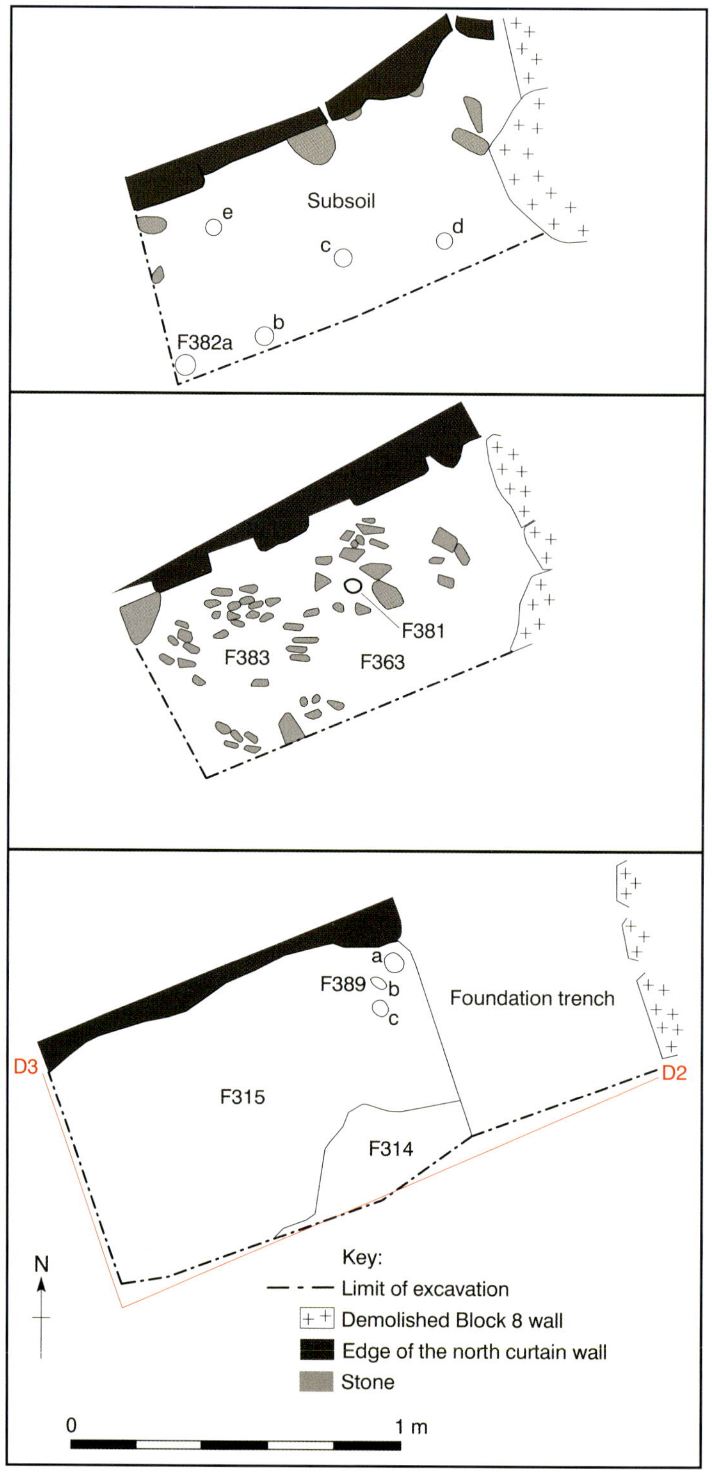

Fig. 3.36 Powder Tower, Cutting 2, Area K features; (Top) Phase 1, (Middle) Phase 2, (Bottom) Phases 15 and 16.

measured 0.8m (east-west) by 0.3m and was *c.* 0.33m deep. There were two main fill deposits, F351 and F328. Fill deposit F351 was buff clay that came away in blocks and contained some charcoal, but otherwise was sterile (Fig. 3.37). Deposit F328 was reddish brown silty clay with some charcoal flecks and flecks of light brown clay, occasional fragmented shell, pebbles and bone. The fill of the pit was sealed with deposit F326, gritty yellow-grey clayey silt with frequent shell and pebbles and occasional bone and larger stones. Deposit F326 contained a lens (F325) of compact sterile grey clay (150mm by 140mm) projecting from the west section.

Phase 11 was established over the sealed Phase 10 pit with layer F329, stratified on Phase 10 deposit F326 and Phase 9 deposit F352. It was pale brown clay up to 40mm deep with occasional shell fragments, but otherwise sterile. It was similar to layer F359 (Phase 6), and pit fill F351 (Phase 10). Deposit F324 was stratified on layer F329. It was compact dark brown charcoal-enriched silty clay with frequent pebbles and shell and contained some patches of sterile clay similar to the underlying F329 layer.

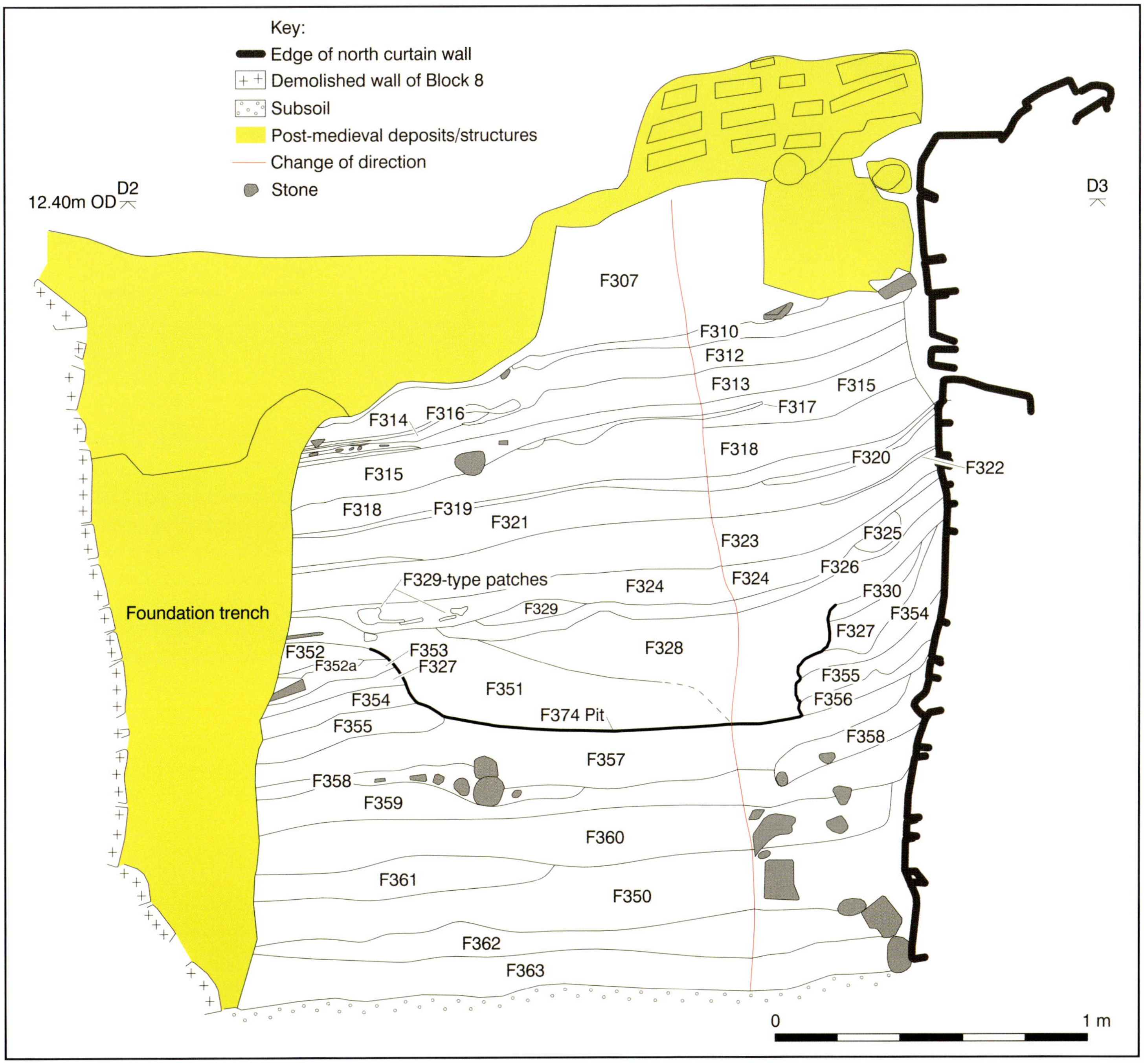

Fig. 3.37 Powder Tower, Cutting 2, Area K; north and east-facing sections (D2-D3) (for location see Fig. 3.36).

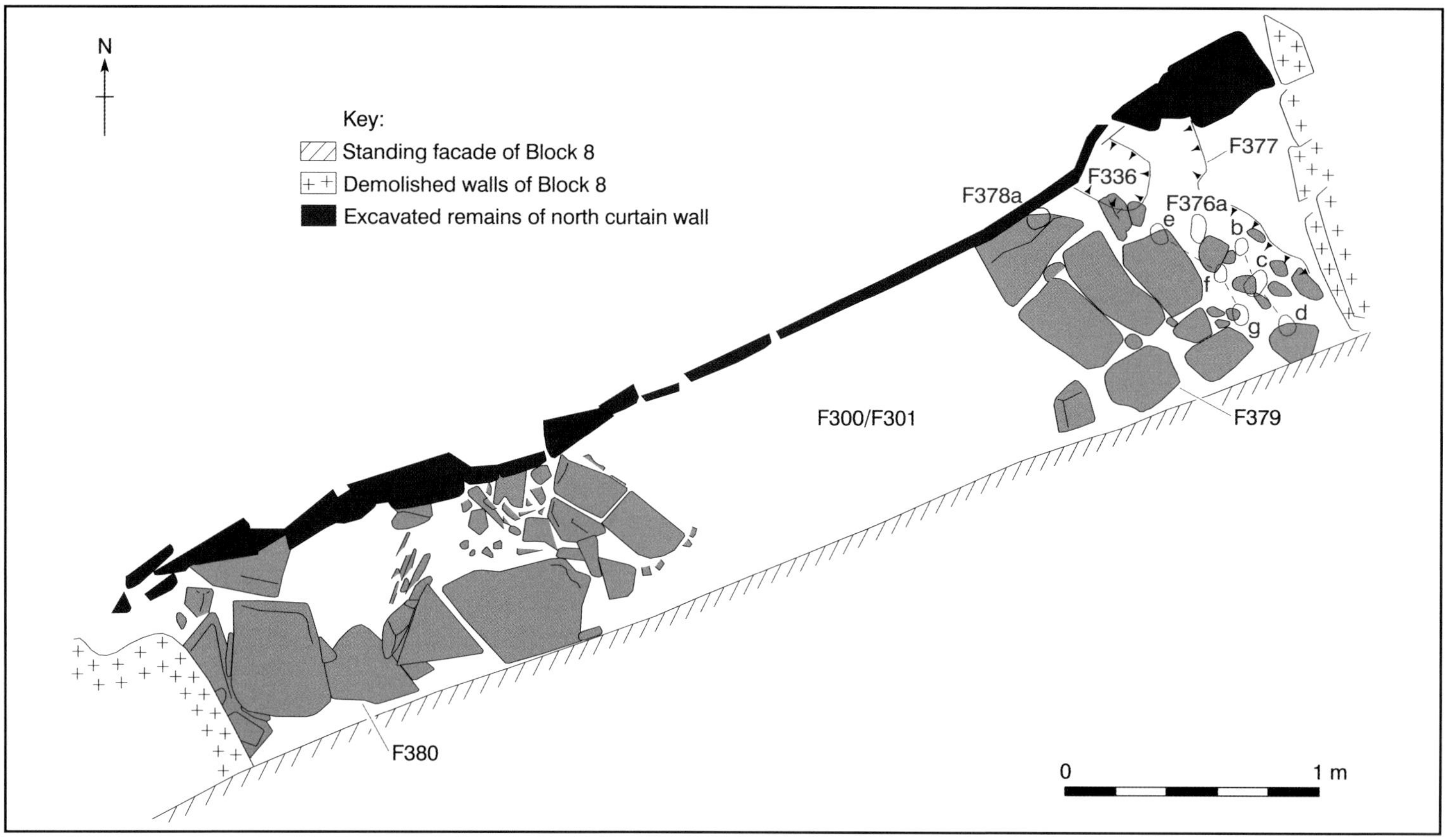

Fig. 3.38 Powder Tower, Cutting 2, Area C; Phase 2 features with Phase 1 features added (see Fig. 3.34).

The stratified sequence continues into Phase 12 with deposit F323 (Fig. 3.37), reddish brown silty clay with flecks of charcoal and occasional shell, bone and pebbles, stratified on Phase 11 deposit F324. It contained a sherd of pottery (E324:9074), a body sherd of Seine Valley white ware with red painted decoration, dated to the late tenth/eleventh century. A thin deposit (F322) of charcoal-enriched clay and ash was stratified on deposit F323.

The upper level of the Area K sequence continues into Phase 13 with layer F321, stratified on Phase 12 deposits F322 and F323. It was in essence redeposited subsoil similar to layer F363 (Phase 2), consisting of compact yellow-grey clay with frequent stones (30–70mm), bone, shell and charcoal flecks. A dark brown burnt clay deposit (F320) was stratified on layer F321. Deposit F319 was stratified on deposit F320 and layer F321; it was dark brown silty clay with frequent bone and pebbles, charcoal patches and occasional fragmented shell.

Phase 14 comprised layer F318, stratified on Phase 13 deposit F319. It was yellow-light brown silty clay that came out in blocks (similar to Phase 6 layer F359 and Phase 4 pit fill F351) and contained thin lenses (5mm deep) of dark brown gritty silty sand.

Phase 15 is represented by layer F315, stratified on Phase 14 layer F318. It was similar to layer F318, consisting of light brown/yellow silty clay with frequent patches of charcoal, bone, shell and pebbles (Figs 3.36, 3.37). A patch (F317) of red ash and charcoal (150mm by 60mm), possibly related to a hearth, was partially stratified on layer F318, partially contained within layer F315. Patches of charcoal were noted in the interface between layers F315 and F318. The surface of layer F315 was cut by three closely spaced stake-holes (F389a–c; Fig. 3.36). The largest (F389a) was 70mm in diameter and 60mm deep; stake-holes F389b/c were 30mm in diameter but were deeper than stake-hole F389a (80mm and 120mm).

The next level of activity, Phase 16, consisted of deposit F313, stratified on Phase 15 layer F315; it was loose, gritty dark brown silty clay with lighter brown flecks throughout, frequent small pebbles, bone and occasional shell (Fig. 3.37). Deposit F313 contained a worked antler tine (E324:8803) and a hollow bone cylinder (E324:1027); it also contained a piece of curved ceramic roof tile (E324:8802), dating from the eleventh century. Two deposits were stratified on deposit F313. Deposit F314 was fine textured dark brown silty clay with occasional shell (Figs 3.36, 3.37). Deposit F316 was composed of very fine bands (10mm deep) of silty clay containing fragments of leaves, twigs and wood, which alternated with thin seams of yellow-brown silty clay similar to the layer F315 material.

Activity continued into Phase 17 with layer F312, stratified on Phase 16 deposits F313 and F314 (Fig. 3.37). It was compact pebbly cream-pale brown/beige silty clay up to 50mm deep and was largely sterile apart from occasional bone and shell fragments. The clay when trowelled came away in blocks, making it very similar to layers F359 (Phase 6), F318 (Phase 14) and F315 (Phase 15) as well as pit fill deposit F351 (Phase 10); a near identical layer (F260) was excavated in Area A (Phase 3). Deposit F310, stratified on layer F312, was buff ashy sediment on a thin seam of charcoal; it contained a body sherd of Ham Green A pottery with applied strip decoration, dated to *c.* 1140–70 (E324:8800/1).

The pre-castle stratigraphy of Area K is concluded at Phase 18 with deposit F307, stratified on Phase 17 deposit F310; it was greenish light brown silty clay up to 0.37m deep with frequent small stones (10–20mm across), shell and occasional bone (Fig. 3.37). Deposit F307 contained a powdery charcoal lens (F309), 0.25m by 0.2m and up to 30mm deep, with associated red sediment. Deposit F307 was the latest pre-castle deposit excavated in Area K. It was discovered under heavy post-medieval rubble overburden (F297) and was truncated by a feature containing a similar body of brick-and-mortar rubble (F370).

Interpretation

Cutting 2 in the Powder Tower area is a long narrow punctuated slice through the deposits of Viking-age Dublin on ground sloping towards the eastern limits of the town at the edge of the Poddle estuary. These deposits were cut into on all sides by later foundations and had dried out, resulting in the loss of organic materials. Areas A, B and C had also been severely truncated by the basement of Block 8, leaving only the lowest layers undisturbed. However, in the tiny Area K, outside Block 8 to the west, a complete series of layers from subsoil up to the late twelfth century was recorded.

A feature common to Phase 1 in all the main areas was the occurrence of a surface with mostly intermittent small stones/pebbles, referred to during the excavation as pebble cobbling. Most of this was not any sort of formal cobbling and much of it could have been a stony layer that forms naturally beneath the sod in permanent grassland. It is possible that the sod was stripped off much of this ground for other purposes such as building and roofing in the initial stages of the settlement leaving this stony layer as a surface. The one clear exception was in Area C, a deliberately laid down surface of small stones 2.2m wide (F392) and running in a north-north-west to south-south-east direction at a slightly lower level than the flanking subsoil. This appears to have been a roadway or street originally using the bare ground, which became eroded and slightly sunken from use and required this metalling of stones to give it a more durable surface. Features at each side of F392 are consistent with it being a roadway between property plots, especially post-holes and lines of stake-holes on the east edge of the road. Also, Alignment 1 of stake-holes in Area A has the same alignment as the roadway.

The existence of a roadway here is supported by the overlying Phase 2 layers, where a paving of large flags covered much of Area C. A puzzle about this paving is that it was missing from a large portion of the centre of the area, which would have been the centre of the road. There are at least two possible explanations: 1) that there had been fine paving flags here but that they were lifted for reuse elsewhere, or 2) that this centre part of the road had a surface of timber planks, which have rotted away. The pathway (F36) beside House III at the Cross Block contained paving stones as well as timbers (see Chapter 3.5). While the Phase 2 paving kept roughly to the same line as the Phase 1 cobbling on the east side, it extended much more on the west side. It is possible that this is fortuitous and merely the paved entrance to a plot on the west side, with the post-hole (F306) holding a gatepost that served both phases. On the limited evidence of Phase 3, the last surviving Viking-age phase in Area C, this road line appears to have gone out of use at that stage.

It is difficult to identify in plan definite evidence for houses in these areas and no clearly defined hearths were uncovered. Some of the post-holes and stake-holes, in particular Alignment 1 in Area A and a double line of stake-holes in Area L (both Phase 1), could have belonged to houses or other buildings but the alignments were too short and fragmentary to be certain in either case. However, what is suggestive of house floors were layers of clay or estuarine mud. A feature of some of these layers is that they came apart in blocks, suggesting that these floors were made up of spade-cut blocks of estuarine mud as has been recorded at other Viking sites as in Cork (Ní Loingsigh 2014). Examples of such layers in Area A were F284 (Phase 2) and F260 (Phase 5). A number of such layers were found in Area K: F359 (Phase 6), F321 (Phase 13), F318 (Phase 14), F315 (Phase 15) and F312 (Phase 17). Other layers found are consistent with being a build-up of occupation debris or deliberate dumping/levelling. An example of deliberate raising of the ground is likely to be F279 in Area A, possibly to form a platform for a house above potential flood levels here, close to the edge of the Poddle estuary.

Radiocarbon dating indicates that at least Phases 1 to 3 belong to the tenth century. Finds from the later phases in Area K indicate that the upper layers here can be dated to the twelfth century. The latest layer here (F307), a thick deposit of clay and stones, was most likely brought in at some point in the latter part of the twelfth century to raise the ground level for some purpose at this time; it is broadly contemporary with the Powder Tower, Cutting 1, Phase 3 level, comprising deposits dumped to raise the ground in that location.

Pl. 3.35 General view of Bermingham Tower excavations; from east. At bottom left is the area enclosed by the base of the square tower where traces of Viking-age deposits had survived. The remains of the thirteenth-century city wall can be seen extending westward from the square tower and is partly overlain by an eighteenth-century wall.

Pl. 3.36 Post-excavation view of gully (F118), later medieval drain (F64) along bottom edge; from east.

Chapter 3.4
The Bermingham Tower area: tenth-century gully and ditch

Introduction

The circular tower known as the Bermingham Tower, which is located at the south-west corner of the castle, was probably the first to be built following the royal mandate of 1204 (Manning 2017–18). A square tower abutted the west side of the Bermingham Tower and the city wall extended westward from the square tower across the castle moat (Fig. 1.1). In 1775 the tower was taken down to *c.*1.7m above the level of subsoil on its west side and was rebuilt with thinner walls. Following demolition of nineteenth/twentieth-century structures, a single large area (BT1, excavation E297) was excavated adjacent to the Bermingham Tower to facilitate the construction of new kitchen facilities to service the castle complex (Fig. 3.39; Pl. 3.35). The excavations covered an area of *c.* 26.7m (east-west) by *c.* 13.7m but for logistical reasons excavation to subsoil within the moat took place only in Trench A and Trenches B1–B4. A short stretch of the lower part of the medieval base of the Bermingham Tower was exposed, together with the adjacent curtain wall that extended northwards. A 10m-long curved stretch of earlier masonry had been incorporated in the thirteenth-century curtain wall, suggesting a pre-1204 masonry structure on the site. The remains of the base of the square tower were uncovered, which were shown to have been constructed by scarping the boulder clay and facing the vertical clay surfaces with mortared limestone masonry. The subsoil left *in situ* within the foundations of the square tower contained the only traces of Viking-age activity recorded in this area (Fig. 3.39).

Viking-age Features

The subsoil (F48) encapsulated within the foundations of the square tower was *c.* 10m OD and comprised a compact mottled clay ranging in colour from yellow to green and orange/red with iron-staining and containing decayed stone. The area of subsoil exposed measured *c.* 4.52m (north-south) by *c.* 4.48m and was delimited on the north and west by the foundations of the tower, on the east by the pre-castle masonry (F30/F40) and on the south by an eighteenth-century wall contemporary with the rebuilding of the upper portion of the Bermingham Tower in 1775. The building of this latter wall (F26) and its associated wide foundation trench (F42) had removed all traces of the south wall of the square tower. A drain (F64) contemporary with the construction of the tower extended north-south across the centre of the exposed subsoil, while an early twentieth-century sewer (F66) had been inserted across the site by tunnelling between a series of open pits (Fig. 3.40).

A linear feature (F118) aligned roughly east-west had been cut into subsoil. It was truncated on the west by the wall of the tower and on the east by the stone-lined drain (F64) (Figs 3.40, 3.41; Pl. 3.36). This feature was *c.* 1.84m long by up to 1.17m wide and 0.25m (max) deep. Two stake-holes (F122a/b), 0.55m apart, were uncovered in the base of the feature close to the west wall. These were 50-60mm in diameter and *c.* 0.18m deep. The fill (F113) of this linear feature was grey/brown silty clay with moderate flecks of charcoal, large stones and occasional mussel shell fragments. It contained frequent animal bones but no artefacts. A radiocarbon date of cal AD 883–1017 (95.4% probability) was obtained from a bone sample (sheep/goat mandible) from the fill.

Pl. 3.37 'Ditch' (F143) visible in section to left of left-hand ranging rod; the 'ditch' was cut by the eighteenth-century foundation trench (F42) as was the footing of the pre-1204 wall (F30) visible at top; from west.

Traces of another feature (F143) cut into subsoil were exposed in the south-east corner of the area. It had been truncated on the south by the foundation trench (F42) for the eighteenth-century wall, on the west by the sewer trench and on the east by the narrow foundation trench (F128) for the early masonry wall (F40). The feature in question survived as a south-facing scarp in the subsoil, just 1m long (east-west) by up to 0.9m wide and 0.85m deep (Figs 3.41, 3.42). The fill (F137) was similar to that of the linear feature F118 and comprised a brown/yellow silty clay with charcoal flecks, shell fragments and frequent animal bone (Pl. 3.37). Artefacts recovered from the fill of this feature included a metal object, a piece of flint and a possible clay mould fragment, but unfortunately these could not be located for the present study.

A bowl-shaped pit (F120) cut into subsoil underneath the thirteenth-century drain (F64) was noted in section (Fig. 3.41). The surviving pit was 0.34m wide by 0.14m deep and the fill (F121) was a rust-coloured silty sand with no inclusions or finds.

A limited number of deposits were stratified on the subsoil in the south-west corner of the interior of the tower (Figs 3.40, 3.41). While these deposits had no direct stratigraphic link with the features described above, they pre-date the construction of the thirteenth-century drain (F64) and may well relate to the Viking-age activity in this area. Deposits F163, F164 were stratified directly on the subsoil and comprised silty yellow clay with occasional charcoal, shell fragments and one stone with mortar adhering to it. The overlying deposits (F162, F161) contained some bone fragments while the uppermost deposit (F138) was similar to the fill of the linear features and contained charcoal flecks, mussel and cockle shells, animal bone and decayed stone (Fig. 3.41).

Pre-Castle Masonry

The excavations exposed a short section (*c.* 1.82m) of the thirteenth-century vertical base of the Bermingham Tower that survived to a height of *c.* 1.65m (Pl. 3.38). At a distance of *c.* 2m north of the tower, a 10m-long curved stretch of earlier masonry had been incorporated in the thirteenth-century curtain wall (Fig. 3.43; Pls 3.38–3.40). This early wall (F40) was constructed with large limestone blocks and had an offset footing (F30) set within a very narrow foundation trench (F128) cut into the subsoil (Figs 3.40, 3.44). The maximum excavated width of this wall was *c.* 1.74m and its full width could not be determined since the foundations of the west wall of the eighteenth-century buildings were built directly on top of it. The early wall was breached to insert the Bermingham Tower the foundations of which were partly constructed on the earlier footing (F30), and a stretch of new masonry (F29) *c.*1.9m long was constructed to fill the gap between the tower and the earlier wall (Figs 3.43, 3.44; Pls 3.38, 3.40). The construction of the early thirteenth-century west curtain wall of the castle incorporated this earlier wall with the addition of an external face and base batter continuing down the east face of the newly dug moat and abutting the north face of the square tower (Fig. 3.44; Lynch *et al.*, forthcoming a).

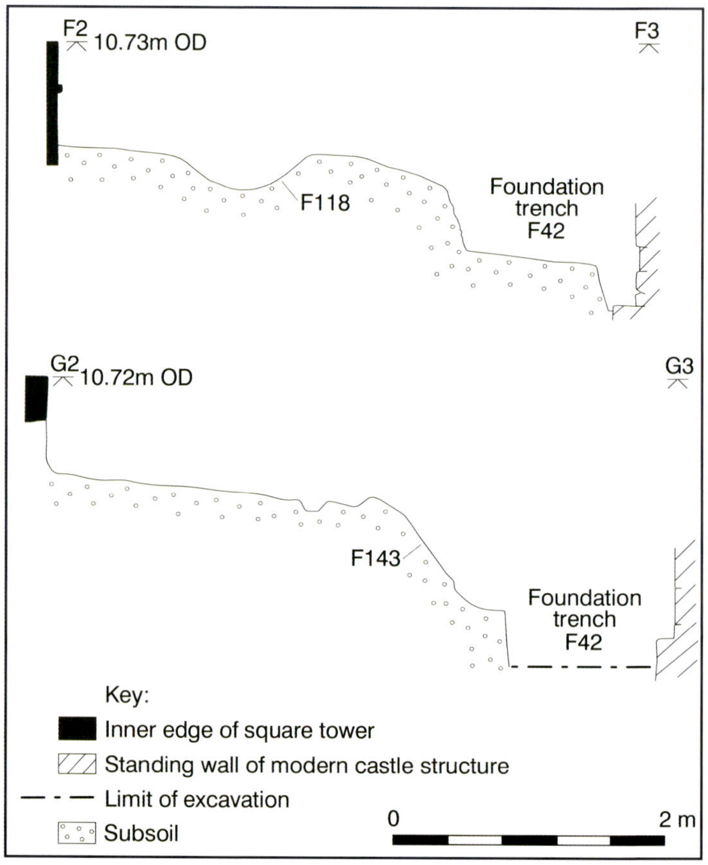

Fig. 3.42 Bermingham Tower; profiles F2-F3 and G2-G3 (for location see Fig. 3.40).

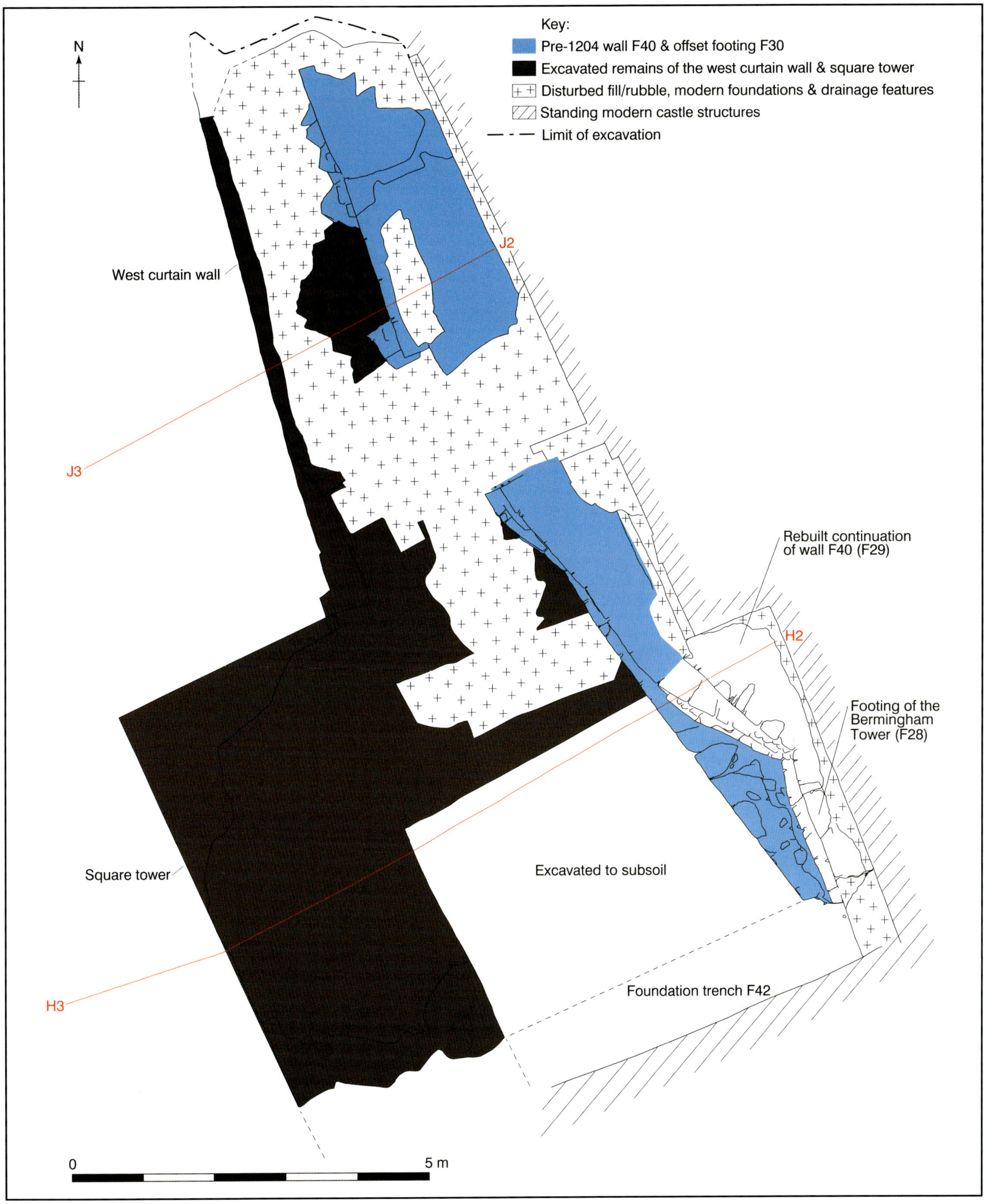

Fig. 3.43 Bermingham Tower; pre-1204 masonry (F40) in relation to later structures.

Pl. 3.38 Western elevation of curving pre-1204 wall (F40) with rebuilt section of the wall (F29) immediately to left of ranging rod and footing (F28) of the Bermingham Tower to the right. All three sit on the footing (F30) of the pre-1204 wall that extends beneath the ranging rod. The north wall of the square tower abuts the early footing at bottom left.

Pl. 3.39 Detail of facing stones of pre-1204 wall (F40) with offset footing (F30).

Pl. 3.40 Remains of pre-1204 wall (F40) with ranging rod lying on abutting thirteenth-century curtain wall; wall of square tower abuts curtain wall, centre right; from north.

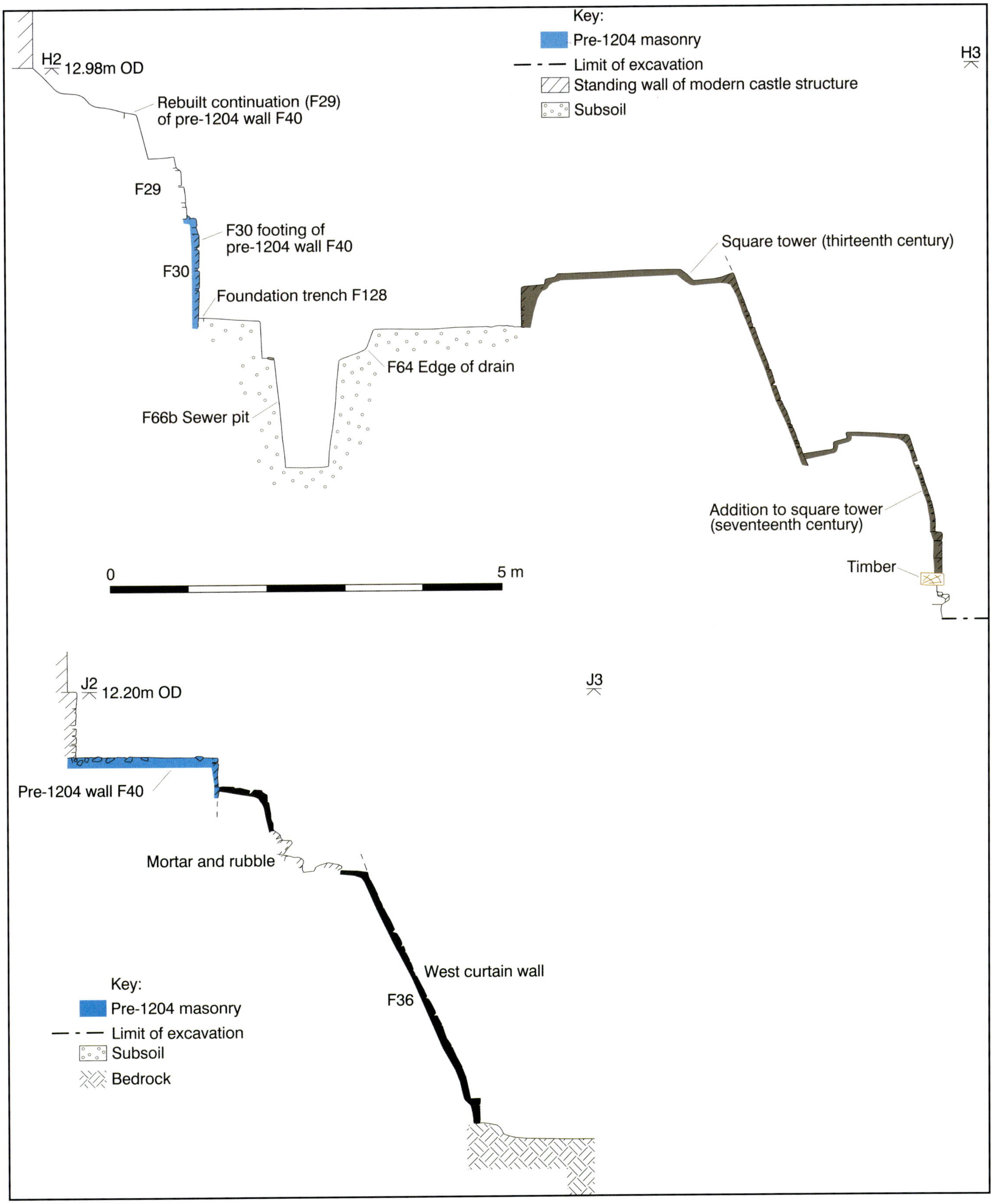

Fig. 3.44 Bermingham Tower; profiles H2-H3 and J2-J3 of pre-1204 masonry and later features (for location see Fig. 3.43).

Interpretation

The ephemeral nature of the features recorded in the subsoil encapsulated within the foundations of the square tower, together with the lack of associated finds, renders their interpretation difficult. Stratigraphically, the linear feature F118 pre-dates the construction of the square tower, while the cut feature F143 pre-dates the early masonry (F40) incorporated into the thirteenth-century curtain wall. This, together with the radiocarbon date centred on the mid-tenth century obtained from the fill of F118, indicates pre-castle Viking-age activity. The small bowl-shaped pit F120 underlying the thirteenth-century drain and adjacent deposits also probably belongs to this period. The date of the early masonry incorporated within the thirteenth-century curtain wall is unclear. Its curving nature suggests an enclosing or *enceinte* wall which could belong to a late twelfth-century Anglo-Norman fortification on the site although a pre-Norman, Hiberno-Scandinavian date cannot be ruled out since the building of substantial defensive masonry walls was well established in Dublin by *c.* 1100 (Wallace 2016, 138). The significance of this early masonry is further considered below in Chapter 9.

Both features (F118, F143) cut into subsoil had similar fills and appear to be of tenth-century date. Their location downslope from the house plots recorded in the Cork Tower area (there is over 2m difference in the level of subsoil) places these features close to the River Poddle and just inside the embanked defences of the Hiberno-Scandinavian town, later replaced by the city wall of medieval Dublin. No evidence of the embanked defences was uncovered within the base of the square tower, in contrast to the Powder Tower, where the remnants of successive embankments had survived (see Chapter 3.2 above). It is possible that houses were not built this close to the Poddle but the extremely limited area available for investigation militates against any such conclusion – extensive housing could, for example, have existed immediately to the west in the area later disturbed by the digging of the castle moat.

The remains of both cut features were aligned east-west, running parallel to the line of the Hiberno-Scandinavian defensive embankment (later superseded by the medieval city wall) with the River Poddle flowing just outside. Feature F118, although up to 1.17m wide, was on average just 0.2m deep and could best be interpreted as a drainage channel or gully. This gully did not extend eastward beyond the thirteenth-century drain (F64) and it appears to widen towards the west, where it was truncated by the foundations of the square tower and where the presence of two stake-holes suggests an associated ephemeral structure. The remains of the second feature (F143), although compromised on three sides by later structures, appears to have been considerably deeper (up to *c.* 0.9m) and may be the edge of a ditch or indeed a large pit. This feature did not extend westward beyond the sewer trench, leaving a gap of *c.* 2m between it and the gully.

Chapter 3.5
The Cross Block area: house plots of the tenth and eleventh centuries

Introduction

In the late seventeenth/early eighteenth centuries the medieval castle was replaced with a commodious quadrangle of buildings. The building forming the east side of this quadrangle, known as the Cross Block, separates the Upper Castle Yard from the Lower Castle Yard of the modern castle complex (Fig. 1.1). In 1961 a decision was taken to demolish and rebuild the Cross Block, as it was deemed to be structurally unsafe. When demolition took place in October of that year it resulted in a large, ragged trench extending from the Record Tower in the south to Block 10 (the site of the medieval Powder Tower) in the north (Pls 3.41, 3.42). It was noted that masonry belonging to the medieval castle had been exposed within this trench, as well as evidence of early habitation in the form of medieval pottery sherds, animal bone, shell, ash and charcoal. The need for an archaeological excavation was recognised, not only to examine and record the evidence for earlier habitation but also to expose and examine masonry remains which might be utilised for foundations. On the recommendation of the Principal Architect of the Office of Public Works, the archaeological excavation was to be carried out by the National Monuments Branch of the OPW and accordingly excavations commenced in November 1961 under the direction of Marcus Ó hEochaidhe and continued until February 1962.

The archaeological investigations were constrained by several factors: the building contractor was already working on site, and it was a proviso that the archaeological excavation should not impede the construction work in any way; the time factor was also important and delays to the construction work had to be kept to an absolute minimum while the time of year, mid-winter, was not ideal for this type of work. As a result, the scale of the investigation was limited to the minimum required to provide an intelligible record of the archaeological content of the areas to be impacted by the rebuilding work. Four separate areas were investigated but Cutting B was the only one where pre-thirteenth-century levels were excavated (Fig. 3.45; Pl. 3.43).

Excavations were suspended in February 1962 at a time when the lowest stratigraphic levels in Cutting B had not been investigated and the exposed section faces had not been fully recorded or interpreted. However, provision was made in the design of the new Cross Block to allow access to these lower levels at a future date and a thick layer of peatmoss was laid over the partially excavated levels in order to keep them damp (J.B. Maguire, pers. comm.). At the time of the 1980s excavations, when Cutting B was still accessible, it was impossible without excavation to judge the state of preservation of features and layers at the base of the cutting, but the sides had dried out and portions had collapsed into the cutting. Access to this area has since been cut off by the insertion of a suspended floor. It would be desirable to undertake further excavation here at a future date.

A preliminary account of the excavations was completed by Ó hEochaidhe in October 1962, a copy of which is lodged in the National Monuments Service Archive. It had been intended to complete the excavation of Cutting B but this did not happen and, as Ó hEochaidhe left the employment of the National Monuments Service in 1970, a full account of the excavations was never published. The preliminary report includes a summary account of the stratigraphy and features uncovered, as well as seven plans, 25 photographs, including one of part of the north section face with the identified horizons/phases indicated (Pl. 3.47) and a preliminary inventory of 106 artefacts recovered from Cutting B. Further searches of the excavation archive located 1779 sherds of medieval pottery not included in the inventory (Papazian and McCutcheon, forthcoming).

Pl. 3.41 Cross Block site following demolition *c.* October 1961; from north. The inner face of the medieval east curtain wall can be seen extending from the bottom left corner towards the Record Tower.

Pl. 3.42 Cross Block site following demolition *c.* October 1961; from south.

Analysis and discussion of the 161 artefacts and a small amount of craft waste material that can be assigned to the Viking-age levels have been included in the finds reports (see Chapter 4 below).

This account of the unfinished 1961–2 excavation of Cutting B under the Cross Block is based on the unpublished preliminary report (Ó hEochaidhe 1962) and on unpublished notes dated 5 February 1962 on a section of stratigraphy (Mitchell 1984). Of particular use in the interpretation of the features were the plans and photographs of the different levels in the preliminary report as well as the short text, which was never intended as a full account of the excavation. The phases identified by the excavator were numbered from the top to the lowest excavated level as Horizon I to Horizon VI. The excavation was stopped before subsoil was reached and, consequently, it is unknown how many phases or layers lay between Horizon VI and the subsoil. Therefore, in the account below, the phases are lettered A to G from the lowest excavated level to the top, in recognition that Phase A is not the earliest phase and to distinguish it from the other excavated areas in Dublin Castle, where Phase 1 was on the subsoil. Horizon VI is here divided into two phases (A and B) resulting in seven phases (A to G) in place of Ó hEochaidhe's six horizons (Table 3.1). Phases A to F belong to the Viking Age, while Phase G appears to date to the period after 1170. The series of hearths have been renumbered chronologically, i.e. from the earliest to the most recent. New numbers have been allocated to the main

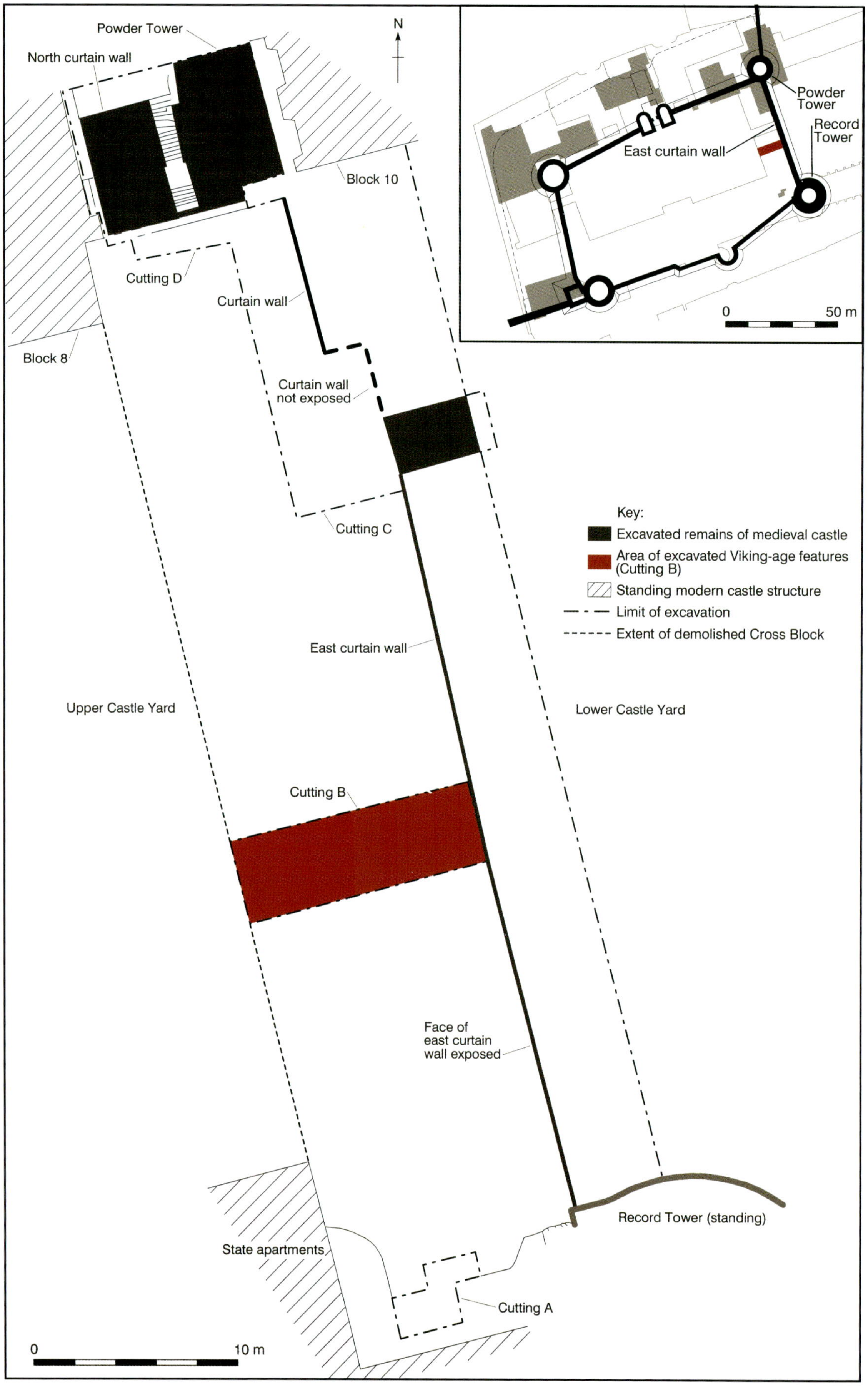

Fig. 3.45 Cross Block; areas excavated and location of Viking-age deposits (Cutting B).

Table 3.1 Concordance between Ó hEochaidhe's numbering of horizons and hearths and the designation of phases, houses and features used in this report.

1961/2 report Horizon	1961/2 report Hearth	Phase	House	Hearth	Features
I		Phase G			F1-F2
II	Hearth 1	Phase F	House V	Hearth 5	F3-F14
III	Hearth 2	Phase E	House IV	Hearth 4	F15-F25
IV	Hearth 3	Phase D	House III	Hearth 3	F26-F41
V	Hearth 4	Phase C		Hearth 2	F42-F43
VI		Phase B	House II		F44-F54
VI	Hearth 5	Phase A	House I	Hearth 1	F55-F75

features (F1 to F75) for ease of description, discussion and reference to the illustrations. Identified houses have been numbered I to V from the earliest to the latest.

Cutting B measured 38 feet (11.58m) east-west by 11 feet (3.35m) north-south and was situated to the south of the archway in the Cross Block that gives access between the two yards of Dublin Castle (Figs 1.1, 3.45; Pl. 3.43). It spanned the width of the then demolished block and this particular location was chosen to cause the least inconvenience to the contractor, who was working on other parts of the site. A substantial wall forming the east end of the cutting was interpreted by the excavator as the east curtain wall of the medieval castle (Pls 3.41, 3.42).

Most of the finds from Horizon II (Phase F) to Horizon V (Phase C) were catalogued in the preliminary report with the numbers B1 to B106 and many were illustrated photographically (Ó hEochaidhe 1962). These have been renumbered for the purposes of publication as E748:1 to E748:106, using a unique excavation number that was more recently assigned to the Cross Block excavation. All, apart from seven, of these finds have survived and there is a photograph of one of the seven missing objects – the iron shackles (E748:90; Pl. 4.15). Other finds from Cutting B in the Cross Block have survived, with numbers between B107 (E748:107) and B154 (E748:154). There are no surviving finds corresponding with fifteen of the numbers in this latter sequence. It is likely that most of these were from Horizon VI (Phases A and B), but there is no certainty about this. Some 868 sherds of pottery were recovered from Horizon I (Phase G) and most of these were numbered by the excavator as B155 to B986 (now E748:155 to E748:986) with a number of sherds in some cases under one number (Papazian and McCutcheon, forthcoming). No catalogue of the finds from B107 (E749:107) to B986 (E748:986) was available to the authors, though labels attached to some of them between B107 and B154 indicated their context. Only two pottery sherds were recorded from phases earlier than G and these were B148 (E748:148) and B149 (E748:149) from Phase D (see Chapter 4.9 below).

The understanding of the features uncovered in this cutting is almost entirely dependent on the plans of the different levels in the preliminary report (Ó hEochaidhe 1962, Figs 2, 3, 4, 5, 6), which have been redrawn here in reverse order as figs 3.46–3.50. There is no signature on the first three of these, which must have been drawn by a member of the excavation team (Figs 3.48–3.50). The last two to be drawn (Figs 3.46, 3.47) were initialled 'R.P.C.' by the late Robert (Bob) Corrigan, who was employed as an architectural assistant/surveyor with the National Monuments Service. He also drew the overall plan of the Cross Block site showing the cuttings (Ó hEochaidhe 1962, fig. 1), on which Fig. 3.45 is based, and the plan and section of the postern gate and steps on the north curtain wall in Cutting D, which he initialled and dated '31/1/'62' (Ó hEochaidhe 1962, fig. 7).

Two other sources throw light on the organisation and progress of the excavation and these are the job diary of J.B. Maguire, who was employed as an architect with the OPW and worked on the project (J.B. Maguire, pers. comm.) and contemporary press clippings relating to the excavation found in the National Monuments Archive. Discussions about carrying out an excavation were held with the National Museum of Ireland and the National Monuments Branch of OPW on 10 October 1961 and the excavation began on Monday 6 November. The excavation team consisted of labourers employed by the building contractor with Mr Coyle and Miss Moran of Schools Section (OPW) seconded to the excavation to assist with recording up to

24 November. Miss Moran had archaeological digging experience. Hearth 3 (Phase D) had been uncovered and the comb with the ogham inscription had been found by 6 December; by 12 January 1962 Houses I and II (Phases A, B) had been uncovered. At a project meeting on 1 January 1962 a decision was made to suspend building work until 7 February and to leave three of the contractor's men working with Mr Ó hEochaidhe (J.B. Maguire, pers. comm.). It would appear, therefore, that Wednesday 6 February was the last day of the excavation, and that Professor Mitchell recorded his profile (see below) on the previous day.

The excavation, although limited in scale and time, excited considerable interest in the press and the earliest of the press cuttings is from the *Irish Independent*, 19 December 1961, where a report included photographs of the comb with the ogham inscription and the 'weaver's comb' and mention of other finds from Phase D. A report in the *Irish Press* of 18 January mentioned the wickerwork levels beneath three stone-kerbed hearths. After excavation ceased there was a report in the *Irish Press* of 10 February based on a press release from Donogh O'Malley, TD, Parliamentary Secretary to the Minister of Finance, on the results of the excavation. In the same issue there was a forum piece titled 'Do we treasure our treasures?' with contributions from Marcus Ó hEochaidhe, P.J. Hartnett, archaeological officer with Bórd Fáilte (the tourist board) and Dr George Little of the Dublin Historical Society. The tourist potential of the discovery was adverted to as well as the desirability of spending public money on such excavations. These discussions mark the beginning of public recognition of the importance of the archaeological deposits that survive beneath the centre of Dublin and the potential of such deposits to contribute to understanding the origins and development of the city. Dr Little's abiding interest was in pre-Viking Dublin and he wrote two further pieces on the subject in the same newspaper on 12 and 13 February. L.S. Gogan was similarly preoccupied in an article in the *Irish Times* of 24 February, where he found the finds 'singularly undramatic' and hoped that the 'fortress of the Eblani' might be found beneath the Viking levels.

Pl. 3.43 Cross Block site; excavation of Cutting B (between the two large tripods) has commenced; from north.

In the following account the description of features is based mostly on the plans in the preliminary report, because no site diary or description of features from the time of the excavation was available to the authors.

Layers below Phase A

An important source of information on this cutting is the profile recorded by Professor G.F. Mitchell on 5 February 1962 as the excavations 'were coming to an end'. The source for this is a single page report typed and signed by Mitchell and dated 8 March 1984 (Mitchell 1984). In this report he attempted to marry his profile with features and horizons recorded by Ó hEochaidhe in the 1962 preliminary report (Table 3.2). A close examination indicates that the two profiles are not even partly comparable and the depths below the top of the cutting that are given by Mitchell show beyond doubt that Mitchell's profile is of an otherwise unrecorded test pit dug below the lowest level of the main excavation at a point recorded by Mitchell as 9' 6" (2.9m) west of the east curtain wall of the castle. This is nearly 2m east of Ó hEochaidhe's Hearth V (Hearth 1), which Mitchell attempted to tie in with his profile. The digging of such a test pit or sondage at this stage of the project would have been essential in attempting to work out what depth remained to be excavated. Though this pit was 0.82m deep, it had still not reached subsoil.

While it is difficult to be sure of interpreting anything in a profile such as this, the identification of wattle in three of the layers might indicate house floors and, consequently, three further possible phases represented by this pit. What further depth there may have been between the ash spread at the base and subsoil is unknown.

Phase A

This was the earliest structural phase that was uncovered in the excavation. It corresponds to the second and third 'wickerwork' (i.e. wattle) levels as named by the excavator (Ó hEochaidhe 1962).

HOUSE I

It is argued here that most of the features referred to in the preliminary report (Ó hEochaidhe 1962) as the second and third wattle levels (Fig. 3.46) are contemporary. Because no accurate levels are recorded in the preliminary report and no drawn section survives it is difficult to be sure of the relative levels of features. A natural fall in the ground here towards the east may have given the impression that Ó hEochaidhe's '3rd Wickerwork' was earlier than his '2nd Wickerwork' to the west.

The remains of a rectangular wattle-walled house of Dublin Type 1 (Wallace 1992) can be identified from the excavation plan and a photograph (Fig. 3.46; Pl. 3.44). The recognisable features of the house are a doorway at the west end with threshold (F61) and jambs (F62), a wattle wall (F67) running southwards from the doorway and continuing around the south-west corner for a short distance (F68); another part of the south wall (F68) at its east end with the south-east corner and part of the east wall and portion of a fine stone-kerbed central hearth (F59, Hearth 1). There were also areas of wattle flooring contemporary with the house: inside the west doorway (F62) and in the south-east corner area (F64). Outside were evenly spaced east-west timber rods (F69), probably the foundation for a paving of timber planks. At the south end of F69 was a small patch of wattle (F71). South of this was an area of stone paving (F72). To the west of F69 was an oval charred patch (F70). Close to the south-east corner and about 0.6m from the south wall of the house was an east-west line of stakes (F73), probably part of a property boundary (Fig. 3.46).

Table 3.2 A profile recorded by Professor G.F. Mitchell in Cutting B at the Cross Block at a point 9 feet 6 inches (2.9m) west of the east curtain wall. It is argued here that this profile relates to a sondage dug below the lowest point reached in the excavation.

Depth below top of cutting	Mitchell's original description of layers dated 5 February 1962
2.40m-2.48m	Hearth? Charcoal and ash.
2.48m-2.54m	Light-brown clayey debris on wattle-floor.
2.54m-2.61m	Green-brown laminated mud?/dung?, with some sand and much debris.
2.61m-2.67m	Dark-brown debris, crumby, sandy.
2.67m-2.77m	Green-brown very fibrous debris, with brown dung?
2.77m-2.81m	Light-brown debris, ashy?, clayey?, associated with wattle-floor.
2.81m-2.85m	Dark green-brown debris.
2.85m-2.86m	Thin band of ash.
2.86m-2.90m	Brown laminated debris, with shell and bone.
2.90m-3.00m	Brown crumbly fibrous debris. At 2.95m wattle floor.
3.00m-3.22m	Brown mixed debris with shell, stone, charcoal, wood and bone. At 3.02m patch of yellow clay.
At 3.22m	Top of extensive ash spread.

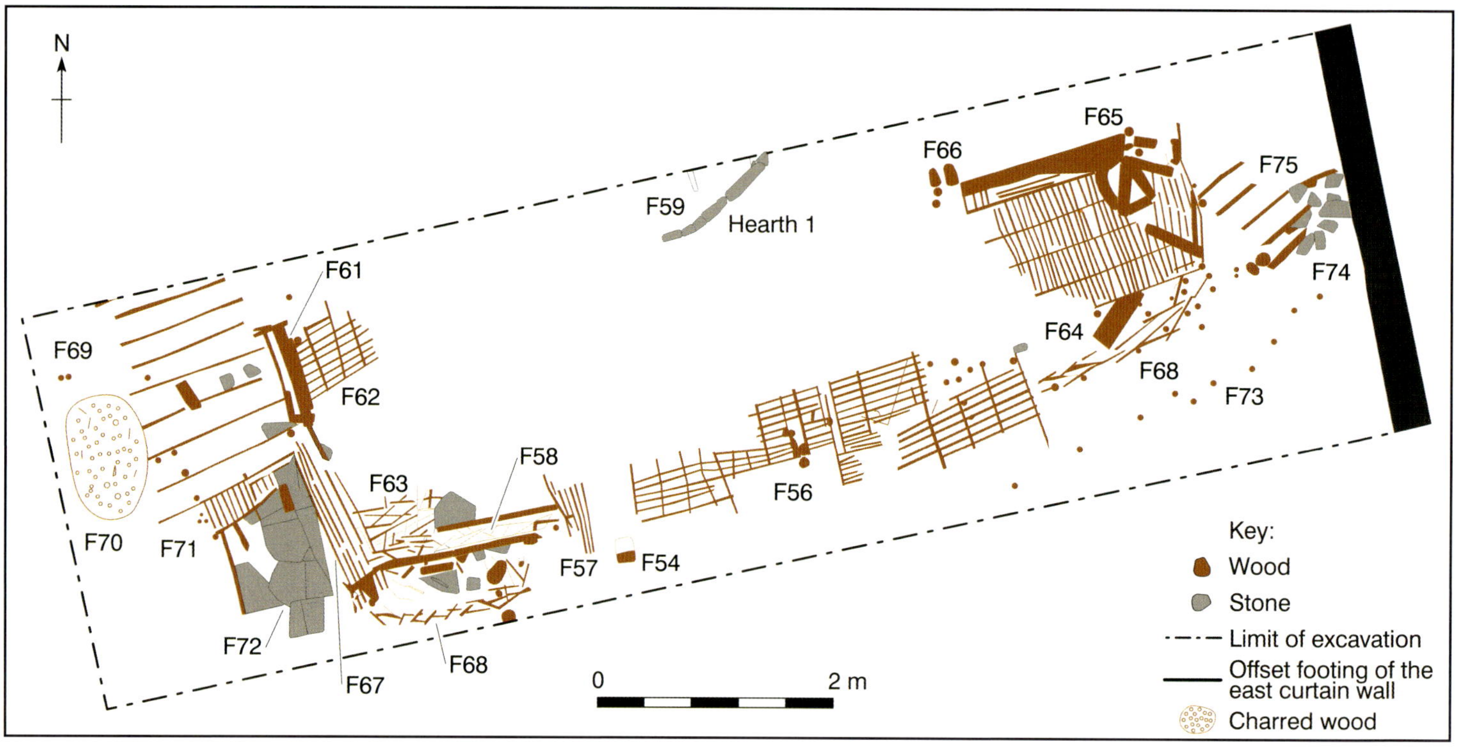

Fig. 3.46 Cross Block, Cutting B; Phase A, House I.

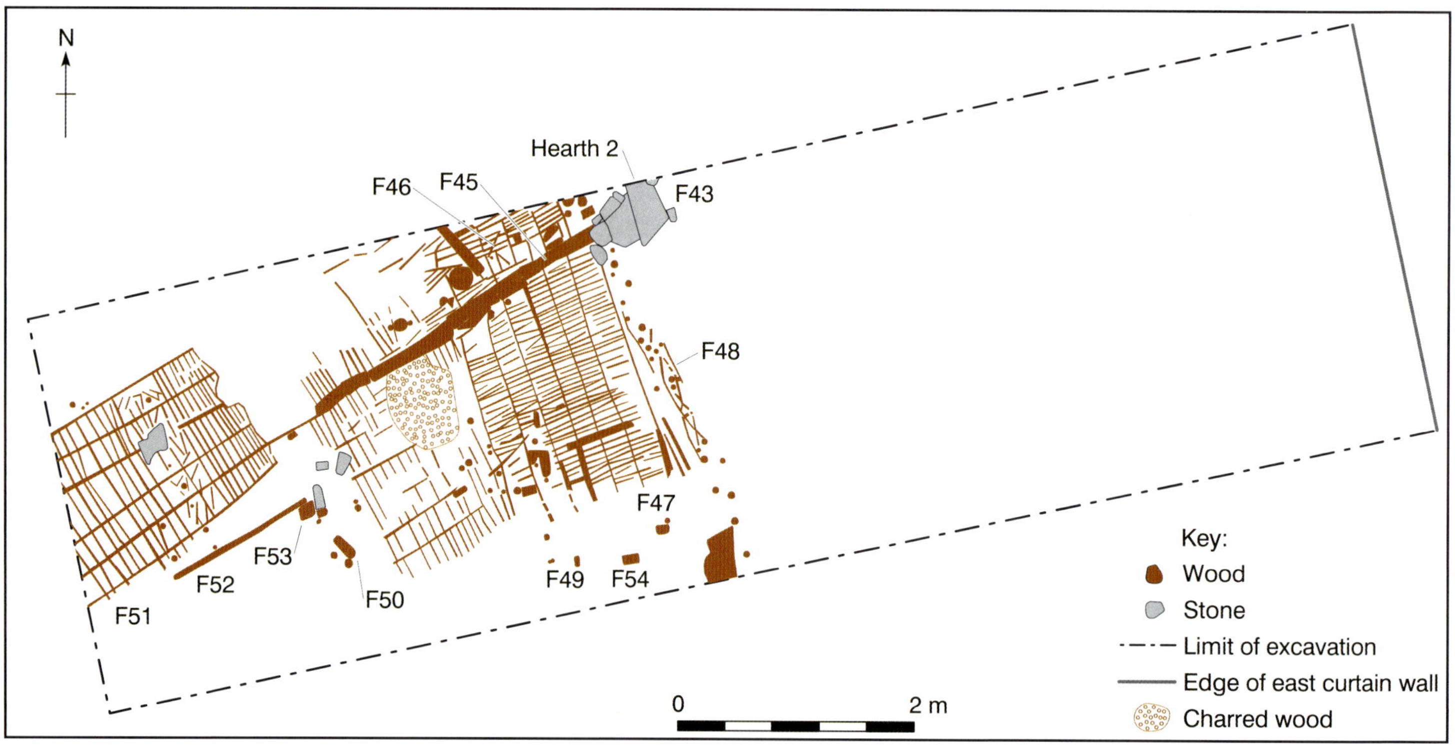

Fig. 3.47 Cross Block, Cutting B; House II (Phase B) and Hearth 2 (Phase C).

Pl. 3.44 Exposed remains of south-west corner of House I (Phase A); excavation of Cutting B was discontinued at this stage. Part of the wattle flooring (F47) from House II (Phase B) is visible at bottom left; from north-west.

The measurements of the house as calculated from the plan are *c.* 7.75m long by *c.* 5.3m wide. The width has been calculated as twice the distance from the centre of the hearth to the line of the south wall, thereby giving a possible floor area of *c.* 41m^2.

Some of the features recorded on plan (Fig. 3.46) belong to a destruction or build-up layer above the floor and other remains of House I. The long flat strips of wattle matting (F56) overlying much of the south wall were part of this layer and may be pieces of demolished wattle walling. There was a dislodged piece of wattle work along with east-west strips of timber (F58) in the south-west corner of the house, while overlying them was another dislodged piece of wattle (F57) aligned north-south (Pl. 3.44). There were no finds from this phase catalogued in the preliminary report, though some of those numbered between E748:107 and 154 may have come from these levels.

Phase B

This corresponds with Ó hEochaidhe's 'first wickerwork' or wattle level of his Horizon VI. It is not clear why this is recorded only in the western half of the cutting (Fig. 3.47). It is possible that the Phase B levels in the eastern half of the cutting were greatly disturbed by the iron-working activity in the subsequent Phase C.

HOUSE II

The remains here can be interpreted as the south-west corner of a large rectangular house with a roughly east-west horizontal timber (F45) defining a partition and a roughly north-south wattle wall (F48) defining another. There was wattle flooring (F47) to the south of F45 and west of F48 (Pls 3.45, 3.46). Remains of further wattle flooring (F46) was

Pl. 3.45 Wattle flooring (F47) within House II (Phase B) bounded on left by post-and-wattle partition wall (F48) and at bottom by horizontal timber (F45); stones of Hearth 2 (Phase C) visible at bottom left; from north-west.

found to the north of F45 in the entrance lobby (Fig. 3.47). It appears that no trace of door jambs was found; these could have been uprooted for reuse or fuel. A possible line of north-south stakes (F50) and one squared post (F53) could be part of the west wall, while the line of the south wall may be indicated by some stakes (F49) and a post (F54). A fine wattle mat to the west (F51) may have been a pathway leading to the door of the house. An east-west timber (F52) is of unknown significance. Hearth 2 (F43) is problematic in that is obtrudes on and overlies F45 (Fig. 3.47; Pl. 3.45). One would expect the hearth belonging to this house to be further to the north and east and indeed outside the area excavated. Therefore, Hearth 2 appears to belong to Phase C. There were no finds from this phase catalogued in the preliminary report, though some of those numbered between E748:107 and 154 may have come from these levels.

Phase C

The preliminary report contained no plan or photograph of this phase, but the level is shown on the photograph of the northern section face (Pl. 3.47). It consisted of a layer some 0.4m deep (F42), which consisted of occupation debris with much evidence of fires and burning but no evidence of structures. Much iron slag (about twenty hemispherical pieces, not retained for post-excavation study) was found throughout the layer, indicating that iron working, most likely smithing, was carried out here during this phase (see Chapter 4.14.1). The annotated photograph of part of the north section face (Pl. 3.47) shows a clearly defined pit with a note indicating that it was filled with pure charcoal. The excavator interpreted this as a store of charcoal for the ironworkers, and ash-filled depressions as the remains of smelting hearths. Part of a stone-lined hearth (Hearth 2, F43; Fig. 3.47) appears to belong to this phase rather than to Phase B.

A considerable number of artefacts were recovered from this layer, including a fragment of Roman window glass (E748:75), a jet or jet-like disc or bead (E748:76), three iron knives (E748:77–9), an iron barrel padlock key (E748:80), a copper-alloy loop-headed ringed pin (E748:86), an iron arrowhead (E748:88), remains of iron shackles (E748:90), two bone spindle whorls (E748:94–5), a whale-bone clamp (E748:103), a wooden stave from a tankard (E748:104) and a decorated copper-alloy strap-end (E748:106).

A piece of unworked blackthorn from this phase, or possibly from Phase A or B, produced a radiocarbon date of cal AD 894–1036 (95.4% probability).

Phase D

This layer (F26) was 0.25m deep, with a recognisable Dublin Type 1 house (House III) and part of a timber pathway outside its south wall (Fig. 3.48).

HOUSE III

Central within the house and fully exposed and excavated within the cutting was a fine stone-kerbed hearth (Hearth 3, F27) (Pl. 3.49). A discontinuous single and, in places, double line of stakes formed the south wall (F35) and parts of the west (F34) and east (F40) walls. The threshold (F30) of the west doorway, but not the jambs, survived (Fig. 3.48). A north-south timber (F29) acted as the sill or threshold between the entrance lobby and the hearth area. There were some east-west timber floor planks (F32) between it and the doorway and others, two of which were aligned north-south (F28), to the east of F29. Further floor planks (F39) were partly exposed at the edge of the cutting near the north-east corner of the house. There was a cluster of

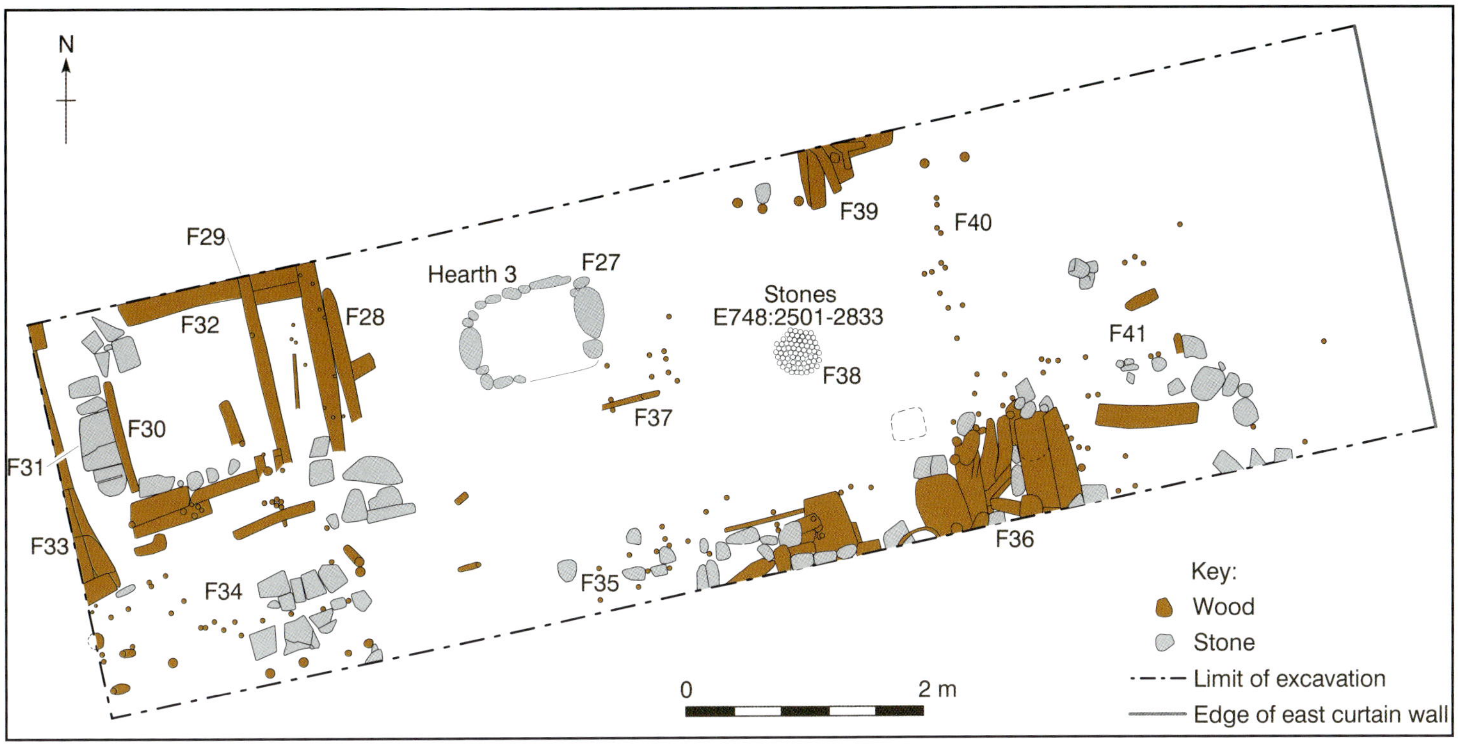

Fig. 3.48 Cross Block, Cutting B; Phase D, House III.

Pl. 3.46 Excavated remains of House II (Phase B); partition wall (F48) at bottom; from east.

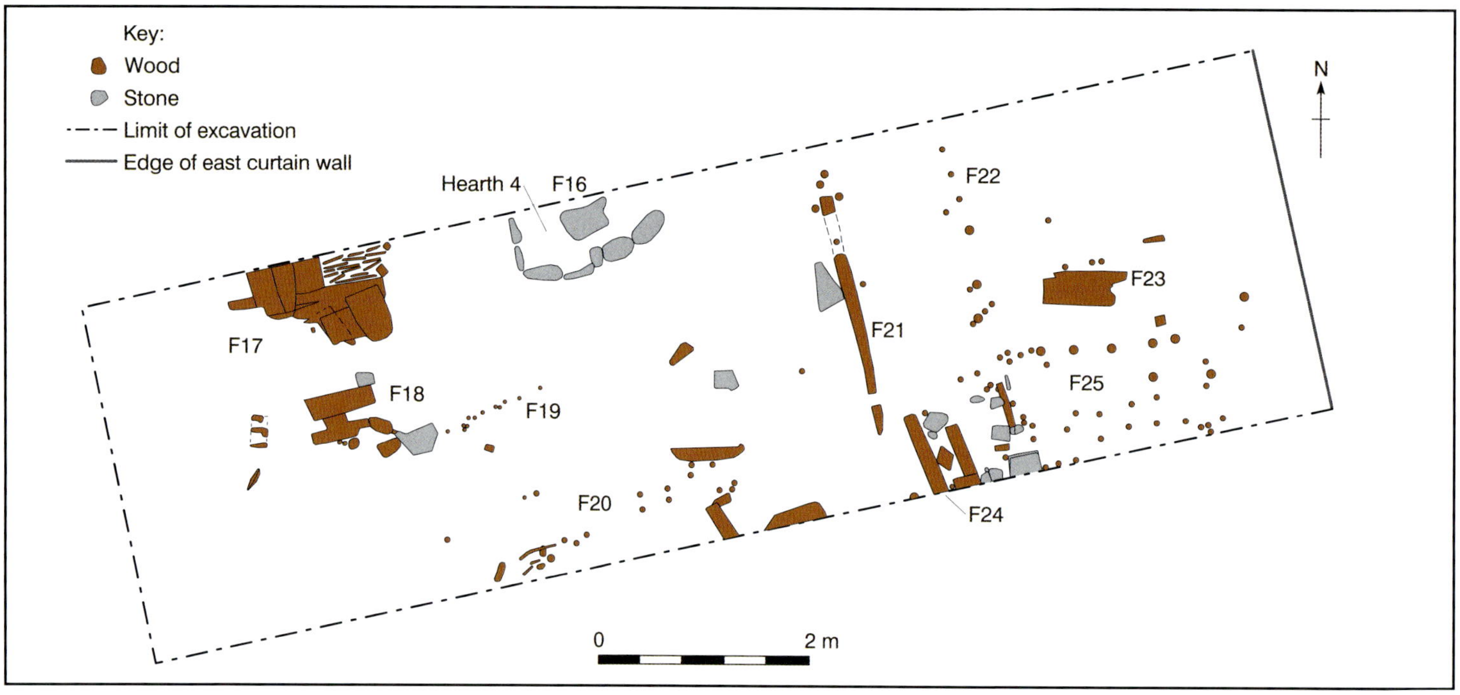

Fig. 3.49 Cross Block, Cutting B; Phase E, House IV.

stakes (F37) to the south-east of the hearth and a cache of what the excavator described as sling stones to the east of the stakes (stone pebbles E748:2501–2833; see Chapter 4.4.1). There was some stone paving (F31) immediately outside the threshold of the west doorway and west of this again the edge of plank paving aligned north-south was uncovered (F33). Immediately outside the south wall of the house, towards its east end and continuing a short distance beyond the corner, was a very well-made plank pathway (F36), the width of which is unknown, as it extended beyond the limit of excavation to the south (Fig. 3.48; Pl. 3.48). It ran in an east-west direction, with its split timbers aligned north-south and pegged into the ground. Beyond this to the east were some stakes, flat timbers and stones (F41). House III was some 7m long and an estimated 4.2m wide, giving a floor area of c. 29m².

Numerous objects were recovered from the associated occupation layer including an iron bridle cheek piece (E748:29), bone pins (E748:33, 40–1, 51–3, 60, 66), iron knives (E748:30, 34, 48, 50), six antler combs (E748:54–9), an iron barrel padlock bolt (E748:47), a copper-alloy stick pin (E748:61), sawn antler tines (E748:42, 49), iron nails (E748:32, 36, 43, 62, 65) and an iron rivet and rove (E748:46). A sherd of Ham Green pottery (E748:149) and a sherd of Redcliffe pottery (E748:148) were also recovered from this phase, although the dating of such pottery suggests the sherds are intrusive to this level (see Chapter 4.9). The find place of one of the antler combs (E748:54, which bears an ogham inscription) is indicated on the photograph of the north section face of the cutting (Pl. 3.63).

Pl. 3.48 Plank pathway (F36), Phase D; from south.

Phase E

This layer (F15) was 0.45m deep with again the remains of a Dublin Type 1 house at its base (Fig. 3.49; Pl. 3.47).

HOUSE IV

The central stone-kerbed hearth (Hearth 4, F16) extended beyond the limit of the cutting to the north. A discontinuous line of stakes (F20) appears to represent the south wall, while another (F22) formed the east wall. A short line of east-west stakes (F19) can be interpreted as an internal partition, while a north-south timber and some stakes (F21) appear to mark another partition. Groups of flat timbers towards the west end of the house (F17 and F18) appear to have been the remains of flooring. No evidence of a doorway was recorded but F17 was probably flooring in the entrance lobby inside the west doorway. Immediately south of the house, towards its east end, some remains of a timber pathway (F24) survived in the same location as the Phase D pathway (F24) beneath it (Fig. 3.49). West of this were stakes (F25) of unknown purpose, though one line continues eastwards from the south-east corner of the house. To the east of the house was a flat timber and some further stakes (F23).

House IV appears to have been about 7m long by an estimated 5.25m wide, giving a floor area of *c.* 36.75m².

Finds from this phase included an iron arrowhead (E748:5), three copper-alloy stick pins (E748:6, 19, 20), a child's copper-alloy bracelet (E748:16), a stone lamp (E748:18) and a glass linen-smoother (E748:17).

A sample of hazelnuts (E748:145) from this phase produced a radiocarbon date of cal AD 907–1147 (95.4% probability).

Phase F

This layer (F3) was about 0.25m deep and had some remains of a house (House V), including a central hearth (Hearth 5, F6) at its base (Fig. 3.50). The preservation of wood, especially stakes, does not seem to have been as good as in the lower layers. A layer of shells in the upper part of F3 is indicated above the level of Hearth 5 in the annotated photograph of part of the north side of the cutting (Pl. 3.47). This appears to have been a localised layer, though it continued beyond the edge of the photograph to the east.

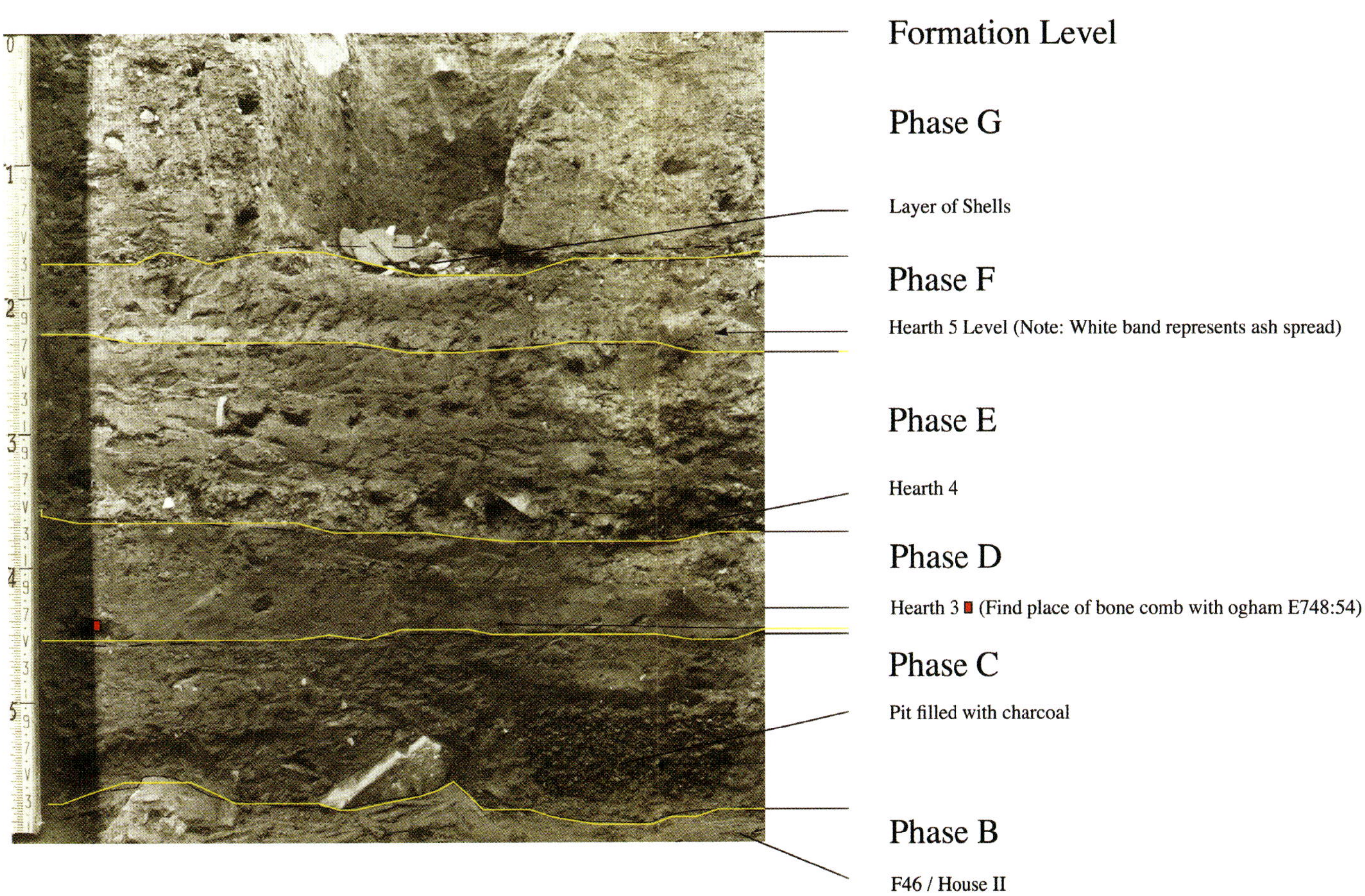

Pl. 3.47 Part of the north section face of Cutting B with stratigraphic divisions marked and annotated by Ó hEochaidhe and with the addition of terminology used in this report. A limited extension was excavated at Phase G level to recover a pair of wooden barrel hoops (E748:21).

HOUSE V

A fine hearth (Hearth 5, F6) with a stone kerb and a base of flagstones was partly exposed at the northern side of the cutting (Pl. 3.50). Attempting to reconstruct the plan of the house is difficult because of the scarcity of stakes marking walls and/or partitions. A few stakes in a rough east-west line (F8) and a timber (F9) in roughly the same alignment may indicate the line of a partition south of the hearth, with the timber possibly being part of a bench or bed frame. A north-south timber (F10) to the east of F9 could be a flooring plank. A large post with smaller adjacent ones (F12) may have been an internal roof support, while a few stakes near it (F11) are of uncertain purpose (Fig. 3.50). Some stone paving to the west (F13) may be associated with a west doorway, while a large flat stone to the east (F14) could be associated with an east doorway. There was an oval spread of ashes (F7) to the east of the hearth and fragments of a quern stone east of this (E748:23). The occupation debris on the house floor was 0.15m to 0.18m deep and included two wooden barrel hoops (E748:21), which partly overlay the hearth. A square extension was excavated into the north section of the cutting to reveal more of the two large hoops (Fig. 3.50); the extension is visible at the top of the photographed section face (Pl. 3.47). If the door locations were as suggested above, House V could have been over 8m long. A suggested width cannot be given because of uncertainty about the location of the walls.

Objects found in this layer included two bone spindle whorls (E847:10, 11), a wooden ripple comb for removing the seed heads from dried flax bundles (E748:14), wooden barrel hoops (E748:21), a quern stone (E748:23) and a fragment of an antler comb (E748:22).

Phase G

This comprised the uppermost 0.45m of deposits and contained no structures or other features (Pl. 3.47). It contained 868 sherds of pottery dating from the eleventh to thirteenth centuries. The lower 0.15m (F2) was distinguished by the excavator as containing mostly pottery of a lighter fabric. The upper 0.3m (F1) mostly contained sherds of green-glazed jugs usually associated with the thirteenth century. There is not enough detail in the preliminary report to be certain of the stratigraphic relationship between this level and the inside of the east curtain wall which formed the east limit of Cutting B. If the Phase G deposits were truncated by the edge of the foundation cut for the wall, it would mean that they pre-date the construction of the castle, and therefore the entire assemblage of medieval pottery could have been included along with other pre-castle sherds in the pottery report of this volume (see Chapter 4.9). However, it is possible that the upper level at least of Phase G was deposited after the construction of the east curtain wall in *c.* 1225. On balance, it was felt the medieval pottery assemblage from the Cross

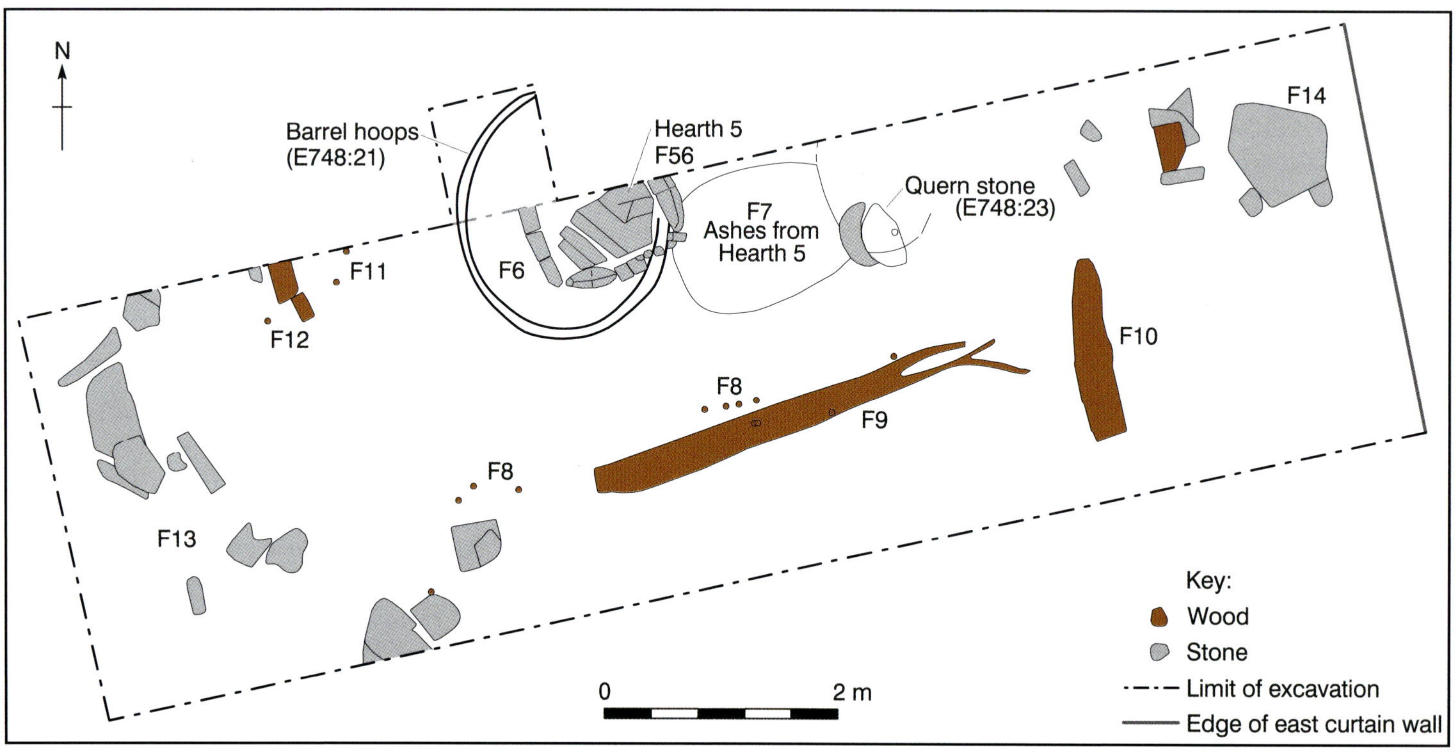

Fig. 3.50 Cross Block, Cutting B; Phase F, House V.

Block is better understood as part of the overall assemblage of medieval pottery from the site, a report on which is to be published in volume 3 of the Dublin Castle excavations series (Papazian and McCutcheon, forthcoming).

Interpretation

Despite the fact that only a preliminary report on this unfinished excavation (Ó hEochaidhe 1962) was available to the authors, it has been possible to provide a reasonable account of the findings because of the good standard, for the time, of this pioneering excavation and the high quality of the plans of the five main phases in the report. It is unfortunate that the excavation of Cutting B was not completed to subsoil, with the result that the number of phases before Phase A is unknown, though likely to be at least four, to judge from Mitchell's profile (Table 3.2). The seven clear phases that were recognised extended from the tenth to the thirteenth century, including the substantial remains of five superimposed Type 1 houses probably dating between the tenth and eleventh centuries. In one tenth-century phase (C) no house appears to have been built and the plot was used for intensive iron working. In the final phase (G), soil and occupation debris including twelfth- and thirteenth-century pottery were dumped here.

A substantial wall at the east end of the cutting was interpreted by the excavator as the east curtain wall of the castle and from its size and position in relation to the Record and Powder Towers there is no reason to doubt this interpretation. Two features of this wall, a 0.3m wide footing projecting eastwards from the lowest exposed level of the wall (Fig. 3.46) and clearly marked as an offset in the preliminary report (Ó hEochaidhe 1962, fig. 1), and the fact that its face was well finished and coursed (*ibid.*, pl. XI), indicate that there must have been a foundation trench cut through the Viking-age levels some 0.3m to 0.5m out from the wall face. This does not appear to have been noted during the excavation but would probably have been noticed if section drawings had been produced. Excavation in the Powder Tower area showed that the north curtain wall was built tight against its foundation trench (Fig. 3.37) as was the inner face of the Powder Tower itself (Fig. 3.28), leading to a rough, uneven and poorly finished face. It is understandable that a wider foundation trench for the east curtain wall at the Cross Block was missed, considering that the main digging appears to have been done by labourers employed by the contractor using spade and shovel. This has implications for the two pieces of later pottery (Ham Green and Redcliffe) found in the Phase D layer in what was described as an undisturbed layer 'near wooden boards at the west end of the cutting under shell'. The fact that the foundation trench for the curtain wall was not recognised opens up the possibility that a pit or other disturbance at the west end of the cutting was missed, which might explain the occurrence of pottery of late twelfth- or thirteenth-century date at this otherwise early eleventh-century level.

Pl. 3.49 Hearth 3 (House III, Phase D) with ash fill partly excavated. The threshold bar (F30) and stone paving slabs (F31) are visible at top; from east.

As argued above, the profile recorded by G.F. Mitchell towards the end of the excavation in 1962 (Table 3.2) is that of an otherwise unrecorded test pit or sondage dug to a depth of 0.82m below what is termed Phase A here. Subsoil was not reached in this test pit and the layers recorded suggest three possible phases as well as what lies beneath the extensive spread of ash at the base of the profile. It gives merely a taste of the lower levels of this unfinished cutting and highlights the necessity of revisiting this excavation and completing it to subsoil. These well-preserved lower levels have the potential to throw considerable light on the earliest Viking settlement around the Poddle estuary as well as early evidence for urban housing and layout in Viking-age Dublin.

In Ó hEochaidhe's excavation the sequence of five houses on a single plot were the chief features uncovered and all appear to have been rectangular aisled structures of Wallace's Type 1. As one might expect, the preservation of wood and organic material appears to have been better in the lower levels and this may explain why horizontal woven wattle rods are not shown in the plans of the three upper houses: III, IV and V (Figs 3.48–3.50). This may be a failure of recording, but it is also noticeable that stakes are more numerous in the lower two houses: I and II (Figs 3.46, 3.47). It is also possible that, as well as the wattle being better preserved and more plentiful in Phases A and B, the excavation team may have become more familiar with it as the excavation progressed.

House I in Phase A with an estimated area of $41m^2$ is the largest of the houses for which a likely size could be calculated though parts of its floor were not fully uncovered when excavation was halted. An early to mid-tenth-century date could be suggested for it in light of the dating of Phase C to the mid- to late tenth century. It had a fine kerbed central hearth, which extended beyond the edge of the cutting.

House II (Phase B), though only part of it survived, could have been the largest of the five houses and appears to have had extensive wattle flooring. Its hearth, if it had one, was outside the cutting.

Though Phase C contained a kerbed hearth, no evidence for a house was recorded and the plot appears to have been intensively used for iron working during this phase. A piece of blackthorn from either this phase or Phases A or B was dated to cal AD 894-1036 (95.4% probability).

House III (Phase D), though a rather small house at $29m^2$, produced some of the best artefacts, including the comb with the ogham inscription. It had a fine kerbed hearth, remains of timber flooring and a finely made corduroy pathway outside its south wall.

House IV (Phase E), also with a kerbed hearth, appears to have been a larger house ($36.75m^2$), again with a corduroy pathway outside its south wall. Hazelnut shells from this level produced a date of cal AD 907–1147 (95.4% probability).

House V (Phase F) is interpreted as a house mainly because of a fine kerbed hearth and some stone paving, stakes and timbers that could be interpreted as relating to a Type 1 house. This was the last house or structure for which there was evidence in this cutting. The context of the earlier radiocarbon date from this cutting is unsatisfactory but the fact that the date for Phase E suggests that it belongs to the early to mid-eleventh century makes it highly unlikely that Phase F could be later than the late eleventh century.

The final phase (G) was represented by a 0.45m layer of dumped habitation material rather than an *in-situ* build-up of such material, and with no record of features or structures. From the suggested likely dating of Phase F (late eleventh century), it appears that houses ceased to be built at least in this plot by around the beginning of the twelfth century. Pottery found in the Phase G level comprises a broad range of Dublin-made and imported types (Papazian and McCutcheon, forthcoming) dating from the eleventh to the thirteenth centuries. The lower 0.15m may have accumulated here in the earlier part of the twelfth century, sealing the remains of House V, but whether the upper 0.3m was deposited before or after the construction of the east curtain wall is uncertain, due to the absence of information on the cut for the, foundation trench for the wall.

Pl. 3.50 Hearth 5 (House V, Phase F) overlain by Phase G deposits, the most recent of the stratified levels recorded during the excavation; from south.

Another issue raised by this excavation is the location of the Viking-age defences at this point. At the Powder Tower these defensive banks were on much the same line as the east curtain wall of the castle and the east wall of the town. The proximity of the houses found at the Cross Block to the castle's east curtain wall and the lack of evidence here for even the inner edge of defensive banks makes it likely that these defences curved out to the east here, possibly following the shore of the Poddle estuary.

In conclusion, this cutting produced remarkably rich archaeology and the questions it raises make it imperative that further excavation should be carried out here in an attempt to answer them.

Chapter 4
The Finds

Chapter 4.1
Introduction

The finds assemblage from Viking-age levels at the castle totals 367, when craft by-products (e.g. metalworking residues, antler and bone waste, etc.) are excluded. This total also excludes intrusive pottery sherds, along with residual prehistoric material, which comprises the small lithics assemblage described below in Chapter 4.5 (Table 4.1; Appendix). Items that can be classified as craft by-products/waste, a total of 85 objects across the sites, are tabulated separately (Table 4.2).

The bulk of the finds derive from the Cork Tower and the Cross Block areas. The total number of artefacts (161) from the Cross Block is somewhat higher than for the Cork Tower (131), but the former is boosted by a larger number of structural finds, specifically iron nails and rivets, related to the timber pathway revealed at the Phase D level. An unusual cache of 333 pebbles from the Cross Block is discussed below (Chapter 4.4.1) and for the purposes of calculating the total number of finds from Viking-age levels, the pebbles are counted as a single item. The two Powder Tower cuttings produced smaller numbers of finds, 44 in the case of Cutting 1 and 31 for Cutting 2 (Table 4.1; Appendix). The only Viking-age context from the Bermingham Tower that produced any finds was the fill of cut feature F143, which contained a metal object and a possible clay mould fragment along with a piece of flint; these finds were not available for study, and since there is no other information on them in the archival records, they are omitted from the tally of finds shown in Table 4.1.

A number of finds from the Cross Block were not available for study, but are included in the relevant reports, since the existence of photographs and drawings allows some observations about them to be made. The objects in question are an iron shackle (Chapter 4.3), two wooden barrel hoops (Chapter 4.7) and the upper stone from a rotary quern (Chapter 4.4).

The evidence for offcuts/waste material and craft by-products is critical to an understanding of what types of artefacts were being produced on the various sites (Table 4.2). The crafts represented are antler/bone working, leatherworking (and possibly tanning), amber working, and metalworking (blacksmithing). Although the overall volume of waste material is small, the distribution of different types of waste across the various sites is significant. A total of *c*. 20 pieces of metalworking waste (iron slag) from the Cross Block was not available for study, but a description contained in the archival report (Ó hEochaidhe 1962) makes it possible for the material to be interpreted in the relevant expert report (Chapter 4.14).

All artefacts have been assigned a unique registration number using the official excavation registration numbers issued by the National Museum of Ireland. In the case of the earlier Cross Block excavation, a registration number has been assigned retrospectively to replace the catalogue numbers used in the preliminary report: Cork Tower area (E296), Powder Tower area (E324) and Cross Block area (E748).

The following abbreviations are used: L.=length, W.=width, Th.=thickness, B.=breadth, H.=height, D.=depth, BL.=blade length, Diam.=diameter, Wgt.=weight.

Table 4.1 Distribution of Viking-age artefacts excluding intrusive pottery sherds and residual prehistoric lithics. The cache of stone pebbles from the Cross Block is counted as a single find.

Artefact material	CT2	PT1	PT2	CB	Total
Antler/bone	37	11	15	49	112
Metal	23	4	0	92	119
Stone	5	1	2	5	13
Jet/jet-like	2	1	1	1	5
Wood	22	2	0	9	33
Leather	6	0	0	2	8
Amber	7	1	1	1	10
Glass	1	0	1	2	4
Textiles	3	0	0	0	3
Ceramic (pottery)	0	14	2	0	16
Ceramic (roof tiles)	0	7	3	0	10
Ceramic (crucibles)	2	1	0	0	3
Ceramic (tuyères)	23	2	6	0	31
Total	131	44	31	161	367

Table 4.2 Distribution of Viking-age craft by-products/waste material.

Waste/by-product type	CT2	PT1	PT2	CB	Total
Antler/horn waste	3	6	8	4	21
Leather waste/offcuts	6	0	1	1	8
Amber waste	4	2	0	0	6
Animal fibres	0	0	0	1	1
Iron slag	23	0	6	c. 20	49
Total	36	8	15	26	85

Chapter 4.2
Antler and bone
Ian Riddler and Nicola Trzaska-Nartowski, with contributions by Ulrich Schmölcke, Fionnbarr Moore and Ken Wiggins

4.2.1
Objects and waste of antler, bone and ivory
IAN RIDDLER AND NICOLA TRZASKA-NARTOWSKI

The Antler Waste
Twenty fragments of antler waste, weighing 459g, were recovered from the three excavations, but the waste was not evenly distributed across those sites. Four fragments of waste came from the Cross Block excavations, two from the Cork Tower and fourteen from the Powder Tower. All of the waste stems from red deer antler. It can be separated into four principal working stages, ranging from the initial dismemberment of the material, secondary reduction of the antler into segments and initial shape of the material to the final finishing of near-complete objects. These stages have been outlined elsewhere for antler waste from early medieval Ireland (Riddler and Trzaska-Nartowski 2014, 44 and forthcoming a). All of the working stages are present in this assemblage, although it is heavily centred on the early ones. Some of the waste provides indications of the nature of the final product, and even of products that are not present in the assemblage of antler objects from the site. Equally, the range of contemporary objects produced from antler, and their relative quantities, can also be related directly to the antler waste. In this case, combs dominate the assemblage of antler objects and all other object types of this material occur only in small quantities (Table 4.3). In general terms, this reflects the image for Dublin as a whole, although the relative use of antler, bone and ivory changes over time within the settlement. Across the tenth and eleventh centuries in Dublin, red deer antler was utilised principally for comb production and that situation is reflected in the antler waste from Dublin Castle.

STAGES OF MANUFACTURE
The red deer antler waste is examined here initially in terms of the assemblage from the Powder Tower, with the small quantities from the Cork Tower and the Cross Block excavation added to the discussion at appropriate points. The first stage of antler working, following the acquisition of the raw material, involved its separation into component parts, namely the beam, crown, tines and burr. The only offcut that can be assigned to this stage is an antler burr (E324:12684: F160; Fig. 4.1:1). This naturally shed burr has been cleanly sawn from several directions across the beam and in a single direction to remove the brow tine. The rear of the burr has been trimmed by knife or drawknife, implying that the surface of the beam had been smoothed beforehand.

In the second stage of working the antler was further reduced into segments that begin to assume their final form, and unwanted pieces, mostly tine ends and sections of crown, were discarded. Most of the Dublin Castle antler waste comes from this stage of working, and this is often the case in assemblages of this date, from both Dublin and elsewhere. It can be seen, for example, at Clonmacnoise and Castlefarm 1, Co. Meath (Riddler and Trzaska-Nartowski 2014, table 1 and forthcoming b). Fourteen of the twenty fragments of antler can be assigned to this stage. Eight of them are tine ends, one of which came from the Cross Block excavation, with the remainder coming from the Powder Tower. At this early stage of working, subtle differences in technique can be seen, which reflect the manufacture of different object types. Five of the tine ends have been cleanly sawn and are not further modified, and a tine end from the Cross Block excavation (E748:42) has

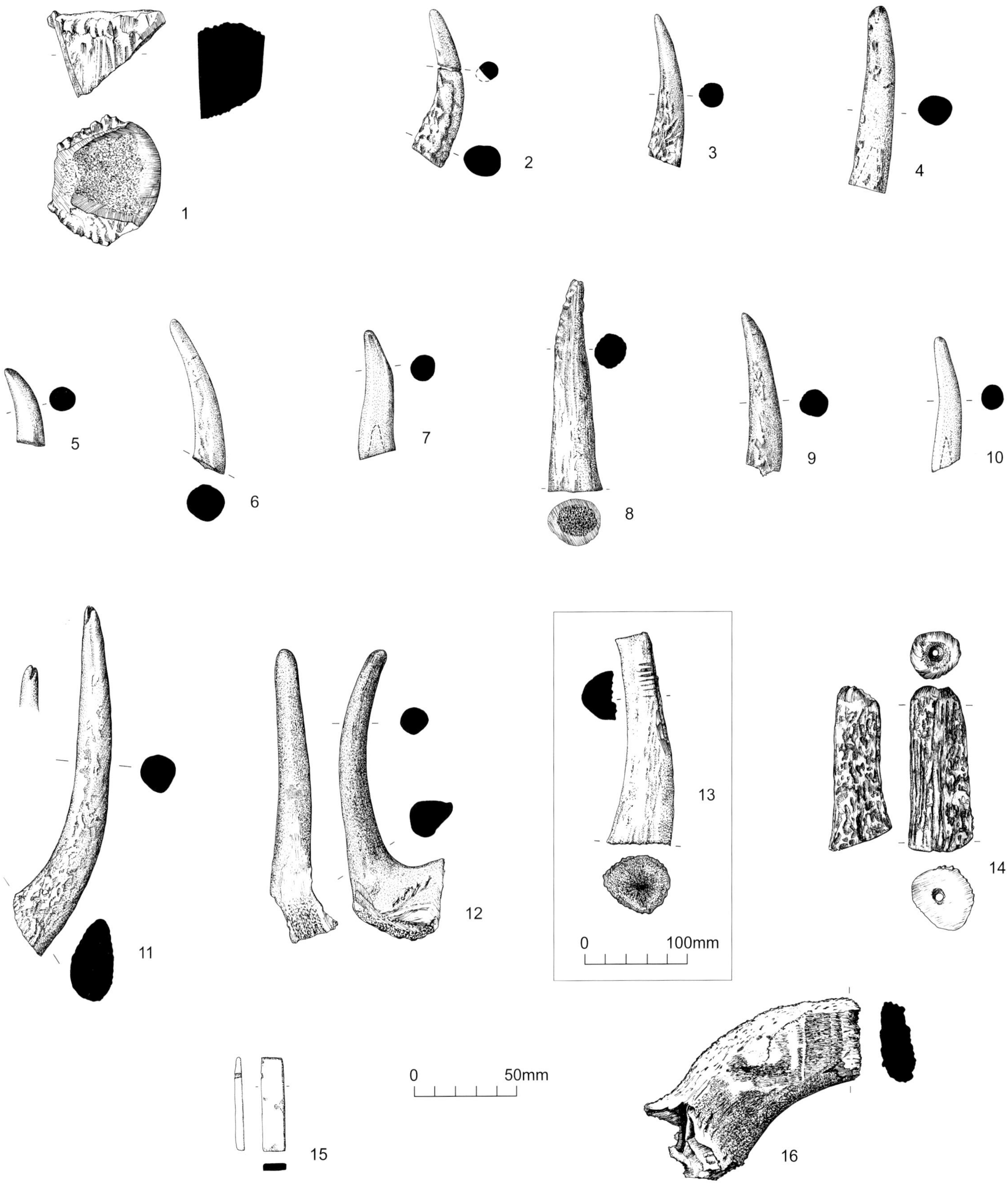

Fig. 4.1 Antler waste (1-15) and horn waste (16).

Table 4.3 Antler/bone artefacts, by functional category.

Category and Object	Bone	Antler	Antler or Bone	Whale Bone	Walrus Skull
Dress Accessories					
Pins	21	1	2	-	-
Personal Possessions					
Comb	-	20	-	-	-
Comb Case	-	1	-	-	-
Axe Blade cover	-	1	-	-	-
Craft Implements					
Saws	-	2	-	-	-
Awl	1	-	-	-	-
Needle	9	-	-	-	-
Needle or Pin	6	-	-	-	-
Needle Case	1	-	-	-	-
Spindle Whorl	9	-	-	-	-
Pin-beater	5	-	-	-	-
Wedge	-	5	-	-	-
Clamp	-	-	-	1	-
Cylinder	12	-	-	-	-
Recreation					
Gaming Piece	-	2	-	-	1
Perforated Pig Metapodia	2	-	-	-	-
Hunting and Fishing					
Pointed Blades	2	-	-	-	-
Miscellaneous					
Polished Bird Bone	1	-	-	-	-
Spacer or Ferrule	-	1	-	-	-
Motif Piece	1	-	-	-	-

been sawn and snapped across the cortile tissue at the centre. Two of the tine ends, both from the Powder Tower (E324:12985:F401 and E324:13387:F501; Fig. 4.1:7 and 10), have been hollowed to depths of 13 to 16mm, and in one case the outer surface has also been smoothed. By comparison with other assemblages, it is likely that they represent waste discarded in the manufacture of antler handles. For this purpose, lengths of antler tines including the tine ends were smoothed and perforated axially, before the tine ends were sawn away to leave unfinished sections of relatively straight antler, of oval or circular section. Thus, the perforation of the tine end belongs to a process relating to the adjacent segment of antler, which was the intended object. Around fifty antler handles are known from the National Museum's excavations in Dublin, stemming mainly from Christchurch Place and the High Street sites.

Tine ends themselves formed the raw material for antler wedges, five of which came from the Dublin Castle excavations. They are described in detail below. All five wedges were recovered from the Powder Tower and four were retrieved from contexts that also produced antler waste, emphasising their close links with antler manufacturing processes. In effect, they can be regarded as tools of the antler worker, produced as required during the antler working processes.

Four fragments of waste from this stage can be identified as sections of tine stemming from the crown area of the antler. Two of them (E324:13029:F217 and E296:48535:F2047; Fig. 4.1:11 and 12) are complete tines, while the other two are tine ends, and one of these (E324:8803:F313) has been hollowed to a depth of 18mm and is pierced also by a small lateral perforation at the tip (Fig. 4.1:4). A small offcut of triangular section from the Powder Tower (E324:8793:F279) also belongs to this working stage. It has been sawn from the beam on one face and subsequently from the tine on the other side, thereby providing the segment of tine with a neat, vertically sawn terminal.

The largest segment of antler waste (E324:12685:F160; Fig. 4.1:13), weighing 125.7g, is a section of beam from close to the area of the burr, sawn cleanly and pared away in part on one side. Some of the outer surface has been smoothed. Its length of 156mm places it within the range of comb connecting plate lengths for Dublin Castle, as noted below, and that may have been its intended purpose. Equally, comb connecting plates could be cut from lengths of antler tines sawn from close to the beam. A comparable (if longer) segment of antler beam from Dublin High Street had been marked in preparation to be sawn to produce comb tooth segments (Riddler and Trzaska-Nartowski forthcoming a).

In the next stage of antler working the material was shaped to form specific objects or their components and was further reduced in size. It is often at this stage that the identity of an object can be determined from the waste. Thus, the sawing and smoothing of a section of antler tine would provide a segment of antler of oval section, and if at this stage a longitudinal slot was cut into it, it could be identified as a rough-out for an axe blade cover, similar to an example from Dublin Castle described below. Three offcuts can be ascribed to this stage, two of which come from the Cross Block and one from the Cork Tower. Two of the offcuts consist of sections of antler tine. One of these (E296:48569:F2074; Fig. 4.1:14) has been cleanly sawn from the beam at one end and burnt to a black colour at the opposite end, where it has been lightly rounded. It includes a neatly drilled axial perforation, 6 to 8mm in diameter. There is some evidence for the burning of areas of antler in prehistory, as an aid to separating the material (Clutton-Brock 1984, 26; Serjeantson and Gardiner 1995, 420–1), but the intended function of this offcut remains unclear. A second offcut (E748:49) is also slightly enigmatic. A slot has been cut into the section of antler tine at one end and this may well represent the vestige of an attempt to saw a section of tine in half, in order to produce tooth segments for combs. This part of the antler tine, which is lightly curved, was then discarded before it had been sawn through entirely. A section of antler tine surface (E748:116) also stems from the same stage of comb manufacture.

The fourth stage of working, seen with comb manufacture in particular, involves the cutting and smoothing of the connecting plates and tooth segments, prior to their assembly. Unfinished comb tooth segments were found at the Powder Tower and the Cross Block. An offcut from the latter site (E748:115) represents an early part of this process, where lengths of antler have been sawn and pared to shape, and the ends of these strips of antler were sawn away and discarded. The tooth segment from the Powder Tower (E324:8808:F335; Fig. 4.1:15) had progressed a little further. It has been sawn on all four edges and includes the vestige of a rivet hole on one of them and thus it comes from a comb that had been assembled and riveted together. The segment has not been tapered along the area of the teeth and it was clearly discarded before the assembled comb reached the next stage and the teeth were cut.

TOOLS OF THE CRAFT

The antler waste provides a small indication of the tools used in the various processing stages. The initial dismemberment was carried out with the aid of a saw, as would be expected. Antler from the second stage of working provided two saw traces, both set into antler tine ends, indicating saw blade widths of 1.7mm and 2.0mm. These can be compared with the gap left for an iron blade on the bow saw from Dublin Castle (E296:48513:F2021; Fig. 4.6), which is 1.7mm in width. It is highly likely that this saw, which is described in detail below, was used to dismember the antler waste found in the excavations. Most of the antler of this stage was dismembered with the aid of a saw but several of the offcuts from the crown area have been sawn in one direction and cut away by knife in the other direction. The admixture of the two methods of dismemberment is characteristic of early medieval assemblages from Ireland, where it is also possible to find offcuts separated entirely with the use of a knife (Riddler and Trzaska-Nartowski forthcoming b).

Analysis of the antler waste from Castlefarm 1, Co. Meath indicated the use of at least two saws, as well as knives, drawknives, a small lathe and several antler wedges (Riddler and Trzaska-Nartowski 2014, 49). The range of evidence from this smaller assemblage at Dublin Castle is more limited, but the use of at least one saw can be postulated, alongside knives, drawknives and wedges.

A BROADER CONTEXT

Small assemblages of red deer antler waste have been found on practically all Dublin sites of this period. As at Dublin Castle, they are clustered in particular areas of the settlement, sometimes associated with specific structures. Among them is an assemblage of thirty fragments of antler waste associated with structure HS 11/2 at High Street, one of the earliest buildings to be identified on Square 2 of that excavation (Murray 1983, 139; Riddler and Trzaska-Nartowski forthcoming a). The structure was considered by Murray to be contemporary with structures HS9/1 and HS8/3, and to date to the early eleventh century. A slightly earlier date of the late tenth- to early eleventh century can be proposed on the basis of the comb assemblage associated with the structure (Riddler and Trzaska-Nartowski forthcoming a). In this case the waste is entirely centred on comb production and belongs to Stages 3 and 4 of the manufacturing process, with nothing from the earlier stages. This almost certainly relates, however, to the sampling methods adopted on site, with the larger fragments of antler removed in bone bags, rather than associated with specific contexts. The working of antler continued in this area into successive structures in the same area, suggesting continuity in the location of the craft over time. These assemblages appear to represent the vestiges of small-scale production episodes, associated with specific structures and not focused on any particular area of the settlement. By the late twelfth century comb manufacture was centred on Dublin High Street, and possibly at Christchurch Place nearby. Prior to that date the craft was more widespread and was not confined to one part of Dublin.

CATALOGUE

STAGE 1

E324:12684:F160 (Fig. 4.1:1). PT1: upper deposit of post-bank levelling; Phase 3. Complete naturally shed red deer antler burr, left side of animal, with part of the coronet surviving. Cleanly sawn in several directions across beam and in one direction to remove brow tine. Rear of burr trimmed by knife. L. 60mm, W. 61.5mm, Th. 39.5mm.

STAGE 2

E748:42. CB: occupation debris under wooden floor west of Hearth 3 (House III); Phase D. Tine end, cleanly sawn in a single direction, partially snapped on one edge. Highly polished, otherwise unmodified. L. 82.5mm, W. 22mm, Th. 20.5mm.

E324:7812:F228 (Fig. 4.1:2). PT2 – Area B: deposit; Phase 1. Complete tine end, cleanly sawn in a single direction and sawn almost through the antler towards the terminal, with saw trace of 1.7mm. Otherwise unmodified. L. 70.5mm, W. 19mm, Th. 16mm.

E324:8791:F285 (Fig. 4.1:3). PT2 – Area A: deposit; Phase 2. Complete tine end, cleanly sawn in a single direction, fractured across one edge, knife marks on one side close to sawn end. L. 70.5mm, W. 16mm, Th. 18mm.

E324:8803:F313 (Fig. 4.1:4). PT2 – Area K: deposit; Phase 16. Complete tine end, stemming from a crown, cleanly sawn at one end and hollowed to length of 17.5mm, pierced also by small lateral perforation at tip. Slight polish throughout. L. 90mm, W. 19.5mm, Th. 17.5mm.

E324:8807:F335 (Fig. 4.1:5). PT2 – Area C: deposit; Phase 1. Complete tine end, cleanly sawn in two directions with remnant stub, otherwise unmodified. L. 36.5mm, W. 14.5mm, Th. 15.5mm.

E324:12683:F160 (Fig. 4.1:6). PT1: upper deposit of post-bank levelling; Phase 3. Complete tine end, cleanly sawn in a single direction with small remnant stub, slight polish, otherwise unmodified. L. 72.5mm, W. 16.5mm, Th. 18mm.

E324:12985:F401 (Fig. 4.1:7). PT1: FW2 deposit of clay and timber bank; Phase 2. Complete tine end, cleanly sawn in a single direction and perforated to a depth of 16.5mm. Smoothed outer surface, highly polished. Possibly waste from handle manufacture. L. 60mm, W. 19mm, Th. 18mm.

E324:13005:F473 (Fig. 4.1:8). PT1: deposit of post-bank levelling; Phase 3. Complete tine end from a crown, cleanly sawn in a single direction, faceted by knife along half of its length, heavily gnawed at the end. L. 101.5mm, W. 26mm, Th. 22mm.

E324:13030:F283 (Fig. 4.1:9). PT2 – Area B: deposit; Phase 2. Complete tine end, cleanly sawn in a single direction with a remnant stub, lightly polished around terminal, otherwise unmodified. L. 74mm, W. 17.5mm, Th. 18mm.

E324:13387:F501 (Fig. 4.1:10). PT1: BW6/7 deposit; Phase 1b. Fragmentary tine end, fractured at broad end, where it is perforated to a length of 13.5mm. Possibly waste from handle manufacture. L. 61mm, W. 15.5mm, Th. 13.5mm.

E324:13029:F217 (Fig. 4.1:11). PT2 – Area C: deposit; Phase 3. Complete crown tine, cleanly sawn in a single direction, polished around terminal with small knife mark there. Otherwise unmodified. L. 155mm, W. 39.5mm, Th. 21.5mm.

E296:48535:F2047 (Fig. 4.1:12). CT2: House 1 deposit; Phase 3. Complete crown tine, sawn vertically from other tines but cut from beam with the aid of a knife. Faceted along part of one side; otherwise unmodified. L. 135.5mm, W. 46mm, Th. 22.5mm.

E324:8793:F279. PT2–Area A: deposit; Phase 2. Complete offcut of wedge form, cleanly sawn on both sides, tapering in section towards one end. From the junction of the tine and beam; otherwise unmodified. L. 14mm, W. 23mm, Th. 18.5mm.

E324:12685:F160 (Fig. 4.1:13). PT1: upper deposit of post-bank levelling; Phase 3. Complete segment of beam from area close to burr, sawn cleanly at both ends and roughly pared in part on one side. Lower end hollowed to depth of 49mm; broad lateral perforation in pared area. Light knife smoothing in one location and series of seven well-spaced lateral narrow knife incisions along part of one edge. L. 156mm, W. 50mm, Th. 43mm.

STAGE 3

E296:48569:F2074 (Fig. 4.1:14). CT2: deposit/surface of subsoil; Phase 1. Section of antler tine form close to beam, cleanly sawn in a single direction and burnt to a black colour at the opposite end, where it is lightly rounded. Pierced throughout by a near, slightly conical, axial perforation, probably drilled. L. 74.5mm, W. 32mm, Th. 29mm.

E748:49. CB: Hearth 3 (House III) level at west end of cutting; Phase D. Complete section of antler tine, lightly curved in profile, cleanly sawn at both ends from several directions. Slot cut into narrow end to depth of 21mm, 2-4mm in width. Outer surface partially smoothed. L. 109mm, W. 27mm, Th. 25mm.

E748:116. CB: context unknown. Section of tine surface, sawn at both ends, roughly pared along sides, cortile tissue largely removed. Lightly curved in profile. L. 62mm, W. 24mm, Th. 6mm.

STAGE 4

E748:115. CB: context unknown. Complete antler tooth segment blank, rectangular in form, lightly curved in section. Sawn laterally at one end, fractured at the other. Pared by knife along sides. L. 11mm, W. 42mm, Th. 5mm.

E324:8808:F335 (Fig. 4.1:15). PT2–Area C: deposit; Phase 1. Complete antler tooth segment blank, rectangular in form, sawn on all four edges with part of a rivet hole remaining along one of them. L. 11mm, W. 45mm, Th. 4mm.

BONE AND HORN WASTE

The majority of the antler waste came from the Powder Tower. An unfinished bone pin, indicative of the manufacture of that object type, was also found on the same site. Evidence for the working of antler, bone and horn is much less evident across the other sites, but it does include the fragment of the lower part of a sawn horn core from the Cork Tower (E296:48566:F2073; Fig. 4.1:16). This is a significant offcut because the upper part of the core has been separated from the remainder with the use of a saw, an implement firmly associated with antler and bone workers, and not used in butchery. The offcut can therefore be identified as waste from the working of horn. It may suggest also that the craftsperson who worked antler also worked bone and horn. This idea is implicit in the *Bretha Nemed*, one of the *Triads* of Ireland, where the comb maker is visualised as 'chanting upon a dunghill so that all antlers and bone and horns that are below come to the top' (Meyer 1906, 17; Kelly 1988, 63; Riddler and Trzaska-Nartowski 2011, 117).

Several of the worked bone objects described below are unfinished. They include a bone pin (E324:12998:F492; Fig. 4.2:1) and an axe blade cover (E296:36958:F1039; Fig. 4.5:3), as well as a small spindle whorl (E748:12). They are described in the relevant sections of the text below.

E296:48566:F2073 (Fig. 4.1:16). CT2: deposit; Phase 1. Lower part of a goat horn core, cleanly sawn across the upper edge and slightly pared on one side. Fractured from skull. L. 118mm, W. 56.5mm, Th. 39mm.

The Antler and Bone Objects

A total of 111 objects of antler, bone and ivory were catalogued and analysed, spread across the three excavations, with 36 from the Cork Tower, 26 from the Powder Tower and 49 from the Cross Block. An unworked bear tooth from the Cork Tower (bringing the overall total of objects to 112) is treated separately at the end of this report. They include pins, combs, needles, cylinders, wedges, spindle whorls, pin-beaters, needle cases, gaming pieces, perforated pig metapodia and pointed blades, as well as a whale bone clamp, a motif piece, an axe blade cover and parts of two antler saws, one of which is substantially complete. Most of these object types are relatively common in Dublin excavations (although some are comparatively rare, both in Dublin and in northern Europe as a whole) yet, in the absence of the full publication of Dublin sites, they remain relatively unknown. Over 8,000 objects of bone, antler and ivory were retrieved from the National Museum excavations in Dublin and only a small fraction of those have been published. The opportunity has therefore been taken to provide full accounts of each object type, relating them as far as possible to finds from other Dublin sites, both published and unpublished.

The objects are described first of all in terms of their material, type and likely date. Broader questions about their manufacture, use and deposition are then examined, within each object type. They have been arranged by functional category, beginning with dress accessories and continuing with personal possessions and craft implements (with textile manufacturing given its own section), and finishing with items of recreation.

DRESS ACCESSORIES

BONE AND ANTLER PINS (FIG. 4.2:1–10; PL. 4.1:1–10)

Twenty-four pins of bone and antler were identified, of which seven came from the Cork Tower, two from the Powder Tower and fifteen from the Cross Block excavations. An unfinished segment of waste from pin-making, recovered from the Powder Tower, is also described here. The overall total is a little low for a central Dublin excavation. The small site at High Street (E43) provided 85 antler and bone pins, while Christchurch Place (E122) and the larger High Street site (E73) each produced over 200 and the total exceeds 500 for the Fishamble Street sites. The pins can be separated into four basic types, on the basis of the form of their heads. One pin (E748:41) is damaged at the head and cannot be identified to type. All of the remaining pins can be placed into the four types, two of which can be sub-divided into four groups, on the basis of the head shape:

1 Undifferentiated Head
2 Lightly Excrescent Heads
  - A: Oval Section
  - B: Shaft Widened Throughout
  - C: Narrow Triangular Head
  - D: Spatulate Head
3 Narrow Spatulate Triangular Perforated Head
4 Broad Expanded Head
  - A: Rounded
  - B: D-shaped
  - C: Bifurcated
  - D: H-shaped

Types 1 and 2 are imperforate, while Types 3 and 4 are perforated. Ten of the pins are perforated and thirteen are imperforate. The four pin types are described here in turn and related to examples from Dublin and further afield, after which broader questions of their use are considered.

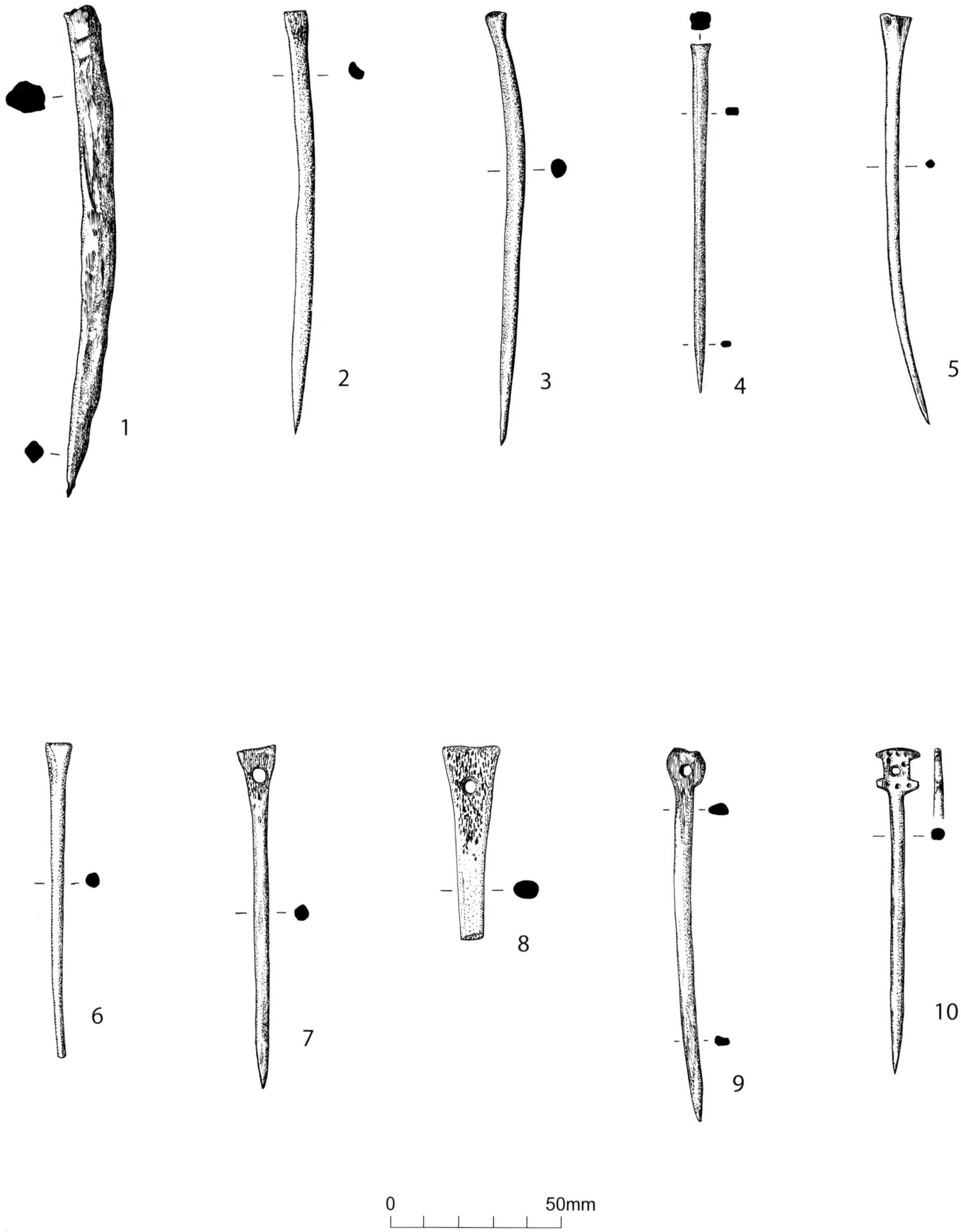

Fig. 4.2 Bone and antler pins. Type 1 (1), Type 2a (2-4), Type 2c (5,6), Type 3 (7, 8), Type 4a (9), Type 4d (10).

TYPE 1: UNDIFFERENTIATED HEAD

Two pins of this form came from the Cross Block excavations (E748:51 and E748:150). Both are made of bone and have straight, polished shafts of D-shaped or circular section, with flat apices. They have no discernible heads. Pins of this type formed Boyle's Class 2a, although his class also included pins with simple expanded heads and those with perforations, as well as several forms of pin with lightly

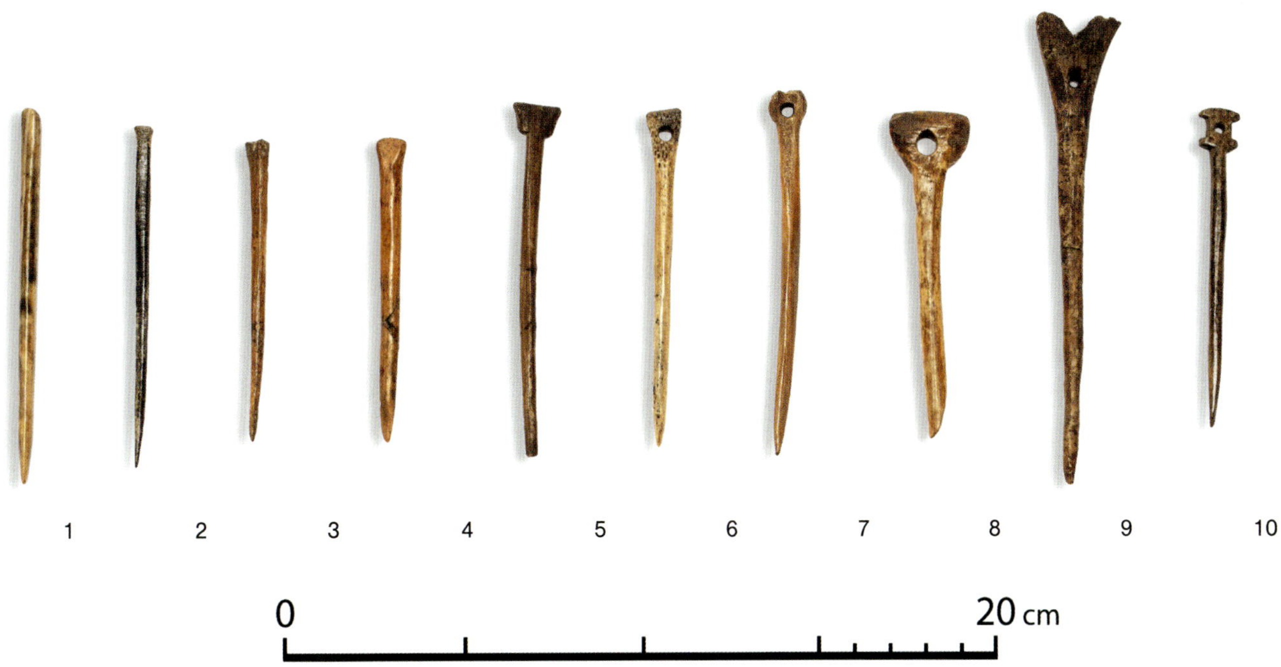

Pl. 4.1 Bone pins: Type 1 (1); Type 2a (2); Type 2b (3); Type 2c (4); Type 2d (5); Type 3 (6); Type 4a (7); Type 4b (8); Type 4c (9); Type 4d (10).

incised decoration (Boyle 2009, 142). The type is restricted here to undecorated, imperforate pins with flat apices and no discernible head. Boyle's sample ranged in length from 82mm to 172mm, emphasising the fact that these are generally long pins (*ibid*., 143).

Small numbers of pins of this type have been found elsewhere in Ireland in pre-Viking contexts extending back to the seventh century, but the majority come from deposits of ninth- to twelfth-century date (Boyle 2009, 152 and 159; Riddler and Trzaska-Nartowski forthcoming c). Outside of Dublin, examples have been found at Beginish, Clonmacnoise New Graveyard, Knowth, Roestown 2 and Waterford (O'Kelly 1955–6, fig 3.5; Riddler and Trzaska-Nartowski 2009a and forthcoming d; Barton-Murray and Riddler 2012a; Hurley 1997b, 672 and fig 17.5.34–6). The type is one of the most common to have been found in Dublin itself, with almost a hundred examples coming from the NMI excavations. Within those excavations there are a few examples from contexts of tenth-century date, but they are much more common in contexts of the eleventh century. Comparable examples are known from Scotland, where they have been described as 'skewer pins'. They occurred in pre-Norse contexts at Skaill (Porter 1997, 99; Hamilton 1956, 115). There is no equivalent of the type within the bone and antler pin sequence from Hedeby, and, although there are numerous examples made of wood, these are regarded as *Stecknadeln* or pack needles, used to secure bundles of cargo (Schwarz-Mackensen 1976; Westphal 2006, 69). At least some of the objects identified as antler and bone long single-pointed pin-beaters, found in York and other sites in England may, in fact, be examples of this pin type (Walton Rogers 1997, 1757). They are not common in England, however, and it is possible that the English examples emanate from Ireland.

An unfinished pin from the Powder Tower (E324:12998:F492; Fig. 4.2:1) has been cut and roughly faceted to shape from the medial or lateral face of a cattle metatarsus. It is lightly curved in section and tapers to a sharp point, with no discernible head. It may well be an unfinished example of this pin form, although it is just possible that a small excrescent head could have been fashioned from the upper end, in finishing the pin. The lightly curved section is not commonly seen on pins of this type, although it does occur occasionally within the Dublin sequence.

Type 2a: Undecorated pins with lightly excrescent heads of oval section

A group of three bone pins, two from the Cork Tower (E296:48520:F2028 and E296:48530:F2045; Fig. 4.2:2 and 3) and one from the Powder Tower (E324:918:F276; Fig. 4.2:4; Pl. 4.1:2) have long curved shafts of circular section and lightly excrescent heads that flow from the shaft and end in flat apices. The head occupies around one-tenth of the length of each pin. The two pins from the Cork Tower are similar in length (120mm and 122.5mm) and retain cortile tissue at the head. Both were probably made from the lateral or medial sides of cattle metapodia, possibly by the same craftsman. The pin from the Powder Tower (E324:918:F276) is shorter, with a length of 98.5mm, and has a straight shaft, circular in section over its lower part and square in section over the upper part.

This small group of undecorated, imperforate pins is closely related to the headless form and is distinguished principally by the presence of a small, subtle head, which is undecorated. Within the Dublin pin sequence this form lies, in effect, between headless pins and those surmounted by a lightly raised, flat disc at the apex. The latter pin type described sometimes as 'nail-headed' (Porter 1997, 99) is not represented at Dublin Castle, but is a common find in Dublin. In the Dublin excavations there are several examples of this lightly excrescent head type that come from early contexts, of early to mid-tenth-century date, including one pin from the High Street and three from Fishamble Street. Several other pins of the type come from contexts of the late tenth century to early eleventh century. It is conceivable, therefore, that this is a relatively early form in Dublin, largely confined to the tenth century. A comparable pin came from Skaill (Porter 1997, fig. 8.3.1031).

Type 2b: Undecorated pins with shafts widened throughout

A related form is represented by two pins from the Cross Block (E748:9 and E748:40). These are pins made from pig fibulae and they widen lightly and consistently from the tip (cut from the proximal end of the bone) to an undifferentiated head with a flat apex. They differ from headless pins for their oval section and continuous taper, which ends in a thin, rectangular section at the head. The nature of the raw material means that they are generally shorter than headless pins or pins with lightly excrescent heads, which are made from other bones, or from antler. In effect, they are similar to headless pins but they are not cylindrical in form and their shafts widen evenly to the head.

These pins resemble pig fibula awls, but the distal end of the bone has been cut away. They also have the appearance of bone spatulae, but the head has simply been cut laterally (sometimes crudely) and they are not shaped to provide either a shallow bowl or a flat terminal. Their close resemblance to headless pins, some of which are made from pig fibulae, suggests that they served as pins. The type is found in small numbers in Dublin and, like the headless pins, it appears to have a fairly wide date range. At least one pin of this type comes from a feature cut into the boulder clay and pre-dating the tenth century whilst other examples were found in tenth- to early eleventh-century contexts. Hamilton illustrated one example from an early Viking-period level at Jarlshof and they are known also from Knowth (Hamilton 1956, fig. 59.3; Barton-Murray and Riddler 2012a).

Type 2c: Imperforate pins with narrow triangular heads

Two pins, both from the Cork Tower, have long curved shafts ending in narrow spatulate heads with flat apices. One of these pins is made from a pig fibula (E296:48559:F2065; Fig. 4.2:5) and the other is antler (E296:48461:F1223; Fig. 4.2:6). The former pin is 117.5mm in length, an impressive size for a pin of that material. It has been skilfully cut to shape in much the same way as the sequence of pig fibula awls described below. Unlike those awls, however, it has a long, thin, curved shaft. The antler pin is 89mm in length but its point has been recut at some point and the pin has been shortened. A related pin of a similar length (E748:66; Pl. 4.1:4) is rectangular in section and the head is narrow and spatulate, but it includes a lightly rounded apex decorated with two dots.

This group of three pins is closely related to the earlier sequences, the form of the head resembling pins of Type 2a, but the triangular shape is flattened on both sides. Once again, they are long, largely undecorated pins. Comparable examples from Dublin excavations cluster markedly around contexts dating from the late tenth to early eleventh century. Complete examples were found at Knowth, as well as Skaill and Pool in Orkney (Barton-Murray and Riddler 2012b, fig. 7.2:16.449; Porter 1997, fig. 8.4.5058; Smith 2007, fig. 8.8.10, pl. 2030 and pl. 2031).

Type 2d: Spatulate head

A fragmentary bone pin (E748:60; Pl. 4.1:5) has a lightly curved shaft and a trapezoidal-shaped head. The head is distinguished from the shaft and the pin has a stylus-like appearance. There are two similar pins from the NMI excavations but neither comes from a securely dated context. The type corresponds closely with Schwarz-Mackensen's Type 7 pins, known from Birka, Lund and Sigtuna, reasonably common in Frisia and found also in Scotland, within contexts of tenth- to eleventh-century date (Schwarz-Mackensen 1976, 35–6; Roes 1963, pls LII.7 and LIII.3; Porter 1997, fig. 8.3.1040–1). It belongs also to Boyle's Type 2b, although this encompasses pins of various different head forms (Boyle 2009, 159–73).

Type 3: Perforated pins with narrow triangular heads

The largest group consists of a series of seven pins (E296:48542:F2049; E324:13228:F191; E748:28; E748:52; E748:102; E748:114; and E748:128), mostly from the Cross Block, made from cattle bone with thick shafts of circular section, narrow triangular-shaped heads and flat apices. Six of the pins are complete or near complete and two are fragmentary. They are long pins, complete examples ranging from 99 to 138.5mm. All of them were produced from cattle-sized long bones, probably from cattle metapodia. Cortile tissue is usually present on one side of the head. All of the pins include single knife-cut perforations and they are undecorated.

Pins of this type and specific raw material are widespread in Dublin and the presence of unfinished pieces indicates that they were made at various locations, including High Street and Fishamble Street. Their dating is more confined than that of headless pins, the other main type of pin from the settlement, extending in this case from the late tenth century to the middle of the eleventh century. The type corresponds in this respect with Schwarz-Mackensen's Type 11, defined as long pins with flat, wide heads, which she placed in the eleventh century, the presence of examples from Schleswig confirming this dating (Schwarz-Mackensen 1976, 44; Ulbricht 1984, tafn 33.1 and 34.1). For Dublin, undecorated pins of this type with narrow heads can be separated from those with wider, more prominent triangular heads, but both types appear to be contemporary and a feature of the eleventh century in particular.

TYPE 4

Each of the four pins of Type 4 has a different head form. In common with the pins of Types 1 to 3, they are all relatively long pins, with straight or lightly curved shafts of oval or circular section. In each case the head is overtly distinguished from the shaft. They are undecorated pins, with the exception of Type 4d.

TYPE 4A: ROUNDED HEAD WITH NEAR-FLAT APEX

A complete pin (E296:48528:F2045; Fig. 4.2:9; Pl. 4.1:7) from the Cork Tower is a pig fibula pin with the head cut from the distal end of the bone and widening in curves from the shaft. The apex appears to be formed from the natural unfused surface of the bone, although it is possible that it was modified slightly to a concave form. Several pins of this type from NMI excavations in Dublin have apices cut to a triangular or concave form, which allows the top part of the pins to resemble animal heads seen in profile, with the jaws wide open. The type is quite rare in Dublin, coming from contexts of the late tenth century to the early eleventh century. There is no equivalent from Hedeby.

TYPE 4B: BROAD EXPANDED D-SHAPED HEAD

A pin from the Cross Block (E748:33; Pl. 4.1:8) has fractured across the straight shaft of circular section and its original length is unclear. The head is D-shaped, widening in curves to a flat apex, with the perforation set low down, close to the shaft. It broadly resembles the pin of Type 4a but has a wider head with a flat apex. A comparable pin from Fishamble Street (E190:6166) came from a context of late tenth-century date. The head form can be seen on an imperforate pin from Birsay, Orkney; it is not a Scandinavian form (Curle 1982, fig. 48.92).

TYPE 4C: BROAD EXPANDED HEAD, BIFURCATED TERMINAL

A bone pin from the Cross Block (E748:53; Pl. 4.1:9) includes a distinctive head with a bifurcated apex; the perforation is set low down, close to the shaft. The form is a very unusual one, not easily paralleled amidst pins recovered from Dublin excavations. Several short pins from Fishamble Street have lightly bifurcated apices (E190:3829 and E172:15096) but otherwise there is nothing comparable to this head form.

TYPE 4D: FLAT RECTANGULAR HEAD WITH TWO SETS OF LATERAL MOULDINGS

A pin from the Cork Tower (E296:48515:F2024; Fig. 4.2:10, Pl. 4.1:10) has a flat rectangular head between two sets of wide lateral mouldings. It is one of the few pins from Dublin Castle to be decorated, with knife-point indentations set within most of the available space. It includes a perforation at the centre of the head. The form is not a common one for Dublin and it is largely localised to High Street. The decoration recurs on a pin from the smaller High Street site that is similar, but for the lack of lateral mouldings (E43:2015). Both lateral mouldings and indentations occur on a pin with a smaller head from the same site (E43:2094), while a further pin from that site has the requisite head form but lacks any decoration (E43:670). A close parallel can be seen also with a pin from Winetavern Street (E81:8868), which has the requisite head form and decoration, but is not perforated. Single sets of lateral mouldings occur on several pins from Fishamble Street (e.g. E190:6345) but the High Street group and the pin from nearby at Winetavern Street are undoubtedly closer in form and decoration. A related design can be seen also on a few pins from Hedeby and Sigtuna, where the upper lateral mouldings are exaggerated and the perforation is set low down, between the lower set of mouldings (Schwarz-Mackensen 1976, 39 and abb 13.7). An undecorated pin from York includes two sets of lateral mouldings, with an additional trapezoidal apex above (Waterman 1959, fig. 14.7).

VIKING PINS, IRISH PINS AND DUBLIN PINS

Smith (2007, 477) rightly noted the difference in length, as well as form, between pre-Viking pins and Viking pins in Orcadian Scotland. The Viking pins are longer and, at Pool at least, they are quite plain. The head forms also differ from earlier pins. On that basis it could be argued that long, plain pins are a Norse innovation to Scotland, but that entirely ignores the Irish component in the equation. In essence, antler and bone pins from Orcadian sites form some of the best parallels for pins from Dublin and from Ireland as a whole. Rather than being viewed as Viking pins, they can be seen as pins of the Irish Sea province.

It is clear from the comparisons cited above that most of the Dublin Castle pin types are not readily paralleled on Viking sites, and neither are many of those from Viking Scotland. Headless pins are a pre-Viking form with origins that go back to the seventh century (Boyle 2009, 143). The form is one of the most common to be seen in Dublin, particularly from the late tenth century onwards, although they can be found in earlier contexts. Boyle was cautious about relating the Scottish examples to Irish pins, but equally they are not a feature of Scandinavian assemblages, casting doubt on his suggestion that they are a Norse introduction to Scotland (*ibid*., 157). Their pre-Viking origins in Ireland militate against any such introduction to there from Scandinavia.

Type 2 pins from Dublin are similar in form to headless pins, with Type 2a belonging essentially to the tenth century and Type 2c being found in contexts of the late tenth to early eleventh century. Type 2b pins appear to have a wide date range. None of these types occur within the pin sequences from Hedeby and their close resemblance to headless pins suggests that they form part of a suite of essentially Irish pin forms. The situation is quite different with the Type 2d pin (E748:60; Pl. 4.1:5), which has a distinctive Scandinavian pedigree, although the form can be seen elsewhere in northern Europe.

Type 3 is a resolutely Scandinavian form. Examples produced from cattle long bones are centred on the eleventh century and may be more common across the first part of that century. Type 4, in contrast, is an insular form spread across the Irish Sea province. Thus, within the assemblage of 24 antler and bone pins, just two types, representing six pins, can be said to show any distinctly Scandinavian influence. The remaining pins can be regarded as Irish forms, the origins of some of which pre-date the Viking settlement of Dublin.

CATALOGUE

TYPE 1: UNDIFFERENTIATED HEAD

E748:51 (Pl. 4.1:1). CB: Hearth 3 (House III) level at west end of cutting; Phase D. Complete bone pin, cattle-sized midshaft, shaft D-shaped in section, tapering lightly and evenly to a rounded point at one end. Highly polished throughout with no discernible head. L. 109mm, W. 9mm, Th. 7mm.

E748:150. CB: context not known. Fragmentary bone pin, cattle-sized long bone midshaft, shaft of circular section with lower part missing. No discernible head. Some polish throughout, slight faceting of the shaft. L. 64mm, W. 5.5mm, Th. 5mm.

E324:12998:F492 (Fig. 4.2:1). PT1: clay and timber bank; Phase 2. Unfinished bone pin, complete, cut from a cattle metatarsus on the medial or lateral face, towards distal end of the bone. Lightly curved shaft, roughly circular in section, tapering to a sharp point. Cut laterally by knife at upper end, some cortile tissue present there and a foramen on one side. Slightly degraded surface in part. L. 140mm, W. 12.5mm, Th. 10mm.

TYPE 2A: UNDECORATED PINS WITH LIGHTLY EXCRESCENT HEADS OF OVAL SECTION

E296:48520:F2028 (Fig. 4.2:2). CT2: House 2 deposit; Phase 5. Complete bone pin, lightly expanded head of sub-triangular shape and flat apex. Upper part of shaft is rectangular in section, lower is slightly curved and circular in section, tapering to a sharp point. Highly polished throughout. L. 119.5mm, W. 7.5mm, Th. 5.5mm.

E296:48530:F2045 (Fig. 4.2:3). CT2: deposit; Phase 4a. Complete bone pin, lightly expanded head of oval section and flat apex. Head has been cut from the proximal end of the bone, with some cortile tissue present, and curves lightly to remainder of shaft, which is straight and circular in section, tapering lightly to a pointed terminal. Polished throughout. L. 122.5mm, W. 7.5mm, Th. 5mm.

E324:918:F276 (Fig. 4.2:4; Pl. 4.1:2). PT2 – Area A: deposit; Phase 3. Complete bone pin with lightly expanded head of rectangular section and flat apex. Upper part of shaft is square in section, lower part is straight and circular in section and tapers to a sharp point. Highly polished throughout. L. 98.5mm, W. 5.5mm, Th. 4mm.

TYPE 2B: UNDECORATED PINS WITH SHAFTS WIDENED THROUGHOUT

E748:9 (Pl. 4.1:3). CB: *c*. 0.96m below formation level in thin dark layer (Hearth 4/House IV); Phase E. Complete bone pin, cut from a pig fibula with the head formed from lower part of the distal end of the bone. Straight shaft of circular section tapers to a sharp point. Upper part of shaft slightly curved in profile, square in section and widening a little to a lightly concave apex. Highly polished throughout with manufacturing marks still visible. L. 86.5mm, W. 8mm, Th. 4.5mm.

E748:40. CB: occupation debris under wooden floor west of Hearth 3 (House III); Phase D. Complete bone pin, cut from a pig fibula with the head fashioned from the distal end of the bone. Straight shaft of oval section tapering to a sharp point. Head not distinguishable from the shaft, knife-cut flat apex. Highly polished with some manufacturing marks visible. L. 90mm, W. 7.5mm, Th. 4.5mm.

TYPE 2C: IMPERFORATE PINS WITH NARROW TRIANGULAR HEADS

E296:48559:F2065 (Fig. 4.2:5). CT2: ash spread; Phase 2. Complete bone pin, cut from a pig fibula with head formed from distal end of the bone. Long curved shaft of circular section tapering over lower part to a sharp point. Head widens from shaft to spatulate form with a knife-cut flat apex. Some polish throughout. L. 117.5mm, W. 9.5mm, Th. 3.5mm.

E296:48461:F1223 (Fig. 4.2:6). CT2: deposit; Phase 2. Incomplete antler pin with shaft of circular section, lightly curved over lower part and tapering to a rounded, reworked terminal. Narrows on two sides and widens lightly to form a spatulate triangular head with a flat apex of rectangular section. Some polish throughout. L. 88.5mm, W. 8mm, Th. 4mm.

E748:66 (Pl. 4.1:4). CB: east end of trench, same level as Hearth 3 (House III); Phase D. Complete bone pin with a straight shaft, the lower part oval in section and tapering to a broad spatulate point. Upper part of shaft is rectangular in section and leads to a slightly widened head with a lightly rounded apex, pierced by two small dots. Some polish throughout. L. 87.5mm, W. 9mm, Th. 4.5mm.

TYPE 2D: SPATULATE HEAD

E748:60 (Pl. 4.1:5). CB: among timbers of wall west of Hearth 3 (House III), at same level; Phase D. Incomplete bone pin with a lightly curved and faceted shaft of circular section tapering towards a point, which is now missing. Upper part of shaft is rectangular in section and widens to a spatulate head with a flat apex. Some polish on the shaft, but not on the head. L. 101.5mm, W. 14.5mm, Th. 5mm.

TYPE 3: PERFORATED PINS WITH NARROW TRIANGULAR HEADS

E296:48542:F2049 (Fig. 4.2:7; Pl. 4.1:6). CT2: House 1 deposit; Phase 3. Complete bone pin, cut from a cattle-sized long bone with cortile tissue visible on one side of the head. Straight shaft of circular section tapers to a sharp point.

E324:13228:F191 (Fig. 4.2:8). PT1: deposit of post-bank levelling; Phase 3. Fragment of a bone pin, cut from a cattle-sized long bone with cortile tissue at the head on one side. Small part of shaft of D-shaped section leads to head of rectangular section, widening lightly and evenly, with a flat sawn apex. Knife-cut oval perforation, no wear visible. Slight polish throughout. L. 55mm, W. 17mm, Th. 7mm.

E748:28. CB: occupation debris of Hearth 5 (House V); Phase F. Complete bone pin, cut from a cattle-sized long bone with cortile tissue visible on one side of the head. Straight shaft of D-shaped section tapers to a sharp point. Upper part of shaft rectangular in section, widens to a triangular head with a lightly rounded apex. Neat knife-cut perforation set at centre of head. Highly polished throughout. L. 123.5mm, W. 17mm, Th. 6.5mm.

E748:52. CB: Hearth 3 (House III) level at west end of cutting; Phase D. Complete bone pin, cut from a cattle-sized long bone with cortile tissue visible on the back of the head. Straight shaft of oval section tapering to faceted, slightly damaged point. Head widens lightly from shaft, rectangular in section with a flat apex. Pierced by a neat knife-cut circular perforation. Highly polished, with rasp marks visible along the shaft. L. 102mm, W. 14mm, Th. 6.5mm.

E748:102. CB: *c.* 76mm under burnt layer; Phase C. Near complete bone pin, cut from a cattle-sized long bone and now in two pieces. Straight shaft of circular section tapers to a rounded point. Head widens lightly and evenly from the shaft, which narrows in width a little. Flat sawn apex and neat, circular knife-cut perforation with slight possible wear on one side. Highly polished throughout. L. 125mm, W. 13mm, Th. 4.5mm.

E748:114. CB: context not known. Fragmentary bone pin, cut from a cattle-sized long bone with cortile tissue visible across one side of the head. Straight shaft of oval section tapering to a sharp point. Upper part of shaft rectangular in section, widening imperceptibly towards head, fractured across a prominent perforation set low down close to the shaft. Some polish throughout. L. 95.5mm, W. 9.5mm, Th. 7mm.

E748:128. CB: context not known. Complete bone pin, cut from a cattle-sized long bone with cortile tissue visible on both sides of the head. Straight shaft of circular section with flattened, lightly indented thumb groove on the upper side. Tapers to broad spatulate point. Head widens imperceptibly to flat angled apex with small knife-cut perforation set well down. Polished throughout, but less on head. L. 138.5mm, W. 14.5mm, Th. 7mm.

TYPE 4A: ROUNDED HEAD WITH NEAR-FLAT APEX

E296:48528:F2045 (Fig. 4.2:9; Pl. 4.1:7). CT2: deposit; Phase 4a. Complete bone pin, cut from a pig fibula, with the shaft oval in section and lightly curved, tapering to a sharp point. Head is rounded to either side of the central knife-cut perforation, with the apex formed from the natural unfused surface of the bone.

TYPE 4B: BROAD EXPANDED D-SHAPED HEAD

E748:33 (Pl. 4.1:8). CB: *c.* 4.41m from east limit of trench, *c.* 1.27m below formation level; Phase D. Fragmentary bone pin, cut from a cattle-sized long bone with cortile tissue across the head on one side. Slightly curved shaft of circular section, lower part missing. Upper part rectangular in section and narrow, head widening in convex curves to a flat knife-cut apex. Neat oval knife-cut perforation set low down on the head. L. 94mm, W. 23.5mm, Th. 6.5mm.

TYPE 4C: BROAD EXPANDED HEAD, BIFURCATED TERMINAL

E748:53 (Pl. 4.1:9). CB: Hearth 3 (House III) level at west end of cutting; Phase D. Complete bone pin, cut from a cattle-sized long bone with cortile tissue visible on both sides at the head. Near straight, slightly sinuous shaft of circular section tapering to a blunt, rounded terminal, sliced diagonally on one side. Upper part of shaft rectangular in section, widening to a forked, bipartite terminal, flat knife-cut apex with V-shaped notch at centre. Oval knife-cut perforation, splayed on both sides. Slight polish to shaft. L. 134.5mm, W. 25mm, Th. 6.5mm.

TYPE 4D: FLAT RECTANGULAR HEAD WITH TWO SETS OF LATERAL MOULDINGS

E296:48515:F2024 (Fig. 4.2:10; Pl. 4.1:10). CT2: House 2 deposit; Phase 5. Complete antler or bone pin with a straight shaft of oval section tapering to a sharp point. Head is rectangular in section and includes flat trapezoidal mouldings to either side of the indented central area, which includes a circular knife-cut perforation. Decorated with indentations on one side across the available space. Lightly rounded apex.

INDETERMINATE TYPE

E748:41. CB: occupation debris under wooden floor, west of Hearth 3 (House III); Phase D. Fragmentary bone pin, cut from a cattle-sized long bone with a lightly curved shaft of circular section tapering to a rounded point. Upper part includes vestige of a groove, possibly cut to separate the shaft from the head. Rectangular section above, seemingly fractured across a perforation set low down. Abraded condition. L. 107mm, W. 5mm, Th. 5mm.

PERSONAL POSSESSIONS

COMBS (FIGS 4.3, 4.4; PLS 4.3, 4.4)

All of the combs conform to types identified in an earlier study of combs and comb making in early medieval Dublin (Riddler and Trzaska-Nartowski forthcoming a). The Dublin typology represents a development beyond the fourteen types of early medieval comb identified by Ashby (2007; 2010), most of which are too broad in scope to be of use here. Combs can be defined within a hierarchy of terms extending from Class and Form to Type and Group. Just one class of comb, the single-sided composite, is present in the assemblage. Combs of this class consist of two antler connecting plates, fastened to two end segments and a series of tooth segments with iron rivets. No rivets of any other materials could be identified. They can be separated into the following seven comb forms:

- paired connecting plate comb cases;
- single-sided composites with broad D-shaped connecting plates;
- Irish single-sided composites;
- single-sided composites with connecting plates of triangular section;
- Middle Period Scandinavian combs;
- single-sided composites with connecting plates of trapezoidal section;
- single-sided composites with narrow D-shaped undecorated connecting plates.

These represent the major comb forms in use within Dublin from the middle of the ninth century to the middle of the eleventh century. It is likely, however, that the comb sequence from Dublin Castle extends merely from the middle of the tenth century to the middle of the eleventh century. The overall dating of the assemblage is considered after each of the comb forms, and the types of comb occurring within each form, are described.

PAIRED CONNECTING PLATE COMB CASE

An antler connecting plate (E324:1024:F285; Fig. 4.3:1) from the Powder Tower, decorated with a loose mesh lattice pattern, can be identified as part of a comb case originally provided with paired connecting plates on each side. This is a fairly common form of comb case and ten further examples are known from the NMI excavations, most of which are fragmentary, as is the situation here. The plate includes two rivet holes that would have secured it to end pieces, as well as an additional perforation, which would have acted as a suspension hole to carry the case. The adjoining upper connecting plates would have been cylindrical in form and an additional perforation through them could retain a peg used to secure the comb to its case. Almost all of the comb cases with paired connecting plates from Dublin include these peg holes. The accompanying comb for this case was relatively short, given that the space between the rivet holes is just 84mm. Its decoration may have matched that of its case, but that is by no means certain. Where combs and their cases of this period have been found together, they do not always have identical decoration (Riddler and Trzaska-Nartowski forthcoming a).

Dating evidence for the Dublin comb cases of this form is centred on the late tenth to early eleventh century, although there is an early fragment of tenth-century date from High Street (E71:10908). Cases from Birka, Hedeby and York all tend to be of this paired connecting plate form, which Waterman considered to be earlier than the single connecting plate type (Waterman 1959, 90). Ulbricht (1984, 51) also regarded the paired plate form as the older form at Schleswig and this was endorsed by Smirnova for Novgorod, where cases with paired plates peaked in the late tenth century while those with single plates were most common in the early to mid-eleventh century (Smirnova 2005, 77).

SINGLE-SIDED COMPOSITE COMBS WITH CONNECTING PLATES OF BROAD D-SHAPED SECTION

Single-sided composites with connecting plates of a broad, D-shaped section represent the most numerous comb form to have come from Dublin Castle, with seven combs altogether, produced in three main decorative designs each, in effect, providing a different comb type. Several of the combs may be Scandinavian in origin. One of them

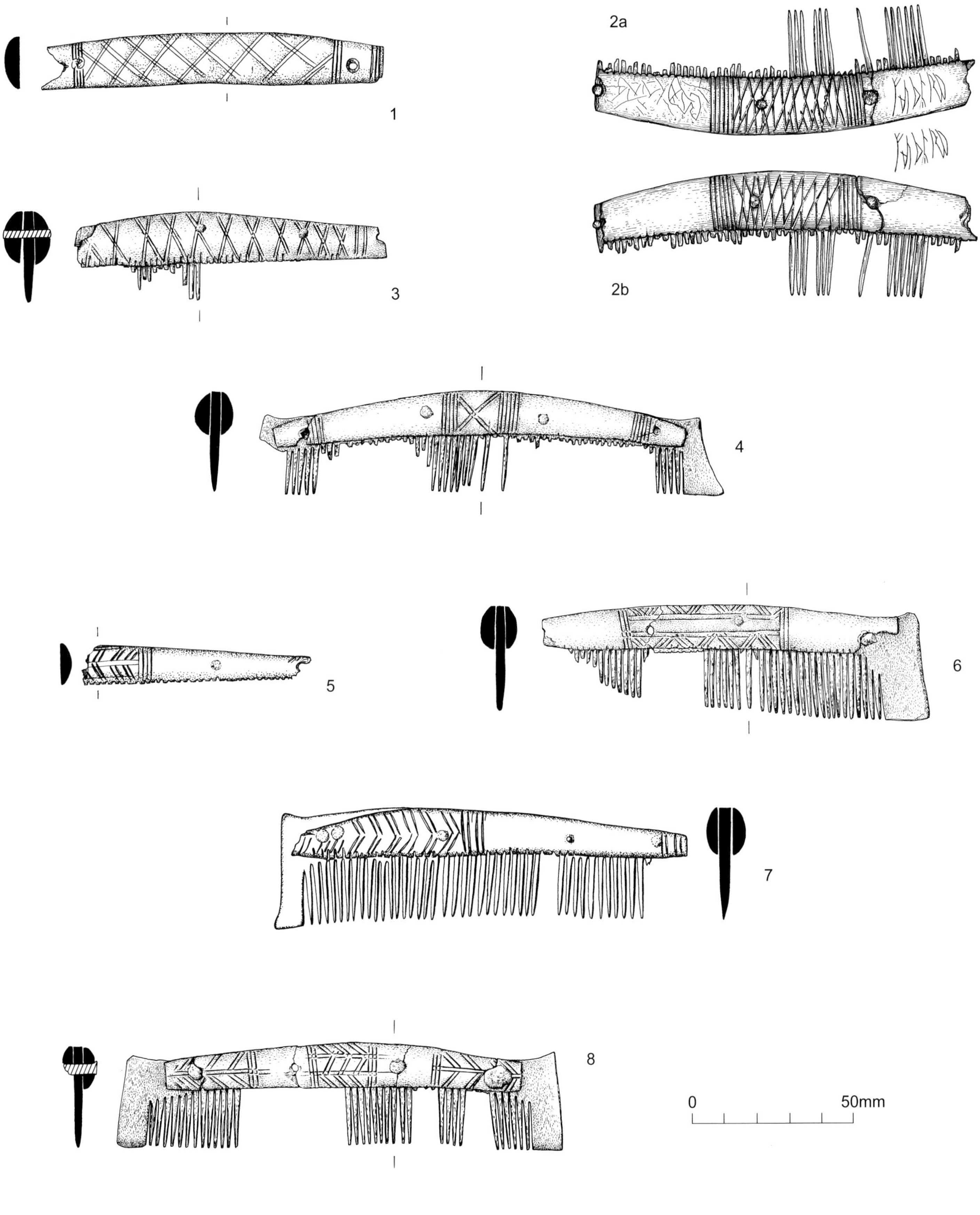

Fig. 4.3 Antler single-sided composite combs including one with runic inscription (2a, 2b) and antler connecting plate from a comb case (1).

Pl. 4.2 Runic inscription on antler comb E296:50058:F1254.

(E296:50058:F1254; Fig. 4.3:2a/b; Pl. 4.2), from the Cork Tower, has been published on several occasions (Barnes *et al.* 1997, 44–5; Lynch and Manning 2001, fig. 7). It consists of a fragment of the central part of a comb, now lacking most of its teeth and decorated on both sides with a single-line loose mesh lattice pattern. There are blank areas to either side of this central design, and one of them includes a lightly incised runic inscription. This inscription has been viewed as an abbreviated futhark with the addition of a single rune monogram, perhaps giving the name *Unnr* or *Uni* (Barnes *et al.* 1997, 45).

It is likely that the comb originally included winged end segments, although they no longer survive. The size and shape of the comb echo examples found in tenth-century contexts across northern Europe and this form appears to develop from the earlier combs of Ambrosiani class B from around *c.* 935 onwards, becoming a standard design of the second half of the tenth century (Ambrosiani 1981, 62–6; Riddler and Trzaska-Nartowski forthcoming a). Combs decorated with single line mesh patterns of this form are not common at this period but have been found in both England and Scandinavia in small numbers. Those from tenth-century contexts, at Hedeby in particular, form close parallels (Tempel 1969, taf 23.95; 1970,43 and abb 4.3) and with this in mind the comb fits very well into Phase 4a of the Cork Tower area.

It is a little surprising, perhaps, that more runes have not been found on combs in Ireland. The fourteen runic inscriptions from Dublin include four carved on wood and ten on antler or bone. Of the latter, three have been cut into unworked rib bones and two into unworked scapulae. One was found on a piece of red deer antler, two come from pins of antler or bone and one from an antler knife handle. Just one has come from a comb. In Frisia, in contrast, six of sixteen runic inscriptions have been found on combs (Düwel and Tempel 1970) and they are also known from several combs and comb cases found in northern England, from both Whitby and York (White 1984; Waterman 1959, 90).

The presence of a runic inscription may indicate that this is a comb owned by a Scandinavian, but that does not necessarily mean that it was actually made in Scandinavia. The comb type was widespread across the northern world and Dublin comb makers emulated Scandinavian comb designs with greater or lesser success across the tenth and eleventh centuries. The presence of a set of lightly incised lines on the same side of the comb, located towards the other end, is paralleled on a number of combs and comb cases from Dublin, as well as on other objects of antler and bone from the settlement. There is nothing overtly Scandinavian about the comb design, although in its decoration the comb is certainly similar to an example from Hedeby, which also lacks its end segments (Tempel 1969, fig. 23.95).

Two small details may be indicative of a southern Scandinavian origin for the comb. The single line loose mesh decoration appears to have been incised over the top of an earlier pattern of short diagonal lines, seen on just one side of the comb, at the centre and a little beyond the runic inscription. This unusual palimpsest of linear patterning can also be seen on several combs from Hedeby, albeit with paired line meshes (Tempel 1969, fig. 23.102–3). It is not a feature seen elsewhere in the Dublin comb corpus. In addition, combs of Scandinavian origin found in Dublin have almost invariably been well-used and considerable wear can be seen on their teeth in particular. The central teeth of this comb are heavily worn on both sides, which would not be out of place on a Scandinavian comb.

A second comb with connecting plates of a broad D-shaped section (E748:57; Fig. 4.3:3) may also be of Scandinavian origin. Once again, it consists of the central part of a comb with the end segments now missing, decorated with an almost continuous loose mesh pattern, formed in this instance from paired crossing diagonal lines and bounded at one end of the comb by two pairs of vertical lines. The connecting plates of this comb are pedimental in form, rising in straight lines to the centre. The decoration extends across most of the surviving parts of the connecting plates, which is unusual for a single-sided composite comb of this type from Dublin, where the decoration is usually confined to the central part of the comb. Combs with decoration across most, but not all, of their connecting plates do occur at Hedeby, however (Tempel 1969, fig. 23.94–5). The most significant characteristic of this comb, in terms of its origins, is the way in which the tooth segments taper from the baseline to the comb back. This is a small and subtle feature but it is seen only on Scandinavian combs, and not on combs of Dublin origin. The teeth of this comb are worn, but not to the extent of the preceding comb. Its central design of paired diagonal lines crossing just once at the centre is a relatively common one, seen upon fifteen combs from the NMI excavations, coming from contexts that range in date from the mid-tenth century to the early eleventh century.

One of the simplest designs to be found on single-sided composite combs with connecting plates of broad D-shaped section is a saltire formed from paired diagonal lines and bounded by bands of vertical incised lines. This decoration can be seen on an incomplete comb from the Cork Tower that lacks a part of one end segment (E296:33418:F1032; Fig. 4.3:4). Five combs from the NMI excavations are decorated in the same way and they stem from contexts that range in date from the mid-tenth century to the early eleventh century. Single or paired saltires provide only a small panel at the centre of the comb, which is not a feature of contemporary comb design in northern Europe, where a greater part of the central area is normally decorated. A similar design can be seen on one side of a comb from Thetford (Rogerson and Dallas 1984, fig. 186.2). An intriguing point about this particular Dublin comb is that it is secured with just four iron rivets, which are widely and evenly spaced. The majority of combs of this class from Dublin possess between five or seven rivets, and only six combs utilise just four rivets.

A common decorative format for Dublin involves the use of chevron patterns in a number of different ways. The chevrons are formed from paired or tripled diagonal lines, which can be put together in a variety of combinations. Some of these designs are suggestive of Dublin provenance, forming a type of decorative 'signature' for the settlement, while other designs are more indicative of origins outside of Dublin; but the situation is never quite that simple. Thus a fragmentary connecting plate from the Cork Tower (E296:48511:F2017; Fig. 4.3:5) includes part of a design with two rows of paired diagonal lines separated by paired horizontal lines at the centre, with single framing lines above and below the diagonals. This decoration is not commonly seen in Dublin and there is only one close parallel for it, seen on a comb from Fishamble Street (E172:14029) recovered from a context of mid- tenth-century date. The decoration can be seen also at Hedeby, Lund, Pool, Sanday and York, providing the possibility that it reflects combs that are not of Dublin provenance (Tempel 1969, taf 27.152, 153 and 155; Blomqvist 1942, bild 21; Smith 2007, fig. 8.8.4., PL5165; Waterman 1959, fig. 16.12 and pl. XVIII.9; MacGregor *et al.* 1999, fig. 886.7582).

Equally, however, the same decoration also occurs on another comb from Dublin Castle, which was catalogued by Dunlevy (1988, 395). The near-complete comb (E748:56; Fig. 4.3:8) includes two different forms of chevron patterning. At either end of the comb there are V-shaped chevrons with paired horizontal lines set between them, reflecting the design of the connecting plate fragment from the Cork Tower. At the centre, however, there are three rows of short paired diagonal lines, with paired horizontal lines between them, producing S-shaped chevrons. This type of patterning is firmly associated with Dublin. Seven further combs from four sites in the settlement include S-shaped chevrons, three of them with paired horizontal lines also present. While this type of decoration occurs across Dublin, it is little known elsewhere, suggesting that it reflects local comb making. The comb may therefore be an amalgam of a local decorative design combined with a design more familiar in northern Europe.

A comb from the Cork Tower (E296:48512:F2021; Fig. 4.3:7) was well used before it was eventually discarded. Around two-thirds of the comb now survives, including the central area, which is decorated with V-shaped chevrons which, in this case, are not separated by paired horizontal lines at the centre. They are bounded by vertical incised lines, which occur also at the ends of the comb. The decoration is closely related to the previous comb from the Cork Tower (E296:48511:F2017; Fig. 4.3:5) and the lack of paired lines at the centre can be seen also on a comb without winged end segments from York (MacGregor *et al.* 1999, fig. 884.7548). It occurs also on a comb from Fishamble Street in Dublin (E172:12826). At some point the Dublin Castle comb fractured across its central area of decoration. It was not discarded, however, but continued to be used in a shortened form, with an end segment (possibly from the fractured part of the comb) secured to the broken end of the modified comb with the aid of two closely spaced iron rivets. The continued use of the comb is reflected in the considerable wear that can be seen on its surviving teeth. The repair was a very basic one and the fractured ends of the connecting plates were scarcely trimmed at all; yet it was sufficient to keep the comb in operation for some time.

An incomplete comb (E748:55; Fig. 4.3:6) includes a central panel with two narrow rows of chevrons formed from triple diagonal lines separated by roughly incised paired horizontal lines and a blank space at the centre. The comb was catalogued by Dunlevy (1988, 395). This type of design is commonly found in Dublin, occurring with doubled, tripled or quadrupled diagonal lines, either with or without the framing bands of horizontal lines. In each case, however, the central area of the design is left blank. Nine combs from the NMI excavations include the horizontal bounding lines and nine further combs lack them entirely. This group of eighteen combs is evenly spread across the main Dublin excavations, coming once again from contexts that range in date from the mid-tenth century to the early eleventh century. This particular comb (E748:55; Fig. 4.3:6) is

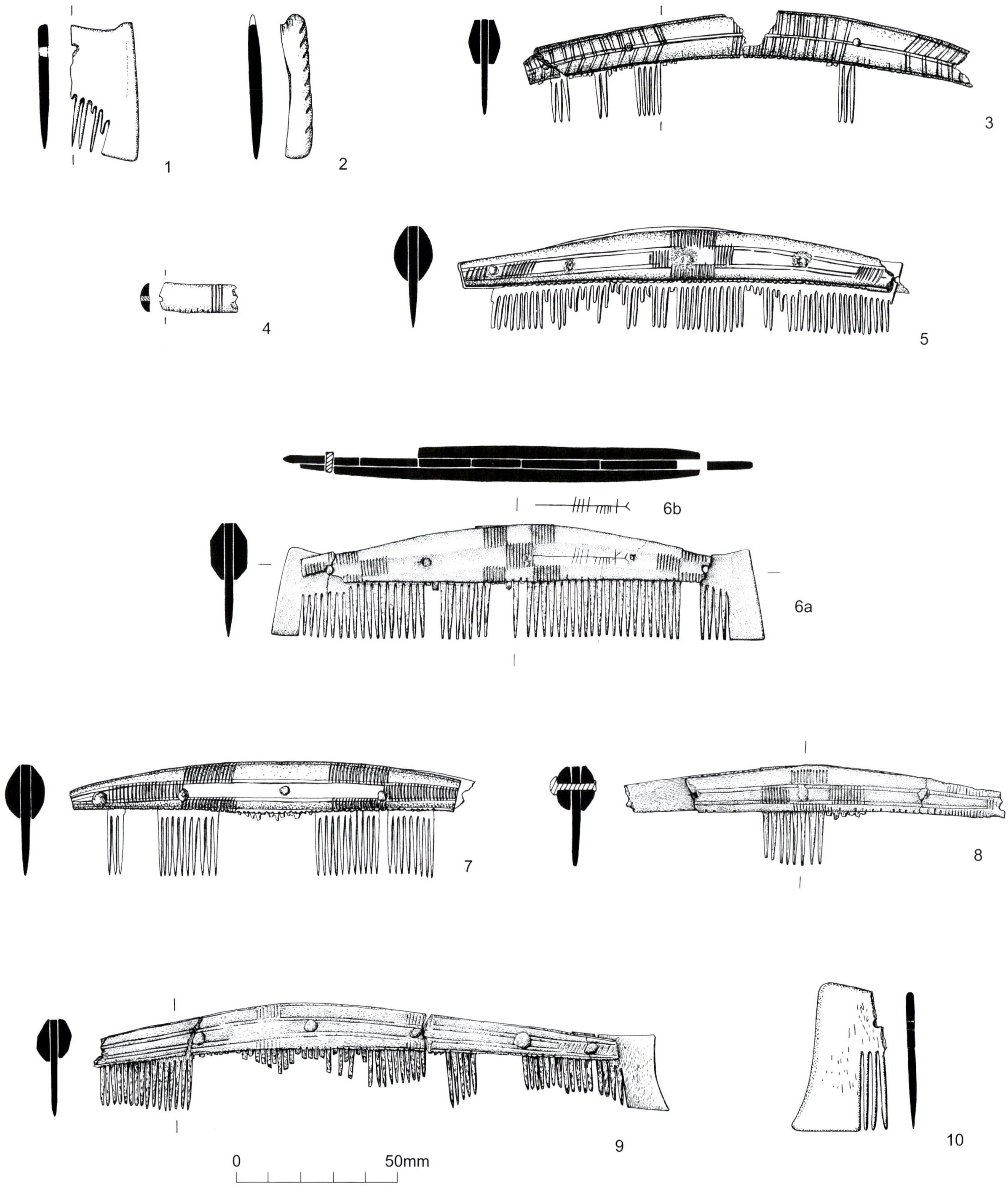

Fig. 4.4 Antler single-sided composite combs including one with ogham inscription (6a, 6b).

relatively stout in its proportions, with a small, stub apex to its winged end segment, which has a near-vertical, concave-curved back edge. These are characteristics of combs of Dublin origin although the decoration can occasionally be seen elsewhere, as at Lincoln, for example (White 1981).

IRISH SINGLE-SIDED COMPOSITES

The single-sided composite combs with connecting plates of a broad D-shaped section can be described as 'Hiberno-Scandinavian' in the sense that they show an admixture of design influences from Scandinavia (which may have arrived directly or via northern England), alongside inherently local practices. Those practices come into sharper relief with Irish single-sided composite combs. These combs lie further towards the Irish end of the spectrum, utilising the single-sided format but revealing continuity in design extending well back into the pre-Viking period. In the case of Dublin Castle, there are just two small fragments of combs that can be related to this comb form, and both of them are merely fragmentary end segments. One of these (E296:48507:F2010; Fig. 4.4:1), from the Cork Tower, includes a stub apex rising in a curve from the comb back, with a convex-curved back edge and curved graduation to the end teeth of the comb. There is an overall emphasis on curved lines in its design. The segment belongs to Dublin Type 3, which is characterised by the stub apex and steep, vertical or near-vertical angle of the back edge (Riddler and Trzaska-Nartowski forthcoming a). The end segment type is associated both with Hiberno-Scandinavian combs and with Irish single-sided composites and may well be another indicator of Dublin provenance. Even less survives of the second end segment (E296:48556:F2062; Fig. 4.4:2), which has a rounded apex and straight back edge, decorated on both sides with short diagonal lines. End segments were rarely decorated at this time and there are just two combs with comparable decoration from Dublin, both of which are Irish single-sided composite combs. One of them came from the larger High Street site, whilst the other was found at Fishamble Street, both coming from contexts of the mid- to late tenth century.

SINGLE-SIDED COMPOSITE COMBS WITH CONNECTING PLATES OF TRIANGULAR SECTION

Just one single-sided composite comb (E324:12980:F410; Fig. 4.4:3), from the Powder Tower, has connecting plates of triangular section. This is not unduly surprising, as this connecting plate section was never widely adopted in the northern world. Tempel noted that their distribution was centred on southern Scandinavia, particularly at Hedeby, and they were quite rare; the Dublin corpus of 28 combs with this connecting plate section (including this example) more than doubles the number known to him (Tempel 1969, 97–8, 126 and 209). V-shaped chevrons were well suited to combs of this section, because they could be set to either side of the raised area at the centre of the connecting plate, which was usually delineated with paired horizontal lines. In this case the comb includes bands of V-shaped chevrons at either end and similar decoration at the centre, where the chevrons are almost vertical, however. Longer, continuous designs of V-shaped chevrons can be seen on two Dublin combs with this connecting plate section, one of which has been published previously (NMI 1973, 32 no. 68 and pl. 9 centre; Dunlevy 1988, 366). A fragmentary comb from the larger High Street site includes part of a chevron design of this type (E71:2293), which can also be seen on a comb from Ballinderry Crannog No. 1 (Hencken 1936, fig. 31E). Tempel (1969, 98) dated the comb type to the tenth century but the earliest of the Dublin series comes from a context of the mid-tenth century and they are not common before the late tenth century, continuing thereafter into the eleventh century. A small, late group of the form can be identified in twelfth-century contexts on the Continent (Tempel 1969, 126) but the Dublin series is centred on the late tenth to eleventh century.

MIDDLE PERIOD SCANDINAVIAN COMBS

There are no early Scandinavian combs among the assemblage from Dublin Castle and few combs can be described as Scandinavian at all, although two examples have been identified above, a relatively high percentage for a Dublin site of tenth- to eleventh-century date. One further possible comb of this origin survives, unfortunately, as a small piece of an antler connecting plate from the Cork Tower that has been burnt to a white colour (E296:31158:F818; Fig. 4.4:4). Given the small size of the fragment, it is difficult to be certain of its form, but it is noticeable that it has a flat baseline and a back that is straight before rising in a low curve. This is not a common shape for the connecting plates of single-sided composite combs from Dublin. The vast majority of them either curve throughout their length or rise in straight lines to an apex at the centre of the comb. The combination of a curved back at the centre leading to narrow, straight terminals is a feature of combs of Scandinavian origin. Three examples from Dublin include a connecting plate from the larger High Street site (E71), part of a comb case from Winetavern Street and a near-complete comb from Fishamble Street. They come from contexts of the late tenth- to early eleventh century, dating that accords well with a comparable example from Lund (Tempel 1969, 98, 210 and taf 38.10; Blomqvist and Mårtensson 1963, fig. 230). A small fragment of this distinctive connecting plate form came from York (MacGregor *et al.* 1999, fig. 884.7948).

SINGLE-SIDED COMPOSITE COMBS WITH CONNECTING PLATES OF TRAPEZOIDAL SECTION

Five combs have connecting plates that are flat at the centre and bevelled to either side, providing what is described here as a trapezoidal section. Several of them were catalogued by Dunlevy (1988, 398). They fall into two distinct types within this form. Four of the combs (E324:3789:F217, E324:13390:F530, E748:54 and E748:58; Fig. 4.4:5, 6a/b, 7 and 8) are relatively short, originally extending to around 170mm in length, secured in each case by five iron rivets. The other comb (E748:59; Fig. 4.4:9) is substantially longer, reaching around 215mm altogether, fastened by seven iron rivets. The four shorter combs have flat baselines and curved or pedimental backs. Two of them (E324:3789:F217 and E748:54) certainly included winged end segments and it is likely that the other two combs were also equipped with them, although they no longer survive. All four combs are decorated in a similar way. Their trapezoidal section is emphasised by two sets of paired horizontal lines, which separate the connecting plate into three long, narrow decorative fields. Single framing lines can be seen along the baseline and comb back. Their decoration is limited to bands of vertical or diagonal incised lines, but it is arranged in a different way in each case. Three of the four combs have unbounded alternating vertical bands at their centres and on the two combs (E748:54 and E748:58) from the Cross Block this pattern is repeated at the ends of the comb. One of the combs (E748:54; Fig. 4.4:6a/b; Pl. 4.3) bears an ogham inscription. The other comb (E324:3789:F217) has long bands of diagonal incised lines at the centre at the end of each connecting plate. The fourth comb (E324:13390:F530; Fig. 4.4:7) effectively reverses the decorative design, keeping the centre entirely blank and placing the alternating bands of vertical lines at either end of the connecting plates.

All four combs can be closely paralleled within the Dublin corpus. The comb form is one of the most common to have been found in Dublin and over 220 examples were recovered from the NMI excavations, extending across the period *c.* 950–1150, but with the majority of examples coming from contexts of *c.* 1000–1125. The four combs from Dublin Castle belong to a standard Dublin type within that form, in terms of their size, decoration and riveting patterns. Around 40 combs from the NMI excavations are of the same general shape and size and are decorated in a similar way; the majority of them come from the Fishamble Street area of Dublin, from contexts of *c.* 975–1075. The pedimental form of connecting plate is not common with this comb form and just four further combs with this shape and connecting plate section are known, spread between High Street, Winetavern Street and Fishamble Street. The abundance of combs of this type within a specific area of Dublin suggests that they may have been made there, although there are no unfinished examples of the comb form that might help to confirm the presence and specific location of workshops.

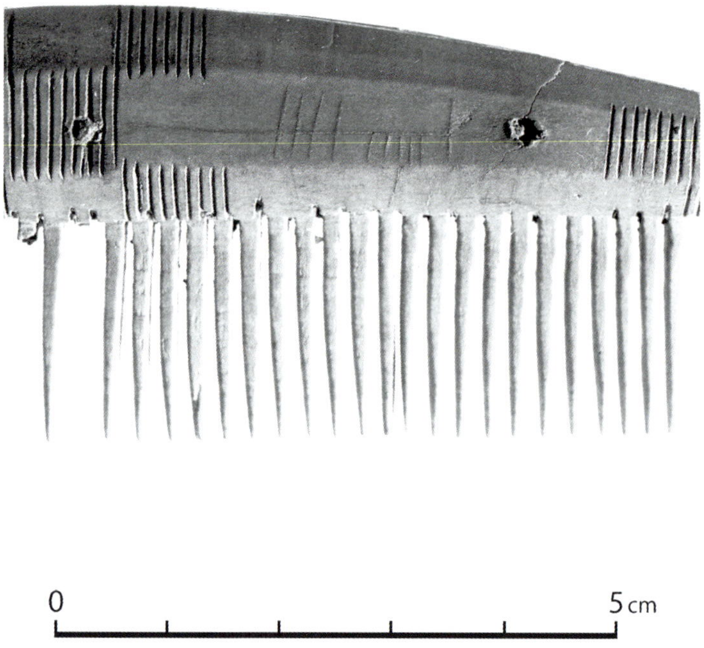

Pl. 4.3 Ogham inscription on antler comb E748:54.

The fifth comb with connecting plates of this section (E748:59; Fig. 4.4:9) differs from the other types in its length, its decoration, and the shape of its connecting plates. The comb has a curved baseline throughout and the comb back rises to the centre and tapers markedly at the ends. The end segments continue this line and are almost horizontal, extending well beyond the connecting plates with curved back edges. The whole comb has an elongated and distinctly different appearance, with a sparse decorative scheme restricted to two rows of knife-point decoration at the centre and single rows of diagonal incised lines at the comb ends. Comparable decoration can be seen on three combs from the NMI excavations, recovered from Winetavern Street, John's Lane and Fishamble Street, in contexts of the early to mid eleventh century. The longer forms of comb of this cross-section appear at this time, and not in contexts of tenth-century date.

The comb type as a whole is likely to be a Dublin innovation. Although it can be seen elsewhere in northern Europe, the numbers of combs involved are relatively low. Tempel was unaware of the Dublin corpus when he considered the type and noted that of just over twenty examples that he recorded from northern Europe, fifteen came from Hedeby (Tempel 1969, 211, Liste 21). It seems likely that some were made there, as well as at Dublin, although it is interesting to note that, while the comb type occurs at Hedeby, it has not been found at the successor site at Schleswig (Ulbricht 1984). Indeed, it is possible that some of the Hedeby examples of the comb type were actually made in Dublin (Tempel 1969, taf 25), a major centre for the production of this comb form.

SINGLE-SIDED COMPOSITE COMBS WITH NARROW UNDECORATED CONNECTING PLATES OF D-SHAPED SECTION

Just one example of a single-sided composite comb with narrow, undecorated connecting plates of a narrow D-shaped section was recovered (E748:22) and it survives only as a fragment. The connecting plates have a flat baseline and lightly curved, rising back, which allows the comb to be assigned to Dublin Type A1. This type consists of single-sided composite combs whose connecting plates have a flat baseline and lightly curved back, with a height at the centre of the comb between 24mm and 34mm, and with 4 to 9 teeth per centimetre, but mostly 5 to 8 teeth per centimetre (Riddler and Trzaska-Nartowski forthcoming a). Over one hundred combs of this specific type were recovered from the NMI excavations, almost half of them coming from the High Street excavations. The overall dating of the comb form is complicated by the lack of twelfth-century deposits in the NMI excavations, but it can be placed at *c.* 1050–1150, with the possibility that it continued a little longer into the twelfth century. As with the single-sided composite combs with connecting plates of trapezoidal section, there is little doubt that the comb form was being produced in Dublin. The large amounts of antler waste recovered from late twelfth-century contexts at Dublin High Street can be related directly to the manufacture of this comb form, if not specifically to this comb type, which may have gone out of use by that time (Riddler and Trzaska-Nartowski forthcoming a). It seems inherently likely none the less that these combs, including the Dublin Castle example, were made on Dublin High Street. The origins of the comb form may lie with similar combs from northern Europe, seen in both Scandinavian and Slavic areas (Riddler, Trzaska-Nartowski and Barton-Murray 2012, 377). The comb form was conceivably exported from Dublin to other sites. Dunlevy listed a number of the examples known from elsewhere in Ireland, to which combs from Beginish, Caherconnell Cashel, Knowth and Rathgureen can be added (O'Kelly and Kavanagh 1955–6, fig. 3.2; Comber and Hull 2010, fig. 10.55:04; Riddler, Trzaska-Nartowski and Barton-Murray 2012, 376–7 and 386–8; Comber 2002, 180 and fig. 17.60). Outside of Dublin, the largest quantity of combs of this form comes from Waterford (Hurley 1997b, 654–61). Few combs of the form can be seen outside of Ireland, with the exception of examples from Durham and Jarlshof (Riddler 2007a; Hamilton 1956, 148 and fig. XXX.3).

COMB TECHNOLOGY, DATING AND IDENTITY

In total, twenty combs and one comb case can be identified from Dublin Castle. Most of them have been described above and placed into different types. There are also two small fragments of combs, including a fractured end segment from a single-sided composite comb of Dublin Type 1 (E324:6100:F217; Fig. 4.4:10), recovered from the Powder Tower, and a tooth segment, originally riveted on one edge, found at the Cork Tower (E296:48508:F2010).

The combs have been placed into one broad class of single-sided composites and separated into seven distinct forms, with a number of types present within those forms. They show comparatively little variation in the way in which they have been put together. Almost all of the combs, irrespective of form, were secured with single rivets through their end segments and rivets on one edge of each tooth segment. This is one of the most common forms of riveting for both Dublin and northern Europe at this period. The two exceptions are combs identified as possibly Scandinavian in origin. The comb with the tapering tooth segments (E296:33418:F1032; Fig. 4.3:4) uses the conventional system but the central tooth segment is secured on both edges. The comb with the runic inscription (E296:50058:F1254; Fig. 4.3:2a/b, Pl. 4.2) has two tooth segments secured on one edge and two on both edges. These variations in common practice do not necessarily confirm that these combs are Scandinavian, as they can be seen with a number of combs from Dublin that are not thought to be of Scandinavian origin. The practice of securing the middle tooth segment a little more firmly with rivets on both edges, for example, occurs on 28 Hiberno-Scandinavian combs from Dublin. Where it does occur, it is usually because the combs include antler rivets, a feature of combs found at Fishamble Street in particular, but it can also be seen on combs fastened with iron rivets throughout. The combination of two tooth segments fastened on one edge, set alongside two fastened on both edges, can be seen on four Hiberno-Scandinavian combs from Dublin, emanating from Winetavern Street and Fishamble Street.

All of the combs have been fastened with iron rivets throughout and this, once again, is a common Dublin situation. Combs with one or more antler rivets, reflecting earlier Irish comb-making practices, also occur at this time and have mainly been found in the Fishamble Street area; they do not occur at Dublin Castle. All the combs have five teeth per centimetre, with just one exception (E324:3789:F217; Fig. 4.4:5), which has six teeth per centimetre. There is some variation in their lengths but it is difficult to assess the significance of this when the sample is a small one. The shortest comb (E748:56; Fig. 4.3:8) would have been just 135mm in length and, compared against the sample of NMI combs, that is suggestive of the dating to the late tenth to early eleventh century applied to the comb on typological grounds. Most of the combs can be measured or estimated at between 150mm and 180mm in length, which is typical for the period as a whole. There are two longer combs. The repaired comb (E296:48512:F2021; Fig. 4.3:7) probably extended to around 200mm in length originally, before it was truncated, and the elongated comb with connecting plates of trapezoidal section (E748:59; Fig. 4.4:9) was around 210–15mm in length. These are reasonable lengths for Dublin combs, but they are not exceptional.

Most of the combs from the Cork Tower and Powder Tower came from separate contexts. An end segment of Dublin Type 3 (E296:48507:F2010; Fig. 4.4:1) and a tooth segment (E296:48508:F2010) came from the same context (F2010) but do not belong to the same comb. An end segment of Dublin Type 1 (E324:6100:F217; Fig. 4.4:10) came from the same context as a comb with connecting plates of trapezoidal section (E324:3789:F217; Fig. 4.4:5) but once again, they are not the same comb.

In many ways, the comb assemblage from Dublin Castle conforms precisely with what would be expected from a site dating to *c*. 975–1050. All of the combs are single-sided composites and they occur in the most common forms of this period, notably with combs with connecting plates of broad D-shaped section and those with connecting plates of trapezoidal section. The presence of just one undecorated comb with narrow connecting plates of D-shaped section indicates that the assemblage does not extend far (if at all) beyond *c*. 1050. There are no combs with connecting plates of rectangular section but these are comparatively rare finds in Dublin. More significantly, the quantity of Irish single-sided composite combs is distinctly low and is confined to two fragmentary end segments. The comb assemblage includes three Scandinavian combs, a case with paired connecting plates and four Hiberno-Scandinavian combs, with several of the latter type including decoration indicative of a Dublin origin. The six combs with connecting plates of triangular or trapezoidal section, alongside the single undecorated comb with narrow connecting plates of D-shaped section, can all be regarded as Dublin products. The assemblage provides a minimum of three Scandinavian combs, representing 13% of the total, a higher figure than is found elsewhere in Dublin at this time.

CATALOGUE

PAIRED CONNECTING PLATE COMB CASES

E324:1024:F285 (Fig. 4.3:1). PT2 – Area A: Phase 2. Incomplete antler connecting plate from a comb case, D-shaped in section, lower back lightly curved throughout and upper baseline also slightly curved. Pierced by two perforations, one iron-stained, and fractured across a third perforation at one end. Central part decorated with a loose mesh lattice of paired crossing diagonal lines, slightly inept with three lines in one area and four in another. Bounded by vertical incised lines set to either side of the perforations. L. 105.5mm, W. 15.5mm, Th. 5mm.

SINGLE-SIDED COMPOSITE COMBS WITH CONNECTING PLATES OF BROAD D-SHAPED SECTION

E296:50058:F1254 (Fig. 4.3:2a/b; Pl. 4.2). CT2: Phase 4b. Fragmentary single-sided composite comb, for which only the central part now survives, with both end segments now missing. Substantial parts of two antler connecting plates of broad D-shaped section secure four tooth segments with three iron rivets, with traces of a fourth rivet hole; comb has fractured across rivet holes at both ends and retains a complete iron rivet at one end. Connecting plates have a lightly curved baseline and curved back and are decorated on both sides at the centre with a dense lattice mesh formed of single crossing diagonal lines, bounded by bands of six vertical incised lines. On one side this pattern overlies an earlier design of short lightly angled lines at the top of the connecting plate. A few of the comb teeth survive, long and rectangular in section, tapering lightly to rounded ends with traces of considerable wear at the centre on one side and towards the end of the comb on the other side. Saw marks are short and discrete on both sides. Blank area beyond central design includes a runic inscription at one end, interpreted as possibly the personal name *Unnr* or *Uni* (see Chapter 9 below) and a series of interlinked lines at the other end. Five teeth per centimetre. L. 117mm, W. 36mm, Th. 12.5mm.

E748:57 (Fig. 4.3:3). CB: occupation debris in immediate vicinity of Hearth 3 (House III) and on same level; Phase D. Fragmentary single-sided composite comb, lacking both ends and consisting of three tooth segments, fastened to parts of two antler connecting plates by three iron rivets, with a further rivet hole also present. Fractured across rivet holes at both ends. Connecting plates have a flat baseline and rising, pedimental back and are decorated across all of the surviving space on both sides by a continuous loose mesh pattern formed from paired crossing diagonal lines. Surviving teeth are long and narrow, tapering to rounded ends with traces of some wear on one side and considerable wear on the other side, leading to beading of the teeth at the centre of the comb. Saw marks of irregular length on both sides; six teeth per centimetre. L. 95mm, W. 32.5mm, Th. 12mm.

E296:33418: F1032 (Fig. 4.3:4). CT2: Phase 4a. Incomplete single-sided composite comb with broad connecting plates of D-shaped section, including two complete connecting plates, fastened to two end segments and three tooth segments by four iron rivets. Connecting plates have a lightly curved baseline and curved back and are decorated by bands of vertical incised lines beside both end rivets, and with a small panel with a saltire formed from paired crossing diagonal lines at the centre, bounded by vertical incised lines to either side. One end segment is complete, the other is fragmentary. Former rises in a curve to a rounded apex with a concave curved outswept back edge, broad flange and no graduation of the comb teeth. Teeth remain only at ends and centre of the comb, the other teeth are now separate. Central teeth show traces of wear on both sides in the form of lateral lines along most of their lengths; end teeth show little or no wear. Very few saw marks on one side of the comb; rather more, of irregular length, on the other side. Five teeth per centimetre. L. 142mm, W. 30.5mm, Th. 11.5mm.

E296:48511: F2017 (Fig. 4.3:5). CT2: House 2 deposit; Phase 5. Fragmentary antler connecting plate from a single-sided composite comb, broad D-shaped section with flat baseline and lightly rising back. Decorated at centre by paired opposed diagonal lines set within single horizontal framing lines at the top and bottom, and paired horizontal lines at the centre, forming a chevron pattern. Bounded by four vertical incised lines. Fractured across rivet holes at either end, with part of an iron rivet surviving towards the centre. Saw marks indicate five teeth per centimetre. L. 69.5mm, W. 11.5mm, Th. 4mm.

E748:55 (Fig. 4.3:6). CB: occupation debris in immediate vicinity of Hearth 3 (House III) and on same level; Phase D. Incomplete single-sided composite comb, consisting of an end segment and three tooth segments, fastened to two connecting plates by four iron rivets. Connecting plates have a slightly curved baseline and lightly curved back and are decorated at the centre on both sides by chevron patterns formed of two sets of short triple diagonal lines in the upper and lower areas, bounded by pairs of horizontal lines, with the centre of the medial area left blank. Design is bounded by triple vertical incised lines to either side, and remainder of each connecting plate is blank. End segment rises to a small rounded apex with a lightly outswept concave curved back edge and a broad flange. Comb teeth are graduated in a sharp, near-vertical curve, and are rectangular in section, tapering over their lower sections to blunt ends. Traces of slight wear on teeth on one side of the comb only. Saw marks of uneven length on both sides of the comb; five teeth per centimetre. L. 121mm, W. 32mm, Th. 12mm.

E296:48512:F2021 (Fig. 4.3:7). CT2: House 3 deposit; Phase 6. Incomplete single-sided composite comb with connecting plates of broad D-shaped section, including one end segment and six tooth segments, originally fastened to two connecting plates by five iron rivets. Connecting plates have a flat baseline and lightly curved back and are decorated at the centre with a band of V-shaped chevrons formed from paired diagonal lines. Design bounded by vertical incised lines, and further paired vertical incised lines lie beyond the end rivet. End segment rises in a curve to a pointed apex with a sinuous back edge and broad flange. Teeth are graduated in a short diagonal line, tapering evenly over their lower sections to blunt or rounded ends with traces of considerable wear leading to slight beading in some areas. Comb has fractured at one end and has been repaired with the addition of two closely spaced iron rivets. L. 130mm, W. 32.5mm, Th. 11.5mm.

E748:56 (Fig. 4.3:8). CB: occupation debris in immediate vicinity of Hearth 3 (House III) and on same level; Phase D. Incomplete single-sided composite comb, including two tooth segments and two end segments, originally fastened to two connecting plates by four iron rivets. Connecting plates have a lightly curved baseline and curved back and are decorated with V-shaped chevrons at either end, formed from paired diagonal lines with paired horizontal lines at the centre. Both designs are bounded by triple vertical incised lines. Central panel includes S-shaped chevrons, also formed from paired diagonal lines, with two sets of horizontal lines, bounded once again by triple vertical incised lines. Upper edge of each end segment sweeps upwards in a curve to a pointed apex, with a slightly convex curved and near-vertical back edge and a broad flange. Segments are slightly different in form. The teeth are graduated in slightly sinuous curves. Both end segments are noticeably long and secured by single iron rivets. Teeth taper over their lower sections to blunt ends with slight wear visible in the form of occasional faint lateral lines. Five teeth per centimetre. L. 135mm, W. 31mm, Th. 11.5mm.

IRISH SINGLE-SIDED COMPOSITES

E296:48507:F2010 (Fig. 4.4:1). CT2: House 3 ash spread; Phase 6. Fragmentary antler end segment from a single-sided composite comb. Near-horizontal upper edge rises to a stub apex, with a slightly convex outswept back edge and narrow flange. Straight diagonal graduation of teeth. Just one tooth remains on the segment (the others are now separate), with some wear apparent on them. Originally five teeth per centimetre. L. 25mm, W. 41mm, Th. 3.5mm.

E296:48556:F2062 (Fig. 4.4:2). CT2: fill of Pit 4a; Phase 4a. Fragment of the back edge, apex and flange of an antler end segment from a single-sided composite comb. Slightly convex back edge with upper edge rising to a rounded apex. Back edge decorated on both sides with diagonal lines, producing a 'feathered' effect. Narrow flange also survives, angled in slightly towards the back edge. Highly polished on both sides. L. 8mm, W. 44.5mm, Th. 4mm.

SINGLE-SIDED COMPOSITE COMBS WITH CONNECTING PLATES OF TRIANGULAR SECTION

E324:12980:F410 (Fig. 4.4:3). PT1: earth and timber bank; Phase 2. Fragmentary single-sided composite comb with connecting plates of triangular section, including parts of two connecting plates, originally fastened to three tooth segments and one end segment by five iron rivets, with traces of a further rivet hole. Connecting plates have a curved baseline and back and are decorated in three areas, at the centre and ends, by narrow bands of paired or tripled diagonal incised lines set above or below the central paired lines. There are also single framing lines at the back and baseline. Noticeable saw marks on both sides, often extending well into the connecting plates, particularly at the centre of the comb. A few teeth survive from one end, tapering lightly and evenly to rounded ends with slight traces of wear in the form of faint lateral lines on both sides. Five teeth per centimetre. L. 150mm, W. 28.5mm, Th. 9mm.

MIDDLE PERIOD SCANDINAVIAN COMBS

E296:31158:F818 (Fig. 4.4:4). CT2: deposit; Phase 1. Due to disturbance of the context (deposit F818) the comb fragment was intrusive to the Phase 1 level of the site. Small fragment of an antler connecting plate from a single-sided composite comb, flat baseline and back that is initially horizontal before rising in a curve. Decorated by a band of four vertical incised lines. Fracture across a rivet hole at either end and burnt to a white colour. Saw marks indicate five teeth per centimetre originally. L. 25.5mm, W. 8.5mm, Th. 3mm.

SINGLE-SIDED COMPOSITE COMBS WITH CONNECTING PLATES OF TRAPEZOIDAL SECTION

E324:3789:F217 (Fig. 4.4:5). PT2 – Area C: Phase 3. Fragmentary single-sided composite comb with connecting plates of trapezoidal section, including substantial parts of two antler connecting plates, now separate from two end segments and six tooth segments, but originally secured with five iron rivets. Both connecting plates lack their ends and have a slightly curved baseline and curved back. Separated into three decorative fields by two sets of paired horizontal lines with single upper and lower framing lines also present. Four bands of vertical incised lines, shorter in the central field than the upper and lower fields, surround the central iron rivet. Further long bands of diagonal incised lines are set in the central fields at either end of the comb. Most of the comb teeth survive, tapering slightly to blunt ends with traces of considerable wear leading to beading across most of them on both sides. Slightly less wear on the end segments, both of which are fragmentary and fractured across rivet holes with the upper edge rising towards the apex. Saw marks largely confined by the lower framing lines, six teeth per centimetre. L. 126.5mm, W. 28.5mm, Th. 11.5mm.

E748:54 (Fig. 4.4:6a/b; Pl. 4.3). CB: occupation debris in immediate vicinity of Hearth 3 (House III) and on same level; Phase D. Near-complete single-sided composite comb with connecting plates of trapezoidal section, consisting of five tooth segments and two end segments, secured to two connecting plates by four iron rivets. Connecting plates have a flat baseline and curved back and are decorated by alternating bands of vertical lines at the centre, with additional bands at either end. One side includes an ogham inscription in the central field, set near to the middle of the comb (see 4.2.3 below). End segments rise in shallow straight lines to apex with straight back edges angled outwards and short diagonal graduations to the teeth. Five teeth per centimetre. L. 152mm, W. 34mm, Th. 11mm.

E324:13390:F530 (Fig. 4.4:7). PT1: BW1; Phase 1b. Fragmentary single-sided composite comb with connecting plates of trapezoidal section, including parts of two antler connecting plates, originally fastened to seven tooth segments by five iron rivets. Connecting plates have a flat baseline and lightly curved back and are separated into three decorative fields by two sets of paired horizontal lines; there are also single framing lines near the baseline and back. Central area is blank, while sides have two long panels of short vertical lines in the upper and lower fields, and an alternating band in the central area. Rivets largely avoid the decoration. Comb teeth survive towards both ends, tapering evenly to rounded or pointed terminals with traces of some wear visible on both sides, more on one side than the other, in the form of lateral lines along most of the length of each tooth. Saw marks largely confined by lower framing lines, five teeth per centimetre. L. 140mm, W. 33mm, Th. 11mm.

E748:58 (Fig. 4.4:8). CB: occupation debris in immediate vicinity of Hearth 3 (House III) and on same level; Phase D. Fragment of a single-sided composite comb with connecting plates of trapezoidal section, including parts of two antler connecting plates, originally fastened to five tooth segments by three iron rivets, with traces of two further rivet holes. Only one tooth segment now remains *in situ*. Connecting plates have a flat baseline and rising, pedimental back and are separated into three decorative fields by two sets of paired horizontal lines; there are no framing lines. Alternating bands of vertical incised lines surround the rivet at the centre and are present in the upper and lower fields towards either end of the comb. Teeth taper evenly to blunt ends with considerable wear visible on the central tooth segment on both sides, which has led to beading and shortening of the teeth. Saw marks are variable in length on both sides of the comb; five teeth per centimetre. L. 116mm, W. 31.5mm, Th. 12mm.

E748:59 (Fig. 4.4:9). CB: occupation debris in immediate vicinity of Hearth 3 (House III) and on same level; Phase D. Incomplete single-sided composite comb with connecting plates of trapezoidal section, including substantial parts of two long connecting plates, fastened to two end segments and nine tooth segments by seven iron rivets. Connecting plates are cut from the end of an antler tine and have a curved back and baseline. Separated into three decorative fields by two sets of paired horizontal lines, and single framing lines are also present. Sparsely decorated with single bands of near-vertical incised lines in the central area at each end of the comb, and two sets of narrow bands of vertical lines in the upper and lower fields at the centre of the comb, with knife-point peck marks between them. One end segment is fragmentary and degraded. The other follows the line of the back of the comb with a horizontal upper edge, leading to a rounded apex set well beyond the connecting plates, concave curved back edge and broad flange, with short diagonal graduation of the comb teeth. Some of the teeth survive but almost all of them are in degraded condition, with their terminals now missing. Saw marks largely confined by the lower framing line on both sides. Five teeth per centimetre. L. 207mm, W. 36mm, Th. 12mm.

SINGLE-SIDED COMPOSITE COMBS WITH NARROW UNDECORATED CONNECTING PLATES OF D-SHAPED SECTION

E748:22. CB: in shells over Hearth 5 (House V); Phase F. Fragment of a single-sided composite comb, including four antler tooth segments, fastened to parts of two connecting plates by three iron rivets. Connecting plates are undecorated, with a flat baseline and straight rising back. Some of the comb teeth survive, tapering evenly to blunt ends with traces of slight wear in the form of faint lateral lines along them. Five teeth per centimetre. L. 76.5mm, W. 29mm, Th. 11.5mm.

END SEGMENTS AND TOOTH SEGMENTS, SINGLE-SIDED COMPOSITE COMBS

E324:6100:F217 (Fig. 4.4:10). PT2–Area C: deposit; Phase 3. Fragmentary antler end segment from a single-sided composite comb, fractured across a rivet hole. Upper edge rises in a straight line to a rounded apex with a concave curved back edge and broad flange. Three long teeth survive, all of the same length, with no graduation. Teeth are long and narrow, tapering over lower sections to blunt ends. Slight wear on display side, in the form of faint lateral lines close to the connecting plate space. Five teeth per centimetre. L. 28mm, W. 44.5mm, Th. 3.5mm.

E296:48508:F2010. CT2: House 3 ash spread; Phase 6. Fragmentary antler tooth segment from a single-sided composite comb, originally fastened on one edge, with its teeth now separate. Narrow connecting plate space with flat baseline and lightly rising, straight back. Teeth show traces of slight wear, with faint lateral lines visible. Five teeth per centimetre. L. 20.5mm, W. 30.5mm, Th. 2.5mm.

CRAFT IMPLEMENTS

BONE CYLINDERS (FIG. 4.5)

Twelve bone cylinders were distributed across two of the three excavations, with two of them coming from the Powder Tower (E324:1027:F313 and E324:13031:F293) and ten recovered from five separate deposits within the Cross Block E748:13, E748:82, E748:83, E748:84 and E748:113). They were mostly recovered as single finds, but E748:113 includes a group of six examples, identified as cylinders a to f.

Bone cylinders are essentially sections of cattle and horse metapodia, sawn at one or both ends. Within Dublin, where over a thousand examples are known from the NMI excavations, three principal forms of bone cylinder can be identified. The first type is cylindrical in form and has been cut from the midshaft of the bone. It includes a central, axial perforation, formed from the natural bone cavity, which has usually been left in an unmodified state. The internal medial line of the bone is often retained with cylinders made from cattle metapodia. The cylinders of this type are usually cleanly sawn at both ends, and those ends are parallel in most cases. The outer surface is generally unmodified and the key characteristic is the cylindrical form. Of the twelve cylinders catalogued here, nine can be assigned to this type (E324:1027:F313 and E324:13031:F293, E748:13, E748:82, E748:83, E748:84 and E748:113c, d and e), the most common form to be seen in Dublin.

The second type has a truncated conical shape, as a result of being cut towards the distal or proximal end of the bone. The central perforation may be modified to remove cortile tissue, allowing the perforation to extend the entire length of the object, and clearly emphasising its importance. Two cylinders can be assigned to this type (E748:113a and f). The third type consists of examples that retain the proximal articulation of the bone, which has usually been perforated axially. They show little other modification. A single example of this type came from the Cross Block (E748:113b).

Bone cylinders were cut from the metapodia of both cattle and horses, and occasionally deer bones were also used. The range of skeletal elements extends, within the Dublin sample as a whole, to the occasional use of cattle radii and tibiae as well. Within the Dublin Castle assemblage one of the cylinders has been made from a cattle metacarpus, nine from cattle metatarsals, one from a horse metacarpus and one from a horse metatarsus. Cattle metatarsals form the dominant material for cylinders, both in this assemblage and elsewhere in Dublin. Within a sample of 132 bone cylinders from Dublin High Street, for example, the relative totals of different bone types reflect the Dublin Castle sample reasonably well. A small number of cylinders were also made of antler, including examples from Cork, Dublin and Waterford, where bone cylinders are none the less still dominant (Hurley 1997b, 685; 2003, 342).

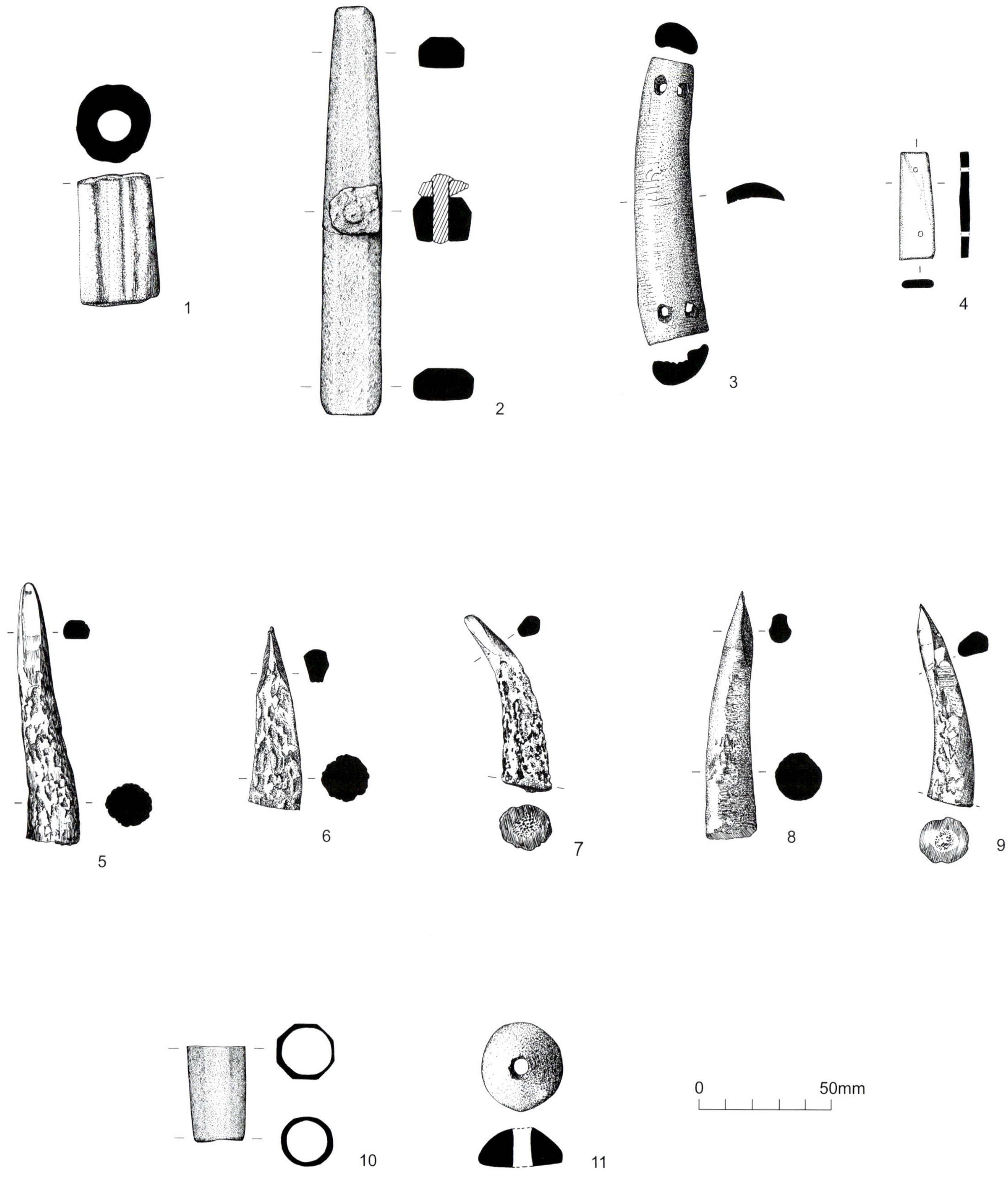

Fig. 4.5 Bone and antler artefacts: Type 1 bone cylinder (1), clamp (2), axe blade cover (3), saw fragment (4), Type 1a wedges (5, 6), Type 1b wedges (7, 8), Type 4 wedge (9), spacer or ferrule (10), spindle whorl (11).

Bone cylinders are common finds on sites of medieval date in Ireland, where the majority of examples have come from urban contexts. They include almost 300 cylinders from contexts mainly of the late eleventh- to twelfth century at Waterford, as well as 39 from twelfth-century contexts in Cork (Hurley 1997b, 685-96; 2003, 342-3). A few examples from recent Dublin excavations have come from contexts of thirteenth-century date (Simpson 1995, 82; Halpin 2000, 172–4; McMahon 2002, 104 and fig. 18.550). Over 1,000 bone cylinders were recovered from the NMI excavations in Dublin, with 560 of those coming from the Fishamble Street excavations and 256 from Wood Quay (E132). Thus the area of Wood Quay and Fishamble Street produced over 800 bone cylinders, while sites further to the south, at Winetavern Street and the High Street, have provided only 272 cylinders.

Bone cylinders have also been found on a few rural sites, including Ardsallagh, Ballynee, Clonmacnoise New Graveyard, Dalkey Island, Farrandreg, Illaunloughlan Island, Knowth, Marshes Upper and Nendrum (Riddler and Trzaska-Nartowski 2009b and forthcoming d; Eogan 2012, fig. 7.4:7.23181 and 23190; Liversage 1968, fig 27.212 and 291–3; Murphy 1998, 271 and fig. 5; White Marshall and Walsh 2005, fig. 96.340:1; Gowan 1992, fig. 18.464; Bourke 2007, 414 and fig. 13.28). The Farrandreg cylinder came from the twelfth-century backfill of a souterrain, several of the Dalkey cylinders came from the primary fill of a ditch sealed by a deposit that included ceramics of thirteenth-century date and the Illaunloughan Island example was retrieved from the fill of a medieval grave (Liversage 1968, 99–100; White Marshall and Walsh 2005, 188). Although this might suggest that bone cylinders are objects of twelfth- to thirteenth-century date, the huge numbers recovered from the Fishamble Street excavations are likely to have come from earlier contexts, going back to the eleventh century, and possibly earlier.

Bone cylinders have not been found in contemporary deposits either in England or Continental Europe, but they do occur in Scotland. Two neatly finished cylinders of square section with pared outer surfaces from Skaill, Deerness, Orkney resemble parallelepiped (four-sided) dice but lack any markings which, as Porter noted, renders that interpretation of their function unsatisfactory (Porter 1997, 101 and fig. 8.8.36 and 72). Other examples are known from the Broch of Burrian and Howe on Orkney (MacGregor 1974, fig. 16.206; Ballin Smith 1994, 170 and fig. 92.2680). A faceted and hollowed section of antler from Foshigarry may also be a cylinder (Hallén 1994, fig. 12.12). The most impressive set of cylinders to have been found outside of Ireland comes, however, from St Ninian's Isle, Shetland. They were described and illustrated as a 'necklace' of bone and antler beads and were thought to be of Iron Age date (Small 1973, 7 and fig. 6).

Bone cylinders have been found both individually and in larger groups of varying numbers. The group of six from Dublin Castle can be compared with an assemblage of eight from Peter Street at Waterford and around twelve from Christchurch Place in Dublin. Sixteen cylinders were found in a single context at Winetavern Street and four cylinders lay together in another group from the same site (Hurley 1997b, 685; Halpin 2000, 172). Thirty-six cylinders from Cork came from the same context, alongside numerous other finds, and thirteen accompanied the St Ninian's Isle Treasure on Shetland (Hurley 2003, 341 and 343; Small 1973, fig. 6).

It has previously been suggested that they functioned either as beads or loomweights, and they have recently been captioned as gaming pieces or textile implements (Liversage 1968, 116; Wallace 2016, fig. 8.39), but none of these interpretations is at all convincing, as noted previously (Hurley 1997b, 685). The precise function of bone cylinders remains to be established, but the objects themselves provide some clues. They are frequently polished on both their inner and outer surfaces. This probably stems from extensive wear and handling, particularly if they were grouped together on a string of cordage or leather, as seen with examples from Dublin and Waterford. A group of seven from Christchurch Place in Dublin were found strung together on a leather strip and a cylinder from Waterford retained a section of cordage through its centre (White Marshall and Walsh 2005, 188; Hurley 1997b, 685). Hurley (1997b, 685) has summarised their possible functions, among the most plausible of which are large beads – which may be borne out by the St Ninian's Isle assemblage but is otherwise unlikely – net spacers and devices for the twisting or rolling of cordage. Less plausible interpretations include counters for an abacus and loomweights. Wallace (2016, 267) has also suggested that they were used as weights (but not as loomweights) and this is possible if their overall weight as a group is considered, rather than the weights of individual pieces. The Waterford sample varies in weight between 17.4g and 71.1g with an average of 26.2g, whilst a group of 93 bone cylinders recorded from the High Street and Christchurch Place in Dublin have weights between 4.3g and 67.7g and an average of 20.4g. The Dublin Castle cylinders vary from 15.1g to 39.6g, with an average weight of 26.5g. More work needs to be done on the metrology of these objects but the wide variation in their weights is notable, although their average weights are reasonably similar. There is a similarly wide variation in their lengths, extending from 11mm to 57mm in the Dublin sample and from 24mm to 49mm in the Dublin Castle assemblage. That may not have been unduly significant, however, if they were used as spacers along the edges of nets, because the different lengths may have coincided with different mesh sizes, and any case, absolute precision in length may not have been important for this function. Their weights suggest that if used in this way they would differ from net floats, of the rolled birch bark type illustrated by Westphal, for example (Westphal 2006, 62–3 and abb 55); they would act instead to sink one part of a net, much like contemporary rolled lead weights but as their counterparts, made of bone. This may also explain why they are such common finds in the waterfront area of Dublin and its damp immediate hinterland but are found in smaller numbers on sites located inland on higher ground.

CATALOGUE

TYPE 1

E324:13031:F293 (Fig. 4.5:1). PT2–Area B: Phase 1. Complete bone cylinder, horse metatarsus midshaft, worked by knife in a rotary motion at both ends to separate it from the remainder of the bone. Cortile tissue remains at one end in the medullary channel. Some polish on the exterior and interior. L. 49mm, W. 30mm, Th. 28.5mm. Wgt. 39.6g.

E324:1027:F313. PT2–Area K: Phase 16. Complete bone cylinder, cattle metatarsus midshaft, neatly sawn at both ends, from several directions on one side. Three notches cut probably by saw on medial or lateral face at one end. Same face also has peck marks across its centre, indicative of its use as a working surface. Highly polished on the exterior, some polish through the medullary channel. L. 23mm, W. 23.5mm, Th. 28.5mm. Wgt.18.6g.

E748:13. CB: occupation debris of Hearth 5 (House V); Phase F. Complete bone cylinder, cattle metatarsus midshaft, sawn from several directions on both sides, with a remnant stub on one side. Lateral saw trace 0.8mm wide on the posterior surface. Exterior surface polished but not the ends or the interior. Slight cortile tissue in the medullary channel at one end. L. 24mm, W. 23mm, Th. 22mm. Wgt. 15.1g.

E748:82. CB: near south section, *c.* 0.15m under Hearth 3 (House III); Phase C. Complete bone cylinder, sawn from the midshaft, towards the distal end, of a horse metacarpus, from several directions on both sides. Worn and highly polished exterior, slight polish also to interior surface. L. 31.5mm, W. 33.5mm, Th. 25mm. Wgt. 32.4g.

E748:83. CB: near south section, *c.* 0.15m under Hearth 3 (House III); Phase C. Complete bone cylinder, cattle metatarsus midshaft, sawn from several directions on both sides with remnant stubs remaining. Highly polished exterior and end faces, some interior polish also. Faint knife line runs along centre of posterior face. L. 33mm, W. 23mm, Th. 25mm. Wgt. 25.8g.

E748:84. CB: near south section, *c.* 0.15m under Hearth 3 (House III); Phase C. Complete bone cylinder, cattle metatarsus midshaft, sawn from several directions on both sides. Highly polished exterior, polished interior, stained black over most of lower surface. L. 33mm, W. 24.5mm, Th. 24.5mm. Wgt. 23.9g.

E748:113c. CB: unknown context. Complete bone cylinder, cattle metatarsus midshaft, cleanly sawn at both ends from the posterior to the anterior face. Slight exterior polish and none visible on the interior. L. 33mm, W. 22mm, Th. 26mm. Wgt. 26.5g.

E748:113d. CB: unknown context. Complete bone cylinder, cattle metatarsus midshaft, sawn from several directions at both ends. Some exterior polish; faint longitudinal knife mark along the centre on the anterior side. L. 33.5mm, W. 25mm, Th. 22.5mm. Wgt. 24.7g.

E748:113e. CB: unknown context. Complete bone cylinder, cattle metacarpus midshaft, sawn at both ends from several directions with a raised remnant stub at one end. Slight exterior and interior polish. L. 28.5mm, W. 31mm, Th. 22mm. Wgt. 22.3g.

TYPE 2

E748:113a. CB: unknown context. Complete bone cylinder, cut from midshaft towards distal end of a cattle metatarsus, sawn cleanly at both ends with a saw trace on the anterior face of 1.12mm. Some exterior and interior polish and edges rounded and worn. L. 40.5mm, W. 26mm, Th. 26mm. Wgt. 27.3g.

E748:113f. CB: unknown context. Incomplete bone cylinder, sawn from a cattle metatarsus midshaft section located close to the proximal end of the bone and split so that only the anterior face now remains, burnt to a light grey colour. Cleanly sawn at both ends with slight polish visible. L. 27mm, W. 22mm (fragment only).

TYPE 3

E748:113b. CB: unknown context. Complete bone cylinder, cut from the proximal end of a cattle metatarsus and including the articulation, which has been trimmed by knife to a cylindrical form and pierced by an axial perforation 3mm in diameter. Sawn from several directions across the opposite end, with a remnant stub remaining. Slight exterior polish. L. 36mm, W. 31.5mm, Th. 30mm. Wgt. 25.8g.

CLAMP (FIG. 4.5:2)

Part of a whale bone clamp (E748:103) was recovered from the Cross Block. It consists of a rectangular strip of whale bone, flat on one side along roughly half of its length but rising up along the other part. It has been faceted to a trapezoidal section and tapers lightly from one end to the other. Part of a substantial iron rivet survives at the centre, set through a square iron washer. Originally a second, companion strip of whale bone would have been attached to this piece with the iron rivet. The two flat surfaces were set together and, when not in use, they were adjoined for part of their length, up to the rivet in the centre. By pressing on the other end the two flat surfaces could be separated and clenched around an object, effectively securing it and allowing it to be held whilst it was worked (Schietzel 2014, 345). The iron rivet could be set in the centre of the clamp, as here, or towards one end.

Clamps are a resolutely Viking implement type. They are known from a small range of sites in northern Europe, including Hedeby, Sandnes, Trelleborg and Trondheim, as well as Birsay in Scotland (Jankuhn 1943, 149 and fig. 74a; Ulbricht 1978, 79; Graham-Campbell 1980, 135, no. 472; Curle 1982, 111 and fig. 50.287; MacGregor 1985, 172 and fig. 91; Nørlund 1948, 131 and pl. 29.1; Simonsen 1953, 113–4; Riddler and Trzaska-Nartowski 2011, 127–8). A clamp was also found in a grave at Ytre Elgsnes in Norway (Simonsen 1953, fig. 3c; Tempel 1969, 39). They were produced in antler and whale bone, as well as iron (Schietzel 2014, 393) and there is one rare example of wood from Dublin (E71:15493). They are not commonplace items. Examples from England, for example, are limited to a few fragmentary examples from Lincoln and York, as well as complete pieces of at least one of the two main components from Dunstable, Earith and Ipswich (Riddler 2013). Intriguingly, the largest collection of clamps from northern Europe comes from Dublin, where there is also some evidence for their manufacture. Ten clamps are known from the two High Street sites and five came from Winetavern Street. Nineteen are known from Fishamble Street and Wood Quay, and twenty from Christchurch Place. Unfinished examples have come from Christchurch Place and the High Street. Dating evidence suggests that the earliest examples in Dublin come from contexts of the late tenth century, and they continue in use into the second half of the eleventh century. Thirty-five of the Dublin sample are made of whale bone and sixteen of antler, providing a ratio of 2:1 in favour of the former material.

Jankuhn initially argued that these implements were both produced and utilised by comb makers, whilst Tempel suggested that they were an implement used by comb makers, but also in other crafts (Jankuhn 1943, 149; Tempel 1969, 39). The Trelleborg example was associated with combs and antler waste, and although the Ytre Elgsnes grave was that of a smith, Tempel noted that tools appropriate for a comb maker were also found there (Tempel 1969, 40). Bayley suggested that they may have been used by metalworkers, while noting that 'there is no positive evidence to associate them with the working of metal rather than other materials' (Bayley 1992, 791). In effect, clamps appear to be implements made by antler and bone workers both for themselves, and for the use of other craftsmen. And it is possible, of course, that the antler and bone worker may have practised other crafts as well, the relationships with iron working and textile manufacture being particularly close.

E748:103 (Fig. 4.5:2). CB: *c.* 76mm under burnt layer; Phase C. One half of a whale bone clamp, consisting of a sub-rectangular strip of whale bone, with a bevelled D-shaped section, tapering slightly towards one end. Pierced by an iron spindle at the centre, with a square rove on the upper surface. Lower surface of clamp is upswept on one side. L. 158mm, W. 23mm, Th. 19mm.

MOTIF PIECE (PL. 4.4)

A segment of cattle-sized rib bone has been roughly fractured at either end, probably in the course of butchering an animal. Subsequently, it formed the raw material for a motif piece (E324:13500:F197). This was a common practice in Dublin, with sections of rib and pelvis forming the most common surfaces utilised for these objects. In this case one side of the rib includes three vertical lines and three horizontal lines, set close to one edge. A pair of curved lines runs between them and there is a sense here that the craftsperson was working on a specific design where broad linear bands were enmeshed with narrower curved bands. A motif piece from the smaller High Street site (E43:4083) includes several versions of a motif that joins straight and curved bands, although the bands of the design are of the same width throughout. It is more likely that both the horizontal and vertical bands formed by the paired lines were intended to form the basis for narrow decorative panels. With most of the motif pieces the frame was created first and was then filled with decoration. In this case the frames have been roughly sketched out, but the design did not progress any further.

The other side of the motif piece includes two rectangular frames. One of these is substantially complete while a small fragment of a design of the same type lies adjacent to it. The design includes a broad frame enclosing three smaller rectangles, with several of the inner lines overlapping in to the outer frame. A motif piece from Christchurch Place (E122:16061) includes an interlace design, set within a large rectangular frame. As with the other side, the frame for the design had been roughly sketched out but was then abandoned. This practice is quite common among the corpus of motif pieces from Dublin, many of which show

Pl. 4.4 Bone motif piece E324:13500:F197.

unfinished designs or, as here, simple frames that have only been sketched out. The same motif piece can include a series of designs ranging from simple frames to complex patterns, as seen on the motif piece noted above (E43:4083).

Around 200 motif pieces have been recovered from Dublin excavations, with well over half of that number coming from Christchurch Place. Smaller quantities, amounting to just under 20 motif pieces, were recovered from the High Street sites and around 40 motif pieces came from the various Fishamble Street excavations. More recent discoveries include motif pieces from Ship Street Little and Temple Bar (Johnson 2004, 54; Simpson 2004) and these are important discoveries, as they widen the area of the settlement within which motif pieces have been found. The majority of these objects can be assigned to the tenth to eleventh century, largely on stylistic grounds.

E324:13500:F197 (Pl. 4.4). PT1: surface of clay and timber bank; Phase 2. Fragmentary motif piece with designs inscribed on to a fractured segment of cattle-sized rib bone. One side has a pattern at one end consisting of four sets of parallel lines, with short curved lines set between two of them. The other side includes an incised square box, formed once again from paired lines, most of which extend beyond the limits of the box itself. A fragment of a second, similar pattern lies at the edge. L. 96mm, W. 44mm, Th. 9mm.

AXE BLADE COVER (FIG. 4.5:3)

A neatly finished antler object from the Cork Tower (E296:36958:F1039) has fractured along its length, but its original form and function can be reconstructed. It includes four perforations, set in pairs at either end, as well as a slot that extends along most of its length. The perforations are angled so that cords could pass vertically across the two ends of the cover. By comparison with similar objects of wood from Hedeby, the object can be identified as an axe blade cover of Westphal's Type 1 (Westphal 2006, 55 and taf 30; Schietzel 2014, 579). This type of cover is essentially rectangular in form, with a lightly curved base and a slot for the axe blade of around 85–115mm in length. This antler example from Dublin Castle is relatively small in its dimensions, the slot extending to 87mm. Axe blade covers of both wood and antler are very rare finds. The ten examples of Type 1 wooden covers from Hedeby are not matched by any antler examples there, whilst the single antler example from Dublin Castle can be compared with another from Fishamble Street (E141:3550), which is roughly finished and may not have been used. There are also two examples in decorated wood from Dublin, described previously as 'scraper handles' (Lang 1988, DW4 and DW61; Wallace 2016, fig. 7.19; Westphal 2006, 55).

E296:36958:F1039 (Fig. 4.5:3). CT2: Phase 4a. Incomplete antler axe blade cover, fractured in half along its length. Formed from a section of antler tine, sawn at both ends, with pairs of knife-cut perforations close to either end. Vestiges of a slot for a blade remain, 87mm long one edge, 84mm on the other. Polished surface with numerous manufacturing marks. L. 107mm, W. 24mm, Th. 11mm.

BOW SAWS (FIGS. 4.5.4, 4.6)

Among the remarkable series of craft tools from Dublin Castle, which include a clamp and an axe blade cover, there is also a near-complete antler saw from the Cork Tower (E296:48513:F2021; Fig. 4.6), as well as a small part of a second example from the Powder Tower (E324:13391:F530; Fig. 4.5:4). The near-complete saw has been published previously (Hall 1996; MacGregor *et al.* 1999, 1945-7; Lynch and Manning 2001, 178 and fig. 6). It has been compared with an antler bow saw from a late ninth- to early tenth-century context at Coppergate in York, with which it shares many similarities. In both cases a long, curved section of an antler tine (probably a brow tine in each case) forms the bow, with a sawn cleft at the narrow end to accommodate the iron saw blade. With the Dublin Castle saw a lateral perforation would originally have retained a peg intended to secure the blade in that position. There is no peg hole on the York saw and trials with a replica indicated that it was not entirely necessary (MacGregor *et al.* 1999, 1947). The Dublin Castle saw includes two rectangular slots, one close to the narrow end and the other towards the broad inner terminal. The latter retains a narrow rectangular antler plate, which has fractured across a perforation at its lower end. A similar plate may originally have been fitted to the narrow end, providing additional support to the blade (Fig. 4.6). A rectangular antler plate from the Powder Tower

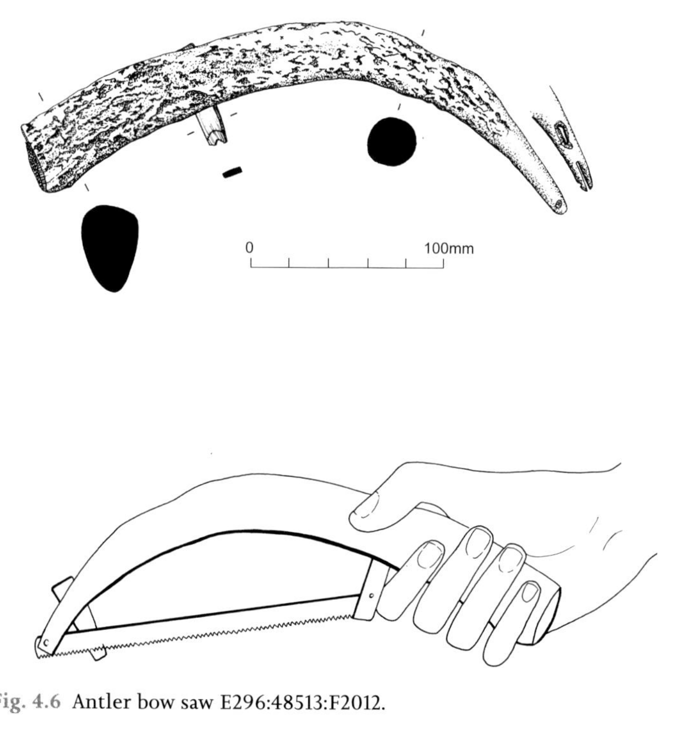

Fig. 4.6 Antler bow saw E296:48513:F2012.

(E324:13391:F530; Fig. 4.5:4) is similar in shape and size to an unfinished tooth segment from a composite comb but it includes two perforations, set in a line towards the centre, and these suggest that it is a segment from a second bow saw. In contrast to the Dublin Castle saw, the York saw has only one slot for a segment, which was secured with the aid of a wedge (MacGregor *et al.* 1999, fig. 906). Whilst the York saw has been smoothed and decorated, the Dublin Castle saw retains much of the outer surface of the antler and has only been lightly trimmed and smoothed.

Both saws can be regarded as possessions of an antler or bone worker, rather than a carpenter. Their shape and size suggest that they were used for the initial dismemberment of the raw material in an early stage of the working process, but what were these saw blades like? Some indication of their widths can be obtained from measurements of saw traces found embedded in antler waste. Six width bands were established for the antler waste of early medieval date from Castlefarm 1, Co. Meath and these have been compared with saw traces from Clonmacnoise New Graveyard and Dublin High Street (Riddler and Nartowski 2014, 44–5). In general, a movement towards the use of finer saw blades over time can be established, with the waste of late twelfth-century date from Dublin High Street sawn with blades using only the three finest width bands of the six established for Castlefarm 1 (*ibid*., fig. 5). Two centuries earlier in Dublin, however, it is likely that the saw blades had widths equating with those from Clonmacnoise New Graveyard. The majority of saw traces lie within the band of 0.8–1.6mm in width, with occasional use of saws with thicker blades. It is likely, therefore, that the saw blade attached to the Dublin Castle saw had a width between 0.8mm and 1.6mm, and this is confirmed by measurement of the slot at its front end, which is 1.7mm in width.

Iron saw blades are also comparatively rare finds and there are not yet enough from Ireland to test the theory of six width bands established for Castlefarm 1. Those from Dublin have been described as 'a series of small blades in which the teeth were arranged in straight lines' (Wallace 2016, 314). It is noticeable that a saw blade from Fishamble Street includes curved, vertical terminals, extending upwards from the flat, horizontal blade (Wallace 2016, fig. 9.3). It could well have been secured to a curved antler tine in the manner of the Dublin Castle saw, although in this case the terminals would have passed through perforations in the antler, with no need for antler strengthening plates.

E296:48513:F2021 (Fig. 4.6). CT2: House 3 deposit; Phase 6. Incomplete antler bow saw, formed from the curved end of a brow or bez tine, which has been lightly smoothed but retains much of the outer surface. Sawn laterally in two directions at the broad end to remove it from the beam. Narrow slot cut through the tine end, with a lateral perforation. Rectangular perforation set into the tine towards the opposite end retains a narrow strip of antler, fractured across a perforation at one end. Second perforation of similar shape and dimensions lies just behind the slot at the tine end. L. 287mm, W. 40mm, Th. 28mm.

E324:13391:F530 (Fig. 4.5:4). PT1: BW1 deposit; Phase 1b. Rectangular strip of antler, tapering towards one end and pierced by two drilled perforations, one along the centre line, the other set to one side. L. 39mm, W. 13mm, Th. 3mm.

ANTLER WEDGES AND NOTCHED WEDGES (FIG. 4.5)

Five antler wedges were retrieved from separate contexts at the Powder Tower. They consist of red deer antler tine ends that have been modified to form blade-like terminals at one end. The opposite end has usually been sawn laterally and the surface tissue of the antler is generally retained and has not been trimmed away. Three of the wedges have thumb grips cut into the antler on one side, just behind the tapered area, and they can be defined as notched wedges. The presence of these notches suggests that these implements (and at least some of the wedges without notched inserts) were not hammered at the broad end, and there are no percussion marks on any of these implements. Rather, they appear to have been held in the hand and either pushed forward or dragged backwards across surfaces. In one case (E324:8792:F283; Fig. 4.5:6), the blade-like point has been slightly damaged from use. The wedges range in length from 74mm to 96mm and the shape of their tapered ends varies from broad, rounded points to sharpened terminals.

Antler wedges are common implements across early medieval northern Europe as a whole. They occur in several different forms and these may reflect different, if related, functions. Within Ireland, five different forms of antler wedge can be identified, on the basis of their tapered ends, and they can be briefly summarised for their main characteristics:

- 1a Straight tine end, cleanly sawn laterally, tapered by knife along part of its length to a sharp or fairly sharp point. Tapered on two faces, sawn laterally or obliquely at the broad end;
- 1b As Type 1a but with a curved tine end rather than a straight one;
- 2 Pared on two faces throughout its entire length, tapering in section to a broad point with the butt end unmodified, aside from paring. Straight or curved in profile;
- 3 Pared on three faces rather than two, over part of its length;
- 4 Straight tine end, sliced and trimmed on four faces, tapering to a rounded point;
- 5 A rare type, sliced only on one side.

The Dublin Castle wedges include two examples of Type 1a, two of Type 1b and one of Type 4. The majority of the 75 antler wedges recorded by the authors from Dublin excavations came from the two High Street sites, with 51 from the larger site (E71), five from the smaller site (E43), four from Winetavern Street (E81) and eleven from Wood Quay (E132). They have not been noted from the Fishamble Street sites, but this may in part be a reflection of the fact that they are often located within antler waste assemblages and they may not have been separately registered. Antler waste assemblages from Fishamble Street remain to be recorded and studied.

Notched wedges are a variant upon the conventional wedge form. In the same way, small numbers of perforated wedges have been noted at Clonmacnoise Steeple Garden and Inis Cealtra, forming another variant on the main type (Riddler and Trzaska-Nartowski forthcoming b). Notched tine implements, another variant that is not seen at Dublin Castle, have been found elsewhere in Dublin in considerable numbers, particularly in the High Street excavations. They utilise the basic, tapering wedge form but include both the notched surface and additional lateral perforations that pass through one surface alone.

The three principal types of wedge implement (wedges, notched tine implements and notched wedges) have rarely been found on rural sites in Ireland. Notched tine implements and notched wedges are known from Clonmacnoise New Graveyard and notched wedges have come from Castlefarm 1, Co. Meath (Riddler and Trzaska-Nartowski 2014, illus. 11). A notched tine implement came from Kilboglashy, Co. Sligo, and two others are known from Drumclay Crannog, Co. Fermanagh (Lucas 1973, 204 and fig. 23; Wood-Martin 1886, 80 and figs 48–52). Outside of Ireland, both ordinary wedges and notched wedges can be seen amidst the antler objects from Hedeby (Ulbricht 1978, taf 45).

CATALOGUE

WEDGES: TYPE 1A

E324:1025:F285 (Fig. 4.5:5). PT2 – Area A: Phase 2. Complete antler wedge, sawn cleanly from several directions with a remnant stub at one end and tapered on two faces to a rounded terminal. Otherwise unmodified. Slightly sinuous in profile. L. 96mm, W. 21.5mm, Th. 20mm.

E324:8792:F283 (Fig. 4.5:6). PT2 – Area B: Phase 2. Complete notched wedge, cut from a red deer antler tine end, separated by sawing laterally from the remainder of the tine. Smoothed and tapered on two faces, with the blade-like point slightly damaged. Notched around the centre on one side, a slight indentation with numerous lateral lines present. Surface tissue largely retained. L. 68mm, W. 20mm, Th. 19mm.

TYPE 1B

E324:8809:F335 (Fig. 4.5:7). PT2 – Area C: Phase 1. Complete antler wedge, sawn cleanly in a single direction with a remnant stub at one end, curved in profile and tapered on two faces close to the terminal to provide a rounded, blade-like point. Otherwise unmodified. L. 113.5mm, W. 24.5mm, Th. 23mm.

E324:8810:F304 (Fig. 4.5:8). PT2 – Area C: Phase 3. Complete notched wedge, sawn laterally from several directions to remove it from the remainder of the red deer antler tine. Tapered on two sides to a blade-like, rounded point. Lightly curved in profile, slightly notched behind the tapered area with numerous closely spaced lateral incised lines. L. 89.5mm, W. 20.5mm, Th. 20mm.

TYPE 4

E324:1023:F228 (Fig. 4.5:9). PT2 – Area B: Phase 2. Complete antler notched wedge, sawn cleanly in a single direction with a remnant stub at one end, tapered on two broad faces and also, closer to the end, on two narrow faces, to provide a sharp point. Notched on one of the curved sides at the junction with the tapered area. Polished throughout. L. 74mm, W. 18.5mm, Th. 16.5mm.

SPACER OR FERRULE (FIG. 4.5:10)

A complete antler implement from the Cross Block (E748:45) has been hollowed from a section of an antler tine and shaped to an octagonal section. It has been hollowed throughout, with almost all of the cortile tissue removed. Its original function is unclear. It may have been intended to fit over a wooden core and to act as a bolster for the front part of an implement handle, but equally it may have been used as an antler spacer. Ulbricht has suggested that these objects could have been suspended from a belt (Ulbricht 1978, 81–2). It falls into a general group of hollowed antler tine segments that are often highly decorated but also include undecorated examples, which are known from a variety of sites of tenth- to twelfth-century date, including Berlin-Spandau, Ely, Hedeby and Mikulčice (Becker 1989, 126–7; Riddler 2009; Ulbricht 1978, 81 and taf 43; Kavánová 1995, 205–9).

E748:45 (Fig. 4.5:10). CB: Hearth 3 (House III) level at west end of cutting; Phase D. Complete antler spacer or ferrule, carefully produced to an octagonal section at one end, tapering slightly to a rounded section at the opposite end. Some polish throughout on the exterior, but not the interior. L. 36mm, W. 22.5mm, Th. 22.5mm.

TEXTILE MANUFACTURE

SPINDLE WHORLS (FIG. 4.5:11)

Nine objects of three bone types can be placed in this object category, no fewer than seven of them coming from the Cross Block. They include spindle whorls cut from the bones of cattle, horse and pig. Six spindle whorls have been cut from the proximal articulation or *caput* of the cattle femur. In most cases they have been sawn from the remainder of the bone, sometimes in several directions, although some of them have been cut away by knife. The upper surface of the whorl is flat, and in two cases (E748:35 and E296:36068:F1045) the edge has been trimmed and bevelled. With one of the whorls (E324:13393:F530) the lower part has been truncated, with the apex of the bone removed. This may have been undertaken in order to reduce the weight of the whorl (an important characteristic, as noted below) or to decrease its size relative to the spindle. The remaining three spindle whorls (E748:10, E748:26 and E748:63) have merely been sawn laterally from the bone and perforated axially. All of the cattle femur *caput* spindle whorls are undecorated and they could have been produced quite quickly and easily from the raw material. The use of a saw does suggest, however, that they were manufactured by antler and bone workers, rather than by the spinners themselves. Subsequent modifications to the whorls, by truncating them or bevelling the upper edge, may have been undertaken by their owners.

Two of the spindle whorls have been produced from smaller proximal articulations of the femur of pigs (E748:94 and E748:95), and one has been manufactured from the corresponding bone of a horse (E748:12). The proximal articulation of the horse is oval in shape, rather than circular, and it would undoubtedly have been much less useful in the spinning process. As a result, it was rarely used for this purpose. A small spindle whorl cut from a pig femur (E748:94) represents another unusual choice of bone for this purpose, given its small size. It is accompanied by a second pig femur *caput* (E748:95), for which part of the outer surface has been modified, but the bone has not been perforated. This may be an unfinished spindle whorl, although it could equally well be a piece of unworked, butchered bone. Small quantities of pig femur *caput* spindle whorls can be seen elsewhere in contemporary deposits, notably at Winchester and York (Woodland 1990, 216; MacGregor *et al.* 1999, 1964).

Given the different materials used there is some variation in the sizes and, correspondingly, in the weights of these spindle whorls. Most of them are complete, the exception lying with a fragmentary whorl (E324:13393:F530) from the Powder Tower. The weights of the cattle and horse spindle whorls vary from 4.9g to 19.1g and in general it can be suggested that they are relatively lightweight. The range of weights can be compared, for example, with 8g to 32g across 85 cattle femur spindle whorls from Ipswich (Riddler *et al.* forthcoming). Two of the Dublin Castle cattle femur spindle whorls weigh less than 10g and one weighs just 10g. All three can be assigned to Henry's lightweight group of spindle whorls (Henry 1999, 72). Three further spindle whorls, two of cattle and one of horse, fall into her median group, of 11g to 29g in weight. The small spindle whorl made from a pig femur (E748:94) weighs just 2.5g. It is possible that the presence of lightweight spindle whorls reflects the spinning of flax, rather than wool and the manufacture of fine fabrics, although the correlation of spindle whorl weight and fabric is not entirely simple and straightforward (Walton Rogers 2007, 106).

Within Fitzgerald's study of spindle whorls from Fishamble Street in Dublin, 86 out of the 102 whorls that she recorded were made of antler or bone, and virtually all of the sample of 86 were cattle femur *caput* whorls (Fitzgerald 2000, 205). There are well over 300 femur *caput* spindle whorls from the NMI excavations in Dublin, almost half of which came from Fishamble Street (a larger figure than the sample recorded by Fitzgerald), and they are well represented at the two High Street sites, with 65 examples, and at Christchurch Place, where 76 whorls of this type and material have been noted. Almost all of those from the High Street sites are femur *caput* whorls, but there are several examples of antler whorls as well. Seven of the nine spindle whorls from Dublin Castle came from the Cross Block, with single whorls from the Cork Tower and the Powder Tower. This suggests that the spinning of flax and wool was largely undertaken in one area of this part of Dublin.

At Waterford all of the spindle whorls of skeletal materials were femur *caput* whorls (Hurley 1997b, 674–5). This is a little surprising, although cattle femur *caput* spindle whorls are well represented in contemporary assemblages in England as well, notably at Thetford, Winchester and York (Riddler 2005, 60; Woodland 1990; Walton Rogers 1997, 1741–3; MacGregor *et al.* 1999, 1964–6). They appear to have been used to a greater extent in Ireland than in Anglo-Saxon England. The development of the femur *caput* whorl in England can be traced from their first occurrence in seventh-century contexts through to their domination of late Saxon urban assemblages (Riddler and Trzaska-Nartowski 2012, 90–1). In Scandinavia, however, the situation is a little different. Antler and bone spindle whorls form a minority of those from Birka, where stone and ceramic whorls are more common, and by no means all of the whorls made of skeletal materials are femur *caput* whorls (Andersson 2003, 74–5). The same situation prevails also at Hedeby, where femur *caput* whorls are less common than discoidal whorls made of antler or bone (Ulbricht 1978, taf 38; Andersson 2003, 118).

CATALOGUE

SPINDLE WHORLS: CATTLE FEMUR CAPUT

E748:35. CB: occupation debris under floor west of Hearth 3 (House III); Phase D. Complete bone spindle whorl, the upper surface sawn from the bone and lightly trimmed around the edges with some light filing marks still visible. Undecorated, with a lightly conical axial perforation. L. 19mm, Diam. 36 x 37mm, Wgt. 10.0g.

E296:36068:F1045 (Fig. 4.5:11). CT2: fill deposit of Pit 6; Phase 4c. Complete bone spindle whorl, produced from the proximal articulation of a cattle femur, cut by knife from the remainder of the bone with a flat, truncated base lipped up in part to the outer surface, and a knife-cut axial perforation. Undecorated and not polished. L. 15mm, Diam. 33 x 33mm, Wgt. 8.5g.

E324:13393:F530. PT1: BW1 deposit; Phase 1a. Fragmentary bone spindle whorl, produced from the proximal articulation of a cattle femur, the flat upper surface seemingly sawn from the bone. Lightly truncated apex, cylindrical axial perforation now visible in section. Burnt to a black colour. Some polish. L. 19.5mm, Diam. 26.5mm, Wgt. 4.7g.

E748:10. CB: occupation debris of Hearth 5 (House V); Phase F. Complete bone spindle whorl, produced from the proximal articulation of a cattle femur, the upper surface sawn from several directions to separate it from the bone. Conical axial perforation, set slightly off-centre, particularly on the upper surface. Undecorated, with slight polish. L. 22mm, Diam. 40.5 x 37.5mm, Wgt. 19.1g.

E748:26. CB: *c.* 0.91m below formation level, near west end of trench, under grey layer on thin dark line; Phase E. Complete bone spindle whorl, cut from the proximal articulation of a cattle femur, with the aid of a knife. Undecorated with an unusual double perforation, possibly intended to enlarge the original hole, the two perforations merged into one oval aperture. L. 20mm, Diam. 42 x 36.5mm, Wgt. 12.2g.

E748:63. CB: near west end of trench at Hearth 3 (House III) level; Phase D. Complete bone spindle whorl, cut from the proximal articulation of an unfused cattle femur, with an uneven upper surface and partially trimmed edges. Conical axial perforation, wider at the base than the upper surface. L. 15mm, Diam. 31 x 30.5mm, Wgt. 4.9g.

PIG FEMUR CAPUT

E748:94. CB: ironworking (smithing) layer; Phase C. Complete bone spindle whorl, cut from the proximal articulation of a pig femur, the epiphyses only partially fused. Upper surface cut by knife and half of it is the natural unfused surface. Undecorated, pierced by a conical central perforation with slight modern damage. L. 12mm, Diam. 23.5 x 23mm, Wgt. 2.5g.

E748:95. CB: ironworking (smithing) layer; Phase C. Small proximal articulation of a femur, probably from a pig, unfused and unmodified but for a small slice cut from the circumference in one area. Not certainly an object. L. 15mm, Diam. 25 x 25mm, Wgt. 3.2g.

HORSE FEMUR CAPUT

E748:12. CB: occupation debris of Hearth 5 (House V); Phase F. Complete bone spindle whorl, cut from the proximal articulation of a horse femur. Plano-convex in section, undecorated, with cortile tissue exposed around circumference in two areas. Upper surface sawn from at least two directions. Central knife-cut axial perforation of conical form. Slight polish around circumference. L. 30mm, Diam. 45.5 x 39mm, Wgt. 18g.

PIN-BEATERS (FIG. 4.7:1–3; PL. 4.5:1 AND 2)

All five of the pin-beaters have all been cut from cattle-sized long bones, identifiable in one case (E324:919:F279; Fig. 4.7:3; Pl. 4.5:2) as the lateral or medial side of a cattle metatarsus. They include three examples from the Cork Tower (E296:48551:F2060, E296:48562:F2069 and E296:49074:F2096), one example from the Powder Tower (E324:919:F279; Fig. 4.7:3; Pl. 4.5:2) and one from the Cross Block (E748:15). One of the pin-beaters (E296:49074:F2096) is fragmentary, whilst the others are complete, although one of these (E296:48551:F2060; Fig. 4.7:1) is an unfinished pin-beater, which shows how they were sliced from the bone after the proximal or distal articulation had been removed, and were then faceted to shape by knife. The complete examples range from 123mm to 149mm in length, which places them around the middle part of the size range, in comparison with the lengths of other examples from early medieval Ireland. They can all be described as single pointed pin-beaters, on the basis that they have one pointed terminal and one blunt end. The pin-beater usually tapers evenly from one end to the other, with cortile tissue often present on one side at the blunt end, indicating that the object had been cut from close to an articulation, usually the proximal end of the bone. It appears that in order to obtain pin-beaters of the requisite length, made of bone, it was acceptable to include some cortile tissue on them.

Two types of single pointed pin-beater can be identified. Just one example (E748:15; Pl. 4.5:1) belongs to Type A, which is distinguished by retaining the same rectangular section from one end of the object to the other (Riddler *et al.* forthcoming). The other complete pin-beaters all belong to Type B, for which the blunt end of the implement is rectangular in section, but the pointed end is circular in section. This type is usually longer than Type A and bears a resemblance to large bone needles. The sense that objects of different functions could closely resemble each other is particularly pertinent within this assemblage, because the single example of a Type A pin-beater looks very much like a Type 4 bone pin. It is undecorated and has a spatulate head with a knife-cut perforation. Unlike pins, however, it has a shaft of rectangular section leading to a blunt, rounded point, and it includes a thumb groove beyond the perforation on one side of the head. Thumb grooves are not a feature of antler or bone pins. Equally, perforations are not normally a feature of pin-beaters, but there are a few comparable examples from contemporary sites in England, including Ipswich, Thetford and York (Riddler *et al.* forthcoming).

Objects of this form have generally been regarded as pin-beaters associated with the vertical two-beam loom, although this interpretation has been questioned on the Continent (Becker 2001; Goret 2009). Brown suggested that the sharpened end of the pin-beater was used to gather groups of warp threads together, behind which weft threads could then be placed. When turned in the hand, the broad end could be used to beat down the weft threads (Brown 1990, 227). In using the warp-weighted loom the textile was produced from the top downwards. With the vertical two-beam loom, in contrast, the textile grew upwards from the base (Brown 1990, 227 and fig. 42; Walton Rogers 1997, 1758–9). The assemblage from Dublin Castle tends to confirm the suggestions for their use put forward by David Brown. The four finished examples are all highly polished and this would have been an essential prerequisite, in order to prevent the implements from snagging on threads. The occurrence of cortile tissue at the blunt ends of all four complete pin-beaters suggests that the object was usually held in the hand with the blunt end in the palm and that most of the work on the loom was carried out with the pointed terminal. Equally, the presence of a thumb groove at the end of the Type A pin-beater indicates that it could be reversed in the hand, with the broad end forming the working surface and the thumb set close to that end.

Outside of Dublin, single pointed pin-beaters have been found at a number of sites, including Baronstown 1, Carraig Aille, Castlefarm 1, Cullahill, Cloghermore Cave, Garrynamona, Knowth, Lagore, Moyne Graveyard and Uisneach, as well as Lough Gur, where one example occurs amidst other items of tenth-century date (Connolly and Coyne 2005, 109 and fig. 31; Riddler and Trzaska-Nartowski 2009a and b; Rynne 1964, 261 and fig. 9.3; Manning 1987, 54 and fig. 10.47; Ó Ríordáin 1949, fig. 14.11; 1954, fig. 26.27, 33 and 40; Fitzgerald 2012, 558–9). The only rural site to have produced more than one example of a single pointed pin-beater, to date, is Drumclay Crannog, where four examples have been identified (Riddler and Trzaska-Nartowski forthcoming c). Unsurprisingly perhaps, the largest quantity of single pointed pin-beaters has come from the NMI excavations in Dublin, where over 70 examples have been recorded, a much larger total than that suggested by Wallace (2016, 268). Even so, this is not a massive total for an urban site of this date, and it compares well with the 80 single pointed pin-beaters recovered from Ipswich (Riddler *et al.* forthcoming). They are not evenly spread across the NMI excavations and they occur only in small quantities at High Street and Winetavern Street, with over half of the sample emanating from Fishamble Street, and particularly from the E172 site (Fishamble Street II, 1978–80). Wallace lists nine examples from Fishamble Street as a whole, but there are at least 40 pin-beaters from the three sites, with 23 of those coming from the E172 excavation. The bias towards Fishamble Street may simply reflect the quantity of objects of all types and materials found in those excavations, but it is also possible that this low-lying and inherently damp area of Dublin was a centre for weaving in the early medieval period. A few of these Dublin pin-beaters are made of antler but the majority are bone, and they are spread across contexts of the tenth to the twelfth century. Several were recovered from contexts of late twelfth-century date at the High Street, while those from Cork and Waterford came from thirteenth-century contexts and are amongst the latest examples to have been discovered in Ireland (Hurley 1997b, 671 and fig. 17.5.8; 2003, 331 and fig. 8.1.5).

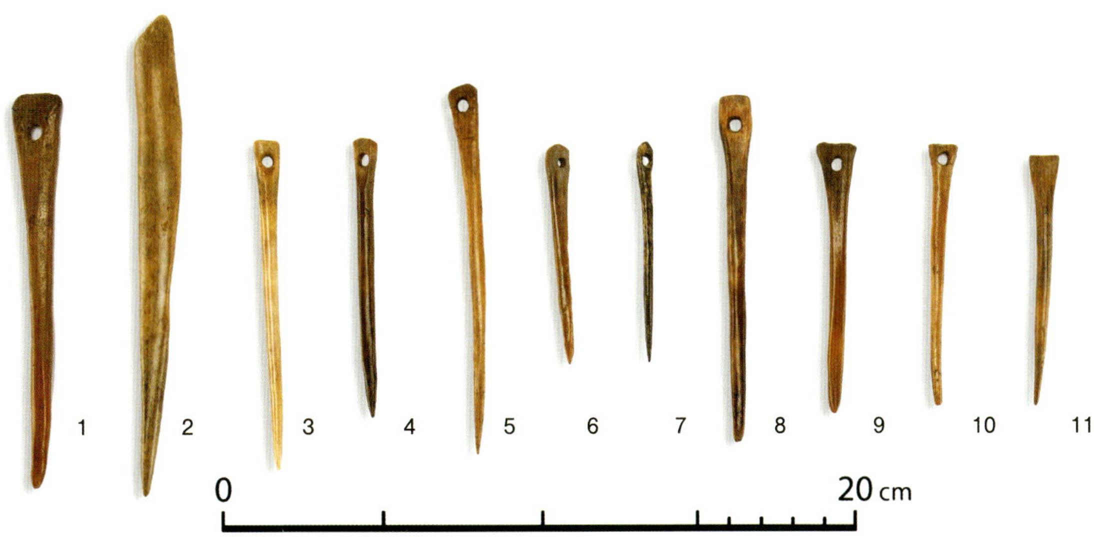

Pl. 4.5 Bone artefacts: Type A pin-beater (1); Type B pin-beater (2); Dublin Type 1 needle (3,4); Dublin Type 2 needle (5); Dublin Type 4 needle (6,7); Dublin Type 5 needle (8); Dublin Type 7 needle (9); Dublin Type 8 needle (10); awl (11).

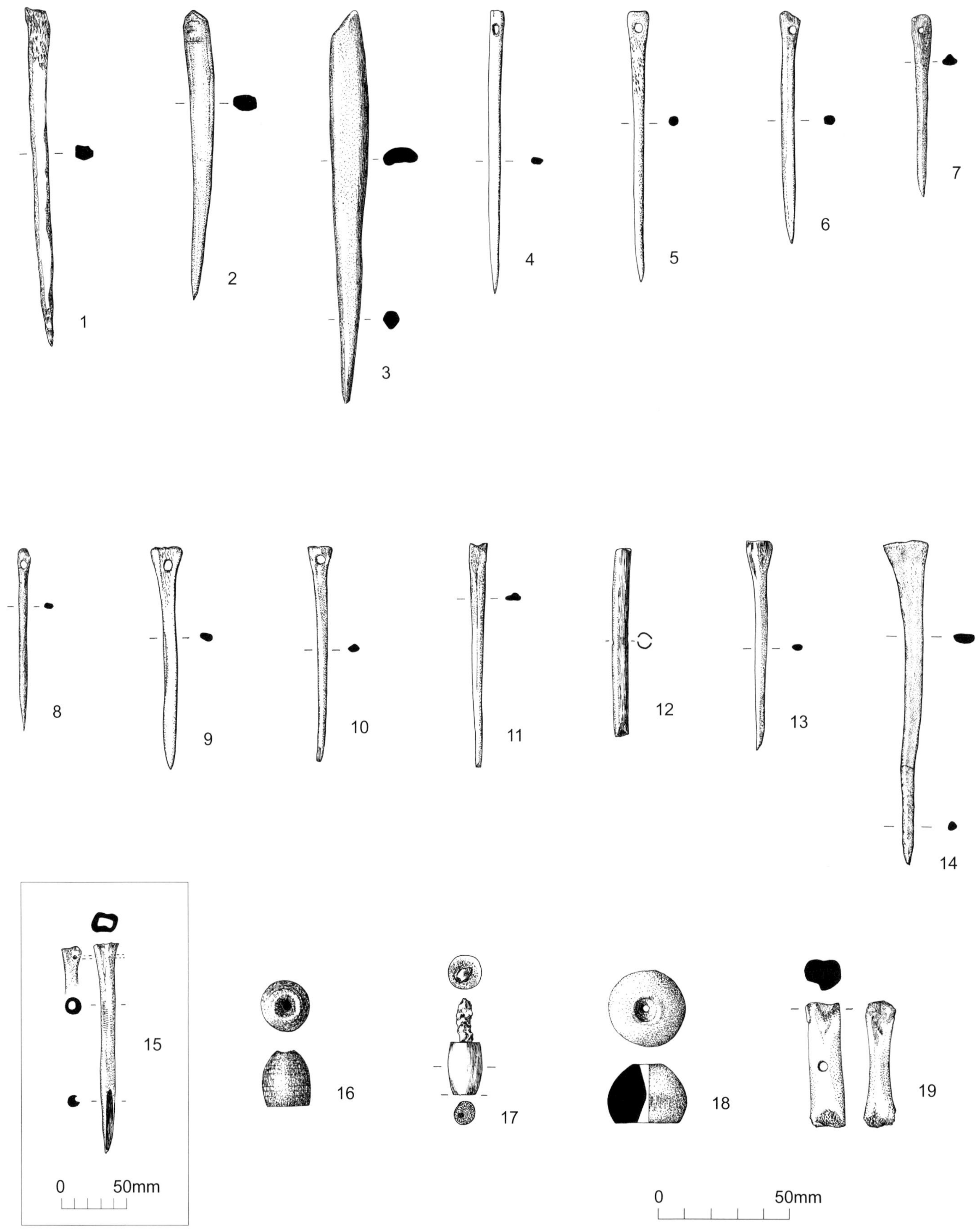

Fig. 4.7 Bone and antler artefacts: Type B pin beaters (1-3), Dublin Type 1 needles (4-6), Dublin Type 4 needles (7,8), Dublin Type 7 needle (9), Dublin Type 8 needle (10), indeterminate type (11), needle case (12), bone awls (13, 14), pointed blade (15), gaming pieces (16-18), perforated pig metapodia (19).

CATALOGUE

PIN-BEATERS: TYPE A

E748:15 (Pl. 4.5:1). CB: occupation debris of Hearth 5 (House V); Phase F. Complete bone pin-beater, cut from a cattle-sized long bone with cortile tissue visible across the head on one side. Lightly curved shaft of rectangular section tapering to a broad, rounded point. Shaft widens evenly and imperceptibly to the head, which has a flat apex with rounded corners and a thumb groove on one side above the knife-cut oval perforation. Highly polished throughout. L. 123.5mm, W. 16mm, Th. 7.5mm.

TYPE B

E296:48551:F2060 (Fig. 4.7:1). CT2: House 1 deposit; Phase 3. Complete segment of cattle-sized long bone, probably from a metapodial, with cortile tissue and part of the inner bone channel visible at one end. Straight, faceted shaft of rectangular section tapering to a sharp point. Natural outer bone surface on one side. Roughly cut diagonal terminal at opposite end. Slightly polished throughout. L. 127.5mm, W. 9.5mm, Th. 8mm.

E296:48562:F2069 (Fig. 4.7:2). CT2: House 1 deposit; Phase 3. Complete single pointed bone pin-beater, cut from a cattle-sized long bone with cortile tissue visible on the reverse at the blunt end. Lightly curved shaft of rectangular section tapers to a sharp point at one end. Opposite end has been cut to a broad triangular point. Undecorated and highly polished throughout. L. 110mm, W. 11mm, Th. 7mm.

E296:49074:F2096. CT2: cut of Pit 4a; Phase 4a. Fragment of one side of a bone pin-beater, cut from the midshaft of a cattle-sized long bone, and including part of the blunt terminal of the object. Segment tapers evenly to a broad terminal, which is curved and has been burnt to a black colour. Corrugated ridging along surface in two areas. Originally rectangular in section and highly polished throughout. L. 54mm, W. 6.5mm, Th. 5.5mm.

E324:919:F279 (Fig. 4.7:3; Pl. 4.5:2). PT2–Area A: deposit; Phase 2. Complete bone pin-beater, cut from a cattle metatarsus on the medial or lateral face, with cortile tissue visible at the broad end on one side. Broad end is rectangular in section with the terminal cut diagonally, and tapers to a point of circular section with a thumb groove at the junction of the two sections. Undecorated and highly polished throughout. L. 149mm, W. 14.5mm, Th. 10.5mm.

NEEDLES (FIG. 4.7:4–11; PL. 4.5:3–10)

Thirteen bone needles were distributed across two of the three sites, with eight examples coming from the Cork Tower and five from the Cross Block. Most of them have been made from pig fibulae (eleven of thirteen examples). This contrasts with the pins, most of which have been made from cattle-sized long bones, probably metapodia, with one example of antler and only three of the twenty-two examples made from pig fibula. Just one of the bone needles is fragmentary and the remainder are complete or near complete and survive in good condition. They all include single perforations, cut with the aid of a blade point, with one exception (E748:110), which has been drilled. They can be separated into five types, based on their head forms. The head is missing from one of the needles (E296:48532:F2045; Fig. 4.7:11), which has fractured across its perforation, and it cannot be assigned to a type. Four of the remaining needles (E296:48501:F2001, E296:48502:F2001, E296:48500:F2001 and E748:110) have narrow heads with parallel sides and flat apices (Type 1) which, in one case, is angled rather than horizontal. Four further needles (E296:48182:F820, E296:48550:F2058, E748:31 and E748:112) are similar in form but have lightly curved apices (Type 4), while one needle (E748:100; Pl. 4.5:5) has a more rounded head (Type 2). With another bone needle (E748:109; Pl. 4.5:8) the head widens around the perforation below the flat apex (Type 5) and one needle (E296:48529:F2045; Fig. 4.7:9; Pl. 4.5:9) retains the unmodified bone of the distal end of the pig fibula as its head (Type 7). The final needle (E296:48523:F2029; Fig. 4.7:10; Pl. 4.5:10) has a spatulate head with a flat apex (Type 8). Altogether, six of the ten types of antler and bone needle seen elsewhere in Dublin are represented in this small sample.

In general terms, although there are copious quantities of needles from Dublin, they fall into a relatively small number of types. Ten principal types can be identified, with three of them represented by fifty or more needles. The same situation can be seen elsewhere within contemporary assemblages, with eight types identified for 342 needles from Ipswich, and just three basic types identified for Birka and Hedeby amidst assemblages of 414 and 302 needles respectively (Riddler *et al.* forthcoming; Andersson 2003, 83 and 127). Moreover, some of the types are closely related. In terms of the heads of the needles themselves, the majority have flat apices (seven of the nine needles) whilst two have rounded apices.

The widths of the heads of the needles vary from 5.6mm to 12.9m and from a simple visual inspection it can be seen that they vary from relatively narrow head forms (E296:48500:F2001; E296:48182:F820; E296:48501:F2001; E296:48502:F2001; E296:48550:F2058 and E748:110) to wider heads of around 10mm (E296:48523:F2029; E296:48532:F2045; E748:100 and E748:112), with three needles (E296:48529:F2045; E748:31 and E748:109) including heads of 11mm to 13mm in width.

It is easy to accept that the bone implements with narrow heads are needles. In contrast, the objects with broad heads of at least 10mm in width have often been described in the past as pins, an interpretation that goes back to the work of Hencken, who described practically all of the pig fibulae objects from Cahercommaun and Lagore as pins

(MacGregor *et al.* 1999, 1950–1; Boyle 2009, 28; FitzGerald 2012, 132; Hencken 1938, 38 and fig. 23; 1950, 194). Plotting the dimensions of the needles against the pins, there is clearly an overlap in terms of their lengths and their head widths, but perforated pins tend to be both larger and longer than bone needles. The subsequent development of functional interpretations of these objects has been outlined in detail elsewhere and the interpretation followed here is based primarily on Continental work, where bone needles and awls have been succinctly distinguished from pins (Westphalen 1999, 60–3; Andersson 2003, 83–7 and 127–30; Struckmeyer 2011, 61–2; Prummel *et al.* 2011, 76–7; Riddler and Trzaska-Nartowski 2011, 139; 2014, 50–1; Riddler *et al.* forthcoming).

These needles should not be regarded merely as sewing implements for the repair of textiles, but rather as objects used in the weaving process, as well as having other functions, as noted by Ulbricht (1984, 54). Penelope Walton Rogers has drawn attention to the fact that bone or antler needles were used with the warp-weighted loom for a variety of purposes within the weaving process itself. Long needles carried thick cords used to stitch the rod to which warp-band is attached on to the cloth-beam, and similar needles were placed into the selvedges and bound to the loom uprights in order to prevent the fabric from being drawn inwards (Walton Rogers 1997, 1757 and 1779). Needles could also be used in the manufacture and repair of nets and sailcloth, in basketry and in loose mesh knitting. It is more appropriate, therefore, to consider them as textile manufacturing implements, rather than simply as needles.

CATALOGUE

NEEDLES: DUBLIN TYPE 1

E296:48500:F2001 (Fig. 4.7:4). CT2: west end wall House 3; Phase 6. Complete bone needle, cut from a pig fibula with the head formed from the distal end of the bone. Long straight shaft of rounded rectangular section tapering to a sharp point. Widest along the shaft, tapering slightly to the head with a prominent oval knife-cut perforation and lightly curved apex. Aperture of perforation slightly splayed on both sides, no wear visible. Some polish throughout, some manufacturing marks visible. L. 108mm, W. 5.5mm, Th. 5.5mm.

E748:110. CB: unknown context. Incomplete bone needle, almost certainly cut from a pig fibula, with a straight shaft of circular section tapering lightly over the lower part towards a point, the terminal now missing. Shaft widens lightly and towards head, which is thin and rectangular in section, with a prominent drilled circular perforation. Flat apex with rounded corners. Slight polish, slight surface degradation. L. 77mm, W. 6mm, Th. 4mm.

E296:48501:F2001 (Fig 4.7:5; Pl. 4.5:3). CT2: west end wall House 3; Phase 6. Complete bone needle, probably cut from a pig fibula, with a straight circular shaft tapering to a sharp point at one end. Head widens slightly from shaft, with a single knife-cut perforation. Near-flat apex with rounded corners. L. 100mm, W. 9mm, Th. 4mm.

E296:48502:F2001 (Fig 4.7:6; Pl. 4.5:4). CT2: west end wall House 3; Phase 6. Complete bone needle, cut from a pig fibula with a short shaft of oval section tapering to a sharp point. Head widens slightly from shaft with an offset circular perforation close to one end and a flat apex cut diagonally. L. 86mm, W. 8mm, Th. 3mm.

DUBLIN TYPE 2

E748:100 (Pl. 4.5:5). CB: *c.* 25mm under burnt thatch layer; Phase C. Complete bone needle, cut from a pig fibula with the head formed from the distal end of the bone. Lightly curved shaft of oval section, faceted throughout, tapering to a sharp hollow point. Upper part rectangular in section, head widening imperceptibly from shaft to a lightly curved apex with rounded corners. Prominent oval knife-cut perforation. Slight polish throughout. L. 115.5mm, W. 10mm, Th. 4mm.

DUBLIN TYPE 4

E748:31. CB: Hearth 3 (House III) level, inside east wall timber; Phase D. Complete bone needle, produced from the midshaft of a cattle-sized long bone, with a lightly curved shaft of rectangular section tapering evenly throughout to a rounded point. Head is not distinguished from the shaft but includes a small part of the inner bone channel, close to the apex, with cortile tissue on one side. Lightly curved apex, cut by knife. Head pierced by a knife-cut circular perforation with traces of wear on one side. Highly polished throughout. L. 101mm, W. 11.5mm, Th. 9mm.

E748:112. CB: labelled 'on wicker rods'; possibly Phase B. Complete bone needle, now in two pieces, produced from a pig fibula with the head cut from the distal end of the bone. Curved shaft of oval section tapering to sharp point. Spatulate head widens lightly from shaft with a crude, lightly curved apex. Knife-cut small circular perforation. Slight polish throughout. L. 104.5mm, W. 9.5mm, Th. 5mm.

E296:48182:F820 (Fig 4.7:7; Pl. 4.5:6). CT2: deposit; Phase 6. Complete bone needle, cut from a pig fibula with a short shaft of triangular to circular section tapering to a sharp point. Head widens slightly from shaft with a rounded apex and a small circular perforation. L. 67mm, W. 8mm, Th. 4mm.

E296:48550:F2058 (Fig 4.7:8; Pl. 4.5:7). CT2: fill deposit of Pit 4a; Phase 4a. Complete bone needle, cut from a pig fibula with a straight shaft of circular section tapering to a sharp point. Head widens slightly from shaft with a rounded apex and prominent circular perforation. L. 68mm, W. 8mm, Th. 2mm.

DUBLIN TYPE 5

E748:109 (Pl. 4.5:8). CB: labelled 'Bone pin 6″ [0.15m] under hearth III [Hearth 3] level (centre)'; Phase C. Near-complete bone needle, produced from a cattle-sized long bone, with a straight shaft of circular section tapering to a broad, spatulate point, with the tip missing. Upper part of shaft is rectangular in section and widens to a head lightly expanded around the circular, knife-cut perforation. Lightly curved apex, highly polished throughout. L. 108mm, W. 11mm, Th. 4.5mm.

DUBLIN TYPE 7

E296:48529:F2045 (Fig. 4.7:9; Pl. 4.5:9). CT2: Phase 4a deposit. Complete bone needle, cut from a pig fibula with the head formed from the distal end of the bone. Straight shaft of rectangular section tapers to a broad, rounded, spatulate point. Head unmodified but for a knife-cut oval perforation. No wear visible. Highly polished throughout. L. 84mm, W. 13mm, Th. 4.5mm.

DUBLIN TYPE 8

E296:48523:F2029 (Fig. 4.7:10; Pl. 4.5:10). CT2: floor deposit, House 2; Phase 5. Incomplete bone needle, cut from a pig fibula with the head formed from the distal end of the bone. Lightly curved shaft of oval section tapering towards a point with the tip missing. Spatulate head of rectangular section widening lightly from the shaft, slightly notched on both sides of the prominent, oval knife-cut perforation. Flat apex cut by knife. Highly polished throughout. L. 81mm, W. 9.5mm, Th. 4.5mm.

INDETERMINATE TYPE

E296:48532:F2045 (Fig. 4.7:11). CT2: Phase 4a deposit. Fragment of a bone needle, cut from a pig fibula with the head formed from the distal end of the bone, with a straight shaft of oval section tapering to a point, the tip now missing. Fractured across a perforation at the opposite end. Faceted by knife in that area, with some polish on the shaft, less around the head area. L. 84.5mm, W. 8mm, Th. 5mm.

NEEDLES OR PINS

Six fragmentary bone objects consist of the lower parts of the shafts of needles or pins. Three of them (E748:111, E296:48462:F1216 and E324:12984:F401) are made from pig fibulae and, on that basis alone, are more likely to stem from needles than pins. Conversely, the other three fragments (E748:105, E296:49423:F1216 and E324:13394:F537) are straight shafts of circular section tapering lightly to sharp points (one of which has fractured away) made from bone, and these may well derive from pins.

NEEDLES OR PINS: PIG FIBULAE

E748:111. CB: labelled 'n[ea]r curtain wall'; context unknown. Fragment of a shaft, probably from a needle, cut from a pig fibula, lightly curved, oval in section, tapering to a rounded point. Some polish throughout with manufacturing marks visible. L. 81.5mm, W. 5mm, Th. 5mm.

E296:48462:F1216. CT2: deposit; Phase 2. Fragment of the lower part of the shaft of a bone pin or needle, probably a needle, cut from a pig fibula, oval in section and straight, tapering to a sharp point. Highly polished throughout. L. 55mm, W. 5mm, Th. 3.5mm.

E324:12984:F401. PT1: FW2 earth and timber bank; Phase 2. Fragment of a shaft, probably a needle, cut from a pig fibula, lightly curved, oval section tapering to a sharp point. Highly polished throughout. L. 55mm, W. 4mm, Th. 3mm.

BONE

E748:105. CB: ironworking (smithing) layer at southern side of trench; Phase C. Lower part of a bone shaft, probably from a pin, circular in section and straight, tapering to a rounded point. Highly polished with some faceting visible and finishing marks. L. 80mm, W. 5.5mm, Th. 6mm.

E296:49423:F1216. CT2: deposit; Phase 2. Fragment of a bone shaft, probably from a pin, circular in section, tapering lightly towards point, with lower part missing. Polished throughout. L. 71.5mm, W. 4.5mm, Th. 4mm.

E324:13394:F537. PT1: slot-trench through stone-faced bank; Phase 1a/b. Fragment of a bone shaft, probably from a pin, cut from a cattle-sized long bone, straight, circular section tapering to a sharp point. Highly polished. L. 47mm, W. 5mm, Th. 5.5mm.

NEEDLE CASE (FIG. 4.7:12)

A complete bone needle case (E324:6097:F279) has been cut from the midshaft of a bird bone, in this case a goose ulna, and it includes a lateral perforation at the centre. It forms one of twelve bone needle cases to have been identified from Dublin. Aside from this example, their distribution is entirely centred on High Street, with two examples coming from the smaller excavation (E43) and nine from the larger site (E71). Context details are unfortunately not available for two needle cases from High Street E71. All but one of the remaining seven needle cases came from high levels on Square 4, equating with deposition in the late twelfth century. The needle cases from the smaller High Street site, in contrast, appear to come from earlier levels, going back to the eleventh century, and possibly earlier. In addition, a copper alloy needle case from the smaller High Street site has been published previously (Curriculum Development Unit 1978, 48, 51 and pl. 6).

Half of the bone needle cases from Dublin have been made from bird bones and the remainder are fashioned from caprine metatarsals. The latter type of needle case can be seen also in contemporary deposits at Dover, and there is a possible example from York (Riddler and Walton Rogers 2006, 282—5; Waterman 1959, fig. 19.12). Needle cases made from bird bones are a common Viking period artefact, noted both from Birka and from various sites in Norway (MacGregor 1985, 193; Petersen 1951, 323 and 325; Mälarstedt 1984; Andersson 2003, 87–8). They have been found in Viking-age contexts in Scotland, notably at Birsay, Jarlshof, Pool, Sanday and Skaill, as well as in several burials (Curle 1982, 61; Hamilton 1956, 123, 146 and fig. 57.3 and 5; Smith 2007, 501–3; MacGregor 1985, 193; Batey 2019a, 254). Smith has noted that in Scotland they have been found predominantly in contexts of the ninth and tenth centuries (Smith 2007, 503), somewhat earlier than most of the examples known from Dublin.

E324:6097:F279 (Fig. 4.7:12). PT2 – Area A: deposit; Phase 2. Complete bone needle case, cut from the midshaft of a bird bone, trimmed at either end with small notches present, lateral oval knife-cut perforation passing through both surfaces at the centre. Polished throughout. L. 70.5mm, W. 6.5mm, Th. 6mm.

BONE AWLS (FIG. 4.7:13 AND 14; PL. 4.5:11)

Two bone awls came from the Cross Block and the Powder Tower (E748:87 and E296:48503:F2001). Both consist of pig fibulae with unmodified heads including the unfused articulation of the distal end, and lightly curved shafts of rectangular section tapering to crudely fashioned points. In essence, they look like bone needles that lack their perforations, but studies of sequences of these objects from elsewhere in Ireland indicate that pig fibula awls are generally longer than needles of the same bone type, and often have wider heads (Riddler and Trzaska-Nartowski forthcoming c). Boyle felt that these objects were unfinished pins but some of them have smoothed shafts polished from use, as well as fractured terminals, indicating that they had been utilised (Boyle 2009, 43). Hallén referred to them as points/pins, viewing them essentially as implements that have been well finished all over but lack the elaboration and decorative value of pins (Hallén 1994, 215). A detailed examination of wear traces on a series of these pig fibula implements from Feddersen Wierde suggested to Struckmeyer (2011, 61–2) that these objects were used with skins, leather or textile, and were probably weaving implements. One of these implements (E296:48503:F2001) was found in association with several bone needles.

They are common implements in early medieval Ireland, occurring in contexts from the sixth century through to the twelfth century, with the latest examples coming from both Waterford and Dublin (Hurley 1997b, fig. 17.5). Around a hundred examples are known from Dublin excavations, almost half of which were recovered from Fishamble Street.

E748:87 (Fig. 4.7:14). CB: *c.* 0.15m under Hearth 3 (House III); Phase D. Complete bone awl, cut from a pig fibula with the head formed from the distal end of the bone. Head has not been modified from natural bone form. Lightly curved shaft of rectangular section tapering to crude, knife-cut point. Shaft has some polish throughout with manufacturing marks but head is not polished. Now in two pieces. L. 123.5mm, W. 18mm, Th. 3.5mm.

E296:48503:F2001 (Fig. 4.7:13; Pl. 4.5:11). CT2: west end wall House 3; Phase 6. Complete bone awl, cut from a pig fibula, the head formed from the natural, unfused distal end of the bone. Straight shaft of rectangular section tapers to an oblique point.

HUNTING AND FISHING

SMALL POINTED BLADE (FIG. 4.7:15)

A single example of a small pointed blade (E296:48504:F2001) came from a context in the Cork Tower. It has been made from a caprine tibia, with the distal end retained although the articulation has been removed, and the midshaft sliced across the anterior face to provide a sharp point. It is highly polished throughout and manufacturing marks are visible along the shaft, mainly in the form of short, lateral 'chatter' marks. The tip is slightly damaged and it has split along the medial face, suggesting that it had been used before it was discarded.

Irish early medieval examples of this object type were expertly gathered together by Clare Mullins (2007), who referred to them as 'socketed longbone points'. However, we have followed northern European terminology in describing them instead as 'small, pointed blades' (as Britnell 2000, 183). The corpus of Irish examples extends from several retrieved from contexts of late prehistoric date to a large series from early medieval sites. It includes eight further examples recovered from NMI excavations, with two from the larger High Street site, one from Christchurch Place, one from Winetavern Street, one from Wood Quay and three from the Fishamble Street sites. All of them have been cut from caprine bones, but whilst the tibia was undoubtedly the preferred bone for the object type across Ireland as a whole and dominates most assemblages (Mullins 2007, 37), within the Dublin sample there are almost equal numbers of tibiae and metatarsals. All of them have hollowed basal terminals, but only some of them have lateral perforations at that end of the implement, as is the case here.

During a period of over a century of debate concerning the function of these implements, two main interpretations emerged. One views them as a form of pin-beater, used in weaving processes, based in part on observations made by O. G. S. Crawford and Elizabeth Crowfoot (Wheeler 1943, 304; Crowfoot 1945). This viewpoint has been developed for the Irish series (Hodkinson 1987). More recently, however, they have been regarded as bone spearheads, though used in hunting and fishing rather than in warfare (Westphalen 1999, 7–8; Olsen 2003, 108–9; Riddler 2007b, 315–6; Mullins 2007, 50–4). This accords well both with the fact that they are hafted implements, originally secured to a wooden shaft, and with experimental attempts at utilising bone implements as projectiles (Pétillon *et al.* 2016).

E296:48504:F2001 (Fig. 4.7:15). CT2: west end wall House 3; Phase 6. Complete bone small, pointed blade, produced from the distal end and midshaft of a caprine tibia, with the distal articulation removed and with a lateral perforation at the basal end, neatly drilled into both surfaces. Midshaft sliced across anterior face to provide a sharp point with slight damage to the tip. Highly polished throughout with manufacturing marks on shaft, including numerous 'chatter' marks. Split along the medial face, probably from use. L. 162mm, W. 21mm, Th. 15.5mm.

LARGE POINTED BLADE

A large pointed blade (E324:6098:F279), cut from the upper midshaft of a cattle or horse tibia (almost certainly cattle) forms an unusual object for an early medieval context in Dublin. Objects of this type were made from splinters of bone midshafts and were roughly trimmed to shape with the intention of providing a broad point at one end. Large, pointed blades, made from cattle-sized bones, can be distinguished from small, pointed blades, made from the bones of caprines. They are familiar, above all, from late prehistoric contexts, where they are comparatively rare, in comparison with small, pointed blades. Just two of the thirty-eight pointed blades from Danebury are cattle-sized and can be described as large, as is just one of the fifty-five bladed implements from Fiskerton (Sellwood 1984, 385; Olsen 2003, table 5.1). The precise function of large implements of this form is unclear. In this case the terminal has been neatly fashioned to form a broad point, more suitable for marking surfaces than for perforating them.

E324:6098:F279. PT2 – Area A: deposit; Phase 2. Complete large, pointed blade, cut from one side of the upper midshaft of a cattle-sized tibia, the narrow ridge of the bone forming the main part of the shaft. Neatly rounded basal end and broad, sharp terminal at the opposite end. L. 120mm, W. 24.5mm, Th. 23mm.

ITEMS OF RECREATION

GAMING PIECES (FIG. 4.7:16–18)

Three gaming pieces were recovered, all of the same basic type, although they vary in size, shape and material. An antler gaming piece from the Cork Tower (E296:31757:F775) has the form of a truncated acorn, with a flat base and apex. It is decorated with lateral incised lines and may well have been made on a lathe. Comparable gaming pieces are known from Knowth and Lagore, and one example from Dublin has also been illustrated (Barton-Murray *et al.* 2012, fig. 7.3:8; Hencken 1950, figs 106.669 and 107.910; Wallace 2016, fig. 11.27). The centre of the gaming piece would originally have included a peg either of antler or of another material, adding a pimple to the apex in the manner of gaming pieces from Knowth and Togherstown (Barton-Murray *et al.* 2012, fig. 7.3:8.349; Macalister and Lloyd Praeger 1931, 79 and pl. XIX.5).

A second gaming piece (E296:48546:F2056), from the same site but a different context, follows the same form and is also made from antler, but it is taller and includes a central peg made of iron, which does not project beyond the flat apex. It illustrates well how the pegs for these gaming pieces extended below their antler bases and enabled them to be fitted into pegged boards with perforations. Celebrated examples of these boards are known from Ballinderry Crannog 1, Co. Westmeath, Knockanboy, Co. Antrim and Waterford (Hencken 1936, 175–81; Simpson 1972; Hurley and McCutcheon 1997, 592 and fig. 16:14:1). An incomplete wooden board came from Christchurch Place in Dublin (E122:186) and fragments of pegged boards made of whale bone from the High Street and Winetavern Street have been identified by the authors (E43:1453 and E81:5843).

The third gaming piece (E324:13392:F530) is a little broader than the other two and considerably heavier, weighing 20g, against 4g and 7g. The shape is the same, if a little more bulbous, with a near-flat base (slightly concave in form) and flat apex. It has been cut, with some difficulty, from the skull of a walrus. An attempt has been made to produce an axial perforation for an accompanying peg by drilling from both ends, and the end result is an hourglass shape. We cannot be certain that the piece ever included a central peg, but it has certainly been heavily used and the base is highly polished from wear. Gaming pieces made from the skull of a walrus are extremely rare and this raw material has seldom been identified anywhere in the past. There is a comparable fragmentary gaming piece of the same material from Fishamble Street (E190:5017), recovered from a foundation layer of early eleventh-century date for structure FS 87.

The form of all three gaming pieces is essentially that of Petersen's Type B (Petersen 1914), which succeeded the domed, hemispherical Type A that can be seen with the gaming pieces from Kilmainham (Harrison and Ó Floinn 2014, 201). Irish examples, however, are distinguished from those found elsewhere by the addition of a central peg, extending below the main body and passing through it, ending with a knop at the apex. Comparable gaming pieces from York, for example, include single holes bored into the base, but these do not project through the entire piece, and the same can be said for gaming pieces from Hedeby (MacGregor *et al.* 1999, fig. 940; Ulbricht 1978, taf 39; Schietzel 2014, 287).

CATALOGUE

E296:31757:F775 (Fig. 4.7:16). CT2: Phase 4b. Complete antler gaming piece of truncated acorn form, circular in section with rounded sides tapering lightly towards the flat apex. Decorated with six lateral incised lines, well-spaced along the body. Base is lightly concave, rather than flat, with an axial perforation through the cortile tissue to accommodate the peg insert, which is now missing. L. 20.5mm, W. 19.5mm, Th. 19mm.

E296:48546:F2056 (Fig. 4.7:17). CT2: fill deposit of Pit 4a; Phase 4a. Complete antler and iron composite gaming piece, near-circular in section and of truncated acorn form, with a flat apex and base. Iron spindle of circular section runs throughout main body and extends below antler component, with a rounded terminal. Antler section is faceted and polished. L. 36mm, W. 15mm, Th. 14mm.

E324:13392:F530 (Fig. 4.7:18). PT1: BW1; Phase 1a. Complete gaming piece, made from the skull of a walrus, hemispherical in shape and of truncated acorn form, with a flat base and apex. Raw material buff to brown in colour, dense and heavy, and undecorated. Pierced at centre by double-splayed hourglass-shaped perforation, cut from both sides with drill marks still visible. Base is smoothed and highly polished from use. L. 22mm, W. 30mm, Th. 29mm.

PERFORATED PIG METAPODIA (FIG. 4.7:19)

Two perforated pig metapodia, one a metatarsus III (E324:13032:F217) and the other a metatarsus IV (E324:12857:F183; Fig. 4.7:19), were recovered from separate contexts in the Powder Tower. Both are unfused bones with single knife-cut lateral perforations through their centres, and with little further modification of the bone. One of them (E324:12857:F183) shows some evidence of wear around the perforation on both sides. Perforated pig metapodia are common finds from Dublin, with just over 250 examples known from the NMI excavations, including over 80 metapodia from both the High Street and Fishamble Street, and almost 60 from Christchurch Place. They have yet to be identified to bone type but it can at least be noted that the small Dublin Castle sample is limited to the inner bones of the pig metatarsals and this reflects the situation seen at Schleswig and across Slavic sites in Mecklenburg, where the metatarsals were preferred to the metacarpals (Ulbricht 1984, 62 and note 29; Lehmkuhl 1982, 214). At Ipswich, in contrast, the quantity of each bone type was relatively even (Riddler *et al.* forthcoming).

Although they have often been regarded as toggles, this is very unlikely. It is not borne out either by wear traces around the perforations, which are quite scarce (although they can be seen on one example here), or by the variety in the choice of bone, and lack of trimming and modification of each bone also indicate that they were produced quickly and easily for a more rudimentary purpose. They are now viewed as simple musical instruments (MacGregor *et al.* 1999, 1981; Riddler 2005, 63). If a cord is threaded through the perforation, they can be made to spin and hum by pulling its ends apart. Heege has suggested that with medieval examples the twine was fastened to wooden handles and these were pulled apart to create the requisite noise, and this may have been the case for Viking period examples as well (Heege 2002, 320 and abb 690). The earliest examples can be found in Slavic contexts of the ninth century, and they are known in England by the tenth century, although the majority of examples are of eleventh-century or later date (Riddler *et al.* forthcoming). It has been suggested that they were a Viking introduction to Britain as a whole and this remains a possibility, although their origins lie firmly in Slavic territories (Spennemann 1988, 27; Lemkuhl 1982, 220). Thereafter they are found in contexts spanning the medieval period.

E324:13032:F217. PT2 – Area C: deposit; Phase 3. Incomplete perforated pig metapodia, metatarsus III, with part of one side fractured away, close to the unfused end. Pierced by a knife-cut lateral perforation, no further modification visible. L. 57mm, W. 18mm, Th. 8.5mm.

E324:12857:F183 (Fig. 4.7:19). PT1: deposit of post-bank levelling; Phase 3. Complete perforated pig metapodial, metatarsus IV, light faceted and trimmed along the shaft and pierced laterally by a knife-cut oval perforation, wider on one side than the other. Slight wear notches on both sides and traces of polish from wear. L. 49.5mm, W. 13.2mm, Th. 12.6mm; perforation 3.6mm by 4.8mm.

OBJECTS OF UNCERTAIN FUNCTION

POLISHED BIRD BONE

A fragmentary goose ulna (E296:48531:F2045) has fractured across the midshaft and shows no signs of working. It is highly polished along the midshaft, however, suggesting that it had been adopted as an implement at some point. Too little survives to be certain of the object type, but the presence of a complete articular surface indicates that it had not been cut to form a whistle or flute, for which a hollowed bone would be required. It resembles the bone pins from Dublin Castle for its form and that may possibly have been its function. Pins made from bird bones have rarely been identified, although there is one example from Ipswich (Riddler *et al.* forthcoming).

E296:48531:F2045. CT2: Phase 4a. Fragment of one end of a goose ulna, including the proximal end, fractured across the midshaft and unworked, but highly polished along part of the shaft. L. 58.5mm, W. 9.5mm, Th. 3.5mm.

4.2.2
The bear tooth (Fig. 4.8)

ULRICH SCHMÖLCKE

Brown bears (*Ursus arctos*) were part of the Irish fauna for many thousand years from the end of the Last Glacial Maximum to the mid Holocene, i.e. up to the Bronze Age. However, the species was never frequent and can be recorded continuously but only rarely in archaeozoological assemblages (Stuart and van Wijngaarden-Bakker 1985). The youngest remains of Irish brown bears are radiocarbon dated to about 1200 BC; they were found in the Poll na mBéar cave, Co. Leitrim and Polldownin cave, Co. Sligo (Edwards *et al.* 2011, fig. 3). Shortly afterwards brown bears must have become extinct in Ireland.

Against this background the find of a bear tooth in pre-Norman layers of the Dublin Castle is remarkable. The object (E296:48534:F2014) is a complete incisive of 53 mm length. While such a bear tooth is unique in the Irish archaeological record, similar finds are relatively common at contemporaneous continental and Scandinavian sites. Typically, they were collected for later perforation and for use as pendants. This tradition is recorded in the Palaeolithic, Mesolithic and Neolithic (Schmölcke *et al.* 2017, 907) and was very persistent: it was, for instance, widespread in parts of Central Europe during the Merovingian dynasty of the Franks AD 450–750 (Wamers 2009, fig. 15) or in Finland, Estonia and Latvia between AD 800 and 1150/1300, with bear remains as one of the most important resources for the production of pendants (Kivisalo 2008; Jonuks and Rannamäe 2018). Even if there could be some overemphasising of the bear in the interpretation of archaeological artefacts (Jonuks 2017), in the second half of the first millennium before Christianisation in many Scandinavian regions and adjacent areas the largest European carnivorous species played a central role in mythology, spirituality, folklore and art (Kurisoo 2018). Perforated but also unprepared bear teeth were used as gifts, as demonstrated for instance in a child's grave in the cemetery of the Viking-age site Birka in central Sweden, where an unmodified bear tooth had been laid on the chest of the child (Gräslund 1973, 170). Additionally, it was a common tradition to bury deceased men and women on bearskins as is argued by Kirkinen (2017), or, in the absence of skins, single bear claws were deposited next to the dead body (Grimm 2014).

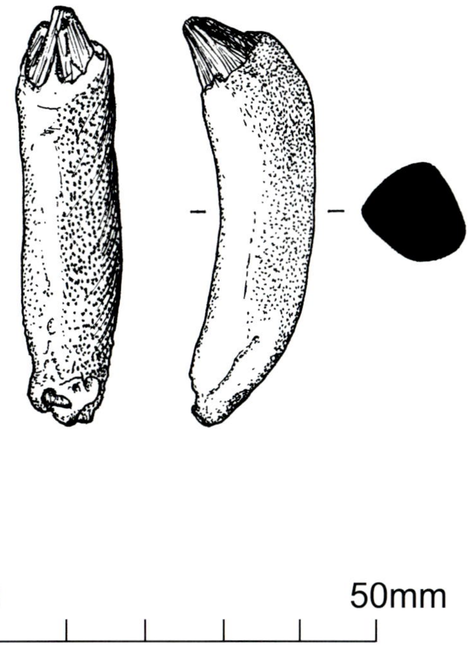

Fig. 4.8 Bear tooth E296:48534:F2046.

The fact that several Anglo-Saxon burials also include bear claws (O'Regan 2018, 9) shows that with settlers from the Continent these traditions reached Britain in early medieval times. Since to date no bear bones other than claws have been identified from British Anglo-Saxon cremations (Bond 1996; O'Regan 2018), it is likely that the bear bones were talismans and used again as substitutes for a skin. In those days, the middle of the first millennium AD brown bears were already nearly extinct in Britain and restricted to only very few and extremely small populations (O'Regan 2018), so that it seems unlikely that the claws were remains of locally hunted animals or of unwieldy imported skins.

To come back to the bear tooth from Viking-age levels at Dublin Castle, it can be supposed that the extraordinary find was part of the raw material of a trader or craftsman who came from Britain and who was an Anglo-Saxon or had contact with Anglo-Saxon communities. Future analyses of the isotope composition of the tooth could prove with scientific methods if the bear was hunted in Central Europe or even in Scandinavia or, less likely, in Britain.

E296:48534:F2046 (Fig. 4.8). CT2: deposit; Phase 4a. Complete incisive bear tooth. Unworked. L. 53mm, W. 14mm, Th. 13mm.

4.2.3 The ogham inscription on comb E748:54

FIONNBARR MOORE AND KEN WIGGINS

Introduction

Ogham is not, as has often been asserted, a cipher based on the Latin alphabet, but is a distinct alphabet in its own right representing the distinct sounds of the Irish language, most likely heavily influenced by Latin grammarians of the second to fourth centuries AD (Moore 2009, 175; 2010, 6). It is most strongly associated with stone monuments, and over 400 ogham inscriptions dating from roughly the fourth to the eighth centuries AD exist on approximately 360 ogham stones from Ireland, the majority of which (252) are from Munster (Moore 2010, 6). Ogham inscriptions are not unique to Ireland, and there are significant numbers of ogham stones in Wales and Scotland, and some examples are known from the Isle of Man and England (Connelly 2015, 39, fig. 1.4, table 1.2).

Ogham letters are usually formed by grouping between one and five parallel lines or notches for each letter alongside or diagonally across the edge of a stone. Sometimes, but rarely, a stem-line is carved on the stone and the ogham inscription carved with respect to it (*ibid.*, fig. 2). The inscription normally gives a person's name (usually male) and an immediate antecedent or a tribal ancestor (Moore 2009, 175). While the monumental, epigraphic, phase of ogham draws to an end in the eighth century, and the Latin alphabet, in semi-uncial book-hand, begins to dominate for memorial and other inscriptions, knowledge of the script is not forgotten and it is often found, as in the case of the bone comb under review here, in what is termed scholastic ogham, mainly in a number of medieval and later manuscripts, with the key to the alphabet and many variations of it preserved in the fourteenth-century Book of Ballymote (McManus 1991, 128–46). As McManus has pointed out, until the demise of the native schools of classical modern Irish 'the ogham system was the framework for the study of Irish letters and was regarded as uniquely Irish' (McManus 2004, 1). According to McManus (*ibid.*, 129), scholastic oghams observe the grammar and orthographical convention of the manuscript tradition, including the use of ogham letter *hÚath* with the value h and the use of the supplementary symbol for E, both of which are rarely attested on the monumental tradition. These factors, taken together with the use of a stem-line and of long scores of equal length to the consonants for vowels, the use of an arrowhead to indicate direction of writing and the separation of words or names, are also part of the manuscript tradition and, according to McManus, are not a direct continuation of the earlier monumental tradition; he would argue these conventions are the 'counterpart on the Og[h]am script to the semi-uncial inscriptions in the Latin alphabet' (*ibid.*, 129). That being said, there is also a possibility that the tradition represented by the scholastic oghams has an antiquity parallel to the monumental epigraphic tradition and in some cases there is overlap between the two with the scholastic style of inscription naturally coming to the fore in the eighth and ninth centuries, being more suited to manuscripts and portable objects. It is highly likely that the ogham script had its beginning as a coded way of communicating messages, preceding its application to stone in the late fourth century and it may be that the scholastic style of the early medieval period echoes the original script in being more suitable for inscribing portable objects. An ogham-inscribed, roughly hewn, short pillar recovered from the well of a Roman house in Silchester, Hampshire, England, observes the basic scholastic form of ogham, drawing two stem-lines and having vowels of equal length to consonants. The context of this nineteenth-century find has recently been re-assessed by the modern excavators of Silchester and they argue convincingly for a late fourth- to fifth-century date which linguistically would not be in conflict with the ogham inscription (Fulford *et al.* 2000, 1–24)

Ogham in its scholastic form is also found on a wide range of portable objects (King 2008, 318–21) sometimes with the name of the owner inscribed or a short prayer and very often the inscription is clearly meant to be cryptic in meaning with a possible curative or talismanic property attached to it (Moore 2017, 278–9). Both scholastic ogham and semi-uncial lettering are employed on the '*Colman bocht*' early medieval grave slab from Clonmacnoise, Co. Offaly (Lionard 1960–61, 98). Ogham occurs in scholastic form as graffiti in the chapel wall of the fourteenth-century Barryscourt Castle, Co. Cork (Moore 2017, 278–80), and a number of names are inscribed in scholastic ogham in the chamber of the eastern tomb of the main mound at Knowth passage tomb, dating to the eighth or ninth century, to give but a few examples (Byrne 2008, 89–119).

The Comb (Fig. 4.4, Pl. 4.3)

An antler comb (E748:54) was found at the Cross Block in 1961–2. The comb is classified above as a single-sided composite comb with connecting plates of trapezoidal section. It was found in a Phase D deposit associated with the House III/Hearth 3 structure (see Chapter 3.5 above). No fewer than five other combs were found in the same deposit: another two single-sided composite combs with connecting plates of trapezoidal section (E748:58 and 59), and three single-sided composite combs with connecting plates of broad D-shaped section (E748:55–7). The date range of the combs with the connecting plates of broad D-shaped section, as discussed above, is typically mid-tenth century to early eleventh century. The combs with connecting plates of trapezoidal section are compared in the above discussion to examples from Fishamble Street dating typically from *c.* 975–1075, but the longer Dublin Castle example (E748:59) is critical to the question of dating, since it is compared in the above discussion to three examples from NMI excavations known to be from contexts post-dating the tenth century. On this basis it is reasonable to suggest that Phase D of the Cross Block mostly likely dates from the early eleventh century, and therefore the ogham-inscribed comb E748:54 can be considered to be a find of roughly early eleventh-century date.

The comb was regarded by its excavator Marcus Ó hEochaidhe as a very significant find from the moment it was discovered in late 1961. Its discovery was first published in the press while the excavation was ongoing. A photograph of the comb appeared in the *Irish Independent* on 19 December 1961, the inscription translated as 'Ena'. The photograph was printed again in another report on the excavation (*Irish Times*, 29 January 1962), the caption correcting the letters to 'ANE'. The image was published for a third time in the *Irish Times* on 24 February 1962, the text of the article speculating that 'Ane may be a personal name (Áine)'. In 1978 Mairead Reynolds published a paper on medieval Irish combs that included a drawing of the E748:54 comb which shows the ogham inscription (Reynolds 1978, fig. 10a). However, the paper does not mention the occurrence of an ogham inscription on the comb as such. A decade later Reynolds included comb E748:54 in the catalogue of a comprehensive study of early Irish combs, noting that it 'was inscribed with the owner's name in ogham' (Dunlevy 1988, 366, 398; comb catalogued as NPM B54). Heather King provides another description of the comb, confirming that the inscription comprises the letters ANE (Áine) (King 2008, 318–9, n. 20; comb referred to by the find no. B54). An arrow (feather mark) at the end of the stem-line, not shown on the drawing of the comb published in 1978, marks the beginning of the inscription, thereby, reading in the direction of the arrow from right to left, confirming the name as ANE (Fig. 4.4; Pl. 4.3).

In the volume on the runic inscriptions of Viking-age Dublin (Barnes, *et al.* 1997, 11-12) it is suggested that the name on the comb may in fact be a Norse personal name, possibly Old Norse Áki, if one interprets the ogham letters as indicating any one of the following: ACE/AQE/AKE. ACE, however, is not possible as C would require only four strokes instead of the five that are present on the comb after A. AQE is only possible if Q is interpreted as mistakenly placed below the stem-line and not to be read as N. With regard to the reading AKE, the ogham symbol for consonantal /K/, which does not occur here, was by as early as the seventh century used to represent vocalic /e/ (McManus 1991, 79, 141-6). Therefore, if a K or CH sound was intended, while it could have been represented by the ogham letter Q, this again is only possible if the five ogham scores representing N are considered to be Q inverted. The fact that the feather mark is not shown on the 1978 illustration of the comb may have influenced Barnes *et al.* in putting forward their suggested reading and while reasonable to suggest it given the information available to them at the time, ANE remains the most plausible reading.

The inscription is lightly incised in the middle of one of the side plates, commencing immediately after the second rivet hole. The inscription is 18mm in length; the vowels A and E, which cross the stem-line are 5mm long each and the consonant N, comprising five scores below the stem-line, is 3mm in length. The stem-line runs on for another 13mm beyond the inscription, indicating that it was incised before the inscription and that perhaps a longer inscription was intended but never finished or added.

Other Portable Objects with Ogham Inscriptions

While there are numerous instances of ogham-inscribed memorial stones in Ireland, examples of portable objects such as comb E748:54 from Dublin Castle that are inscribed with ogham lettering are very rare. Johnson's study of portable inscribed objects from Britain and Ireland identifies a corpus of sixteen ogham-inscribed objects (including the comb from Dublin Castle), half of which are from Ireland, the others from the Scottish Isles and two from England (Johnson 2019, 55, 62, chart 3.2). However, the discovery of a wooden ogham-inscribed weft-beater from Lemanaghan Bog, Co. Offaly, increases the number to seventeen (Sikora and Moore 2020). Such objects include a silver penannular brooch from Ballyspellan, Co. Kilkenny, dated to the ninth century, which bears successive names of its owners in ogham (Macalister 1945, 32; Raftery 1969, 169; King 2008, 318). A bronze hanging bowl from Kilgulbin East, Co. Kerry, has two personal name inscriptions (Raftery 1966, 30–3; fig. 2). A perforated amber bead from Ennis, Co. Clare, for generations in the possession of a family named O'Connor and used as an amulet for the cure of sore eyes as well as being considered to be 'efficacious' in childbirth cases, has a cryptic inscription in ogham (Graves 1856, 149–50; Macalister 1945, 57; King, 2008) – a definite example of ogham being regarded as having talismanic or prophylactic properties. A wooden 'weaver's sword' from Littleton bog, Co. Tipperary, 'probably dating to the late tenth century', has a series of letters along its spine in ogham (Raftery 1969, 162). A few ogham-inscribed bone objects other than the Dublin Castle comb are known: a sheep's metacarpal from Cahercommaun, Co. Clare is inscribed with ogham lettering and other forms of decoration (Hencken 1938, 66; Macalister 1945, 56; King 2008, 318), and an antler knife handle bearing a cryptic ogham inscription, found during excavations in 1996 at Clonmacnoise, Co. Offaly, is interesting in that it employs notches for the vowels which is the custom in the monumental ogham tradition (King, 2008; figs 1 and 2). A bone dice found on the excavations at Ballinderry Crannog, Co. Offaly, in early medieval levels, has the letter V in ogham inscribed on one side of it, representing the number 5 (Hencken 1942, 55, fig. 22). An antler tine found at Moynagh Lough Crannog, Co. Meath in the late nineteenth century also bears a cryptic ogham inscription (Bradley 1991, 7). Most intriguingly, an inscription in the monumental form of the ogham script was found on a fragment of bronze sheet in an area that produced first- to fourth-century Roman coins, close to the perimeter of the great mound at Newgrange, providing possible evidence for the use of the monumental form of the script on portable objects contemporaneously with its earliest application to stone (Carson and O'Kelly 1977, 53; E56:1715).

Examples of portable objects with ogham inscriptions from locations beyond Ireland include an ogham-inscribed bone plaque recovered from an unstratified context during the excavation of Mound 1, Bornais, South Uist in the Outer Hebrides (Forsyth 2012). The excavation of a Pictish farmstead at Buckquoy, Orkney, dating from the seventh to the tenth centuries, produced a spindle whorl made from chalk/limestone with a circular ogham inscription (Ritchie 1976–7, 222) which has most recently been interpreted by Katherine Forsyth to contain a blessing in old Irish, possibly indicating an Irish presence in Orkney prior to the Viking invasions (Forsyth 1995, 677–96).

Conclusion

Comb E748:54 from Dublin Castle is significant as an important addition to the very small assemblage of portable ogham-inscribed objects from Ireland. It is the only artefact from Viking-age Dublin with such an inscription, and the only antler comb with ogham markings. It is, of course, impossible not to compare this find to another antler comb in the Dublin Castle assemblage (E296:50058:F1254; see above; Fig. 4.3:2a/b; Pl. 4.2). This find is also unique in being the only bone/antler comb in the Dublin corpus inscribed with Viking runes. The inscription has been tentatively interpreted as a personal name, perhaps that of the comb's owner (*Unnr*), but alternatively it could be taken as a monogram of the personal name *Uni* (Barnes *et al.* 1997, 45). The runic comb is a single-sided composite comb with connecting plates of broad D-shaped section (see above), and as such is of the same category as three other combs (E748:55–7) from the Phase D Cross Block deposit that contained the ogham-inscribed comb E748:54. As outlined above, the runic inscription on E296:50058:F1254 tells us that the comb belonged to a Scandinavian, and there are indicators to suggest that the comb itself could have been manufactured in Scandinavia, although this is not absolutely certain. In contrast, the ogham-inscribed comb belonged to an Irish person, and the comb itself was of a type that was most likely made in a Dublin workshop (see above).

Two bone/antler combs from the Dublin Castle assemblage, E748:54 and E296:50058:F1254, are a remarkable pair of similar functional artefacts, although distinguished by contrasting cultural markings. The objects illuminate the underlying processes of collaboration and integration at work in the late tenth to early eleventh century, as an urban community was forged through the mixing together of people of Scandinavian and Irish backgrounds in the melting pot that was Viking-age Dublin. The person who owned comb E748:54 was part of the new order of things, but, while familiar with the customs particular to Scandinavian society, nevertheless chose to assert in an unexpected way clear evidence of a strongly held Irish identity.

Similar cultural connections are evident elsewhere in areas of Scandinavian influence, the inscribed stone discovered in the wall of the enclosure around Killaloe Cathedral, Co. Clare being a case in point, bearing both an ogham and runic inscription of possible eleventh-century date (Macalister 1945, 58–9). The stone was originally a cross, the upper part of which was lost in antiquity. It has a runic inscription on one face with a small cross above it and the inscription reads [TH]ORGRIM RISTI [KR] USTHINA which translates as 'Thorgrim carved this cross'. On the sinister side of the stone is a two-line inscription in scholastic ogham reading BENDACHT [AR] THORGRIM which translates as 'A blessing upon Thorgrim'. There is a crucifix carved on the opposite face to the runic inscription (*ibid.*, 59). The stone, which clearly commemorates a Christianised Viking, is unique in being our only bilingual runic and ogham inscription and, like the two combs from Dublin Castle, one with a name in Viking runes and the other in ogham, also dating from the tenth to eleventh centuries, it again attests to the strong cultural links between native and 'foreigner' that had developed by this time in areas of strong Viking influence like Dublin, and, in the case of the cross base from Killaloe Cathedral, the wider Limerick area. The ogham-inscribed comb, while on the face of it a somewhat insignificant looking find, speaks volumes for the cultural milieu of Dublin in the tenth and eleventh centuries.

Chapter 4.3
Metal artefacts
Órla Scully and Louise Nugent

Introduction

The assemblage consists of 119 objects, 105 of which are iron (two of which are coated in tin or silver), thirteen copper alloy and there is a single lead object. Approximately 75% of the metal artefacts were recovered from the Cross Block with most of the remainder coming from the Cork Tower area (Table 4.1). Since the majority of the artefacts (excluding the nails and rivets) were personal items it is not surprising that they were found within the domestic house plots. The presence of tools associated with leather working suggests this craft activity was carried out within one of the houses at the Cross Block and this is discussed further in Chapter 9 below. For the purposes of discussion, the objects have been divided into nine groups according to their function. All measurements are given in millimetres.

Domestic Items

In this group are two iron needles and a set of shears. One needle (E748:107) has a silver or tin coating still evident. Needles were precious objects and often kept in needle cases to prevent loss in what was a poorly lit environment. Plating with non-ferrous metal provided 'a corrosion resistant surface, enhancing the appearance of the object [and] giving a suitable surface' (Ottaway 1992, 486). A tin or tin-lead alloy has been found on dress fitting, spurs, strap-ends and pins in Anglo-Scandinavian levels at Coppergate, York. The objects would have been immersed in a bath of molten metal with a suitable flux (such as tallow): 'for a good result a clean oxide-free surface would be required. Filing the surface of the object immediately before immersing it would have this effect and many plated objects from 16–22 Coppergate appear to have fine grooves or striations on their surfaces' (*ibid.*, 491). The needle from Dublin Castle (E748:107) does indeed appear to have longitudinal striations.

Both needles are circular in section. Only a vestige of the bifurcation of the longer needle (E748:107) is left, but the straight shaft has a sharp point. The eye of the second needle (E748:117) has partially survived. It is punched as opposed to Y-eyed. In production, a punch would have been used to slightly flatten the top of the needle, 'leaving a thin membrane in the eye. This would then have been removed with an even more delicate punch' (Ottaway 1992, 544). In the absence of the entire eye in the Dublin examples, it is not possible to definitively state whether they were formed by punching, or by splitting the shank, but evidence from early levels at Coppergate, York yielded about 40 iron examples of which all but three have punched eyes (*ibid.*, 547).

The shears (E748:1) has a looped bow with no recesses at the junction of the arm and blade and the tops of the blades are sloped inwards (Pl. 4.6). These are classed as Type 2a, well known in medieval contexts in Britain (Goodall

Pl. 4.6 Iron shears E748:1.

2011, 112, fig. 8.6). A similar shears was recovered from the backyard of a post-and-wattle house in Waterford, dated to the mid to late twelfth century (Scully 1997b, 459). Shears first came into use in the Iron Age (de Neergaard 1987, 60) and have been found at native sites such as Garryduff, Co. Cork (O'Kelly 1962, 45) and Lough Gur, Co. Limerick (Ó Ríordáin 1949, 77). They were in more common usage than scissors which were rare during the medieval period and were used for a range of domestic activities such as cutting hair, cloth, finishing cloth and for agricultural purposes like sheep shearing (Goodall 1990a, 861). The size of shears E748:1 indicates it was probably used for domestic purposes.

CATALOGUE

E748:107. CB: unknown pre-castle context. Iron and tin needle. Eye does not survive but vestige of bifurcation visible, shaft is straight and tapered to sharp point. Evidence of silver-coloured coating is possibly tin. L. 82.5mm, Diam. 3mm.

E748:117. CB: found beside timbers at east end of the cutting; depth below formation level not known. Iron needle. Eye is partially intact, aperture almost 2.5mm, appears to have been punched, circular-sectioned shaft tapered to point. L. 52mm, W. 3.5mm, Th. 3mm.

E748:1 (Pl. 4.6). CB: *c.* 0.3–0.45m below formation level at western end of the cutting; Phase G. Iron shears with looped bow and rectangular cross sectioned blade arms, the blade tops taper gently at shoulder, flat triangular blade with triangular section, one blade detached (L. 52mm, W. 11mm, Th. 5mm). L. 156mm, 22.5mm, Th. 7mm.

Dress Accessories

PINS (FIG. 4.9:1–6; PL. 4.7:1–7)

The majority of the fourteen finds in this category are pins used as dress fasteners, of which there are eleven examples. Three of these are ringed pins (Fig. 4.9). Two of the ringed pins are made from iron and both examples came from the Cork Tower area (E296:48568: F2073; E296:50005: F2046). They are loop-headed pins in which the top of the shank is flattened and rolled over to hold the ring. The ring is missing from one example (E296:48568: F2073). The third ringed pin is copper alloy and was recovered from the Cross Block (E748:86) and its form is similar to the complete iron example.

The earliest ringed pins were spiral-ringed pins and have been found in seventh-century contexts at Garryduff I, Co. Cork (O'Kelly 1962, 32) and Lagore Crannog, Co. Meath (Hencken 1950, 71). Spiral rings most often have baluster-shaped pin heads, through which the spiral ring was threaded. The early medieval Irish sites also produced plain-ringed pins, which had complete rings, sometimes thinned at the point of articulation and which were most often combined with loop-headed pins, as opposed to baluster-headed pins. At Garryduff I the earliest strata yielded only spiral-headed pins; once use of the looped form of pin became widespread the replacement of spiral rings by plain rings seems almost to have been inevitable (Kelly 1986, 195). Iron ringed pins are known from other native settlement sites such as Feltrim Hill, Co. Dublin, where both copper alloy and iron ring-headed pins were found in the habitation layers of a stone enclosure dating to the early medieval period (Hartnett and Eogan 1964, 23). The corpus of ringed pins used by Fanning (1994) to devise his classification was mostly of copper alloy. The iron examples were confined to two classes: 'plain-ringed loop-headed', of which forty-five of the sixty examples were iron, and 'plain-ringed polyhedral-headed', of which there was a total of eighty-one examined, only five of which were iron. In total, of the 263 ringed pins examined by Fanning, only fifty were made of iron, the overwhelming majority of these being plain-ringed loop headed types, like those from Dublin Castle. This was the simplest form of ringed pin, which made them particularly suitable for smithing (*ibid.*, 15,16). Seventy-three per cent of the iron plain-ringed loop headed types in Fanning's study are dated to the tenth century. Both of the Dublin Castle iron ringed pins came from the Cork Tower, one from a late ninth-century deposit (E296:48568:F2073), the other from a deposit of the mid/late tenth century (E296:50005:F2046). The copper alloy example from the Cross Block (E748:78) is also from a context dating to the mid/late tenth century. Examples of this type of loop-headed ringed pin have been more recently found in mid to late ninth-century Viking habitation deposits in Temple Bar West, Dublin (Simpson 1999, 27). Seven examples of ringed pins have been identified from Viking graves in Ireland (Harrison and Ó Floinn 2014, 154), including Woodstown, Co. Waterford, where two iron ringed pins were also recovered from other contexts within the settlement (Johnson 2014, 118).

The ringed pins were adopted by the Vikings on arrival in Ireland and have been described as 'possibly the most emblematic objects produced in the Viking-period Irish Sea region' and are found across the western Viking world (Griffiths 2010, 152).

The manner in which these pins were worn as initially suggested by Fanning (1994, 125) is with the point facing upwards, and examples have been found with cord attached to the ring which would have looped around the pin to guard against loss. The reason for the point facing upward was to avoid self-injury when bending over. An ancient Irish law stipulated that 'passers-by injured by projecting pins were entitled to have their case adjudged by the criminal law' (Whitfield 1997, 496). Fanning (1994, 1) notes that by the late twelfth century the ringed pin had been replaced as a dress-fastener by the annular brooch or the stick pin which was shorter and had a solid head of multiple forms.

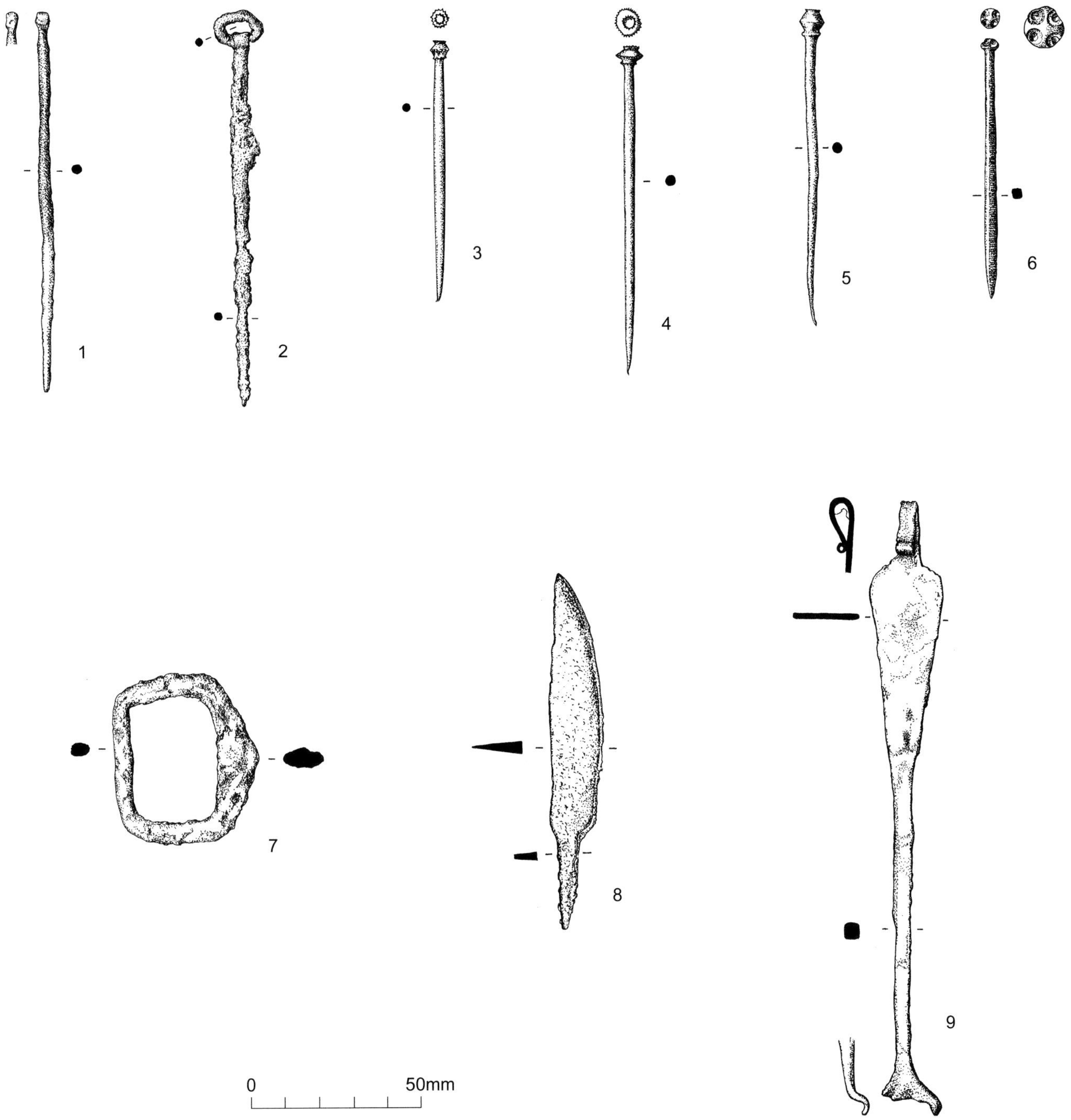

Fig. 4.9 Copper alloy and iron artefacts: iron loop-headed ringed pins (1, 2), Class 2 copper alloy watch-winder pins (3,4), copper alloy Class 9 club-headed pin (5), copper alloy Class 8 stud-headed pin (6), iron buckle (7), Type E iron knife (8), barrel padlock key (9).

The classification of stick pins used here is from O Rahilly (1998). Despite the increased numbers of stick pins recovered from development-led excavation in more recent years, O Rahilly's classification does seem to stand the test of time. On the whole, it would appear that the Dublin Castle stick pins follow the sequence, although some of the examples from the assemblage appear slightly earlier in the timeline. O'Rahilly (*ibid.*, 33) suggests that the change from ringed pins to stick pins reflects changes associated with the emergence of an urbanised society but this is refuted by Wallace (2016, 289), who points out that this phenomenon goes back probably to the end of the ninth century. Wallace does, however, seem to agree that the demands of a more urbanised and cheap market could have resulted in the mass production of stick pins.

A total of eight stick pins were recovered from across all areas of excavation and six of O Rahilly's types are represented. Two examples of watch-winder pins belong to Class 2 (E296:48450:F1206 and E296:48601:F2058) and a semi-watch-winder pin is from a sub-group of Class 2 (E748:61). There is one Class 4 crutch-headed stick pin (E748:19), two stud-headed stick pins (Class 8: E324:7352: F452 and F748:6), a Class 9 club-headed stick pin (E324:13398:F535), and one Class 11 barely differentiated-headed stick pin (E748:20).

The watch-winders have two superimposed circular components or 'wheels' with notched edges, the lower projecting horizontally and of greater diameter. This is an attractive and practical decoration which must have aided grip while pushing the pin through layers of cloth. These are the amongst the earliest of the stick pins (along with the semi-bramble-headed) according to O Rahilly, who based her classification on examples recovered from the excavations in High Street and Winetavern Street in Dublin (O Rahilly 1998, 23). The semi-watch-winder has the same date range as the full watch-winder – from the last quarter of the tenth century to towards the end of the eleventh century. These have only one serrated edge around the circumference of the head, without the upward 'crown'. Both watch-winder pins from the Cork Tower (E296:48450: F1206; E296:48601: F2058) are from mid/late-tenth century pit fills. The Cross Block example (E748:61) is from an eleventh-century layer over a timber pathway.

The crutch-headed pin from the Cross Block (E748:19) has a T-shaped head, albeit quite a small one, which is a little misshapen. O Rahilly (1998, 26) suggests a date range from the eleventh to mid-twelfth century for this type and this example was found in a mid-eleventh-century context. One stud-headed pin from the Powder Tower (E324:7352: F452) is decorated on the head with ring and dot motifs. The second stud-headed pin (E748:6), from the Cross Block, is also decorated on the head with deep punched circles dividing the head into a trefoil pattern. The date range for stud-headed stick pins is from the end of the eleventh century and 'appears to have lasted to the mid-thirteenth century' (*ibid.*, 28).

The club-headed stick pin (E324:13398: F535) is a fine example of its type. This Class 9 example is a typological development of and contemporaneous with the stud-headed pin (O Rahilly 1998, 28). The example from the Powder Tower has a knob-shaped head with a sloping underside and below the head there is a collar. The shank is decorated with dots and vertical lines. A club-headed pin decorated underneath the head with oblique lines was recovered from pre-reclamation levels at the Civic Offices, Winetavern Street, Dublin (Halpin 2000, 169).

BUCKLE (FIG. 4.9:7)

A plain rectangular-shaped iron buckle (E296:48567:F2073) without its pin was found in a late ninth-century context at the Cork Tower. The outer edge has a pointed pin rest. Buckles have been in use since Roman times and there is great variety in the size and form used in the early and later medieval period. Diversity in form reflects the multiplicity of functions, with smaller buckles used on both men and women's clothing, as well as stirrup buckles. Larger buckles were often used as part of horse equipment or used with swords and occasionally for men and women's waist belts (Egan and Pritchard 2002, 50). An identically shaped bronze buckle was found in late tenth/early eleventh-century deposits at Exchange Street Upper/Parliament Street, Dublin (Gowen with Scally 1996, 10; pl. 6c). There is also an iron buckle pin (E324:13388:F506) in the assemblage with circular-sectioned shaft which expands at one end. The attachment loop is missing.

STRAP-END (PL. 4.8)

A very well preserved copper alloy strap-end (E748:106) was found in a mid to late tenth-century context in the Cross Block area. It is a solid piece with a split at the wider end where the leather was inserted. Two rivet holes survive at either side of the split end, allowing the strap to be riveted in place. The rectangular body of the strap-end is decorated with interlace panels bordered by single lines of ring and dot motifs. Above this is a circular panel with a cruciform motif around a central aperture. The areas between the arms of the cross are stippled, and the circular area is defined by a circle of ring and dots. The strap-end tapers to a zoomorphic head, which terminates in a rounded knop, with two raised bosses on the shoulders above the circular panel, giving a zoomorphic representation of eyes and a projecting nose. The reverse side of the object is also decorated but in a much simpler style with the outline of panels again defined by a linear arrangement of dot and circle motif.

Strap-ends first appear in the archaeological record in Britain during the late Roman period and remained a common 'class of multi-purpose strap fitting until the later Middle Ages' (Thomas 2003,1). During the time period AD 750–1100, large numbers of strap-ends were produced relative to other classes of dress accessories, with production peaking during the ninth century. Strap-ends were attached to the ends of straps/belts to prevent them from fraying or curling and could be added to waist-belts, sword-belts and harness-fittings or purse- and satchel-fittings. When used on costume items they added 'weight to make them hang down attractively (*ibid.*, 1).

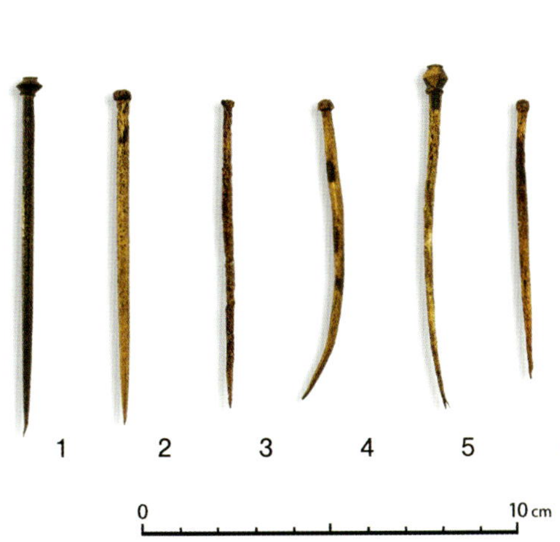

Pl. 4.7 Copper alloy stick pins and ringed pin: watch-winder stick pin (1); semi watch-winder stick pin (2); crutch-headed stick pin (3); stud-headed stick pin (4); club-headed stick pin (5); barely differentiated-headed stick pin (6); loop-headed ringed pin (7).

Pl. 4.8 Copper alloy strap-end E748:106.

Zoomorphic strap-ends are relatively common in Anglo-Saxon contexts in Britain and continued in use well into the twelfth century. Thomas (2003; 2004) identified seven variants of strap-ends from the period 750–1100, which he divides into classes A to G. The Dublin Castle example belongs to his Class F: a strap-end with 'split-end, zoomorphic terminal and double-sided decoration featuring a roundel and panels of interlace' (Thomas 2004, 4). This class is believed to have originated in Ireland and was produced from the late ninth to the eleventh century. Several features of these strap-ends are drawn from insular metalworking traditions, including elements such as 'distinctive animal-heads with triangular ears and 'whiskers', a type featured on the hinge-plates used to secure the carrying straps of eighth- and ninth-century Irish house-shaped shrines, and the combination of incised roundels with panels of interlace. The roundels which may be perforated or plain, are likely to be in imitation of the decorative bossed rivets common to buckles and bridle-fittings produced within the same cultural milieu' (*ibid.*, 4). Citing similarities between zoomorphic strap-ends and buckles found in Dublin and at Meols (NW England) and other sites on the west coast of Britain, Griffiths (2010, 151) also argues for an Irish Sea, possibly Dublin, origin.

A copper alloy strap-end of similar style to the Dublin Castle example was found in Dunmore cave, Co. Kilkenny in 1999 in association with a coin hoard of late tenth-century date (Hall 2007, 121). A tenth-century strap-end found within a midden beside a ninth-century Viking house, with associated later burial at Truska, Co. Galway, provides an additional parallel (Kelly 2010, 179–80, fig. 17.3). In Waterford city a very similar strap-end was recovered from occupation deposits in an urban Viking context (O Hara and Scully forthcoming). Another example of this type of strap-end was found in Christchurch Place, Dublin (E122:17157) and its outline is very similar to the Dublin Castle example, though the basal panel is simpler in the former (Lang 1988, fig. 118).

CATALOGUE

E296:48568:F2073 (Fig. 4.9:1). CT2: deposit; Phase 1. Iron loop-headed ringed pin. Loop-headed pin, i.e. terminal is folded over to form small loop; ring missing, circular-sectioned shank is slightly curved and tapered to a point. L. 111mm, W.4.7mm, Th. 3mm.

E296:50005:F2046 (Fig. 4.9:2; Pl. 4.7:7). CT2: deposit; Phase 4a. Iron loop-headed ringed pin. Plain ringed loop-headed pin, shank complete and tapered to a point. L. 108mm, W. 14.5mm, Th. 5mm.

E748:86. CB: in black layer *c.* 0.12m under Hearth 3 (House III) and just south of it; Phase C. Copper alloy loop-headed ringed pin. Ring absent; top of shank is rolled over on itself to form loop; complete shank is sub-rectangular in section, tapered to point. L. 103.5mm, W. 4.5mm, Th. 3.5mm.

E296:48450:F1206 (Fig. 4.9:3). CT2: fill deposit of Pit 4a; Phase 4a. Copper alloy watch-winder stick pin. Complete with flat head edged with cog-like tiny upright spikes, widening out to second horizontally serrated edge, with a plain collar, no decoration on shank, gold colour due to chalcopyrite. L. 75.5mm, W. 5.5mm, Th. 3mm.

E296:48601:F2058 (Fig. 4.9:4; Pl. 4.7:1). CT2: fill deposit of Pit 4a; Phase 4a. Copper alloy watch-winder stick pin, with flat head surrounded by upright tiny spikes with head expanded with concentric cog-like spikes horizontally positioned around the widest point; complete. L. 97mm, W. 9mm, Th. 3mm.

E748:61 (Pl. 4.7:2). CB: east end of cutting, immediately over level of pathway; Phase D. Copper alloy semi watch-winder stick pin. Complete shank with undecorated but pitted surface. Head is flat-topped with evenly serrated edge. L. 89mm, W. 5mm, 3.3mm.

E748:19 (Pl. 4.7:3). CB: *c.* 1.03m below formation level on thin black layer, *c.* 3.96m west of east curtain wall; Phase E. Copper alloy crutch-headed stick pin. The head is T-shaped, and the ring and dot decoration appears to extend all over the object, though pitting has occurred. Dots on either side of the head are reminiscent of sockets for ring. L. 82m, W. 4mm, Th. 2.7mm.

E324:7352:F452 (Fig. 4.9:6). PT1: deposit of post-bank levelling; Phase 3. Stud-headed stick pin. Head has ring and dot decoration, patina on shank, no decoration evident; circular-sectioned shank tapers to a faceted rectangular sectioned point, complete. L. 75mm, W. 5mm, Th. 3mm.

E748:6 (Pl. 4.7:4). CB: *c.* 0.96m below formation level in thin dark layer. Hearth 4 (House IV) , Phase E . Copper alloy stud-headed stick pin. Stud head decorated with dot and circle motif forming trefoil pattern on surface of head. Plain shank. L. 80mm, W. 4.5mm, Th. 3.2mm.

E324:13398:F535 (Fig. 4.9:5; Pl. 4.7:5). PT1: BW2 deposit; Phase 1a. Copper alloy club-headed stick pin. Complete pin, with knob-shaped head with flat top, rounded edges with sloping top and underside. Collar beneath head, shank decorated with vertical lines and dots, not clear due to wear or corrosion. Gold colour from chalcopyrite. L. 91mm, W. 7mm, Th. 4mm.

E748:20 (Pl. 4.7:6). CB: *c.* 1.03m below formation level on thin black layer, *c.* 3.96m west of east curtain wall; Phase E. Copper alloy barely differentiated-headed stick pin. Complete pin with shank expanded to form blunt head. Head and shank decorated with ring and dot motif deepest on head. L. 74mm, W. 4mm, Th. 3mm.

E296: 48567:F2073 (Fig. 4.9:7). CT2: deposit; Phase 1. Rectangular-framed iron buckle with one side of frame expanded to rest pin, frame has rectangular cross-section. L. 50mm, W. 43mm, Th. 6mm.

E324:13388:F506 . PT1: BW5/6 deposit; Phase 1b. Iron buckle pin. Incomplete circular-sectioned pin with one end expanded. L. 33mm, W. 5mm, Th. 3mm.

E748:106 (Pl. 4.8). CB: east of line of posts of Hearth 3 (House III) *c.* 2.13m west of east curtain wall and *c.* 1.57m below top of south section. In ironworking (smithing) layer under Hearth 3 level; Phase C. Copper alloy strap-end. Ornate, flat, tapered strap split at wider end (leather still intact inside) with rivet holes either side. The Interlace decoration is in panels, bordered by ring and dot. The object widens around a circular panel with a central cruciform motif which has a central aperture; tapers to rounded knop, which, combined with bosses on the shoulders above the circular panel, gives zoomorphic representation of eyes and protruding nose. Reverse is less ornate, with outline of panels picked out by dots; same zoomorphic design on reverse, both sides having six rows of tiny dots in the space between the 'eyes' and the end of the 'nose'. L. 45mm, W. 15mm, Th. 4mm.

Horse Equipment (Pl. 4.9)

Although a large variety of equine artefacts have been recovered from Viking-age levels in Dublin, including harness trappings, bridle bits, stirrups, spurs, pommels or harness bows and horseshoes (Kavanagh 1988, 101–2), only a single piece of horse equipment was recovered from the Cross Block in Dublin Castle in addition to a horseshoe nail from the Cork Tower (E296:48565: F2071). The Cross Block find is an iron bridle cheek piece (E748:29) that formed part of a snaffle bit and was recovered from a probable eleventh-century context (Pl. 4.9). The piece has a central ring, at either side of which projects straight bars with flared terminals. It would have been part of a pair, one on either side of a snaffle bit. A snaffle bit consists of 'a mouth piece, either a plain bar or made up of jointed links...fastened (usually with a with a swivelling joint) to cheek-pieces which are basically ring form, often extended into wings or bars; to the rings are attached both the straps of the headstall, holding the bit in place in the horse's mouth, and the reins by which the rider controls it' (Clark 1995, 46). The original typology by Ward Perkins (1940) classified cheek pieces A to E. The Dublin Castle example is a Type B which is found in Scandinavia as early as the ninth century (e.g. a grave-group in the Museum of Cultural History, Oslo. Museum, No. C20168), but not all the British examples are considered to be as early (*ibid.*, 80). This typology is retained by Goodall (2011, 365) who has modified the Type B from straight bars to curved, matching the only example in his catalogue, which has arms with out-turned tips. The Type B example given by Goodall is from the twelfth century, as is an example from Waterford

Pl. 4.9 Iron bridle cheek piece E748:29.

in which the ends of the bars extending from the ring are curved (Scully 1997b, 477; fig. 15.15, 8). The illustration of a Type B cheek piece in the London Museum Catalogue (Ward Perkins 1940, 80, fig.19a), which has flat arms, thickening slightly towards the terminals, is a perfect parallel to the Dublin Castle example.

Cheek pieces with short stops were recovered from a Viking horse burial at Athlumney, Co. Meath, which had a complete bridle bit in which 'each of the snaffle rings has a pair of stops to prevent the cheek-pieces from turning completely in the mouthpiece' (Kavanagh 1988, 101). This bridle bit is considered to be an earlier type than those represented in the Dublin finds of the tenth century (*ibid.*, 103). The cheek pieces were part of a two-link cast copper alloy bit and consisted of rings with pairs of opposed projecting knob-ended stops. The projections on the Athlumney cheek piece are a lot shorter than the Dublin Castle example. A cheek piece found in the Viking boat burial at Balladoole, Isle of Man also differs from the Dublin Castle example in that the ends of the extended bars are turned out (Bersu and Wilson 1966, 19–20).

An intact cheek piece of similar form, 'a ring…which has a strip projecting from it that is flattened and widened towards the tip' was found at Coppergate, York (Ottaway 1992, 706) from Anglo-Scandinavian levels. Ottaway classes this as a Type B. This, and the example illustrated by Ward Perkins (1940, 80, fig. 19a) are the closest parallels to the Dublin example.

A single horseshoe nail (E296:48565: F2071) was recovered from a late ninth-century context at the Cork Tower. Its flattened rectangular shaft expands to what is most likely the remains of a fiddle-key head. These would have been used with horseshoes with countersunk holes for the nail heads in an early type which have been recorded from ninth- and tenth-century contexts in Britain (Clark 1986).

CATALOGUE

E748:29 (Pl. 4.9). CB: *c.* 0.3m west of Hearth 3 (House III); Phase D. Iron bridle cheek piece. Circular sectioned iron bar with central circular opening (internal diam. 20mm), wider at terminals, side piece of bridle. L. 120mm, W. 27mm, Th. 9mm.

E296:48565:F2071. CT2: deposit; Phase 1. Iron horseshoe nail. Rectangular-sectioned head formed by expansion of shaft, which is flat, rectangular-sectioned and almost complete. L. 41mm, W. 13mm, Th. 4mm.

Knives (Fig. 4.9:8; Pl. 4.10:1–4)

A total of twelve complete knives, which includes a knife blade separated from its tang, as well as two isolated tangs (E748:48 and E748:121) form the knife collection from the Viking levels. The knives were mostly recovered from the Cross Block (E748:2; E748:4; E748:8; E748:30; E748:34a/b; E748:50; E748:77; E748:78; E748:119; E748:120) and two were recovered from the Cork Tower (E296:50004:F2012 and E296:48574:F2080). The most relevant typologies of knives are by Ottaway (1992) based on Anglo-Scandinavian knives from Coppergate in York and the updated typology of medieval knives published posthumously, bringing together the medieval studies of Goodall (2011). All but one of Ottaway's knife types have angled blade backs and the typology is largely based on the angles of the rear blade back in relation to the front part of the blade back (Ottaway 1992, 563).

All the knives are iron with whittle tangs. Whittle tang knives have pointed projections which were inserted into bone, antler or wooden handles. Some of the knives can be compared with examples from Ottaway's typology of Anglo-Scandinavian knives, which divides whittle tang knives into three groups (A to C) based on the blade back form. Types A and C are further subdivided into three sub-groups (Ottaway 1992, 561–5). Other examples are best paralleled by Goodall's medieval types, based on medieval examples throughout Britain.

The only example of an Ottaway Type A1 knife (E748:77) from Dublin Castle was found in a probable mid/late tenth-century context at the Cross Block. In this type, the rear part of the blade back is parallel to the cutting edge and then slopes to the tip. Almost 40% of the York Type A1 knives come from mid/late ninth to early tenth-century contexts (*ibid.*, 563).

Four of the knives (E748:2; E748:4; E748:8; E748:30) approximate to Ottaway's Type A3. In this type, the rear part of the blade slopes slightly downwards and the change in plane is very slight. The only example from Coppergate in York is from a mid-ninth-century context. 'Blades with either downward sloping or horizontal rear parts are not common, but other examples occur in the middle Anglo-Saxon period…and in a late eleventh century context at Flaxengate, Lincoln' (*ibid.*, 565). It could be argued there is no change in plane in some of the Dublin examples, but perhaps this could be the result of wear.

One knife (E748:78) approximates to an Ottaway Type C1, in which the rear of the blade runs horizontal then becomes convex, curving down to the tip. As with the Type A3 blades, the example from Dublin does not have a pronounced angle at the downturn on the blade back.

Three of the knives (E748:34a/b; E748:119 and E748:120) are not comparable with any of the Ottaway typology. They resemble more closely a Type C from Goodall's medieval typology. In this type, there is a straight blade back parallel to the cutting edge, which rises close to the tip to meet the back. This knife form occurred in large numbers at Winchester within excavated deposits dating between the eight to sixteenth centuries, with the majority dating from between the tenth and thirteenth centuries (Goodall 1990b, 835).

Finally, three blades (E748:50; E296:48574:F2080 and E296:50004:F2012) with no angles on the blade back, but instead having a generously curved blade back, conform to Goodall's Type I (formerly his Type E). One example was recovered from a late ninth-century context at the Cork Tower while the remaining two came from early/mid eleventh-century contexts. This type has a curved blade back and variously formed cutting edge. It has been found at Winchester in deposits dating from the tenth to the fifteenth centuries (Goodall 1990b, 850). Three similar knives were recovered from the Viking site at Woodstown, Co. Waterford, though these are not from dated contexts, having been recovered from metal-detected topsoil from test and excavation trenches (Scully 2014, 132). Knives of Type I are of eleventh- to fourteenth-century date (Goodall 2011, 107). One of the examples from the Cork Tower (E296:48574:F2080) belongs to the late ninth century, which is earlier than this range, as must be the similar knives from Woodstown, as the settlement there is likely to have been abandoned at the end of the ninth century (Russell and Hurley 2014, 19).

Knives were considered essential personal possessions. They were used for a variety of functions, by both men and women in crafts and everyday work such as skinning and cutting up animals to the preparation and eating of food. According to de Neergaard (1987, 55), until the fourteenth century only favoured guests could expect to be provided with a knife at mealtimes and all others had to provide their own or share. While some knives have characteristics of a speciality use, the size and form of the Dublin Castle knives indicates everyday usage.

Pl. 4.10 Tanged iron knife blades: Ottaway Type A1 (1); Ottaway Type A3 (2); Goodall Type C (3); Goodall Type I (4).

CATALOGUE

OTTAWAY TYPE A1 (FIGURE 1)

E748:77 (Pl. 4.10:1). CB: *c.* 0.15m under level of Hearth 3 (House III) in occupation debris; Phase C. Iron whittle-tanged knife. Flat blade back angles towards tip halfway along its length, sloped shoulder and curved blade edge, tang set centrally, complete. L. 111mm, W. 15mm, Th. 6mm.

OTTAWAY TYPE A3

E748:2. CB: *c.* 0.3–0.45m below formation level at western end of the trench; Phase G. Iron whittle-tanged knife. Blade back slopes from back to tip, blade edge is curved, possibly due to wear. Short, sloped shoulder, short tang set low, thick blade possibly due to flaking, corroded. L. 110mm, W. 17mm, Th. 11mm.

E748:4. CB: *c.* 0.3–0.45m below formation level at western end of the trench; Phase G. Iron whittle-tanged knife. Long tapered tang, raised shoulder blade back slopes to point, blade straight. L. 91mm, W. 9mm, Th. 4.5mm.

E748:8 (Pl. 4.10:2). CB: *c.* 0.96m below formation level in thin dark layer. Hearth 4 (House IV) level, Phase E. Iron whittle-tanged knife. Straight blade backed knife with short incomplete tang, set centrally, blade edge is fairly straight and slopes up to point. L. 157mm, W. 19mm, Th. 6mm.

E748:30. CB: Hearth 3 level, inside east end wall of House III; Phase D. Iron whittle-tanged knife. Triangular-sectioned blade with blade back sloping to tip, which is missing, straight blade edge, raised shoulder, tapered flat rectangular-sectioned tang is complete. L. 75mm, W. 17mm, Th. 5mm.

E748:78. CB: *c.* 0.15m under level of Hearth 3 (House III) in occupation debris; Phase C. Iron whittle-tanged knife. Small with flat back angled to tip, which is missing, straight blade edge, sloped shoulder with tang set low. L. 87mm, W. 12mm, Th. 5mm.

GOODALL TYPE C

E748:34a/b. CB: *c.* 4.41m from east limit of trench, *c.* 1.27m below formation level; Phase D. Iron whittle-tanged knife. (a) Flat blade back with parallel blade edge which slopes up to point near tip, which is missing. L. 98mm, W. 12mm, Th. 3mm. (b) Long narrow rectangular-sectioned tang, tapered to a point; part of E748:34a. L. 63mm, W. 7mm, Th. 3mm.

E748:119 (Pl. 4.10:3). CB: unknown pre-castle context. Iron whittle-tanged knife. Straight blade back with sharp short shoulder, blade is very worn, presenting as roughly parallel to blade back. Tang is set low and intact, point missing. L. 98mm, W. 10mm, Th. 4mm.

E748:120. CB: unknown pre-castle context. Iron whittle-tanged knife. The tang is complete, rectangular and tapered, but the blade is broken off. What remains has a straight blade back, with a very slight sloped shoulder, the cutting edge is parallel. L. 56mm, W. 12mm, Th. 5mm.

GOODALL TYPE I KNIVES

E296:48574:F2080 (Fig. 4.9:8). CT2: deposit; Phase 1. Iron whittle-tanged knife. Curved blade back, sloped shoulder, short, tapered tang set low and straight cutting edge. L. 104mm, W. 15mm, Th. 3.5mm.

E748:50 (Pl. 4.10:4). CB: Hearth 3 (House III) level at west end of trench; Phase D. Iron whittle-tanged knife. Complete with blade back curved and straight blade edge, tang set centrally. Type E. L. 130mm, W. 19mm, Th. 5mm.

E296:50004:F2012. CT2: northern side wall of House 3; Phase 6. Iron whittle-tanged knife. Straight blade back with curved cutting-edge set, tang set high, tip missing, corroded, broken into 3 pieces. L. 111mm, W. 26mm, Th. 12mm.

KNIFE TANGS

E748:48. CB: Hearth 3 (House III) level at west end of trench; Phase D. Iron knife tang; part of whittle-tanged knife. Long tapered tang, rectangular cross-section, dull point, broken at larger end. L. 69mm, W. 5mm, Th. 3mm.

E748:121. CB: unknown context. Iron knife tang. Most probably from a knife, rectangular tapered bar. L. 60mm, W. 7.5mm, Th. 6mm.

Locks and Keys (Fig. 4.9:1, Pl. 4.11:1–3)

Two components of barrel padlocks were recovered from the Cross Block area, one of which (E748:47) was from a probable early eleventh-century context. The bolt with double-leaf springs (E748:47) has a circular closing plate still in place which indicates it probably belonged to a Type 1 lock which is attached rigidly to the case and extends parallel to it (Goodall 2011, 232). In this example the keyhole may have been a T-shaped slot in the outer case of the lock, or the keyhole may have been at the opposite end to the plate. The key was inserted into the keyhole and the open bit surrounded and compressed the leaf springs attached to the bolt, allowing the bolt to be released from the padlock. The second fragment of a barrel paddock (E748:130) was a U-shaped bolt of such a lock.

These locks, which were universally used to secure chests, caskets, gates, doors and shutters, are generally known from pre-eleventh-century contexts. Irish sites that have yielded similar barrel padlocks include the ringforts at Garryduff, Co. Cork (O'Kelly 1962, 55), Cahercommaun, Co. Clare (Hencken 1938, 46, fig. 29) and Lagore Crannog, Co. Meath (Hencken 1950, 80, fig. 20).

A total of five barrel padlock keys (E748:24; E748:80; E748:118; E748:132 and E296:48518:F2028) were identified, all except one recovered from the Cross Block area. According to the classification by Goodall (1990c, 1005), barrel padlock keys are classified according to the relationship of the key shank to the bit. Type A examples have the bit set laterally to the stem; the Type B form has the bit set centrally to the stem, and in Type C the bit and stem are in line.

A large Type A key (E296:48518:F2028) recovered from a late tenth/early eleventh-century context in the Cork Tower area is almost complete, but whether the bit was originally closed or open cannot be determined (Fig. 4.9:9). A second Type A key (E748:118) has the bit set laterally but the details of the internal wards of the bit are obscured. Type A padlock keys are the most common and continued in usage into the post-medieval period (Goodall 1990c, 1006). One key (E748:80) has a looped bow expanding to a pear-shaped flattened expansion on the stem but is without a bit. Also missing its bit is a key (E748:24) which has a rectangular stem and looped bow. The remaining key (E748:132) also has a looped bow, with the partial remains of a square-sectioned stem.

Finally, a bar forming a triangular-shaped link may have functioned as a hasp (E748:81).

CATALOGUE

E748:47 (Pl. 4.11:3). CB: Hearth 3 (House III) level at west end of cutting; Phase D. Iron barrel padlock bolt. U-shaped staple complete attached to incomplete closing plate, one spine with double-leafed spring, complete except for damage to closing plate. L. 78mm, W. 26mm, Th. 21mm.

E748:130. CB: unknown pre-castle context. Iron barrel padlock bolt. U-shaped padlock bolt, rectangular in section with one arm tapered to point. L. 48mm, W. 16.5mm, Th. 5mm.

E748:118. CB: unknown pre-castle context. Iron barrel padlock key. Rectangular stem which broadens into slightly expanded terminal with partial rear looped hook. Rectangular bit set centrally to stem with detail obscured by corrosion. L. 113mm, W. 14mm, Th. 10mm.

E296:48518:F2028 (Fig. 4.9:9). CT2: House 2 deposit; Phase 5. Iron barrel padlock key. Large barrel padlock key, most probably Type A. It has a looped bow, with the upper part of the stem flattened to form a round-shouldered plate; below this the stem has a square section, with incomplete bit set laterally to stem. L. 179mm, W. 21mm, Th. 10mm.

E748:24 (Pl. 4.11:1). CB: *c.* 0.91m below formation level; Phase E. Iron barrel padlock key. Rectangular stem with looped bow, stem is damaged, and bit does not survive. Stem tapers towards former bit, but this may be due to corrosion, rather than indicating a point. L. 117mm, W. 12, Th. 7mm.

Pl. 4.11 Iron artefacts: barrel padlock key, side and front views (1); barrel padlock key (2); barrel padlock bolt (3); tweezers, front and side views (4).

E748:80 (Pl. 4.11:2). CB: *c.* 50mm under Hearth 3 (House III) level near south section of trench; Phase C. Iron barrel padlock key. Rectangular stem which broadens from the centre to create a flat pear-shaped plate with looped bow. Bit set laterally to stem with open-ended rectangular aperture. Rear of stem decorated with two sets of three horizontal incised lines. L. 100mm, W. 15mm, Th.2.5mm.

E748:132. CB: among timbers of pathway; Phase D. Iron barrel padlock key. Looped bow with partial remains of square cross-sectioned stem, incomplete. L. 47mm, W. 11mm, Th. 7mm.

E748:81. CB: *c.* 0.15m under Hearth 3 (House III) level; Phase C. Iron hasp. Flat rectangular-sectioned bar, forming an opened-centred triangle with a small break at base. L. 69mm, W. 35mm, Th. 5mm.

Personal Items (Pls 4.11:4, 4.12)

Tweezers have been in use since Roman times and along with bone combs and ear spoons were an essential part of the personal grooming kit of the Viking era. A set of tweezers (E296:48539:F2047) was recovered from early/mid-tenth-century levels at the Cork Tower. It consisted of a folded-over thin narrow strip of iron that tapered to both terminals (Pl. 4.11.4). The tweezers are undecorated, but traces of tinning survive on its surface (see pins above). A folded-over band of copper alloy acted as a slide. In Winchester, the earliest slide tweezers were found in an early tenth-century context (Biddle 1990, II, 690). Though tweezers are known from Roman times, no Roman example with a slide has been recovered to date. Three pairs of similarly shaped tweezers, all with twisted wire suspension hoops, were found in Anglo-Scandinavian levels at Coppergate, York, two of which had slides (Mainman and Rogers 2000, 2600). A beautiful silver toilet set complete with tweezers, nail file and ear scoop were found in Viking levels at Fishamble Street, Dublin (Simpson 1999, 32; pl. XVI).

A decorated child's bracelet (E748:16) made from copper alloy was recovered from an early/mid-eleventh-century context at the Cross Block (Pl. 4.12). The bracelet has flattened abutting terminals and an internal diameter of only 43mm. It is decorated with stamped ring and dot motifs. The dots are in pairs on the half of the bracelet nearest the terminals which themselves have two central dots. The cross-section of the bracelet is sub-lozenge-shaped, with the inner profile being gently rounded, and the outer surface has a slight central ridge.

A remarkably similar copper alloy bracelet with punched dot decoration (E173:3370) was found at John's Lane, Dublin and is currently on display in the National Museum of Ireland. The entire outer surface is decorated with two parallel rows of stamped dots and the band has pointed and faceted terminals.

CATALOGUE

E296:48539:F2047 (Pl. 4.11:4). CT2: House 1 deposit; Phase 3. Iron and tin tweezers. Folded-over strip with central overlapped binding strip of copper alloy, terminals missing. L. 45mm, W. 6.5mm, Th. 5mm.

E748:16 (Pl. 4.12). CB: *c.* 1.03m below formation level on thin black layer; Phase E. Child's copper alloy bracelet. Small bracelet formed by bending lozenge-shaped bar into sub-circular band. Terminals flattened and decorated with ring and dot motif. More pronounced ridge on outer surface. Ext. diam. 47.5mm, Int. diam. 43mm.

Pl. 4.12 Decorated copper alloy bracelet E748:16.

Structural Items (Fig. 4.10:1–10; Pl. 4.13:2)

There are thirty-six nails in various states of preservation and twenty rivets, fifteen of which retained the rove. Thirty of these, fifteen nails and fifteen rivets (E748:124a-dd) were found in association with an eleventh-century wooden pathway at the Cross Block and these are catalogued separately in Table 4.4. Nails are one of the most common finds from medieval archaeological sites and their morphology is influenced very much by the different functions for which they were used (Bill 1994, 55; Zori 2007, 32). Ottaway (1992, 607) identifies five groups of nails based on their heads and sizes. Those with flat or roughly flat heads were the most common type in Anglo-Saxon contexts in England. Of the twenty-eight heads that survive on the nails from Viking-age levels in Dublin Castle, all had round roughly flat heads and square or sub-square shafts.

A rivet differs from a nail in that it is inserted through aligned holes in the pieces to be joined and then hammered on the protruding end to form a second burred head. A rove is a plate with a central hole, placed over the end of the rivet which is hammered or 'clenched' to secure the rivet holding the timbers together, hence the term 'clench nail', often used for a rivet and rove. A simple way to differentiate between a nail and a rivet (where the rove or burred terminal does not survive) is by its bulk. If it would be impracticable to hammer it through timbers, then it is a rivet, which necessitated drilling a hole before insertion.

Ships' nails used in conjunction with clinker-built boats would have had circular-sectioned shafts, to reduce ingress of water. Of the 566 possibly Viking or medieval nails from Woodstown, Co. Waterford, a high proportion have shanks that are round in section and a high proportion also have roves, leading Bill (2014, 154) to conclude that since the clench nails with round shanks were restricted to Scandinavian Viking-age contexts it indicated the probability that it was the use of Scandinavian vessels at the site that produced the nail deposits. Of the twenty rivets from Dublin Castle Viking levels, fifteen have round shafts; since making a round shaft is more labour intensive, it suggests specialisation suited to shipbuilding in the community.

Two perforated strips of iron in the assemblage are likely to have functioned as strap hinges (or hinge straps). Both artefacts were recovered from mid to late tenth-century deposits at the Cross Block. These rectangular bars are not complete, but both have rivet holes, one with a rivet *in situ*. The smaller one has a tapered outline, while the longer piece is straight, both forms which are considered by Goodall (2011, 166) to be the most common form of medieval hinge. Similar objects are also known from Anglo-Scandinavian York and, according to Ottaway (1992, 623), were probably used in the site's timber buildings or on wooden artefacts.

Finally, E748:91 is a wall hook (Pl. 4.13:2). Such hooks with tapering shanks were driven into timber or into masonry joints. This object has the hook projecting beyond the end of the shank and is of a type found as early as the ninth and tenth centuries in Winchester (Goodall 1990e, 328).

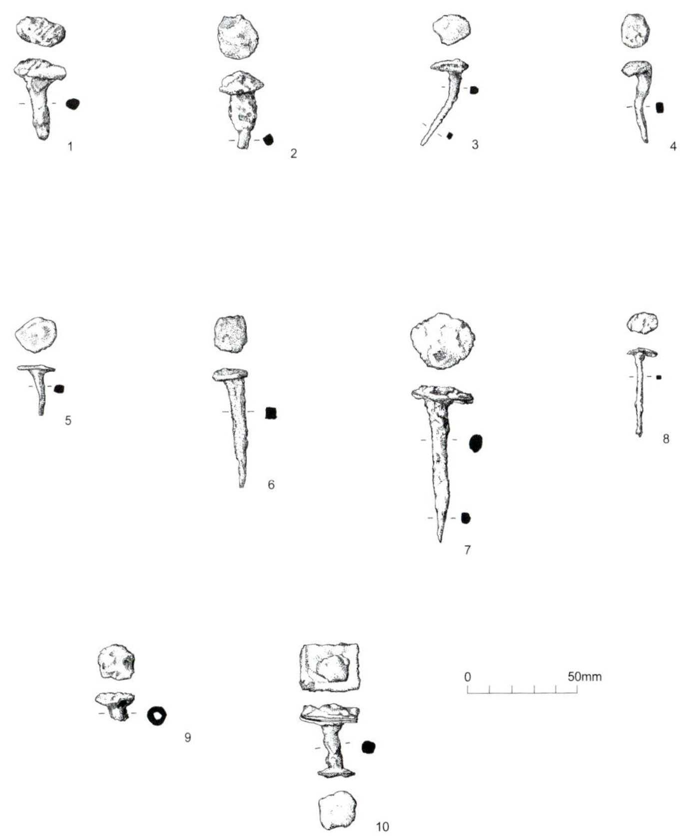

Fig. 4.10 Iron nails (1-9), iron rivet and rove (10).

Table 4.4 Iron nails and rivets (E748:124a-dd) from the Phase D plank pathway (F36) at the Cross Block.

Find	Type	Description	Measurements
E748:124a	Nail	Large flat round head with rectangular-sectioned shaft, badly bent though complete.	L. 59mm, W. 23mm, Th. 7mm.
E748:124b	Nail and strap	Round flat head tapered rectangular shaft, nail has penetrated a short iron rectangular strap with one rounded end and one broken.	L. 53mm, W. 29mm, Th. 23mm.
E748:124c	Nail	Round flat but damaged head, straight tapered rectangular-sectioned shaft, tip missing.	L. 57mm, W. 18mm, Th. 6mm.
E748:124d	Nail	Large flat partially intact round head, rectangular-sectioned shaft tapered to tip.	L. 74mm, W. 47mm, Th. 9mm.
E748:124e	Nail	Small round headed nail with tapered square-sectioned shaft.	L. 42mm, W. 18mm, Th. 4mm.
E748:124f	Head of nail	Large flat round head with vestige of rectangular shaft remaining.	L. 22mm, W. 22mm, Th. 13mm.
E748:124g	Nail	Round flat head with twisted rectangular-sectioned shaft.	L. 48mm, W. 18mm, Th. 5mm.
E748:124h	Nail	Tapered rectangular-sectioned shaft no head, fine point.	L. 63mm, W. 6mm, Th. 5mm.
E748:124i	Nail	Round flat head with tapered rectangular shaft.	L. 38mm, W. 17mm, Th. 9mm.
E748:124j	Nail	Round flat head with tapered rectangular shaft, point missing.	L. 26mm, W. 19mm, Th. 5mm.
E748:124k	Nail	Flat head tapered rectangular shaft, complete.	L. 52mm, W. 26mm, Th. 8mm.
E748:124l	Nail	Round flat head with robust tapered rectangular shaft, incomplete and splitting.	L. 25mm, W. 22mm, Th. 10mm.
E748:124m	Nail	Round head with robust tapered rectangular shaft, incomplete and splitting.	L. 16mm, W. 14mm, Th. 9mm.
E748:124n	Nail	Round flat head with tapered rectangular shaft, point missing.	L. 36mm, W. 18mm, Th. 7mm.
E748:124o	Nail	Square tapered shaft, head missing.	L. 43mm, W. 5mm, Th. 5mm.
E748:124p	Rivet and rove	Round flat head with circular-sectioned shaft and incomplete rectangular rove intact.	L. 37mm, W. 18mm, Th. 25mm.
E748:124q	Rivet and rove	Round flat head with circular-sectioned shaft and incomplete rectangular rove intact.	L. 33mm, W. 16mm, Th. 25mm.
E748:124r	Rivet and rove	Round damaged head with circular-sectioned shaft and incomplete rectangular rove intact.	L. 32mm, W. 25mm, Th. 30mm.
E748:124s	Rivet and rove	Round damaged head with circular-sectioned shaft and relatively large diamond-shaped rove intact.	L. 32mm, W. 20mm, Th. 38mm.
E748:124t	Rivet and rove	Round flat head with circular-sectioned shaft and diamond-shaped rove intact.	L. 31mm, W. 20mm, Th. 24mm.
E748:124u	Rivet and rove	Round flat head with square-sectioned shaft and small diamond-shaped rove intact.	L. 35mm, W. 13mm, Th. 16mm.
E748:124v	Rivet and rove	Round flat head with circular-sectioned shaft and diamond-shaped rove attached.	L. 51mm, W. 18mm, Th. 26mm.
E748:124w	Rivet and rove	Only vestige of head remains probably round, circular shaft and diamond-shaped rove attached.	L. 32mm, W. 16mm, Th. 24mm.
E748:124x	Rivet and rove	Small circular head, circular shaft and diamond-shaped rove intact.	L. 41mm, W. 15mm, Th. 25mm.
E748:124y	Rivet and rove	Domed head with circular-sectioned shaft and damaged diamond-shaped rove.	L. 31mm, W. 19mm, Th. 21mm.
E748:124z	Rivet and rove	Part of circular-sectioned shaft with diamond-shaped rove attached.	L. 25mm, W. 26mm, Th. 23mm.

Find	Type	Description	Measurements
E748:124aa	Rivet and rove	Round head with rectangular-shaped rove or strap fragment immediately underneath head. Shaft rectangular in section, tapered to blunt point.	L. 51mm, W. 19mm, Th. 24mm.
E748:124bb	Rivet	Large flat round head with circular-sectioned shaft, gently tapered to blunt point.	L. 52mm, W. 27mm, Th. 9mm.
E748:124cc	Rivet	Large flat round head with circular-sectioned shaft, gently tapered to blunt point.	L. 58mm, W. 25mm, Th. 9mm.
E748:124dd	Rivet	Flat round head, incomplete, with circular-sectioned shaft, gently tapered to point.	L. 62mm, W. 19mm, Th. 9mm.

CATALOGUE

E296:48506:F2001 (Fig. 4.10:1). CT2: west end wall House 3; Phase 6. Iron nail. Damaged flat head with tapered rectangular-sectioned robust shaft. L. 36mm, W. 23mm, Th. 10mm.

E296:48509:F2015 (Fig. 4.10:2). CT2: deposit; Phase 6. Iron nail. Round head, tapered square-sectioned shaft corrosion products adhering. L. 34mm, W. 21mm, Th. 13mm.

E296:48510:F2016 (Fig. 4.10:3). CT2: House 2 deposit; Phase 5. Iron nail. Small round flat head tapered rectangular shaft, complete. L. 40mm, W. 12mm, Th. 5mm.

E296:48519:F2028 (Fig. 4.10:4). CT2: House 2 deposit; Phase 5. Iron nail. Flat round head with tapered rectangular shaft, damaged but complete. L. 35mm, W. 15mm, Th. 6mm.

E296:48538:F2047 (Fig. 4.10:5). CT2: House 1 deposit; Phase 3. Iron nail. Round flat, tapered incomplete rectangular-sectioned shaft. L. 22mm, W. 18mm, Th. 5mm.

E296:48543:F2050 (Fig. 4.10:6). CT2: fill deposit of Pit 4a; Phase 4a. Iron nail. Flat sub-square-headed nail with rectangular shaft, tapered to tip. L. 53mm, W. 19mm, Th. 9mm.

E296:48555:F2062 (Fig. 4.10:7). CT2: fill deposit of Pit 4a; Phase 4a. Iron nail. Large round flat head tapered rectangular shaft, complete. L. 68mm, W. 25mm, Th. 10mm.

E296:48572:F2076 (Fig. 4.10:8). CT2: wattle lining of Pit 4a; Phase 4a. Iron nail. Small round flat head tapered rectangular shaft, complete. L. 40mm, W. 13mm, Th. 3mm.

E324:12983:F401 (Fig. 4.10:9). PT1: FW2 deposit of clay and timber bank; Phase 2. Iron nail. Nail head, flat round head of nail, vestige of shaft remains. L. 12mm, W. 17mm, Th. 9mm.

E748:79. CB: east end of the cutting *c.* 0.15m under level of Hearth 3 (House III) in occupation debris; Phase C. Iron nail. Small round head and narrow tapered rectangular shaft, complete. L. 33mm, W. 12mm, Th. 4mm.

E748:93. CB: metalworking layer; Phase C. Iron nail. Shaft, vestige of circular head visible at one end of rectangular bar. L. 38mm, W. 9mm, Th. 7mm.

E748:96a. CB: metalworking layer; Phase C. Iron nail. Rectangular tapered shaft, stone accreted to tip, and no head. L. 58mm, W. 7mm, Th. 6mm.

E748:96b. CB: metalworking layer; Phase C. Iron nail. Narrow tapered rectangular shaft, head and point missing. L. 34mm, W. 5mm, Th. 3mm.

E748:96c. CB: metalworking layer; Phase C. Iron nail. Narrow tapered rectangular shaft, head missing. L. 46mm, W. 6mm, Th. 4mm.

E748:122a. CB: under pathway; Phase C. Iron nail. Small round-headed nail with tapered rectangular-sectioned shaft. L. 39mm, W. 11mm, Th. 5mm.

E748:32. CB: Hearth 3 (House III) level, inside east end wall of the house; Phase D. Iron nail. Small round head and tapered rectangular shaft, tip missing. L. 36mm, W. 14mm, Th. 6mm.

E748:36. CB: occupation debris under floor west of Hearth 3 (House III); Phase D. Iron nail. Large round flat head and tapered rectangular shaft, complete. L. 57mm, W. 23mm, Th. 8mm.

E748:43. CB: occupation debris under floor west of Hearth 3 (House III); Phase D. Iron nail. Flat round-headed nail with tapered rectangular shaft, tip missing. Diam. 15mm, L. 42mm, W. 9mm.

E748:62. CB: near pit (F38) containing 'sling stones', House III level; Phase D. Iron nail. Round flat head, tapered rectangular shaft. L. 19mm, W. 9mm, Th. 5mm.

E748:65. CB: east end of trench, same level as Hearth 3 (House III); Phase D. Iron nail. Tapered shaft, rectangular cross-section, head and tip missing. L. 48mm, W. 7mm, Th. 6mm.

E748:25. CB: *c.* 0.91m below formation level, Phase E. Iron nail. Large round flat head and tapered rectangular shaft complete. L. 74mm, W. 20mm, Th. 6mm.

E296:48571:F2076 (Fig. 4.10:10). CT2: wattle lining of Pit 4a; Phase 4a. Iron rivet and rove. Small round-headed rivet with sub-rectangular-sectioned shaft and rectangular rove *in situ*. L. 33mm, W. 27mm, Th. 19mm.

E748:122b. CB: under pathway; Phase C. Iron rivet. Iron. Partial round flat head with sub-square straight shaft; no rove survives but terminal is hammered. L. 36mm, W. 20mm, 9mm.

E748:123. CB: east end of cutting, *c.* 0.6m below top of pavement: Phase C. Iron rivet and rove. Round head, surface missing with short sub-circular shaft with rectangular rove in place. L. 31mm, W. 32mm, Th. 12mm.

E748:125. CB: south-east corner of cutting outside pathway in occupation debris; Phase D. Iron rivet. Large round slightly domed head with square shaft and partial remains of diamond-shaped rove. L. 40mm, W. 23mm, Th. 23mm.

E748:46. CB: Hearth 3 (House III) level; Phase D. Iron rivet and rove. Round head with short sub-circular shaft with rectangular rove in place. L. 31mm, W. 19mm, Th. 19.

E748:97b. CB: metalworking layer; Phase C. Iron strap hinge. Flat rectangular strap expanded at one end with round-headed rivet with rectangular truncated shaft *in situ*. L. 52mm, W. 29mm, Th. 10mm.

E748:101. CB: *c.* 76mm under burnt layer; Phase C. Iron strap hinge. Rectangular flat strap with crescent-shaped half rivet hole at one end, opposite end broken. L. 105mm, W. 25mm, Th. 3mm.

E748:91 (Pl. 4.13:2). CB: metalworking layer; Phase C. Iron wall hook. Pointed bar with rectangular cross-section with a small hook projecting from beyond the shank. L. 47mm, W. 11mm, Th. 5mm.

Tools (Pl. 4.13:1 and 3)

There are four awls in the assemblage, all recovered from the Cross Block (E748:3; E748:124ee; E748:124gg and E748:124ff). These tools were used in leatherworking, and there are many different forms according to their specific task. The working ends may have either round, square or diamond-shaped sections, depending on the type of hole required and the stitch to be used (Goodall 2011, 68). They normally taper at either end, and all awls would have had square or diamond-sectioned tangs, to prevent the tool turning in the handle. Three of the awls come from the same stratigraphic level, among the timbers of a pathway belonging to Phase D (*c.* early eleventh century), which also contained many nails and rivets. The longest example (E748:124ee) is over 100mm long, has a sub-square-sectioned tang and the body of the awl is rounded in section (Pl. 4.13:3). Another example from that context (E748:124ff) is tapered at both ends, both of which are diamond-shaped in cross-section. The third example from that context (E748:124gg) is a tapered rectangular bar with one end incomplete. The occurrence of three awls from a single context may indicate a leatherworking craftsman in the location. Another awl (E748:3) has an elongated square-sectioned tang, with a shorter circular-sectioned blade. There are five such awls, with one arm with round cross-section and the other rectangular, from Anglo-Saxon levels in York (Ottaway 1992, 554).

An unusual object is also likely to be a tool of the leatherworking trade. It is an incomplete creaser (E748:97a), a tanged tool originally bifurcated into two 'tipper arms'. It was recovered from a mid to late tenth-century context at the Cross Block. Similar but complete examples are known from Anglo-Saxon levels in Coppergate, York (Ottaway 1992, 555). Creasers were 'used to finish the outer edge of leather goods such as straps, compressing the edge to harden it and enable it to resist wear, and in doing so, embellishing the leather with a slightly darker, shiny line. It was also used to imprint a line as a guide or shallow channel for sewing' (Goodall 1990d, 249).

There is a single punch from the Cross Block (E748:92). This is a mason's punch, rectangular in section and tapered to a damaged or missing terminal. The wider end is flattened by hammer action. Such a punch would have been used for the dressing of stone into its final shape.

A well-preserved file (E748:98) has a short rectangular tang and the long rectangular-sectioned body of the tool retains the worn teeth of the file (Pl.4.13:1). The teeth appear closely set and this would indicate its use in metalworking (Goodall 2011, 11), which would be consistent with its recovery from the metalworking level at the Cross Block.

Pl. 4.13 Iron file (1); wall hook (2); leatherworking awl (3).

A robust wedge-shaped object (E748:99a –c), although in a poor state of preservation and in three pieces, may have functioned as a wood splitting aid. The object is rectangular and tapered to a blunt point. Usually wedges for wood felling or splitting have a chisel-like terminal, as the desired objective was to split the timber, not to become embedded in it. As such, the identification as a wedge is not definite. A trapezoidal-shaped wedge was recovered by metal-detecting from the Viking-age site at Woodstown, Co. Waterford (Scully 2014, 139).

CATALOGUE

E748:124ee (Pl. 4.13:3). CB: in timbers of pathway; Phase D. Iron leatherworking awl. Long shaft tapered to point with sub-square cross-section becoming rounded halfway along its length; sloped flat terminal at wider end. L. 101mm, W. 6mm, Th. 5mm.

E748:124gg. CB: in timbers of pathway; Phase D. Iron leatherworking awl. Iron. Square-sectioned bar, tapered, unevenly, at both ends, one for hafting (this end broken), the other pointed for boring, crisply defined edges. L. 42mm, W. 5mm, Th. 5mm.

E748:124ff. CB: in timbers of pathway; Phase D. Iron leatherworking awl. Diamond-sectioned bar, tapered at both ends, one for hafting, the other for boring. L. 52mm, W. 6mm, Th. 5mm.

E748:3. CB: *c.* 0.3–0.45m below formation level at western end of the trench; Phase G. Iron leatherworking awl. Straight with long rectangular tang, with circular-sectioned shorter working end, with blunt tip. L. 76mm, W. 5mm, Th. 4mm.

E748:97a. CB: metalworking layer; Phase C. Iron leatherworking creaser? Iron. Originally double-armed with point of break evident, flat rectangular tipper arm with tapered rectangular-sectioned tang. L. 104mm, W. 10mm, Th. 6mm.

E748:92. CB: metalworking layer; Phase C. Iron punch. Rectangular robust gently tapered bar with flattened burred head, tip damaged. L. 56mm, W. 8mm, Th. 5mm.

E748:98 (Pl. 4.13:1). CB: metalworking layer; Phase C. Iron file. Rectangular bar tapered at either end, one of which is a tang; the body of the tool has a scored textured surface on all four sides. L. 137mm, W. 8mm, Th. 6mm.

E748:99a–c. CB: metalworking layer; Phase C. Iron probable wedge fragment. Wedge-shaped short robust tapered bar, corroded and flaking, in three parts: (a) L. 53mm, W. 19mm, Th. 13mm; (b) tapered piece of wedge: L. 41mm, W. 16mm, Th. 9mm; (c) tapered rectangular tip: L. 27mm, W. 13mm, Th. 8mm.

Weapons and Shackle (Fig. 4.11; Pls 4.14:1–3, 4.15)

Weaponry is represented in the assemblage by three arrowheads recovered from the Cross Block and a spearhead found at the Cork Tower. One of the two arrowheads (E748:5) has a miniature blade and a very long shaft relative to the size of the blade (Pl. 4.14:1). These are classified as Type 5 arrowheads and may have functioned as incendiary devices (Halpin 2008). Flammable material was wrapped around the iron stem and ignited before the arrow was discharged; the 'long, solid stem effectively replaces the wooden shaft for some 100–300mm below the blade' (*ibid.*, 115). There are eleven known examples from Dublin and both tanged and socketed examples are represented (*ibid.*, 111). The arrowhead from Dublin Castle is broken at the terminal, so its method of hafting is unknown. Comparable examples were found in Viking-age levels at Christchurch Place, and the majority of Type 5 arrowheads have been recovered from contexts dating to between the middle of the tenth century and the end of the twelfth century (*ibid.*, 112).

The second arrowhead from the Cross Block is a tanged elongated leaf-shaped blade (E748:88) with midrib, and sloped shoulders (Pl. 4.14:2). The blade has a rectangular-sectioned tang and is a well-preserved example of Halpin's Type 1 projectile head in which the blade and tang are separated by a short, concave stem or 'stopper' (Halpin 2008, 81). The third example is also a Type 1 tanged arrowhead (E748: 89) but it has a more curved entry and run (Pl. 4.14:3). This also has a stem between the blade and the tang. The presence of this stem, or 'stopper', between the tang and the blade 'seems to have been designed to prevent the arrowhead splitting the shaft on impact' (Harrison and Ó Floinn 2014, 130). The function of arrowheads is determined by the blade width, with broad blades of 18mm or more deemed to be hunting arrows, and those blades less than 14mm wide thought to have been used to pierce armour. The example from Dublin Castle is 17mm wide and probably had a military function.

An iron shouldered spearhead (E296:48516:F2024) was recovered from a late tenth/early eleventh-century level at the Cork Tower (Fig. 4.11). The spear blade was complete, having a central rib and gently sloping narrow rounded shoulders, set close to the socket neck. The tang of the spear is missing but was probably socketed. After arrowheads, spearheads were the next most common weapon type found in settlement type assemblages in Hiberno-Norse Dublin and Waterford (Halpin 2010, 127-8). Spears were used for hunting as well as warfare. They were easier to manufacture than swords and were a prime offensive weapon for short range combat, delivering a heavy piercing blow. Throwing spearheads seem to have been smaller and lighter and most of the known spearheads from Dublin are of this type. 'An emphasis on small, light spears, presumably intended for throwing rather than hand-to-hand combat, is perfectly understandable in the context of medieval Irish warfare which …was characterised by mobility rather than by solidity, and by fast-moving skirmishes rather than pitched battles' (*ibid.*, 128).

Pl. 4.14 Iron arrowheads: Type 5 (1); Type 1 (2, 3).

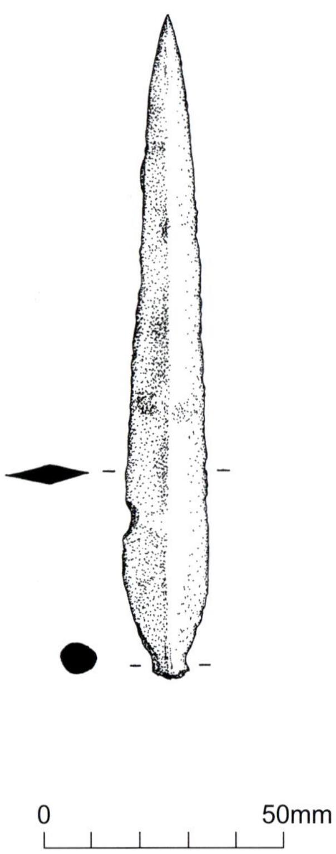

Fig. 4.11 Iron spearhead E296:48516:F2024.

The majority of Dublin spearheads are socketed and since Halpin (2008, 132) calculates that sockets normally account for 30 to 40% of the total length, it is likely that the total length of the Dublin Castle example would have been *c.* 192mm. With a blade length of 134mm, it fits in a grouping of medium- length blades that accounts for about one-third of recorded examples from Dublin, and it also fits into a subgroup of these which have very slender blades. This type of slender-shouldered blade compares well with an example from Fishamble Street (DWP 599, *ibid.*, 133; Wallace 2016, fig. 9.32) which may have come from a tenth-century context, and which conforms to Type VII.2B of Solberg's Norwegian typology of spearheads (Halpin 2008, 136). Other spearheads with slender blades of medium length have been recovered from excavations at Christchurch Place and Fishamble Street and appear to date mostly from the tenth century (*ibid.*).

A similarly shaped spearhead, albeit considerably longer with a blade length of 319mm, was recovered from a Viking burial at Woodstown, Co. Waterford, which probably dates to the second half of the ninth century (Harrison 2014a, 100; 2014b, 161). On the basis of its size, Harrison (2014b, 161) argues that this spearhead is Scandinavian in origin, as contemporary Irish examples are considerably smaller. A second spearhead closer in size to the Dublin Castle example was found in plough soil within the Woodstown enclosure. Another parallel to the Dublin Castle spearhead was recovered from a Viking burial in Kilmainham (Harrison and Ó Floinn 2014, 109). The smaller sizes of the Dublin spears are interpreted as a cultural factor by Halpin, who postulates that the Hiberno-Norse may have adapted to Irish patterns of warfare and Irish weapon standards (Halpin 2010, 128).

The iron shackle (E748:90) recovered from a mid/late tenth-century context at the Cross Block also provides potential evidence for conflict and confinement. The object is not available for study, but some general observations can be made based on an archival black and white photograph (Pl. 4.15). It consists of a rounded open-sided cuff with looped terminals, both of which have looped links attached. The main loop of the shackle has an internal diameter of *c.* 80mm (100mm externally), which is ample for a wrist, but quite small for an ankle. It has one figure-of-eight loop (formed by cinching the loop near its centre) and another shorter loop in the perforate terminals. The shorter link is attached to the partial remains of a second shackle. It compares closely with a Roman iron shackle from Norfolk, comprising a C-shaped bar (Diam.140mm) with loops or 'eyes' at both ends, one broken, the other holding a long curved ovoid loop (British Museum and Amgueddfa Cymru–National Museum of Wales, Record ID: NMS-3924D6). A second example of an almost identical object is also from a Romano-British context at Liverpool Street in

London (Marshall 2018, 15–16; fig. 4). It is described as an iron shackle component, internal diameter 81mm, which 'cannot have been securely attached to a hand or arm but may have been attached to a leg as part of a set of fetters'.

Evidence from seventh-century Lagore Crannog, Co. Meath of a decorated slave collar and a leg iron (Hencken 1950, 116) attests to the practice of slavery or hostage-taking long before the arrival of the Vikings. Wallace (2016, 323) mentions a pair of iron cuffs from Fishamble Street: one with sub-rectangular links in both terminal loops, the other with an elongated barrel padlock, which 'must be regarded as a pair of manacles'. In the same publication, he mentions a 'slave collar' from material bulldozed in Fishamble Street that 'probably ought now [to] be regarded as a hobble for tethering/impeding horses'. The Dublin Castle shackle was found in a domestic setting and was more likely used for securing captives. The taking of slaves was a key component of Viking warfare, and the importance of Dublin as a slave-market is well documented (Holm 1986). A very similar, but complete shackle with its shackle chain and barrel padlock attached was found in Winchester, Hampshire, dating from the late tenth to eleventh-century levels. The object is described as limb shackles (Goodall 2011, 250). The distance between the shackle loops in that example suggests they were used on wrists. The diameter of the shackle loop in the Dublin Castle example also suggests their use as manacles.

CATALOGUE

E748:89 (Pl. 4.14:3). CB: *c.* 3.11m west of east curtain wall, *c.* 1.62m below formation level; Phase C. Tanged leaf-shaped shouldered arrowhead. Small and complete, with curved entry and run, with rectangular-sectioned stop, or stem, terminating in short tang, which is bent. L. 89mm, W. 15mm, Th. 5mm.

E296:48516:F2024 (Fig. 4.11). CT2: House 2 deposit; Phase 5. Shouldered iron spearhead. Complete blade with central rib, tapered to point with gently sloped shoulders, broken at point where blade meets socket which does not survive L. 134mm, W. 18mm, Th. 7mm.

E748:5 (Pl. 4.14:1). CB: *c.* 0.96m below formation level in thin dark layer. Hearth 4 (House IV) level, Phase E. Miniature iron arrowhead. Tiny triangular blade with horizontal shoulders. Blade is flat, with a disproportionately long circular-sectioned shaft which widens slightly towards the terminal, which shows signs of breakage. Almost intact, blade has small nick on one side; an incendiary device. L. 138.5mm, W. 13mm, Th. 5mm.

E748:88 (Pl. 4.14:2). CB: *c.* 3.11m west of the east curtain wall, *c.* 1.57m below formation level; Phase C. Iron tanged broad-blade arrowhead. Tanged arrowhead with elongated leaf-shaped blade with midrib, sloped shoulders tapered to sub-circular which reduces to narrower rectangular tang. L. 131mm, W. 17mm, Th. 7.5mm.

E748:90 (Pl. 4.15). CB: *c.* 0.1m below Hearth 3 (House III) level, near Hearth 3; Phase C. Iron shackles. Item unseen.

Miscellaneous

A thin triangular piece of copper sheet (E296:48544:F2051) was possibly used as a casket mount. The wafer-thin sheet is perforated with round holes. It was probably part of a longer strip used to decorate a casket or even a bucket, as is the case with a highly decorated stave-built bucket from the Viking ship burial at Oseberg, Norway (Holck 2006), which has concentric bands of appliqued copper alloy strips with perforations. A curved rectangular-sectioned iron bar (E296:48553:F2061) is most likely incomplete and as such its function is unknown. Three thin strands of copper wire (E296:50003:F2031), one of which was in two pieces, were recovered from the Cork Tower. Wire was used for a variety of tasks but, given the delicate nature of these lengths of wire, they may have been used in craftwork or in decoration of jewellery.

CATALOGUE

E296:48544:F2051. CT2: deposit; Phase 4a. Copper alloy casket mount. Very thin triangular flat sheet with multiple circular perforations. L. 57mm, W. 15mm, Th. 0.8mm.

E296:48553:F2061. CT2: deposit; Phase 3. Iron bar. Short curved rectangular-sectioned bar. L. 72mm, W. 5mm, Th. 4mm.

E296:50003:F2031. CT2: House 2 deposit; Phase 5 (*c.* late tenth/early eleventh century). Copper alloy wire. Three similar lengths of wire (one in two pieces), all curved to crescent shape. L. 48mm, Diam. 0.4mm.

E748:37. CB: occupation debris under floor west of Hearth 3 (House III); Phase D. Lead off-cut. Rectangular flat blank with slight ridging. L. 36mm, W. 20mm, Th. 3mm.

Pl. 4.15 Iron shackle E748:90.

Chapter 4.4
Stone
Anne Carey, with a contribution by Stephen Mandal

4.4.1
Artefacts
ANNE CAREY

Introduction
Twelve stone artefacts were recovered from Viking-age contexts, comprising five hone stones, one possible hone stone, one rotary whetstone, two stone discs, one gaming piece, a stone lamp and the upper stone of a rotary quern. In addition, a large cache of unworked pebbles was recovered as a single context find at the Cross Block, and the significance of this is discussed. The stone objects were recovered predominantly from the Cork Tower and Cross Block areas with just three items recovered from the Powder Tower. A petrographical analysis of the stone artefacts is included in Chapter 4.4.2 below.

Hones (Fig. 4.12:1–6)
Five hone stones and one possible example were examined. Hone stones were used to sharpen metal implements, resulting in one or more smooth surfaces on the stone. Occasionally scoring or deeper indentations are present resulting from sharpening needles or points. These artefacts are also known as whetstones in the archaeological literature. The Dublin Castle examples were made from a variety of stones: three from metamorphic rocks and one each from limestone, slate and sandstone (see Chapter 4.3.2). A small, finely made hone (E324:915:F277) recovered from the Powder Tower has a perforation at one end; Graham-Campbell has classified such perforated sharpening stones as 'pendant whetstones' (Graham-Campbell 1980, 49–50) and O'Connor called them 'perforated whetstones' (O'Connor 1991, 51). The perforation for suspension suggests that the hone stone was worn and would most likely have been highly prized by its owner. A perforated whetstone from Lagore, Co. Meath was found with a bronze ring through the perforation (*ibid.*, 47). While small, perforated hone stones are uncommon, they are known from Viking-age sites in Ireland, with a fine example coming from the furnished burial at Woodstown, Co. Waterford (Harrison 2014b, 169). Small hones can also have notches at one end allowing the stone to be securely tied (Carey 2014, 316–7). Hone stones are not good chronological indicators, having a wide date range.

CATALOGUE

E324:915:F277 (Fig. 4.12:1). PT2: Area A: fill of Pit F281; Phase 3. Hone, perforated, broadly hourglass-shaped due to wear on all surfaces. Small circular perforation for suspension at one end. A shale water-rolled cobble, L. 52mm, W. 7mm, Th. 4mm.

E296:48517:F2028 (Fig. 4.12:2). CT2: deposit of House 2; Phase 5. Trapezoidal-shaped hone, with an irregularly shaped broader end. Smooth on all surfaces. A water-rolled schist cobble, L. 154mm, W. 30mm, Th. 18mm.

E296:48533:F2045 (Fig. 4.12:3). CT2: deposit; Phase 4a. Hone, triangular in section. Very smooth on one side and with occasional light scoring on other surfaces. A water-rolled limestone cobble, L. 122mm, W. 31mm/33mm/30mm.

E296:48563:F2071 (Fig. 4.12:4). CT2: deposit; Phase 1. Roughly rectangular hone, with unworked ends. There are two working surfaces, comprising one convex smooth broad surface and a very smooth surface on one narrow side, part of which is stained red. The other narrow side and broad surface are rough and unworked. A water-rolled slate cobble, L. 77mm, W. 45mm, Th. 94mm.

E324:11889:F174 (Fig. 4.12:5). PT1: post-bank levelling; Phase 3. Roughly rectangular-shaped hone, with smooth working surfaces on the central part of one broad surface

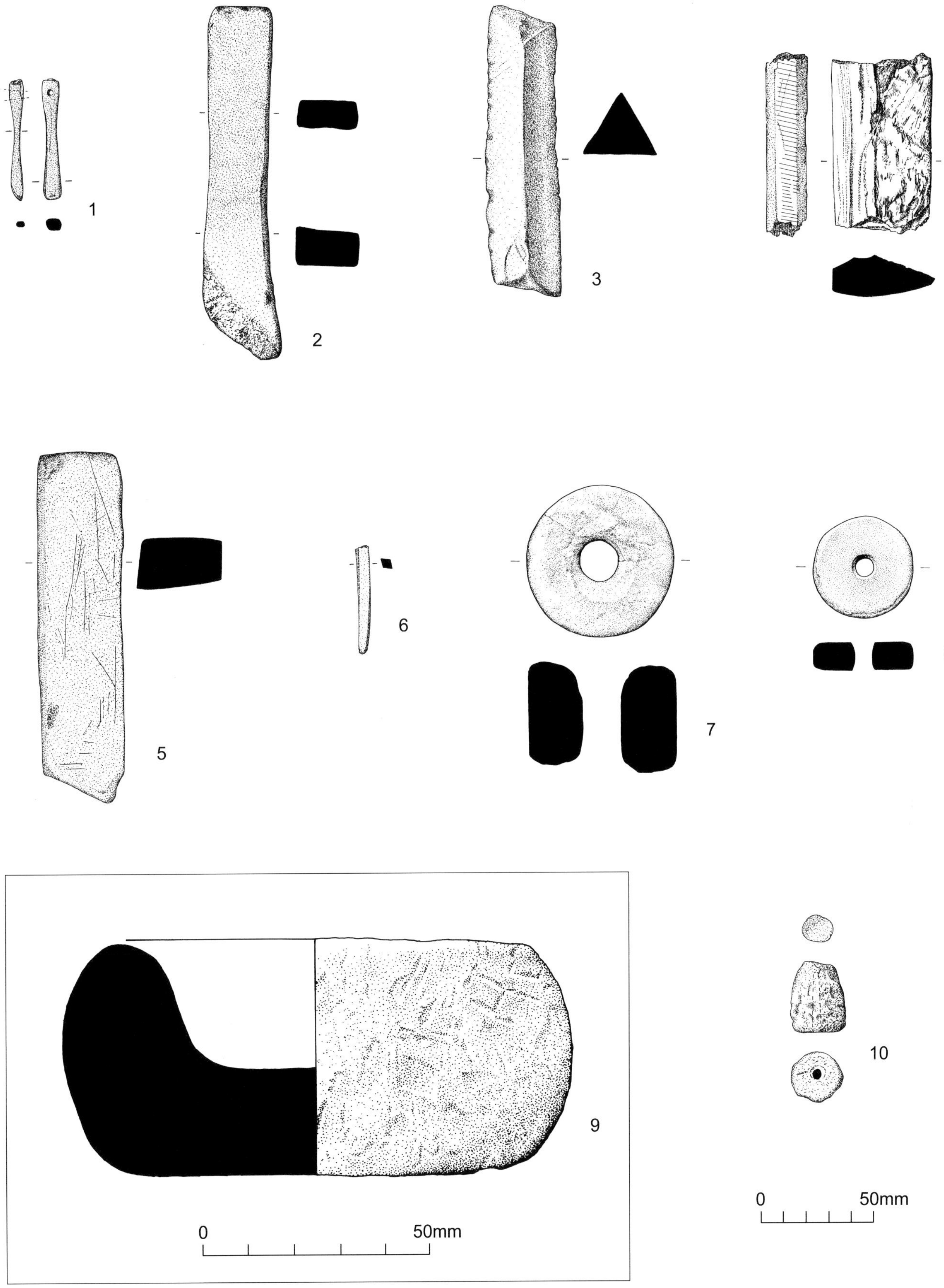

Fig. 4.12 Stone artefacts: hone stones (1-6), rotary whetstone (7), spindle whorl (8), lamp (9), gaming piece (10).

and one narrow side which also has light scoring. The remaining broad surface and narrow side are unworked. A water-rolled sandstone cobble, L. 150mm, W. 34mm, Th. 20mm.

E296:48603:F2036 (Fig. 4.12:6). CT2: fill of Pit 4b; Phase 4b. Small trapezoidal-shaped possible hone. The stone is smooth, which may indicate use. The artefact is likely to be a rough-out of a small hone. There is some discolouration to the final 10mm of the narrow end of the stone. Meta-sediment, L. 46mm, W. 5.5mm, Th. 4mm.

Rotary Whetstone (Fig. 4.12:7)

One complete rotary whetstone was recovered from the Cork Tower area. These small cylindrical artefacts were used to sharpen tools by continuous rotary motion. To achieve this, they are mounted on an apparatus that allows them to rotate, giving their outer edges a characteristic smooth worn appearance. Rotary whetstones have been found in significant numbers on Viking-age sites in Britain and Ireland. At Woodstown, Co. Waterford sixty-two examples were recorded (Carey 2014, 299) and twenty-nine examples were found at Coppergate in York (Mainman and Rodgers 2000, 2479).

E296:48484:F1184 (Fig. 4.12:7). CT2: Phase 4b. Complete cylindrical rotary whetstone with central circular perforation that widens to one surface, that may indicate it was drilled from one side only. The upper and lower surfaces are roughly dressed and the central perforation is worn through use. Sandstone, Diam. 65mm, Diam. central perforation: 25mm, L. 45mm.

Rotary Quern

Roughly half of the upper stone of a rotary quern was excavated at the Cross Block. This object was not available for study but it was drawn on one of the original site plans close to the hearth of House V (Fig. 3.50). It appears to have had a central perforation but no evidence of a handle hole was recorded which would have allowed it to be placed in Caulfield's (1969) classification.

E748:23. CB: between two ash deposits near Hearth 5 (House V); Phase F. Rotary quern. Item unseen. Roughly half of upper stone with central perforation. Diam. *c.* 0.55m.

Stone Discs/Spindle Whorls (Fig. 4.12:8)

Two perforated stone discs were recovered from the Cross Block area. Perforated stone discs can belong to a number of different artefact types, including spindle whorls, loom weights and gaming pieces. The Dublin Castle examples are most likely spindle whorls, which were used in hand spinning to add weight to the wooden spindles which allowed the spindle to keep its spinning momentum (Walton Rogers 1997, 1731). Nine bone examples, seven of which also came from the Cross Block are described in Chapter 4.2 above. The diagnostic features of the stone whorls relate particularly to the weight of the stone and the size of the central perforation. Both Dublin Castle examples conform well to the Form B classification for stone spindle whorls from the 16–22 Coppergate excavations in York, where 78 stone spindle whorls were examined from Anglo-Scandinavian contexts and where the Form B examples dated to between the tenth and twelfth centuries (*ibid.*,1736–41). The Coppergate disc-shaped whorls had weights of between 10g and 55g and the central perforations had a diameter of 9–11mm. Both the Dublin Castle examples have perforation diameters of 10mm and they weigh 35g (E748:64) and 45g (E748:11). Stone spindle whorls from Viking-age Waterford averaged 18.3g in weight, the diameter of the central perforations averaged 8mm and the diameter of the discs averaged 32mm, suggesting slightly smaller examples (McCutcheon 1997, 404).

CATALOGUE

E748:11 (Fig. 4.12:8). CB: layer of occupational debris associated with Hearth 5 (House V); Phase F. Spindle whorl. Finely made stone disc with a smooth-sided central perforation. The upper and lower surfaces are flat and the sides are regular. Sandstone, Diam. 44mm; Diam. of central perforation 10mm, Th. 10mm.

E748:64 (not illustrated). CB: east end of trench at Hearth 3 (House III) level; Phase D. Spindle whorl. Sub-circular stone disc, edge partly damaged. All surfaces are roughly shaped and slightly irregular. There is evidence of burning on one face of the disc. Granite, Diam. 40mm; Diam. of central perforation 10mm, Th. 10mm.

Stone Lamp (Fig. 4.12:9)

Stone lamps are defined by Moore as 'a stone with a cup or reservoir for the liquid fuel and some sort of handle which makes it easy to carry' (Moore 1997, 432). The example recovered from the Cross Block comprises a simple roughly dressed flat-based stone bowl and does not strictly fulfil the definition of a stone lamp due to the absence of a handle, but the internal base and sides have dark staining, indicating burning consistent with its use as a lamp (M. Moore, pers. comm.). It is very similar to two others in the National Museum of Ireland: NMI 1915:65 (unprovenanced) and NMI 1915: 13 from Knocktemple, Co. Wexford (Moore 1977, 78–9, 143, fig. 26, M10 and M11).

E748:18 (Fig. 4.12:9). CB: *c.* 1.11m below formation level, in wood layer of House IV; Phase E. Sub-circular stone lamp with a reservoir with slightly sloping, smooth sides and a flat base. The sides and base of the lamp are roughly dressed.[2] Sandstone, Height 51mm, depth of reservoir 26mm, internal Diam. 72mm, external Diam. 115mm.

Gaming Piece (Fig. 4.12:10)

Games using gaming pieces are widely known since prehistoric times throughout Europe, using a variety of materials including antler, stone and wood. The earliest known gaming piece from Ireland is of Viking date (Hurley 1997b, 666) and gaming boards, such as the remarkable wooden gaming board from Ballinderry 1, have been extensively studied (Graham Campbell 1980, 23). The particular setting of peg-holes on the boards and the prevalence of gaming pieces with peg-holes on their flat bases are consistent with games of the *tafl* group (Simpson, 1972, 64). The stone gaming piece recovered from the Powder Tower has a peg-hole in the base and is shaped but not decorated. Its shape is similar to the two antler gaming pieces from the Cork Tower and described above (Chapter 4.2) as 'truncated acorn' in form. A third more bulbous form in walrus bone was also recovered from the Powder Tower. It is likely that all the Dublin Castle pieces had central pegs for use on a pegged board perhaps similar to an incomplete wooden board found at Christchurch Place and the fragments of pegged boards made from walrus bone from High Street and Winetavern Street (Chapter 4.2 above).

E324:2928:F248 (Fig. 4.12:10). PT2 – Area A: deposit; Phase 7. Gaming piece. A roughly cylindrical gaming piece, narrower at the top than at the base. There is a centrally placed perforation (6mm in width) in the flat base and a smooth, slightly curving top to the piece. The sides are roughly shaped with pecking marks in evidence. There is a small depression in one of the sides which may be natural. Possible metasedimentary stone, Diam. 23mm, L. 32mm.

Stone Pebbles

INTRODUCTION

A cache of 333 stones was found at the Cross Block and were classified by the excavator as 'sling stones'. The stones were clustered on the floor of House III *c.*1.6m east of Hearth 3 (Fig. 3.48), but there is no information on the nature of the deposition, whether the stones were highly mixed or stratified, or if they were placed in a pit or were simply sitting on the house floor (see Chapter 3.5).

HISTORICAL CONTEXT

The excavator, Marcus Ó hEochaidhe (1962, fig. 4), described these stones as 'sling stones'. While the history of slings has been described as 'frustratingly hard to trace' due to the perishable nature of the organic material the sling would have been made from, the use of slings and sling stones is known throughout the world, from the earliest times (York and York 2011, 5). There are many references to the sling in the Bible (Sellers 1939, 41), the best-known being David felling Goliath with a sling shot and the sling is also widely referenced in the Classical world (Vigors 1888). Slings were thought to have four main functions: as weapons of war, as hunting tools, to scare scavengers and as toys (Lindblom 1940, 5). The most important feature of a sling stone was its weight, with an optimum weight range of between 28g and just under 1kg (Seager-Thomas 2013). They were made using natural or lightly modified spherical or sub-spherical stones, with bi-conical stones being prevalent in prehistory (York and York 2011, 10). In their wide-ranging study of slings and sling stones, York and York state that the bi-conical sling stone is 'the only design that we can place with some confidence as definitive for sling missiles', with stones having spheroidal or sub-spheroidal shape possibly used as hand-hurled missiles (*ibid.*).

The practice of identifying spheroidal or sub-spheroidal stones from excavated contexts as sling stones was widespread in excavations in southern England, based on an assumption that caches of well-sorted beach pebbles, particularly if they were outside their natural distribution, were most likely used for defensive purposes (Seager-Thomas 2013, 1). A large quantity of stones that were identified by the excavators as sling stones were found at the Iron Age hillforts of Maiden Castle, Dorset, Danebury, Hampshire and Caburn, East Sussex. A reanalysis of some of these sites has cast doubt on this classification, with the suggestion that, in the absence of evidence, the interpretation of these stones should be left open (*ibid.*, 12).

2 Photographs of the lamp, showing the exterior markings in detail, were sent to Professor Michael Barnes to determine whether any of the numerous tool marks could be interpreted as Viking runes. Nothing could be identified as runic for certain, although one or two lines are suggestive of runic shapes, but these could well be chance. Professor Barnes concluded that there is nothing that can be woven into a runic text and certainly nothing meaningful on the exterior surface area of the lamp.

SLING STONES IN IRELAND

Early literary references to the sling in Ireland can be found in the *Táin Bó Cúailnge*, where the skill of Cúchulainn is shown through his accuracy with the sling (O'Rahilly 1967). The *Aided Meidbe*, also from the Book of Leinster, tells of the death of Medb (Maeve) by a slingshot (Hull 1938, 61).

A review of the literature in Ireland shows the classification of finds as 'sling stones' was favoured particularly in the nineteenth century to explain the presence of small stones on archaeological sites. Sir William Wilde described small stones in the upper portion of the cairn at Dowth, Co. Meath, as 'sling stones' (Cooke 1903, 96), Walter Bernard described finding 'sling stones' on the Grianán of Aileach, Co. Donegal (Bernard 1879) and E.A. Conwell, excavating in Loughcrew, Co. Meath in 1864, discovered 'sling stones' in Carin V (Conwell 1866, 374). Vigors, writing in 1888, said the use of the sling in Ireland was 'well established' but he was cautious on this point due to the lack of finds from Irish sites. He described two sites at which sling stones were found (a rath at Dunbell Big, Co. Kilkenny, and a crannog at Drumdarragh, Co. Fermanagh) but he also noted the existence of a metal mould, possible for clay sling-shot, in the Royal Irish Academy Museum (now the National Museum of Ireland) (Vigors 1888, 360–1). He quotes a description (probably by W.F. Wakeman) of the finds at the crannog in Drumdarragh townland as being 'from the size of an orange to a moderately-sized plum, some formed by art, others merely water-worn pebbles' (*ibid.*, 361). O'Curry gave the first detailed classification of slings in his series of lectures published in 1873 as 'On the Manners and Customs of the Ancient Irish', describing two types of sling used in Ireland. The first is the more common type, the *Deil Clis*, comprising two leather thongs joined to a piece of leather to hold the stone. The second type was a *crann-tabaill*, or a 'wood sling', using a long rod or staff of wood with one thong (O'Curry and Sullivan 1873, Vol. 1, 456–60). These classifications were described by Joyce in 1906, but he calls the *Deil Clis* the *teilm* and *taball* and he notes 'numerous' sling stones, 'many perfectly round' were found in raths and crannogs (Joyce 1906). In an article published in 1906, Power notes that sling stones found with 'stone chalices' at the site of an early medieval church in Decoy, Co. Tipperary (Power 1906, 146–7). Power wrote more extensively on the sling and sling stones in 1915, describing different types of sling and citing examples from Swiss lake dwellings as well as Egyptian and Roman examples (Power 1915, 119). Four specimens were found at Armagh (Emania), Budore and Rathmore, both in Co. Antrim (Bigger 1925). A further reference in the 1960s stated that the sling was familiar from archaeological contexts in the Iron Age (Jackson 2011, 32).

Despite the wealth of literary references, the evidence for slings from archaeological contexts in Ireland is limited to a small number of examples. There are three leather artefacts from Fishamble Street (E180:7033, E190:6006 and E190:7007) tentatively identified by Halpin as slings of the *crann tamall* type (Mould *et al.* 2003, 3409–10). There have been no independent studies of sling stones on excavated sites and the use of the term 'sling stone' to describe natural or curated stone pebbles from archaeological sites appears to have fallen out of use from the mid-twentieth century onwards. The term is not currently used by the National Museum of Ireland unless the finds are associated with a known battle site or a castle (Sharon Weadick, NMI, pers. comm.). The National Museum has a record of four sling shots, three of which were sourced by Sir William Wilde and are unprovenanced, the other from a lakebed in Mahanagh townland, Co. Leitrim, acquired in 1945.

The term 'stone balls' is used by the National Museum to describe pebble- or cobble-sized stones, of either natural or altered type, from archaeological contexts. While this classification could potentially include stones for use in slings, the majority of these finds in the Museum are stone balls of Neolithic date. Three stone balls are included in the finds catalogue from the excavations of the late Bronze Age hillfort, Dún Aonghasa on Inis Mór, Aran Islands, Co. Galway, all of which were sub-spherical and were probably deliberately shaped (Cotter 2013, 104).

A review of early medieval sites excavated in the period 1930–2004 was carried out by the Early Medieval Archaeology Project (EMAP) and their report did not include any references to stone ammunition (O'Sullivan *et al.* 2014). These sites included ringforts and crannogs, which were seen by antiquarians of the nineteenth century as the most productive in terms of sling stones.

THE DUBLIN CASTLE PEBBLES (PL. 4.16)

The 333 pebbles are rounded due to water rolling and comprise two main lithologies, coarse-grained granite and fine-grained limestone with small amounts of sandstone and mudstone; they do not exhibit any signs of wear (see Chapter 4.4.2 below). The slightly more numerous fine-grained pebbles range in size from 30mm x 25mm x10mm to 57mm x 50mm x30mm. The smallest stone weighs 17g, the largest 157g. The coarse-grained examples range in size from 30mm x 23mm wide x15mm deep to 60x 35mm x30mm. The stones have a weight range of between 23g and 187g.

Pl. 4.16 Pebbles E748:2501-2833 from House III, Cross Block. (left) 147 coarse-grained granite stones; (right) 186 fine-grained limestone / sandstone stones.

The pebbles were stockpiled in the centre of House III, with the plan showing a circular arrangement of unknown depth (Fig. 3.48). Given the domestic context of the pebbles, it is unlikely that they were used as sling stones. It is, however, difficult to assign a function to them. It is clear that they were curated but uniform sizes were not chosen, and the stones were not altered beyond their natural appearance.

E748:2501–2833 (Fig. 3.48; Pl. 4.16). CB: in tightly packed circular cluster, Diam. 0.4m, near Hearth 3 (House III) level; Phase D. The stones comprise 147 coarse-grained granite pebbles and 186 fine-grained limestone/sandstone water rolled pebbles. The collection largely comprises irregularly shaped pebbles, roughly ovoid or elongated oval in shape. Thirteen of the stones are coarse-grained pebbles with a more regular appearance than the others but this may be due to natural weathering. None of the stones have evidence of wear.

4.4.2 Petrographical analysis

STEPHEN MANDAL

Introduction

This report is based on the macroscopic (hand specimen) examination of stone objects found during archaeological excavations undertaken at Dublin Castle. The objects consist of six hone stones, a rotary whetstone, two spindle whorls, a perforated stone (gaming piece) and a stone lamp.

A visual inspection of the 'sling stones' (E748:2501–2833) was also undertaken as part of the analysis.

The purpose of the study was to identify the rock types from which the stone objects were made, to highlight potential sources for them, and to comment on their possible function. It is important to note that macroscopic petrographical studies have been considered of limited value in comparison to microscopic (thin section and geochemical analysis) studies. On the other hand, macroscopic studies provide an excellent preliminary assessment tool and have proven to be of considerable value in petrographical studies (e.g. Mandal 1997; Cooney and Mandal 1998).

Solid Geology Glacial Tills And Soils Of The Site

The bedrock underlying the site at Dublin Castle is Carboniferous Age limestone, known as the Lucan Formation. This is part of a large expanse of limestone which was deposited about 340 million years ago in a deep marine basin. The Lucan Formation, which comprises dark limestones and shale and is known as calp, is bounded to the south by the Dublin/Wicklow mountains, but extends as far west as Loughrea, Co. Galway and as far north as Navan, Co. Meath (for a more detailed description of the Lucan Formation, see Marchant and Sevastopulo 1980).

Dublin city is extensively urbanised and the River Liffey has had quay walls in place since the 1850s, such that bedrock, glacial tills and soils are not exposed. However, in medieval times the glacial tills as shown in Fig. 4.13 would have been close to the surface and exposed in places. Limestone bedrock may also have been exposed in places close to the river. On the north side of the river and in patches to the west of the site, glacial deposits consist of till derived from the underlying limestone bedrock. Gravels, also derived from the underlying limestone, occur to the south of the site and in a lens to the north of the river opposite the site. There are abundant patches of alluvium on either side of the river and running parallel to its course.

Results

(See Table 4.5 for detailed petrographical and function identifications)

HONES

The assemblage includes five hone stones and a possible hone. Three are made from metamorphic rocks (E296:48517:F2028–schist; E296:48563:F2071–slate; E296:48603: F2036–meta-sediment), the remaining three from limestone (E296:48533:F2045), shale (E324:915:F277) and sandstone (E324:11889:F174). Five are made from water-rolled cobbles and exhibit evidence of wear, consistent with having been used as a hone (E296:45817:F2028; E296:48533:F2045; E296:48563:F2071; E324:915:F277 and E324:11889:F174). Hone E324:915:F277 has been perforated at one end, indicating it may have (also) served as a pendant.

Hone E296:48603:F2036 is unusual, both in rock type (some sort of meta-sediment) and in shape, comprising a thin sliver of stone with flat sides that appear natural. It is square in cross-section, tapering to a point. The faces are worn with a sheen consistent with rubbing with an iron blade. It is very small to have been used as a hone but does appear to have had some sort of sharpening function.

ROTARY WHETSTONE

There is one grinding stone (E296:48484:F1184), made from grey, medium-grained, micaceous sandstone. It appears to have been modified from an elongate water-rolled cobble, with both ends broken off and a perforation added. The ends are uneven and rough. The circumference is ground but contains subtle parallel grooves at an angle of *c.* 30 degrees to the vertical.

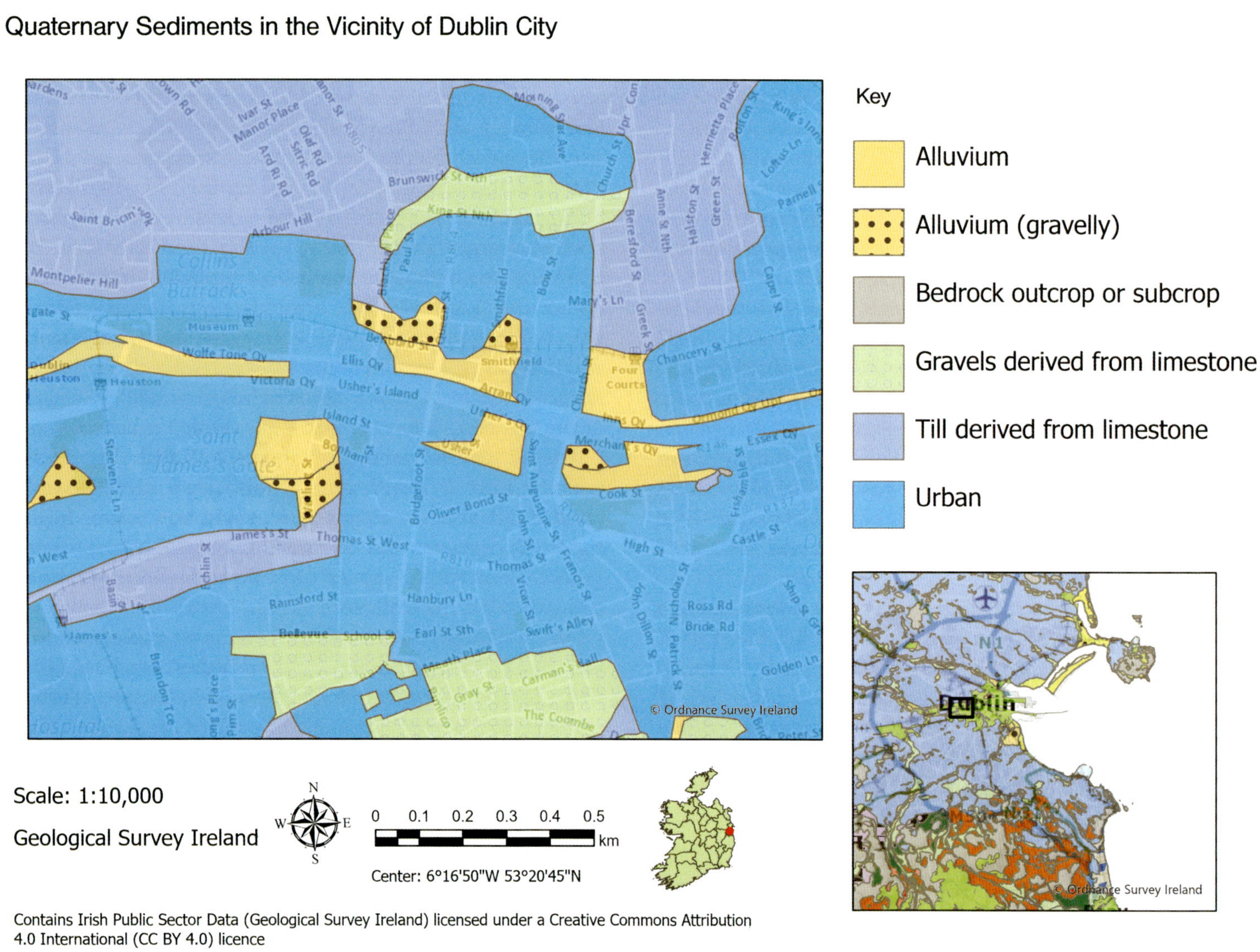

Fig. 4.13 Quaternary sediments in the vicinity of Dublin Castle (Geological Survey Ireland).

Table 4.5 Petrographical identifications of stone finds.

Find No	Rock type	Description	Artefact type	Observations
E748:11	Sandstone	Dark grey, fine-grained, thin parallel bedded, micaceous sandstone	Spindle whorl	Made from modified cobble. Circumference appears natural. Faces are natural bedding planes. Perforated. Appears burned.
E748:18	Sandstone	Green greywacke	Lamp	Modified from flat water-rolled cobble. Lower and upper faces are bedding planes, laminae visible on sides. Circumference extensively marked with thin vertical grooves which appear random. There is a deep concave hole in the top giving the object a bowl-like appearance. It is stained black (charcoal) on the inside, with some patches on the outer sides. The base has been damaged.
E748:64	Granite(?)	Banded, meta-granitic (difficult to identify due to weathering)	Spindle whorl	Possibly a modified cobble. Circumference appears natural. Faces are flat. Perforated. Appears to be burned, especially on one face.
E296:48517:F2028	Schist	Dark green grey fine-grained mica schist	Hone	Modified from water-rolled cobble. Natural with rectangular cross section/flat sides and faces. Both sides and both faces are very smooth but there are no obvious grinding striations. This is consistent with use as a hone stone rather than a grinding/sharpening stone.
E296:48484:F1184	Sandstone	Grey, medium-grained, micaceous	Rotary whetstone	Probably a modified elongate water rolled cobble, with both ends broken off and a perforation added. The ends are uneven and rough. The circumference is ground but contains subtle parallel grooves at an angle of *c.* 30° to the vertical.
E296:48533:F2045	Limestone	Dark grey	Hone	Fortuitous (natural) triangular in section, with flat faces. The edges are highly chipped. One face is considerably smoother than the other two, consistent with use as a hone stone.
E296:48563:F2071	Slate	Dark green/grey, micaceous	Hone	Modified broken cobble. Elongate, both ends broken off. Upper face is worn. One side is worn to a facet with unusual red staining (which is a stain as opposed to weathering).
E296:48603:F2036	Meta-sediment (?)	Dark grey green, fine-grained, dense meta-sediment (difficult to identify due to wear / weathering)	Hone, possible	Sliver of stone with natural flat sides. Square in cross-section, tapering to a point. Faces are worn with a sheen consistent with rubbing with an iron blade. However, this is very small to have been used as a hone.
E324:915:F277	Shale	Dark grey, fine-grained, parallel laminated	Hone, perforated (pendant)	Modified water-rolled cobble with perforation at one end. Waisted due to use as a hone.
E324:11889:F174	Sandstone	Fine-grained greywacke sandstone	Hone	Cleaved cobble with flat sides, faces and ends. Bottom face and one side are rough. Top face and other side are smooth, consistent with use as a hone. Lots of random fine scratch marks.
E324:2928:F248	Meta-sediment (?)	Chalky textured meta-sediment (difficult to identify due to weathering)	Gaming stone	Thimble-shaped stone, which has been weathered.
E748:2501–2833	Limestone (48%) Granite (46%) Sandstone (6%)	Fine-grained, grey Coarse Fine-grained, red/grey	'Sling stones'	Water-rolled pebbles of fine-grained limestone and sandstone, and coarse-grained granite.

SPINDLE WHORLS

The assemblage includes two spindle whorls. E748:11 has been made from a modified cobble of dark grey, fine-grained, thin parallel-bedded, micaceous sandstone. Its circumference appears natural and its faces are natural bedding planes. It has a perforation and appears burned. E748:64 also appears to have been made from a modified small cobble, of what appears to be a banded meta-granite (it is difficult to identify reliably due to surface weathering). As with E748:11, the circumference appears natural and it is perforated and has been burned. The faces are flat.

GAMING PIECE

The assemblage includes a partially perforated stone (E324:2928:F248), made from what appears to be a chalky textured meta-sedimentary rock (identification was difficult due to extensive weathering).

STONE LAMP

The assemblage includes a green greywacke sandstone lamp (E748:18), which has been modified from a flat water-rolled cobble. The lower and upper faces are bedding planes, with laminae visible on sides. It is stained black on the inside, with some patches on the exterior.

STONE PEBBLES

The assemblage of stone pebbles as described above comprises two main lithologies, granite and limestone, with lesser amounts of fine-grained sandstone and mudstone. They have been rounded due to water-rolling and are remarkably consistent in size and weight.

Potential Sources And Conclusions

The only widely available local source is limestone – the bedrock in the area and the stone dominating the local glacial deposits. Hone E296:48533:F2045 is made from such material, as are over half of the possible sling shots.

With the exception of the spindle whorl (E748:64), hone (E296:48603:F2036) and gaming piece (E324:2928:F248) (see below), it is likely that the sources for the remaining stones are derived from riverine deposits associated with the River Liffey, or from the glacial tills/sub-soils to the south of the site. There are abundant sources for sandstone, slate and schist in the southern part of County Dublin (and into County Wicklow). The Silurian sedimentary rocks and their metamorphic counterparts relating to the Leinster Granite and Ordovician volcanics that occur in south Dublin and Wicklow contain widespread rocks of these descriptions.

The choice of sandstone, schist and meta-sediments for the manufacture of grinding and sharpening tools is typical. These coarse-grained rock types are relatively hard rock types with good erosive qualities. Because they are relatively soft rocks, it is unusual (but not unprecedented) for limestone and slate to be used as a material for making hones.

It is possible that the three objects – spindle whorl E748:64 made from meta-granite (?), hone E296:48603:F2036 and gaming piece E324:2928:F248 made from meta-sediments (?) – are exotic, as they are certainly of unusual lithology. However, they are badly weathered and detailed microscopic analysis would be unlikely to identify exact sources.

In conclusion, it is not possible to determine a definitive source for these objects based on macroscopic examination alone. It can be stated that the materials from which the majority of these objects were manufactured are available within the glacial tills of the wider area. Thus, it is probable that these objects derived from these sources. It is also possible to say, in particular in the case of the possible sling shots, that the non-local stones such as granite and meta-sediments were deliberately selected for their geological properties, be it density or abrasive qualities.

Chapter 4.5
Flint lithics
Siobhán Scully

Introduction
Seven lithic artefacts were recovered from Viking-age contexts in the Cork Tower, Powder Tower and Cross Block areas. All of the artefacts are of flint and include a core, a side scraper, an awl/borer, a retouched blade, a possible retouched flake and two pieces of debitage. The terminology used in this report is after Andrefsky (1998) and Woodman *et al.* (2006).

Raw Materials
The colour of flint can vary due to the different minerals that the flint may have absorbed (Dillon 1997, 33). The flint from Dublin Castle has variations of grey and brown. The cortex is the outer layer of the flint that has formed through chemical and weathering processes. The amount of cortex remaining on the dorsal side can be used to indicate the reduction stage of a tool (Andrefsky 1998, 101). Flakes are expressed as being primary (100% cortical cover), secondary (100%>x>0% cortical cover) or tertiary (0% cortical cover). Four of the flint artefacts from Dublin Castle can be described as secondary with some cortical cover and three are tertiary with no cortical cover. There are no primary flakes. Two of the flint artefacts are fresh, four are weathered, although one of these (E324:12986:F401) may have been heat-affected, and one (E296:48549:F2056) is possibly burnt.

Technology
Only three of the flint artefacts from Dublin Castle have features which indicate the technology used to remove flakes, in the case of the amorphous core (E324:13400:F530), or to produce them, in the case of the retouched blade (E296:48469:F1216) and the awl/borer (E324:12986:F401). Percussion flaking was employed with all three artefacts where force was applied either directly or indirectly.

Typology
CORE
The core (E324:13400:F530) is an amorphous core which has had flakes removed from a number of different directions but not in a systematic way. It is an irregularly shaped nodule of flint which is grey/beige in colour and has some patches of light grey cortex. At least two flake scars are visible where the flakes have been removed using percussion flaking. The nodule is slightly weathered so it is possible that there may have been more flake scars which have become worn.

SIDE SCRAPER
There is one side scraper (E324:13399:F535; Fig. 4.14:5) in the assemblage. It was made on a tertiary flake of light grey flint but the flake has shattered and only the medial fragment remains. The flake received semi-abrupt retouch on one lateral edge. Scrapers had a wide range of uses in prehistory such as scraping, boring, chopping and projectile use and could be used on a number of materials such as hides, bone, wood and antler (Andrefsky 1998, 193–4). Similar types of implements may have had different uses and a single scraper may have been repurposed during its functional history (Woodman *et al.* 2006, 156).

AWL/BORER
There is one flint awl or borer (E324:12986:F401; Fig. 4.14:4). It was made on a secondary flake where the distal end of the dorsal face had been trimmed to form a point. There is little typological information available on awl/borers and it is possible that these artefacts would have served a number of different functions (*ibid.*, 172).

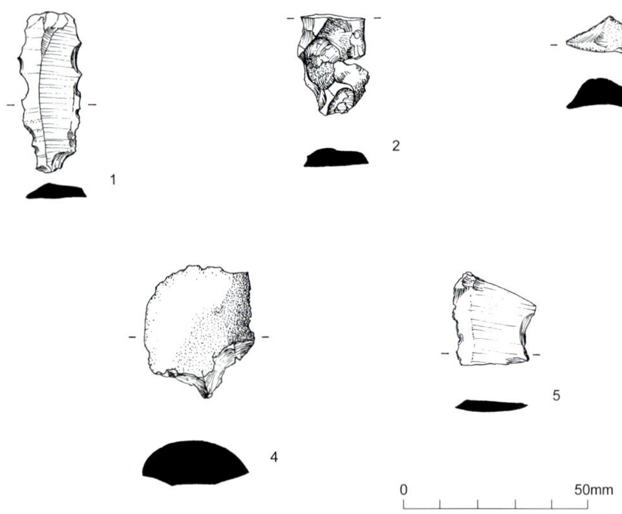

Fig. 4.14 Flint: retouched blade (1), possible retouched flake (2), debitage (3), awl or borer (4), side scraper (5).

RETOUCHED BLADE AND FLAKE

There is one retouched blade (E296:48469:F1216; Fig. 4.14:1) and one possible retouched flake (E296:48549:F2056; Fig. 4.14:2) in the assemblage. Blades are flakes which are at least twice as long as they are wide. The retouched blade (two fragments) was made on a tertiary flake and has abrupt retouch on the dorsal face along the right edge of the blade, at the distal end of the left edge and at the distal end of blade. There is some possible semi-abrupt retouch on the right and left edges of the fragments. This flake is fragmentary with only the proximal and distal ends of the flake remaining. The medial area of the flake is missing but the two fragments, recovered from the fill of a pit, are thought to belong to the same flake due to the similarity of the colour of the flint and the cortex and both fragments having the same thickness.

DEBITAGE

There are two pieces of debitage in the assemblage. These are detached pieces which did not receive any further working and were discarded. One piece of debitage (E748:68) is a secondary flake which has a flat striking platform and a recognisable ventral and dorsal face and a patch of grey cortex at the distal end of the flake. The other (E324:12981:F410; Fig. 4.14:3) is a piece of angular shatter which does not have a ventral and dorsal face and has no cortex remaining.

Discussion

It is likely that the small assemblage of lithics from Dublin Castle represents residual prehistoric finds. It has been noted, however, that flints recovered from excavations of early medieval sites, particularly rath sites, may not be of prehistoric date but are rudimentary struck flint implements of early medieval date that may have functioned as strike-a-lights, scrapers or knives. Flint artefacts recovered from excavations at Clea Lakes Crannog, Co. Down, and enclosures at Crossnacreevy, Co. Down and Ballyutoag, Co. Antrim have all been interpreted as possibly being early medieval in date, particularly in the case of Ballyutoag, where hundreds of small flint fragments were recovered from all phases of occupation recorded at the site and were thought to have been used as strike-a-lights (Collins *et al.* 1959, 98; Harper 1973–4, 37; Williams 1984, 46). A flint chunk (02E441:2256:15) associated with a sword blade and spearhead from a Viking grave at Woodstown, Co. Waterford was interpreted as being a possible strike-a-light which would have been used in conjunction with a metal blade to produce a spark (Harrison 2014b, 170). Three of the flint artefacts from Dublin Castle (E296:48469:F1216; E324:13399:F535 and E748:68) have steep edges which would have been suitable for such a purpose but they do not, however, have any evidence of use-wear to support such an interpretation and therefore the initial suggestion that the flint artefacts from Dublin Castle represent residual prehistoric finds is the most probable.

CATALOGUE

E296:48469:F1216 (Fig. 4.14:1). CT2: deposit; Phase 2. Retouched blade. Tertiary flake. Brown in colour but also completely covered in grey weathering. Flat striking platform. Bulb of percussion. Feathered termination. Abrupt retouch on the dorsal face along right edge, at distal end of left edge and at distal end of blade. Weathered. L. 42mm, W. 18.2mm, Th.6mm; Wgt. 4.8g.

E296:48549:F2056 (Fig. 4.14:2). CT2: fill deposit of Pit 4a; Phase 4a. Possible retouched flake. Only distal and proximal ends of flake remain, the medial area of the flake is missing. Secondary flake. Red-brown in colour with dark purple cortex. Possible semi-abrupt retouch on right and left lateral edges. Burnt? Two pieces: (1) L. 14.8mm, W. 17mm, Th. 4mm; (2) L. 15.6mm, W. 19mm, Th. 4mm; Wgt. 2.4g.

E324:12981:F410 (Fig. 4.14:3). PT1: layer within clay and timber bank; Phase 2. Debitage. Angular shatter. Light grey in colour. Fresh. L. 21.5mm; W. 10mm, Th. 6.2mm; Wgt. 1.1g.

E324:12986:F401 (Fig. 4.14:4). PT1: FW2 deposit of clay and timber bank; Phase 2. Awl/borer. Secondary flake. Light brown/dark brown in colour with light grey/grey cortex on most of dorsal face except at distal end. Flat striking platform. Bulb of percussion with large eraillure scar. Distal end of dorsal face has been trimmed to a point. Weathered/heat-affected. L. 35mm, W. 30.6mm, Th. 12mm; Wgt. 14.5g.

E324:13399:F535 (Fig. 4.14:5). PT1: BW2 deposit; Phase 1a. Side scraper. Tertiary flake–medial fragment of flake. Light grey in colour. Semi-abrupt retouch on one lateral edge. Fresh. L. 23.7mm, W. 22.6mm, Th. 3.2mm; Wgt. 2.4g.

E324:13400:F530. PT1: BW1 deposit; Phase 1a (*c.* early/mid tenth century). Amorphous core. Irregularly shaped flint nodule. Grey/beige in colour with patches of light grey cortex. At least two flake scars where flakes have been removed from different platforms (Flake 1: L. 22mm, W. 33.5mm. Flake 2: L. 12mm, W. 11mm). Slightly weathered. L. 109mm, W. 64mm, Th. 58mm; Wgt. 477.7g.

E748:68. CB: east end of trench, same level as Hearth 3 (House III); Phase D (*c.* early eleventh century). Debitage. Secondary flake. Grey/beige/black in colour with patch of grey cortex at distal end of dorsal face. Flat striking platform. Plunging termination. Weathered. L. 51mm, W. 27.8mm, Th. 4–11mm; Wgt. 12.9g.

Chapter 4.6
Jet and jet-like artefacts
Paul Stevens

Introduction
Five artefacts of jet/jet-like material were recovered from tenth / eleventh-century contexts in the Cork Tower, Powder Tower and Cross Block areas. This assemblage comprises two bangle fragments, two finger-ring fragments and a disc or bead and represents items of personal jewellery. The assemblage is typical of the Viking-age period in Ireland and similar discoveries have been made on sites including Fishamble Street and Temple Bar West in Viking Dublin, as well as Baldoyle, Co. Dublin, Knowth, Co. Meath and Woodstown, Co. Waterford (Simpson 1999; Hunter and Sheridan 2014, 320; Wallace 2016, 297–8; Duffy 2014; Stevens 2017, 263, table 1).

Scientific Analysis
Scientific analyses of British, Norwegian and (more recently) Irish archaeological material have successfully identified a broad range of raw materials with similar properties that were used in the manufacture of early medieval hard black highly polished jewellery. Carboniferous organic and inorganic materials used in the manufacture of such jewellery from the early medieval period in Ireland have included true jet (including Whitby jet), lignite, oil shales and coals, and although true jet is not in the geology of Ireland, the other material types can be sourced in a limited number of outcrops and seams throughout the island (Lanigan 1964, 4–10; Hunter 2008; 2016; Patrick Orr, pers. comm.). A suite of non-destructive analytical and visual assessment techniques is well established in Britain and Scandinavia, but not commonly applied to archaeological material from early medieval Ireland (Allason-Jones and Davis 2002; Allason-Jones and Jones 2001; Hunter *et al.* 1993; Penton 2008; Plahter 2011). This study utilised three analytical techniques (x-ray, FTIR and SEM/EDX) on four of the five jet-like artefacts in this assemblage. In addition, a small number of geo-reference samples were used for comparative purposes, including raw and archaeological materials from counties Dublin, Antrim, Fermanagh, Meath and Offaly, and Yorkshire in England. The remaining artefact (E748:76) was not analysed as this was a late addition to the study, and the techniques were unavailable to the author at that time.

X-ray analysis mainly differentiates the level of organic matter present in a material by the opacity visible. This was undertaken on the artefacts by conservator Susannah Kelly in the National Museum of Ireland. The results showed all the Dublin Castle jet-like artefacts could be classified as having a moderate to low opacity – indicative of an organic material, such as lignite or jet. Although inconclusive as a stand-alone technique, as can be seen below, it was more effective when used in conjunction with other analyses.

Fournier Transform Infrared (FTIR) is a highly sensitive and accurate multi-spectral analysis technology, used widely in the geochemical and petrochemical industries. It can be used to identify pure organic compounds. Although it is not widely used in archaeology, the advantages of this technique have been demonstrated in several high-profile experimental papers (Hunter *et al.* 1993; Watts and Pollard 1998; Penton 2008; Plahter 2011; Hunter and Sheridan 2014). Four artefacts were analysed by FTIR by the author, at the School of Chemistry, University College Dublin under the supervision of Dr Dermot Noonan. While this technique demonstrated high levels of precision, it is better suited to a powder or solution. The nature of the archaeological material and the limitations of the measuring device required readings from small areas, with clean breaks and a smooth surface. Furthermore, contamination from surface treatments, attrition and past use, common to archaeological objects, contributed to highly complex results. As a consequence, a definitive match with the geological reference samples was not possible, and no definition on the source of the materials was forthcoming.

Finally, due to lack of availability, only one artefact (E296:48487:F1222) was subject to spectroscopic analyses by scanning electron microscope (SEM) and energy dispersive x-ray (EDX). Analysis was carried out by Prof. P. Orr, School of Geoscience, University College Dublin. This technique can be used on a very small target area, at a very high microscopic resolutions, which avoids contamination and erroneous adherent materials, and can provide an elemental and quantitative material composition. The results were highly encouraging and revealed a possible match to the Whitby jet sample material.

The results of the combined geo-chemical and scientific analyses revealed only one object was positively identified as a true jet, likely to be Whitby jet. Of the remaining jet-like materials represented, two were identified as lignite, and one was inconclusive, but possibly lignite. Although the source of the lignite could not be provenanced in this study, lignite is a raw material indigenous to both Scotland and Ireland, and commonly found around parts of counties Armagh and Antrim. It was evident that the artefacts were not carved from any one source material.

Results of the Scientific Analysis

E296:48487:F1222 (Fig. 4.15:3; Pl. 4.17:3): Finger ring fragment. Material: Dull matt-black colour, laminar fracture, visible pores and pitting. X-ray has a moderate to low opacity, SEM showed a very abrasive and mottled microscopic surface with visible linear cracks and with Si, Al and K adhesions (e.g. iron pyrite) adhering particles of soil, EDX measured high levels of Carbon and Sulphur, with intrusive Iron Pyrite particles, FTIR analysis indicates a broad O-H bond stretch between 3653–3566cm-1, and an aromatic C=C stretch at 1558–1507cm-1, carbonates at 1419 and silicated at 605–425cm-1. The combined analyses indicated the raw material is most likely to be a true jet.

E296:48525:F2031 (Fig. 4.15:1; Pl. 4.17:1): Unfinished bangle. Material: black, laminar almost crystalline, hackneyed non-conchoidal fracture, regular woody grain pattern visible on the exterior, interior is pitted and pored throughout. X-ray has a low opacity, FTIR analysis indicates a broad O-H bond stretch between 3902–3566cm-1, and a C=O stretch at 1749–1698cm-1, carbonates at 1419 and 1396cm-1 and silicates at 546–425cm-1. The combined analyses indicated the raw material is most likely to be lignite.

E324:12989:F470 (Fig. 4.15:2; Pl. 4.17:2): Bangle. Material: Black, slightly hackneyed fracture, very pitted interior, tight irregular structure; X-ray has a moderate to low opacity, FTIR analysis indicates a broad O-H bond stretch between 3689–3566cm-1, and a C=O stretch at 1733–1698cm-1, carbonates at 1418 and 1398cm-1 and silicates at 545–420cm-1. The combined analyses indicated the raw material is most likely to be lignite.

E324:3715:F296 (Fig. 4.15:4; Pl. 4.17:4): Finger ring fragment. Material: Black, laminar fracture, hackneyed surface. X-ray has a moderate opacity, FTIR analysis is inconclusive, and indicates a C=O stretch at 1733–1698cm-1, carbonates at 1418 and 1398cm-1 and silicates at 669–420cm-1. The combined analyses were inconclusive.

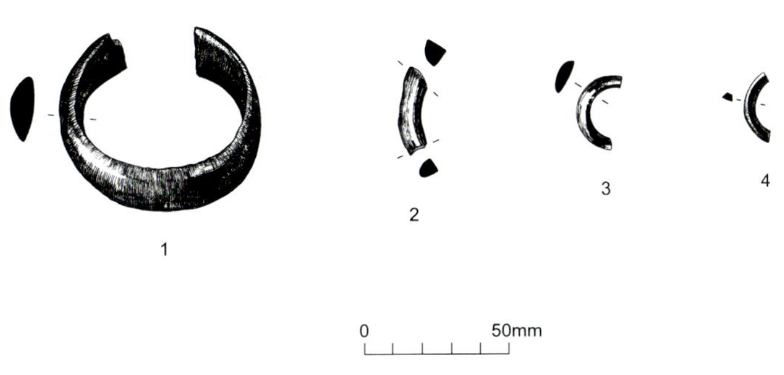

Fig. 4.15 Jet / jet-like artefacts: bangle fragments (1, 2), finger ring fragments (3, 4).

Pl. 4.17 Jet/jet-like artefacts. Bangles (1, 2); rings (3, 4); disc or bead (5).

Discussion

In Ireland, jet-like jewellery (e.g. beads, bangles and bracelets) can be found from the Early Bronze Age to the early medieval period, although finger rings are normally limited to the later first millennium AD (Hunter 2008, 104–6; Hunter and Sheridan 2014, 320; Stevens 2017, 251–8). The example found in in the clay and timber bank at the Powder Tower (E324:12989:F470) was a small bangle fragment of a typology distinctive to the early medieval period in Ireland, *c.* AD 400–1100. The example found within House 2 at the Cork Tower (E296:48525:F2031) is an almost complete bangle of a distinctive broad, narrow-style of arm jewellery that appears to date exclusively to after the ninth century and is associated with Viking settlements (Hunter 2008; Wallace 2016, 297, 371, figs 8.29 and 10.22; Stevens 2017, 255).The two finger ring fragments recovered from the Cork Tower and Powder Tower (E296:48487:F1222; E324:3715:F296) are far rarer, as this type of jet-like jewellery does not appear in early medieval assemblages in Ireland until after the ninth/ tenth century (Stevens 2017, 255). Finally, the flat bead or perforated disc (E748:76) recovered from House III at the Cross Block is of a type recovered in considerable numbers in stone from Viking-age levels elsewhere in Dublin (Wallace 2016, 297, fig. 8.29), although its function is unclear; jet-like examples are known from Drumclay Crannog, Co. Fermanagh (Stevens 2019).

Jet or jet-like material is the most common medium used in Irish early medieval arm jewellery along with other materials including stone, glass, silver and gold (Doyle 2014, 67–8). Evidence from Viking graves in the Orkney Islands and on mainland Scotland shows that arm bangles were worn by females (e.g. burials from Lamba Ness, Westness, Rousay, Newark, Orkney Is. and Castletown, Caithness) but beads were worn by both sexes (e.g. Drimore Machair, S. Uist [male] and Cruach Mhor, Eigg, Argyll and Bute [female]) (Hunter 2008, 109, 114–5). There is no reliable data currently available for how finger rings, hair or ankle rings were worn (Hunter 2008, 104–6; Hunter and Sheridan 2014, 320). Recent evidence from graves in Ranelagh, Co. Roscommon, revealed incomplete fragments of bangles in graves of an adolescent male and adult female and an infant (Stevens forthcoming a). There are no references in early Irish literature to the use of jet or jet-like material although the Roman writer Pliny the Elder and the Venerable Bede, who died in AD 735, refer to its medicinal and occult uses, among others (Rackham 1952, 141–2; Coulter 2015, 117; Stevens 2017, 246–7).

Manufacture of jet-like jewellery took place at various locations throughout Ireland from the beginning of the fifth century to the end of the twelfth century (Stevens 2017, 251–7). Irish material was carved by hand, using a knife or gouge to remove a central biconical waste core or disc, followed by a smooth polishing by stone to produce a high gloss lustre (*ibid.*, 243–6, fig. 3a). This technique was universally adopted in Ireland and in parts of western Scotland alongside earlier native techniques (Hunter 2016, 294–8). However, jet/jet-like jewellery was not popular in Anglo-Saxon England, despite access to sources of the raw material, and was only reintroduced at York by the Scandinavians, following initial raids on Britain and Ireland, and adapted by them to their own style (Hunter 2008; Stevens 2017, 255).

There appears to be a strong association between early ecclesiastical sites and production, with significant demand for jet-like jewellery evidenced at the larger monasteries, such as Armagh and Clonmacnoise in Ireland and Whithorn in Scotland. These artefacts are also well represented on Irish royal sites such as Knowth and Lagore and Dunadd in Scotland and on urban settlements like Viking Dublin (Stevens 2017, 250). However, the majority (83%) of jet-like jewellery occurs in small numbers (fewer than five pieces) on early medieval sites (*ibid.*, 258). Finds are scattered across a range of sites types and geographical regions, although regional clusters occur in Armagh and the north-east, Clonmacnoise and the midlands and counties Dublin and Meath in the east – possibly indicative of production centres and/or the availability of raw materials, and a measure of control in supply (*ibid.*).

Identification of the raw material(s) used has important economic, social and cultural implications, such as recognition of indigenous exploitation and possible external contacts and trade (Stevens 2017, 258; 2018, 174–97). This study has identified jet/jet-like jewellery made from both imported jet and potentially indigenous lignite materials from Viking-age levels at Dublin Castle. Similar findings are noted at other Viking settlements in Kaupang, Norway and Woodstown, Co. Waterford, where an even more extensive range of materials was found in the jet-like jewellery assemblage (Plahter 2011; Hunter and Sheridan 2014). This emerging trend would appear to undermine the suggestion that Whitby was the sole source of 'jet' supplied to Scandinavian-run towns such as York and Dublin (Wallace 2016, 297–8), and introduces more complex economic possibilities – e.g. trade in lignite between Armagh and Dublin (Stevens 2018, 159). Furthermore, the diagnostic 'Viking-style' bangle fragment (E296:48525:F2031) was lignite rather than jet, and this is also the case with a similar unfinished bangle recovered as a residual find in later levels in Dublin Castle (E323:5244:F192; Stevens, forthcoming b).

Conclusion

Although relatively small and fragmentary, the collection of jet/jet-like artefacts from Viking-age levels at Dublin Castle tells us something about economic and social activity of the time. In terms of style, the objects display both insular and Scandinavian characteristics. The study suggests that raw material was sourced in north-east England and potentially north-east Ireland / south-west Scotland. This finding shows that the manufacture of jet-like jewellary was the product of developed trading links between Ireland and Britain.

CATALOGUE

E296:48525:F2031 (Fig. 4.15:1; Pl. 4.17:1). CT2: House 2; Phase 5. Unfinished Viking-style bangle (in three parts); 87.5% survives. Elongated narrow D-section, interior almost flat, exterior semi-circular, hoop is circular but irregular in thickness and circumference is asymmetrical. One small section missing, ends snapped, one straight, one stepped along a linear crack, partly split lengthwise. Also broken into three during excavation, also snapped straight. Dull burnish and unpolished. Hand carved, transverse saw marks visible on the interior and linear scratches on the exterior are grinding marks rather than from use-wear. Raw material likely to be lignite. L. 72.73mm, W. 22.61–21.22mm, Th. 9–7.15mm; Est. int. diam. 56.56mm.

E324:12989:F470 (Fig. 4.15:2; Pl. 4.17:2). PT1: clay and timber bank; Phase 2. Bangle fragment; 20% survives. D-shaped. Interior flat, exterior curved. Incomplete, split along full width and both ends snapped cleanly. Dull lustre and polished exterior, very worn with scratches. Raw material is likely to be lignite. L. 30.09mm, W. 5.17–7.18mm+, Th. 7.72-8mm; Est. int. diam. 43mm.

E296:48487:F1222 (Fig. 4.15:3; Pl. 4.17:3). CT2: deposit; Phase 2. Finger ring fragment; 50% survives. Elongated D-section. Interior flat, exterior asymmetrical and tapering – likely worn on the right-hand ring finger. Snapped at both ends and exterior has hairline surface cracks. Dull lustre, handcarved with visible transverse interior cut marks and exterior is well-worn from use. Raw material is likely to be true jet. L. 25.09mm, W. 12.19–10.93mm, Th. 4.27mm; Est. int. diam. 17.36mm.

E324:3715:F296 (Fig. 4.15:4; Pl. 4.17:4). PT2 – Area B: Phase 1. Finger ring fragment; 40% survives. D-section. Small, very thin slightly asymmetrical band. Incomplete, split along full width and snapped cleanly at both ends. Dull lustre, polished both sides, interior has multiple hairline cracks and exterior is very worn, scratched and nicked. Hand cut, faint carve marks evident as interior transverse striations together with the irregular circumference. Raw material likely to be lignite or some other unknown material. L. 22.73mm, W. 2.88mm, Th. 3.45mm; Est. int. diam. 18.72mm.

E748:76 (Pl. 4.17:5). CB: under Hearth 3 (House III); Phase C. Flat thin perforated circular disc or bead; 100% survives. Exterior very slightly asymmetrical, with a uniform thickness – and symmetrical central perforation and slightly bevelled edges, particularly more curved on one side. Dull lustre, slightly more polished on the one (obverse) face, slightly worn on both sides. Handcarved, particularly noticeable around the perforated edges; hole is cut from two sides. Diam. 10.98–10.77mm; perforation diam. 2.91mm; Th. 1.81mm. Material: Dull matt-black colour, no visible breaks, laminations or fractures. Raw material is likely to be cannel coal or oil shale, however, no scientific analysis was conducted on this object.

Chapter 4.7
Wood
Aidan O'Sullivan and Caitríona Moore, with a contribution by Aonghus Moloney and Ellen OCarroll

4.7.1
Wooden artefacts

AIDAN O'SULLIVAN AND CAITRÍONA MOORE

Introduction

The assemblage comprises 33 artefacts ranging in species, size and function, of which 31 were examined, and two were not available for study. Twenty-two artefacts were recorded by Aidan O'Sullivan in 1990/1 and a further eleven artefacts were recorded by Caitríona Moore in 2018 when an update of the original report was undertaken. The majority (22) were recovered from the Cork Tower area with just two recorded from the Powder Tower, where soil conditions were less conducive to survival of organic material. Although a small sample by the standards of other artefact assemblages, it is a comprehensive collection, indicative of a wide range of crafts and activities. The perishable nature of wood requires that it be deposited in anaerobic conditions, free from the activities of wood rotting organisms and fungi. While not technically 'wet', urban sites, due to the rapid build-up of successive layers of settlement deposits, sometimes have these necessary conditions. The wood from the collection varied greatly in state of preservation, according to where it was deposited and the species of the wood itself, as some types of wood react differently to taphonomic processes. This report outlines the methods of examination, and the organisation of the catalogue is summarised, with a discussion of each section and finally the extent to which different species are used is examined.

The Dublin Castle wooden material is restricted in quantity but varied in type and provides a valuable contribution to knowledge concerning the use of wood in Viking Dublin. The material was divided according to artefact form, depending in part on the manufacturing methodology. In this way ten artefacts associated with the craft of cooperage were recognised, including staves, hoops and parts of composite and unitary discs. Three artefacts were related to textile production. A fragment of a plate worked on a pole lathe was found. Small functional items such as pegs, pins and nails accounted for seven pieces. A miscellaneous category contained twelve items of uncertain function. The species used in the manufacture of the artefacts were dominated by yew, with alder, ash, hazel, oak and willow also used. Fourteen artefacts have not been identified to species.

WOOD SPECIES IDENTIFICATION

Species identification was attempted firstly by the naked eye. When the presence of oak was suspected, a surface was cleaned off with a blade. The distinctive early wood vessels and medullary rays of this species make identification relatively easy. Otherwise, the wood was identified by taking thin slivers from various sections and examining them under magnification. A total of 24 of the 33 artefacts were identified. Most oak identifications were carried out by Aidan O'Sullivan, with additional identifications, including some of oak, carried out by Aonghus Moloney and Ellen OCarroll. Most of the wood was in excellent condition at the time of original recording and was relatively free of algal growth.

ORGANISATION OF THE CATALOGUE

The terminology used in the catalogue is derived from a number of sources, which are referenced. The catalogue is organised under a series of headers: textile production; cooperage; turned objects; pegs/pins; and miscellaneous objects including objects of uncertain function.

Some problems arose in the compilation of the catalogue; in a small number of cases the prolonged immersion in water since discovery has made the labels difficult to read, while a

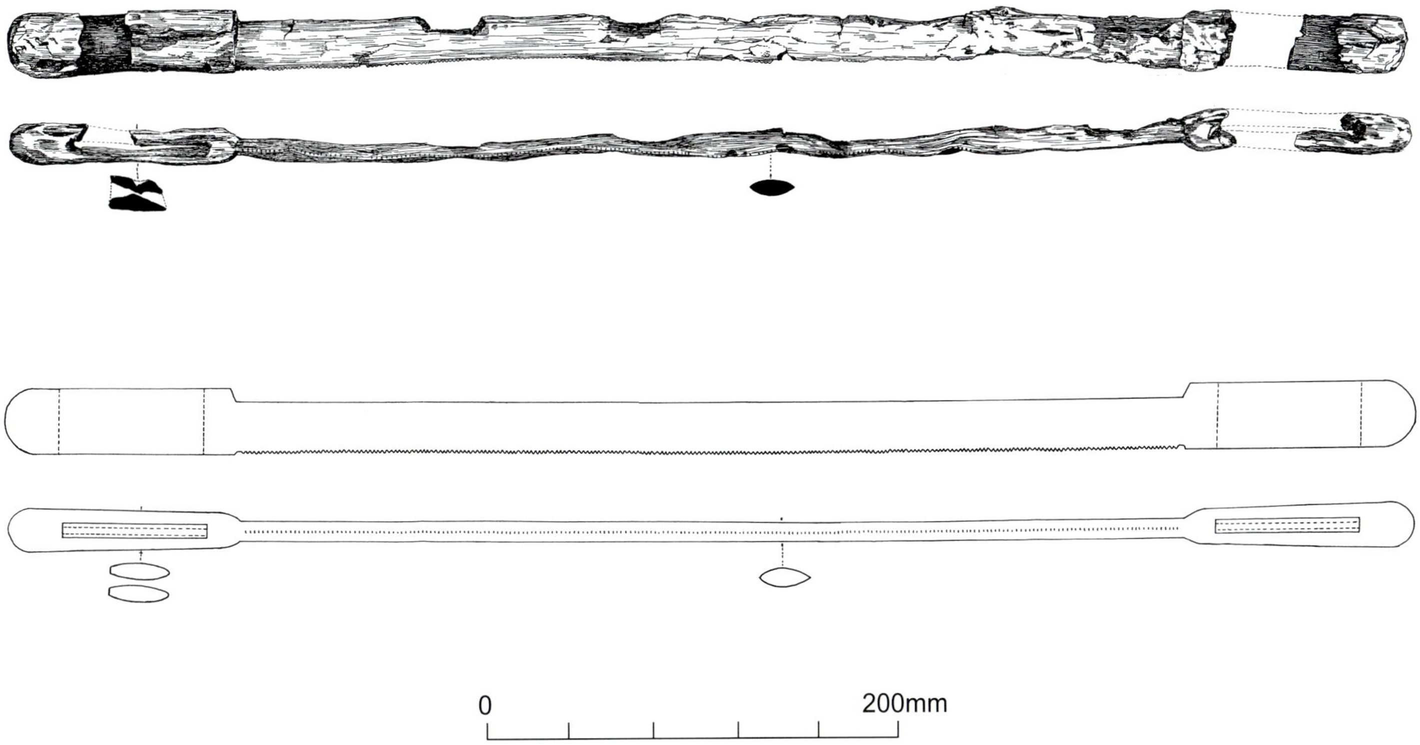

Fig. 4.16 Wooden possible loom piece E296:48591:F2055.

small number of samples had no information included with the bag. One or two descriptions do not fit with the material found in the bag. A record of one artefact was generated from site plans/photographs while an additional two were generated from artefact drawings.

Objects Associated with Textile Production

Three artefacts are associated with textile production: a probable loom piece found at the Cork Tower and a flax ripple comb and a spindle from the Cross Block. These three items are important evidence of textile production in Viking Dublin. The ripple comb (sometimes referred to as a rippler) was used to process flax at one of the earliest stages of linen production, while the spindle would have been used to spin either prepared fibres or wool into thread. The loom represents the final stage whereby the spun threads were woven into cloth.

POSSIBLE LOOM PIECE (FIG. 4.16)

This artefact (E296:48591:F2055) is a morticed beam made from alder which may have been part of a loom. It is *c.*0.67m long and the mortices at each end were clearly designed to hold tenons or shafts. However, they narrow towards the centre, which would make any such components very thin and weak. This internal narrowing could also be due to anisotropic shrinkage rather than an original design of manufacture. The mortices are nonetheless small and narrow, indicating the use of the beam in a lightweight composite frame. The notching along the length of the thin edge of the shaft is done carefully and at regular spacing. Despite its severely degraded condition, there is little evidence for wear along this shaft, or no evidence of material having been tied around the notches which could indicate that the piece was not extensively used.

This artefact was clearly part of a lightly built frame of some description and cord or threads were either tied around the shaft or draped across it. It may be part of a two-beam vertical loom in which the tension is maintained on the warp by means of a beam. A loom of this form and scale may have been used to make sprang (Dolores Kearney, pers. comm.), a type of open weave-like netting, evidence for which has been found in Viking Dublin (Wincott Heckett 2003, 109). Made entirely from wood, looms are elusive in the archaeological record. Artefacts similar to this include a loom from the ninth-century Oseberg ship burial and later examples from fourteenth/fifteenth-century levels in York (Morris 2000, 2335).

E296:48591:F2055 (Fig. 4.16). CT2: on wattle mat in House 1; Phase 3. Finely worked flat thin shaft, expands in width and thickness at either end, best preserved end is L. 110mm,

W. 30mm, Th. 20mm. Ends are rectangular in cross-section with mortices through the centre of their narrow edges. The mortises are hourglass in section and the best preserved is L. 68.5mm, W. 7mm, narrowing internally to 2.5mm. The ends are rounded slightly by knife cuts and unworn. The shaft (L. 46mm, W. 22mm, Th. 13mm) is pointed oval in cross-section, with a rounded edge and a sharp edge. The latter is worked continuously along its length, evidenced by over 200 shallow, narrow notches 1mm wide and 8mm deep, regularly spaced 4mm apart. Taken from central heartwood of sapling, the wood is degraded. Function: the piece is possibly part of a frame. Because of their internal narrowing, the mortices must have held only a very thin wooden tenon or textile. The shaft is unworn, but the notches were most likely for holding threads of some description. Alder (*Alnus glutinosa*). L. 670mm (approx.), W. 22mm (shaft) to 30mm (end), Th. 12mm (shaft) to 20mm (end).

Pl. 4.18 Ripple comb (or rippler) E748:14.

RIPPLE COMB (PL. 4.18)

A ripple comb (or rippler) was a comb-like tool used to remove the seed heads from dried flax bundles. The perforation through one end of this example (E748:14) would originally have held a separate handle set perpendicularly to the teeth. A flax ripple comb from thirteenth-century York, although broken, is very similar to this artefact, while a large wooden comb from High Street, Dublin may represent a closer parallel (Morris 2000, 2325-6).

E748:14 (Pl. 4.18). CB: occupation debris of Hearth 5/House V level; Phase F. Approximately triangular in shape. Located 44mm from the narrow end is a circular perforation 13mm in diameter. From this point the comb gradually increases in width to a maximum of 111mm. Edges are slightly curved. On both sides, adjacent to the edge is a narrow chamfer. At the widest end are seven teeth (L. 47–57mm). The teeth are unevenly sized and taper to rounded tips. The narrowest tapers from W. 8–4mm, the widest from W. 16–4mm. Some minor surface damage and cracks. Teeth are sharp and unworn. Function: ripple comb (or rippler) for flax processing, apparent sharpness of teeth suggests little use. Yew (*Taxus baccata*); species identification by Ellen OCarroll. L. 268mm, W. 18–111mm, Th. 5–29mm.

Pl. 4.19 Wooden artefacts: spindle (1); stave (2); pegs (3,4); unknown function (5); small peg? (6).

SPINDLE (PL. 4.19:1)

A carved object, circular in cross-section with an elongated biconical shape (E748:138) is almost certainly part of a spindle used to spin fibres into thread. Spindles of this form have been found on several Viking sites in Dublin and on contemporary rural sites such as crannogs (Earwood 1993, 135–6). Cut at both ends, E748:138 is incomplete and may have been destined for reworking into another smaller item.

E748:138 (Pl. 4.19:1). CB: unknown context. Carved object. Elongated shape, circular in cross-section. Widest in centre (Diam. 15mm) but curvature is slightly uneven, more pronounced on one side. Ends are cut flat. Surface covered with linear knife marks (average W. 2–3mm). Function: possible spindle fragment, reworked/cut down? Yew (*Taxus baccata*); species identification by Ellen OCarroll. L. 89mm, Diam. 7.5–15mm.

Wooden Objects Associated with Cooperage

Ten pieces in the assemblage are products of the craft of cooperage including staves, disc fragments and binding hoops. Seven were found at the Cork Tower, three at the Cross Block.

STAVES (FIG. 4.17:1 AND 2, PL. 4.19:2)

Three well-made staves of mid-late tenth-century date were present. E296:48588:F2039 and E748:104 are from conical vessels wider at the base than the rim. The third, E296:48522:F2060, is from an inverse conical vessel in which the rim was wider than the base. All of the vessels were open-topped. Close to the base of each stave is a small disc-locating groove. These vary slightly in form (see Comey 2010, 42, Types A and C) and would have been carefully cut to receive a base with a corresponding edge profile. The grooves are narrow and the associated discs would have been very thin. The staves are concavo-convex or plano-convex in cross-section, the surfaces shaped with a drawknife and the rims angled with a slight internal bevel. On the exterior of all three are marks of external binding hoops, most likely of wood but possibly of metal. Tiny peg holes (Diam. 2mm) close to the base of E748:104 indicate where the hoop was fixed in place with a small peg, probably metal.

The conical staves measured 92mm and 176mm in height and were likely components of small open-topped drinking vessels. A bevel around the upper edges of E748:104 suggests that it may originally have had a vertical handle. The inverse conical stave was 156mm in height and had the corroded remains of a metal fitting and ring for holding a metal handle. This suggests it took the form of a bucket-type vessel, but one small enough to have functioned as a piece of domestic tableware. Small to medium-sized drinking and serving vessels were the most numerous stave-built vessels in Viking Dublin (Comey 2010, 183; chart 6:1), with these examples falling at the smaller end of the scale.

With only single staves surviving it is difficult to assess the volume of the original vessels. It is likely that they were made to well-established specifications, each volume depending on height and diameter and carrying a name.

CATALOGUE

E296:48522:F2060 (Fig. 4.17:1). CT2: House 1 deposit; Phase 3. Small, finely made stave. Trapezoidal in shape, widening from base to top. Straight longitudinal profile, concavo-convex cross-section. Base flat and slightly worn, rim has slight internal bevel. Equilateral V-shaped disc-locating groove cut 10mm from base. Two hoop marks on outer surface. Uppermost (W. 13mm) is 73mm from base, lower (W. 2mm) is 12mm from base. The corroded remains of a metal handle or fitting (L. 62mm, W. 17mm) is attached to the exterior. It is trapezoidal in shape, widening and thickening towards the top where it loops over the rim forming a ring. It is attached to the stave with a rivet set 58mm below the rim. Function: stave from finely made tankard, which widens from the base to its top. Bound with a wide hoop in the middle and a narrower one at the base. Yew (*Taxus baccata*). L. 156mm, W. 35mm (base) 43mm (rim), Th. 7mm (base) 5mm (rim).

E296:48588:F2039 (Fig. 4.17:2). CT2: House 2 deposit; Phase 5. Small, finely made stave. Trapezoidal in shape, narrowing from base to top. Straight longitudinal profile, concavo-convex cross-section. Base flat and slightly worn, rim has slight internal bevel. Equilateral V-shaped disc-locating groove cut 17mm from base. Three external wear marks made by binding hoops. Top and bottom marks are narrow (W. 4–5mm), centre mark is wider (W. 17mm). Function: stave from small finely made tankard with narrowing diameter towards top. Bound with three hoops probably made of wood, although middle hoop may have been metal. Narrow groove would only allow a thin base. Yew (*Taxus baccata*). L. 176mm, W. 33mm (base) 23mm (rim), Th. 12mm (base) 10mm (rim).

E748:104 (Pl. 4.19:2). CB: ironworking layer; Phase C. Stave, trapezoidal in shape, narrowing from base to top. Straight longitudinal profile, plano-convex in cross-section with flat interior and slightly convex exterior. Edges flat, slightly angled towards the interior. Base is flat; 10mm above it on interior is a disc-locating groove (W. 5mm, D. 2mm) the upper and lower edges of which are bevelled. Rim is damaged; bevelling on edges suggests presence of a vertical handle. Interior is smooth with possible scorching close to rim. Faint hoop marks on exterior at rim and base. The stave is perforated by a tiny peg hole (Diam. 2mm) 1mm above the disc-locating groove, and by a second peg hole (Diam. 2mm) 8mm above the base. Two fine longitudinal cracks close to base. Function: stave from a small tankard type vessel with narrowing diameter towards top. Bound with hoops at rim and base, tiny peg holes indicate fixing of hoop to vessel at base. Yew (*Taxus baccata*); species identification by Ellen OCarroll. L. 92mm, W. 23mm (base) 19mm (rim), Th. 5–7mm.

WOODEN DISCS (FIG. 4.17:3–5)

Wooden discs formed the bases and heads of coopered vessels. They are divided into composite discs made from two or more split pieces, and unitary discs made from a single piece, usually carved but occasionally turned. Fragments of a composite disc, a unitary disc and two possible unitary discs were recovered from mid to late tenth- and early eleventh-century levels at the Cork Tower.

Part of a cant (E296:48592:F1208), the outermost board of a composite disc, was found at the Cork Tower. Made from yew, it has flat surfaces worked smooth by a thin, flat-sectioned blade, most likely an adze. Bevelled outer edges were made to fit in a corresponding disc-locating groove. The inner edge contains three dowels which would have

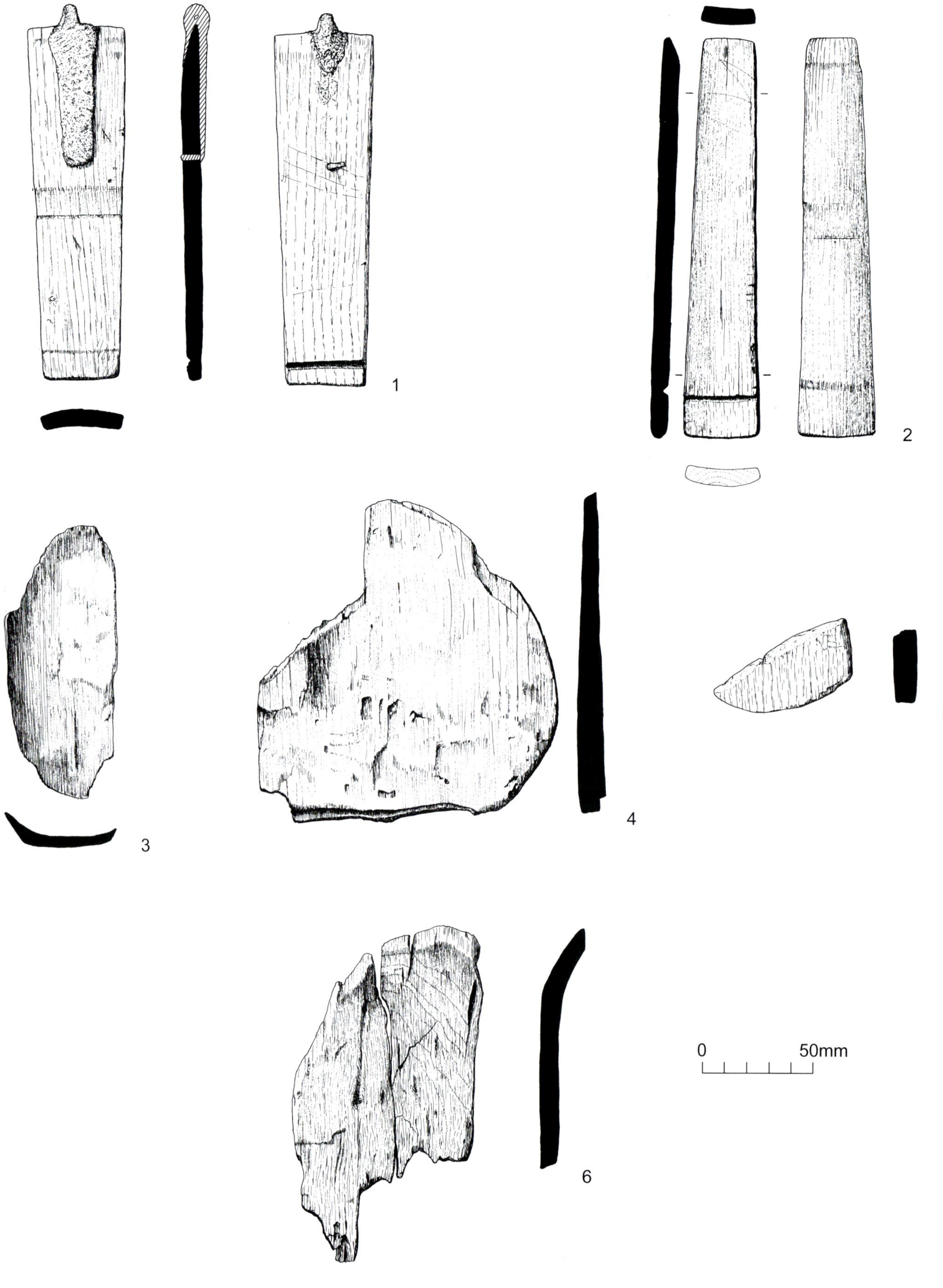

Fig. 4.17 Wooden artefacts: staves (1, 2), disc (3), unitary discs (4, 5), fragment of turned plate (6).

secured it to the adjacent middle board. The estimated original diameter of the disc is 480mm and at 27mm thick in the centre and 15mm at the edge, it was part of a fairly large and heavy disc, likely used in a substantial vessel such as a keg or cask.

Approximately one quarter of a unitary disc (E296:48454:F1208). The estimated original diameter of this disc is 300mm and at 11mm thick in the centre but only 8mm at the edge, it is much smaller and lighter than the cant and was perhaps used in a bucket or small keg. Finally, E296:48585:F2025 and E296:48581:F2008 are both small fragments of possible unitary discs carved respectively from ash and oak.

CATALOGUE

E296:48592:F2062. CT2: fill of Pit 4a; Phase 4a. Very large, thick cant. Inner straight edge with three dowel holes, haphazardly placed on different alignments 25–170mm apart. All retain dowels (L. 43–82mm, Diam. 13–16mm). Outer edge curved. Bi-planar in cross-section with both outer edges bevelled, but predominantly on one. Surfaces worked smooth by thin, flat-sectioned blade. Both damaged by burning, extensively on one surface revealing end of dowel in hole. Small traces of metal corrosion on both surfaces. Function: cant from barrel head or base. Yew (*Taxus baccata*). L. 450mm, W. 155mm, Th. 27mm (centre) 15mm (edge); estimated original Diam. 480mm.

E296:48581:F2008 (Fig. 4.17:3). CT2: deposit external to House 3; Phase 6. Disc fragment. Thin fragment, curved in width section. Slightly thicker at base of curve, thinning to edges. Worn condition. Function: possible fragment of a unitary disc. Oak (*Quercus*). L. 120mm, W. 50mm, Th. 6mm.

E296:48454:F1208 (Fig. 4.17:4). CT2: fill deposit of Pit 4a; Phase 4a. Fragment, possible quarter of a unitary disc, approximately triangular in shape. Plano-convex in cross-section. Short section of original outer edge bevelled on convex side only, other edges broken. Function: disc, base or lid. Yew (*Taxus baccata*). L. 140mm, W. 135mm, Th. 11mm (centre) 8mm (edge); estimated original Diam. 300mm.

E296:48585:F2025. (Fig. 4.17:5). CT2: stones covering fill of Pit 4b; Phase 5. Fragment with section of original curved edge, other edges broken. Uniform thickness. Function: possible fragment of disc. Ash (*Fraxinus excelsior*). L. 67mm, W. 29mm, Th. 10mm.

WOODEN BINDING HOOPS

To form a vessel the side staves had to be bound together using wooden or occasionally metal hoops. Wooden hoops may be made from longitudinally split rods or carved laths, the former most commonly used by Dublin's coopers (Comey 2010, 64). The hoop ends overlap and are secured using a variety of fastenings with additional pegs along the length used to hold the hoops in place.

Binding hoop E296:41286:F1240 was made from a half-split yew branch with its bark removed and ends tapered to flat terminals. Through one of the terminals are drilled two small perforations (Diam. 5mm) through which pegs would have secured the hoop to the vessel staves. Although damaged when recorded, its estimated original diameter is 310mm, indicating a medium-sized vessel such as a bucket. The remaining two hoops, F748:21, were recorded only from site plans (Fig. 3.50). Both appear to have been very large with diameters of *c.* 2m and a possible overlap and fixing at the ends. Even allowing for the fact that these hoops were likely 'open' when drawn, they must have been for use with a very large vessel such as a cask.

CATALOGUE

E296:41286:F1240. CT2: incorporated within south side wall of House 1; Phase 3. Split branch bent into near circular curve. Semi-circular cross-section. Bark removed from external surface with knife leaving flat, narrow facets. Internal split surface is flat. Tapers in thickness at terminals to flat ends. At one end are two small perforations (Diam. 5mm), the external surface is flat at this area. The other end, which probably overlapped the former, is broken, with remains of perforation and a small notch in one edge. Function: hoop for binding vessel staves together. The overlapping ends were attached by means of small pins inserted through drilled perforations and also by tying together with help of small notches. Shape of hoop indicates bucket widening towards top. Yew (*Taxus baccata*). L. 680mm, W. 15mm, Th. 7mm; circumference of original bound hoop 635mm.

E748:21 (Fig. 3.50). CB: in shells over Hearth 5 (House V); Phase F. Items unseen (recorded from site plan). Two barrel hoops in occupation deposit above Hearth 5. Possible overlap and fixing at ends. Function: hoops of large stave-built vessel. Diam. 2m (external), 1.9m (internal), W. *c.* 5mm.

VIKING-AGE COOPERING

The evidence for cooperage in Viking-age Dublin has been the subject of extensive and detailed study (Comey 2010). The Dublin Castle assemblage, while small, adds to the published corpus. No complete vessel is represented, only broken or damaged components, including individual staves, portions of discs and two binding hoops. It is difficult to reconstruct the volume of a vessel from a single stave, but general statements about the size of the vessels represented can be made. Coopering involves the making of circular, wooden containers of joined staves bound together by hoops of wood or iron and fitted with a separate disc base and sometimes head. There are three forms of traditional coopering. Wet coopering, the most skilled version, involves the use of precise measurements and tight fitting of staves to make liquid-tight vessels. The products of dry coopering, which are vessels to hold solid goods, are not as carefully finished.

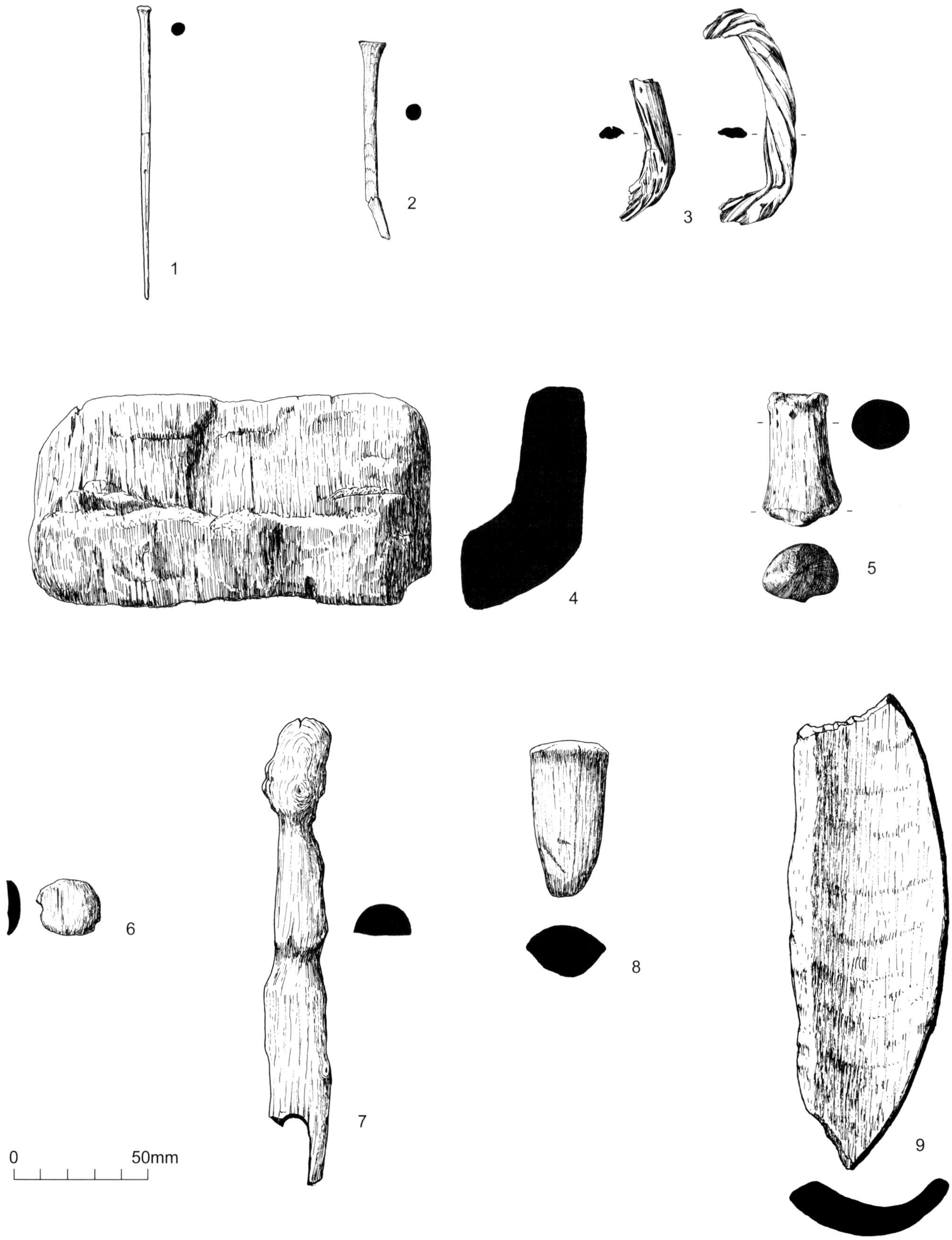

Fig. 4.18 Wooden artefacts and rope fragments: wooden pin (1), wooden nail (2), rope fragments (3), wooden block (4), wooden peg or dowel (5), unidentified wooden objects (6, 7, 8, 9).

E286:48605:F2061 (Fig. 4.18:5). CT2: deposit; Phase 3. Small wooden object. Appears to be carved from a larger stem, circular in cross-section. Broken (?) at one end, the opposite expanded slightly to a rounded head (Diam. 28mm). Function: peg or dowel? Species cannot be determined. L. 49mm, Diam. 22–28mm.

E324:13402:F474 (Fig. 4.18:6). PT1; deposit of clay and timber bank; Phase 2. Possible disc. Tiny, very thin fragment or disc, oval to circular shape. Flat on one surface, slightly convex on opposite; thickest in centre. Function: unknown, may only be wood chip. Species not identified. Diam. 21–24.5mm, Th. 45mm (centre).

E296:48584:F2023. CT2: deposit; Phase 5. Twelve small pieces of broken burnt wood. Some bear remains of tool marks on surfaces. The sides of some are curved, possibly the remains of perforations. The pieces may derive from a perforated board (Th. 18mm). Function: part of perforated board. Ash (*Fraxinus excelsior*). L. 25–55mm, W. 20–45mm, Th.18–20mm.

E296:48586:F2027 (Fig. 4.18:7). CT2: House 2 deposit; Phase 5. Split and carved object. Half-split, semi-circular in cross-section. Outer natural surface is gnarled. Apparently worked at one end to form neck and head. Opposite end notched to form two prongs (L. 25mm), broken at time of record. Function: unknown. Yew (*Taxus baccata*). Slightly charred. L. 172mm, W. 28mm, Th. 21mm.

E296:48590:F2046 (Fig. 4.18:8). CT2: deposit; Phase 4a. Small wedge-shaped carved object, oval in cross-section. Flat top, possibly hammered. Tapers to blunt, rounded tip. Function: unknown, possible dowel or peg? Species not identified. L. 61mm, W. 32mm, Th. 21mm.

E296:48596:F2015 (Fig. 4.18:9). CT2: deposit; Phase 6. Thick fragment, approximately rectangular in shape. Slightly curved in length, sharply curved cross-section. No original edges. Smooth outer surface. Inner surface ribbed, possibly from wood growth. Function: unknown, resembles part of pipe stave or spout. Willow (*Salix*). L. 174mm, W. 57mm, Th. 13mm.

E748:27 (Pl. 4.19:5). CB: near hoops (E748:21) under shells (House V); Phase F. Finely carved object. Central shaft (L. 26mm), square in cross-section (W. 6mm, Th. 5mm) which at one end curves sharply forming an angled L-shape. This part is rectangular in cross-section (W. 8mm, Th. 4mm). At the opposite end the shaft expands to a roughly triangular shape, the tip of which is elongated and circular in cross-section (Diam. 4mm). The apex is rounded. Surfaces smooth with faint traces of chamfering on narrow edges. Function: unknown. Yew (*Taxus baccata*); species identification by Ellen OCarroll. L. 69mm, W. 14–36mm, Th. 4–6mm.

E748:44 (Pl. 4.19:6). CB: occupation debris under wooden floor of House III; Phase D. Carved, elongated bi-conical shape, semi-circular in cross-section. Flat side trimmed with occasional long narrow knife marks. A small ridge across the centre may be a knot. The opposite convex side is roughly trimmed with long flat knife cuts (max. L. 37mm, W. 7mm). One end trimmed almost flat, the opposite cut to a small wedge point with opposing faces. Function: small peg or possible unfinished knife handle. Yew (*Taxus baccata*); species identification by Ellen OCarroll. L. 76mm, W. 10–16mm, Th. 8–13mm.

Species Selection

Six species are represented in the 24 artefacts which have been identified to species level. These are oak (*Quercus robur*), sessile oak (*Quercus petraea*), yew (*Taxus baccata*), ash (*Fraxinus excelsior*), hazel (*Corylus avellana*), alder (*Alnus glutinosa*) and willow (*Salix*). The two artefacts identified above as oak are not distinguished as either *Quercus robur* or *Quercus petraea* as this cannot be done microscopically. The significance of the presence of these species must be assessed by comparisons with macro-botanical and palynological evidence from the site, as well as the general species report (see Moloney and OCarroll below). Nevertheless, it can be stated that general mixed woodland as well as a number of disparate environments are represented in the sample.

SPECIES PROPERTIES

Penduncculate oak prefers lighter, well drained soils while sessile oak grows on heavier wetter soils. Oak wood has always been preferred for building purposes, but the ease with which it splits also makes it suitable for furniture and coopering. Yew grows singly on lime-rich soils or singly in oak woodland. Its wood is extremely dense and durable, and the difference in colour between the creamy sapwood and amber-coloured heartwood is an aesthetic quality that was probably recognised and exploited. Ash is a light demanding species and grows well on well-drained soils. Its wood is very versatile, elastic and easily worked, well suited to handles, shafts and poles. Hazel grows in a variety of conditions, and responds well to management, thus being commonly used for wattles. Its wood is soft and easily worked, tough and flexible, but when exposed, dries quickly. Alder prefers not too acid soils with some movement of water and is typically found on riverbanks. Its wood is light, straight and durable, useful in water-logged conditions. All willows prefer wet conditions, and its use depends on its species, as some are shrubs while others are trees. Willow osiers are used in basketry and it is also commonly used in wood turning. These species were no doubt available to some extent near to the site, but of course the portability of artefacts means that local woodland composition cannot be clearly defined by the record (see also following Chapter 4.7.2). It is more pertinent to examine how the species were used.

USE OF SPECIES

Yew dominates the artefacts as it is the preferred wood of coopers (Comey 2010). Yew was used for the manufacture of the staves, hoops, discs and a nail. It is easily the hardest wood available, especially when seasoned, influencing its use as a treenail. It is the single most common identified species in the early Dublin decorated wood assemblage (Lang 1988, 100). Yew, because of its close grain and dense texture, is an extremely tough and durable wood. Although not easy to work, it does hold its surface well and is particularly useful for making small items. Its lustrous red colour which weathers to a rich orange is an aesthetic quality which probably influenced its choice for finer artefacts. Although not well represented in the pollen record, this is probably more to do with its pollen production, and it would have flourished in association with oak woodland or indeed as woodland on its own.

Ash, hazel and willow were also well-established native species. Ash was used in the making of the perforated board and for a simple peg. Hazel was used for small items like pegs and dowels while willow was used for the possible spout. Alder was used in the making of the loom piece.

4.7.2 Structural wood

AONGHUS MOLONEY AND ELLEN OCARROLL

Introduction

A total of 31 structural wood samples were analysed from property boundaries, pit lining, house posts and embanked defences, all dating to the tenth / eleventh centuries (Table 4.6). Eighteen wood samples from nine different Cork Tower contexts were analysed by Aonghus Moloney in 1990. The results of this analysis are included in the report below along with thirteen wood samples from a further seven Cork Tower contexts and from four Powder Tower contexts submitted to Ellen OCarroll for analysis in 2018.

The samples from the Cork Tower derived from post and wattle property boundaries, the lining timbers, posts and fill of Pit 4a (Phase 4a) from a stone-kerbed hearth (Phase 4a) and from Houses 2 (Phase 5) and 3 (Phase 6). The analysed wood samples from the Powder Tower derived from breakwater (BW) structures of Phase 1b as well as the clay and timber bank (Phase 2).

The study of the range and age of tree types used for structural purposes on an archaeological site offers an indication of the composition of local woodland at the time and any selection policies for particular species. Medieval communities were mainly dependent on woodland resources for the construction of nearly all buildings, pathways, fences and also for most domestic and industrial utensils and implements. The woods in a surrounding catchment area were exploited and often managed to provide an essential raw material for the community.

The analysis presented here concentrates on species identification, species selection and the composition of the local woodland during the Viking Age in Dublin city and its hinterland.

Methods

WOOD IDENTIFICATION AND PRESERVATION

The identification of wood, whether it is charred, dried or waterlogged, is carried out by comparing the anatomical structure of samples with known comparative material or keys (Schweingruber 1990). A wood reference collection from the National Botanic Gardens in Glasnevin, Dublin was also used in this instance. The wood was in a very poor state of preservation when the author (Ellen OCarroll) received the samples in 2018. The samples were dried out and shrivelled and very hard to identify. A large majority of the samples were indeterminate as to species due to the poor preservation.

Results and Analysis

There were four species types present and the most commonly occurring one was oak (*Quercus* spp.) followed by ash (*Fraxinus excelsior*), birch (*Betula* spp.) and then hazel (*Corylus avellana*) (Fig. 4.19).

When the results are plotted by feature type there is a preference for ash in relation to the pit-lining timbers and posts of Pit 4a, oak in association with the property boundaries and hazel in relation to the Powder Tower Phase 2 clay and timber bank (Fig. 4.20). A variety of taxa were present in relation to the house posts (birch, oak and hazel).

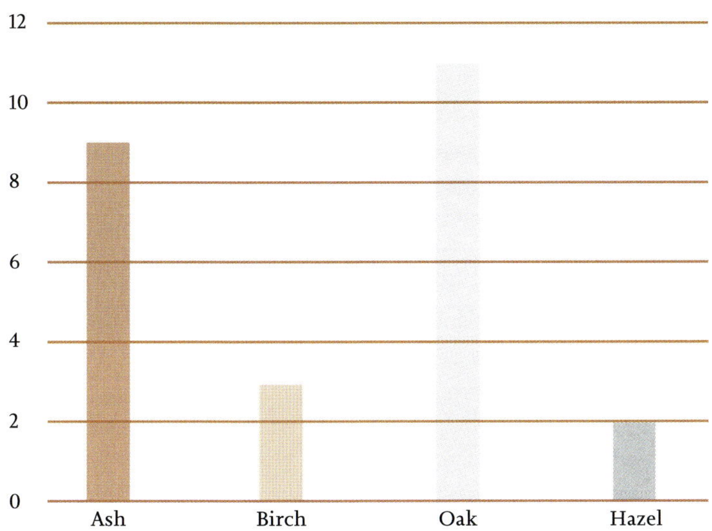

Fig. 4.19 Wood samples: all species identified.

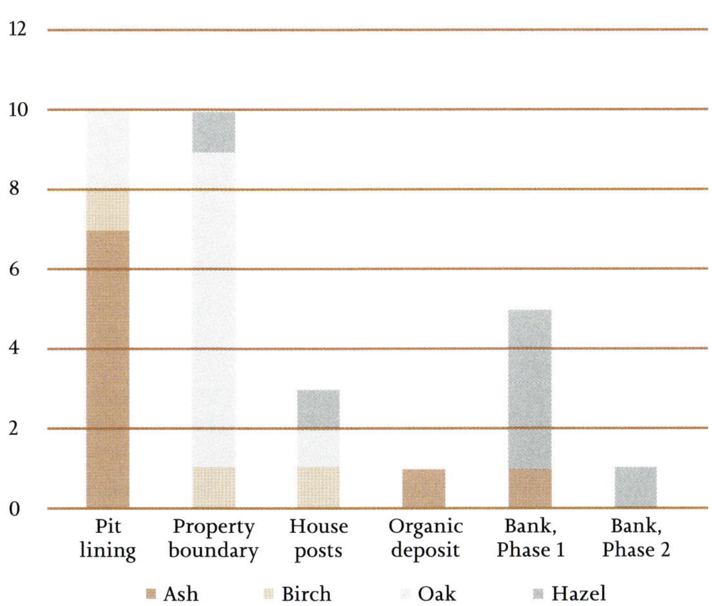

Fig. 4.20 Wood samples: species distribution by feature type.

Pit-lining timbers and posts of Pit 4a (Cork Tower area)

Samples of four of the lining timbers (Timbers 1–4) and two structural posts (F2099 and F2100) of Pit 4a were analysed (Fig. 3.5; Pls 3.9, 3.11). Timber 1 was ash, three pieces of which (a–c) were submitted for analysis. Heartwood could be seen in all three samples of Timber 1 and it was evident that it had been cut tangentially to give an acute oval shape. This ranged from 52mm by 90mm to 24mm by 107mm in section. This cross-sectional size was common to many of the timbers recorded from Dublin Castle and would have allowed for maximum strength in the timber while providing a narrow plank-like shape. Timber 2, also ash, had no evidence of tangential splitting but the timber was still similarly shaped (50mm by 124mm). This timber was naturally shaped to this size and was deliberately selected. The birch timber (Timber 3) as well as the oak timber (Timber 4) were roughly the same shape as the two ash timbers (Timber 3 was 66mm by 108mm in section; Timber 4 ranged between 55mm by 78mm to 60mm by 100mm in section). The oak timber (Timber 4) was over a hundred years old and was clearly selected from a mature tree. Timber F2099 measured 148mm in diameter and was identified as ash, with 75 tree rings present. Timber F2100 was also an ash post measuring 70mm in diameter and containing 73 annual tree rings. These two posts had similar growth patterns.

Property boundaries (Cork Tower area)

One birch, seven oak and a hazel timber were identified from the Phases 3 / 4a property boundary F1194–6; and another oak timber from the Phase 5 boundary F204 (Fig. 4.20). The oak stakes/posts were between 23 and 82 years old; the hazel stake was recorded as 27 years old and no rings were recorded on the birch timber post.

House posts (Cork Tower area)

A hazel and an oak post were identified from the structural timbers of House 2 (F1126 and F2014; Phase 5). A birch post and an ash threshold bar were identified from the structural timbers of House 3 (F1113 and F2003; Phase 6). The wood remains were too degraded to count the rings (Fig. 4.20).

Organic deposit (Cork Tower area)

An ash wood timber measuring 30mm in diameter was identified from an organic deposit in House 2 (F2016; Phase 5) (Fig. 4.20).

Phase 1b breakwater structures and Phase 2 clay and timber bank (Powder Tower area)

Four hazel posts were identified in the BW3 (F547; Phase 1b) structure, and an ash post in BW4 (F509; Phase 1b). Hazel was identified in the framework timbers (FW1a) of the clay and timber bank (F495; Phase 2) (Fig. 4.20).

AGE, SIZE AND GROWTH PATTERNS

Size and growth pattern graphs were generated by Moloney in relation to the wood samples analysed in 1990 (Figs 4.21, 4.22). Analysis shows that the size and shape of the timbers were the governing factor in relation to wood selection rather than species or age. Steady growth was recognised from most of the timbers in relation to the annual rings counted. However, in several cases, there was a marked decrease in growth over the final twenty years. This may reflect a period of relatively poor climate prior to the cutting of the timber.

The two structural posts (ash) from Pit 4a (F2100 and F2099) show a similar growth pattern whereby there was a marked decrease in growth rate over the final years of growth, indicative of a period of poor climate preceding cutting (Fig. 4.21).

Many of the oak timbers, such as stakes F1195a and d from the Phase 4a property boundary, displayed different growth patterns, which suggests that the stakes could have been made from more than one oak tree (Fig. 4.22).

Some stakes, such as the hazel specimen F1195h from the Phase 4a property boundary (Fig. 4.22) showed signs of bruising which would seem to indicate two stakes being forced against each other and hammered into position.

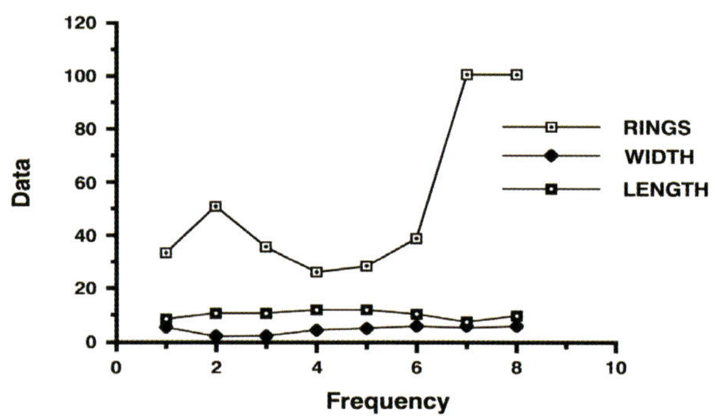

Fig. 4.21 Wood samples: evidence for selection by size.

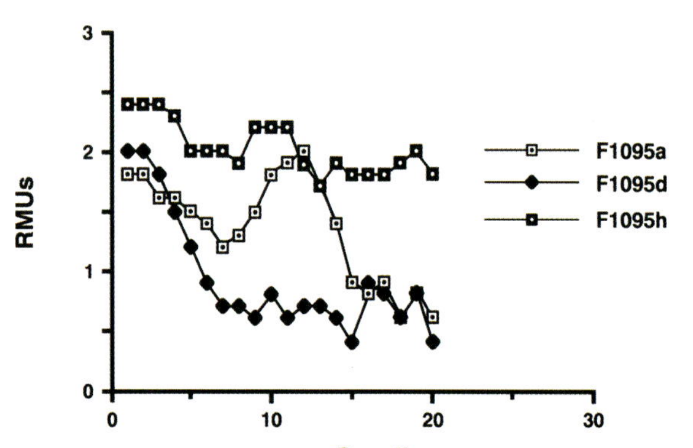

Fig. 4.22 Wood samples: differing growth patterns from Phase 4a property boundary F1195.

Discussion

Four taxa were identified from the assemblage with oak and ash being the most common followed by birch and hazel.

WOOD SELECTION BY TYPE

There were two variables at play with regard to wood selection. Wood was selected based on size and shape as well as specific properties associated with a certain wood species. Identifications revealed that there was some selection of wood types in relation to many of the features analysed. Ash was mostly used (along with one example of birch and oak) for the lining and posts of Pit 4a and may have been deliberately selected for the construction of the pit, as it is easily worked and split (Hurley and McCutcheon 1997). Analysis of the wood samples suggests that there was deliberate wood selection, reflecting a preference for narrow, plank-like timbers, which were either selected as such or trimmed accordingly. The ash timbers used for the lining of Pit 4a were oval in section, providing strong yet pliable timber ideal for construction.

Oak, hazel and birch were used for the posts of the post-and-wattle walls of Houses 2 and 3 at the Cork Tower. The posts were selected from suitably sized trees from a mixed woodland. This result agrees with that obtained by O'Sullivan (1994) from a post-and-wattle Type 1 house excavated in Back Lane, Dublin as well as posts identified from Hiberno-Norse levels at Dean Street, Dublin (OCarroll 2018). Analysis of samples from these sites found that alder was the most predominant species, but hazel, ash, oak, holly and willow were also used in the manufacture of posts (O'Sullivan 1994, 86). Similar species were used for post-and-wattle structures in other areas of Viking Dublin and elsewhere in Ireland (Stuijts 2001; O'Donnell 2010; OCarroll and Moore 2013).

Hazel was the preferred taxa for use as posts in association with the Phase 2 clay and timber bank at the Powder Tower.

Oak was used more frequently for the property boundaries in the Cork Tower area. We know from the *Bretha Comaithchesa* that oak fences were very important in the medieval period to withstand animals and humans. Descriptions of these fence structures record that they were six feet high, stout and dense (Ó Corráin 1983). The tenth-century inhabitants on the site of Dublin Castle may have adopted the traditional ways of manufacturing these boundary fences using oak posts which are stronger and longer lasting than other species. The evidence suggests that boundary fences called for construction using wood that was more robust than the wood type used in the making of the post-and- wattle walls of houses, where hazel was generally preferred (O'Sullivan 1994).

WOODLANDS SURROUNDING DUBLIN IN THE VIKING AGE

The limited number of timber samples retrieved from Dublin Castle throws little light on the woodland present during the Viking Age. However, other wood reports and insect evidence in relation to Viking-age Dublin have helped to fill in some of the gaps (Reilly *et al.* 2016).

Wood analysis undertaken at Viking-age sites at Temple Bar West (Stuijts 2001) and Fishamble Street (O'Donnell 2004) present a somewhat similar picture where alder and ash respectively constituted a large proportion of the structural timbers. Oak was insignificant (apart from artefacts at Fishamble Street) and it has been suggested that it was in short supply during the ninth/tenth and eleventh centuries in Dublin. These results are corroborated vis-à-vis the insect evidence from Temple Bar and Fishamble Street, whereby there were surprisingly few specialist wood-borers or old woodland indicators despite many samples being examined from many different feature types. Oak may have been more valuable for charcoal, artefacts, sturdy long-lasting structures and ship building (Reilly *et al.* 2016). The use of oak within the Cork Tower property boundaries must be related to its deliberate selection for strong fences.

The range of species identified from Viking-age levels at Dublin Castle includes large trees, small trees, scrub and species from wetland environments, indicating that a range of habitats would have been exploited for collection of timbers. The growth patterns observed on the timber samples analysed in 1990 indicate that they grew on good soils in favourable condition. Ash is a species native to Ireland, preferring lime-rich freely draining soils and would have been abundant in the limestone-rich soils of County Meath and north County Dublin. The narrow growth rings noted at the latter stages of growth and prior to the felling of the ash trees may be indicative of deteriorating climatic conditions. Alternatively, the narrow growth rings may simply have been symptomatic of restricted growth due to the less open nature of the surrounding environment as the ash trees grew and expanded into denser woodlands.

It is clear from the analysis that some oak woodlands were accessible in the surrounding hinterland. However, as noted above, the use of oak may have been restricted to specific features which required strength and longevity and hence the lack of oak identified from other structures analysed from Dublin Castle and other Viking sites in Dublin during this time period.

Hazel wood was used for posts associated with the Phase 1b breakwater structure (BW3) and Phase 2 clay and timber bank at the Powder Tower, as well as for uprights for House 2 and a property boundary at the Cork Tower. Hazel posts associated with the property boundary and west end wall of House 2 were older and stouter, while the posts associated with the embanked defences were smaller and younger, although they were incorporated into the body of the bank and were not associated with a wattle structure on top of the bank. Hazel coppiced wood was required for the construction of all wattle structures of which there were many in Viking Dublin. It has been estimated that over 900 houses were in use over any given time period and most were constructed of hazel wattle (Reilly *et al.* 2016; Wallace 2016, 234). Consequently, due to the sheer quantities of hazel wood required for the construction of wattle structures, fences and paths, hazel coppice woods must have been accessible and managed in the hinterland of Dublin. Evidence from recent work completed in relation to Viking-age wattle structures at Dean Street, Dublin certainly points towards a hazel coppice management regime on a short rotation, as nearly all hazel rods used were of a similar age (OCarroll 2018). Hazel coppice woods managed on a short rotation must have been accessible and within easy reach of Viking Dublin. The use of coppiced hazel has been noted from other Viking-age structures including at Back Lane, Dublin, where an extraction system in the underwood was identified, mainly including coppice rotation cycles of five and eight years (O'Sullivan 1994). At Winetavern Street, Dublin when thirteenth-century post-and-wattle waterfront structures were examined, the extraction of underwood at four, seven/eight and ten/eleven years was recorded, while at the medieval settlement site of Irishtown, Kilkenny, a coppice rotation cycle at six years of age was identified from the site (O'Donnell 2010).

The ash and oak were probably selected from areas of woodlands where good soils prevailed. Mixed drier woodlands of oak, hazel and ash could have been found in a number of locations, such as in the hilly landscape to the south of the city and along the upper slopes of the River Liffey valley (O'Sullivan 1994). Birch would have been growing along the shores of the Liffey and Poddle rivers and would have been easily accessible for use as posts.

Chapter 4.8
Leather
John Nicholl

Introduction

A total of sixteen leather finds were recorded from Viking-age levels: three from the Cross Block and, with the exception of one from the Powder Tower, the remainder were recovered from the Cork Tower area. The drier soil conditions at the Powder Tower were not conducive to the survival of organic remains. The leather from the Cross Block was not illustrated at the time of excavation but had survived in a dried-out condition. The leather from the Cork Tower and Powder Tower was examined by Dáire O'Rourke shortly after excavation when a draft report was prepared for the entire assemblage (O'Rourke 1990). Only five of the Viking-age finds have survived and are in a very fragile state. The following descriptions and catalogue were compiled by combining a close examination of the surviving material with the details originally recorded of the unseen items.

Leather Production in the Viking Age

The production of leather and the processing of skins for fur was an important craft industry in the Viking Age. The leather artefacts recovered from the Viking-age levels of the Dublin Castle excavations include examples of tanned leather and processed skins. The methods for producing both were different in both the scale of effort involved and the duration of the actual process.

Leather Tanning

Once the animal was skinned and the hide cleaned, the tanning sequence began, with the fresh or salted hides being pegged in a river or stream and left for a number of days to wash (Cherry 2001). Once the skins were clean of dirt and excess fats, the next stage involved the removal of any hair or fur. There were different ways of doing this, including hanging the hide in a warm, damp room or shed, or sprinkling the hides with urine, after which they were folded and piled in a warm space until the hair began to loosen (*ibid.*, 296). Salt could also be used instead of urine. Another method involved immersing the hides in a variety of solutions, some acidic, others alkaline, in order to open the pores and loosen the hair. The most commonly used solution was a mixture of lime and water. Once the hair was removed, the hide had to be thoroughly washed to remove all traces of lime, which would otherwise hinder the tanning (*ibid.*; Reed 1972; Morfitt 1852).

The final stage of the process, the actual tanning of the hides, involved the immersion of prepared hides in a pit or barrel of tanning liquor for at least twelve months. The liquor was a mixture of water and tree bark. The bark of the oak tree was the bark of choice but other tree bark such as hazel or ash could be used if oak was not available. The hides would be placed in layers in the pit with crushed oak bark between each layer. The pit was then filled with water. The hides would be removed for inspection and then replaced at intervals until the required degree of tannage had been achieved (Forbes 1966).

Fur Production

Unlike tanning, which requires the removal of all the animal's hair from the hide, the production of fur needs to retain the hair intact. The most likely method to have been used in the Viking Age is known as braintanning, a process which utilises the animal's brain to preserve the skin.

Once the animal is slaughtered, the skinner must immediately remove all fat and flesh residue from the skin in order to prevent damage to the fur from putrification. The brain is then cooked with a small amount of water and mixed to form a soup-like liquid. This is then rubbed into the flesh side of the skin to preserve it. Following this, the skin needs to be softened by stretching over a beam or a log. It is then smoked over a low fire to complete the process.

An alternative to braintanning used salt, alum and organic oils such as egg yolks to treat the skin. This process, known as whittawing, involved stretching the skin on a wooden frame. The flesh side was then salted which drew any remaining fluids out of the skin and dried it. It was then treated with a dressing of alum and organic oils and fats to preserve and soften it (Cherry 2001).

Off-cuts and waste

The manufacturing process generated a variety of waste pieces of differing size and shape, which Mould *et al.* (2003, 3245–7) classified as primary, secondary and tertiary waste. Primary waste was generated in the preparation of hides for leatherworking and can be recognised as flesh-shavings, fur trimmings or off-cuts of rough leather trimmings from the edge of a hide.

Secondary waste was produced when individual parts were being cut to shape and such waste is frequently recognised as regular geometrically shaped off-cuts of various sizes. A particularly significant off-cut piece, a triangular shape with one concave side, is usually the product of soles being cut from a hide. Such intersectional off-cuts are a good indicator of footwear manufacture in particular.

Tertiary waste is composed of narrow strips of leather, which were trimmed from artefacts in the final stages of assembly (*ibid.*).

Footwear manufacture in the Viking Age

There were two principal methods of footwear manufacture in this period, the one-piece shoe in which sole and uppers are shaped from one piece of leather and the composite shoe or boot which utilised separate parts for sole and upper. Both types of footwear used the turn-shoe method of construction where the shoe was shaped inside-out and stitched with thread or thong, possibly with the aid of a last and then turned right way round for wearing. This placed the seams on the inside of the shoe protecting them from wear-damage through contact with the ground.

The composite shoe or boot was composed of separate upper and sole parts. The upper was generally made as a single piece where vamp and quarters were cut from one piece of leather, which wrapped around the foot with a seam at the heel or to one side. A triangular-shaped insert was often needed to complete this side seam, which was generally stitched as an edge/flesh butt seam.

Uppers and soles were stitched together using linen thread, animal sinew or leather thong. Generally, the upper and sole were joined using a combination of upper grain/flesh stitch and sole edge/flesh stitch. Sometimes a rand, a narrow strip of thin leather, was stitched between the upper and sole to give a tighter and more water-resistant seam.

Shoes and boots were fastened to the foot in a number of ways, the most common being a length of thong threaded through keeper slots along the top edge, with the ends tied across the instep to secure the shoe. Alternatively, multiple or single pairs of toggle and fastening loops, anchored either side of the ankle, could be used. Once the foot was placed in the shoe, the toggle was passed through the opposing loop and tightened to secure the shoe or boot. The toggle could be of wood or bone or, more frequently, a narrow strip of leather which was rolled at one end to form a toggle and anchored securely to the quarters at the other (Goubitz 2001).

Cross Block Finds

Despite the small number of finds recovered, it is still possible to draw some conclusions concerning the processing of skins and hides and the use of the leather produced as a result.

The two surviving finds, E748:67 and E748:69, are evidence for the two traditional methods of tanning and whittawing for treating skins and hides for leather production. However, it is not possible to say whether the finds in question were actually processed on site or in the vicinity.

Lacing/suspension thong

E748:67, two interlaced pieces of leather thong, is an example of tanned leather and may originally have functioned as a lacing thong or suspension cord on any number of the items mentioned by Aelfric (Watkins n.d.). The manner in which the two lengths have been interlaced through slits cut in each piece would have made for a very secure fastening. Similar lengths of leather thonging were recovered from the lower levels of Drumclay Crannog and functioned as fastenings on ankle boots (Nicholl 2016). Slotted strips of leather were also recovered at 16-22 Coppergate in York and in London from tenth- to mid-eleventh-century contexts. Such strips were interpreted as serving a function of suspending sheaths or scabbards (Mould *et al.* 2001, 3401).

E748:67 (Pl. 4.20:1). CB: Hearth 3 (House III) level, east end of trench; Phase D. Two lengths of leather lacing-thong threaded together through narrow slits to form a knot. The longer length measures L. 154mm, W. 7mm and the shorter length measures L. 30mm, W. 7mm. Both lengths are Th. 3mm.

Fur trimming

E748:69, on the other hand, has not been tanned in the same manner. Clumps of a dark brown hair are still attached to the skin. It is possibly a very rare example of the process of skin treatment which was used to produce furs for clothing

Chapter 4.9
Pottery
Clare McCutcheon

Introduction
A total of 63 sherds were presented for study having been selected as relevant to the Viking-age/pre-castle levels at Dublin Castle. Following identification and some reassembly this was reduced to a total of 59 sherds. In the course of this process 39 sherds from eight different Viking-age contexts at the Cork Tower were judged most likely to have derived from deposits related to the moat of the medieval castle. As explained above (Chapter 3.1), the sloping outer edge of the moat cut the eastern edge of the investigated Viking-age area, creating a high risk of contamination of habitation deposits of tenth/eleventh-century date from abutting/overlying moat-fill deposits of thirteenth/fourteenth-century date. On that basis, the 39 sherds in question have been separated from the Viking-age pottery assemblage and will be included in the report on medieval pottery post-dating the construction of the castle in the early thirteenth century (Papazian and McCutcheon forthcoming). That leaves twenty sherds of pottery: eighteen from the Powder Tower and two from the Cross Block.

Methodology
The material has been identified visually and the detailed information is presented in Table 4.7, including the minimum number of vessels (MNV) present and the minimum vessels represented by the sherds (MVR).

Discussion
The initial study of the medieval pottery from the Dublin Castle excavations was completed in 1989 by Cliona Papazian for her MA thesis from University College Cork (Papazian 1989). In the intervening 30+ years, more detailed

Table 4.7 Pottery identifications.

Fabric	Sherds	MNV	MVR	Form	Centuries/ date range
Seine valley whiteware	4	-	2	Jars	10th-11th
Seine valley highly decorated wares	4	-	1	Jug	13th
Ham Green A ware	2	-	1	Jug	1140-1170
South-east Wiltshire	1	-	1	Jug	12th
Redcliffe	1	1	1	Jug	1250-1400
Leinster Cooking Ware	2	-	2	Cooking jars	Late 12th-mid 14th
Dublin-type ware	2	1	1	Jug	13th
Portuguese redware	2	-	1	Costrel	13th
Saintonge ware	1	-	1	Jug	13th-mid 14th
Langerwehe	1	-	1	Jug	14th-16th
Total	20	2	12		

information on pottery fabrics and their dating has been developed. While some fabric types are unchanged, although with amended dates, others sherds have been reassigned, and the Dublin-type wares have been renamed for easier reference (McCutcheon 2000).

All of the imported wares have been found both in the Dublin area and in the other medieval port cities of Ireland, especially Waterford, Cork and Limerick (Gahan and McCutcheon 1997; McCutcheon 2003 and 2006; Whyte 2016).

Seine Valley Whitewares

Previously known in British and Irish publications (Ponsford 1998; Gahan and McCutcheon 1997, 304) as Normandy smooth and gritty wares, the term Seine valley is now preferred by French ceramic researchers. The very wide date range of tenth to fifteenth centuries can also be narrowed, based on decoration, rim form and vessel form where these can be distinguished. All of the sherds in the current group from Dublin Castle would fall into the smooth ware group. The most notable is a rim sherd (E324:13406:F160), with some variation in date, centring on the eleventh to twelfth centuries.

E324:13406:F160 (Pl. 4.21:1). PT1: upper deposit of post-bank levelling; Phase 3. Rim, decorated with applied strip, stamped with saltire cross or Cross of St Andrew (Lecler and Calderoni 1999, 53, fig. 132): eleventh–twelfth century.

E324:13226:F182 (Pl. 4.21:2). PT1: deposit of post-bank levelling; Phase 3. Rim, square in section: eleventh century.

E324:9074:F323 (Pl. 4.21:3). PT2–Area K: deposit; Phase 12. Body, two lines trailed red paint: late tenth–eleventh century.

E324:12817:F417 (Pl. 4.21:4). PT1: deposit of post-bank levelling; Phase 3. Body, white clay, slight trace of red clay paint: late tenth–eleventh century.

Seine Valley Highly Decorated Ware

These were previously listed as Rouen-type wares (Ponsford 1998, Gahan and McCutcheon 1997, 306), but the style of decoration is typical of a wider area, in much the same way as what is understood as classic Saintonge mottled green glazed ware can be found in the towns of Cognac and Bergerac. These highly decorated wares, dating to the twelfth century in Ireland, come in both fine pink and sandy white clays and both are present in this assemblage.

E324:12681:F160 (Pl. 4.22:1). PT1: upper deposit of post-bank levelling; Phase 3. Body, white clay, pale green glaze, evidence of red clay applied strip.

E324:12682:F160 (Pl. 4.22:2). PT1: upper deposit of post-bank levelling; Phase 3. Rim, white gritty clay, red painted under rim.

E324:11895:F177 (Pl. 4.22:3). PT1: deposit of post-bank levelling; Phase 3. Body, pink clay with applied thumbed strip in white clay.

E324:12855:F447 (Pl. 4.22:4). PT1: deposit of post-bank levelling; Phase 3. Body, white clay, applied red clay strip, diagonal scoring, pale green glaze on body, sooting.

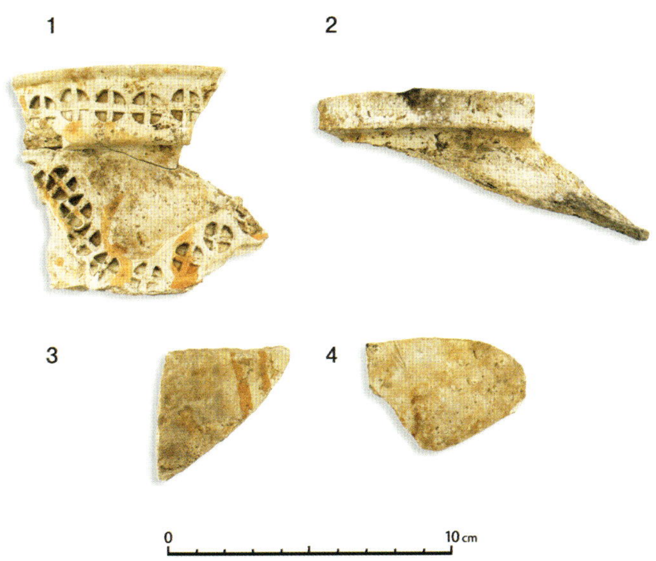

Pl. 4.21 Seine valley white ware (1-4).

Pl. 4.22 Seine valley highly decorated ware (1-4).

Ham Green A Ware

These hand-built wares from Bristol were widely found in Ireland through the early twelfth to mid-thirteenth century. Ham Green A dates from *c.*1140–70 while Ham Green B ware dates from *c.*1170–1250 (Barton 1963; Ponsford 1991).

E324:8800/1:F310 (Pl. 4.23:1). PT2: deposit; Phase 17. Body with applied strip, diamond rouletting, glaze pooled in diamonds.

E748:149. CB: according to the site record, the sherd was 'f[oun]d n[ea]r wooden boards at the W end of cutting under shell. Undisturbed layer', which places it at the Hearth 3 (House III) level; Phase D (*c.* early eleventh century). Body, ridged decoration. Although the excavator regarded the layer as undisturbed, a sherd of this type must be intrusive to a context of this date.

South-East Wiltshire Wares

The earliest glazed wares generally found on Irish sites are the pitchers from south-east Wiltshire. The fabric colour can be white to mid-grey and even red but the single most visible characteristic is the inclusion of abundant quartz, giving the ware an even, pimply finish. The exterior is glazed in a thin lead glaze giving a generally muddy green finish. These wares have been dated to the late eleventh and twelfth centuries although they were thought not to have been exported until the later twelfth century (Vince 1988, 264).

E324:13224:F182 (Pl. 4.23:2). PT1: deposit of post-bank levelling; Phase 3. Body, pink 'pimply' clay, unglazed.

Redcliffe Ware

By the mid-thirteenth century, this wheel-thrown ware from Bristol appears to have largely put Ham Green wares out of business (Ponsford 1991, 95). There is certainly a clear change in the import pattern to Ireland, with Redcliffe replacing Ham Green wares, although the hand-built wares continued to be produced in Bristol until the end of the century (*ibid.*).

E748:148. CB: according to the site record the sherd was 'f[oun]d n[ea]r wooden boards at the W end of cutting under shell. Undisturbed layer', which places it at the Hearth 3 (House III) level; Phase D (*c.* early eleventh century). Rim/strap handle, light grey/grey/cream in section, mottled green. Although the excavator regarded the layer as undisturbed, a sherd of this type must be intrusive to a context of this date.

Leinster Cooking Ware

This micaceous, hand-built ware 'is the single most widespread medieval pottery type in Leinster' (Ó Floinn 1988, 340). It has been found in varying quantities on both urban and rural sites from Dungarvan to Dublin and further north. The fabric contains large plates of mica, quartz grits and other inclusions such as decomposed feldspar (*ibid.*, 327) and the vessels are unglazed. While similar clay can be found in Dublin-type cooking ware and other locally made unglazed wares of the period, the method of construction and firing leaves the Leinster Cooking Ware vessels with an easily recognisable sand-pitted base. The sherds from Dublin Castle represent a cooking jar which, on the basis of its context, can be dated to the late twelfth/early thirteenth century.

E324:12675/7/8/9:F160 (Pl. 4.23:3). PT1: upper deposit of post-bank levelling; Phase 3. Rim, flat top.

E324:12676:F160. PT1: upper deposit of post-bank levelling; Phase 3. Rim from the same vessel as 12675 above.

Pl. 4.23 Ham Green A ware (1); South-east Wiltshire ware (2); Leinster Cooking Ware (3).

Dublin-Type Glazed Wares

The designation of a fabric with the suffix '-type' is recommended in pottery studies to indicate that a ware has been consistently found in a particular area while evidence for a production centre or kiln has not yet been discovered (Blake and Davey 1983, 39–40). The general term 'London-type', for example, has been adopted to describe wares that share general traditions and clay sources (Pearce *et al.* 1985, 2). A fuller discussion of the names of the Dublin-type glazed wares has been detailed elsewhere (McCutcheon 2000, 120–3; 2006) and only a general outline is included here. The relative dating of the Dublin-type glazed wares has been developed as a result of consistent recovery in the stratigraphic levels of the Dublin excavations, and the absolute dating is developing by the association with imported wares, and the dating information from coins and dendrochronology. Dublin-type coarseware, a hand-built ware, was certainly in production by the 1180s and a broad date of thirteenth century has been determined for the wheel-thrown Dublin-type ware, with the Dublin-type fineware dating to the end of the thirteenth and into the mid-fourteenth century.

E324:11985:F174. PT1: deposit of post-bank levelling; Phase 3. Dublin-type ware. Body, grey clay, dark green glaze.

E324:12988:F422. PT1: deposit of post-bank levelling; Phase 3. Dublin-type ware. Body, spots of glaze on interior, some green glaze on exterior.

Portuguese Redware

Formerly known as Merida ware 'a misnomer for Portuguese coarsewares of characteristic brick-red fabric with quartz and mica inclusions, which were probably manufactured in the High Alentejo, an area extending inland from Lisbon and to the east' (Gutiérrez 2007, 64).

Medieval pieces dating to the thirteenth and fourteenth centuries tend to be rougher and brown while the sixteenth- and seventeenth-century fabric is harder, finer and usually red-brown to red (Hurst *et al.* 1986, 69).

E324:12680:F160. PT1: upper deposit of post-bank levelling; Phase 3. Body, red interior, blackened exterior, fine mica evident.

E324:13397:F537. PT1: slot-trench through Phase 1a clay bank (early/mid tenth century) and Phase 1b stone-faced clay bank (mid/late tenth century). Body, red interior, blackened exterior, fine mica evident. While the sherd was found during the excavation of the slot-trench through the earliest embanked defences of the site (Phase 1a/b clay bank/stone-faced clay bank; see Chapter 3.2), a sherd of this type must be intrusive to this level of the stratigraphy.

Saintonge Ware

Mottled green glazed and unglazed jugs were drawn from a wide area upstream from Bordeaux and were widely distributed with the trade in wine, especially when the English moved south to Aquitaine following the loss of Normandy in 1204.

E324:13225:F182. PT1: deposit of post-bank levelling; Phase 3. Body, pink clay, mottled green glaze.

Langerwehe Ware

While this ware was extensively traded to Britain from the Northern Rhine area close to Belgium in the second half of the fourteenth and first half of the fifteenth centuries (Hurst *et al.* 1986, 186), it is rarely found in Ireland, with single sherds recorded from both Waterford (Gahan and McCutcheon 1997, 320, fig.11:15.5) and Wood Quay, Dublin (McCutcheon 2006, 168).

E324:13299:F197. PT1: upper deposit of clay and timber bank; Phase 2. Body, purple stoneware, interior dark ginger brown, exterior iron wash, creamy brown. In light of the dating of pottery of this type the sherd must be intrusive to the context.

Chapter 4.10
Ceramic roof tiles
Joanna Wren

Introduction and Methodology

A small assemblage, comprising ten sherds from curved roof tiles, was recovered from Viking-age levels at the Powder Tower. They were made in soft earthenware that had been completely oxidised and fired to a light pink. Curved and flanged tiles made in this fabric are currently confined to sites in Dublin (Wren 2002, 98; Wren 2006, 181; Wren forthcoming a) and this group is referred to as DCT (Dublin Curved Tile).

Two of the sherds were recovered from deposits (F458 and F464) related to the Phase 2 clay and timber bank that comprised part of Dublin's eleventh-century urban defences. The other five sherds were from Phase 3 deposits (F160 and F198) of the later twelfth century, post-dating the embanked defences. The remaining sherds came from habitation deposits dating to the eleventh century (F327), with one small fragment was found in a twelfth-century layer (F313).

Discussion

Curved tiles like these are one of the oldest forms of clay roofing. They may have been used along the roof ridge but were mostly used on the body of the roof, in combination with interlocking, flatter flanged tiles. The flanged tiles were placed with their flanges facing upwards. The curved tiles then faced downwards and fitted over two adjacent flanges, sealing the tiles together. One tile (E324:8795/6/9:F327) has the remains of a peg-hole through which a peg would have attached the tile to laths on the roof (Fig. 4.23:3).

This form of tiling originated in Greece and Turkey in the sixth / early seventh century BC (Davey 1961, 149) and by the late seventh century it had been introduced to Italy. From there it spread throughout the Roman Empire, reaching Britain by the first century AD. Even after the fall of the Roman Empire it continued to be used on some

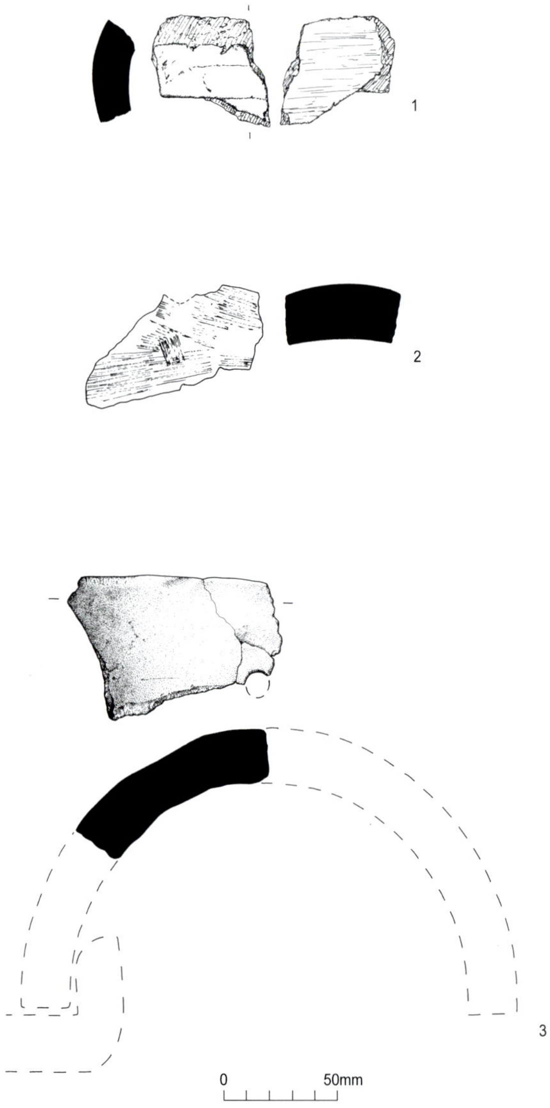

Fig. 4.23 Ceramic curved roof tiles.

European sites. In Flanders examples are known from sites in the fifth–tenth centuries (F. Verhaeghe, pers. comm.) and in Paris they were used to roof the fifth–sixth-century monastic buildings at the Abbey of St Denis (Walters 1985, 189; UASD). In Britain, however, the evidence suggests that curved tiling went out of use in the fifth century AD and was not reintroduced until the Norman invasion, in the late eleventh century (Cornish 2015, 27).

In Ireland curved tiling originated in the early eleventh century, before the arrival of the Normans. The tiles in DCT fabric from Dublin Castle are some of the earliest examples of the form. They are heavy and it seems likely they would have been used on substantial stone or wooden buildings, probably prestigious buildings in the medieval town. The earliest examples came from sites which can be linked to pre-Norman ecclesiastical foundations at Bride Street, Fishamble Street, St Peter's Church and Hammond Lane.

At Bride Street the curved tiles were found in a burial horizon which included a skeleton with a radiocarbon date range from the late ninth to the early eleventh centuries (cal. AD 877–1001) (Wren 2002, 97). This deposit is believed to have formed part of a tenth- / eleventh-century graveyard at the church of St Michael le Pole (McMahon 2002, 4). Burials of this date were also uncovered beneath the twelfth-century stone church and round tower on this site (Gowen 2001, 51). A deposit of lime mortar at the same level as the burials could indicate the presence of earlier stone buildings at the site (*ibid.*, 48) and the tiles might have been used in roofing one of these.

At Fishamble Street curved tiles first occurred in contexts dated numismatically to the early eleventh century (P.F. Wallace, pers. comm.). Tiles from here and from Winetavern Street are likely to have been used at nearby Christ Church Cathedral. The original cathedral building was founded by Sitriuc Silkenbeard, Hiberno-Norse king of Dublin and erected in 1028–30 (Stalley 2010, 53; Bradley 1992, 48). It was probably made of timber (Simms 1990, 47), but it could still have been substantial enough to support a tiled roof. In Scandinavia from the eleventh century onwards there was a fashion for building large, elaborate timber churches (Jensenius 2000, 10), some of which were durable enough to survive today.

A single sherd of curved tile was recovered near St Peter's Church, during excavations at Longford Street Little, Dublin (Wren forthcoming b). The first reference to this church is in 1179 when it was listed amongst the possessions of Christ Church Cathedral (Bradley 1992, 50), but it may have originated in the pre-Norman era (Clarke 1990, 60). The tile came from the upper fill of a ditch, possibly part of a pre-Norman church enclosure (Ó Neill 2004).

Curved tiles were also found during excavations on the north side of the River Liffey at Hammond Lane (Wren forthcoming a). Most of the tiles at this site were deposited in occupation debris beneath a flood bank, which ranged in date from the early eleventh to the mid twelfth centuries (cal. AD 1021-1156). The site was located just 50m from St Michan's Church, which was probably founded in the late eleventh century (AD 1095–6) (Phelan 2010, 165) and the curved tiles presumably came from there.

There are two possible sources for the curved tiles found at Dublin Castle: Christ Church Cathedral and the church of St Mary del Dam both lay within a minute's walk from the site. St Mary del Dam was closer, lying just outside the castle wall by the Powder Tower. Although first mentioned in 1179, this church is believed to have been founded before the twelfth century (Gilbert 1859, 1). St Mary del Dam was demolished at the beginning of the seventeenth century, however (Culliton 1987, 4), and it is impossible to verify that the tiles came from there.

There are indications, however, that medieval building material from Christ Church Cathedral was deposited at the castle. The medieval floor tile assemblages from the two sites are closely comparable (Eames and Fanning 1988, 63; Lynch *et al.* forthcoming b). While the Dublin Castle floor tile fragments were found in much later post-medieval moat fill, they do indicate a pattern of deposition from one site to the other. It is possible that the curved tiles in the pre-Norman levels at Dublin Castle also represent debris from Christ Church Cathedral, like those found at Fishamble Street and Winetavern Street. The evidence suggests that these curved tiles were used on Dublin's ecclesiastical buildings in the later pre-Norman period. Introduced in the early eleventh century, they appear to have gone out of use during the twelfth or the early thirteenth century, when they occur in large bulk deposits throughout the city, probably as a result of the dismantling of entire roofs (Wren 2010, 141). It seems likely that they were first used to roof Christ Church Cathedral, given the scale of that building project, and the fact that the dates for the Fishamble Street tiles coincide so closely with its foundation.

Samples of curved roof tile from Fishamble Street have been subjected to ICP-OES (inductively coupled plasma optical emission spectomatry) analysis (McCutcheon 2006, 156). Recent analysis of the sample results indicated that the clay used to make the tiles was sourced locally (Badreshany forthcoming) and that they were probably made in Dublin. They represent a significant departure from earlier organic forms of roofing found in Ireland, however, and it is probable that they came to be used in Dublin as a result of outside influence. Britain would seem an obvious source, but curved tiling seems to date later there and it has been linked to the Norman Invasion (Cornish 2015, 24). Instead, Dublin's use of tiled roofing in the pre-Norman period may be unique in these islands and could reflect influence from elsewhere in Continental Europe.

CATALOGUE

E324:13006:F464 (Fig. 4.23:1). PT1: lens associated with FW2 timbers of clay and timber bank; Phase 2. Curved roof tile made in DCT fabric.

E324:8797/8:F327 (Fig. 4.23:2). PT2–Area K: deposit; Phase 9. Curved roof tile made in DCT fabric.

E324: 8795/6/9:F327 (Fig. 4.23:3). PT2–Area K: deposit; Phase 9. Curved roof tile made in DCT fabric with the remains of a peg hole.

E324:12686:F160. PT1: upper deposit of post-bank levelling; Phase 3. Curved roof tile made in DCT fabric.

E324:12687:F160. PT1: upper deposit of post-bank levelling; Phase 3. Curved roof tile made in DCT fabric.

E324:2086:F198. PT1: deposit of post-bank levelling; Phase 3. Curved roof tile made in DCT fabric.

E324:2087:F198. PT1: upper deposit of post-bank levelling; Phase 3. Curved roof tile made in DCT fabric.

E324:12088:F198. PT1: upper deposit of post-bank levelling; Phase 3. Curved roof tile made in DCT fabric.

E324:8802:F313. PT2–Area K: deposit; Phase 16. Curved roof tile made in DCT fabric.

E324:12931:F458. PT1: upper deposit of clay and timber bank (same as deposit F197); Phase 2. Curved roof tile made in DCT fabric.

Chapter 4.11
Amber artefacts
Cecily Cropper

Introduction

Although small in number, the ten amber items from Viking-age contexts cover most known artefact designs typical of the material within the Viking period. Magnus's 'standardised catalogue of amber objects for all Scandinavian settlements' (Magnus 2003, 130) includes beads, pendants and rings as well as hemispherical game pieces and most of these, if not all, are represented. The majority (six) were recovered from the house plots in the Cork Tower area.

The small assemblage also indicates amber working, evidenced by flakes, unfinished objects and possibly fractured rejects. The castle assemblage sits alongside a significant centre for amber working already known within Dublin, where, according to Wallace (1987b, 215), the excavation of amber workshops in Fishamble Street has gifted the city with one of the largest assemblages of Viking amber in Europe. As yet unpublished, the assemblage from Fishamble Street is, however, referred to within the Woodstown, Co. Waterford report, where Harvey (2014, 285–6) compares amber items within a broader Dublin typology.

Outside of Ireland, York has produced the largest Anglo-Scandinavian amber-working assemblage in England, dating from approximately the mid-ninth century and continuing into the eleventh (Mainman 2000, 2500–17). As with the Fishamble Street assemblage, the items from Dublin Castle are comparable, as are the techniques used during the working process (Panter 2000, 2501-3). Magnus (2003, 131) notes that the workshops in Dublin and York produced more 'artistic' artefacts than those made in Scandinavia during the Viking period, a fact that also supports Dublin as a major artisan centre for amber working that would have supplied a wider external market (Wallace 1987b, 216).

Beads (Fig. 4.24:1 and 2; Pl. 4.24:1)

A globular and a disc-shaped bead were recovered. Both types are found in Early Christian contexts in Ireland, though those that are so highly polished and potentially worn, and also complete, seem to be relatively unusual, even from the large assemblages from York and Dublin. Harvey catalogues a smaller disc-shaped example from Woodstown (2014, 286–7; no. 02E0441:2173:42, fig. 8.10) and compares it to others from Fishamble Street (*ibid.*, 286). While the perforation on the complete bead (E324:3989:F279) is even and straight, that for the bead fragment (E296:48522:F2029) has an hour-glass cross-section, indicating working from both sides of the perforation, a technique used to dissipate the build-up of excess heat (Panter 2000, 2502).

CATALOGUE

E324:3989:F279 (Fig. 4.24:1; Pl. 4.24:1). PT2 – Area A: deposit; Phase 2. Bead, disc-shaped, translucent yellow-orange, flattened D-shape cross-section. Perforation even and straight. Concentric lathe-turning marks on each flattened surface, chips and wear around perforation entrances. Rounded edge polished. Diam. 20mm; Diam. of perforation 5mm; H. 6mm.

E296:48522; F2029 (Fig. 4.24:2). CT2: House 2 deposit; Phase 5. Item unseen. Fragment of amber bead. Polished and with an hour-glass perforation. Diameter approximately reconstructed 13.5mm (description taken from the Dublin Castle excavations archive). Dimensions (based on illustration): Diam. *c.* 11.5mm, W. *c.* 5mm, H. *c.* 4mm.

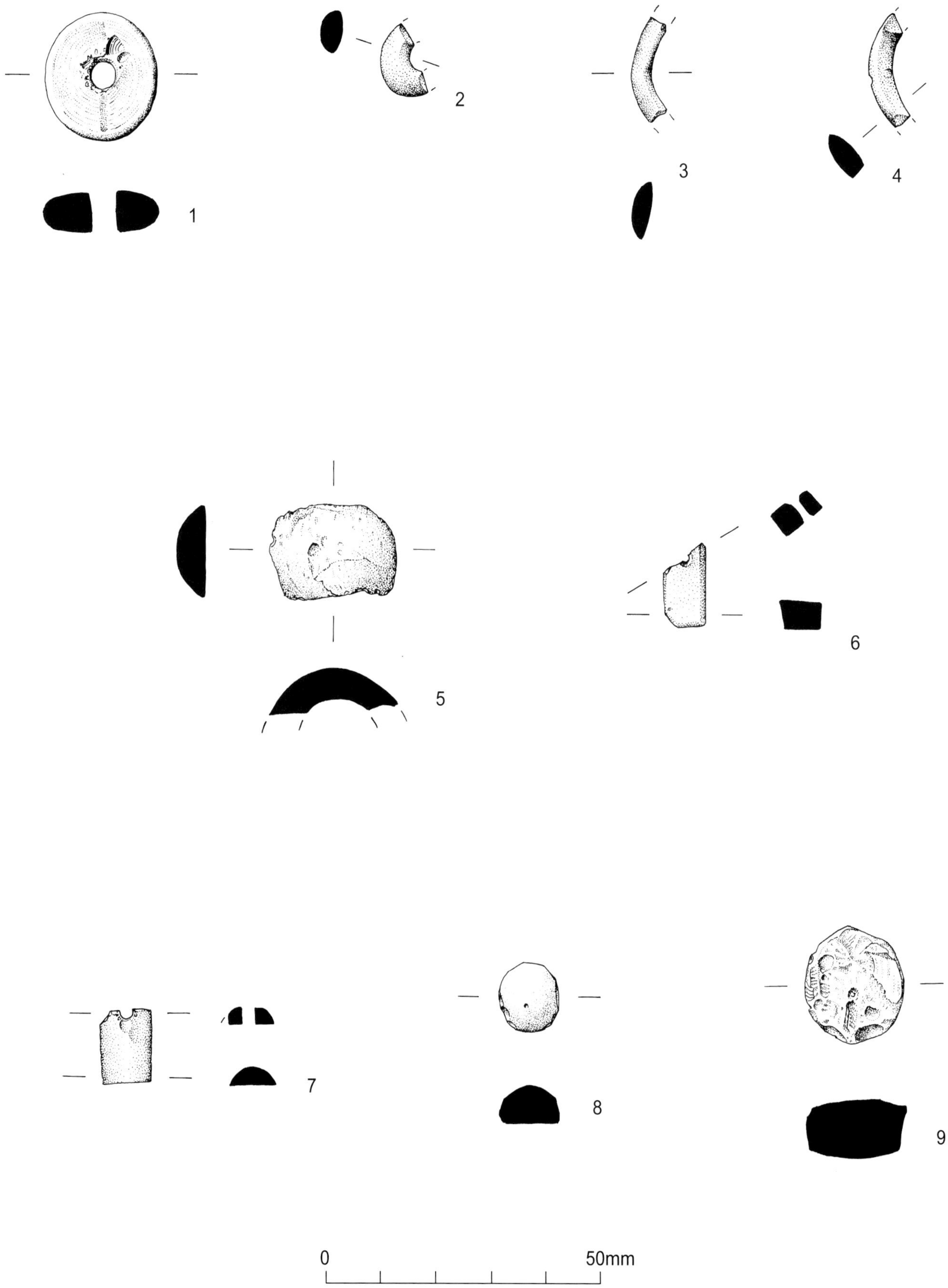

Fig. 4.24 Amber artefacts: beads (1, 2), ring fragments (3, 4, 5), pendant fragments (6, 7), possible inset (8), unfinished piece (9).

Rings (Fig. 4.24:3–5; Pl. 4.24:2 and 3)

Four ring fragments were recorded and fragments E296:48560:F2066 and E748:136 show evidence of having been worked with a knife, indicated by both tell-tale striations and the remnants of ovoid-shaped pits left as small fragments of amber are removed through the working process (Panter 2000, 2501). Polishing on the internal surface has occurred after working. Ring E748:136 is much deeper than E296:48560:F2066, and this, together with the angular internal section, suggests an alternative function to that of personal adornment.

CATALOGUE

E296:48560:F2066 (Fig. 4.24:3; Pl. 4.24:2). CT2: area of burning; Phase 2. Ring fragment, opaque orange-yellow. Flattened, D-shaped cross-section. Highly polished external surface and a less polished and slightly angular, unevenly worked internal surface. Diam. *c.* 25mm, W. 3.5mm, H. 10mm.

E296:48557:F2064 (Fig. 4.24:4). CT2: remains of wattle mat associated with House 1; Phase 3. Item unseen. Broken amber ring with attempted re-use as pendant? There are attempted bore holes on both sides of the ring. Cloudy yellow colour. Width maximum 6.5 mm (description taken from the Dublin Castle excavations archive). Dimensions (based on illustration): Diam. *c.* 22mm, W. *c.* 6–8 mm, H. 12–15mm.

E296:48564:F2071. CT2: deposit; Phase 1. Item unseen. Broken amber ring, cloudy yellow colour (description taken from the Dublin Castle excavations archive).

E748:136 (Fig. 4.24:5; Pl. 4.24:3). CB: unknown context. Ring fragment, translucent yellow-orange. Flattened D-shaped cross-section, worked and polished surfaces. Internal diameter quite angular on one side. Diam. *c.*25mm, W. 6mm, H. 14mm.

Pendants (Fig. 4.24:6 and 7)

Both pendants are partial and broken through the perforation and both would appear to be from narrow pieces, which makes them comparable to examples from York (Mainman 2000, 2589; fig. 1283, nos 9932–3). E296:48526:F2038 is a typical rectangular or possible wedge shape and of a highly polished and even thickness. E324:13000:F491 has, however, a more unusual D-shaped cross-section, unreferenced within the York assemblage but hinted at within the Woodstown catalogue description by the 'apex of a convex pendant' (Harvey 2014, 286; 02E0441:2173:41, not illustrated). It is interesting to note that both pendants have fractured, not just through a completed perforation, but also after having been highly polished. This would seem to indicate the hazardous nature of working with this particular organic material at each stage of production.

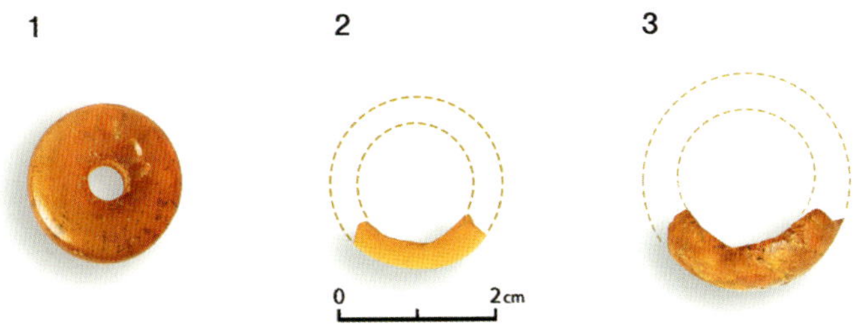

Pl. 4.24 Amber artefacts: bead (1); ring fragments (2,3).

CATALOGUE

E296:48526:F2038 (Fig. 4.24:6). CT2: deposit associated with House 2; Phase 5. Pendant, rectangular end-fragment from a longer object of orange-yellow 'bastard' amber. Polished on all flat sides, one corner oblique, fractured through perforation. Perforation has hour-glass cross-section, one side more flared than the other. L. 13mm, W. 8mm, H. 4.5–5mm; Diam. of perforation 1.5–2.5mm.

E324:13000:F491 (Fig. 4.24:7). PT1: deposit of clay and timber bank; Phase 2. Pendant, rectangular fragment with a D-shaped cross-section, translucent orange-yellow. Polished on all worked sides, fractured through even perforation. Flat sides display fine parallel striations lengthways from polishing. L. 11.5mm, W. 9mm, H. 3mm; Diam. of perforation 2.5mm.

Possible Inset (Fig. 4.24:8)

The overall polished surface of E296:28479:F779 supports this being a finished object. Although it is opaque, the shape and size suggest its role as either a cabochon or inset.

E296:28479:F779 (Fig. 4.24:8). CT2: deposit; Phase 4b. Semi-hemispherical-shaped object. Opaque, mottled matt, black colour with dirty white/cream patches (possibly burnt). Polished all over, but still showing subtle faceting on sides from initial shaping, some pock marks. The uneven base has been polished flat where possible. Diam. 11mm, H. 6.5mm.

Unfinished Piece (Fig.4.24:9)

E296:48505:F2001 is a typical unfinished proto-bead, seen in examples from York (Mainman 2000, 2505; fig. 1219, nos 10728, 10733). The piece has been worked into a shape with two flat sides and a partially polished narrow edge. The indent and slight gouge on one flat surface may indicate either where the piece was held in order to work the outer edge, or possibly the initiation of a perforation. If the latter, this piece would fit within Panter's Stage 2 of production (2000, 2504) and it is possible at this point that the piece was then abandoned. The fine parallel striations within one facet on the same side are of note, indicating a tool mark or marks during production.

E296:48505:F2001 (Fig. 4.24:9). CT2: deposit associated with west end wall of House 3 (partly disturbed); Phase 6. Unfinished piece, mixed translucent/opaque yellow-orange. Disc-shaped with two roughly flat sides, possible proto-bead. Displays multiple facets resulting from initial shaping including very shallow, parallel rectangular grooves, *c.* 0.5mm in width, displayed within one larger facet on one of the flat sides. Evidence of polishing on edge. One flat side shows a centralised indent. Diam.17mm, H. 9 mm.

Waste

Fragments of production waste are common from amber-working sites in north-west Europe (Coulter 2015, 110), comprising small flakes which could not be reused that have been fractured off larger cores (Mainman 2000, 2509).

CATALOGUE

E296:48453:F1189. CT2: deposit; Phase 4a. Waste flake, some original skin, translucent orange-yellow. L. 9mm, W. 4.5mm.

E296:48417:F1197b. CT2: deposit; Phase 3. Waste flake, some original skin, translucent orange-yellow. L. 10mm, W. 5mm.

E296:48602:F2061. CT2: deposit; Phase 3. Waste flake, some original skin, translucent yellow. L. 11mm, W.8mm.

E296:48548:F2056. CT2: lower fill deposit of Pit 4a; Phase 4a. Waste flake, translucent orange-yellow. L. 14mm, W. 10mm.

E324:13395:F537. PT1: slot-trench through Phase 1a clay bank and Phase 1b stone-faced clay bank. Waste flake, some cortex, opaque yellow. L. 11mm, W. 7mm.

E324:13389:F530. PT1: BW1 deposit contemporary with clay bank; Phase 1a. Chip. Item unseen. No description available.

Chapter 4.12
Glass
Cecily Cropper, with a contribution by Laura W. Adlington

4.12.1
Artefacts
CECILY CROPPER

Introduction
Four glass items, comprising a decorated bead, a stud or inset, a linen-smoother and a window glass fragment, were recovered from Viking-age contexts ranging in date from the early tenth to the mid-eleventh century. A fifth item, a fragment of crucible with adhering vitreous material from an early tenth-century context, is also included.

The production of natron-based glass ceased at around the ninth century, but analysis has shown that the crucible fragment was being used to work this type of glass at this location some one hundred years later. The presence of a first- to fourth-century Roman window fragment supports proof of the continued recycling of this early, durable glass and adds further evidence for this process in Britain and Ireland. This tenth- and eleventh-century industry would have produced the translucent stud/inset and added colourants such as cobalt, in the form of tesserae, to produce beads and soda-based window glass that survives so well. Additional evidence from Fishamble Street in Dublin shows that this city, along with York, was simultaneously embracing the working of a new lead-rich dark glass that was used to make linen-smoothers as well as beads and rings.

Bead (Fig. 4.25:1; Pl. 4.25:1)
The fragment of bead (E296:48527:F2039) has weathered opaque and has some surface iridescence on the broken edges, obscuring the original colours. The body of the bead appears to be of dark glass and has been formed on a metal rod. The decoration is of a chain pattern consisting of two intersecting wavy lines with eyes, one of which appears to be spiral and the other a single solid dot of glass. Each chain appears to be of least two different colours that have been coupled with each other, but not woven. One chain is of opaque white glass and a light blue-grey colour and the other broader chain appears to be of opaque yellow, again with the light blue-grey. Within the diamond shape created by the intersecting waves is a spiralling eye of at least two different colours, including the opaque white and a dark colour. The solid eye may be of opaque yellow but this is difficult to ascertain securely.

In terms of typology, the bead fits within Callmer's (1977, 45–51) broad series of decorated Type B beads and then within his Group Bm (*ibid.*, 86–7) characterised by intersecting wavy lines forming a chain pattern with eyes. He also notes that individual lines on black beads are often of different coloured glasses. The most directly comparable are the Type B080s (*ibid.*, colour plate 1). Callmer describes these types of decorated beads as 'archaic', possibly originating from western or central Europe (and therefore potentially imported into Scandinavia) particularly during the periods AD 790–820 and AD 915–50 (*ibid.*, 86–7; 97). By 'archaic', he is referring to the longevity of this type of design, which within Britain and Ireland begins with comparable Iron Age examples such as those of Guido's Class 6B (Colchester-type), combining spirals of opaque white and yellow between swags of wavy lines (Guido 1978, 53–7).

The bead does not fit within a type found more commonly within Ireland, such as, for example, the collared blue and white beads. Comparable examples, though not exact, come from the Viking cemetery at Kilmainham-Islandbridge, Dublin (Armstrong 1921, 73; fig. 2 (m) and (n)) and Cush in Co. Limerick (Ó Riordáin 1940b, 146–7, no.302), the latter having a similar design although of white trailed waves and spiral eyes on a bead of light blue glass. A group of polychrome beads from Coppergate, York (Mainman and Rogers 2000, 2595–6, fig. 1289) are also broadly comparable.

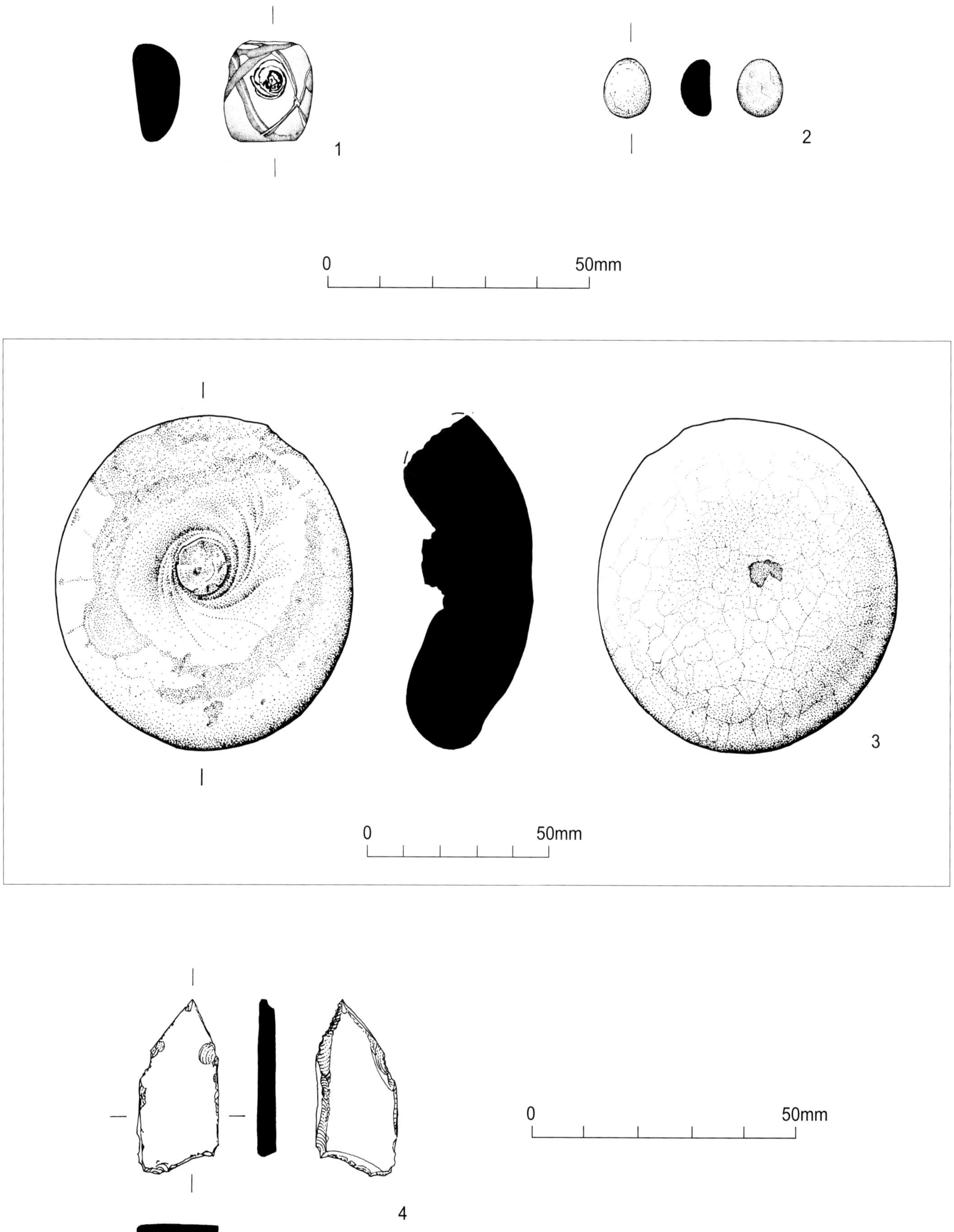

Fig. 4.25 Glass artefacts: bead (1), stud / inset (2), linen smoother (3), window glass (4).

Pl. 4.25 Glass artefacts: bead fragment (1); stud / inset (2).

The inability to class this bead as either a truly Scandinavian or Irish type supports O'Sullivan's interpretation of diverse sources for glass beads as indicated from a number of Viking graves within Dublin (O'Sullivan 2014, 147).

E296:48527:F2039 (Fig. 4.25:1; Pl. 4.25:1). CT2: deposit associated with House 2; Phase 5. Bead fragment, globular, polychrome and decorated with intersecting wavy lines and eyes. Weathered opaque. Diam. *c.* 22mm, H. 16mm; Diam. of bore *c.* 4–7mm.

Stud/Inset (Fig. 4.25:2; Pl. 4.25:2)

This object (E324:916:F277; Fig. 4.25:2; Pl. 4.24:2) would have acted as a cabochon and been placed within a mount as part of a piece of jewellery or another valuable item. The smooth, rounded convex upper surface contrasts with the flattened under surface that has a textured impression. Formation would most likely have been on a rod, the end of which provided a platform on which the glass would have sat during heating and shaping. The textured surface corresponds with that platform and is also very slightly countersunk due to the shaping of the convex side on a surface. Concentric scratches are present around approximately two-thirds of the perimeter of the inset, suggesting where the mount was in direct contact with the glass.

Comparable plain glass studs or insets were recovered from Woodstown, Co. Waterford, all of similar transparent, colourless slightly tinted glass. Although described as 'drops', the two ovoid examples are almost certainly for mounting within a composite object (Cropper 2014, 283–4). A green-tinted inset, with an almost identical description, was recovered from Movilla Abbey, Co. Down and analysis showed this to be of soda-lime-silica 'Roman' glass (Henderson 1984, 99, fig. 15.1). Decorated glass studs in this tinted translucent glass have been found at Garryduff I, Co. Cork (O'Kelly 1962, 119) and at Lagore Crannog (Hencken 1950, 129–30, fig. 52, no.1302b), although these were produced in moulds. At Dunmisk, Co. Tyrone an unfinished glass stud of a translucent blue glass and with curvilinear design was found (Henderson 2000, 146). The use of this soda-based translucent tinted glass for these objects is common within both simple and complex decorated insets, obviously giving the gem-like quality required.

E324:916:F277 (Fig. 4.25:2; Pl. 4.25:2). PT2 – Area A: upper fill of Pit F281; Phase 3. Glass stud or inset, slightly elliptical, 'cabochon'-shaped, transparent and colourless with a slight blue-grey tint. The flat surface has an indented pattern, slightly countersunk. Slight concentric scratching around some of the perimeter. Diam. 9.5–10mm, H. 5.5mm; flattened under surface 9mm by 8mm.

Linen Smoother (Fig. 4.25:3; Pl. 4.26)

Glass linen smoothers are well attested in the archaeological record from as early as the Roman period until as late as the nineteenth century (Pritchard 1991, 173). They are commonly found in Viking contexts, either secular such as at York (Mainman and Rogers 2000, 2534) or within graves such as at Townfoot Farm, Cumbria (Watson *et al.* 2011, 59). Of particular note, however, is the linen smoother from Kilmainham-Islandbridge, just west of medieval Dublin, recovered from the site of the Viking cemetery and described as a 'boss' that had been found alongside 'Danish weapons.' (Coffey and Armstrong 1910, 120, fig. 17). In 1940 however, Bøe re-termed this a linen smoother (Bøe 1940, 49).

Glass linen smoothers, or slick-stones, were used to smooth wet linen or other receptive textiles, and to bring up a natural gloss to the material. The linen smoothers of this period, and up until around the sixteenth century, are characterised by the countersunk stump with a telltale twist to the glass, formed during the shaping process and on removal from the rod it would have been gathered upon. Charleston (1984, 38) notes that the earlier examples are smaller in diameter, ranging from 65mm to 90mm. Both the Dublin Castle (E748:17) and the Kilmainham-Islandbridge smoothers sit comfortably within these dimensions, directly comparable with those from, for example, Birka and Hedeby (Andersson 2003, 127), York (Walton Rogers 1997, 1775) and, more recently, the East Mound longhouse on Orkney (Batey 2019b, 265–6).

Analyses of the smoothers from Coppergate, York showed the majority to contain high levels of lead, and one of nine from unpublished sites in Dublin has a comparable composition (Bayley 2009, 257). Analysis of contemporary examples from France showed a lead-rich composition close to that of lead-smelting slag, this being potentially recycled into linen smoothers from the Carolingian silver-smithing area of Melle, western France (Batey 2019b, 266).

Weathering evident on the Dublin Castle example is complex; the overall surface has weathered opaque and dark brown in colour, with signs of strain cracking appearing in the form of lighter coloured striations. The loss of this external weathered surface on the most convex area displays internal strain cracking shown by a 'sugary' appearance

(Newton and Davison 1989, 156). Additionally, the chipped surface reveals a depth of alteration to the glass that has weathered to a crystalline, almost stone-like appearance. This is a temporal effect on an original defect, known as devitrification, introduced during the glass-working process when crystals are formed within the glass due to insufficient viscosity, or heat control (*ibid.*, 4).

The loss of weathered surface on the convex areas of both sides is notable and corresponds with the areas receiving most wear. The larger convex surface would have been in contact with the material being smoothed, and under closer scrutiny it is possible to see fine striations radiating outwards from the central part. These have also been noted on a Viking example from York (Walton Rogers 1997, 1777, fig. 828a) and are created by the long-term movement of the smoother over textile. On the countersunk side, wear is seen on the circular convex ring around the cracked-off pontil. It is likely that this was in contact with a hard surface, most likely during storage, much like the base of an early wine bottle. A Viking-type smoother from Orkney displays the same wear patterns (Hunterian Museum, Glasgow, GLAHM.B.1914.861).

E748:17 (Fig. 4.25:3; Pl. 4.26). CB: *c.* 1.04m below formation level, *c.* 3.96m west of east curtain wall; Phase E. Linen smoother (slick-stone) of dark glass, circular with a flattened kidney-shaped cross-section, large chip on external curve. Devitrification present. Wear pattern on countersunk side with surface loss. Wear pattern on apex of convex side of fine radiating striations. Diam. 80mm, Th. 31mm.

Window Glass (Fig. 4.25:4; Pl. 4.27:1)

The fragment of window glass E748:75 is Roman in date with a composition typical of natron-based Levantine glass produced between the first and fourth centuries AD (see Chapter 4.12.2 below). The analysis points out further elemental similarities with Levantine 1b glass, produced from the fourth century and containing manganese (MnO) only as a trace element. This type of glass has been shown to be relatively less common within Romano-British assemblages than the more dominant contemporary fourth-century glass, HIMT, from Egypt (Foster and Jackson 2009, 194–5). The same study also found that Levantine 1 glass was more likely to be in a newly manufactured state, as is the Dublin Castle fragment, rather than HIMT glass that commonly appears to have been recycled (*ibid.*, 196).

Pl. 4.26 Glass linen smoother E748:17.

In terms of Roman glass found in Ireland as a whole, it does not stand alone; most are fragments but there is also a small number of complete vessels from Roman and later contexts (Bourke 1994). In Viking-age Dublin, at least thirteen fragments have been recovered from tenth- and eleventh-century contexts within excavations at Fishamble Street and Christchurch Place (Bourke 1987). Fragments listed comprise window and bottle fragments from forms common to the first and second centuries AD (Price and Cottam 1998). Notably, excavations at 35–39 South Main Street, Cork also produced an assemblage from eleventh to twelfth-century contexts of natron-based fragments consistent with first- to third-century Roman glass (Phelps 2011). Detailed scientific analysis of composition showed that these fragments had already been through a recycling process (*ibid*., 16–7).

The double-glossy nature of this particular piece of window glass indicates manufacture by the cylinder method, a technique that becomes more common during the third century (Allen 2002, 109). The complete fragment is produced by cutting and grozing, both processes being employed to create the right dimensions of glass for apertures and practised during the Roman period (*ibid*., 106). A large and significant stash of Roman glass cullet, including window glass fragments with the remains of grozed edges, was recovered from Basinghall Street, London (Shepherd and Wardle 2009, 37). It cannot, however, be determined whether the Dublin Castle piece was an original Roman shape or was reworked and reused within the window of a later structure.

E748:75 (Fig. 4.25:4; Pl. 4.27:1). CB: near/immediately under Hearth 3 (House III); Phase D. Window glass fragment, blue-green tint, double glossy. Leaf-shaped with three cut edges and the rest grozed. No evidence of paint. Both sides weathered with very fine pitting, scratching and slight iridescence in places, otherwise preservation is good; one side appears slightly more weathered than the other. L. 30mm, maximum W. 15.5mm; Th. uniform, just under 3.25mm.

Crucible Fragment (Pl. 4.27:2)

Initial microscopic analysis of metallurgical debris (see Chapter 4.14.2) singled out one fragment of ceramic crucible (E296:S1029:F1223) with adhering vitreous-like material. It had no metals present and was therefore not associated with metalworking. It was proposed that this crucible fragment was used in the production of non-lead glass, as suggested by a high level of sodium within the ceramic (see Chapter 4.14.1). Given this, subsequent SEM analysis (see Chapter 4.12.2 below) indeed provided more concrete evidence that the vitreous material was a soda-rich slag resulting from glass-working. More specifically, this analysis was able

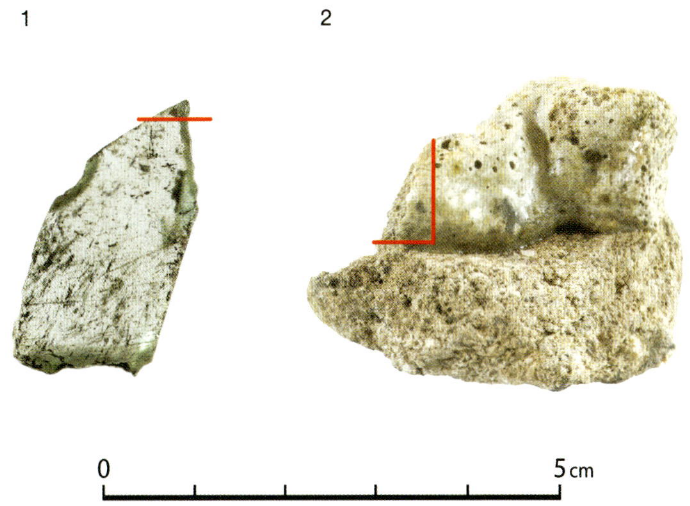

Pl. 4.27 Fragment of window glass (1); crucible fragment (2) viewed in cross-section. Waste material in the form of a thick glassy accretion can be seen on top of the fabric of the crucible. Red lines indicate location of samples taken for SEM-EDS analysis (see Chapter 4.12.2).

to propose that the type of glass being worked contained natron (soda) as a flux and was therefore 'Roman' in recipe.

The natron-based glass industry was long-lived, with glass produced in primary glass-making sites in Egypt and the Levant up to around the mid-ninth century AD (Schibille and Freestone 2013, 11). An increase in chemical analyses on glass from the second half of the first millennium has supported the model of these primary production sites continuing to supply fresh cullet to secondary working sites certainly as far west as Britain (Freestone 2004, 3).

A level of recycling is inherent within the glass industry as a whole, and certainly was carried out throughout the first millennium, but the process appears to pick up considerably from the late seventh or early eighth century particularly within Europe (Freestone 2015, 35).

Evidence of glass-working activity in Ireland during the early medieval period is well attested though limited. Different types of objects, from unfinished glass studs and beads to rods and droplets, come from a range of settlement sites and indicate the probability of glass working (Henderson 2000, 143). Crucible fragments on the other hand, although rare, prove that glass was worked. They have been found at the early medieval sites at Dunmisk, Co. Tyrone (Henderson 1988, 117, no.13) and from an industrial area at Cathedral Hill, Co. Armagh (Gaskell-Brown and Harper 1984, 146, fig. 19, no. 113). Henderson (1988, 124) also includes an unpublished crucible fragment from Scotch Street, Co. Armagh with comparable glass to Cathedral Hill. Analysis of the Dunmisk fragment has shown that the colourant lead-tin oxide, used to create opaque yellow, was added to a soda-lime-silica glass before being incompletely melted, potentially with the aim of creating frit to be used in either bead decoration or in enamelling (Henderson 2000, 150). Both sites cover a period between the late sixth and late ninth century AD, the earlier part of this range associated with the establishment or re-founding of monasteries and ecclesiastical centres in the later seventh and eighth centuries (Willmott and Welham 2013, 234). It was during this time that glass-working was introduced at English sites including Glastonbury Abbey, the monastery site of Jarrow and possibly the early minster site at Barking Abbey, although an early to mid-tenth-century date of a burnt context beneath the furnace at Barking conflicts with the destruction date by Danish raiders in 870 (*ibid.*, 234). Natron-based soda-lime-silica glass was used at Glastonbury and at both the sites of Monkwearmouth and Jarrow. Analysis of material from Glastonbury and the Northumbrian sites shows compositions comparable to both fresh imported Levantine 1 cullet from the production sites of fourth- to seventh-century Palestine, and to recycled Roman first- to fourth-century glass (*ibid.*, 236).

This sets the context for glass-working in both Ireland and Britain from the late seventh to the ninth centuries with the predominant natron-based glasses. But a new type of glass, rich in lead, was introduced, probably from Eastern Europe, during the tenth and eleventh centuries and used to make beads, rings and linen-smoothers (Bayley 2009, 255). Although tenth- and eleventh-century glass-working in Ireland is elusive, it has actually already been evidenced in Dublin. Analysis undertaken on material from various unpublished sites within the city includes a crucible fragment from Fishamble Street that contained a dark, lead-rich glass (*ibid.*, 256). There is more evidence from Britain. At York, two contemporaneous activities were identified: the actual making of high-lead glass, introduced at some point in the tenth century, and the working of low-lead, or Roman-style soda-based glass (Bayley and Doonan 2000, 2528). Although it is not entirely clear what the high-lead glass was being made into on these specific sites, the soda-based glass was being worked into beads. Other evidence of high-lead glass-working during these two centuries comes from crucibles containing yellowish glass from both Flaxengate, Lincoln (Bayley 2008, 4) and Westgate Street in Gloucester (Bayley 2009, 257).

The most prolific early medieval Irish site for crucibles is the ringfort at Garranes, Co. Cork (Laing 2006, 114). Crucibles were used in both copper-working and glass-working 'and it seems likely that the same craftworkers would have been involved in both activities' (Edwards 1996, 92). Two crucible fragments from Viking-age levels are part of the metalworking assemblage from Dublin Castle (see Chapter 4.14). It is noted that 'characteristically their fabric contained much quartz' and that they were made of 'local clay' (Laing 2006, 114–5). The analysed crucible fragment indicating glass-making at Dublin Castle could be similar to a hemispherical type from Garranes (*ibid.*, fig. 46.3; 116, 342, n. 5), but not enough of the fabric survives to determine its full profile.

E296:S1029:F1223 (Pl. 4.27:2). CT2: deposit, Phase 2. Rim sherd of a crucible. Upright, rounded rim form. Translucent pale yellowish glass mixed with porous opaque white vitreous material on inner surface and a thinner more translucent amount extending over crucible lip onto the exterior surface. Fabric is pale grey-buff with quartz inclusions, coarse and blackened on the external surface. Th. 10mm; Wgt. 8g.

4.12.2 Microscopical analysis of window glass and crucible fragment

LAURA W. ADLINGTON

Introduction

Two artefacts from Dublin Castle were submitted for analysis by scanning electron microscopy with an energy dispersive spectrometer (SEM-EDS) for major element characterisation.

The first, a fragment of window glass (E748:75, Pl. 4.27:1), was excavated from an early eleventh-century context at the Cross Block. The fragment was tentatively identified as possibly Roman in origin, and then submitted for analysis to determine the composition and approximate date of the glass.

The second artefact is a fragment of a crucible (E296:S1029:F1223, Pl. 4.27:2) with a blob of thick, greenish material adhered to its inner surface, which was excavated at the Cork Tower and dates from *c.* early tenth century. Crucible fragments from Viking levels of Dublin Castle, along with tuyère fragments and pieces of slag, were treated as evidence for metalworking. In the course of the preparation of the metalworking report for this volume (Chapter 4.14.1), crucible fragment E296:S1029:F1223 along with three others was submitted for analysis by stereomicroscope and SEM-EDS; the latter analyses were carried out non-destructively without invasive sampling or carbon coating (see Chapter 4.14.2). The results for this crucible fragment revealed no presence of metals associated with non-ferrous metalworking, but the ceramic was high in sodium. Possible explanations for these results included the use of a different source of clay, or that the crucible was used for glass-working. Upon further discussion, it was decided to sample the material inside the crucible for identification.

Methodology

A small sample was removed from the window glass fragment (E748:75) using a diamond cutter and pliers and a sample was removed from the waste material adhered to the interior of the crucible fragment (E296:S1029:F1223) using a Dremel drill (Pl. 4.27). The latter sample crumbled upon removal and two parts were prepared for analysis.

The samples were mounted in epoxy resin with the cross-sections exposed. The resin block was polished to 1µm and vacuum-coated with carbon. The samples were analysed at the University College London (UCL) Institute of Archaeology Wolfson Archaeological Laboratories using a Hitachi S-3400 scanning electron microscope with an attached Oxford INCA energy dispersive spectrometer (SEM-EDS), with an accelerating voltage of 20kV, with deadtime between 30 and 40%, probe current of 56µA, a working distance of 10mm and a live time of 120 seconds.. The data were normalised and reported as oxides, in weight per cent.

Corning A and B were analysed as secondary standards. Relative accuracy is better than 5% for Na_2O, SiO_2, and MnO; better than 10% for K_2O, CaO and Fe_2O_3; and better than 20% for other elements present in concentrations above 0.5 wt%.

Window Glass Fragment E748:75

RESULTS

The window glass fragment E748:75 is transparent green-blue and is in excellent condition, an observation which led to the initial identification of the glass as a probable Roman natron-type glass.

The mean results of five analyses across the cross-section are reported in Table 4.8. The window glass fragment has a soda-lime-silica composition and is consistent with natron production, with low magnesia and phosphate. The glass has low iron (0.36% Fe_2O_3), and MnO contents of about 0.3%. Alumina contents are at the lower part of the range of Roman natron compositions (e.g. Schibille and Freestone 2013, fig. 2) at 2.2% Al_2O_3.

DISCUSSION

Glass production during the Roman period until the eighth or ninth century (Shortland *et al.* 2006) was based on the exploitation of natron (evaporitic sodium carbonate found

Table 4.8 Mean and standard deviation of analyses (n=5) on the cross-section of window glass fragment (E748:75), reported as oxide weight per cent.

	Mean	St. dev.
NaO_2	14.61	0.07
MgO	0.36	0.03
Al_2O_3	2.24	0.10
SiO_2	73.48	0.07
Cl	0.91	0.03
K_2O	0.48	0.03
CaO	7.27	0.04
MnO	0.29	0.04
Fe_2O_3	0.36	0.05

at Wadi el-Natrun in Egypt), as the flux. Primary production was centred in Egypt and the Levant, and the raw glass was exported widely to secondary workshops (Foster and Jackson 2009; Foy *et al.* 2003; Freestone *et al.* 2000; Phelps *et al.* 2016; Rehren and Freestone 2015). The small number of primary production sites and the use of different sands, lime sources and decolourisers (Sb and Mn) have resulted in various chemical markers that can help distinguish provenance, approximate date, and recycling practices.

The presence of MnO and the low Sb_2O_3 concentrations (below detection), as well as the lime, alumina and iron concentrations, are overall similar to Roman Mn-decolourised glass production in the Levant (first to fourth centuries AD); the low TiO_2 (below detection) is also consistent with Levantine production (Foster and Jackson 2009; Foy *et al.* 2003; Freestone 2003; Silvestri *et al.* 2008). Of particular interest for comparison is the study by Foster and Jackson (2009), in which natron glass from Romano-British contexts was studied. Glass fragment E748:75 found at Dublin Castle is similar in composition to the 'Levantine 1b' group in that paper (characterised by lower iron and soda, higher lime, moderate to low MnO contents, and are usually tinted blue-green), which appeared in mid-fourth-century Romano-British contexts before HIMT glass (high iron, manganese and titanium) became dominant by the late fourth century onwards. The presence of MnO in the Dublin Castle fragment also points to a pre-fifth-century date, as after this date manganese was no longer used to decolourise Levantine glass (Foy *et al.* 2003; Schibille *et al.* 2016).

Decolourised glass that has been recycled through re-melting of cullet can be identified compositionally due to the elevated trace concentrations of various colourant elements (e.g. Fe, Cu, Co, Pb, from the accidental inclusion of coloured cullet in the melt) and/or elements associated with fuel ash from repeated re-melting (e.g. Mg, P, K). In this glass fragment, the MgO, P_2O_5, K_2O, and Fe_2O_3 contents are all low, and CuO, CoO and PbO were below detection limits, consistent with fresh or minimally re-melted glass.

In summary, the chemical composition of the glass fragment from Dublin Castle suggests the glass was produced in the Levant around the fourth century. If re-melted for recycling, it was minimally so (i.e. fewer episodes of re-melting). The glass may have originated in a pre-Viking building and was then reused at a later date (*c.* seventh century or later; Cecily Cropper, pers. comm.), a practice documented at other sites dating from the late first millennium (e.g. Schibille and Freestone 2013).

Table 4.9 Mean of four analyses on the silicate matrix of crucible fragment (E296:S1029:F1223).

	Mean	St. dev.
NaO_2	6.66	0.96
MgO	0.73	0.44
Al_2O_3	7.88	1.90
SiO_2	71.88	1.28
P_2O_5	0.20	0.30
SO_3	0.21	0.18
Cl	0.57	0.15
K_2O	5.02	0.50
CaO	2.36	0.74
TiO_2	0.54	0.07
MnO	1.03	1.75
Fe_2O_3	3.03	2.01

Substance Adhered to Crucible E296:S1029:F1223

RESULTS

Close visual inspection of the crucible fragment (E296:S1029:F1223) revealed a coarse, porous ceramic with several large inclusions of quartz. The fragment appears to be the lip of the crucible, with a large blob of a porous substance adhered to the interior surface and a thinner layer adhered to the exterior surface as a glaze (Pl. 4.27:2). The sample was taken from the larger deposit on the interior surface.

Examination of the cross-section under the scanning electron microscope reveals a heterogeneous, porous material (Pl. 4.28). Analyses identified a silicate material with variable concentrations of soda, magnesia, alumina, phosphate, lime, and iron (mean concentrations and standard deviations of the matrix are reported in Table 4.9); some areas analysed were identified as very high silica, with all other elements below detection (excluded from results reported in Table 4.9). Inclusions and phases rich in calcium phosphate were also identified (Pl. 4.28). No elements associated with non-ferrous metalworking, such as copper, were detected.

DISCUSSION

The material appears to be slag (i.e. a waste product) from glass-working. The chemical contents of the slag derive from the contents of the crucible (soda-rich glass), the fuel ash, ceramic, and possibly the gathering rod or blowpipe. The fuel ash may have contributed to the concentrations of Mg, P, S, K, Ca, and Mn. The high alumina and iron contents derive from the ceramic, although the high iron contents (3% Fe_2O_3) could also suggest the use of an iron stirring rod or blowpipe. Previous experimental studies in Roman glassmaking have demonstrated the contribution of several factors to the composition of the final glass product as well as waste materials (including fuel ash, waste gases, ceramic crucibles and furnace lining, and iron gathering rod; Paynter 2008).

The porous, heterogeneous structure of the slag derives from the incomplete mixing of the components and slow cooling, which allows the formation of phases. While the lime contents of the silicate matrix are lower than might be expected for a glass-working slag, it appears that the lime segregated to form calcium phosphate, resulting in the inclusions and crystalline phases shown in Pl. 4.28.

Although it is impossible to determine the composition of the glass melted in the crucible from this sample, the soda concentrations and the low magnesia and phosphate contents (despite the contribution of the fuel ash) suggest a natron glass.

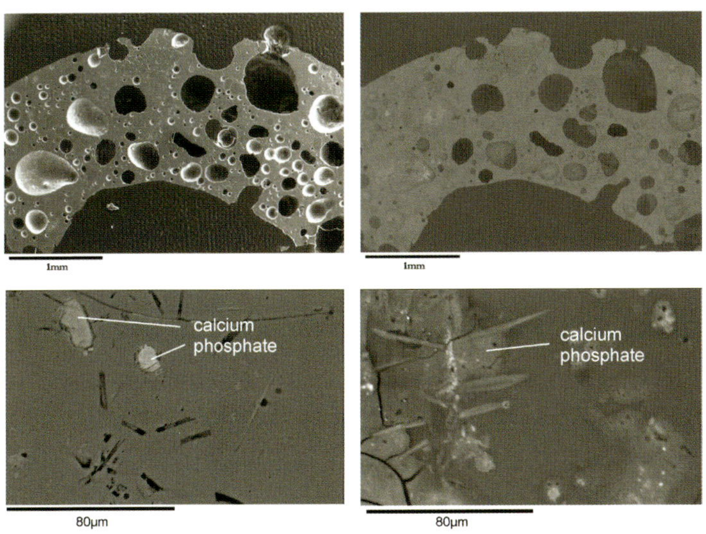

Pl. 4.28 Secondary electron (top left) and back-scattered electron (top right) images of the crucible waste material in cross-section, showing porosity and heterogeneity; (bottom left, bottom right) the waste material in cross-section, showing calcium phosphate inclusions and crystalline phases. (UCL, Institute of Archaeology).

Conclusions

E748:75 is a fragment of window glass which is comparable to Roman natron glass production in the Levant of the fourth century. There are no chemical indicators of re-melting and therefore it appears this glass originated in an earlier structure and was reused at a later date.

E296:S1029:F1223 is a fragment of a crucible which has a large blob of material adhering to its surface. Analysis suggests this substance is a slag (waste product) from glass-working, with a heterogeneous composition derived from the glass, ceramic, fuel ash and iron tools (e.g. gathering rod or blowpipe). The crucible appears to have been used for melting natron glass.

Although this report is based upon the analysis of only two artefacts from different tenth- to eleventh-century contexts, it appears that Roman natron glass was collected for re-use and/or re-melting in the Viking town where Dublin Castle later came to be established. This practice is documented elsewhere during the earlier medieval period and has been attributed to a severe decline in east-west trading activity in the Mediterranean towards the end of the first millennium (Schibille and Freestone 2013).

Chapter 4.13
Textiles and animal fibre
Elizabeth Wincott Heckett and Aislinn Collins, with a contribution by Penelope Walton Rogers

4.13.1
Textiles (Fig. 4.26; Pls 4.29–32)
ELIZABETH WINCOTT HECKETT AND AISLINN COLLINS

Three textile pieces and a group of animal fibres were recovered from Viking-age levels at Dublin Castle. The three textile finds came from the Cork Tower. Two date from the early/mid tenth century (E296:48595:F2053 and E296:48600:F2045); the third from the late tenth/early eleventh century (E296:48598:F2001). The fourth item consists of a collection of animal fibres (E748:85) that were recovered from a probable early eleventh-century context at the Cross Block. Dye analysis was carried out on one of the textile pieces.

Pl. 4.29 Wool tabby weave cloth E296:48595:F2053.

E296:48595:F2053 (Pl. 4.29)
This is a group of plain (tabby) weave wool fragments that appear to be from the same piece of cloth, with Z/Z spinning of the yarn, found within House 1 at the Cork Tower (Fig. 4.26:1). The yarn is regularly spun and has been combed so that the fibres lie parallel with each other resulting in a strong fine thread which can be made into cloth with a clearly defined weave. Since there are eight threads per cm in one system and seven in the other, and only a slight difference in the diameter of the threads used for the two systems, the weave is balanced. With average yarn diameters of *c.*1.17mm (system 1) and *c.* 0.95mm (system 2), the cloth is quite lightweight but not an open weave. Yarn densities of eight and seven to the centimetre designate the cloth as coarse, but the fineness of the yarn and the tight, regular weave contribute to improved quality and the piece was technically well produced. Some fragments have become frayed. The fabric is carbonised and blackened, so no sample was taken for dye analysis because traces of dye do not survive in such textiles (P. Walton, pers. comm.).

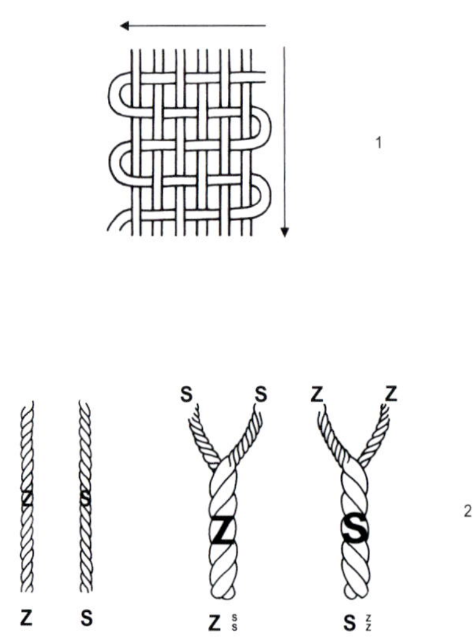

Fig. 4.26 Diagrams of tabby or plain weave (1), Z and S spin and Z and S ply (2).

Tabby cloth has been found generally in Viking-age contexts; examples have survived in England (York and London) (Walton 1989b, 319; Pritchard 1984, 51); Sweden (Aarhus and Lund) (Lorenzen 1971; Lindstrom 1982, 182); Poland (Gdansk) (Kaminska and Nahlik 1958); and Russia (Stara Ladoga and Novgorod) (Nahlik 1964; 1965). However, many of the tabbies are in Z/S spinning rather than Z/Z, although there are a few finer quality pieces with the latter spinning combination including WAT 78 from the Late Saxon excavations in Milk Street, London which is Z/Z spun, with 13/13 threads to the centimetre, yarn diameters of 0.5/0.5mm and combed yarn used to make the thread (Pritchard 1984, 52). Another tabby, 1460b, comes from York, also Z/Z with combed yarn but here the quality is finer, with 24 by 16 threads to the cm and the weave is unbalanced in contrast to the Dublin Castle piece (Walton 1989b, 319).

There is a large group of Z/Z almost balanced weave tabbies from Fishamble Street and St John's Lane, Dublin (Wincott Heckett 1987, 160) but these average 16 by 13 threads to the cm, and the combed yarn used is much finer (ranging between 0.09 to 0.34mm). The type of cloth in the Fishamble Street pieces is therefore much lighter and with much better draping qualities; 41 of these pieces are identified as headscarves and caps (Wincott Heckett 2003).

Balanced tabby weaves have also been found in Waterford (Wincott Heckett 1997, 748) and Cork (Wincott Heckett and Janaway 1997, 341–2; Wincott Heckett 2010, 556–8). However, these are mostly quite coarse with only two or three threads to the cm in both warp and weft. The three pieces from Waterford are Z/Z, while nine from Cork are woven from two-ply S-spun Z-plied yarn. Both groups were found close to docks and trading areas, suggesting commercial or industrial use. Coarse tabby woven cloth had many domestic and commercial uses, including cloaks, blankets, shrouds and packaging for goods during transport or for burial.

Two other pieces found at Christ Church, Cork are better quality: E146:27022.2 has a similar thread density to the Dublin Castle example, 6 to 8 threads to the centimetre; the other piece has 10 to 12 threads. It is suggested that these are dress fabrics (Wincott Heckett and Janaway 1997, 342).

E296:48598:F2001 (Pl. 4.30)

This is a remnant of thick wool with a braided wool cord stitched to the selvedge (woven edge) and was found in association with House 3 in the Cork Tower area. Not enough of the cloth remains to ascertain the weave but it may well have been tabby. It must have been quite a substantial cloth since it is 2.43mm thick. The cord is tightly braided from six two-ply (S-twisted) threads and is tubular in shape with a diameter of 3.2mm. The cord is whip-stitched to the cloth with Z-spun, S-plied (two-stranded) yarn. The stitching is even and regular, consisting of straight parallel stitches. There are 3 to 4 stitches to the cm, with 23 stitches in 8cm. The length of stitch ranges between 4.06mm and 4.36mm.

Pl. 4.30 Detail of wool cloth with cord attached using wool thread E296:48598:F2001.

The cloth and cord are both a dark reddish brown in colour. Samples from warp and weft systems and the cord were sent to Penelope Walton, Textile Research Associates (now The Anglo-Saxon Laboratory) for analysis (see Chapter 4.13.2). The two former showed traces of madder dye from *R. tinctorum* L. and the latter a possible trace of the same. Cloth dyed with madder is known from the Viking-age excavations in Fishamble Street/St John's Lane, Dublin (Wincott Heckett 1987, 161; Wincott Heckett 2003, 128–9) and 19 wool textiles from Anglo-Scandinavian levels at York showed traces of the same dye (Walton 1989b, 396; Walton 1988). Indeed, remains of madder plants were found at Coppergate, York, together with dyer's greenwood and clubmoss, showing that in a similar settlement to Dublin cloth was being dyed (Walton 1989b, 400).

Cords and braids were used to strengthen and protect seams and garment edges, as well as for decoration. Two wool caps found in Fishamble Street, Dublin (Wincott Heckett 2003, 56–60) have edging cords similar to the Dublin Castle piece. The cords on DHC30 and DHC33 are 3mm and 5mm (respectively) in diameter and made from six strands of Z-spun, S-plied (two-stranded) yarn. The cords on both caps are sewn to the edge using stitches that are 4–6mm long with 3 to 4 stitches to the cm. However, the cord on DHC30 is sewn directly onto the selvedge, like the Dublin Castle piece, while the cord on DHC33 is attached to a hemmed edge.

Pl. 4.31 Fragments of wool yarn E296:48600:F2045.

E296:48600:F2045 (Pl. 4.31)

This consists of five short pieces of wool yarn recovered from an organic deposit belonging to Phase 4a at the Cork Tower. They are loosely Z-spun and quite thick, measuring about 3.8mm in diameter. It is possible that the yarn is the unravelled remains of cloth since the threads are kinked as if from being formerly woven. Alternatively, the strands may have been plied together; there is a slight suggestion of S-plying. No samples were sent for dye analysis.

Animal fibres

E748:85 (Pl. 4.32)

Five short pieces and one triangular clump of animal hair were recovered from under Hearth 3 at the Cross Block. The pieces are partially encased in organic matter and the visible fibres appear coarse and close to their natural state. The pieces vary from 3mm to 17.5mm in diameter. Unlike the wool yarn in the other artefacts, these pieces are all S-spun, albeit very loosely. No samples were sent for dye analysis.

Animal hair appears regularly in medieval town sites including Cork, Waterford, and High Street in Dublin, and may be connected with tanning activities (Wincott Heckett and Janaway 1997, 342; Wincott Heckett 1997, 757).

Catalogue

Technical details listed in the catalogue are as follows – the fibre used and the weave are followed by the dimensions of the textile. The warp system is always listed before the weft system where these can be identified. Where warp and weft cannot be differentiated the terms 'system 1' and 'system 2' are used. System 1 is always listed first and is more likely to represent the warp system. Fibres spun or twisted to the left are designated 'Z', and those spun or twisted to the right are designated 'S' (Fig. 4.26:2). The direction of the spin and measurements of yarn diameter are given together with the densities of thread per centimetre. Colour gradings according with the Munsell Colour Charts are also given, with the verbal description first and then the gradings for hue, value and chroma.

E296:48595:F2053 (Pl. 4.29). CT2: matted organic material in House 1; Phase 3. Fragments of wool cloth. Wool tabby, very regular, tight weave, fragile and carbonised; 30 by 25mm, 23 by 28mm and ten fragments; no selvedge; density of threads per cm (system 1) 8/(system 2) 7-6; one

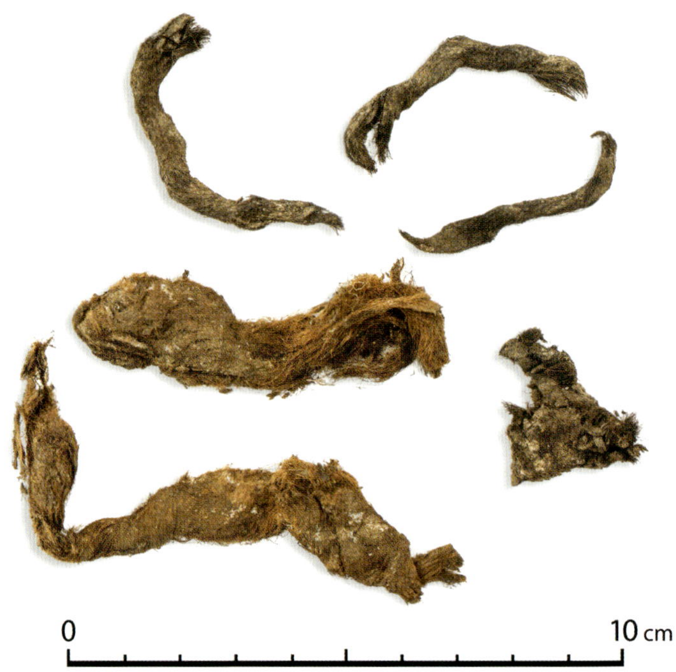

Pl. 4.32 Fragments of animal hair E748:85.

thread in one count of 6 per cm is doubled; worsted type Z/Z spun yarn in both systems; degree of spin loose/loose; yarn diameter 1.17/0.93. Dark reddish brown 5YR 2.5/2; and black 5YR 2.5/1.

E296:48598:F2001 (Pl. 4.30). CT2: west end wall of House 3; Phase 6. Wool cloth with cord attached with wool thread. Cloth: wool tabby (?) regular, balanced weave and yarn, 110 by 10mm; selvedge; density of threads per cm, warp (too few threads to determine)/weft 3-4; thickness of cloth 2.43mm; yarn diameter 1.71/1.90; worsted type Z/Z spun yarn in both systems, degree of spin loose/loose. Cord: wool, 140mm (175mm including unravelled ends); firmly braided from six Z-spun S-twisted two-ply threads, tubular in shape; diameter of cord 3.2mm. Thread: wool yarn, Z-spun two-ply, S-twisted, diameter 1.88mm. Whip-stitched; stitches are even, regular and parallel, 3-4 stitches to cm, 23 stitches to 8cm; length of stitch *c.* 4mm. Dark reddish brown 5YR 3/3; dyed with madder, *R. tinctorum*. Very dusky red 2.5YR 2.5/2. Dark reddish brown 5YR 3/2.

E296:48600:F2045 (Pl. 4.31). CT2: organic clay deposit; Phase 4a. Five pieces wool yarn: 110mm, 90mm, 80mm, 60mm and 63mm in length; loose Z-spun; yarn diameter between 3.24mm and 3.88mm. Dark brown 7.5YR 3/4.

E748:85 (Pl. 4.32). CB: *c.* 0.15m under Hearth 3 (House III); Phase D. Six fragments of animal hair. Five pieces are 64mm, 53mm, 50mm, 70mm and 106mm in length; loose S-spun; diameter between 5mm and 17mm. The sixth piece is a triangular clump 29 by 26 by 24mm.

4.13.2 Dye analysis

PENELOPE WALTON ROGERS, THE ANGLO-SAXON LABORATORY

Three samples taken from the warp, weft and corded edging of E296:48598:F2001 were subjected to the tests for dye which were current in 1989. Essentially, these were solvent extraction followed by absorption spectrophotometry (using a Perkin-Elmer UV-Visible 402 spectrophotometer) and thin-layer chromatography, or TLC (Walton 1988; Walton and Taylor 1991). Although more refined forms of chromatography, such as HPLC, have been developed since then, the results obtained in 1989 should still be sound.

Spectrophotometry showed that a red madder or bedstraw dye had been used for the warp and weft (Walton 1989a). A trace of similar dye was detected in the cord, although this was very weak in concentration and may have bled from the adjacent dyed element. When the samples were tested with TLC, the dye of the warp and weft proved to contain alizarin and purpurin in a similar ratio to that of dyes derived from dyers' madder, *Rubia tinctorum* L.

Madder dye, probably from France, was traded into high-status sites in the Irish Sea region in the seventh century (Walton Rogers 2005; Campbell 2007, 32-50, 80), but proved to be comparatively rare in a sample of 56 textiles from Viking Dublin (Walton 1988). Lichen purple was more common in Dublin, at any rate in wool textiles, while madder was better represented in the Anglo-Saxon textiles of the same date (Walton 1988). It is possible, therefore, that the makers of textile E296:48598:F2001 were using an imported dye, or that the textile itself was an import.

Chapter 4.14
Metalworking
Paul Rondelez, with a contribution by Lorna Anguilano

4.14.1
Metalworking remains
PAUL RONDELEZ

Introduction
Metalworking remains dating from Viking-age contexts were found at the Cork Tower and the Powder Tower. The material, with a total weight of just over 8.6kg, consisted nearly exclusively of slag and vitrified clay fragments. About twenty hemispherical pieces of ironworking waste were recorded from Phase C of the Cross Block, but this material is not available for study (see Chapter 3.5).

All the diagnostic material, smithing hearth cakes and tuyère front fragments, is identifiable as the waste from secondary blacksmithing. The best preserved tuyère front is of a type not yet recorded from Ireland but is well known from the Viking Age in Scandinavian countries.

Two crucible fragments, one from the Cork Tower (E296:48545:F2055) and another from the Powder Tower (E324:13396:F537), indicate that non-ferrous metals were also processed near those areas. Another crucible from the Cork Tower (E296:S1029:F1223) was related to glass manufacture (see Chapter 4.12 and Chapter 4.14.2 above).

The Cork Tower
Most of the material related to metalworking was recovered from the Cork Tower area.

PHASE 1
The earliest phase of Viking-age activity included a truncated pit measuring 2.4 by 1.6m and a depth of 0.3m (Fig. 3.2). This pit (cut F2105 and fill F2078) yielded eight complete smithing hearth cakes (Pl. 4.33:1), with weights ranging from about 200 to 700g, and one partial one. Most of the smithing hearth cakes had adhering, or inclusions of, charcoal fragments while one also had adhering burnt bone. A further 1.4kg of slag was included in this assemblage.

From the same context, multiple vitrified clay tuyère fragments were recovered. The most complete piece had a flat edge, a corner and a curved edge (Pl. 4.34:3). Its maximum preserved dimensions were 160 by 115mm. Another tuyère fragment from the same context consisted of a curved edge (Pl. 4.34:2).

Although pit F2105/F2078 is recorded as having traces of burning, it is very large compared to early and late medieval Irish smithing hearths (Rondelez 2014, 170). It is possible that part of the pit was used as a smithing hearth but there is not enough evidence to conclude that this was the case.

PHASES 2–5
A small piece of slag and a possible tuyère fragment were recovered from deposit F1070 belonging to Phase 2 (early tenth century). Contemporary deposits F1081 and F1223 yielded one, possibly two, smithing hearth cakes, vitrified tuyère material and a crucible fragment related to the production of glass. Among this material was also a nice example of a so-called 'slag beard': an accumulation of slag dripping from the lower front of the tuyère (Pl. 4.33:2). Another Phase 2 deposit (F2066) yielded a further fragment of vitrified tuyère material.

Small amounts of slag and possible tuyère material were recovered from deposits F1068 and F1090 belonging to Phase 3 (early / mid tenth century). Some of the slag from F1068 was covered with a powdery white crust (Pl. 4.33:3). Two contexts of wattle, F2055 and F2064, related to House 1 (Phase 3), yielded a crucible fragment (Pl. 4.35) and some possible tuyère material.

Pl. 4.33 Smithing hearth cake, plan and side views (1); slag beard (2); slag with powdery white crust (3).

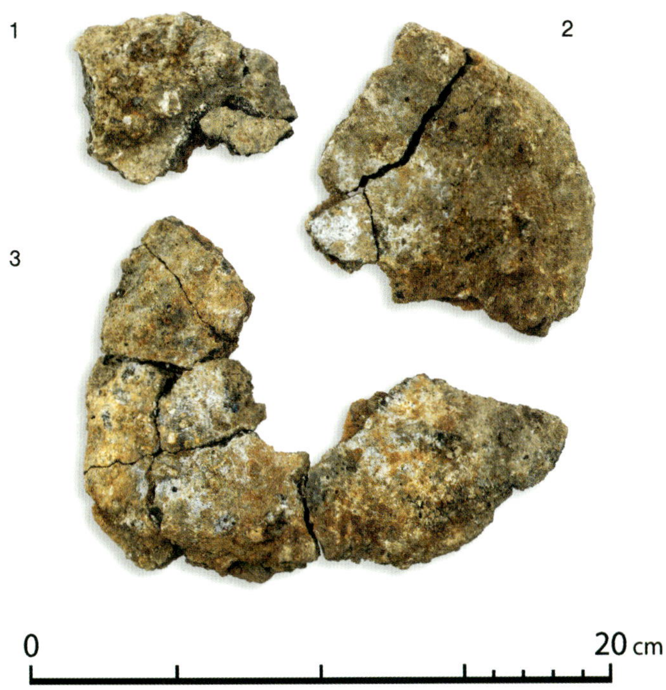

Pl. 4.34 Fragments of vitrified tuyère fronts (1-3).

All the material related to metalworking belonging to Phase 4 (later tenth century) came from Pit 4a (fill deposits F2056, F2058 and F2076) and recut Pit 4b (fill deposit F775). This consisted of further small pieces of slag and (possible) tuyère fragments.

An unstratified smithing hearth cake was also recorded from the Cork Tower area.

Pl. 4.35 Crucible base fragment E296:48545:F2055; exterior surface (left) and section view (right).

A single fragment of vitrified tuyère material came from deposit F1170 in Phase 5 (early eleventh century). Also in Phase 5, five pieces of slag and a fragment of vitrified tuyère front were found within House 2.

The Powder Tower

The metalworking material from Viking-age levels inside the base of the Powder Tower all belonged to Phases 1a/1b, when an initial clay bank (Phase 1a) was replaced with a more substantial stone-faced clay bank (Phase 1b); wooden breakwaters were constructed on the external side of the embankment, the earliest (BW1 and 2) in Phase 1a and later versions (BW3–7) in Phase 1b. Six small fragments of possible tuyère material were retrieved from deposits contemporary with BW2 in Phase 1a (F535) and BW6 in Phase 1b (F501). A crucible fragment (E324:13396:F537) was found in slot trench (F537) which was excavated across the Phase1a/b clay banks.

Viking-age metalworking remains were found in only two of the four areas excavated along the inside of the north curtain wall to the west of the Powder Tower (PT2 – Areas A and B).

Within Area A, two partial smithing hearth cakes and four fragments of likely tuyère were retrieved from a deposit F279 (Phase 2). From Phase 3 within that same area, two more smithing hearth cakes and four (possible) tuyère fragments were found within two deposits (F276 and F277). Deposit F277 was part of the upper fill of Phase 3 Pit F281, while lower fill deposit F282 of the same pit yielded six possible tuyère fragments.

A small piece of slag was recovered from deposit F229 (Phase 2) within Area B.

Discussion

THE SLAG (TABLE 4.10)

Apart from small undiagnostic pieces, all the slag is recognisable as partial or complete smithing hearth cakes. Smithing hearth cakes form below the iron during smithing and are accumulations of lost iron, clay from the bellows protectors and impurities within the hearth/fuel. The assemblage includes a good example of a so-called slag beard or pro-tuyère tongue: slag dripping from the lower tuyère front (Pl. 4.33:2).

The weights of the smithing hearth cakes, varying between *c.* 100g and *c.* 700g, are typical of secondary ironworking. Assemblages related to primary bloom processing generally include cakes weighing several kilograms. At the ninth- to tenth-century Viking-age site at Woodstown, Co. Waterford, the assemblage included much material related to bloom processing, with the largest smithing hearth cake weighing over 6kg (Young 2014, 106).

Some of the slag pieces from deposit F1068 (Cork Tower Phase 3) had an unusual white crust (Pl. 4.33:3). A piece was submitted for chemical analysis (E296:S586:F1068; see Chapter 4.14.2 below; Table 4.13). Only qualitative results were obtained but the presence of both sulphur (S) and calcium (Ca) could indicate that the material is gypsum ($CaSO_4 \times 2H_20$). If this is the case, the crust would be the result of the conditions in the surrounding soil and not of an unusual composition of the slag.

It is unclear if the burnt bone included in one of the smithing hearth cakes from F2078 (Cork Tower Phase 1) was added intentionally as a source of calcium (Ca) or phosphorus (P). Burnt bone was also found adhering to smithing slag from the Viking-age site at Woodstown, Co. Waterford (Young 2009). Tuyères were recovered from Viking-age layers during other excavations in Dublin (Wallace 2016, 334) but have not been described in detail.

Some pieces of slag showed flow structure. While flow structure is typical for smelting slag, it is also frequently observed with assemblages related only to smithing.

Table 4.10 Catalogue of slag.

Sample	Description
E296:S87:F2078 (Pl. 4.33:1). CT2: fill of metalworking feature F2105; Phase 1 (*c.* late ninth century).	Rather well-formed dense smithing hearth cake. The upper surface is rather smooth and the lower surface has adhering heat-affected sand, suggesting that the cake formed at the base of the hearth. Inclusions of charcoal. Wgt. 698g.
E296:S87:F2078. CT2: fill of metalworking feature F2105; Phase 1 (*c.* late ninth century).	Irregular-shaped smithing hearth cake with adhering vitrified ceramic material. This material has a flat surface and is likely tuyère. Adhering charcoal and a piece of burnt bone. Wgt. 368g.
E296:S87:F2078. CT2: fill of metalworking feature F2105; Phase 1 (*c.* late ninth century).	Small bun-shaped smithing hearth cake. Inclusions of charcoal. Wgt. 228g.
E296:S87:F2078. CT2: fill of metalworking feature F2105; Phase 1 (*c.* late ninth century).	Small irregular-shaped smithing hearth cake. Wgt. 202g.
E296:S87:F2078. CT2: fill of metalworking feature F2105; Phase 1 (*c.* late ninth century).	37 small lumps of rather light to dense slag. Some with charcoal inclusions. Wgt. 990g.
E296:S88:F2078. CT2: fill of metalworking feature F2105; Phase 1 (*c.* late ninth century).	Well-shaped near-circular rather light smithing hearth cake. Corroded. Flat upper surface and irregular lower surface. Inclusions of charcoal. Wgt. 701g.
E296:S88:F2078. CT2: fill of metalworking feature F2105; Phase 1 (*c.* late ninth century).	Well-shaped near-circular rather dense smithing hearth cake. Somewhat corroded. Many charcoal fragments included/attached. Wgt. 415g.
E296:S88:F2078. CT2: fill of metalworking feature F2105; Phase 1 (*c.* late ninth century).	Rather irregular bun-shaped rather dense smithing hearth cake. With an upstanding ridge on one side. Many charcoal fragments included/attached. Inclusion of possible tuyère material. Wgt. 442g.
E296:S88:F2078. CT2: fill of metalworking feature F2105; Phase 1 (*c.* late ninth century).	Rounded rather dense smithing hearth cake with charcoal inclusions. Wgt. 249g.
E296:S88:F2078. CT2: fill of metalworking feature F2105; Phase 1 (*c.* late ninth century).	Approximately 50% of a rather dense, bun-shaped smithing hearth cake. Charcoal inclusions. Wgt. 148g.

Sample	Description
E296:S88:F2078. CT2: fill of metalworking feature F2105; Phase 1 (*c.* late ninth century).	Ten lumps of rather light to dense slag. Some with charcoal inclusions. Wgt. 474g.
E296: S777:F1070. CT2: deposit; Phase 2 (*c.* early tenth century).	Small piece of rather dense slag. Wgt. 10g.
E296:S784:F1081. CT2: deposit; Phase 2 (*c.* early tenth century).	Small bun-shaped, rather dense smithing hearth cake. Wgt. 118g.
E296:S784:F1081. CT2: deposit; Phase 2 (*c.* early tenth century).	Piece of rather dense tuyère-influenced slag. Wgt. 57g.
E296:S1023:F1081. CT2: deposit; Phase 2 (*c.* early tenth century).	Lump of heavily weathered and encrusted rather dense slag. Likely smithing hearth cake. Wgt. 89g.
E296:S1025:F1081 (Pl. 4.33:2). CT2: deposit; Phase 2 (*c.* early tenth century).	Slag with adhering ceramic material. Good example of a 'slag-beard'. Wgt. 116g.
E296:S1030:F1217. CT2: deposit; Phase 2 (*c.* early tenth century).	Three pieces of rather dense, heavily weathered slag. Wgt. 144g.
E296:S586:F1068 (Pl. 4.33:3). CT2: deposit; Phase 3 (*c.* early/mid tenth century).	Two largish and several smaller pieces of light porous slag. All have a powdery white coating. Wgt. 9g.
E296:S791:F1090. CT2: deposit; Phase 3 (*c.* early/mid tenth century).	Fragment of dense, heavily weathered slag. Wgt. 32g.
E296:S80:F2056. CT2: fill deposit of Pit 4a; Phase 4a (*c.* mid-tenth century).	Weathered piece of rather dense slag. Wgt. 37g.
E296:S85:F2056. CT2: fill deposit of Pit 4a; Phase 4a (*c.* mid-tenth century).	Two smallish pieces of rather dense iron slag with flow structure. Wgt. 35g.
E296:S83:F2106. CT2: floor level between threshold and hearth associated with House 2; Phase 5 (*c.* mid/late tenth century).	Five pieces of weathered rather light to rather dense slag. Wgt. 127g.
E296:S84:F2107. CT2: unidentified context.	Smithing hearth cake heavily encrusted with charcoal-rich material. Wgt. 832g.
E324:S109:F279. PT2–Area A: deposit; Phase 2 (*c.* early/mid tenth century).	Partial smithing hearth cake (*c.* 70% preserved), dense slag. Thin body with a slag ridge on upper surface. Wgt. 145g.
E324:S109:F279. PT2–Area A: deposit; Phase 2 (*c.* early/mid tenth century).	Fragment of smithing hearth cake with more fluid material on the upper surface. Wgt. 62g.
E324:S1:F229. PT2–Area B: deposit; Phase 2 (*c.* early/mid tenth century).	Small piece of rather dense drippy slag. Wgt. 24g.
E324:S12:F276. PT2–Area A: deposit; Phase 3 (*c.* early/mid tenth century).	Encrusted smithing hearth cake. Wgt. 222g.
E324:S12:F276. PT2–Area A: deposit; Phase 3 (*c.* early/mid tenth century).	Six fragments of dense slag. Wgt. 75g.
E324:S11:F277. PT2–Area A: upper fill deposit of pit F281; Phase 3 (*c.* early/mid tenth century).	Slightly curved, rather dense smithing hearth cake. Wgt. 108g.

THE TUYÈRES (TABLE 4.11)

The evidence for the early and late medieval period in Ireland points to smiths consistently using clay bellows protectors. In the early medieval period these were tuyères generally with a circular front. In the late medieval period, native Irish smiths appear to continue to use the round tuyères while their Anglo-Norman counterparts had a perforated clay wall around part of the top of the smithing hearth (Rondelez 2014, 289–90). A more complicated type, an oval tuyère with an oval blowhole, perhaps indicating that it was used by two bellows, is known from the, as yet undated, site at Roscrea, Co. Tipperary (Rondelez 2016).

The best preserved tuyère from the Dublin Castle excavations, from Cork Tower pit F2105 (fill F2078), however, has a flat edge, a corner and a curved edge. This shape is reminiscent of the semi-circular or D-shaped tuyères which are characteristic for smithing during the Viking period in Scandinavia. In most cases, these Viking tuyères were made from stone but ceramic varieties are known from Hedeby (Haithabu), formerly part of Denmark, now in Germany (Gustafsson 2009, Westphalen 1989, 74–80). The two tuyère fragments from Woodstown, Co. Waterford described as having a 'flattish base' (Young 2009) possibly indicate that a similar type of tuyère was also in use at that site. Tuyères were also found during excavations at Wood Quay, Dublin (Wallace 2016, 334) but are not described in detail.

Table 4.11 Catalogue of tuyère fragments.

Sample/find	Description
E296:S82:F2073. CT2: deposit; Phase 1 (*c.* late ninth century).	Rather dense piece of either heavily vitrified ceramic material or slag with high content of ceramic material. Possibly tuyère-related. Wgt. 56g.
E296:S88:F2078 (Pl. 4.34:1). CT2: fill of metalworking feature F2105; Phase 1 (*c.* late ninth century).	Fragmented part of a tuyère front. Wgt. 50g.
E296:S88:F2078 (Pl. 4.34:3). CT2: fill of metalworking feature F2105; Phase 1 (*c.* late ninth century).	Fragmented tuyère front with a corner, a strongly rounded edge and a less rounded, near straight edge. The clay is fine grained and has inclusions of stony material and charcoal. L. 160mm, W. 115mm, Wgt. 264g.
E296:S88:F2078 (Pl. 4.34:2). CT2: fill of metalworking feature F2105; Phase 1 (*c.* late ninth century).	Fragmented part of a tuyère front with a rounded edge and with part of its side preserved. 110 by 90mm. Wgt. 230g.
E296:S88:F2078. CT2: fill of metalworking feature F2105; Phase 1 (*c.* late ninth century).	Fragments of vitrified tuyère fronts and a piece from the side. Wgt. 344g.
E296:S88:F2078. CT2: fill of metalworking feature F2105; Phase 1 (*c.* late ninth century).	Five fragments of vitrified tuyère material and a piece of slag heavily influenced by tuyère material. Wgt. 46g.
E296:S777:F1070. CT2: deposit; Phase 2 (*c.* early tenth century).	Piece of heavily vitrified material. Possibly tuyère fragment. Wgt. 7g.
E296:S1023:F1081. CT2: deposit; Phase 2 (*c.* early tenth century).	Small piece of vitrified ceramic material. Possible tuyère fragment. Wgt. 9g.
E296:S1025:F1081. CT2: deposit; Phase 2 (*c.* early tenth century).	Two small pieces of vitrified ceramic material. Tuyère fragment. Wgt. 6g.
E296:S1030:F1217. CT2: deposit; Phase 2 (*c.* early tenth century).	Small piece of vitrified ceramic material. Possible tuyère fragment. Wgt. 6g.
E296:48561:F2066. CT2: area of burning; Phase 2 (*c.* early tenth century).	Fragment of vitrified tuyère material. Wgt. 7g.
E296: S601:F1068. CT2: deposit; Phase 3 (*c.* early/mid tenth century).	Piece of vitrified ceramic material. Tuyère fragment. Wgt. 5g.
E296: S787:F1085. CT2: deposit, same as F1068; Phase 3 (*c.* early/mid tenth century).	Small piece of vitrified ceramic material. Most likely tuyère fragment. Wgt. 2g.
E296:S86:F2055. CT2: wattle mat associated with House 1; Phase 3 (*c.* early/mid tenth century).	Small fragment of heavily vitrified ceramic or stony material. Could be tuyère-related. Wgt. 1g.
E296:48558:F2064. CT2: wattle mat associated with House 1; Phase 3 (*c.* early/mid tenth century).	Small fragment of vitrified tuyère material. Wgt. 3g.
E296:S79:F2056. CT2: fill deposit of Pit 4a; Phase 4a (*c.* mid-tenth century).	Small fragment of heavily vitrified ceramic material. Could be tuyère-related. Wgt. 5g.
E296:S80:F2056. CT2: fill deposit of Pit 4a; Phase 4a (*c.* mid-tenth century).	Three small fragments of heavily vitrified ceramic material. Could be tuyère-related. Wgt. 5g.
E296:48547:F2056. CT2: fill deposit of Pit 4a; Phase 4a (*c.* mid-tenth century).	Fragment of vitrified tuyère material. Charcoal fragments adhering to the outside. Wgt. 34g.
E296:S81:F2058. CT2: fill deposit of Pit 4a; Phase 4a (*c.* mid-tenth century).	Lump of heavily vitrified ceramic material. Could be tuyère-related. Wgt. 30g.
E296:48570:F2076. CT2: remains of wattle lining of Pit 4a; Phase 4a (*c.* mid-tenth century).	Piece of vitrified tuyère material. Wgt. 14g.
E296:S817:F775. CT2: fill deposit of Pit 4b; Phase 4b (*c.* mid-tenth century).	Piece of vitrified ceramic material. Tuyère fragment. Wgt. 5g.
E296:S1031:F1170. CT2: Deposit, Phase 5 (*c.* mid/late tenth century).	Piece of vitrified ceramic material. Tuyère fragment. Wgt. 14g.
E296:S83:F2106. CT2: floor level between threshold and hearth associated with House 2; Phase 5 (*c.* mid/late tenth century).	Fragment of vitrified ceramic tuyère material. Wgt. 38g.
E324:S204:F535. PT1: BW2 deposit; Phase 1a (*c.* early/mid tenth century).	Four small fragments of heavily vitrified ceramic material. Could be tuyère-related. Wgt. 19g.

Sample/find	Description
E324:S202:F501. PT1: BW6 deposit; Phase 1b (c. mid/late tenth century).	Two pieces of heavily vitrified ceramic material. Could be tuyère-related. Wgt. 26g.
E324:S109:F279. PT2–Area A: deposit; Phase 2 (c. early/mid tenth century).	Four pieces of heavily vitrified ceramic material. Possibly tuyère fragments. Wgt. 32g.
E324:S12:F276. PT2–Area A: deposit; Phase 3 (c. early/mid tenth century).	Two pieces of heavily vitrified ceramic material. Possibly tuyère fragments. Wgt. 28g.
E324:5799:F276. PT2–Area A: deposit; Phase 3 (c. early/mid tenth century).	Fragment of vitrified tuyère front. Wgt. 27g.
E324:S11:F277. PT2–Area A: upper fill deposit of pit F281; Phase 3 (c. early/mid tenth century).	Fragment of vitrified, slightly convex ceramic material. Tuyère material. Wgt. 12g.
E324:S10:F282. PT2–Area A: lower fill deposit of pit F281; Phase 3 (c. early/mid tenth century).	Piece of straight, vitrified ceramic material. Likely tuyère material. Wgt. 9g.
E324:S10:F282. PT2–Area A: lower fill deposit of pit F281; Phase 3 (c. early/mid tenth century).	Five pieces of heavily vitrified ceramic material. Likely tuyère-related. Wgt. 66g.

THE CRUCIBLES (TABLE 4.12)

The three crucible fragments were too small to enable the identification of their original types. All three fragments were subjected to non-destructive SEM-EDX analysis (see Chapter 4.14.2 below; Table 4.13).

Only for fragment E324:13396:F537 could the analytical data be presented as quantitative values (see Chapter 4.14.2 below). The surface of this fragment was covered with a glaze which gave high values for lead (Pb) and lower ones for copper (Cu) and tin (Sn) (Fig. 4.27).

The relationship between the proportion of metallic elements in crucibles and moulds compared to the composition of the original alloy is complex. The following is based on the findings of the experimental work by Kearns *et al.* 2010.

Due to its high volatility, lead will be present in exponentially higher quantities in crucible surfaces compared to copper and tin. In the case of a copper-tin bronze, the proportions of these elements will be reflected more or less equally in the receptacle. When a copper-tin-lead (80-10-10) alloy is used, however, the crucible will show very high quantities of lead, over 90%, while copper and tin make up the rest with tin levels proportionally higher compared to a non-lead bronze. This means that the metal melted in crucible E324:13396:F537 was likely a bronze with average tin content (c. 10%) with a few percentages of added lead.

Crucible fragment E296:48545:F2055 (Chapter 4.14.2 below), for which only qualitative values could be obtained, showed the presence of lead, copper and zinc. Zinc is even more volatile than lead, leading to even higher proportional quantities being present in crucibles as opposed to the original alloy. Here the original alloy was possibly a bronze with lower or no tin content and very small proportions of lead and zinc.

Table 4.12 Catalogue of crucible fragments.

Sample/find	Description
E296:S1029:F1223. Deposit, Phase 2 (c. early tenth century).	Crucible fragment (Th. 10mm). Distinguished by a thick blob of yellowish vitreous material adhering to its inner surface. Initial analysis of the accretion showed a lack of non-ferrous metals. Further analysis confirmed that the crucible was used for the production of non-lead glass. The crucible fragment is discussed in more detail in the glass finds report (Chapter 4.12). Wgt. 8g.
E296:48545:F2055 (Pl. 4.35). CT2: wattle mat associated with House 1; Phase 3 (c. early/mid tenth century).	Crucible fragment (Th. 8mm). Possible base fragment. The fabric is heavily vitrified and consists of two layers. The outer layer is light grey, has largish air cavities and some inclusions of stony material. The inner surface is dark grey with smaller air cavities. There is some charcoal adhering to the inner surface. Wgt. 2g.
E324:13396:F537. PT1: slot trench through clay bank and stone-faced clay bank; Phase 1a (c. early/mid tenth century) and Phase 1b (c. mid/late tenth century).	Small fragment of a crucible rim (Th. 9mm). Inner and outer surface covered in a red and grey glaze. Wgt. 1g.

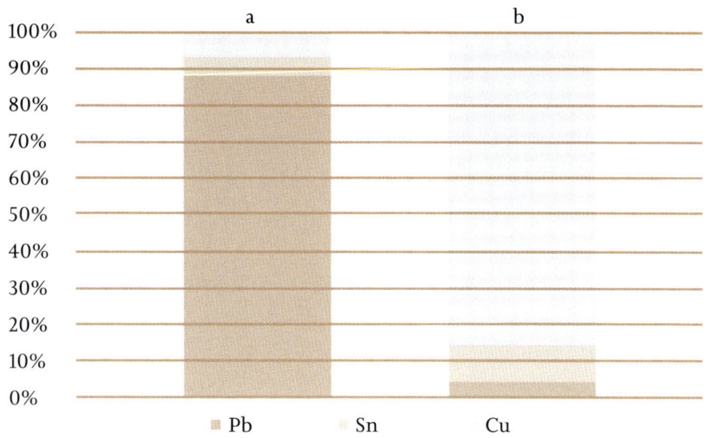

Fig. 4.27 (a) Relative average % of Cu (copper), Sn (tin) and Pb (lead) in crucible fragment E324:13396:F537 and (b) estimated composition of metal used in the crucible.

Crucible fragment E296:S1029:F1223 (Chapter 4.14.2 below) had a blob of yellowish vitreous material adhering to its inner surface and the analysis of this piece showed a lack of non-ferrous metals. This strongly suggested that this crucible was used for the production of non-lead glass, an interpretation confirmed by SEM analysis of the same piece, which recorded high levels of sodium, a common component of early glass (see Chapter 4.12.2 above). The crucible fragment is discussed in more detail in the glass finds report (Chapter 4.12).

Conclusions

Most of the metalworking waste was recovered from the Cork Tower, Phase 1 level. It is unclear if the pit (cut F2105/ fill F2078) was the location of the activity, but it is clear from the nature of the residues, consisting of smithing hearth cakes and tuyère fragments, that this activity was iron smithing. Re-fitting of the fragments of one tuyère front shows that it was of a type known from Scandinavian Viking smithing contexts, but which is new for Ireland.

It is unclear if the ironworking waste from the subsequent Cork Tower phases are residual from the Phase 1 activity or if they are related to continued smithing in the vicinity. No evidence for copper production was included in the Phase 1 material, while a crucible fragment recovered from a Phase 3 context perhaps suggests that copper production was carried out at a later date.

Limited evidence of ironworking and a crucible fragment from the Powder Tower area suggests that smithing and copper production was also carried out near that area during Phase 1 and possibly later. Although ironworking waste was recovered from Phase C of the Cross Block, this material is not available for study. The excavator considered the material to be related to smelting activity (see Chapter 3.5). However, the hemispherical lumps of iron noted at the time are most likely smithing hearth cakes.

4.14.2
Microscopical analysis of metallurgical debris

LORNA ANGUILANO

Introduction

Four samples were analysed by the Experimental Techniques Centre (ETC), Brunel University, London. The samples underwent non-destructive analysis using SEM-EDX, the analyses were to be performed directly on the surface of the samples and the aim of the analyses was to identify the metals present on the surface to inform on the potential metallurgical activity (i.e. type of metal processed) from which the samples derived.

Analysis

The samples were investigated using stereo-microscopy and were then analysed using a Zeiss Supra 35VP field emission scanning electron microscope equipped with an EDXA Octane energy dispersive X-ray analyser. EDX analysis was carried out with the SEM set to 20kV for 45 seconds live-time, and a 3.84 amplitude time.

Results and Discussion

The stereomicroscope observation results are set out in Table 4.13.

SEM ANALYSES OF THE SAMPLES

CRUCIBLE FRAGMENT E324:13396:F537

The glaze indicates a lead silicatic composition. The ceramic shows a calcium, potassium alumino silicatic composition. In the glaze, copper and tin were detected, and also iron and nickel (Table 4.13; Fig. 4.28). As iron and nickel are visible when copper and tin are detected it might be inferred that the origin of these elements is the same and they are not part of the ceramic body. Lead is highly volatile and it might be derived from the melting of leaded bronze. However, while the presence of lead added to a bronze as noble metal collector cannot be ruled out, none of the analyses indicated the presence of noble metals.

Table 4.13 Metalworking analysis: stereoscopic observations.

Sample	Side A	Side B	Notes
E324:13396:F537 (crucible)	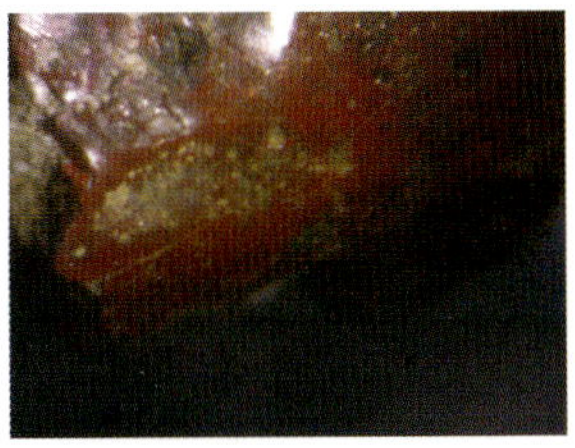		The surface of this sample is of interest because of the dark red glazing. Some areas of the glazing are degraded by pitting, exposing part of the ceramic underneath. The other side of the fragment showing the ceramic, indicates a light ceramic matrix with quartz grain inclusions (white) and some darker inclusions of similar size (~1mm).
E296:48545:F2055 (crucible)	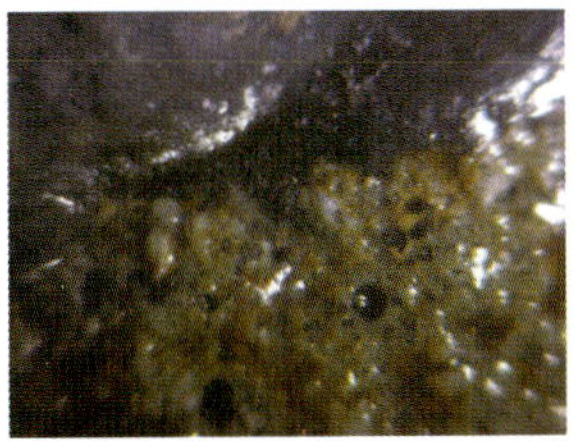	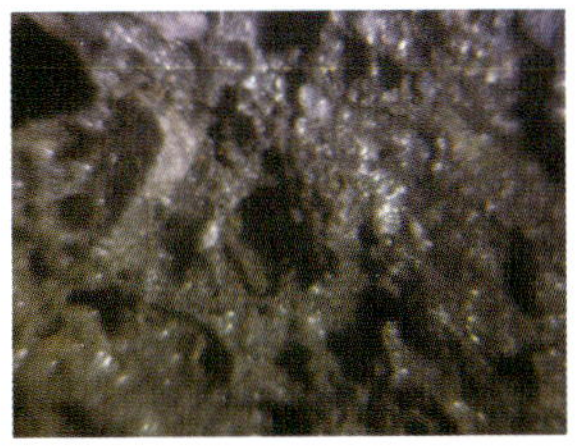	The surface of this sample shows translucent-yellow glazing of about 0.5mm thickness. The ceramic is dark grey and shows very high porosity.
E296:S1029:F1223 (crucible)			Very similar to sample E296:48545:F2055, this sample also shows a yellowish glazing. The ceramic is though of lighter colour, and large dark inclusions are visible. The porosity in the ceramic is less intense than in sample E296:48545:F2055.
E296:S586:F1068 (slag)	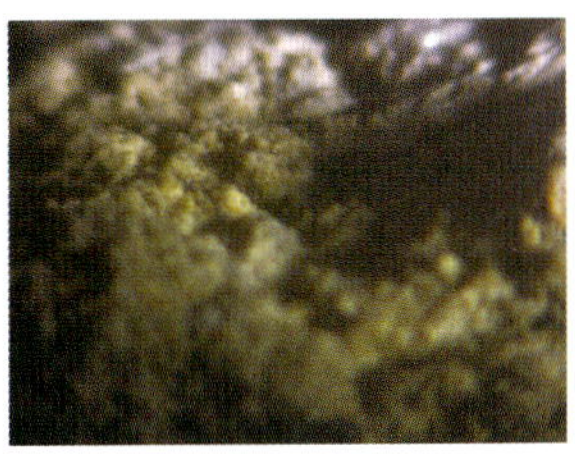	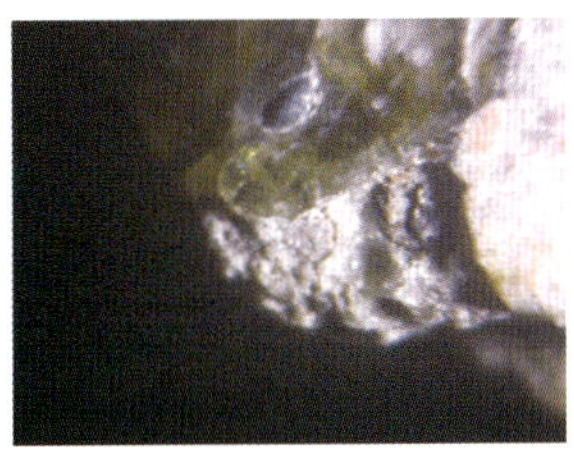	This sample again shows a similar yellowish glazing, in this case the thickness is about 0.3mm. Part of the glaze appears more opaque and more yellow.

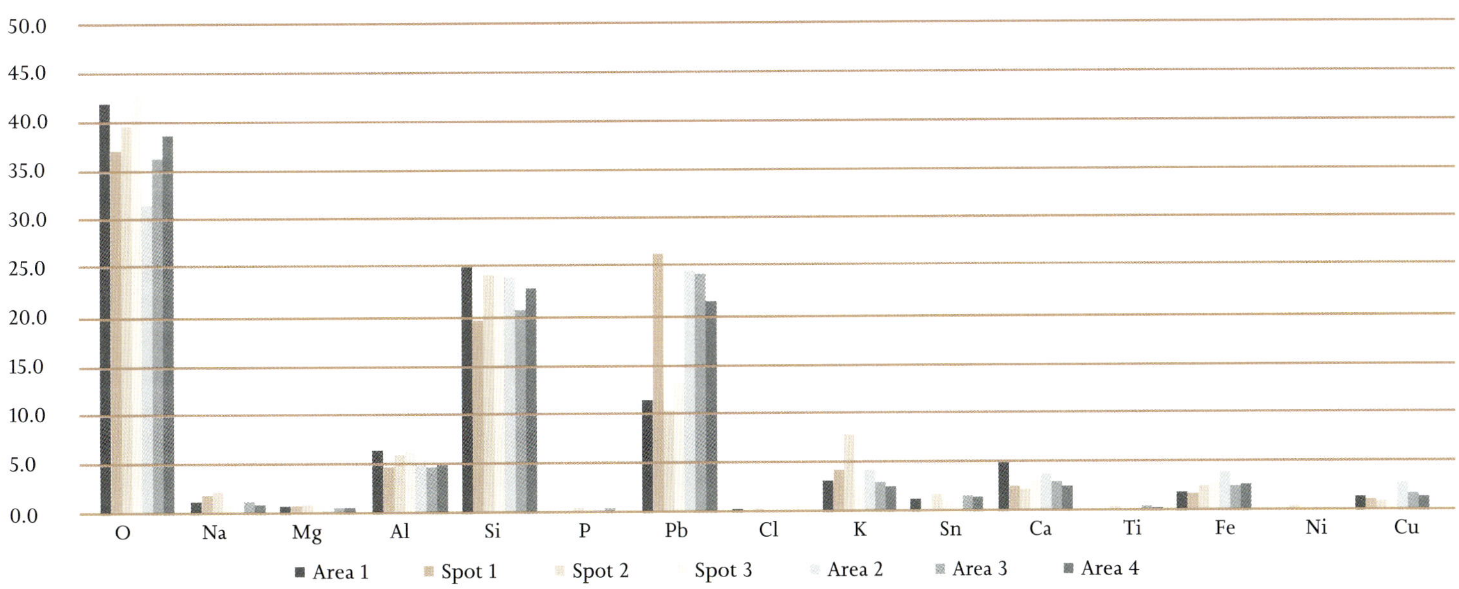

Fig. 4.28 Crucible E324:13396:F537: concentration of the different elements in the points analysed. There is a clear relationship between copper and iron (and tin) and lead and copper, aside from spot 1 which shows a high enrichment of lead but not followed by copper. However, the same point shows a decrease in silicon indicating the possibility that this is a lead oxide area possibly indicating a degradation of the glaze.

CRUCIBLE FRAGMENT E296:48545:F2055

This sample shows traces of copper and zinc, as well as diffused iron (~ 2%) and sulphur (below 1%). The copper is around 0.5 to 1% in weight as detected in the bulk area (Fig. 4.29), however their distribution is inhomogeneous and only some areas show indication of the two metals. However, a more detailed observation of the areas where copper and zinc were detected (Fig. 4.30) shows small areas of enrichment of copper and zinc, in association with lead. Also in those areas the iron concentration increases as in the crucible fragment E324:13396:F537. In this case the glazing is mostly vitrified ceramic, and the metal-enriched glazing is limited to some spots.

CRUCIBLE FRAGMENT E296:S1029:F1223

No metals were detected in this sample. The ceramic is porous with pore sizes around 0.5 to 1mm. The ceramic composition is more enriched in sodium compared to the previous two samples (Fig. 4.31). In this case the sulphur detected was confirmed to be linked with calcium forming a gypsum cement deposited on some areas of the sample from the soil surrounding it.

SLAG E296:S586:F1068

This sample also did not show any metal (Fig. 4.32). The matrix was again potassium/calcium alumino silicate presented low sodium. High iron was visible in this sample, and at close investigation the iron (and sulphur) were observed to derive from debris present on the surface of the sample as pyrite debris. The gypsum and iron sulphide are related to the surrounding soil.

Conclusions

The crucible fragments E324:13396:F537 and E296:48545: F2055 show presence of copper alloys, copper/tin in sample E324:13396:F537 and copper/zinc in sample E296:48545:F2055 in association with lead. Iron is also observed in association with the metals. The crucible fragment E296:S1029:F1223 does not show metals; however, the ceramic seems enriched with sodium, indicating the possible use of two different sources of clay for different types of crucible. The slag E296:S586:F1068 also does not show metallic particles on its surface, the glassy surface composition confirms an iron/calcium silicatic matrix common in ironworking slags. Sulphur is also present and evaluation of the surface particulates is identified as newly crystallised pyrite, which indicates an acidic aggressive soil and possible leachate of iron-rich salts from the slag.

It cannot be determined with these non-invasive analyses if the crucibles are for alloying of leaded bronzes, or for cementation of brasses. Further cross-sectional analysis may confirm the type of process undertaken in the vessels.

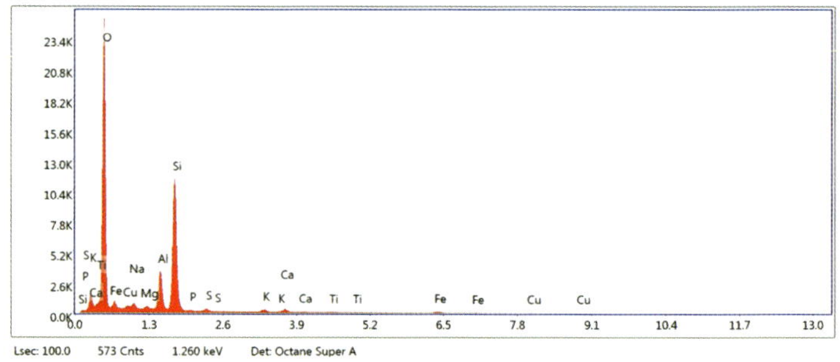

Fig. 4.29 Crucible E296:48545:F2055: representative spectrum of the bulk area showing traces of copper.

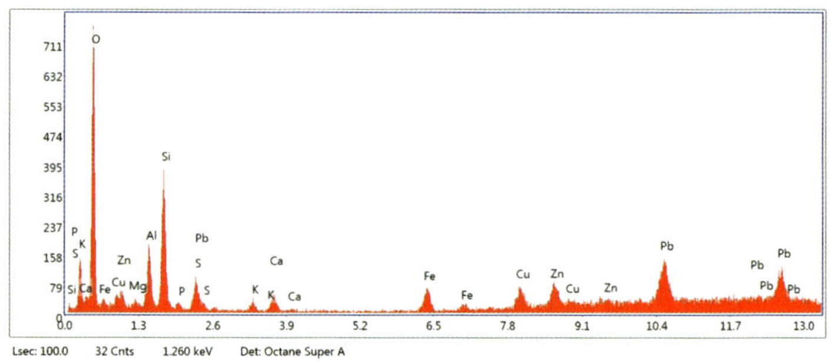

Fig. 4.30 Crucible E296:48545:F2055: representative spectrum of the areas analysed. These analyses indicate spots enriched in copper, zinc and iron in association with lead.

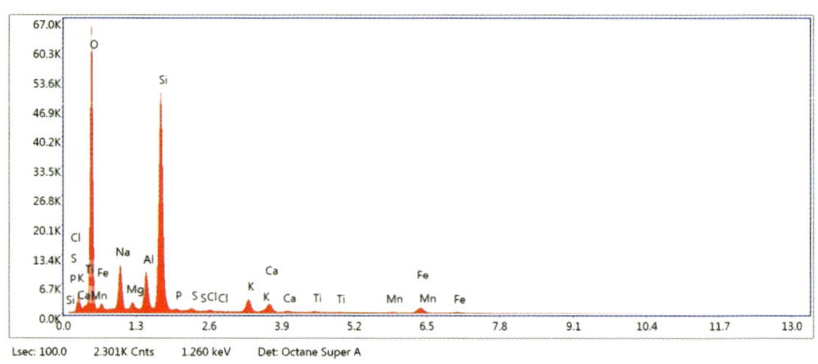

Fig. 4.31 Glass-working crucible E296:S1029:F1223: representative composition of the ceramic matrix, showing high sodium (Na).

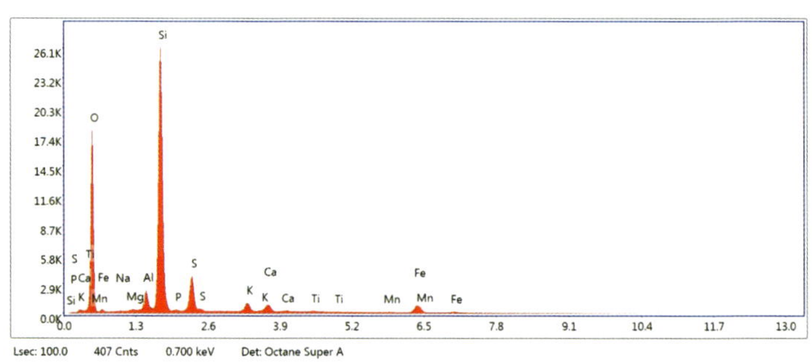

Fig. 4.32 Slag E296:S586:F1068: representative analysis of the surface of the sample. The surface glazing shows a potassium/calcium, alumino-silicate composition and enrichment in iron and sulphur can also be observed.

Chapter 5
Human remains

It was possible to estimate the sex of three of the adult individuals (E296:F2028:BN17, E296:F2077:BN20, and from the F160 assemblage in PT1) and these skulls or skull fragments belonged to males in each case. It is not possible to estimate the sex of non-adult individuals. The estimates of age-at-death were more problematic as these are based on the general size of the bones for the non-adults and on cranial suture closure for the adults. Neither approach is ideal and, as a result, the age-at-death data should be treated with some caution. Assuming that no individual is represented by remains in more than one context, the entire collection has an MNI of ten. Of these, three (E296:F779:BN5, E296:F2069:BN19, and one of the F160 individuals from PT1) and possibly four (Individual 1 of E296:F2069:BN19) were non-adults at the time of death. The youngest of these was probably the individual (Individual 2) represented by the frontal bone in E296:F2069:BN19 who may have been aged about ten years. The other non-adults were adolescents. Among the adults, on the basis of cranial suture closure, all but one appear to have been younger adults. The exception to this is the adult whose skull vault was recovered in the F160 human bone assemblage at the Powder Tower, who was probably a middle or older adult.

Due to the fragmentary nature of the remains, the orbits of just two individuals were available for inspection: the two frontals from E296:F2069:BN19. Both individuals have the distinctive pitting of cribra orbitalia and this is mild in both cases. A number of different possible causes have been suggested for this pitting of the orbital bone of the frontal but the consensus is that it is an indicator of physiological stress of some form, possibly nutritional or related to the intestinal parasites that would have been endemic in pre-industrial populations. Pitting of the outer surface of the skull vault, porotic hyperostosis, is considered to be a related condition with similar causes. This condition was noted in three individuals (E296:F2077:BN20; the older individual of the E324:F160 remains; and E324:F506:HB1). Given the small sample size, the distribution of these conditions suggests that physiological stress of some form was common in the population at large or at least in the cohort of same from which these individuals were drawn.

Evidence of trauma was noted in two individuals, both of whose remains were recovered from layer F160 of the Powder Tower site (PT1). One was blunt force trauma from which the individual had recovered while the other was sharp force trauma that was inflicted at the time of death. Another possible case of blunt force trauma was noted in the single Powder Tower bone E324:F506:HB1. The latter case may represent post-mortem damage to the bone or it may be a perimortem linear depressed fracture. It is possible to be more definitive about the second case of blunt force trauma as this had healed. This injury occurs in the remains of the adolescent from the F160 Powder Tower human bone assemblage and a rectangular portion of bone on the right side of the forehead was broken and slightly punched in. The detachment involved both outer and inner table bone. This potentially serious skull fracture had occurred some considerable time before death, with a sufficient time interval for the bone to heal. In the modern clinical management of skull injuries, fractures to the frontal bone are relatively uncommon (Thiagarajan 2013) and falls and assault are the common causes among adults while abuse is a common cause in children (Hobbs 1984).

The middle or older adult male whose remains were recovered from layer F160 (PT1) had sustained at least three wounds from a sharp cutting blade. These were perimortem injuries and one of them may have been the cause of death. This was the deep cut to the inferior portion of the right parietal. The full impact of this wound cannot be assessed due to the fragmentary nature of the bone but it is clear that the weapon penetrated the skull in the area behind and above the right ear. Less lethal are the two glancing blows to the back of the head, on either side of the midline. These wounds are almost symmetrical and each removed a shallow plaque of outer table bone only. Only fragments of skull vault from this individual were recovered so it is possible that he suffered other injuries as well as these three wounds. The glancing blows to the back of the head are suggestive of attempted decapitation.

The profiles of the remains from these contexts at Dublin Castle–skull fragments of adult males and adolescents, some with evidence of trauma including attempted decapitation, are reminiscent of the isolated heads found in association with the Viking-age banks that surrounded the settlement. I have argued elsewhere (O'Donnabhain 2011) that at least some of these heads were mounted on the boundaries of the settlement as a warning to potential malefactors. The Powder Tower findings appear to be consistent with this interpretation. The tower was built on the remains of the embanked defences of the Viking-age settlement of Dublin, and it superseded the twelfth-century wall of the Hiberno-Scandinavian town. The Phase 1b bone (E324:F506:HB1) was in a deposit abutting the stone-faced clay bank, while layer F160, which contained all the other human bone from the Powder Tower, was part of the Phase 3 material deposited on the Phases 1–2 banks and was adjacent to the line of the first stone wall. The bone specimens recovered from five contexts at the Cork Tower are more difficult to account for, since the habitation evidence uncovered on the site was some distance to the north of the town's defensive boundary, and we can only speculate on the processes whereby human heads were broken down to become randomly scattered fragments embedded in the detritus of everyday living in Viking-age Dublin.

Chapter 6
Faunal remains

Chapter 6
Faunal remains
Margaret McCarthy

Introduction

Faunal material associated with Viking-age occupation was recovered from the Cork Tower and Powder Tower areas. No faunal material had been retained from the Cross Block excavations undertaken in 1961/62. Much of the pre-Norman levels were truncated by the construction of the castle in the thirteenth century and as a consequence a certain degree of disturbance and redeposition of faunal material occurred. Animals that could with a reasonable degree of confidence be linked to the pre-castle settlement were recovered in almost equal quantities from a range of features at the Cork Tower and from deposits both within and adjacent to the Powder Tower. Altogether, an assemblage of 4,865 bones was recovered, representing a collection of primary butchery debris and discarded food waste from Viking-age households. In studying the remains, the aim was to provide an account of the animals, birds and fish that were exploited during this earliest period of occupation and to determine how the growth of the Viking town influenced the rural economy in the surrounding hinterland. The assemblage constitutes one of the few Hiberno-Scandinavian assemblages of animal bone to be examined in Ireland and it is important to compare the results with evidence from other contemporary sites both in Dublin and other Viking urban settlements.

Methods

The bones were identified to species using the reference collection in the Department of Archaeology, University College Cork and in the Natural History Museum, Dublin. Identifications were taken to species where possible and those fragments for which specific identification could not be made were classified in terms of size and morphological character. The material recorded as 'large mammal' (LM) in the tables and text, for instance, is likely to belong to cattle but was too small to eliminate the possibility of horse and red deer. Similarly, specimens that in all probability were sheep but which could also have originated from goat, pig or large dog were recorded as 'medium mammal' (MM). Where possible, sheep were distinguished from goats using the guidelines of Boessneck (1969) and Prummel and Frisch (1986). The ovicaprid bones are all referred to as 'sheep' in this report as many of them were definitely identified to this species by anatomical features, and just a few bones, mostly horn cores, were identified as goat. Ageing data were determined using the procedures outlined by Silver (1969) for long bones and Grant (1975a and b) for mandibles. The relative proportion of the different species was assessed using the fragments total (NISP) and the minimum number of individuals (MNI) represented (Figs 6.1–6.4).

Condition and Recovery

In common with most deeply stratified urban assemblages, the preservation of the faunal material is considered excellent with most fragments retaining fine surface detail that allowed for easy recognition of butchery marks and other traces of utilisation. Several immature long bones and vertebrae survive with their epiphyses and there is a large assemblage of indeterminate material. The assemblage contains a relatively high frequency of gnawed specimens indicating that some bones were made available to dogs before being disposed of, though not for so long that they had become abraded through trampling and weathering. The major upper and lower limb bones of cattle are the most commonly affected by dog gnawing. Faunal material retrieved from the pits in the backyards of the individual house plots is particularly fresh in appearance, indicating that meat waste was discarded into these features almost immediately following butchery and food consumption. Some of the pits appeared to have originally functioned as latrines while others were used specifically for the disposal of general household waste. Bone specimens incorporated, deliberately or otherwise, into the defensive earthen bank at the Powder Tower exhibit a significantly higher incidence of gnawing and erosion, suggesting a more mixed origin for this material. Despite the overall good state of preservation of the bones, the assemblage is nonetheless very fragmented, a condition often associated with prolonged exposure to weathering, gnawing and poor preservation. Other reasons for the high fragmentation rate could be the cooking and food preparation processes which may have led to the deliberate breakage of bones, to facilitate inclusion in stew cauldrons for example. Fracturing of bones may also be related to industrial and craft activities such as glue manufacture, soap and oil production, horn-working and bone-working, all of which could have been conducted at this location in the Viking town.

Retrieval of faunal remains at Dublin Castle was almost entirely by normal hand collection; due to time constraints animal bones were not retained during the second phase of excavation at the Cork Tower Viking area (VA2). While there is no doubt that the bones were recovered and handled with care, the lack of a sampling and sieving programme designed specifically for animal bones means that the assemblage is probably biased not only towards larger animals but towards the larger elements in their skeletons. A sieving strategy initiated for the recovery of plant remains (see Chapter 7) indicated that the sorted residues contained small peripheral bones such as the phalanges of sheep/goats, pigs and dogs as well as some very small fish vertebrae. These sieved samples, however, represent just a tiny proportion of the whole assemblage and are of limited value when assessing the ratio of component parts for the livestock animals. It is likely that the assemblage is wholly biased by the recovery methods towards larger species and elements, with the remains of birds and small mammals being considerably underrepresented. The rate of loss of fish bones is probably more serious and the bones of those species collected by hand during the excavation cannot represent the full range and size of fish species that would have been available to the occupants of Viking-age Dublin.

The Cork Tower

The faunal material from pits and occupation deposits in two house plots in this area is described under the headings of chronological Phases 1 –4 (Table 6.1). In all, a total of 2,472 animal bones was examined from Phases 1 to 4a–c of the pre-castle period; most of the archaeological evidence for the two latest phases (5 and 6) derived from the second (rescue) phase of excavation, and since animal bones were not retained in the course of this excavation, there was not enough material from contexts dating from these phases to warrant inclusion in the study. The relative proportions of the identified species are presented graphically (Figs 6.1 and 6.2) and the variation of the principal stock animals across each phase is shown in Table 6.2.

Table 6.1 Distribution of Cork Tower animal bones by occupation phase.

Phase	Number of Bones	%
Phase 1	339	14
Phase 2	411	17
Phase 3	257	10
Phase 4a	693	28
Phase 4b	374	15
Phase 4c	398	16

Table 6.2 Variation of principal stock animal fragments from the Cork Tower, by occupation phase.

Phase	Horse	Cattle	Pig	S/G*	TNIF*
Phase 1	-	85%	11%	4%	193
Phase 2	1%	77%	15%	7%	222
Phase 3	2%	71%	15%	12%	124
Phase 4a	0.1%	64%	29%	7%	546
Phase 4b	-	55%	40%	5%	167
Phase 4c	-	58%	36%	6%	225

S/G* Sheep/Goat TNIF* Total number of identified fragments

Fig. 6.1 Cork Tower–number of individual specimens (NISP).

Fig. 6.2 Cork Tower–minimum number of individuals (MNI).

PHASE 1 (c. LATE NINTH CENTURY)

Three features from Phase 1 were chosen for analysis: a cesspit (Pit 1: F1041) and spreads of occupation material (F1228 and F1229) as described in Chapter 3.1. In all, 339 bones were examined of which 152 came from the cesspit, originally used to contain human excrement. The recovered bones are stained dark brown and a number have faecal concretions on the shaft surfaces. The botanical analysis indicated that a considerable quantity of blackberry/raspberry seeds had also been present in the cess (see Chapter 7). As the Phase 1 bone sample is relatively small and as there are no significant differences in species composition between the pit and the general occupation layers, the results are presented together in the following description. In all, 193 bones were taken to species level with the unidentifiable sample mostly comprising tiny bone fragments from large and medium-sized ungulates. The three main livestock animals are the only species to be identified in this earliest phase of Viking occupation (Table 6.2). The analysis shows that cattle are by far the most numerous species present, accounting for 85% of the identifiable material and representing at least six individuals. Cattle bones significantly outnumber those of pig, and sheep are the least well represented of the main stock animals. An examination of the distribution of skeletal elements indicates that while most parts of the skeleton are present, the sample is dominated by vertebrae with additional high proportions of major meat-bearing bones, particularly upper forelimb (humerus, scapula) and hindlimb (pelvis, femur). Peripheral foot elements such as phalanges and metapodials are less well represented and a few horn cores are also present.

Pig is the only other species to be represented in any quantity, accounting for 11% of the identifiable bones and representing at least two individuals. In contrast to the cattle sample, pigs are represented by more bones from the best meat cuts from the hindlimbs as well as cuts from the shoulder. It may be tentatively suggested that dressed carcasses of pig are present and that the primary butchery of these animals occurred at a different location. The most common elements, including femur, tibia, humerus, skulls and mandibles, are those which preserve well and, while some elements such as peripheral foot bones are considerably less frequent, the overall skeletal part distribution indicates the presence of complete skeletons. Some pigs were probably kept by householders in pens in the backyards while others would have been driven live into the town where they were slaughtered and butchered.

Fewer than ten of the identified bones are from sheep and just one individual is represented, mostly by upper limb bone fragments including pelvis, tibia, radius, ulna and mandible.

PHASE 2 (C. EARLY TENTH CENTURY)

This phase saw the erection of a boundary fence between two separate plots (see Chapter 3.1). The faunal material selected for examination came from general occupation debris on both sides of the property division. Initially, it was hoped that an examination of the samples from each plot might reveal differences in diet between the two households but as there proved to be no noteworthy variation between both areas, the results are described together. The total sample amounted to 411 bones and these are generally well preserved with just a few exhibiting traces of gnawing by dogs. Cattle bones are again very well represented, contributing 171 (77%) fragments to an identifiable sample of 222 bones and representing at least nine individuals. While most parts of the skeleton are represented, the sample is dominated by vertebrae, major and minor meat-bearing bones and phalanges.

Pig remains account for 15% of the identified sample and these mostly comprise good meat-bearing elements from the forelimbs and hindlimbs of at least two individuals. Sheep are present in small numbers, making up just 7% of the identifiable sample and, as a result, comparisons of the differing proportions of anatomical elements must be tentative. However, although limited in number, the sheep remains indicate a higher proportion of major meat-bearing bones. Horse is the only other species represented, with two bones being recovered from occupation debris associated with Plot 1. These are identified as a worn molar from a mature individual and a mandible fragment that had not been butchered.

PHASE 3 (C. EARLY/MID TENTH CENTURY)

Animal bones belonging to this phase came from a bedding area within House 1, from deposits which accumulated outside the house and from backyard material associated with Plot 2. The analysis suggests that this material consisted of domestic refuse and primary butchering debris. A total of 257 bones were examined, of which 124 are identifiable to species. As in the two earlier phases, cattle fragments comfortably outnumber those of pigs and sheep, accounting for 71% of the identified assemblage and representing at least seven individuals. All the common skeletal elements are represented, indicating that the slaughter and dismemberment of cattle continued within the vicinity of the house plots. Vertebrae and cranial elements including teeth, skull and mandible fragments are most frequent followed by butchered portions of the better meat-bearing bones.

Pigs and sheep are relatively evenly distributed throughout the deposits but in considerably lower proportions than cattle. In fact, the species ratios show a higher value for sheep (12%) than for all other phases, but this may be biased by the small sample. At least two adult sheep are represented and the range of elements includes humerus, scapula, femur, pelvis, vertebrae and teeth. Two adult male pigs are attested based on their distinctive canines and the sample also includes major meat-bearing elements such as femur, pelvis, scapula and vertebrae as well as many teeth and mandibles. An older female is represented and the recovery of two piglet bones indicates that some breeding sows were kept by the occupants of this plot in a backyard pen. Three horse bones (a scapula and two vertebrae) were found in the backyard of Plot 2; the bones belong to an adult individual and there is no evidence that they were butchered for food processing.

PHASE 4A (C. MID/LATE TENTH CENTURY)

Various organic layers that accumulated as backyard deposits during Phase 4a of habitation contributed the greatest quantity of material to the Viking-age assemblage from the Cork Tower. The assemblage comprises 693 bones and the three main livestock species are represented throughout. Cattle again dominate the identified sample both in terms of NISP (64%) and minimum number of individuals present with at least eight individuals being estimated from distal tibia. The range of skeletal elements indicates that virtually all parts of the skeleton are present, with bones from the head and the lower regions of the limbs being the most common. In contrast to the three earlier phases, cattle horn cores are notable by their absence, suggesting that these elements were removed to another location, perhaps to a nearby hornworkers' shop. A high proportion of pelvis and scapula fragments show evidence of butchery, including a portion of an illium with evenly spaced knife marks, suggesting that numerous slices of beef had been cut from it.

Pigs account for 29% of the identifiable sample representing at least five individuals, and while most parts of the carcass are identified, there is a bias to cranial elements and vertebrae. Nonetheless, the overall pattern of skeletal elements indicates that slaughtering and primary butchery of pigs was carried out in the vicinity of the households. Sheep are represented by just 37 complete or near complete bones, including radius, femur, scapula, vertebra and metapodials. At least one female goat is represented by two horn cores and there is a single horse bone, a humerus fragment. The overall impression gained is that this, the largest sample of Viking-age bone from the Cork Tower, is composed not only of food refuse but also of waste from the slaughter and subsequent butchery of the three main livestock animals within the immediate vicinity of the house plots.

PHASE 4B (C. MID/LATE TENTH CENTURY)

Faunal material associated with this sub-phase of habitation came from general dump layers (e.g. deposit F1141) and from two refuse pits (Pits 4b and 5) (see Chapter 3.1); Pit 4b also contained a large number of edible shellfish varieties. Sieved material from the pits indicated that they were used by the occupants to contain a variety of food waste including fruit, eggs, fish, shellfish and nuts. Together, the features yielded 411 bones of which 227 could be positively identified. The sample is interpreted as a concentration of bone derived principally from the butchery and consumption of cattle and pig carcasses. Cattle predictably form the bulk of the identifiable bones, accounting for 58% of the identified sample assemblage and representing at least seven individuals. All parts of the body are present, the most numerous elements being vertebrae and major meat-bearing forelimbs and hindlimbs. Some of the skull fragments appear to have been smashed during brain extraction.

A total of 91 of the identifiable mammal bones are identified as pig, accounting for 40% of the assemblage with vertebrae and cranial bones proving to be the most commonly occurring elements. At least three adult individuals are represented. As with previous phases of occupation, sheep remains form only a very small proportion of the collection accounting for just 7% of the identified sample and representing one individual. No bones are specifically identified as goat. The most noteworthy aspect of the assemblage is the appearance of red deer, *Cervus elaphus*, for the first time in the Viking-age assemblage. This is identified as the sawn tip of an antler tine from the craft industry. Its presence does not necessarily indicate that venison was consumed by the Hiberno-Scandinavian occupants as it could have been cut from a naturally-shed antler beam.

PHASE 4C (C. MID/LATE TENTH CENTURY)

The faunal sample from Phase 4c came from Pit 6 (F1246). The recovery of moss and human coprolites from the pit indicated that it was originally used as a cesspit. The mammalian component consists of 194 bone fragments comprising the remains of the three principal stock animals. Very little gnawing or weathering was observed on the bones, indicating that they represent a primary deposit of food waste. Cattle bones account for 59% of the identifiable material and the majority of these are vertebrae and upper limb bone fragments although the consistent presence of non-meaty peripheral elements indicates that the pits were used both for the disposal of primary butchery waste and leftovers from the kitchen and table. An estimate of the minimum number of individuals indicates the presence of at least two cattle, including the remains of a calf less than four months old at slaughter.

The only other animal to be present in significant proportions is pig with 57 (29%) of the identifiable bones being from this species. Most skeletal elements are represented with vertebrae, metapodial and cranial elements being predominant. The pig sample also includes two femora from a neo-natal individual, providing further evidence for the keeping of breeding sows in pens in the backyards of the house plots. There are negligible amounts of sheep, just thirteen bones being identified. The only clear evidence for goat is two horn cores which had been chopped horizontally at the base during removal of the sheaths for horn-working.

The Powder Tower

In general, the Powder Tower bones are less well preserved than those from the Cork Tower suggesting that they had been exposed for a longer period of time to the effects of weathering and gnawing, although the drying out of the deposits is also a factor. There are more eroded bones and loose teeth than from the Cork Tower assemblage and, as is often the case in conditions of poor preservation, the assemblage is dominated by cattle and the larger bones from these animals (Figs 6.3, 6.4). The poor quality of the environmental samples from the Powder Tower is also borne out by the macrofossil analysis where preservation and representation of species was considerably less than at the Cork Tower (see Chapter 7). The greater part of the

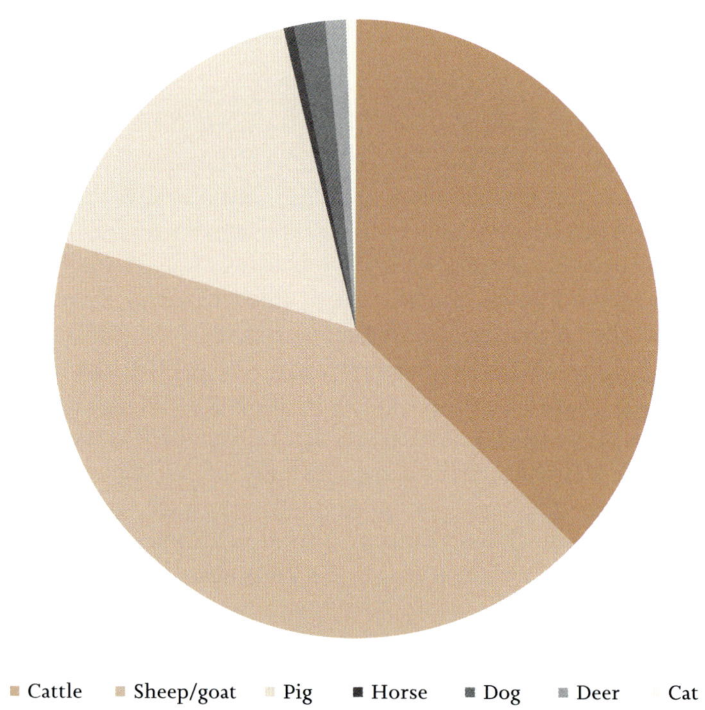

Fig. 6.3 Powder Tower–number of individual specimens (NISP).

Fig. 6.4 Powder Tower–minimum number of individuals (MNI).

Powder Tower assemblage is from within the tower (PT1), recovered from successive layers forming a two-phase bank which was on the line of the early defences of the Viking town. A further assemblage of bone was recovered from a series of pits and habitation layers in Areas A, B, C and K (PT2) excavated along the inside of the north curtain wall adjacent to the tower (Tables 6.3 and 6.4).

POWDER TOWER 1

PHASE 1A/B (EARLY/MID TENTH CENTURY)

This earliest phase of activity consisted of the construction of a low clay bank (Phase 1a) subsequently developed as a more substantial stone-faced clay bank (Phase 1b: F427) which survived to a height of 2.7m (see Chapter 3.2). The bank material included butchered animal bone which probably originated from nearby house plots. Domestic waste was also discarded on the external side of the bank, where a succession of post-and-wattle breakwaters were constructed (Phase 1a/b) to protect the exterior of the embankment from damage by the tidal action of the River Poddle, resulting in a build-up of deposits and a heightening of ground level along the river frontage. The state of preservation of the recovered animal bone, with a higher incidence of gnawing and erosion than was noted in the Cork Tower assemblage, suggests a more mixed origin for the material. In all, 826 animal bones were examined and it was possible to identify 455 fragments to species level. The highest proportion of meat eaten derived from cattle; this livestock animal contributes 331 bones (73%) to the identifiable sample and represents at least seventeen individuals. The distribution of body parts indicates the presence of primary butchery debris as well as table waste from meals.

Table 6.3 Distribution of Powder Tower animal bones by area, occupation phase and feature type.

Area/Phase	Number of Bones	%
PT1		
Phase 1	826	35
Phase 2	580	24
PT2-Areas A-C and K		
Pits	271	11
Habitation layers	716	30

Table 6.4 Variation of principal stock animal fragments from the Powder Tower, by excavation area and occupation phase.

Phase	Horse	Cattle	Pig	S/G*	TNIF*
PT1					
Phase 1	0.2%	76%	16%	7.8%	435
Phase 2	0.3%	69%	21.7%	9%	324
PT2-Areas A-C and K					
Refuse pits	-	81%	14%	5%	171
Habitation layers	0.4%	70%	25%	4.6%	449

S/G* Sheep/Goat TNIF* Total number of identified fragments

Pigs (15%) are second in importance both numerically and in terms of minimum numbers of individuals present (10) and, as with the cattle remains, there is a relatively even distribution of body parts suggesting that pigs were slaughtered and butchered locally. Despite the limited sample size, the distinctive canine teeth indicate that young male pigs are more frequent than females, suggesting a local pig husbandry that focused on the supply of young animals to the town's butchers' shops and market. Sheep again are in the minority (7%) and there is no evidence for goat. The 33 identified specimens consist primarily of the major and minor meat-bearing bones and vertebrae and at least three individuals are represented. Along with the main food mammals, there is also evidence for dog, cat and horse. The single horse bone from these deposits was probably worked rather than butchered, as a sharp knife had been used to perforate the joint surface area of the metatarsus. Other evidence for object manufacture from this phase of activity was noted in the form of a cattle horn core which had its tip sliced off, and four small fragments of red deer antler represent waste from the craft industry. Dogs appear for the first time in reasonable quantities with fourteen bones being identified, representing at least three individuals, of which one could only have survived for a couple of months. The estimated shoulder heights (0.54m–0.69m) are well within the range observed in dogs from other Viking sites in Ireland (McCormick 1997). There are just two cat bones, a humerus and an ulna. Both bones are from an individual less than a year old and very fine knife marks on the humerus are consistent with this individual being killed for its pelt. The resources of the sea are poorly represented, just eleven fish vertebrae were found and these were identified as hake, *Merluccius merluccius* and ling, *Molva molva*.

PHASE 2 (ELEVENTH CENTURY)

A timber-reinforced earthen bank was constructed over the earlier stone-faced bank for continued defensive purposes (see Chapter 3.2). Bone material and other domestic refuse were again deliberately used for the construction of this bank, an exercise that demonstrates the practical use of domestic waste generated by the occupants of the town. The bones, not surprisingly, given the context of the finds, are rather poorly preserved and many had clearly been exposed to the effects of weathering and trampling before being sealed within the bank. Altogether, a total of 580 fragments were examined and these are characteristic of domestic refuse, consisting largely of the butchered remains of the three major livestock animals. Cattle bones are again in the majority accounting for 69% of the total number of identifiable bones and representing at least eight individuals. Skeletal element distribution shows a bias towards meat-bearing fragments consisting mainly of food waste from the table. The single horn core may represent the by-product of craft working, as it was chopped at the base in an effort to remove the sheath.

Pigs are second in importance numerically, contributing 70 fragments and representing at least four individuals. The sample is dominated by loose teeth and mandible fragments and a wide range of the primary and secondary meat-bearing bones. The only other mammalian species present is sheep, which accounts for just 9% of the total identifiable sample. There is also evidence for two goat bones and the recovery of two neonatal caprine bones suggests that the occasional goat was kept to supply fresh milk to the households. Horse is represented by a heavily gnawed and severely eroded fragment of a pelvis and non-edible mammals include the remains of dogs and cats. Eight dog bones represent two individuals, one of which was sixteen months of age at death. The single cat bone is from a small kitten which could scarcely have been more than eight to ten weeks old. Evidence of craft activity can be seen in a sawn antler tine from a red deer and a cow horn core carefully chopped at the base during the removal of the sheath.

POWDER TOWER 2

The pre-castle levels were cut away on the north side by the thirteenth-century curtain wall and moat and on the south side by eighteenth-century foundations, but small narrow pockets of Viking-age deposits survived and were excavated in Areas A, B, C and K (see Chapter 3.3). A total of 987 bones was examined of which 628 were identifiable to species level. Not surprisingly, the sample is dominated by the bones of the three main livestock animals representing a mixed accumulation of waste from the slaughter yard, kitchen and table. The remains of cattle and pigs are the most common, contributing 76% and 24% respectively to the identified sample. There was also evidence for two calves indicating that either these young animals were driven into the town to be slaughtered for veal or that a certain number of cows were kept within the precincts of the houses to provide a ready supply of milk. The most frequent elements in the collection are loose teeth, humeri, femora, tibiae, vertebrae, skull fragments and metapodials. Higher frequencies of peripheral foot and cranial elements suggest that this large assemblage represents live animals that were slaughtered here before being distributed to the butchers' shops and markets in the town. The recovery of two neonatal piglets continues to provide evidence that breeding sows were kept by the occupants of nearby house plots. Sheep are again characterised by their small numbers and there is evidence for very young lambs or goats, indicating that sheep or goats were kept by the households for the supply of milk. A single horn core from a male goat was chopped at the base and relates to bone-working activity. The habitation layers and pits also provided evidence for the keeping of dogs in small numbers. Fine knife marks on the dorsal surface of a thoracic vertebra indicate that the pelt may have been removed from this animal. A cat mandible represents a single mature individual which may have been kept to control the vermin population while horse is identified from a portion of a first phalanx and an extremely worn first molar. The only other point of particular interest in the sample is the identification of an immature cetacean vertebra. The finding of this bone may indicate that the occasional stranded whale was exploited for its food potential and there are records of whales being eaten in times of need (Kelly 2000). In addition to food waste, there is evidence for bone-working waste in the form of a cow metatarsus which was sawn horizontally across the distal end of the midshaft. Four sawn fragments of red deer antler also represent waste from craft working.

Table 6.5 Cattle ageing data.

Bone/end	Approx. age at fusion	Unfused total	Fused total
Scapula D	10 months	3	27
Humerus D	18 months	-	33
Radius P		1	31
Phalanxes 1 & 2 P		-	20
Metapodial D	2–2.5 years	13	41
Tibia D		8	26
Femur P	3.5 years	9	7
Calcaneum P		2	8
Humerus P	3.5–4 years	3	9
Radius D		8	18
Ulna P		6	6
Femur D		9	12
Tibia P		5	11

D = distal; P = proximal

Table 6.6 Pig ageing data.

Bone/end	Approx. age at fusion	Unfused total	Fused total
Scapula D	10 months	2	5
Humerus D		3	7
Radius P		1	4
Phalanxes 1 & 2 P		-	1
Metapodia D	1.5–2 years	18	3
Tibia D		13	9
Ulna P	2.5–3 years	11	1
Femur P		1	-
Calcaneum P		6	1
Radius D		7	-
Humerus P	3–3.5 years	4	-
Femur D		2	-
Tibia P		10	1

D = distal; P = proximal

Ageing Analysis

If the sample of animal bones chosen for analysis is typical of the cattle husbandry methods employed by farmers living in the vicinity of Dublin during the Viking age, the indications are that the fattening of cattle solely for meat production was not commonly practised. While allowing for the fragile nature and hence the poor survival rate of immature cattle bones, the ageing evidence suggests that that the majority of the animals eaten by the Hiberno-Scandinavian occupants were fully grown individuals with 79% being older than three years at slaughter. Most of the mandibles have Grant numerical values of over 30 and all those with values of 37 and above have completed their tooth eruption sequence and are well in wear, suggesting individuals at around five years of age (Grant 1975a and b). The less reliable epiphyseal fusion method of ageing also indicates that mature individuals are better represented, although calf bones from individuals less than four months of age were found at both the Cork Tower and the Powder Tower sites, indicating that veal appeared in the town's markets on occasion. No neonatal mortalities were found, suggesting that calves may not have been reared in the town (Table 6.5).

Ageing analysis for pigs indicates that these animals were generally killed at a younger age than cattle and sheep, a pattern replicated in many faunal assemblages and typical of animals that are exploited entirely for meat. Most pigs were between one and two years old at slaughter and the presence of piglets less than three months old indicates that suckling pig was eaten on occasion. The few complete pig mandibles recovered indicated that none of the mandibles had gone beyond the stage of early wear on the third molar and most had reached the stage where the second molar had come into wear (Table 6.6).

Ageing analysis established from the state of fusion of the long bones indicates that most sheep were killed between two and five years of age, which suggests a mixed local economy aimed at the production of wool, woolfells and meat. There is evidence for all age groups in the collection including young lambs and sub-adults. Limited tooth wear evidence indicates that most of the complete mandibles were from animals probably over four years of age and again the indications are that wool production was significant to the local economy. This is also borne out by an assessment of the rate of epiphyseal fusion of the long bones. There is evidence for a neonatal mortality which may represent the offspring of a female goat kept in the town for the supply of fresh milk.

Biometrics

Metrical analysis was limited, but the general small size of the cattle bones is typical of the cattle recovered from contemporary Viking sites both in Dublin and elsewhere in Ireland (McCormick 1997, McCormick and Murray 2007). An estimation of the shoulder height of twelve complete cattle long bones ranged from 1.032m to 1.282m with a mean value of 1.13m. Cattle horn cores were recovered in a reasonably large amount and these indicate that cattle were all of a short-horned breed and a range of males, females and castrates was identified. The mean withers height calculated from sheep metacarpals and metatarsals is 0.549m and 0.552m respectively. Very few measurements could be taken but the limited metrical data showed that the sheep were of the small, slender-limbed type common on sites in Ireland contemporary with Viking-age levels at Dublin Castle.

Pathology

There are a number of instances of pathologically-altered bone. Five cattle femora are so severely affected by arthropathy that a very obvious area of eburnation is present on the articular surface, indicating that these individuals were subjected to considerable strain during their working lives. There were four instances of pathology on cattle bones recovered from the two-phase defensive embankment in the Powder Tower area. These include two instances of eburnation on the femoral caput, a distally splayed metacarpal with lateral osteophytic growth and a healed fracture of a pelvis resulting in serious eburnation around the rim of the acetabulum. Additionally, there was evidence for eburnation and pitting on the cranial surface of a cow lumbar vertebra. A number of cattle first phalanges also show eburnation and grooving on the proximal joint surface, and these are either indicative of advanced age or some form of arthropathy resulting from heavy use. Evidence for trauma is noted in a number of instances. A pig fibula from the Phase 4b deposits in the Cork Tower area had fractured and healed which may indicate pigs were hobbled in an effort to control them. The ascending ramus of a pig jaw from outside House 1 (Cork Tower, Phase 3) was severely fractured which resulted in complete displacement of the bone. The animal survived the trauma but not without experiencing some distress as well as the loss of its third molar.

Butchery

Cattle carcasses were more heavily utilised than those of other livestock, with butchery marks being recorded on 32% of the postcranial bones. In general, the pattern of butchery is similar to that noted in contemporary assemblages (McCormick and Murray 2007) with the most common butchery marks being associated with the disarticulation of the elbow and the hip joints. Traces of chopping linked to disarticulation are noted on proximal humerus and proximal femur, and disarticulation cuts and chops are also to be found on distal scapulae, mandibular ramus, pelves, metapodials, calcaneus and astragalus. Most of the vertebrae were split laterally and transversely, probably on the ground, although the presence of vertebrae that were split axially suggests that some carcasses were dismembered after being suspended following slaughter. Some of the bones exhibit knife marks made during skinning, disarticulation and filleting while other knife marks seem to have been made during severing the tendons at the articulations. Fine knife marks on fragments of scapulae, pelves and vertebrae are linked to the stripping of meat from these bones. In addition, the process of marrow extraction seems to have been significant, as evidenced by the large number of the major long bones that were chopped and split. Cut marks indicative of skinning and stripping meat from major long bones, pelves, scapulae and vertebrae were also recorded and the overall fragmented nature of the sample suggests that products other than meat, such as fat, grease and marrow, were also targeted during the processing of cattle carcasses. Some of the bones, notably the metapodials and the upper limb bones, exhibit clear evidence of having been split longitudinally to facilitate the extraction of marrow. All of the skulls had been cleaved in two and smashed and broken, most probably to gain access to the nutritious brains.

Butchery marks on pig and sheep bones are less common, which is not surprising, as these are smaller animals and require less chopping and division into suitable cooking portions. Cut and knife marks are the most common and are associated with the division of the carcass into manageable portions for cooking. A few superficial knife marks on metapodials are related to skinning and the removal of hides from the animals. Knife cuts associated with the stripping of meat were also observed on the blades of scapulae and pelves and also on a few vertebrae. There is little evidence for chop marks that could be linked to the extraction of marrow. Cut marks relating to the removal of the horn sheath, most probably for craft working, were noted on a number of goat horn cores. Most common are chop marks and cut marks relating to the disarticulation of the hip and shoulder joints from the main trunk of the body.

Bird Bones

The bird bone assemblage from the Viking-age levels is quite small and derived mostly from the cess pits where advantageous conditions ensured their preservation. Just 124 bones were recovered and domestic fowl are by far the most common species, accounting for 50% of the identified assemblage. Measurements taken on the bones indicated that there was little variation in the size of the fowl present and the differences which do exist are more likely to reflect sex and age. The bones are generally from mature individuals, suggesting that they were kept as much for their eggs as their meat. The recovery of a few immature bones indicates that hens were reared in the backyards of the houses and the occurrence of medullary bone, a bony deposit that builds up in hens during the laying period, provides supporting evidence for the keeping of poultry. The long bones were compared for build with fowl from Wood Quay (O'Sullivan 1990) and from a number of medieval sites (McCarthy 1988); most fell well within the range of measurements obtained for these sites and indicated that they were considerably smaller than present-day birds.

The limited evidence suggests that geese were second in importance to fowl as an avian food source and at least three individuals were identified from a limited sample of 45 bones. Most of the birds seem to have been reared to maturity as useful suppliers of eggs and down as well as meat. The majority of the few gosling bones presumably represent premature death. Aside from the importance of geese for the supply of eggs, down and meat, the best pens were made from primary quills plucked from live geese in the spring. Goose feathers were also used for fletching arrows.

The remains of all other species are extremely scarce. Remains of duck (*Anas* sp.) are represented by nine fragments. The problems of distinguishing domestic duck from its wild ancestor, mallard (*Anas platyrhynchos*) are well documented although the scarcity of their remains from Dublin Castle suggests that the bones originated from the wild form of the duck. McCormick (1997) and McCormick and Murray (2007) have reported on the relatively small amount of duck from other Viking sites in Ireland and it is only in the later medieval period that domestic duck becomes more frequent. Two other duck species were identified: the small teal (*Anas crecca*) and possible widgeon (*Anas penelope*). Both are common in the Dublin region today and would have been readily available in wetland areas in the vicinity. The only other bird species identified is white-tailed eagle (*Haliaeetus albicilla*), two wing bones being recovered from one of the cess pits (Pit 6) at the Cork Tower. The disproportionate amount of white-tailed eagle wing bones from Viking and medieval sites across Ireland and Britain has been interpreted as providing evidence for the trading of eagle wings from Scandinavia to provide fletching for arrows (O'Connor 1989). A preponderance of wing bones was found at Wood Quay, Dublin (O'Sullivan 1990), Fishamble Street, Dublin (McCormick and Murray 2007), Wexford (McCarthy 1992), York (O'Connor 1989) and Hedeby (Reichstein and Tiessen 1974). Serjeantson (2009) has suggested that an excess of carpo-metacarpii and wing digits of birds may also indicate that wings were used as dusters and to provide primary feathers for use as quill pens.

Discussion

The Viking-age features identified during excavations at the Cork Tower and Powder Tower produced a moderate amount of animal bones which became incorporated into general habitation spreads and deposits in the backyards of houses. Additionally, bone waste was discarded into backyard pits, some of which were intentionally used for food disposal while others seem to have originally functioned as cesspits before being filled with domestic waste. At the Powder Tower (PT1) the build-up of the defensive banks included discarded bone waste and other domestic debris.

There is little doubt that the assemblage of bones examined represents the remnants of the systematic slaughter, processing and reduction of cattle and pig carcasses, carried out for the most part, it would seem, in the immediate vicinity of the households. The recovered animal bones therefore provide a basis for investigating diet in Dublin during the tenth and eleventh centuries. The individual samples from the Cork Tower and Powder Tower are similar in size and the remains appear to represent a mixture of primary and secondary butchery waste and domestic household refuse, as well as waste from industrial and craft activities. In general, the frequency of body parts across the various features is relatively even and no significant variation in the distribution of different elements could be discerned. It can be concluded from this that beef and pork derived from complete carcasses, from cattle and pigs bred in the hinterland of the town and driven live into the town's markets to be sold and subsequently slaughtered and dismembered by resident butchers. Products other than meat were also of commercial interest to a variety of craftsmen. The overall low proportion of cattle horn cores, for instance, suggests that these elements were removed from the skulls during the primary stage of butchery and dispatched to the horn worker, who would then have removed the valuable horn sheath by soaking it in water. Similarly, fresh hides may have been removed from the carcass soon after slaughter and transported to the tanner and tawyer for curing; the relatively low proportions of terminal limb elements in some collections from the Viking-age levels suggest that these elements were left attached to the hide, as it would have been a labour-intensive process to bone them out for little reward. The bones of domestic cattle, sheep and pigs seem to represent the waste from a range of activities not just involving meat consumption but other secondary industrial or craft activities linked with hide preparation, horn working, bone and antler working, and probably glue production.

A provisioning exercise based almost entirely on cattle suggests a well organised supply of these animals to the town from the hinterland. While the evidence is admittedly limited by the small sample size and the retrieval methods, cattle formed the greater part of the assemblages at both the Cork Tower and Powder Tower and the patterning of finds suggests that the slaughter, preparation and consumption of these animals was undertaken within the vicinity of the households. Cattle account for over 80% of the identified fauna in the earliest levels, followed by lesser amounts of pigs and very small numbers of sheep. Pigs increase in significance at the expense of cattle in the later phases (4a–c) of settlement at the Cork Tower. Analysis of tooth wear and epiphyseal fusion rates shows that the majority of cattle were adult, i.e. over four years of age at death, and the low proportion of neonatal individuals suggests that the recovered animal bones represent livestock brought to market by producers located outside the town. While a small number of livestock may have been kept to provide fresh milk, the Viking-age town was essentially a consumer and market centre that would have relied on the surrounding rural hinterland to supply the bulk of its food requirements. The presence of large numbers of adult animals is consistent with their multi-purpose use in the countryside for meat, dairying and traction and the age profile suggests that the Viking-age town was not sufficiently large to overly influence animal husbandry practices. Mutton and lamb seem to have had a relatively insignificant role in the meat diet and, with the exception of a small quantity of horn cores and two possible kid bones, there is no other evidence for the keeping and consumption of goats. Traces of cut marks and working on goat horn cores suggest that these elements were detached from the skulls and dispatched to horn workers' shops in the town. There is evidence that a certain number of goats were kept by the occupants of the town to provide milk but the disproportionate numbers of horn cores suggests that these elements may have been deliberately traded by rural producers with craft workers in the town. Pigs were principally kept for their meat, although lard and hide were also significant by-products of these animals. Limited data from pig bones indicate an age profile consistent with intensive pork production, i.e. large numbers of sub-adult animals. Approximately 60% of pig post-cranial remains are from animals estimated to have been killed between twelve and 24 months. The presence of neonatal remains from both excavated areas suggests that some breeding sows were kept and bred within the town. Pigs are ideal animals for keeping in pens in the backyards and they would also have been useful recyclers of household refuse. The presence of bones of young pigs echoes the pattern observed at many contemporary urban sites (McCormick 1997) and indicates that a certain number of pigs were reared within the town for breeding. However, the high proportion of adult pigs cannot represent surplus animals from backyard production alone and it would seem that the majority of pigs were driven live into the town's markets.

The low frequency of all other species means that they are of little interpretative value. Horse is present in small numbers throughout all Viking-age phases of occupation and the remains represent animals that were kept for light work and transportation around the town. Dog bones were also found in moderate amounts and represent disarticulated individuals, with no evidence from any phase of the deliberate burial of these animals. Of interest is a thoracic vertebra showing evidence of cut marks on the dorsal surface, suggesting that some dogs were processed for their pelts. The very low frequency of cat bones in the assemblage is pertinent to the debate on when cats became common as pets in Ireland. Cat bones are also rare finds in contemporary Viking assemblages (Bourke 1995, McCormick 1997). One bone bearing cut marks associated with skinning demonstrates that cat furs were of value for sale and export.

The lack of a systematic sieving programme precluded a representative collection of small mammals, birds and fish, the latter usually being a prominent feature of urban assemblages. Some evidence of the fish consumed, however, was recovered during the sieving of organic samples retained for macrofossil analysis and these included herring, eel, whiting, salmon, ray, trout, hake and ling (see Chapter 7). There is no evidence that wild species of animals living in the vicinity of the town were captured and red deer is represented only by sawn antler which could have been collected in the countryside in early spring and traded for commercial gain in the town's markets. The available data therefore from Dublin Castle suggest that venison did not make a significant contribution to the food supply in the town but what the assemblage does indicate is that within range of Dublin, in the pre-Norman period, there was a live population of red deer whose antler was highly valued by craftsmen resident in the town. The only other evidence of the exploitation of wild fauna is the recovery of a butchered vertebra from an immature cetacean that probably washed up in a nearby coastal area and was subsequently processed for its meat. Wild boar was not identified among the remains, and apart from a few finds scattered unevenly across the deposits, wild species of birds were also very rare, despite what must have been a plentiful locally available resource of native wildfowl including winter migrants. Accumulations of refuse or stored foodstuffs would have attracted scavengers such as corvids, birds of prey and smaller passerines and the riverfront site must have provided an ideal habitat for rodents.

The faunal assemblage from the Viking-age levels at Dublin Castle is an important addition to a rather limited number of pre-existing published Viking assemblages from Dublin (McCormick and Murphy 1997, McCormick and Murray 2007), Waterford (McCormick 1997) and Wexford (Bourke 1995). When set against the results from contemporary sites, it would seem that Viking diet relied on a narrow economic base focusing almost exclusively upon large-scale cattle butchery with some evidence for the consumption of pork and mutton and little input from either wild mammals or wild species of birds. Domestic livestock alone accounted for 99% of the identified faunal assemblage at Fishamble Street, Dublin (Wallace 2016, 215–7; McCormick and Murray 2007). In contrast to Dublin Castle, an estimate of the minimum number of individuals at Fishamble Street indicated that pigs were by far the most dominant animals (McCormick and Murray 2007). There was also a disproportionate amount of neonatal and young individuals in the recovered assemblage, which was interpreted as an indicator of a certain degree of self-sufficiency on the part of occupants. The preponderance of cattle at Dublin Castle fits well with the pattern observed at most other Viking settlements and there is no doubt that beef was generally the most commonly consumed meat. Sheep are the least important of the three main livestock species in the Dublin sites and this is also the case at Waterford (McCormick 1997) and Wexford (Bourke 1995, McCarthy 1992). Where specific identifications were possible, sheep bones outnumber those of goat at all sites, the latter being represented almost entirely by horn cores. Many of the sheep in the Dublin Castle samples were mature and represent wool producers that were slaughtered when no longer required for this purpose; the meat from such animals would not have been very tender. The numbers of sheep are also low at all other Irish Viking sites (McCormick and Murray 2007) and it would appear that mutton was a limited resource, eaten on a less regular basis than beef or pork. The recovery of bones of newborn goat kids and piglets at most of the sites also implies some limited husbandry within the town. There is little to suggest that the occupants of Irish Viking towns enjoyed a richness of diet through a wide range of fish, wild birds and wild fauna (McCormick 1997; Bourke 1995; McCarthy 2011). In general, if one takes the recovered bones from Dublin Castle as indicators of the diet of the Viking-age occupants of Dublin, the picture is one of a somewhat dull diet with no great indicators of wealth and status.

There is some evidence that the bone assemblage contains more than simply food waste and other aspects of a Viking urban way of life can be inferred from the remains. The presence of horse bones is a reminder that horses had an important role to play in the Viking town in terms of the transport of people and goods. The recovery of a range of dog sizes, probably representing guard dogs and pets, is a sign too that dogs were an everyday feature of life in the urban community. Fine knife marks on the thoracic vertebra of one dog bone is linked to the occasional exploitation of these animals for their hides but there were no signs of chop marks on the dog bones as was recorded on over 10% of the canid sample from Fishamble Street, Dublin which McCormick (2007) links to a possible time of food shortage. In terms of the avian remains, a marked over-representation of white-tailed eagle bones is suggestive of the importation of the wings of these birds for fletching. The disproportionate amount of goose wing bones may indicate their use as dusters, as was common practice in Ireland until recent times. The size and character of the cattle bone assemblage is suggestive of a commercial butchery regime and its waste was included in the general domestic waste used in the construction of this part of the Viking town's defences. Overall, it is clear that there was a noteworthy preponderance of cattle over other livestock species throughout all the phases of Viking/Hiberno-Scandinavian settlement and while accepting that there may have been a certain degree of loss due to the methods of collection, there is no doubt that there was a dietary preference for beef over other meats during the period of urban habitation preceding the construction of Dublin Castle.

Chapter 7
Plant and insect remains

Chapter 7

Plant and insect remains

Brenda Collins and Nikolah Gilligan

Introduction

All organic deposits exposed in the Viking levels at Dublin Castle (excluding the Cross Block investigations) were sampled during excavation; environmental analyses were carried out by Brenda Collins between 1987 and 1991, the findings of which are detailed in reports lodged in the National Monuments Service Archive (Collins 1988). Following an initial assessment of the potential of each bulk sample, sub-samples of 500ml were chosen for detailed analysis and where separate fills were recorded in certain features (e.g. pits) a subsample of 500ml was examined from each fill. Environmental indicators including seeds, fruit stones, nut shells, faecal remains, fish bones, shellfish, moss, fly puparia, insects, charcoal, straw, mites and eggshell were recorded. Seed identification was carried out using a reliably identified reference collection and the manuals of Katz, Katz and Kipiani (1965), Beijerinck (1947), Bertsch (1941) and Berggren (1969; 1981). The nomenclature used follows Scannell and Synnott (1987). The following report, updated by Nikolah Gilligan, incorporates the results of this work and places it in a national and international context in light of findings from excavations in the thirty years since the original analyses.

The archaeological contexts from which environmental indicators were retrieved ranged from cess/rubbish pit fills and occupation deposits within houses in the Cork Tower area to waste material associated with the clay embankments in the Powder Tower area and ranged in date from the late ninth century to the early eleventh century (Table 7.1). The level of preservation of the Cork Tower samples was considered very good, with the exception of the cesspit fill contexts from Phase 1. The preservation of organics in the Powder Tower samples was moderate at best, which may be attributed to the exposed nature of the site and the fluctuating water table caused by the ebb and flow of the nearby Rivers Liffey and Poddle. A small portion of the assemblage was charred. The stated objectives of the original analyses included an examination of the foods eaten in Viking-age Dublin, the materials used within the houses, the degree of infestation that was part of everyday living, the general environmental conditions within the town and the identification of the origin and nature of the dumped deposits used in building the clay embankments, including the influence (if any) of the nearby River Poddle. The results are combined in this revised report.

Cork Tower: Cess/Rubbish Pits

The pits comprised a mixture of cesspits and rubbish pits. As noted above, preservation in the Phase 1 pits was poor, while in the Phase 4 pits it was excellent (Table 7.2). Environmental indicators such as seeds, fruit stones, nutshells, faecal remains, fishbones, shellfish, mosses, fly puparia, insects, charcoal, straw, mites and eggshell were abundant and well represented. Pit 1 (F1041), Pit 2 (F2075), Pit 4b (F2092) and Pit 6 (F1246) were classified as cesspits because they include typical indicators of such features as described by Smith (2013). These include the nature of the feature itself, the presence of cess or faecal waste, the typical food waste and 'fruit-salad' (Greig 1982, 52) of edible seeds, such as wild strawberry (*Fragaria vesca*), apple (*Malus sylvestris*), sloe (*Prunus spinosa*), frochan/bilberry (*Vaccinium myrtillus*) and blackberry/raspberry (*Rubus fruticosus/idaeus*), which are commonly present in cesspits, as well as the insect remains such as fly puparia. The Phase 4 pits also contained mosses which was probably used for wiping.

Cesspits and rubbish pits are an extremely important source of information because they normally contain a variety of well-preserved material, reflecting different aspects of town life. Containing decomposing matter and usually exposed to the elements, pits are also catchment

Table 7.1 Samples analysed for environmental indicators.

Cork Tower, Cutting 2		Powder Tower	
Feature	**Context**	**Feature**	**Context**
F1041	Phase 1 Cesspit fill (Pit 1).	F562	Phase 1a Dump layer in clay bank.
F2075	Phase 1 Cesspit fill (Pit 2).	F561, F556, F563 F559	Phase 1b Dump layers in stone-faced clay bank.
F2053	Phase 3 Organic deposit in NW corner of House 1.	F542, F548, F551, F550, F546	Phase 1a Deposits associated with breakwaters BW 1 and 2.
F2061	Phase 3 Occupation layer on floor of House 1.	F544	Phase 1b Deposit associated with breakwater BW 4.
F2086	Phase 4a Fill of stone-lined post-pit.	F491, F492	Phase 2 Deposits in timber-reinforced clay bank.
F2096	Phase 4a Fill of rubbish pit (Pit 4a).	F482, F474, F458	Phase 2 Deposits associated with timber frameworks FW 1b and 2.
F2092	Phase 4b Cess/rubbish fill (Pit 4b).		
F1246	Phase 4c Cess/rubbish fill (Pit 6).		
F2045, F2046, F2051	Phase 4a Occupation layers.		
F2033	Phase 5 Organic deposit on wattle panel outside House 2.		
F2013	Phase 5 Sod deposit within House 2		
F2016	Phase 5 Deposit on floor of House 2.		

sites for seeds, especially those produced in the vicinity of the pits. However, given the complexity of mechanisms by which seeds arrive in pits, the interpretation of these assemblages should be approached with caution, and the grouping of particular species into specific habitats is not necessarily absolute. They do, however, offer an insight into how people disposed of their rubbish and yield information about past diet.

The food remains in the Cork Tower pits indicated a varied and high-fibre diet. Evidence for the consumption of fruit, eggs, shellfish, nuts and meat was present. Bread was probably eaten and charred cereal grains of wheat as well as cereal bran were identified. Seeds cannot provide information on every aspect of diet however, as vegetables, soups, herbs and beverages leave no trace in a seed assemblage.

FOOD PLANTS

Foodstuffs were primarily represented by the seeds of cultivated cereals and gathered scrubland fruits. Wild strawberry, apple, sloe, frochan/bilberry, blackberry/raspberry, and rowan were present. The latter two species were found within human faecal pellets (Pit 4b/F2092) and provide direct evidence for the consumption of these fruits. Apple and rowan were only found in Pit 6, while bilberry was also found in Pit 6 and on a wattle screen (F2033) just outside House 2.

The highest representation of sloe stones came from Pit 6 (F1246) in Phase 4c. Notes taken during excavation remark on the reddish-purple colour of the soil associated with the fruit stones in the pit. A layer of branches, wattle and pieces of wood, laid down over the accumulation of fruit stones acted as a sealing layer. This would have had the effect of providing a new and dry surface within the pit, which continued to be used for the disposal of general domestic waste. The accumulation of such large amounts of sloe stones may reflect residue from fruit processing dumped into the pit as waste.

Hazelnuts (*Corylus avellana*) were also collected and eaten. Hundreds of discarded hazelnut shells were found in all of the pits. Bog myrtle (*Myrica gale*), used in brewing for flavouring (Atkin *et al.* 1985; Mitchell 1987), was represented by one seed in Pit 4a/F2096 (Phase 4a). Black mustard (*Brassica nigra*) was present although represented by only two seeds. The seeds of this plant can be used as a mustard and was described as a garden plant by Albertus Magnus in the thirteenth century (Robinson 1987).

Table 7.2 Cork Tower; plant remains from cess/rubbish pits.

Cork Tower Cutting 2 (CT2)							
Feature Number		F1041	F2075	F2086	F2092	F2096	F1246
Volume (mls)		500	500	500	500	500	500
Binomial classification	**English/common**						
Cultivated							
Avena sp. L	Oat		1		6	4	2
Hordeum sp. L.	Barley		1	1	22	17	5
Linum usitatissimum L.	Cultivated flax				2	43	4
Triticum sp. L.	Wheat species				1	1	
Gathered							
Fragaria vesca L.	Strawberry				1	3	1
Malus sp.	Apple						9
Prunus sp.	Various						3
Prunus spinosa L.	Blackthorn/sloe		4	1			567
Rubus fruticosus L. *agg./ideaus* L.	Blackberry/raspberry	>1000	98		6	45	428
Sorbus aucuparia L.	Rowan						66
Vaccinium sp.	Various						2
Vaccinium myrtillus L.	Bilberry						38
Grassland							
Alchemilla sp.	Lady's mantle					4	12
Linum catharticum L.	Fairy flax			1	14	1	
Plantago lanceolata L.	Ribwort plantain					1	1
Plantago media L.	Hoary plantain				2		
Prunella vulgaris L.	Self-heal		1	1	40	12	6
Dry places/bare ground							
Rumex acetosella L.	Sheep's sorrel						1
Tread-resistant plants							
Coronopus squamatus (Forskål) Ascherson	Swinecress			1			
Plantago major L.	Greater plantain						1
Poa annua L.	Annual meadow-grass				1	1	
Polygonum aviculare L.	Knotgrass		70	32	21	30	11
Disturbed ground							
Aethusa cynapium L.	Fool's parsley		1			2	
Anagallis arvensis L.	Scarlet pimpernel		2	3	26	10	2
Anthemis cotula L.	Stinking chamomile			13	81	5	42
Aphanes arvenvsis L.	Parsley-piert		6	5	4	7	5

Binomial classification	English/common						
**Atriplex* cf. *patula* L.	Common orache	1	16	3	36	93	33
Brassica nigra (L.) Koch	Black mustard					2	
Brassica rapa L.	Wild turnip	1	1		2	8	
**Chenopodium album* L.	Fat hen	5	74	13	34	85	84
Chenopodium rubrum L.	Red goosefoot		85	57		42	9
**Daucus carota* L.	Wild carrot					1	
Euphorbia helioscopa L.	Sun spurge					1	
Galium aparnine L.	Cleavers				1		
Hyoscyamus niger L.	Henbane		1				
Lapsana communis L.	Nipplewort	1	6	2	30	23	46
Papaver rhoes/dubium L.	Common/long-headed poppy						5
**Polygynum persicaria* L.	Redshank		5		2	1	3
Ranunculus acris/repens L.	Meadow/creeping buttercup		4	2	8	29	18
Raphanus raphanistrum L.	Wild radish						1
**Sambucus nigra* L.	Elder				1	2	
Solanum nigrum L.	Black nightshade		3				1
Sonchus arvensis L.	Perennial sow-thistle				3	1	
Sonchus asper (L.) Hill	Prickly sow-thistle		2	1	15	1	4
Stellaria media (L.) Vill.	Common chickweed		22	20	11	52	15
Thlaspi arvense L.	Field penny-cress						1
Urtica dioica L.	Common nettle		9	10	8	23	6
Urtica urens L.	Small nettle		47	24	31	13	6
Damp and wet places							
Alisma plantago-aquatica L.	Water-plantain					1	
Carex cf. *disticha* Huds.	Brown sedge						1
Carex cf. *flacca* Schreber	Glaucous sedge				19	34	8
Carex riparia Curtis	Greater pond-sedge	2				3	1
Carex rostrata Stokes/*vesicaria* L.	Bottle sedge/Bladder sedge		4	6	5		9
Eleocharis palustris (L.) Roemer & Schultes	Common spike-rush				2	6	8
Juncus bufonius L.	Toad rush		24	2	9	28	32
Montia fontana L.	Blinks				2	43	7
Potentilla anserina L.	Silverweed				5	1	1
Potentilla cf. *palustris* Scop.	Marsh cinquefoil				1		
Potentilla erecta (L.) Rauscel	Tormentil				3	1	
Ranunculus cf. *lingua* L.	Greater spearwort				1		
Ranunculus flammula L.	Lesser spearwort				4		7
Ranunculus scleratus L.	Celery-leaved buttercup					3	1
Scirpus setaceus L.	Bristle club-rush			1	1	23	2
Stellaria palustris Retz.	Marsh stitchwort					1	

Binomial classification	English/common						
Salt marsh							
Aster tripolium L.	Sea aster				1	2	
Arable weeds							
Agrostemma githago L.	Corncockle						p
**Fallopia convolvulus* (L.) Á.Löve	Black bindweed				1	8	
Valerianella dentata (L.) Pollich	Narrow-fruited cornsalad				1		
Viola arvensis Murray/*tricolor* L.	Field pansy/wild pansy					3	2
Miscellaneous							
Crataegus monogyna Jacq.	Hawthorn						1
Labiatae	Various						1
Unidentified		2	1		2	6	
Species identified to genus level							
Agrostris sp.	Bent				1	1	1
Alnus sp.	Alder						1
Alopecurus sp.	Foxtail				1		
Apium sp.	Various				1		
Arctium sp.	Burdock				1		
Atriplex sp.	Orache				9	10	
Brassica sp.	Various				1		5
Carex ssp.	Sedge		4	4	23	23	18
Chenopodium ssp.	Goosefoot	5	3		5	2	1
Cirsium sp.	Thistle				2	2	1
Galeopsis sp.	Hemp-nettle					3	1
Hypericum sp.	St. John's Wort		1				
Juncus ssp.	Rush	4	10		8	11	17
Leontodon sp.	Hawkbit			2	15		2
Mentha sp.	Mint						1
Polygynum sp.	Various					1	1
Potentilla sp.	Various		4	1		1	
Rumex ssp.	Dock		4	3	7	14	6
Silene sp.	Campion						1
Solanum sp.	Various					1	
Sonchus ssp.	Sow-thistle					2	

p means present
* represents possible food plants

Cultivated plants included charred grains of wheat (*Triticum* sp.), barley (*Hordeum* sp.) and oat (*Avena* sp.). Charred cereal grains, when found in small numbers in pits, usually reflect accidental burning during the drying process or may represent threshing debris. The disaggregation of faecal remains from Pit 4b/F2092 (Phase 4b) revealed that the excrement was crammed with cereal bran of either wheat or rye (*Secale* sp.), pointing to a high-fibre diet.

Evidence for cultivated flax (*Linum usitatissimum*) in the form of seeds and capsules was found. Flax seeds and capsules are waste materials resulting from the processing of flax stems into linen yarns (Pals and van Dierendonck 1988) and their presence in the pits may be evidence for the production of linen. The seeds of cultivated flax are also used in the production of linseed oil which has culinary uses.

DISTURBED GROUND

CEREAL WEEDS AND GRASSLAND

Without the use of herbicides, weeds grow freely within the cereal crop and are harvested with it. In the past, cereal weeds were common and some like fat-hen (*Chenopodium album*), oraches (*Atriplex ssp.*), black bindweed (*Fallopia convolvus*) and knotgrass (*Polygynum aviculare*) may have been purposely harvested and eaten (Godwin 1975; Mitchell 1987). Cereal weeds may also have come into the town with the straw used for thatching or litter. However, some weeds are characteristic of disturbed ground generally and can grow freely in cereal fields and towns. Given the large number of fat-hen seeds in the deposits it is likely that this plant grew as a weed in the town.

The majority of disturbed ground species are likely to have originated from within the town itself. Generally, the species present are those which thrive in disturbed nitrogen-rich soil, conditions one would expect to find in the vicinity of open pits. Most of the weeds are annuals. The disturbed conditions in towns would have been ideal for the growth of annuals, where perennials, which need a stable environment, would have found it more difficult to get established. Species like small nettle (*Urtica urens*), black nightshade (*Solanum nigrum*) and fat hen (*Chenopodium album*) are common garden weeds and might have grown in plots within the town. Plants capable of withstanding trampling were also present and included knotgrass, annual meadow grass (*Poa annua*), greater plantain (*Plantago major*) and swine cress (*Coronopus squamatus*). These species probably grew on pathways and were repeatedly trampled upon by the townspeople and the animals.

Species common to grassland were present in the pits. Seeds, unlike pollen, do not travel very far from the site of production and so grassland species are likely to have arrived by indirect means. The use of cut sods for roofing might help to explain the presence of some of the grassland species in the pits. Ribwort plantain (*Plantago lanceolata*), self-heal (*Prunella vulgaris*) and hoary plantain (*Plantago media*) can be found on the short turf of pastures (Salisbury 1961) and may have been introduced into the town with cut turf. Ribwort plantain, however, is a variable species and might have been growing in the town as a weed. Hay, used to feed cattle and horses, would have similarly contained weed seeds. Once in the town, the seeds would have dispersed quite easily, some ending up in the pits.

PLANTS OF WET PLACES

The proximity of the Rivers Poddle and Liffey and the salt marshes and sand banks which accompanied them (Mitchell 1987) account largely for the presence of wetland seeds in the pits. Sea aster (*Aster tripolium*), a plant found in coastal salt marshes, was present. Natural dispersal, together with the accidental transportation of seeds by man and animal, explain how these seeds came into the town. In many cases they would have been transported with waterside vegetation, for example, for use as litter, and their inclusion in the urban organic make-up is to be expected. Some of the plants, however, may have found niches, such as ditches and puddles, within the town. Hall *et al.* (1983) suggested this might be the case for celery-leaved buttercup (*Ranunculus scleratus*) and toad rush (*Juncus bufonius*), both of which were represented by large amounts of seeds in the York deposits.

OTHER REMAINS

Human faecal concretions were found in two of the pits (Pit 6/F1246 and Pit 4b/F2092; Phase 4). Mosses were present in all of the pits from Phase 4 and the species were identified as *Thuidium tamariscinum* and *Eurhynchium striatum* (identified by Alan Hall, Environmental Archaeology Unit, York). A pit, possibly serving as a latrine, and containing large quantities of mosses, faecal remains and seeds, was found at Winetavern Street, in Dublin (Mitchell 1987) and mosses were also recorded in cesspits of Hiberno-Scandinavian and Anglo-Norman date in Waterford (Tierney and Hannon 1997, 882). The mosses were interpreted as wiping material and the moss in the Cork Tower pits may have served a similar purpose.

Bones of herring (*Clupea harengus*), eel (*Anguilla anguilla*), whiting (*Merlangius merlangus*), salmon (*Salmo salar*) and ray (*Raja* sp.) were noted in the pit fills, as well as fragmented shells of mussel and cockle. Fragments of poultry eggs were also recorded.

A small amount of charcoal was examined from Pit 4a/F2096 and Pit 6/F1246 in Phase 4. Hazel, sloe, alder (*Alnus* sp.), ash (*Fraxinus* sp.) and willow (*Salix* sp.) were identified, all of which could have been growing locally. Their presence in the pits probably reflects their use as firewood.

Beetle remains were also examined from the pits with a view to establishing if pests of stored products, such as grain, flour and dried fruits were present. *Trox*, a genus often, not entirely, associated with dry materials of animal origin such as skins, hooves, feathers, bones, etc. was present in Pit 6/F1246 and Pit 4b/F2092 (Phase 4), and could have come into the pit with waste of that nature. Beetles associated with rotting vegetable matter were also present. Fly puparia of the common housefly (*Musca domestica*) were abundant, the pits offering ideal conditions for their development. Remains of a human flea (*Pulex irritans*), beautifully preserved in Pit 6/F1246, was probably thrown out with bedding or other material and points to the less than ideal living conditions in the town.

Cork Tower: House Interiors

Floor deposits along the side walls of House 1 (F2061; Phase 3) and House 2 (F2016; Phase 5) were sampled (Table 7.3). These deposits probably belonged to bedding areas within the houses that also functioned as seating areas during the day. Both deposits contained well-preserved environmental indicators. Organic material embedded in a wattle screen in the north-west corner of House 1 (F2053) and a sod deposit (F2013) in House 2 were also examined.

HOUSE 1

The floor deposit in House 1 (F2061) consisted of a compacted mass of vegetable matter including fern, feathers, straw, wood chips and mosses. A lot of coarse-grained sand was also present. The small number of food remains recorded included blackberry seeds, sloe fruit stones and hazelnut shells; one grain of charred wheat was noted.

Weeds (grasslands and wetland species), already represented in 'outdoor' seed assemblages, were present in the floor deposits. Weed seeds, plentiful in the town, could have blown through open doors and were easily incorporated into the floors when they fell from clothing and shoes. Vegetation, used as flooring material in the houses, naturally would have contained many weed seeds and could explain the representation of wetland plants. However, rush seeds (*Juncus* ssp.) were abundant in House 1 with more than five hundred seeds (including toad rush), present and point to the use of rushes in bedding material, mats and suchlike.

An abundance of charcoal, probably debris from the hearth, and food remains were present. It is probable that when sweeping the central living area, bits and pieces would have easily gathered in corners and in deposits along the side walls.

Shellfish fragments and animal bone were also noted, as well as three chips of amber that may have fallen from one of the occupant's work clothes.

A wattle mat (F2055) had survived in the north-west corner of House 1 (Fig. 3.4). A thick organic layer (F2053) containing twigs, leaves, straw, mosses, fern and wood was matted into the screen. The organic mass was examined with a view to ascertaining the function of this corner of the house. The seed assemblage (Table 7.4) differed little from the bedding / seating area. Hazelnut shells, fragments of crushed leaves, wood chippings, straw and feathers were also present. However, charcoal, which littered the bedding/seating area was absent from this context suggesting that the corner was closed off from the rest of the house. Bones of flat fish, herring (*Clupea harengus*) and trout (*Salmo trutta*) were identified from the deposit.

The remains of beetles were also identified in this deposit (Table 7.5). A single elytron (wing case) of *Gnathoncus* sp. was present. All of the four species found in Britain live in birds' nests and poultry sheds (Harde 1984). They are not necessarily restricted to these habitats, however, and feathers present in these deposits were not in amounts that would substantiate evidence of the housing of fowl. Its presence may simply indicate that birds were nesting in the roof of the house. Environmental indicators specifically associated with the keeping of animals in House 1 were not present.

Artefacts associated with this mat consisted of a piece of woollen fabric, part of a crucible, a leather strap and a fragment of a wooden loom. The artefactual evidence would suggest the use of this corner of the house as a craft work/storage area.

HOUSE 2

The floor deposit (F2016) in the north-west corner of House 2, in what was probably the bedding / seating area, was highly organic and consisted of a compacted mass of vegetable matter including fern, feathers, straw, wood chips and mosses. The small number of food remains which were noted included charred cereal grains, especially barley (*Hordeum* sp.) and waterlogged blackberry seeds, sloe fruit stones and hazelnut shells. Weeds (grasslands and wetland species) similar to those of House 1 were also noted in House 2.

Table 7.3 Cork Tower; plant remains from floor deposits of House 1 (F2061) and House 2 (F2016).

Cork Tower Cutting 2 (CT2)			
Feature Number		F2061	F2016
Volume (mls)		500	500
Binomial classification	**English/common**		
Food/Useful plants			
Avena sp. L	Oat		3
Hordeum sp. L.	Barley		9
Linum usitatissimum L.	Cultivated flax		2
Rubus fruticosus L. *agg./ideaus* L.	Blackberry/raspberry	18	4
Prunus spinosa L.	Blackthorn/sloe		4
Triticum sp. L.	Wheat species	1	6
Grassland			
Leucanthium vulgare Lam.	Ox-eye daisy	2	6
Prunella vulgaris L.	Self-heal		2
Disturbed ground			
Anagallis arvensis L.	Scarlet pimpernel	10	
Anthemis cotula L.	Stinking chamomile	7	44
Aphanes arvenvsis L.	Parsley-piert		8
**Atriplex* cf. *patula* L.	Common orache	21	16
Brassica cf. *rapa* L.	Wild turnip	1	
**Chenopodium album* L.	Fat hen	28	19
Chenopodium rubrum L.	Red goosefoot	23	3
Lapsana communis L.	Nipplewort	2	7
**Polygynum aviculare* L.	Knotgrass	50	6
**Polygynum persicaria* L.	Redshank	1	2
Ranunculus acris/ repens L.	Meadow/creeping buttercup	8	1
Sonchus arvensis L.	Perennial sow-thistle	1	
Sonchus asper (L.) Hill	Prickly sow-thistle		4
Stellaria palustris Retz.	Marsh stitchwort	11	
Urtica dioica L.	Common nettle	3	
Urtica urens L.	Small nettle	46	16
Binomial classification	**English/common**		
Damp and wet places			
Carex cf. *flacca* Schreber	Glaucous sedge	3	1
Carex rostrata Stokes/ *vesicaria* L.	Bottle sedge/Bladder sedge		4
Eleocharis palustris (L.) Roemer & Schultes	Common spike-rush		3
Juncus bufonius L.	Toad rush	>100	23
Montia fontana L.	Blinks		1
Ranunculus flammula L.	Lesser spearwort		1
Scirpus setaceus L.	Bristle club-rush	2	
Species identified to genus level			
Carex ssp.	Sedge	7	7
Chenopodium ssp.	Goosefoot		6
Cirsium sp.	Thistle		2
Juncus ssp.	Rush	>500	10
Leontodon sp.	Hawkbit		7
Mentha sp.	Mint		2
Rumex sp.	Dock	7	4
Viola sp.	Violet	1	
Miscellaneous			
Gramineae	Grasses		4

* represents possible food plants

A sod deposit (F2013), closely associated with the floor deposit (F2016) was also examined. Preservation was poor. Common chickweed (*Stellaria media*; one seed), bristle club-rush (*Scirpus setaceus*; one seed), blinks (*Montia fontana* ssp. *chondrosperma*; 121 seeds), together with many mites, were all that survived. Large quantities of blinks, together with other grassland indicators, were present in sods examined from Fishamble Street, Wood Quay (Geraghty 1996). The sod layer in House 2 may represent a foundation layer or 'mattress' upon which straw, mosses and other vegetation were placed or gradually accumulated. At Wood Quay turves and brushwood formed benches along the side walls of the houses and these also served as beds (Wallace 1984). Alternatively, the sods in House 2 could have collapsed from the roof or the walls of the house and subsequently became incorporated into the house floor.

Table 7.4 Cork Tower, House 1, plant remains from north-west corner compartment deposit F2053.

Cork Tower Cutting 2 (CT2)		
Feature Number		F2053
Volume (mls)		500
Binomial classification	**English/common**	
Food/Useful plants		
Rubus fruticosus L. *agg./ideaus* L.	Blackberry/raspberry	2
Grassland		
Leucanthium vulgare Lam.	Ox-eye daisy	1
Prunella vulgaris L.	Self-heal	3
Disturbed ground		
Aethusa cynapium L.	Fool's parsley	1
Anthemis cotula L.	Stinking chamomile	3
**Atriplex* cf. *patula* L.	Common orache	7
**Chenopodium album* L.	Fat hen	2
Lapsana communis L.	Nipplewort	1
**Polygynum persicaria* L.	Redshank	1
Ranunculus acris/repens L.	Meadow/creeping buttercup	28
Sonchus arvensis L.	Perennial sow-thistle	1
Stellaria palustris Retz.	Marsh stitchwort	3
Urtica dioica L.	Common nettle	1
Urtica urens L.	Small nettle	1
Binomial classification	**English/common**	
Damp and wet places		
Calluna vulgaris (L.) Hull	Ling	1
Carex cf. *flacca* Schreber	Glaucous sedge	15
Carex riparia Curtis	Greater pond-sedge	1
Carex rostrata Stokes/*vesicaria* L.	Bottle sedge/ Bladder sedge	6
Eleocharis palustris (L.) Roemer & Schultes	Common spike-rush	1
Juncus bufonius L.	Toad rush	11
Lycopus europaeus L.	Gipsywort	1
Ranunculus flammula L.	Lesser spearwort	1
Stellaria palustris Retz.	Marsh stitchwort	1
Woods and Shady Places		
Glechoma hederacea L.	Ground ivy	3
Species identified to genus level		
Atriplex sp.	Orache	2
Carex ssp.	Sedge	20
Cirsium sp.	Thistle	2
Galeopsis sp.	Hemp-nettle	2
Juncus ssp.	Rush	6
Leontodon sp.	Hawkbit	4
Rumex sp.	Dock	2
Viola sp.	Violet	2

* represents possible food plants

Beetles, extracted from subsamples primarily analysed for plant remains, were identified (Table 7.6). Generally, the beetles present can be found in all kinds of decaying organic matter living on and in animal excrement (e.g. *Hister* ssp., *Aphodius* ssp.) and rotting organic plant material (e.g. *Cercyon analis* (also found in waterside debris) and *Philonthus* ssp.). Dung beetles could have been introduced with the cow dung used to plaster the walls of the houses for insulation purposes (Buckland *et al.* 1974). Beetles which inhabit decaying organic matter of various kinds were similarly abundant in samples from Viking deposits in York (Hall *et al.* 1983). Deposits would have accumulated rapidly within these houses. Fresh, dry material such as straw would have become mouldy and stale with use and unless frequently and thoroughly removed would have decomposed *in situ*. The constant addition of dry fresh straw onto the floor and its subsequent decomposition with time, together with other plant debris and waste, resulted in ideal conditions for beetles to breed and survive. Beetles could also have been introduced with the flooring and bedding material itself, and as such represent an 'outdoor assemblage' (e.g. *Amara* ssp.).

Fly puparia, including those of the common housefly, were present in the bedding/seating area of both houses. These could have come into the houses with flooring material and did not necessarily hatch indoors. The common housefly is closely associated with man, successfully reproducing where food and waste is exposed, thriving in the absence of hygiene.

Pieces of slag and two coprolites, probably of canine origin, were present in the floor deposits of House 2, as well as shellfish and animal bone.

Table 7.5 Beetle remains within House 1 deposit F2053.

Cork Tower Cutting 2 (CT2)	
Feature Number	F2016
Volume (mls)	500
	MNI
Carabidae	
Calathus sp.	1
Hydrophilidae	
Cercyon analis (Paykull)	5
Histeridae	
Acritus nigricornis (Hoffmann)	3
Gnathoncus sp.	1
Ptiliidae	
Ptenidium sp.	1
Staphylinidae	
Anotylus cf. *rugosus* (Fabricius)	1
Gyrohypnus angustatus Stephens	1
Gyrohypnus fracticornis (Muller)	2
Philontus ssp.	2
Quedius sp.	2
Scarabaeidae	
Aphodius granarius (Linnaeus)	2
Rhizophagidae	
Monotoma cf. *picipes* Herbst	1
Anthicidae	
Anthicus sp.	1

Table 7.6 Beetle remains within House 2 deposit F2016.

Cork Tower Cutting 2 (CT2)	
Feature Number	F2016
Volume (mls)	500
	MNI
Carabidae	
Notiophilus sp.	1
Amara sp.	1
Hydrophilidae	
Cercyon analis (Paykull)	8
Cercyon unipunctatus (Linnaeus)	2
Cercyon sp.	1
Megasternum obscurum (Marsham)	4
Histeridae	
Hister merdarius group *	3
Leoididae	
Leoides sp.	1
Staphylinidae	
Platystethus arenarius (Fourcroy)	1
Othius sp.	1
Leptacinus sp.	1
Gyrohypnus fracticornis (Muller)	3
Xantholinus linearis (Olivier)/*longiventris* Heer	3
Philontus ssp.	2
Quedius sp.	1
Scarabaeidae	
Aphodius ssp.	2
Dascillidae	
Dascillus cervinus (Linnaeus)	1
Melyridae	
Malachius sp.	1
Cryptophagidae	
Cryptophagus sp.	1

* *Hister merdarius* group includes *Hister cadaverinus* Hoffmann, *merdarius* Hoffmann, *striola* Sahlberg

Cork Tower: Urban Environment

The urban environment was assessed by examining the series of rich organic occupation layers which had accumulated outside the houses; three layers were sampled (Phase 4a: F2045, 2046, 2051). Clay with organic content (F2033) which had gathered outside House 2 (Phase 5) within a wattle panel was also examined. It is not clear whether this panel was part of a walkway or whether it had been part of the structure of House 2 (Fig. 3.8).

The seeds from the organic occupation deposits (Table 7.7) reflect plant remains also present in the cesspit and rubbish pit fills discussed above. Plant food remains included charred cereal grains, fruit seeds and hazelnut shells. The abundance of weed species confirms the high profile that weeds and ruderals had in the town; the organic nature of the material, like the pit fills, acted as a catchment site for seeds dispersed in the vicinity. Grassland and wetland plants were represented. Wild celery (*Apium graveolens*) was represented by one seed. Found in damp grassy places, mostly near the sea, this plant can be eaten as a vegetable and used as a flavouring. Other macrofossil remains included straw, bits of wood bark, mosses, fern tips, leaves and charcoal. Food remains included fishbone, eggshell and cockle and mussel shells. Organic layers of build-up are characteristic of medieval towns and similar deposits are present; for example at York (Hall *et al.* 1983) and at Wood Quay, Dublin (Geraghty 1996).

Fly puparia were abundant in these layers, especially those of the common housefly (*Musca domestica*); masses of decomposing organic matter, including food waste, provided ideal conditions for the development of larvae into adult flies. Conditions appear to have been far from ideal and infestation and disease must have caused major problems to health. No human faecal material was present, confirming its disposal was confined to designated cesspits or perhaps the nearby river.

An organic layer (F2033) overlying a wattle panel outside the north-west corner of House 2 was also examined. The panel was less than a metre from the wall of the house, just north-west of the doorway (Fig. 3.8). Seeds extracted from this deposit are listed in Table 7.8. Pathways, especially when outside a house, will collect mud and dirt and need to be swept and maintained on a regular basis. It would appear that this panel, probably because of its proximity to the house, was relatively well maintained and large masses of organic build-up were not in evidence. Instead, there was a thin layer of organic material embedded into the wattle.

The seeds in this deposit may have arrived in a variety of ways and food remains dropped accidentally or swept out of the house would account for the presence of blackberry (*Rubus fruticosus*), sloe and frochan (*Vaccinium myrtillus*). Hazelnut shells and shellfish were also present. Flax is well represented and may indicate that processing was carried on nearby. Other seeds could have fallen from the shoes of passers-by or have been blown from plants growing in the vicinity. Weeds and ruderals of disturbed ground, which seemed to infiltrate all contexts, were again present. These included cereal weeds like corn marigold (*Chrysanthemum segetum*) and black bindweed (*Fallopia convolvulus*), together with weeds like common nettle (*Urtica dioica*) and stinking chamomile (*Anthemis cotula*), which probably grew in the nutrient-rich deposits alongside the houses and around the pathways. Greater plantain (*Plantago major*), a plant capable of withstanding trampling, probably grew up between the wattle strands of the pathway itself.

The presence of grassland and wetland plants in town deposits has already been discussed above in the context of the cesspit assemblages. Cut sods used for roofing and the proximity of the River Poddle and River Liffey, together with salt marsh in the locality, explain why these habitats are represented in the town. Salisbury (1961), when discussing the dispersal of weed seeds, concludes that while wind is the most widespread and effective natural agent of dispersal, animals are also important in this respect. In his work, droppings of cattle, horses, pigs, goats and birds contained, among other species, creeping buttercup (*Ranunculus repens*), chickweed (*Stellaria media*) and oxeye daisy (*Leucanthemum vulgare*). Many of the species he lists were in the pits and walkway samples and, given the organic nature of deposits within the town, the deposition of cow and horse manure was likely. Other remains included fly puparia of the common housefly, fragments of animal bone, straw, charcoal, wood chippings and fern. The presence of fly puparia, often associated with dung, is further evidence for the presence of animals in the town.

Powder Tower: Earthen Banks and Associated Deposits

Samples were taken from the Phase 1a clay bank (F562) and a larger stone-faced clay bank that superseded it in Phase 1b, comprising layers of dumped material F561, F556, F563 and F559 (see Chapter 3.2). Additional dumping continued in the area, associated with post-and-wattle breakwaters set up to protect the embankment from the flow of the Poddle. Dump deposits accumulated on and beyond the Phase 1a bank (deposits F542, F548, F551, F550 and F546), and the Phase 1b bank (deposit F544), resulting in a build-up of deposits and a heightening of ground levels in the area. A Phase 2 timber-reinforced clay bank (deposits F491, F492) was constructed over the earlier Phase 1a/b deposits, as an alternative to replacing the breakwaters when they became damaged. Samples were examined with two objectives in mind: 1) to define the origin and nature of the make-up of the earthen banks and associated deposits and 2) to determine the effect of the River Poddle in the area and examine to what extent its movements can be traced in the archaeological deposits.

Table 7.7 Cork Tower, plant remains from Phase 4a organic habitation deposits F2045, F2046 and F2051.

Cork Tower Cutting 2 (CT2)				
Feature Number		F2045	F2046	F2051
Volume (mls)		500	500	500
Binomial classification	**English/common**			
Food/Useful plants				
Avena sp. L	Oat			1
Fragaria vesca L.	Strawberry		1	
Hordeum sp. L.	Barley	1		
Rubus fruticosus L. *agg./ideaus* L.	Blackberry/ raspberry	9		5
Grassland				
Linum catharticum L.	Fairy flax		2	4
Prunella vulgaris L.	Self-heal	5	37	11
Disturbed ground				
Aethusa cynapium L.	Fool's parsley	3		
Anagallis arvensis L.	Scarlet pimpernel	1	4	5
Anthemis cotula L.	Stinking chamomile	33	18	29
Anthriscus caucalis Bieb.	Bur chervil		2	
Aphanes arvenvsis L.	Parsley-piert		4	2
**Atriplex* cf. *patula* L.	Common orache	27	14	12
Brassica cf. *rapa* L.	Wild turnip		14	
Chenopodium rubrum L.	Red goosefoot	11	3	15
**Daucus carota* L.	Wild carrot			1
Hyoscyamus niger L.	Henbane	1		
Lapsana communis L.	Nipplewort	12	8	6
Odontites verna (Bellardi) Dumort.	Red bartsia			3
Ranunculus acris/ repens L.	Meadow/creeping buttercup	12	30	5
Solanum nigrum L.	Black nightshade			2
Sonchus arvensis L.	Perennial sow-thistle	7	1	2
Sonchus asper (L.) Hill	Prickly sow-thistle	20	2	3
Sonchus oleraceus L.	Smooth sow-thistle	1		
Stellaria media (L.) Vill.	Common chickweed	11	9	3
Urtica dioica L.	Common nettle	7	6	13
Urtica urens L.	Small nettle	3	50	14
Binomial classification	**English/common**			
Damp and wet places				
**Apium graveolens* L.	Wild celery		1	
Carex cf. *flacca* Schreber	Glaucous sedge		3	2
Carex riparia Curtis	Greater pond-sedge		1	
Carex rostrata Stokes/ *vesicaria* L.	Bottle sedge/ Bladder sedge		2	2
Eleocharis palustris (L.) Roemer & Schultes	Common spike-rush			1
Juncus bufonius L.	Toad rush	12		30
Potentilla anserina L.	Silverweed		1	
Potentilla erecta (L.) Rauscel	Tormentil		1	1
Ranunculus flammula L.	Lesser spearwort		1	
Scirpus setaceus L.	Bristle club-rush			2
Stellaria palustris Retz.	Marsh stitchwort	1	1	2
Species identified to genus level				
Carex ssp.	Sedge	3	2	8
Chenopodium ssp.	Goosefoot	1		
Cirsium sp.	Thistle		1	
Eleocharis sp.	Spike-rush			1
Galeopsis sp.	Hemp-nettle	2		2
Hypochoeris sp.	Cat's ear		1	
Juncus ssp.	Rush	2		20
Leontodon sp.	Hawkbit	5	14	1
Mentha sp.	Mint		1	1
Potentilla sp.	Various		2	1
Ranunculus sp.	Various		1	
Rumex sp.	Dock	1	1	6
Sonchus ssp.	Sow-thistle	1		
Stachys sp.	Woundwort		1	
Taraxacum sp.	Dandelion		1	
Viola sp.	Violet		1	3

* represents possible food plants

Table 7.8 Cork Tower, plant remains from deposit F2033 on wattle panel outside House 2.

Cork Tower Cutting 2 (CT2)		
Feature Number		F2033
Volume (mls)		500
Binomial classification	**English/common**	
Food/Useful plants		
Linum usitatissimum L.	Cultivated flax	14
Prunus spinosa L.	Blackthorn/sloe	2
Rubus fruticosus L. *agg./ideaus* L.	Blackberry/raspberry	4
Vaccinium myrtillus L.	Bilberry	3
Grassland		
Leucanthium vulgare Lam.	Ox-eye daisy	2
Prunella vulgaris L.	Self-heal	38
Disturbed ground		
Anagallis arvensis L.	Scarlet pimpernel	3
Anthemis cotula L.	Stinking chamomile	63
Anthriscus caucalis Bieb.	Bur chervil	7
Aphanes arvenvsis L.	Parsley piert	3
**Atriplex* cf. *patula* L.	Common orache	9
Brassica cf. *rapa* L.	Wild turnip	1
**Chenopodium album* L.	Fat hen	10
Euphorbia helioscopa L.	Sun spurge	1
Lapsana communis L.	Nipplewort	13
Plantago major L.	Greater plantain	1
Ranunculus acris/repens L.	Meadow/creeping buttercup	17
Sonchus arvensis L.	Perennial sow-thistle	3
Sonchus asper (L.) Hill	Prickly sow-thistle	6
Stellaria media (L.) Vill.	Common chickweed	1
Urtica dioica L.	Common nettle	11
Urtica urens L.	Small nettle	4

Binomial classification	English/common	
Damp and wet places		
Carex cf. *flacca* Schreber	Glaucous sedge	8
Carex rostrata Stokes/*vesicaria* L.	Bottle sedge/Bladder sedge	4
Eleocharis palustris (L.) Roemer & Schultes	Common spike-rush	1
Juncus bufonius L.	Toad rush	27
Montia fontana L.	Blinks	22
Potentilla anserina L.	Silverweed	1
Ranunculus flammula L.	Lesser spearwort	5
Stellaria palustris Retz.	Marsh stitchwort	29
Arable weeds		
Chrystanthemum segetum L.	Corn marigold	2
**Fallopia convolvulus* (L.) Á.Löve	Black bindweed	1
Species identified to genus level		
Carex ssp.	Sedge	17
Cirsium sp.	Thistle	2
Galeopsis sp.	Hemp-nettle	1
Juncus ssp.	Rush	23
Leontodon sp.	Hawkbit	7
Myosotis sp.	Forget-me-not	2
Potentilla sp.	Various	1
Rumex ssp.	Dock	14
Senecio sp.	Various	2
Stachys sp.	Woundwort	1
Miscellaneous		
Gramineae	Grasses	4
Unidentified		2

* represents possible food plants

EARTHEN BANKS AND ASSOCIATED DEPOSITS (TABLES 7.9, 7.10)

All of the deposits examined associated with both Phase 1 and Phase 2 contained domestic and food waste indicating that refuse from the town had been incorporated within the make-up of the earthen banks throughout the tenth and eleventh centuries.

FOOD WASTE/USEFUL PLANTS

Generally, the food refuse present in the earthen banks was similar to the remains associated with the domestic and cesspit deposits in the Cork Tower area. Fruits, probably gathered from local scrubland, include blackberry/raspberry, strawberry and sloe. Blackberry/raspberry, along with fat hen and orache, were found in all deposits except F556. Very small amounts of charred barley, wheat, oat and rye were present, apart from F542, which contained the greatest number of charred cereals and food remains. The charred cereal remains probably represent grains accidentally burnt, perhaps during the drying process, and later thrown out with other rubbish. Fragments of hazelnut shell were scattered throughout the deposits. Elderberry (*Sambucus nigra*), another edible species often found in association with occupation deposits, was also present. Elderberry is a durable seed and can withstand the aerobic conditions other seeds will not tolerate. Hall *et al.* (1983) interpreted it as a common urban plant whose seeds were readily dispersed by birds in Anglo-Scandinavian Coppergate (York) contexts and its interpretation as a food source, when based on seed remains alone, evidently requires further substantiation. Cultivated flax, although represented here by only one seed, is another plant frequently found in occupation contexts (Geraghty 1996; Hall *et al.* 1983). Flax seeds when found in association with spindle whorls and loom weights on archaeological sites can be interpreted as evidence for the linen industry although their use in linseed oil production cannot be eliminated. Fragments of a bone spindle whorl (E324:13393) were found in dump material (F530) associated with a breakwater feature (BW1) in Phase 1a (see Chapter 4.2.1).

Phase 2 deposits did not contain much evidence for food refuse; blackberry/raspberry and strawberry seeds, fat hen and one grain each of wheat and barley were noted in the deposits (Table 7.10).

DISTURBED GROUND

Species indicative of disturbed ground were well represented in both phases, although more were found in Phase 1 deposits. One of the problems interpreting these species in archaeological contexts is the differentiation between weeds of arable land and those of waste ground, both of which are disturbed habitats. Equally, these seeds were cultivated in the past as food grains, for gruel or coarse bread, as Mitchell (1987) suggests for fat hen and species of *Polygonum*. Also, chickweed (*Stellaria media*), common orache (*Atriplex patula*), fat hen (*Chenopodium album*) and stinking chamomile (*Anthemis cotula*) are plants which, although found in association with arable land, were not necessarily confined to it in the past and could have thrived as weeds in towns.

The interpretation of disturbed ground species as indicative of waste ground therefore may be more plausible, given that the disturbed conditions associated with dumping clearly would have encouraged the development of an annual weed flora. The settlers could also have taken advantage of these plants as sources of food. The question remains, however, to what extent these wasteland species represent *in-situ* growth, and the possibility remains that these seeds could have been introduced with rubbish originating from the town. However, it is clear from the disturbed ground seed assemblage that most, though not all, of the species present are annuals, e.g. small nettle (*Urtica urens*), red goosefoot (*Chenopodium rubrum*), poppy (*Papaver rhoeas/dubium*), knotgrass (*Polygonum aviculare*), etc., indicating that the environment was not stable enough to encourage perennials to establish themselves.

GRASSLAND

Grassland species are poorly represented. Self-heal (*Prunella vulgaris*), fairy flax (*Linum catharticum*) and some of the weeds were probably deposited with rubbish from the town.

PLANTS OF WET PLACES

Plants of wet places, for example sedges (*Carex* spp.), common spike-rush (*Eleocharis palustris*), (*Juncus* spp.) and celery-leaved buttercup (*Ranunculus scleratus*), were noted; the last-mentioned was the most commonly noted plant of wet places in both phases, while rushes were the second most commonly identified. These have all been found in Viking towns (Geraghty 1996; Hall *et al.* 1983) and the introduction of at least some of these species with refuse cannot be overlooked. The use of waterside vegetation for litter and daub might explain their presence in dumped refuse (Hall *et al.* 1983). The representation of wetland species in the deposits is also to be expected, given the influence of the nearby River Poddle.

Fragments of cockle shell and mussel were also abundant and these, together with the hazelnut shells and fruit seeds, appear to reflect food waste thrown out with other domestic refuse. The dumping of large quantities of unfragmented cockle shells was evident in one of the dump layers (F483; see Chapter 3.2) which made up the earthen bank in Phase 2 and may indicate commercial waste. Small amounts of fishbone vertebrae were present. Preliminary investigations identified the majority of these as herring (*Clupea harengus*) although salmon (*Salmo salar*), eel (*Anguilla anguilla*) and flat fishes were also represented. Other waste included eggshell, charcoal and tiny fragments of waste amber.

Table 7.10 Powder Tower, Cutting 1, plant remains from deposits associated with Phase 2 clay/timber bank.

Powder Tower Cutting 1 (PT 1)						
Feature Number		F492	F482	F474	F458	F491
Volume (mls)		500	500	500	500	500
Binomial classification	**English/common**					
Food/Useful plants						
Fragaria vesca L.	Strawberry					10
Hordeum sp. L.	Barley				1	
Rubus fruticosus L. *agg.*/*ideaus* L.	Blackberry/raspberry	10	7	1	19	17
Triticum sp. L.	Wheat species				1	
Disturbed ground						
Aethusa cynapium L.	Fool's parsley	1				
Anagallis arvensis L.	Scarlet pimpernel					1
**Atriplex* cf. *patula* L.	Common orache	1	2			1
**Chenopodium album* L.	Fat hen	1	16		25	
Chenopodium rubrum L.	Red goosefoot	8		2	51	
Euphorbia helioscopa L.	Sun spurge					1
Hyoscyamus niger L.	Henbane	2				3
Lamium purpureum L.	Red dead-nettle					1
Potentilla anserina L.	Silverweed					2
Ranunculus acris/*repens* L.	Meadow/creeping buttercup		1		3	
**Sambucus nigra* L.	Elder				3	
Solanum nigrum L.	Black nightshade	1				
Stellaria media (L.) Vill.	Chickweed					2

Discussion

The analysis of macrofossils from organic deposits in the Cork Tower and Powder Tower areas has provided some insights into the diet and lifestyle of the inhabitants of Viking Dublin between the late ninth and early eleventh centuries. Given the truncated nature of the archaeological remains, the limited number of samples does not allow for analysis of changes through time and consequently all results are combined for discussion purposes below.

CEREALS

Small quantities of barley, oat and wheat grains were recovered and bran of either wheat or rye was also identified. Barley is found in most Hiberno-Norse sites, including Fishamble Street, Dublin (Geraghty 1996), Peter Street/Arundel Square, Waterford (Tierney and Hannon 1997), as well as on contemporary sites further afield in York, England (Hall and Kenward 2004) and Hedeby (Haithabu), Germany (Behre 1983). The barley found in Dublin Castle was unidentifiable to species, but it was probably six-row hulled barley (*Hordeum vulgare* ssp. *vulgare*) which was noted in Fishamble Street (Geraghty 1996, 48). This is also the most commonly identified grain in Irish early medieval assemblages (McClatchie *et al.* 2015, 182) and was ubiquitous across early medieval Britain (Hagen 2010, 33). This barley is high in protein, but is coarse and produces low yields (Moffett 2009, 49). The hulls tightly adhere to the grain, protecting it against infestation and decay, but they require removal if the grains are to be used for the preparation of food products. However, the crop does not have to be

Binomial classification	English/common					
Thlaspi arvense L.	Field penny-cress					1
Urtica dioica L.	Common nettle	3				
Urtica urens L.	Small nettle					10
Plants of wet places						
Carex cf. *flacca* Schreber	Glaucous sedge	1	2	1		
Carex rostrata Stokes/*vesicaria* L.	Bottle sedge/Bladder sedge				1	
Eleocharis palustris (L.) Roemer & Schultes	Common spike-rush			1		1
Juncus bufonius L.	Toad rush	5		4		1
Montia fontana L.	Blinks	2				
Ranunculus scleratus L.	Celery-leaved buttercup	68		12		
Scirpus setaceus L.	Bristle club-rush			1		
Arable weeds						
Valerianella dentata (L.) Pollich	Narrow-fruited cornsalad					9
Seeds identified to genus level						
Atriplex sp.	Orache	2			1	1
Brassica sp.	Various					2
Carex ssp.	Sedge	2	1		3	
Chenopodium ssp.	Goosefoot				4	
Cirsium sp.	Thistle					1
Juncus sp.	Rush		8			20
Potentilla sp.	Various	1				1
Rumex ssp.	Dock				1	
Senecio sp.	Various					1
Viola sp.	Violet					1

* represents possible food plants

threshed or processed further if it is to be used for animal fodder or brewing (Cappers and Neef 2012, 273). Analysis of breads/biscuits found in Viking-age cremations and inhumations at Birka and on Börkö, Sweden indicated that hulled barley was among the list of ingredients (Hansson 1996; Hjelmqvist 1984). Dental attrition present on skeletal teeth could also have been the result of tough inclusions such as glumes (Power 1994). No evidence for malting, for example coleoptile or coleorhizae growth (Stika 1996, 83) was noted in the Dublin Castle assemblage.

The presence of oats in the assemblage is also typical for this period in Ireland (McClatchie *et al.* 2015; Monk 1991). It was the main crop noted in the floor deposits of Viking houses uncovered during recent excavations in the Coombe, Dublin (Stone 2018), as well as dominating the assemblage of the tenth-century corn-drying kiln in the Viking site of Golden Lane, Dublin (Sara Halwas in O'Donovan 2008, 56) and the Hiberno-Norse kiln in Arundel Square, Waterford (Johnston 2018). It has been identified on international Viking sites, including Kaupang, Norway (Barrett *et al.* 2007) and Gammel Lejre, Denmark (Robinson 1991), although in much smaller amounts than in Ireland. It is also the main ingredient of the only archaeological cereal product identified in Ireland: a fragment of an oat and whey biscuit retrieved during the excavation of a seventh-century ringfort in Lisleagh, Co. Cork (McLaren *et al.* 2004). Not all oat caryopses in an assemblage are identifiable to species, however, and it is difficult to differentiate between cultivated oats (*Avena sativa*) and wild oats (*Avena fatua*) when the floret base and distinctive attachment scar are missing

(Cappers and Neef 2012, 267). Unfortunately, the chaff of certain cereals does not preserve well when charred, which occurs when cereals are deposited into a hearth or corn-drying kiln (Boardman and Jones 1990). Interestingly, the oats found within the kiln in Arundel Square, Waterford were still within glumes when they were imported into the town, thus providing evidence for the processing of cultivated oats within an urban context (Johnston in Hughes *et al.* 2018). Wild oat also commonly grows in arable fields (Jones *et al.* 2004) and it is likely to have formed a large component of assemblages as it is of a similar morphology to its domesticated counterpart and would therefore have been difficult to remove. It is edible and was also consumed in the past. The eleventh-century Irish parody *Aislinge Mheic Conglinne* (The vision of Conglinne), which contains a large amount of information regarding foodstuffs, lists wild oats as consumed grains alongside oats, rye, wheat and barley (Sayers 1994, 3).

Growing mixtures of cereals together would have mitigated against crop failure and it has been suggested that the barley and oats retrieved from the Fishamble Street site were grown in a dredge (combining spring barley and oat) where it is believed that the ratio represented a clean and purposefully mixed crop (M.A. Monk, pers. comm. in Geraghty 1996, 49). Geraghty also suggests that this may have been the case with the assemblage retrieved from the pits in Plot 11 of Fishamble Street. There is no evidence to suggest that the barley and oats found in Dublin Castle were grown in this way, but it would not have been unusual. Both crops have fairly low growth requirements and hardiness to tough conditions (Riehl 2009; Murphy and Potterton 2010, 311). They are both hulled and therefore require similar processing techniques. Both are highly nutritious and lend themselves to various types of cooking, although oat appears to have been used in more varied ways (Sexton 1998).

Very small amounts of wheat were noted, although no chaff survived and therefore it is not clear whether the caryopses were those of a free-threshing (naked) or of a glume (hulled) subspecies. The latter comprises caryopses which are tightly enclosed by glumes (bracts), which allows protection from decay or infestation. This type of wheat can grow in adverse conditions, but it requires additional processing to remove its glumes (Cappers and Bekker 2013). Free-threshing or naked wheats have been bred to produce grains which sit loosely in the chaff, thereby allowing easier harvesting. However, the lack of a protective cover renders the grains susceptible to decay or infestation, especially in the temperate oceanic climate of north-western Europe where there is no dry season (Peel *et al.* 2007). The data gathered during the Early Medieval Archaeology Project (EMAP) indicated that naked wheat, typically that of bread wheat (*T. aestivum*) with evidence for a *T. aestivum/T. aestivum compactum* (club-wheat), was the most commonly encountered wheat in rural assemblages (McCormick *et al.* 2011, 56; McClatchie *et al.* 2015, 182). Wheat was also found on the Fishamble Street site but it was not identifiable to species and bread-wheat was found in Peter Street/Arundel Square (Tierney and Hannon 1997). It was also consumed by inhabitants in Gotland, Sweden (Kosiba *et al.* 2007) and Ribe, Denmark (Jensen *et al.* 1991). The increased cultivation of free-threshing wheats throughout the medieval period probably led to the decline in glume wheats such as emmer; and perhaps, as Griffin and Rowlett (1981) note the complete replacement of other grasses like Lyme grass (*Elymus arenarius*).

Bran of either wheat or rye was identified in faecal material. This is similar to findings from cesspits excavated in Waterford (Tierney and Hannon 1997) and York (Hall and Kenward 2004, 395). Cereal bran (wheat/rye) was also found in Viking Cork (McClatchie 2003). Rye is present in small amounts in early medieval Ireland, albeit in all regions (McClatchie *et al.* 2015), and in the ninth-century law text *Bretha Déin Chécht* it is recorded that rye was the second highest-valued grain, below bread-wheat, and was for 'a superior king' (Binchy 1966, 23). Rye was suited to unfavourable soils and would have lent itself well to cultivation in Ireland, although it is susceptible to the ergot fungus (*Claviceps purpurea*) which sprouts in damp weather, and which can cause painful swellings and even death (Youngken 1947). Rye was cultivated throughout early medieval Europe and still remains an important grain for baking various breads; it produces an excellent sourdough (Hansson 1994, 10).

Cereals formed a large part of the early medieval diet across Europe and references to products appear in contemporary literature such as the Irish and Welsh law tracts (Owen 1841; Binchy 1938; 1966). However, the small amounts of cereals present in Irish urban deposits has been noted by Geraghty (1996), Mitchell (1987) and Lyons (2015). This scarcity may be explained by preservation biases or taphonomy, as well as processing and consumption practices.

Flax seeds were found in most of the domestic deposits of the Dublin Castle excavations. Flax has been cultivated in Ireland from at least the Bronze Age (Monk 1985) and formed a significant part of the diet in medieval Europe, in both seed and oil form. Its oil was also used for cooking and lighting and the plant was also grown to produce fibres for the manufacture of linen. Little work has been carried out on flax cultivation and preservation in Ireland and it is not clear whether different varieties were grown in the past to produce the different products. It is not clear whether flax was grown in a small plot or within fields in a similar manner to crops. Contemporary Welsh laws indicate that it was grown in a garden (Owen 1841, 561), while the same is suggested for Viking-age Sweden (Rohde Sloth *et al.* 2012). Flax seeds are often found on early medieval and Hiberno-Norse/Viking sites, in the form of single seeds and capsules (Monk 1991; McCormick *et al.* 2011). Flax was known to be a crop which required little attention during growing, resulting in overgrown and weedy plots or fields (Smyth 2012, 161). It is not always clear from the archaeobotanical record whether the plant was cultivated for its seeds and oil or for linen production, although morphometric studies have been undertaken in this area (Lodwick 2017; Herbig and Maier 2011). However, there are sometimes clues regarding its use as a culinary ingredient, such as the seeds present in the breads excavated in Birka (Hansson 1996).

The crops which have been identified on Hiberno-Norse sites also reflect the general trend of contemporary Irish assemblages and suggest that there was no discernible desire for particular foods from the Scandinavian homelands; rather the newcomers consumed what was available and what was cultivated in the locality. This creolisation or Irish/Insular character has been noted in Hiberno-Norse settlements (O'Sullivan *et al.* 2014, 120) including Fishamble Street, Dublin (Geraghty 1996), Winetavern Street, Dublin (Mitchell 1987) and Bride Street, Wexford (Bourke 1995).

GATHERED FOODS AND ARABLE WEEDS

Arable weeds grow within plots of cultivated grains. They are often gathered with the grain and, while some are removed during pre-processing cleaning of the crop (Hillman 1981), others are mistakenly included in the foodstuffs produced. Some arable weeds are tolerated as food, i.e. 'secondary cultivated plants' (Behre 2008, 65). Those associated with the latter category include fat hen and common orache, both of which were commonly noted within the Powder Tower and Cork Tower assemblages.

Fat hen was found in most of the samples retrieved from Dublin Castle and was also present in large numbers in other Viking excavations in the vicinity (Mitchell 1987, 23). Evidence for its consumption is suggested by its inclusion within a latrine pit at Winetavern Street, where it was present within a faecal mass of foodstuffs which had been ground to flour. It was also present within another faecal mass associated with the pelvis of a young girl on High Street. Fat hen has also been found extensively on other Viking sites including Cork (McClatchie 2003) and Gammel Lejre, Denmark (Robinson 1991). It is considered a cereal weed today but was consumed in the past and there are finds of large numbers of the seeds on sites across Europe. It is not clear whether it was tolerated as a weed among cereals or if it was purposely cultivated, as it grows widely on disturbed ground. Experimental work based upon the gathering of fat hen seeds as a crop indicates that it would have been a suitable food source; the seeds are gathered and processed as easily as cereals and would have provided a sufficient calorific return to have been a viable food product (Stokes and Rowley-Conwy 2002). Mitchell (1990, 171) suggests that the seeds and leaves were consumed alongside *Polygonum* (meld) to supplement the diet of the lower classes.

Common orache was noted in most of the deposits in Dublin Castle and is also found on early medieval sites (McCormick *et al.* 2011) and Hiberno-Norse settlements in Ireland, including Dean Street, Dublin (Stone 2018) and Baldoyle, Co. Dublin (Gilligan 2015); the latter may have had an association with Viking settlement in the hinterland. It is also found across Europe, on sites such as Kaupang, Norway (Barrett *et al.* 2007). Similar to fat hen, orache grows in fields and gardens and evidence for its consumption appears to be widespread. It was probably eaten in both seed and leaf form. Serra and Tunberg (2013) treat it as a consumable green alongside nettles and goosefoot, while the Anglo-Saxons also treated it as a vegetable, along with mallow, spinach and fat hen (Hagen 2010, 50). Orache, similar to nettle, is rich in both vitamins and biologically active compounds and would have provided much nourishment as a condiment or within a stew (Zeipiņa *et al.* 2015, 30).

Wild fruits and nuts, such as wild strawberry, blackberry/raspberry, sloes, bilberries and hazelnut, grow within scrubby hedgerow and would have provided additional nutrition and taste to the diet. These types of seeds, such as *Rubus* species, survive well due to their hard endocarp. However, in certain cases they produce numerous seeds per drupe and may therefore lead to overrepresentation. The most visible wild seeds of this type in the Dublin Castle assemblage were strawberry and blackberry/raspberry. One of the earliest cesspits (Cork Tower, Phase 1; Pit 1/F1041) contained over a thousand blackberry/raspberry seeds, alongside few other taxa. They are commonly found on sites of the same date, such as in Dean Street, Dublin (Stone 2018) and Wexford (Bourke 1995). Sloes were also found in almost all the deposits. Behre (1983) suggests that sloes may have been cultivated near Hedeby; however, there is no reference to the cultivation of sloes in early medieval Ireland. Geraghty (1996, 33) suggests that, despite their sourness to modern palates, fresh sloes were consumed whole. They were also probably processed further to produce jams and preserves that would have provided extra flavour during the winter months when no fresh fruit or vegetables were available (Davidson 1999). The contents of Pit 6 (Cork Tower, Phase 4c, F1246) possibly provide evidence for such processing; a large number of sloe stones and blackberry/raspberry seeds were present and the surrounding soil was stained red/purple. This deposit was covered with branches, wattle and pieces of wood which would have sealed the deposit and prevented the attraction of pests. It is possible that the stones were discarded after the sloes were processed. Evidence for fruit processing was suggested for the deposition of a large amount of fruit-stones, some with remaining pulp adhering, in an eleventh- century pit in Winetavern Street (Mitchell 1987, 25). A possible collapsed wooden loft and chute, which was packed with the remains of pulpy fruit, including sloes and bilberries, was also found in High Street, Dublin (*ibid.*, 27) and, albeit of a later twelfth-century date, provides further evidence for the large-scale processing of such fruits.

Hundreds of fragments of hazelnut shells were encountered in almost all contexts within the Dublin Castle assemblages. Those noted in the Powder Tower assemblage were fragmented and had been included in the domestic refuse used in the construction of the earthen embankments. Hundreds of shells were also found within the cess/rubbish pits at the Cork Tower and were most likely deposited after consumption. They were also present in the build-up occupation deposits of Phase 4, the floor deposits of House 2 and in deposit F2053 (House 1), which indicates their widespread consumption. A small quantity of hazelnut shells was found in the Cross Block excavation, one of which provided a radiocarbon date of cal. AD 907–1147 (see Chapter 8). Hazelnuts were found in Dublin sites such as Fishamble Street (Geraghty 1996), South Great George's Street (Penny Johnston, pers. comm.) and Winetavern Street (Ó Ríordáin 1971), as well as Wexford (Bourke 1995) and Waterford (Tierney and Hannon 1997). Some of those noted in Fishamble Street contained evidence for damage by the nut weevil *Curculio nucum*, which appears to be extinct in Ireland today (Geraghty 1996, 44). There was no such damage noted in the Dublin Castle assemblages. Hazelnuts appear to have been a valuable food source since prehistory (Geraghty 1996, 43). The nuts could have been consumed raw or roasted, although roasting improves their bioavailability (Locatelli *et al.* 2015). The unripe nuts are also soft enough to process and consume fresh (Moscetti *et al.* 2012) and could have been used in a type of early medieval muesli alongside fruits and honey (Sexton 1998).

Apple pips were found only in Pit 6 (F1246; Phase 4c) at the Cork Tower. The lack of pips elsewhere is unusual given the importance and ubiquity of apples in early medieval Ireland (Lyons 2015; McGrath 2010; Brady 2011). However, perhaps, as today, the cores were not typically consumed and the presence of pips within a cesspit is not to be expected. An apple endocarp was found on Fishamble Street (Geraghty 1996, 32), while pips have been found in most Hiberno-Norse assemblages, including Waterford (Tierney and Hannon 1997) and Wexford (Bourke 1995) as well as on sites such as Novgorod, Russia (Monk and Johnston 2001) and Hedeby, present-day Germany (Rohde Sloth *et al.* 2012). Evidence for crab apples has been found on prehistoric sites in Ireland (McClatchie *et al.* 2016) and by the early medieval period there appears to have been a distinction between sour (wild) and sweet (cultivated) varieties. It is not clear as to which variety the Dublin Castle pips belonged; analysis of their DNA could shed more light on this and indicate whether apples were gathered as a wild food or cultivated as a food source (Cappellini *et al.* 2010).

Bilberries were found in only two of the deposits at the Cork Tower: cesspit Pit 6 (F1246, Phase 4c) and deposit F2033, embedded in a wattle panel outside House 2 that may have formed part of a walkway. Bilberries are not as commonly noted on Hiberno-Norse sites as other wild fruits, though they were recorded at Fishamble Street, Dublin (Geraghty 1996) and in Wexford (Bourke 1995). They are commonly found on other early medieval sites and their absence from the Hiberno-Norse sites could be an indicator of cultural preferences (Lyons 2015). Their importance in early Ireland was indicated by the traditional gathering of bilberries/ *frochans* at the end of July, coinciding with the Festival of Lughnasa and the ritual ascension of 'holy mountains' such as Croagh Patrick. The bilberries and sundew would have been sourced from uplands in the vicinity of Dublin.

As noted above, no edible leaves, buds or flowers had survived in the samples analysed and neither were roots or rhizomes recorded. Consumption of vegetables is noted in the historical texts, including brooklime, onions, etc. (Kelly 2000, 250–9; 310–1) and their absence in the archaeological record is probably due to the fact that they break down in the gut and also that the soft parts are harvested before seed production and tend to disintegrate easily (Karg and Robinson 2002). However, a recent multi-proxy analysis of medieval latrines in the Netherlands and northern Belgium indicated that pollen analysis supplemented the information provided by macrofossils (Deforce *et al.* 2018), showing the presence of plants mentioned in historical texts but which did not survive as macrofossils. Identification of phytoliths present in dental calculus and in burial plots can also serve to augment the picture (Fox *et al.* 1996) and this may be a worthwhile analysis to undertake should Viking skeletal remains be uncovered during future excavations. Equally, skeletal remains already found in Hiberno-Norse excavations could be reassessed. Such analyses can augment existing proxy information; for example, isotopic analysis indicates a terrestrial and marine intake by Viking Dublin inhabitants (Knudson *et al.* 2012). Further analyses could seek to understand nutritional stresses noted by M. Delaney (pers. comm. in Geraghty 1996, 67), which could be associated with the consumption of poisonous weeds, such as corncockle.

PLANT-BASED FOOD PRODUCTS

The cereals identified in Viking Dublin could have been consumed in a variety of ways such as breads and pottage. A seventh-century oat and whey flat cake was found in Lisleagh, Co. Cork (McLaren *et al.* 2004), while grave-breads have been found at Birka and Björkö, Sweden (Hansson 1996; Hjelmqvist 1984). The latter comprised a variety of ingredients, including grains and legumes and the addition of seeds such as flax which would have added flavour and moistness. Cesspits have also provided direct information as to consumed products; they vary from ground cereals, legume testae and seeds to wild fruits (Mitchell 1987). The charred and waterlogged macrofossils found in Dublin Castle and in various contemporary contexts indicate that there would have been a great variety of flours and carbohydrates available, including oats, wheat, barley, rye, dock, goosefoot and legumes, both wild and cultivated.

Oats, wheat, barley and rye were also used for the production of beer across medieval Europe; (Behre 1999) and Kelly (2000, 334) note an early medieval reference to an Irish wheat beer. It is possible that sloes and other hedgerow fruits were pressed to create juice or alcoholic drink, as noted above in Winetavern Street (Mitchell 1987, 25).

ENVIRONMENT

Hall and Kenward (2004) have noted that it can be difficult to reconstruct the environment from the remains found in medieval towns such as Dublin. The mix of food remains, cess and dung and the movement of people, plants and animals result in very specific deposits particular to that town.

Analyses of the Dublin Castle assemblages suggest that there are differences between the outdoor and indoor plant and insect taxa. The plants which were noted outside were those which grow in trampled and nitrogen-rich areas, especially those associated with the cesspits, such as the small nettle (*Urtica urens*), knotgrass, annual meadow-grass (*Poa annua*) and greater plantain (*Plantago major*). The cess was limited to pits and it would appear that an effort was made to maintain the pits. Indoor indicators of dung were noted in the house floor deposits (see below). Outdoor fauna associated with the cesspits comprise those found on decaying matter and excrement, such as fly puparia (*Musca domestica*) and are similar to those found in York (Hall *et al.* 1983). A flea (*Pulex irritans*) was noted in Pit 6 (Cork Tower, F1246), which may have been discarded with use of the latrine; it could have been a vector of disease for the inhabitants. Another species, *Trox*, which is often associated with dry materials of animal origin such as skins, hooves, feathers, bones, etc., was present in Pit 4b (F2092) and Pit 6 (F1246). This was also present in Novgorod, Russia (Reilly 2012) and Kaupang, Norway (Barrett *et al.* 2007). Interestingly, no evidence of intestinal parasites was detected in the cesspits.

Taxa associated with the general occupation layers of both assemblages included domestic waste such as charred cereal grains, fruit seeds, hazelnut shells, fishbone, eggshell and cockle and mussel shells. This decomposing organic matter attracted the common housefly (*Musca domestica*), indicating that some of the conditions within the town would have been less than pleasant and is similar to the build-up noted in other medieval towns, such as York (Hall and Kenward 2004) and Riga (Banerjea *et al.* 2017).

Both assemblages in Dublin Castle contained the seeds of plants associated with damp habitats, such as celery-leaved buttercup (*Ranunculus scleratus*) and rushes which may have originated from the vicinity of the nearby Rivers Liffey and Poddle but could also have grown in certain niches within the town. Brackish species were noted in the form of mare's tail (*Hippuris vulgaris*) and sea aster (*Aster tripolium*), which indicate nearby saline conditions.

It would appear that an attempt was also made to keep the areas alongside the houses and the space within the houses themselves clean; there was minimal build-up alongside the possible wattle walkway outside House 2 and only small sweepings of food remains were noted, including blackberry (*Rubus fruticosus*) and sloe. Taxa which thrive in disturbed ground were prevalent, such as stinking chamomile (*Anthemis cotula*) and greater plantain (*Plantago major*). Only 3% of the outside organic material (Cork Tower, Phase 4a deposits F2045, F2046 and F2051) comprised plant food remains in the form of oat, strawberry, barley and blackberry/raspberry, suggesting that this area of town was kept fairly clean from general food deposition.

The flora and fauna noted inside the houses were similar to those identified elsewhere (Reilly 2014; Geraghty 1996). Beetles which were noted in the floor of House 2 were those which would have been introduced from the outside; they were associated with animal excrement (e.g. *Hister* ssp., *Aphodius* ssp.) and rotting organic plant material (e.g. *Cercyon analis*). *Aphodius* sp. were also noted within the floor deposits of Structure Kappa, Deer Park Farms, Co. Antrim (Kenward *et al.* 2000). The presence of *Cercyon analis* may suggest that animals, especially pigs, were kept close by. This was also the case with Essex Street, Dublin (Reilly 2003), where archaeological and entomological evidence for the presence of animal pens was noted.

Small mites were noted in the bedding area of House 2, as well as fly puparia; the latter were also noted in the bedding area of House 1. Interestingly, in contrast to Deer Park Farms (Kenward *et al.* 2000, 515), there was a lack of lice within the bedding areas in Houses 1 and 2. However, this was also the case for Fishamble Street and may perhaps be associated with taphonomy.

The beetles in the north-west corner compartment of House 1 (deposit F2053) were similar to those of the rest of the house, apart from the presence of *Gnathoncus* sp., which indicates an association with fowl. This complements the evidence for egg consumption provided by the eggshells in the assemblage.

In general, the local environment was similar to that of contemporary towns and settlements, such as York (Hall and Kenward 2004) and Kaupang (Barrett *et al.* 2007). The plants and insects indicate a town which was located close to fresh and saline water, the resources of which were no doubt exploited.

RIVER PODDLE

The nature and course of the River Poddle changed considerably with the development of the city (Ronan 1927; 1948; Clarke 1977; Andrews 1983). Fluvial detail for the Poddle during early medieval times is unknown and information on tidal activity and its effect on the Poddle foreshore at this time is, as a result, hypothetical. In this respect archaeological deposits in the Powder Tower are of interest.

Although the Poddle was almost certainly tidal in the vicinity of Dublin Castle, the obstruction of sand banks and saltmarshes on the Liffey would have slowed down and eased the effect of rising tides in this area (G.F. Mitchell, pers. comm.). The absence of significant amounts of sorted fluvial sediment in the Powder Tower excavation indicated that flooding was by 'low energy or slow moving water' (Hall *et al.* 1983). Within the reach of high spring tide, material was being constantly removed and re-deposited, and sediments, together with botanical and other material from upstream, would have been mixed in with the general accumulation of dumped material on the site.

In the samples analysed there was generally a low incidence of aquatic/waterside plants. All species except two, water crowfoot (*Ranunculus* subgenus *Batrachium*) and mare's tail (*Hippuris vulgaris*), were also present in the Cork Tower area, where they were thought to reflect the use of wetland plants in litter and suchlike. A terrestrial source of origin, therefore, must be considered for at least some of the wetland species present, some of which would have been introduced with domestic rubbish. Water crowfoot is a freshwater aquatic (Fitter 1987) and must have been washed into the deposits together with other wetland species. Brackish species such as mare's tail and sea aster (*Aster tripolium*) were recorded in both areas and they indicate saline conditions. Ostracods (aquatic crustaceans with calcium carbonate (calcite) shells) and *foraminifera* (single cell protists) identified from two Hiberno-Norse Dublin sites at Golden Lane and Hammond Lane confirm association with a saltmarsh or marginal marine setting at this time (Kontrovitz and Snyder 2008).

The location of the central river channel of the Poddle in relation to the excavated area (PT1) is not known. Although clearly the excavated area was not permanently below water, it would have been inundated from time to time following heavy rains and flash floods in the Liffey and at high spring tide. Consequently, the deposition of aquatic biota would have been minimal. It should also be kept in mind that the continuous dumping of waste material in the area had the effect of raising the ground level which in turn reduced the effect of the Poddle there.

HINTERLAND

There are hints within the assemblages about the hinterland and the resources it provided. As noted above, cereals may have been cultivated in the vicinity but as the settlement expanded, additional arable land must have been needed. Although the number of samples in this study was small, there appears to have been an increase in the presence of cereals (including the appearance of wheat) in the later phases of the site. Geraghty (1996, 65) notes that an estimate of *c.* two million kg of grain would have been required for food supplies, including seed for storage, in Viking Dublin. This would have required at least 10,000 acres of land which was probably located in the hinterlands. It is not clear whether food was traded between Hiberno-Norse Dublin and native Irish farmers or rural Hiberno-Norse settlers. *Dyflinnarskiri* (Dublin-Shire), the Viking-controlled rural lands outside Dublin, are believed to have extended from the contemporary north Co. Dublin town of Lusk as far south as Dalkey, an area within which there would have been a wide choice of lands suitable for cultivation. Evidence for Viking settlement has been recorded at Cabinteely, south Dublin (Conway 1999), Finglas, north Dublin (Sikora 2010), Baldoyle, north Co. Dublin (Duffy 2016) and Ninch, Co. Meath (McConway 2003).

The floor deposits and bedding / seating areas within Houses 1 and 2, as well as the corner deposit F2053 in House 1, contained organic matter including ferns and moss. A sod layer in House 2 contained a large number of grassland seeds, including blinks (*Montia fontana* ssp. *chondrosperma*), which was similar to a bedding deposit noted in Fishamble Street (Geraghty 1996) and suggests imported turves. Other taxa which are associated with grassland were probably introduced with hay and thatch; ribwort plantain (*Plantago lanceolata*) and self-heal (*Prunella vulgaris*), for example, grow on the short turf of pastures (Salisbury 1961).

Wild fruits and nuts such as wild strawberry, blackberry/raspberry, sloe and hazelnut grow within and around scrubland and would have been gathered from lands close to the settlement. Two species of moss present in Pit 6 (Phase 4c) at the Cork Tower, identified as *Thuidium tamariscinum* and *Eurhynchium striatum* would have been gathered in woodland. Apple and rowan appear only in this pit, while bilberries are noted only here and in the assemblage of the Phase 5 deposit F2033 immediately outside House 2. The latter grow in acidic soil and damp upland areas and could have been gathered in the uplands south of Dublin.

Summary

Organic deposits exposed in the Viking levels at Dublin Castle were sampled and analysed for the presence of environmental indicators. The analysis was undertaken between 1987 and 1991 and the results are presented here together with an updated discussion and consideration of the results within a broader context. The environmental indicators identified included seeds (mostly waterlogged), fruit stones, nut shells, faecal material, fish bones, shellfish, moss, fly puparia, insects, charcoal, straw, mites and eggshells. The contexts from which this material was recovered ranged in date from the late ninth century to the early eleventh century and included cess/rubbish pits, house interiors, external occupation deposits and waste material incorporated within earthen defensive banks and associated deposits. The limited number of samples did not allow for a study of changes through time and all results have been combined for discussion purposes.

The evidence suggests a varied and high-fibre diet was enjoyed by the inhabitants of this corner of Viking Dublin. The cereals present include barley, oats and, to a lesser extent, wheat, all represented by charred seeds. Disaggregation of faecal material from one of the cesspits revealed large quantities of cereal bran of either wheat or rye, indicating a high-fibre diet. Seeds and capsules of cultivated flax were found in most samples and, while these could be interpreted as evidence for the production of linen, the seeds could also have been used to produce linseed oil for consumption, cooking or lighting. Foraging and collection of wild fruits and nuts appears to have been prevalent, as evidenced by the significant amounts of wild strawberry, blackberry/raspberry, sloes, rowan and hazelnuts recovered. A large deposit of sloe stones and blackberry/raspberry seeds in one of the cess/rubbish pits could represent the discard from processing of the fruits for the production of juice, jams or preserves. A small number of bilberry seeds was identified and these may have been gathered from as far afield as the Dublin/Wicklow mountains. Apple pips were found in just one cess/rubbish pit and probably belong to the wild crab apple. Other plants identified that could have had culinary uses included bog myrtle (used for flavouring in brewing) and black mustard. Weed species including fat hen, orache, black bindweed and knotgrass may have been purposely harvested and eaten but could also have grown as weeds in the town. In addition to the plant macrofossils, other environmental indicators point to the consumption of poultry eggs, cockles and mussels and a wide variety of fish including herring, whiting, salmon, ray and trout.

Although the house remains were fragmentary, the survival of some floor deposits has provided insights into the living conditions of their inhabitants. The abundance of rush seeds in House 1 suggests the use of rushes for floor covering and perhaps bedding. Straw, mosses, ferns, twigs and leaves had also accumulated within a corner of the house where beetle remains suggest the presence of poultry or, more likely, a bird nesting in the roof space. The organic remains in the bedding / seating areas of House 2 were similar and included fern, feathers, straw, wood chips and moss. Sods taken from a grassland area were also present and may have formed part of the make-up of the bedding / seating area or could represent collapse from the roof of the house. Coprolites of probable canine origin were present in the floor deposits of House 2. Flies, including the common house fly together with mites were present in both houses. A human flea perfectly preserved in one of the cess / rubbish pits provides evidence of less-than-ideal living conditions.

Weeds appear to have been plentiful in the areas surrounding the houses and the earthen embankments. Grassland and wetland plants were present and species including the common nettle and stinking chamomile probably grew in the nutrient-rich soils around the houses and pathways. Some of the wetland plants may have found niches such as ditches and puddles within the town. Brackish species such as mare's tail and sea aster were also recorded and must have originated in the nearby tidal reaches of the River Liffey.

Chapter 8
Radiocarbon dates
Cormac McSparron

Introduction

There are fifteen dates available for analysis, primarily from samples of animal bone and from five separate locations at Dublin Castle (Table 8.1). These can simply be calibrated, which gives a reliable chronological range for each dated sample (Table 8.1; Fig. 8.1). There are, however, a number of different types of analysis, beyond simple calibration, which can be carried out on these dates.

The analysis in this report is based around the implementation of Bayesian statistical principles in OxCal 4.3 (Bronk Ramsey 2019) using the IntCal 13 calibration curve (Reimer *et al.* 2013). Bayes's theorem can be rendered as follows:

> Posterior belief = standardised likelihood x prior beliefs (Buck *et al.* 1991).

It has been summarized as 'revising current beliefs in the light of new information...a formal way of dealing with life's ubiquitous problem of learning from experience' (*ibid.*). You take the data that you already have, comprising the standardised likelihood (in this case radiocarbon dates), and interpret them using information you believe to be correct, i.e. prior beliefs (such as, for example, a stratigraphic sequence, a dated artefact, or a series of dated events which frame the activity), leading to a new understanding – the posterior belief (modelled calibrated date ranges).

There are many ways in which Bayesian principles can be integrated into archaeological interrogation of radiocarbon dates. Commonly the 'prior' is a stratigraphic sequence, or some similar, hopefully robust, chronological model which can either be tested by the radiocarbon dates for its reliability as a model, or, if it is believed to be reliable, used to constrain/modify the dates provided by the radiocarbon data.

In addition to Bayesian analysis one can stand back from the site-specific sequences and stratigraphy and look cumulatively at the radiocarbon dating evidence as a proxy for human activity at the Dublin Castle site. In this case calibration and other information from OxCal 4.3 was reanalysed using the ArchaeoPhases software to obtain a Tempo Plot (Dye 2016).

The radiocarbon analysis of the Dublin Castle excavation uses these approaches to make a number of inferences.

The analysis demonstrates that:

- at the Cork Tower there may be a lot of residual deposition of material from Phases 1 and 2 in Phases 3 and 4.
- at the Powder Tower (PT2) it is possible to constrain the calibrated ranges of Phases 3 and 4 dates to *c.* 70-year periods.
- there were fluctuations in the overall levels of activity revealed by an analysis of the radiocarbon dates from Dublin Castle as proxies for human activity. This reveals that there
    - may have been pre-Viking activity, although it is possible that none of the features excavated at Dublin Castle are pre-Viking, but that rather an animal bone from earlier activity has become incorporated into later strata;
    - that there is more intense activity at Dublin Castle from the late ninth century, with possible dips in the level of activity which may tally with historical events; there is very little evidence of activity after the early eleventh century.

Table 8.1 All dates calibrated. The calibrated date ranges in this table are those reported by the 14 Chrono Centre at Queen's University Belfast and have been obtained using Calib Rev 7.0.0 (Stuiver and Reimer 1986-2013) using the IntCal 13 calibration curve (Reimer *et al.* 2013). The calibrated ranges, both unmodelled and modelled in the other tables in this report have been calculated with OxCal 4.3 (Bronk Ramsey 2019) using the IntCal 13 calibration curve (Reimer *et. al.* 2013). Any small discrepancies apparent in the calibrated ranges between Table 8.1 and subsequent tables are the result of the different algorithms used in each programme and are not significant.

Lab no.	Context	Species	Element	C14 yrs	+/-	68.3% cal AD	95.4% cal AD
UBA-35661	CT Phase 1; F1228	Pig	Pelvis	1172	32	777 - 892	770 - 966
UBA-35660	CT Phase 2; F1227	Pig	Radius	1067	32	905 - 1017	895 - 1022
UBA-35659	CT Phase 2; F1217	Sheep / goat	Radius	1061	32	908 - 1019	896 - 1024
UBA-35658	CT Phase 3; F1202	Cow	Horn core	1215	22	770 - 867	719 - 885
UBA-35657	CT Phase 4a; F1193	Pig	Tibia	1144	30	780 - 969	777 - 975
UBA-35656	CT Phase 4b; F999	Pig	Metacarpus	1120	30	893 - 969	778 - 994
UBA-35665	PT2 Phase 1; F295	Sheep / goat	Vertebra	1052	36	969 - 1022	895 - 1030
UBA-35663	PT1 Phase 1b; F509	Ash	Wattle	1047	24	988 - 1017	904 - 1025
UBA-35662	PT1 Phase 2; F495	Hazel	Rod	1004	27	995 - 1033	984 - 1149
UBA-35666	PT2 Phase 2; F301	Deer	Antler	1078	45	900 - 1014	779 - 1032
UBA-35664	PT2 Phase 3; F281	Sheep / goat	Metacarpus	1104	29	897 - 981	885 - 1012
UBA-35669	PT2 Phase 4; F361	Sheep / goat	Metacarpus	1098	32	897 - 986	888 - 1014
UBA-35671	BT; F113	Sheep / goat	Mandible	1099	34	897 - 986	883 - 1017
UBA-35672	CB Phase C; E748:135	Blackthorn	Twig	1046	38	970 - 1024	894 - 1036
UBA-35675	CB Phase E; E748:145	Hazel	Nuts	1020	31	991 - 1026	907 - 1147

Methodology

The radiocarbon dates were modelled and calibrated with OxCal 4.3 (Bronk Ramsey 2019) using the IntCal 13 calibration curve (Reimer *et al.* 2013). OxCal 4.3 contains a number of powerful statistical tools for analysing radiocarbon dates. It is possible in OxCal 4.3 to build models using additional, non-radiocarbon information, such as stratigraphy from an excavation, a known calendrical date, or an assumed sequence of events. OxCal 4.3 can estimate how possible these models are when compared to the actual radiocarbon dates available. OxCal 4.3 cannot *prove* that a model is correct, since more than one possible model can fit the data, but it can reject models which are incompatible with the radiocarbon evidence.

In addition to being able to tell which models are compatible with the radiocarbon evidence OxCal 4.3 has a number of tools for estimating the start, end or span of defined phases. These estimates are informed by the order, stratigraphic or calendrical, of information built into the model.

OXCAL COMMANDS AND STRUCTURES

The following is a brief description of the basic OxCal 4.3 programme structures and commands implemented in the models presented below.

A *Sequence* is an OxCal 4.3 programme structure which orders events or groups of events.

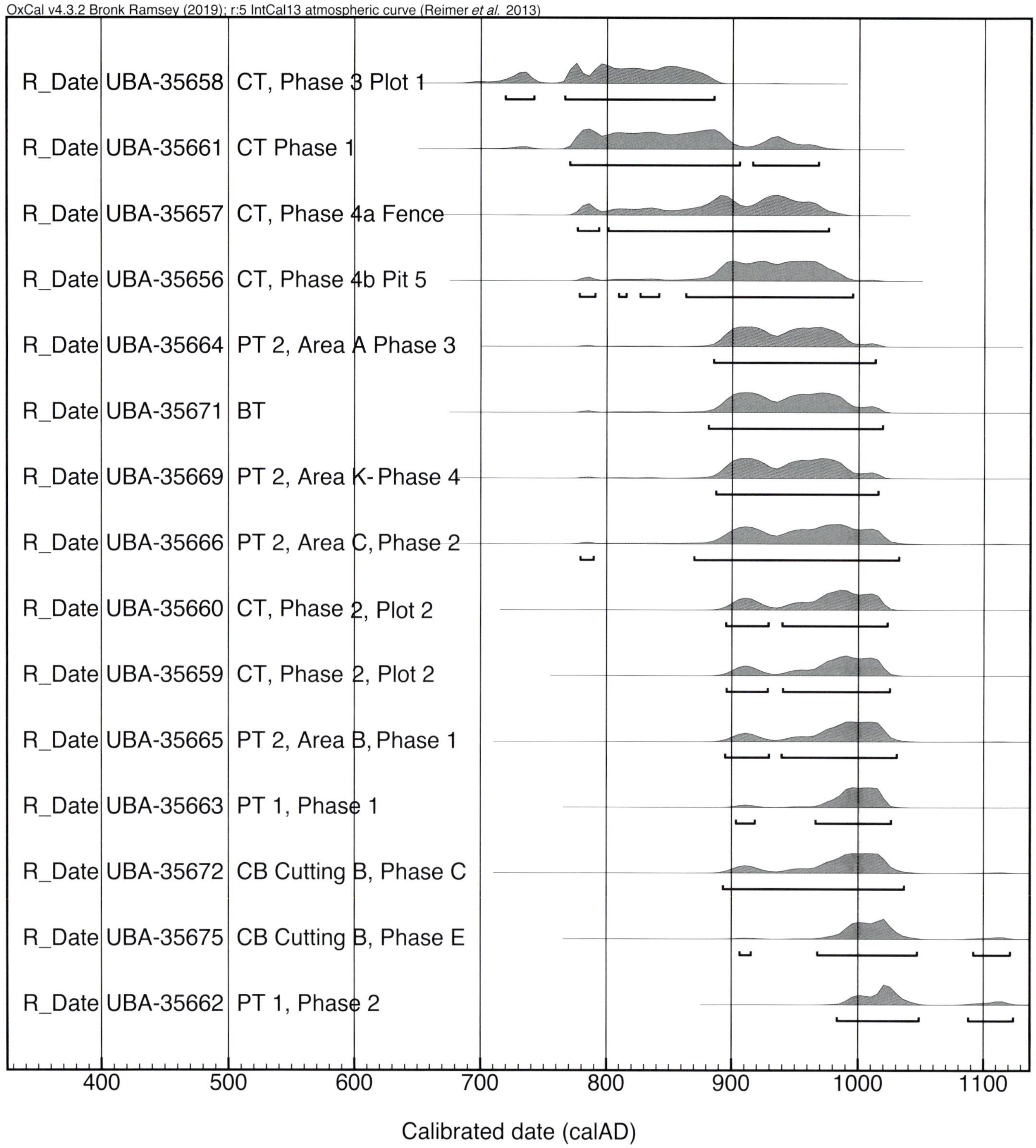

Fig. 8.1 All dates calibrated.

Table 8.2 Cork Tower Sequence.

Name	Unmodelled (BC/AD)						Modelled (BC/AD)						Indices Amodel 11.8 Aoverall 12.8
	from	to	%	from	to	%	from	to	%	from	to	%	Acomb
Sequence													
Boundary Start Cork Tower Sequence							846	926	68.2	784	945	95.4	
R_Date UBA-35661	777	892	68.2	770	968	95.4	868	926	68.2	829	945	95.4	89.7
Phase													
R_Date UBA-35660-Phase 2	905	1017	68.2	895	1023	95.4	901	927	68.2	889	942	95.4	59.9
R_Date UBA-35659-Phase 2	908	1019	68.2	896	1025	95.4	901	927	68.2	889	943	95.4	47.4
R_Date UBA-35658-Phase 3	770	868	68.2	719	885	95.4	926	941	68.2	890	952	95.4	1.6
R_Date UBA-35657-Phase 4a	780	969	68.2	776	976	95.4	930	950	68.2	921	970	95.4	138.1
R_Date UBA-35656-Phase 4b	893	970	68.2	778	995	95.4	936	966	68.2	924	988	95.4	114.3
Boundary End Cork Tower Sequence							937	985	68.2	890	1042	95.4	

A *Phase* is an OxCal 4.3 structure for grouping a series of radiocarbon dates together which are believed to belong to the same era but which have no stratigraphical or other information that can be used to further order them relative to each other. Internally, therefore, the phase is unordered, but externally each phase can be ordered relative to other phases, radiocarbon dates or calendrical events.

A *Boundary* is an OxCal4.3 command which estimates the beginning and end of phases and sequences. The model code presented below creates a sequence, a series of dates and/or dated events in the order they are believed to have occurred. The boundaries defined at the top and bottom of the sequence estimate date ranges for its beginning and end.

One point which should be noted is that, in phases and sequences with small numbers of dates, such as in this analysis, the boundary function produces *very* wide start and end date ranges, often larger than what is already known from archaeological knowledge (Bronk Ramsey 2000, 201). This is because OxCal 4.3 makes the assumption that, with a small number of samples, it is possible that the earliest and latest dated samples may not be truly representative of the phase's real duration, consequently, it extends its estimate of the boundaries to encompass this uncertainty. This can be seen in the analyses carried out below where only a small number of dates are available, and the estimated start and age date ranges are very wide. If there had been more available dates, the OxCal 4.3 boundary command would have given a much narrower estimate of the beginning or end of a sequence or phase.

The *Agreement Index* is OxCal 4.3's estimation of how well the radiocarbon dates fit the model. An agreement index of less than 60% is usually thought of as denoting a model which does not agree well with the available radiocarbon dates. An agreement index of more than 60% is thought of as compatible with the radiocarbon dates. Of course, a high agreement index does not prove a model is correct, just that it is possibly correct. It is always conceivable that another model could be constructed to fit the radiocarbon dates just as well. In this respect it is like other, less quantitative, archaeological evidence.

Agreement index is reported in several different ways by OxCal 4.3. The *Aoverall* agreement index is the combined degree of agreement of the dates to the sequence; the *Amodel* is an estimation of the level of agreement of the model used in the sequence. There is also an agreement index for each individual date in the sequence. The *Aoverall* and *Amodel* values tell us about the degree of compatibility of the dates and model and vice versa, and typically will have similar values, but the agreement index of the individual dates allows the user to spot specific dates which do not fit a sequence which may be broadly in agreement with the other dates in the analysis.

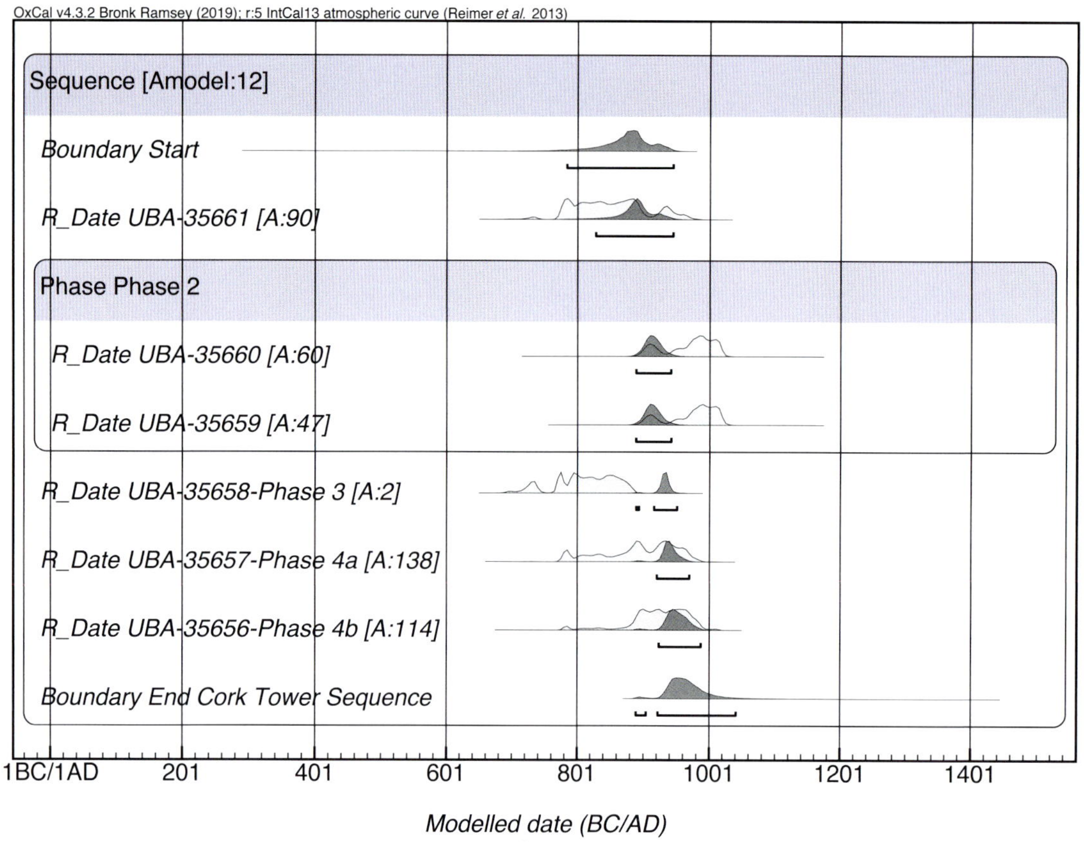

Fig. 8.2 Cork Tower sequence.

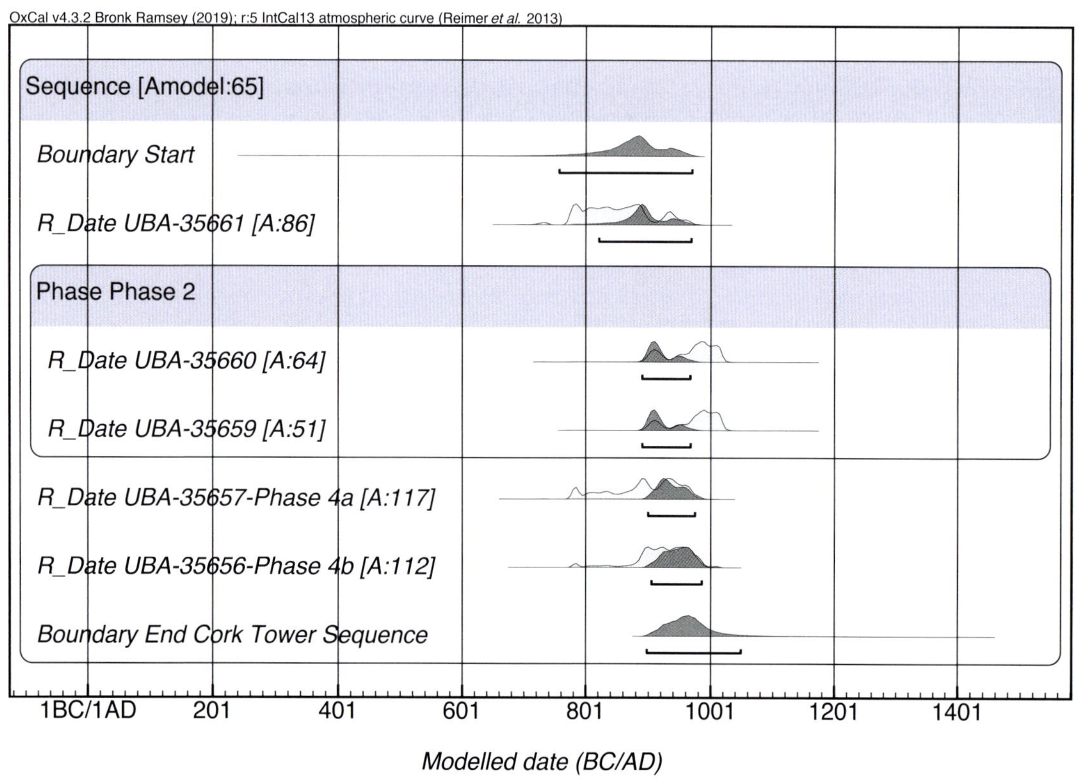

Fig. 8.3 Cork Tower sequence minus UBA-35659 from Phase 3.

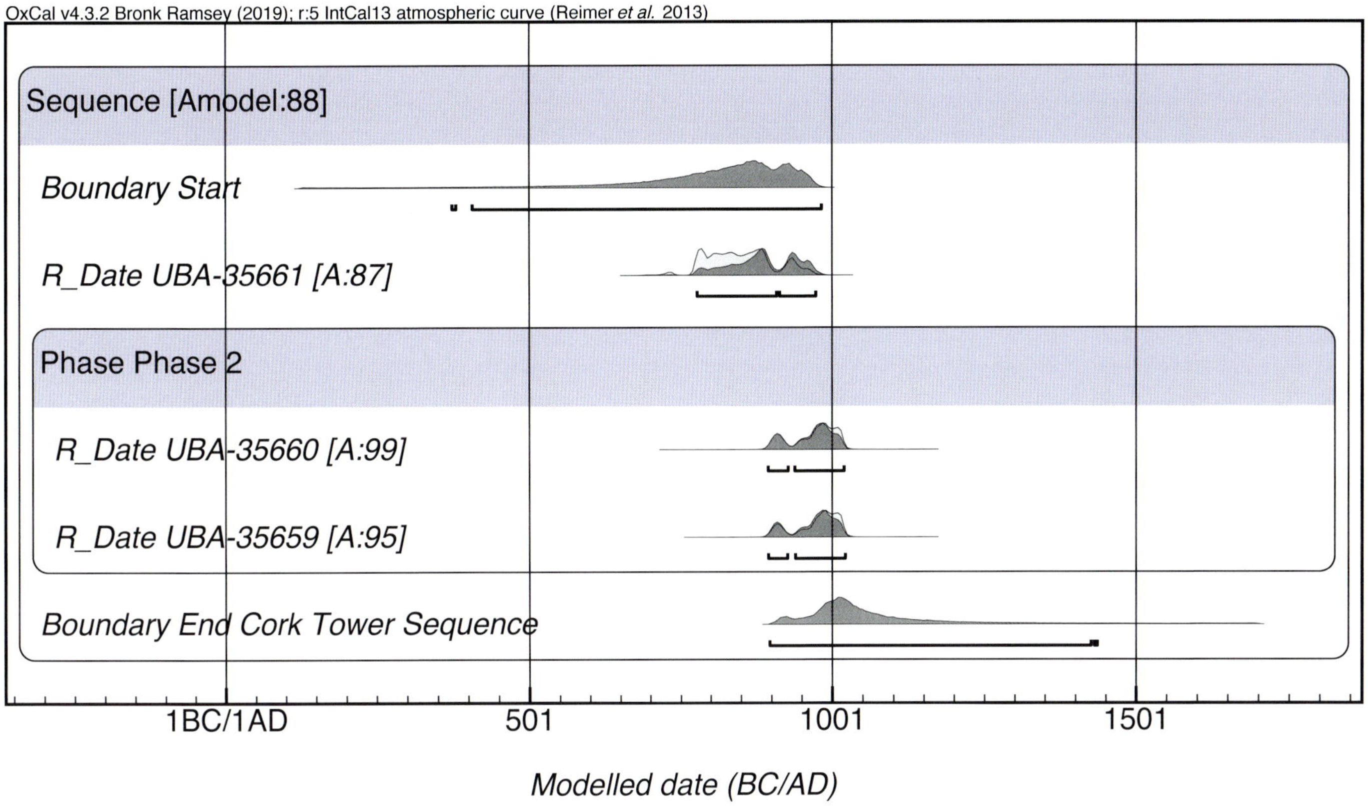

Fig. 8.4 Cork Tower sequence using only Phase 1 and 2 dates.

OXCAL ANALYSIS

The analysis in OxCal 4.3 took two forms: the basic calibration of dates, and the sequencing of those dates using a chronological information provided by stratigraphy and other chronological information. When the OxCal 4.3 script for the analysis of dates is informed by a chronological model, the individual sequences are altered for their specific chronological model and their dates.

TEMPO PLOTS AND ACTIVITY PLOTS

The 'tempo plot' was first proposed by Dye (2016) as a way of looking at long-term chronological patterns. It takes the results of the Markov Chain Monte Carlo (MCMC) routine in OxCal 4.3, where hundreds of thousands of individual iterations of date calibrations are calculated within the constraints of the suggested chronological model, and graphically represents the mean and standard deviation of the posterior distribution of a subset (in this case 1000) of these iterations. The tempo plots in this analysis are implemented using the ArchaeoPhases software package developed by Anne Philippe and Marie-Anne Vibet of the Laboratoire de Mathématiques Jean Leray, Université de Nantes, France, which is available to use in R software (https://cran.r-project.org/web/packages/ArchaeoPhases/index.html) or as a stand-alone web-based application (https://archaeology-bayesian-modelling.shinyapps.io/ArchaeoPhases/).

Analysis of the Radiocarbon Dates

THE CORK TOWER

There were six dates from the Viking-age levels of the Cork Tower (CT2), from Phases 1, 2, 3, 4a and 4b. All of the dates were obtained from animal bone, ruling out any possible 'old wood' effect (Warner 1990).

Initially all the dates were arranged in an OxCal 4.3 sequence model according to their position within the site stratigraphy, from the earliest Phase 1 date to the latest Phase 4b date (Table 8.2; Fig. 8.2). Unfortunately, this model, with an overall agreement index (the combined degree of agreement of the dates to the sequence) of only 12.8%, and the model agreement index of 11.8%, fell well below the 60% agreement index acceptable threshold, indicating that the chronological model of five distinct sequential phases is not supported by the radiocarbon dates. It was also apparent that three of the individual radiocarbon dates, UBA-35659, UBA-35660 and UBA-35658, had individual agreement indices below 60%, with one (UBA-35658) having an agreement index of only 1.6%.

Table 8.3 Cork Tower sequence minus UBA-35659 from Phase 3.

Name	Unmodelled (BC/AD)						Modelled (BC/AD)						Indices Amodel 64.7 Aoverall 63.7
	from	to	%	from	to	%	from	to	%	from	to	%	Acomb
Sequence													
Boundary Start Cork Tower Sequence							842	945	68.2	757	970	95.4	
R_Date UBA-35661	777	892	68.2	770	968	95.4	865	946	68.2	822	969	95.4	86
Phase													
R_Date UBA-35660-Phase 2	905	1017	68.2	895	1023	95.4	895	926	68.2	891	968	95.4	64
R_Date UBA-35659-Phase 2	908	1019	68.2	896	1025	95.4	895	926	68.2	891	968	95.4	50.7
R_Date UBA-35657-Phase 4a	780	969	68.2	776	976	95.4	913	960	68.2	900	975	95.4	117.1
R_Date UBA-35656-Phase 4b	893	970	68.2	778	995	95.4	925	971	68.2	906	986	95.4	111.7
Boundary End Cork Tower Sequence							925	988	68.2	898	1050	95.4	

This implies one of two things: either a) that the model is not a valid interpretation of the archaeological sequence of the site, or b) that some of the radiocarbon dates have been displaced from their original chronological location, either through later deposition of an earlier artefact or earlier strata being disturbed by activity during later archaeological periods. Since the model was based on what appears to be a reliable stratigraphic sequence, it was thought that displacement of material which was subsequently dated was more likely.

Two new revised versions of this sequence were analysed. In the first sequence the assumption was made that UBA-35658, the date from Phase 3 with the lowest agreement index, was residual, probably disturbed from earlier strata, and removed from the sequence (Table 8.3; Fig. 8.3).

In the second revised version it was assumed that three samples, UBA-35658 from Phase 3, UBA-35657 from Phase 4a and UBA-35656 from Phase 4b, were residual (Table 8.4; Fig. 8.4).

Both models reach and exceed the necessary 60% agreement index, for both the model and the overall agreement, to be considered an acceptable match between model and dates, although in the first model (Table 8.3; Fig. 8.3) there is still a single date, UBA-35659, where its individual agreement index is only 50.7%. With the second model (Table 8.4; Fig. 8.4), all the agreement indices exceed the 60% threshold. Unfortunately, with only three dates for analysis, the suggested start and end ranges for this site are significantly elongated. This is because OxCal 4.3 makes the assumption that, with a small number of samples, it is likely that the earliest and latest dates in the phase are unlikely to be truly representative of the phase's real duration; consequently, it extends its estimate of the boundaries.

The results of these analyses indicate that the dated samples from Phase 3, Phases 4a and 4b probably are material disturbed from earlier strata.

THE POWDER TOWER

There were four dates from the excavations at the Powder Tower (PT2). These were from four stratigraphic phases, Phases 1, 2, 3 and 4. When the four dates were initially sequenced the overall agreement index for the model, *Amodel*, was 80.4% and for the overall sequence, *Aoverall*, was 81.3%. The Phase 1 date, UBA-35665, however, had an individual agreement index of only 54.1% (Table 8.5).

The reason for this low agreement index appears to be because of the similarity between dates UBA-35665 and UBA-35666, even though the model suggests that they are distinct phases. Layer F301, which contained the sample for UBA-35666, was stratified above a layer of cobbles, F392, in Area C, which were set into subsoil, whereas F295, the layer from which the sample for date UBA-35665 came, lay directly on the subsoil in Area B. It is possible, therefore, that there is little chronological distance between these phases, although they do appear stratigraphically distinct (see Chapter 3.3).

Table 8.4 Cork Tower sequence only using Phase 1 and 2 dates.

Name	Unmodelled (BC/AD)						Modelled (BC/AD)						Indices Amodel 87.8 Aoverall 89.1
	from	to	%	from	to	%	from	to	%	from	to	%	Acomb
Sequence													
Boundary Start Cork Tower Sequence							767	961	68.2	374	984	95.4	
Phase													
R_Date UBA-35661-Phase 1	777	892	68.2	770	968	95.4	848	968	68.2	778	974	95.4	87.1
R_Date UBA-35660-Phase 2	905	1017	68.2	895	1023	95.4	904	1013	68.2	895	1020	95.4	98.6
R_Date UBA-35659-Phase 2	908	1019	68.2	896	1025	95.4	905	1015	68.2	896	1022	95.4	95.3
Boundary End Cork Tower Sequence							915	1102	68.2	898	1437	95.4	

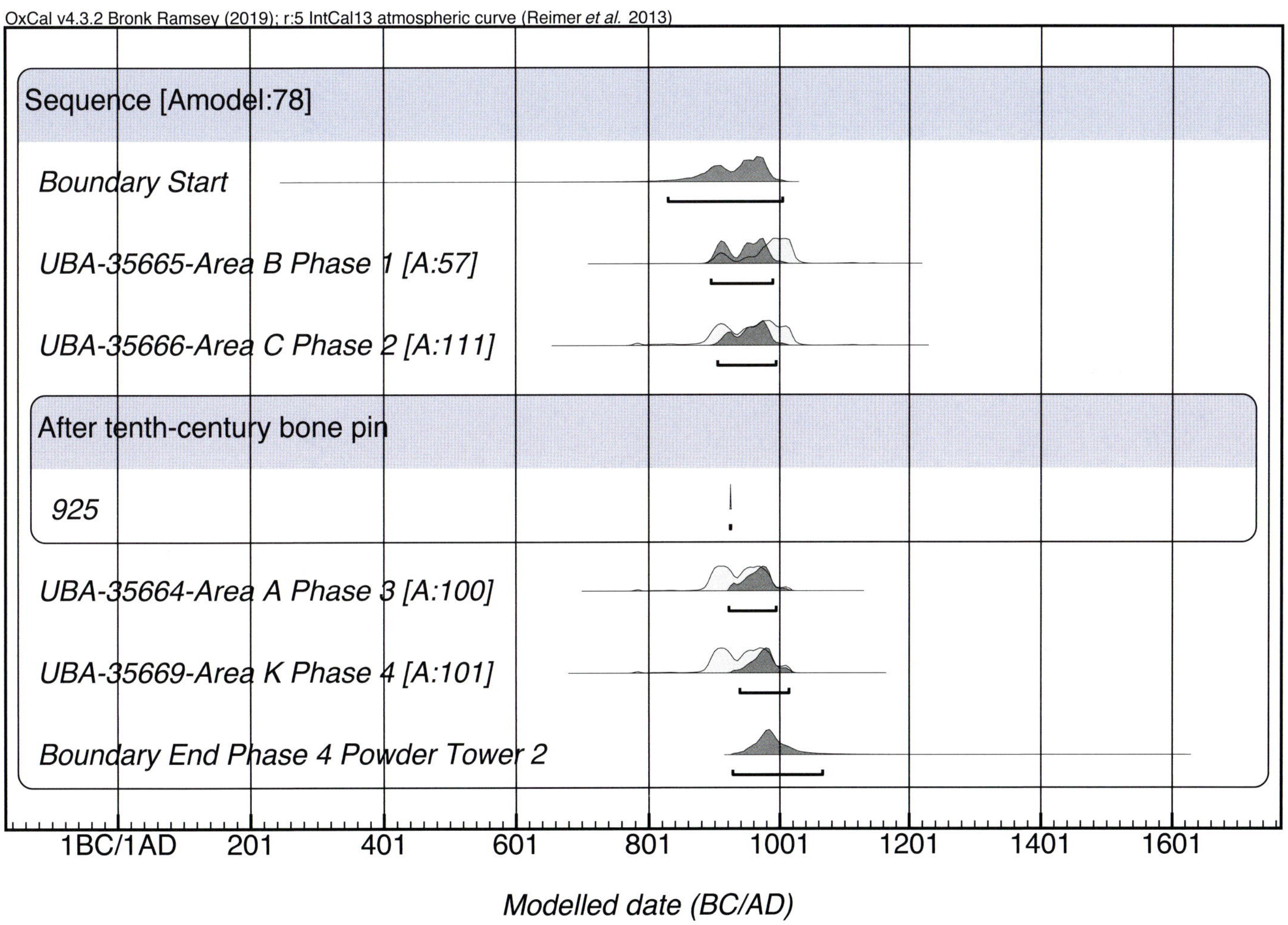

Fig. 8.5 Powder Tower 2 sequence including bone pin E324:918:F276.

Table 8.5 Power Tower, Cutting 2, sequence.

Name	Unmodelled (BC/AD)						Modelled (BC/AD)						Indices Amodel 80.4 Aoverall 81.3
	from	to	%	from	to	%	from	to	%	from	to	%	Acomb
Sequence													
Boundary Start Powder Tower 2							886	981	68.2	827	996	95.4	
R_Date UBA-35665-Area B Phase 1	970	1022	68.2	895	1030	95.4	897	980	68.2	891	990	95.4	54.1
R_Date UBA-35666-Area C Phase 2	900	1014	68.2	779	1032	95.4	904	983	68.2	898	990	95.4	111.9
R_Date UBA-35664-Area A Phase 3	898	980	68.2	885	1013	95.4	910	987	68.2	901	995	95.4	105.2
R_Date UBA-35669-Area K Phase 4	898	986	68.2	887	1015	95.4	913	994	68.2	906	1011	95.4	103.8
Boundary End Phase 4 Powder Tower 2							913	1009	68.2	901	1061	95.4	

Within Phase 3, layer F276, there was a bone pin which was dated to the early to mid-tenth century (E324:918, see Chapter 3.3 and 4.2). It can be added to the sequence, using the OxCal 4.3 command *After*, as a *terminus post quem*, for activity in Phase 3 and beyond. It was modelled as dating to AD 925 or later (Fig. 8.5). This has the effect of considerably constricting OxCal 4.3's estimations for the calibrated ranges for the dates UBA-35664 and UBA-35669, in Phases 3 and 4 respectively, reducing them to approximately 70-year calibrated ranges at 95.4% certainty (Table 8.6). The agreement index for UBA-35665, the Phase 1 date, was still just below the 60% threshold at 56.5%.

MODELLING ACTIVITY AT DUBLIN CASTLE

It is possible to model human activity at Dublin Castle during the early medieval period by looking at the general distribution of radiocarbon dates from the site and graphically displaying them using a tempo chart (Fig. 8.6) and the related activity chart (Fig. 8.7). These two charts suggest that activity at Dublin Castle could have commenced as early as the later eighth century and continued at approximately the same level of intensity until the later ninth century, when there was a sudden increase in activity. This more vigorous phase of activity paused in the middle decades of the tenth century, before recommencing in the later tenth century and continuing until the early eleventh century when activity at the site seems to have ceased. The hiatus in the eleventh century may have been the result of later truncation, and/or the sampling strategy employed during the excavation, such as the absence of radiocarbon dates from Phases 5 and 6 from the Cork Tower. The early start of activity proposed by this chart is interesting, in that it suggests activity at this site may pre-date what is conventionally believed to be the commencement of Viking Dublin (see Chapter 2.1), with more intensive activity having commenced in the last quarter of the ninth century. Also interesting is the apparent dip in activity in the mid-tenth century, before a more intense period of activity in the late tenth and early eleventh centuries (Fig. 8.7).

Discussion

The analysis of the radiocarbon dates seems to suggest, very tentatively, a number of things. It suggests that at the Cork Tower there is residual material from Phases 1 and 2, redeposited in Phases 3 and 4. This redeposited material was sampled and dated.

By building a model of the stratigraphy at the Powder Tower (PT2) and including the information from a dated bone pin, it is possible to constrain the date of Phase 3 from AD 922 to 995 and Phase 4 from AD 939 to 1015.

The most exciting possibilities come not from an analysis of the sequence of the dates directly, but from modelling the dates in a tempo plot as a proxy for human activity at Dublin Castle. This highlights the possibility that there may have been activity at this site from the last quarter of the eighth century. As noted above (Chapter 2.1), there is reason to believe that Scandinavian settlers were making camp in Dublin from the 790s, although this has conventionally been thought to be some distance away, at *Duibh Linn*, to the south of Dublin Castle. The evidence, of this analysis at least, leaves open the possibility for earlier activity at the Dublin Castle site as well.

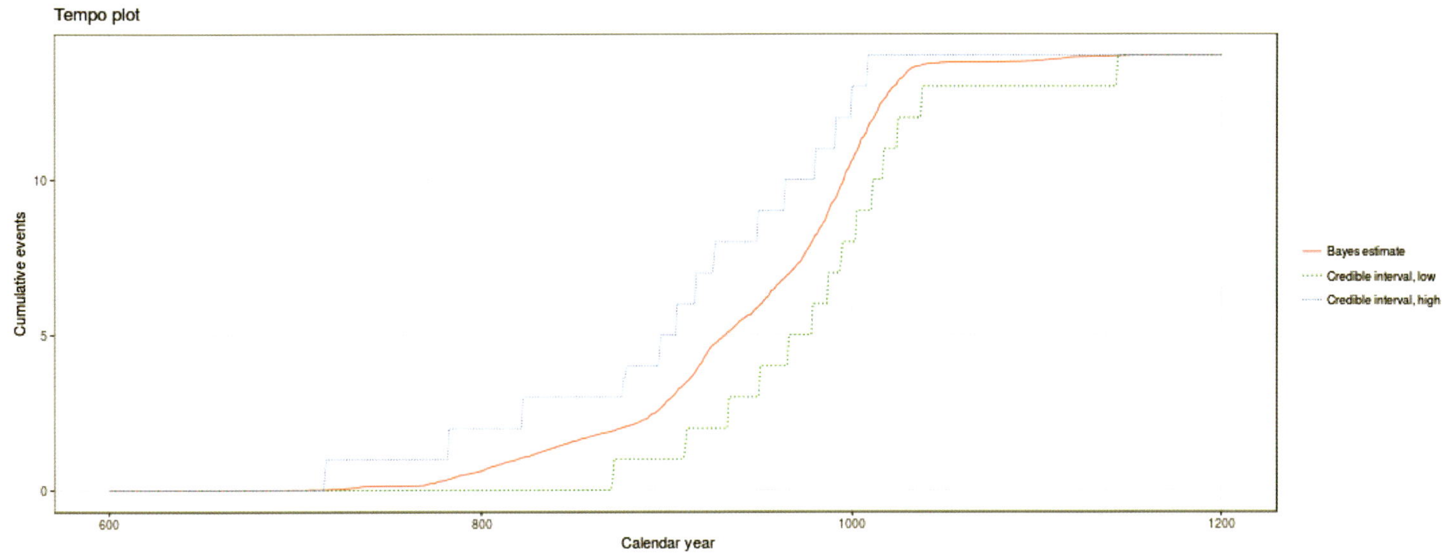

Fig. 8.6 Tempo plot of all dates (unmodelled).

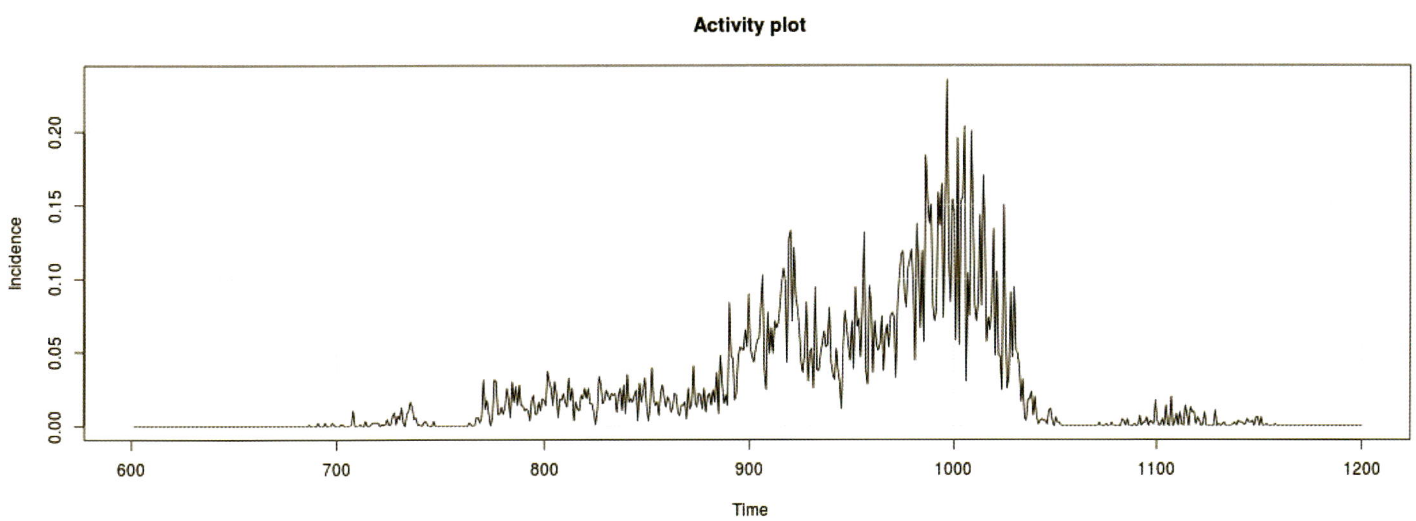

Fig. 8.7 Activity plot based on radiocarbon dates (unmodelled).

The tempo plot analysis also seems to indicate that this early settlement continued at a fairly even rate until the later ninth century when there was a rapid increase in the level of activity on the site of Dublin Castle. This may be an indication of more activity in Dublin, perhaps occasioned by Amlaib and Ímar's arrival with 200 ships in Dublin in 871 (see Chapter 2.1).

The indications of oscillations in activity at the site in the tenth century are potentially very interesting. There appear to be, after an initially vigorous start, hints of a lessening of activity at Dublin Castle in the middle decades of the tenth century, with a recovery in the last quarter of the tenth century. The mid tenth century was a period of intense warfare between the Irish and the Hiberno-Scandinavian inhabitants of Dublin (see Chapter 2.1), with an apparent destruction of the town, slaughter of the male inhabitants and enslavement of the women and children in 944. It is possible that this lessening of activity hinted at by the radiocarbon record could be linked to these events.

Table 8.6 Powder Tower, Cutting 2, sequence with dated mid tenth-century pin (E324:918:F276).

Name	Unmodelled (BC/AD)						Modelled (BC/AD)						Indices Amodel 78 Aoverall 79.4
	from	to	%	from	to	%	from	to	%	from	to	%	Acomb
Sequence													
Boundary Start Powder Tower 2							892	983	68.2	830	1005	95.4	96.6
R_Date UBA-35665-Area B Phase 1	970	1022	68.2	895	1030	95.4	904	981	68.2	895	990	95.4	98.4
R_Date UBA-35666-Area C Phase 2	900	1014	68.2	779	1032	95.4	945	985	68.2	905	995	95.4	99.1
After tenth-century bone pin	925	...	68.2	925	...	95.4							
925							924	925	68.2	924	925	95.4	100
R_Date UBA-35664-Area A Phase 3	898	980	68.2	885	1013	95.4	950	987	68.2	922	995	95.4	99.5
R_Date UBA-35669-Area K Phase 4	898	986	68.2	887	1015	95.4	956	993	68.2	939	1015	95.4	99
Boundary End Phase 4 Powder Tower 2							959	1009	68.2	928	1067	95.4	96.7

Conclusions

These results of the analysis of the C14 dates leave open the possibility that there was activity at the site of the castle from the pre-Viking later eighth century. They also indicate that there was more intensive use of the site from the later ninth century, continuing through the tenth century and into the early eleventh century. There are intriguing hints of more detailed patterning within the data, but the scale of the analysis is too small to allow meaningful conclusions to be drawn. A wider meta-study of the radiocarbon dating evidence from the entirety of Viking Dublin could, however, be of huge benefit. Such a study could take the form of this analysis, using a combination of Bayesian sequencing and tempo plots, and could look at localised models as well as cumulative information from all the excavated sites.

Chapter 9
Discussion and conclusions

Chapter 9
Discussion and conclusions

Introduction

The findings from the Viking-age levels at Dublin Castle are informative about the nature of the settlement and defences of Dublin, particularly in the tenth and eleventh centuries. Though individually small in area and mostly heavily truncated, the areas excavated throw light on the nature of the settlement that preceded the great stone castle that was built in the south-east corner of the medieval walled town in the early thirteenth century.

The first investigation of Viking-age settlement remains in Dublin took place at Dublin Castle in 1961/2 under the direction of Marcus Ó hEochaidhe and while this limited excavation was superseded by the subsequent large-scale excavations by the National Museum of Ireland (1962–81), it is perhaps fitting that the first of these excavations to be fully published are those where the archaeological investigation of Viking Dublin started. The rich discoveries at Dublin Castle in 1961/2 and the depths of deposits and quality of preservation justified future archaeological campaigns by National Museum archaeologists.

The areas where the Viking-age deposits survived were very limited, including just outside the outer edge of the castle moat in the Cork Tower area, inside the curtain wall of the castle in the Powder Tower 2 area and at the Cross Block and under the floors of the Powder Tower and the square tower attached to the Bermingham Tower. The surviving depth and quality of preservation of the deposits varied greatly from one area to another. Organic deposits were best preserved by waterlogged anaerobic conditions at the Cross Block, less so at the Cork Tower and at Powder Tower 1. In all three areas the lower deposits had survived best. At the Bermingham Tower only a few features cut into subsoil can be attributed to this period. At Powder Tower 2, the narrow strip of deposits surviving between the foundations of the medieval castle wall and a later eighteenth-century wall had dried out, and wood and other organic materials did not survive. These deposits were also heavily truncated, except in one very small area where a full sequence of deposits between subsoil and the late twelfth century survived. Radiocarbon dating and some datable artefacts have made it possible to suggest a chronology linking the individual phases of activity in these disparate areas (Table 9.1).

Earliest Evidence for Settlement

The date and location of the earliest Viking settlement at Dublin, and its evolution from a seasonal ship-camp (*longphort*) to a more permanent settlement on the ridge between the Liffey and Poddle have been the subjects of debate over recent decades using both historical and constantly evolving archaeological evidence.

The discovery of ninth-century habitation evidence and four male Viking warrior burials at a site on South Great George's Street (Simpson 1999; 2005), when combined with the name 'Dublinn', points to the pool on the Poddle estuary immediately south of Dublin Castle as the focus of early Viking settlement, with the location of the *longphort* in close proximity (Fig. 1.2). However, evidence for settlement dated to about the mid-ninth century has also been found at Parliament Street and Essex Street West on the north-eastern side of the ridge between the Liffey and Poddle (Simpson 1999; 2005) (Fig. 2.2). While Clarke (2002, 2) has argued for a second *longphort* on this ridge, it is possible that these habitations represent a growth of settlement outside the confines of the *longphort* at the pool. The Dublin Castle excavations, though admittedly limited in extent and, in the case of the Cross Block, not completed to subsoil, did not produce evidence of early or mid-ninth-century habitation but did uncover remains of late ninth-century habitation in Phase 1 at the Cork Tower. Also, a cow horn from Phase 3,

Table 9.1 Schematic representation of the phases of activity described in this volume.

	Cork Tower	Powder Tower 1	Powder Tower 2	Bermingham Tower	Cross Block
Post-1204 (1204–c. 1230)		Pre-Powder Tower ground level (Phase 3)			Upper dump deposits (Phase G)
Pre-1204 (c. 1170–1204)		Upper dump deposits (Phase 3)	**Truncated above this level** Dump deposits (Phase 18)	Pre-1204 wall?	Upper dump deposits (Phase G)
c. 1100–c. 1170		Lower dump deposits (Phase 3) *Contemporary with the Hiberno-Scandinavian stone wall found on other sites*	House floors (Phases 13-17)	Pre-1204 wall?	Lower dump deposits (Phase G) *Contemporary with the Hiberno-Scandinavian stone wall found on other sites*
Eleventh century	**Truncated above this level** House 3 (Phase 6) House 2 (Phase 5)	Phase 2 bank	House floors (Phases 7-12)		House V (Phase F) House IV (Phase E) House III (Phase D)
Tenth century	Refuse/cess pits (Phase 4) House 1 (Phase 3) pathway, cess pits (Phase 2)	Phase 1b bank Phase 1a bank	House floors (Phases 3-6); House floor, paved street (Phase 2); street, structures (Phase 1)	**Deposits truncated above this level** Gully/ditch?	Iron working (Phase C) House II (Phase B) House I (Phase A)
Ninth century	Cess/refuse pits (Phase 1)				**Not excavated below Phase A**
Pre-Viking (eighth century)	Cow horn (residual in Phase 3)				

clearly residual in that context, produced a radiocarbon date centring around 800, indicating some activity on the ridge at this time.

While house structures were not found in Phase 1 at the Cork Tower, the habitation evidence uncovered was undoubtedly in close proximity to dwellings. It is likely this late ninth-century activity belongs to an early phase of settlement on the ridge, outside the enclosed confines of the *longphort* and associated settlement around the pool to the south. This fits well with Halpin's (2005) model for the development of the town, with the entire east end of the ridge forming Stage 1 of that development in the ninth century. The move northwards from the *longphort* on the shores of the pool to the ridge makes sense in that the ridge, with water on three sides, was more easily defended and was a more suitable, drier location for settlement. The earliest phases at the Cork Tower show that this move was underway in the late ninth century, gradually leading to the establishment of the town with its defences, streets and house plots. Evidence that appears to be out of step somewhat with this narrative, however, is the late tenth-century date suggested by Byrne (2015) for the earliest phase of settlement on a site in Castle Street, immediately north of the Cork Tower area. This date is based on coin hoards dating to the very end of the tenth century and could indicate an area within the Hiberno-Scandinavian town that was kept free of habitation while settlement expanded both to the north and south.

Fig. 9.1 Conjectural reconstruction of the tenth-century stone-faced defensive bank along the shore of the Poddle estuary at the eastern end of the town with a street and houses behind (artist Matthew Ryan).

The Defences

THE POWDER TOWER AREA

The deposits contained by the walls of the circular Powder Tower, though only 5.95m in diameter, revealed significant information on the defences of pre-Norman Dublin. These were the eastern defences of the Hiberno-Scandinavian town built along the edge of the tidal Poddle estuary at the tail end of the ridge between the Liffey and the Poddle (Fig. 1.2). An insubstantial clay bank (Phase 1a) dating from *c.* 900 was replaced by a more substantial clay bank with an external stone facing (Phase 1b) and this in turn was reinforced by a clay bank with timber lacing (Phase 2). These banks, while having a unique stone-facing feature (Phase 1b), can be compared with the series of banks excavated at other sites in Dublin, including the fine series of defences excavated at Wood Quay/Fishamble Street (Wallace 2016, 124–5).

The earliest banks found at other locations in Dublin compare well with the Phase 1a bank in being relatively low, possibly non-defensive features. Where located close to high-tide level, these banks could also have served as flood barriers; elsewhere they may have served only as a town boundary. Bank 1 at Wood Quay/Fishamble Street is a good parallel. Bank 2 at that site had wattle breakwaters set in the foreshore in front of it, as at the Powder Tower, where successive breakwaters constructed in front of the Phase 1a and 1b banks also served to retain material to diminish the erosive action of tidal and flood water. Both Banks 1 and 2 at Parliament Street, directly north of the Powder Tower, were interpreted as non-defensive in character (Scally 2002, 15–16). Excavations at Ross Road to the west of the castle also uncovered an early bank (Bank 1), which was interpreted as non-defensive; it is clearly not a flood bank, given its elevation above the Poddle. Bank 2 here was built on top of Bank 1 and evidence of burning, the excavator argued, might have been caused by a recorded burning of Dublin in 936 or a destruction in 944 (Walsh 2001, 101). It is interesting that the surface of the Phase 1a bank at Dublin Castle had a layer of charcoal on it, possibly associated with the same event.

It is, of course, possible that the Phase 1a bank at Dublin Castle was not the earliest bank, which, on the analogy of Parliament Street, could have been slightly further in from the water's edge. If there was such an earlier bank, there would have been a similar sequence to Parliament Street and Ross Road, with the first two banks being slighter features and the third bank (possibly built after the burning of 936) being a more seriously defensive feature, having, at least in the area of the later Powder Tower, a stone facing as well.

The interpretation of the Phase 1a and 1b banks at Dublin Castle is limited by the fact that only the lower outer faces of the banks survived. The full height of both banks is unknown, as is the nature of any timber/wattle palisade on their crests or revetment of their inner faces (Fig. 9.1). The stone facing of the Phase 1b bank at the Powder Tower is unique among the banks excavated in Dublin and may have been necessary because its base was constructed below high tide level and therefore subject to considerable water erosion. The fact that it was built on shelving bedrock meant that there was a good supply of easily quarried stone to hand, while the exposed bedrock would also have made it more difficult to embed a protective upright timber facing.

The Phase 2 bank at Dublin Castle was built against the Phase 1b stone-faced bank and incorporated material retained by successive wattle breakwaters. While the outer eastern face was beyond the area of surviving deposits, evidence of timber lacing was found within it, similar to Bank 3 at Fishamble Street, which contained a series of long poles laid at right angles to its long axis and was a substantial defensive bank (Wallace 2016, 129–30). The equivalent at Parliament Street is probably Bank 3, identified as a defensive bank, and Bank 4 at Ross Road (Walsh 2001, 106). The criss-cross timbers of the framework in the Phase 2 bank at the Powder Tower were probably well secured by wooden pegs to each other and to a strong wooden facing that would have been necessary at its exposed front to withstand the erosive effects of tidal water in the Poddle estuary. A radiocarbon date from a timber belonging to this bank centres on the mid-eleventh century.

All of these earthen and timber defences at Dublin were replaced by a substantial mortared stone wall which is thought to have been built sometime around 1100. This was best preserved on the Wood Quay/Fishamble Street site, where it had an average surviving height of *c.* 2m (Wallace 2016, 138) and where a part of it can still be viewed *in situ*. It is likely that this major piece of defensive infrastructure would have formed a complete circuit of the town including the area of the later castle. No trace of it was found in the small area excavated at the Powder Tower and it is unknown whether its line here was to the east or west. Phase 3 at the Powder Tower consists of layers of dumped material dating from the twelfth and early thirteenth century, which could have either been dumped inside or outside this wall. The proximity of the Hiberno-Scandinavian houses excavated at the Cross Block to the east curtain wall of the later castle would suggest that both the shore of the Poddle estuary and the pre-Norman defensive banks curved out here to the east close to the bend in the Poddle (Fig. 1.2). It is possible that the straightening out of this line happened first when the *c.* 1100 wall was built, and this might explain the lack of evidence for twelfth-century houses in Cutting B at the Cross Block.

By the second quarter of the tenth century Dublin had become a very wealthy trading centre, a lucrative target to be raided by Irish kings. Domination of it was also contested by Scandinavian kings. It is not surprising, therefore, that the town needed defences. When the settlement was destroyed by the kings of Brega and Leinster in 944, 400 people were reported as killed in what the Irish annalists called the '*dún*' of Dublin. This was the first time the word *dún* had been used to describe Dublin, and Duffy (2022) has argued that in this context it signifies a fortified town. The Phase 1b bank at the Powder Tower was probably in existence in 944, a conclusion that is supported by a radiocarbon date for one of its protective breakwaters.

THE BERMINGHAM TOWER AREA

The small area with pre-castle features within the square tower attached to the Bermingham Tower was truncated to such an extent that no archaeological deposits survived above subsoil. The exact nature of the two main features cut into the subsoil here and the level from which they were dug are uncertain. One survived as an east-west shallow gully while the other was a deeper feature, either a pit or a ditch terminal. It is likely that these features were located just inside the southern defences of the Hiberno-Scandinavian town and may be in some way related to them. At Ross Road to the west, a number of gullies were found close to the banks. Radiocarbon dating to the mid-tenth century of a bone from the gully at the Bermingham Tower is consistent with such an interpretation.

A POSSIBLE HIBERNO-SCANDINAVIAN STRONGHOLD OR AN EARLY ANGLO-NORMAN CASTLE?

An intriguing feature is the early masonry wall found close to the Bermingham Tower. This clearly pre-dated the early thirteenth-century Bermingham Tower and adjacent square tower and had been incorporated into the west curtain wall of the castle.

This slightly curving early wall with an offset footing and no base batter was built directly on subsoil. Only its west face was uncovered and just *c.* 1.2m of its height had survived. The style of masonry with bedding planes of large blocks forming the facing is common in early masonry churches in Ireland from the tenth to the thirteenth centuries and also in some buildings constructed soon after the Anglo-Norman invasion of 1169. Mortared masonry is extremely rare in surviving secular buildings that pre-date the arrival of the Anglo-Normans. Two examples are the earliest town walls of Dublin (Wood Quay) and Waterford built around 1100. The town wall at Wood Quay had vertical faces while that at Waterford narrowed with height. The pre-1204 wall at the Bermingham Tower curves slightly to the north-east and is roughly at a right angle to the line of the southern defences of the town; it cannot therefore be part of the town wall that was built *c.* 1100. It could, however, be contemporary with the town wall and be part of an internal defensive enclosure built close to the south-east corner of the Hiberno-Scandinavian town. Though there is no direct reference to such a stronghold at Dublin prior to 1170, there was likely to have been a strongpoint within the walled town to facilitate the holding of Dublin by Irish kings in the late eleventh and early twelfth centuries (Duffy 2022, 13). There was also undoubtedly a high-status residence of the Hiberno-Scandinavian king of Dublin, the location of which is also unknown. It has recently been suggested, based on similar foundations in Britain and on the Continent (Bhreathnach 2020, 159), that after nearby Christchurch was founded by King Sitriuc in the early eleventh century, the king's residence and that of the bishop would probably have been close to the cathedral.

The location, nature and size of the castle built by Hugh de Lacy on the orders of Henry II on his departure from Dublin in 1172 is unclear and will be further discussed in volume 3 (Lynch *et al.* forthcoming a/b). The only reference to its location is the grant of a burgage plot to Savaricus the saddler sometime between 1173 and 1176 that refers to the gate of the castle (Duffy 2022, 22). The plot is described as being in front of St Mary's, extending the same length as that church's cemetery and with its front 'in the route which is opposite the castle gate'. While the present-day City Hall is on the site of the church of St Mary del Dam, a lack of knowledge about the detailed urban topography of this part of Dublin at that time does not allow for absolute certainty on the location of the plot. Differing interpretations of this grant could place the early castle either to the south within the footprint of the post-1204 castle or alternatively, on the north side of Castle Street.

If the early wall found at the Bermingham Tower was part of a defended walled enclosure built *c.* 1100, this enclosure could have been adapted and modernised as the inner ward of the 1172 castle. The outer ward could have extended as an earth and timber bailey roughly co-extensive with the post-1204 castle with a gateway onto Castle Street. The inner stone-walled ward, possibly D-shaped or polygonal, may have covered only a quarter or a sixth of the total area of the castle. It is interesting to compare this possible arrangement of polygonal inner ward at one corner of a large roughly rectangular outer ward with that at Ludlow Castle, the principal castle of the de Lacy's in England and obviously very familiar to Hugh de Lacy (Shoesmith and Johnson 2000). The reuse of an earlier stronghold is a pattern seen in many Anglo-Norman castles in Ireland, where sites important to previous rulers were chosen because of the inherited political, military and social power associated with them. There is also the practicality of being able to reuse a suitable location and defensive features already in place.

An alternative interpretation of the Savaricus grant suggests that the 1172 castle could have been located on the west side of Cork Hill and on the north side of Castle Street. This could explain a substantial ditch of early Anglo-Norman date which was excavated at this location (Byrne 2015, 351) and that may have been part of a rectilinear enclosure associated with that castle. Another possibility, if this ditch is indeed part of an enclosure, is that it formed part of a temporary fortification constructed within the town after it was captured in 1170 and that remained in use until the 1172 castle was completed.

The discovery of a short stretch of pre-1204 masonry close to the Bermingham Tower has brought into focus the debate about the possible location of a Hiberno-Scandinavian stronghold and the early Norman castle built on foot of an order given by Henry II in 1172. This question will be considered in more detail in volume 3 of this series in the context of a broader discussion of the development of the castle between 1170 and the early thirteenth century.

Houses, Property Plots and Pathways

The infrastructure of Viking-age Dublin comprised property plots that ran perpendicular to the streets and contained houses, pathways, outhouses, workshops and associated structures. In his seminal work on the Viking-age buildings of Dublin, Wallace (1992) identified five different house types with his Type 1 accounting for about three-quarters of all known house remains at that time. This house type was considered to be the Dublin house *par excellence* throughout the tenth and eleventh centuries, possibly enduring until the arrival of the Anglo-Normans in the late twelfth century (Figs 9.2 and 9.3). The remains of Type 1 houses have also been identified in Wexford (Bourke 1995), Waterford (Scully 1997a) and Cork (Ní Loingsigh 2014; Murray 2018) and, based on excavations up to 2006, almost a half (227) of all known Viking-age buildings in Ireland have been classified as Type 1 (Boyd 2015, 332).

The Viking-age deposits recorded within the footprint of Dublin Castle were disjointed, truncated and cut away on all sides; the deposits underneath the Cross Block were not fully excavated and due to health and safety restrictions, an important area close to the Cork Tower was investigated as a salvage operation. Nevertheless, important insights have been gained into the nature and chronology of early settlement in this area.

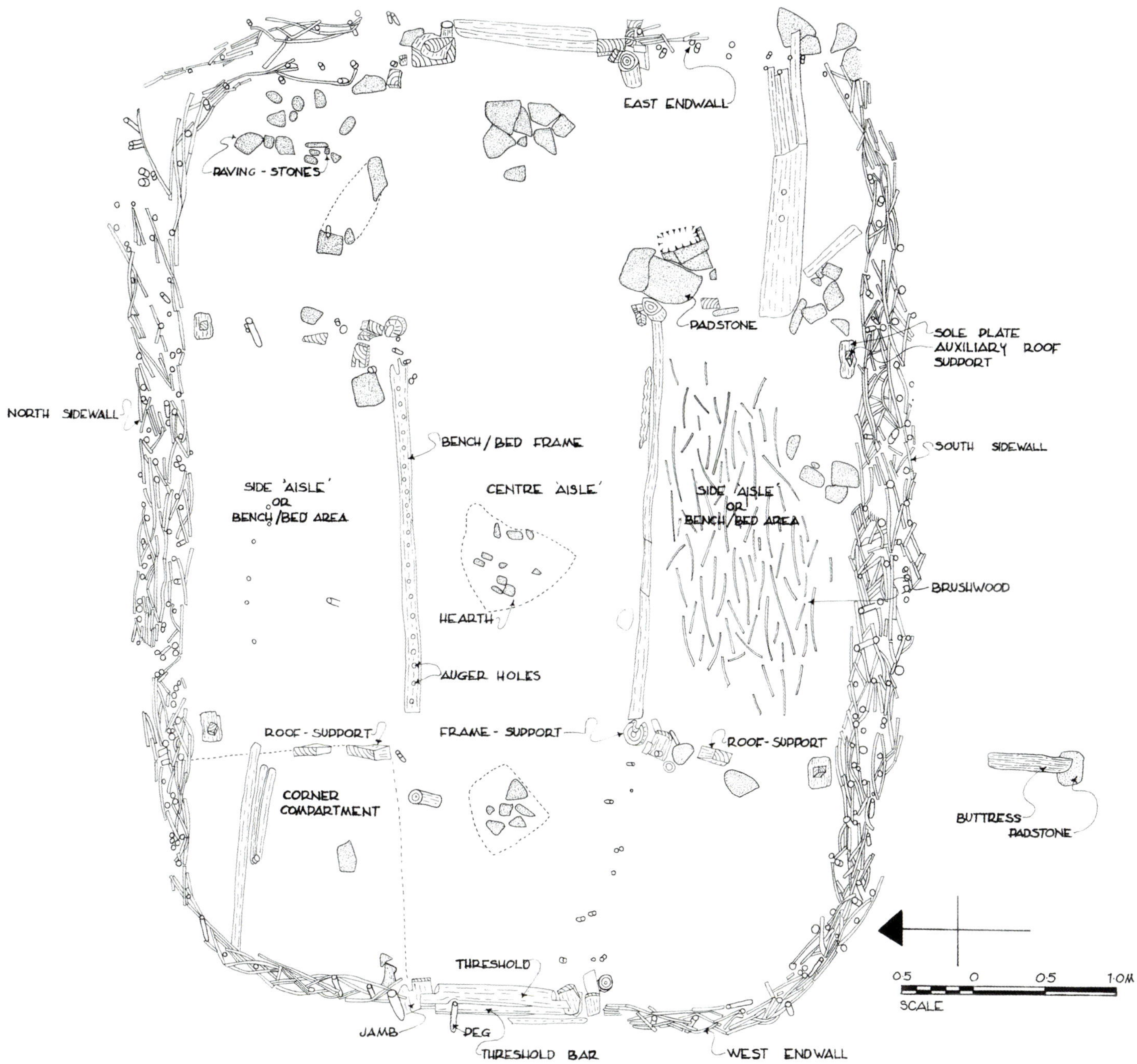

Fig. 9.2 Plan of a Dublin Type 1 house (after Wallace 1992, Part 2, fig. 183; © National Museum of Ireland.)

NINTH-CENTURY HABITATION

A hint of possible activity in the last quarter of the eighth century in the vicinity of the Cork Tower is provided by a cow horn dated to cal. AD 719–885. This, however, was recovered from a later Phase 3 deposit and must be considered the result of residual deposition. The earliest evidence for actual settlement belongs to Phase 1 in the Cork Tower area, where a series of pits (including a large cesspit), a hearth, metalworking debris, timber posts and other ephemeral features were recorded at subsoil level. Animal bone associated with these deposits has returned a date centring on the late ninth century. Although no trace of a house was present, the density and nature of the features suggest that they were in close proximity to habitation. Two further

as House 1 in Phase 3, it is more likely that this was the established layout within the plot and for some reason there was a hiatus in house building in Phase 4. The possibility that the Cork Tower houses were built in the backyard behind the primary dwellings was also considered, as many of the plots at nearby Fishamble Street and John's Lane had more than one building (*ibid.*). These secondary structures, however, were usually smaller buildings and there is only one instance of a Type 1 house in such a location (P.F. Wallace, pers. comm.).

Approximately 125m downslope to the south-east, a sequence of five houses uncovered underneath the Cross Block also relate to a single plot. The long axes of these houses were aligned roughly east-west, similar to the Cork Tower houses, and a line of stake-holes just to the south of House I is the only surviving evidence of a possible property boundary. In spite of the limited area excavated, traces of pathways were recorded at several levels. Just outside the west doorway of House I a series of evenly spaced timber rods are interpreted as the foundations for a timber pathway which, further south, appears to have incorporated a wattle mat and an area of stone paving. A fine mat of wattle was uncovered just outside the probable site of the west doorway in House II while there was stone paving immediately outside the threshold of House III and a well-made plank pathway ran along the south side of the house. Traces of a timber pathway were found along the same line at a higher level outside House IV. Given that the east curtain wall of the thirteenth-century castle, which formed the east end of the Cross Block cutting, must have been close to the line of the earlier defences, then the houses excavated were built on one of the most easterly plots within the Viking-age town. The west doorways of these houses must have been linked by pathways to a street that ran roughly north/ south which, if extended northwards, would intersect with the area of habitation uncovered in the Powder Tower 2 area where, in the two earliest phases, remnants of what appears to have been a street surface were uncovered on a similar alignment. The putative clay house floors, together with the many post-holes and stake-holes, are consistent with property plots bordering this street. The evidence for such a street is unusual in Viking-age Dublin, as the modern street pattern tends to follow the line of the ancient streets and consequently these areas have not been subjected to excavation.

CHRONOLOGY OF HABITATION

The archaeology of the different areas excavated within Dublin Castle has been divided into chronological phases based on stratigraphic evidence and a limited number of radiocarbon dates that have been subjected to Bayesian modelling has allowed a broad chronological framework to be established for settlement within the site as a whole (Table 9.1). Six radiocarbon dates were obtained for deposits in the Cork Tower area but the modelling has indicated that three (relating to Phases 3, 4a/b) are in fact the result of residual deposition and, although indicating activity in the ninth century, they cannot be used for dating the phases of housebuilding in the area. The remaining three dates as a result have end ranges that are 'significantly elongated' (see Chapter 8 above). The earliest evidence of settlement, at subsoil level, can be reliably dated to the latter half of the ninth century. Following a phase of less intense activity, dated to the earlier part of the tenth century, the first house (House 1) was constructed. A hiatus in house building occurred when the area was again used for the disposal of cess and refuse in the mid/late tenth century before the construction of House 2, probably in the early eleventh century. The fire-damaged House 2 was replaced immediately by House 3, the construction of which incorporated some of the undamaged post-and-wattle walls of the earlier house. Composite antler combs from both of these houses have decoration that is closely related and a design feature of a comb found in House 2 parallels one found in House III (Cross Block), suggesting probable contemporaneity. The surviving evidence for Viking-age habitation in the Cork Tower area therefore appears to span the period from the latter half of the ninth century to the early eleventh century. Later Viking-age layers in this area were truncated by eighteenth-century house building and other activity.

The earliest house (House I) exposed underneath the Cross Block and that which replaced it (House II) are tentatively assigned to the first half of the tenth century on stratigraphic evidence, although it should be noted that, because this cutting was not fully excavated, it is likely that habitation in this area commenced earlier, possibly as early as the ninth century. Following a period of ironworking dated to the mid/late tenth century, house building recommenced when Houses III, IV and V were constructed in the early/mid eleventh century, after which there was no further evidence of house building.

The construction of a roughly cobbled street on subsoil in the Powder Tower 2 area can be dated to the early/ mid tenth century. Despite the very limited size and compromised nature of the excavation area, traces of timber structures and a succession of possible clay house floors were identified on either side of this street. Approximately four phases of activity were recorded on the east side of the street but in one very restricted area (Area K) a series of up to 18 phases of habitation extending into the late twelfth century were identified.

While acknowledging that establishing the average life span of Dublin Viking houses is simply guesswork in the absence of a comprehensive series of dendrochronological dates, Wallace (1992, Part 1, 8) tentatively suggests that houses lasted for between ten and twenty years. This was based on a few tree-ring determinations, numismatic evidence and artefact associations. The fragmentary and disjointed nature of the evidence from Dublin Castle and the lack of dendrochronological dates means that we cannot estimate the life span of the houses with any degree of certainty. The general impression from the Cork Tower and Cross Block houses is that throughout the tenth century there were approximately three separate phases of habitation, while in the Powder Tower 2 area the succession of clay house floors suggests more intensive settlement.

The deposits and structures found at Dublin Castle can be paralleled at other large sites excavated within the walled town such as Fishamble Street and Essex Street West / Exchange Street Upper (Temple Bar West). The strong evidence for occupation and structures datable to the ninth century at Temple Bar West was not replicated at Dublin Castle nor indeed at Fishamble Street. However, the layout of plots in relation to streets and the preponderance of Type 1 houses from the tenth century on are features that are common to all three sites (Fig. 9.4). The manner in which the houses were used, the industrial and craft work carried out and the types of finds recovered are generally similar. Full publication of the excavations of the Fishamble Street and Temple Bar West sites will allow more detailed comparisons to be made between them.

Fig. 9.4 Reconstruction of buildings, yards and street layout on Fishamble Street (after Wallace 2016, fig. 2.27; drawing by Michael Heffernan © National Museum of Ireland).

HISTORICAL CONTEXT

The linking of Hiberno-Scandinavian settlement features at Dublin Castle with historically recorded events is not always possible because of the broad timespans of chronology based on radiocarbon dating and artefactual evidence. However, broader historical trends do seem to be reflected in the archaeological record. The change of settlement focus from the pool with its *longphort* to the ridge between the Liffey and Poddle, likely to be reflected in the change of name in the Irish annals in the late ninth century from Duiblinn to Áth Cliath (Duffy 2022), finds support in the radiocarbon dating of Phase 1 at the Cork Tower. The first use of the word *dún* by the Irish annalists in 944, interpreted as indicating both stronger defences and a stronger urban identity (*ibid.*), is reflected in a more congested and affluent settlement with more clearly demarcated plot boundaries and the building of houses as at the Cork Tower. That this is an organised urban settlement continuing up to the arrival of the Anglo-Normans in 1170 is clearly indicated in both the historical record and in the archaeological deposits at Dublin Castle and elsewhere in the city.

Material Culture

Approximately 370 artefacts were recovered that relate to the pre-castle occupation of the site of Dublin Castle between the late ninth and early thirteenth centuries. This assemblage of artefacts supports the view of a vibrant town with craftwork and small-scale industry carried out within the domestic housing plots. There is evidence for trade with Scandinavia and northern Britain, but everyday objects were manufactured within the town using locally-sourced raw materials. The majority of artefacts, including waste material generated by various craft activities were recovered from the house plots at the Cork Tower and the Cross Block (Tables 4.1, 4.2; Appendix) and, although the surviving deposits were limited in scale and no complete house plan had survived, it appears, based on the quality of the material culture, that the occupants of the houses uncovered underneath the Cross Block were more prosperous than the inhabitants of those upslope in the Cork Tower area.

CLOTHING AND PERSONAL ITEMS

No recognisable items of clothing were recovered. A few fragments of woollen fabric and scraps of fur trimming were found in the Cork Tower houses and the small leather assemblage includes two shoe parts and fragments of straps or belts including one decorated strap-end. Dress fasteners include three ringed pins (two of iron and one of copper alloy) and ten copper alloy stick pins while the most common dress accessory was the bone/antler pin, 24 examples of which were recovered. The most impressive item relating to dress is the highly decorated copper alloy strap-end recovered from a deposit of ironworking debris at the Cross Block.

Items of personal jewellery were found throughout all areas. In common with other Viking-age sites, amber imported from the Baltic region was used for the manufacture of finger rings, beads and pendants, although the assemblage comprises only ten pieces in total. Objects made from jet or jet-like material include a finger ring made from jet sourced in Whitby, north-east England. A decorated copper alloy bracelet from the Cross Block probably belonged to a child, indicating a family of some status. A glass bead and a glass inset (probably part of a piece of jewellery) are of interest, given the evidence for possible glass manufacture in the Cork Tower area in the early tenth century.

Composite antler combs were in widespread use in Viking-age Dublin (more than 2,000 have been recorded to date) and nineteen examples were recovered from Dublin Castle, ranging in date from the mid tenth to the early eleventh century, including two with incised inscriptions. One of three combs possibly imported from Scandinavia was recovered from a mid / late-tenth century deposit at the Cork Tower and has a runic inscription interpreted as possibly the personal name *Unnr* or *Uni*, perhaps that of the comb's Scandinavian owner. The second inscribed comb was associated with House III in the Cross Block area and dates to the early eleventh century. In this instance, an ogham inscription is read as the personal name 'ANE', suggesting the comb belonged to a woman of ethnic Gaelic connection. These two personal items bear testimony to the diverse ethnicities within late tenth / early eleventh-century Dublin.

Hints of pastimes are provided by the four gaming pieces, one of which is a very rare example fashioned from a walrus skull. Two perforated pig metapodia and a polished bird bone have been interpreted as simple musical instruments. A bear tooth recovered from the Cork Tower area is unique in an Irish context and must have been a treasured possession, possibly kept as a talisman.

CRAFT PRODUCTION

Viking-age Dublin was a vibrant hub of commercial activity that included a thriving craftworking industry. The recovery of antler waste and some unfinished bone objects indicates local production. Much of the antler working was concerned with the production of combs, as evidenced by the many unfinished comb tooth segments found. The near-complete example of an antler bow saw and part of a second are likely to have been among the tools used by an antler or bone worker, while a clamp fashioned from a whale bone is a rare and important implement that could have been used by a range of craftworkers. Amber was worked in the Cork Tower area, as evidenced by the recovery of waste flakes and the amber chips found inside House 1. Products of the craft of cooperage were also recovered from the Cork Tower area and the Cross Block.

Textile workers were also living in this area of the Viking-age town. The spinning of wool and flax is evidenced by the nine spindle whorls recovered, and the five examples of single-pointed pin beaters would have been used in the weaving process. The relatively light weight of the spindle whorls could reflect the spinning of flax rather than wool and the manufacture of fine fabrics. A glass linen-smoother and a wooden ripple comb used for removing the seed heads from dried flax bundles provide further evidence for the production of linen. Needles manufactured from bone and iron would have had many uses related to textile manufacture and repair. A fragile wooden artefact recovered from House 1 has been interpreted as part of a loom frame, possibly a two-beam vertical loom used for the manufacture of a light fabric such as sprang (a type of open weave similar to netting) or perhaps a small-scale tapestry. An iron shears may have been used in the textile industry or other domestic activity. A small number of leather offcuts were found and leatherworking tools, including iron awls and a creaser, were recovered from the Cross Block area.

Evidence for metalworking was present throughout all phases of occupation and seems to have been concentrated in the Cork Tower area. Slag resulting from iron smithing has been identified in addition to fragments of clay tuyères that would have been used as bellows protectors by the ironworkers. Fragments of two ceramic crucibles used for non-ferrous metalworking were also recovered. Analysis of residues indicates the melting of copper with a very low tin content and, in one case, the addition of lead or zinc was recorded. It is probable that the traces of lead noted relate to the alloying of leaded bronzes rather than the production of lead artefacts. Leadworking was widely practised in Viking-age Dublin, including at nearby Fishamble Street, where a considerable quantity of waste lead was found in tenth- and eleventh-century levels, including spillages of molten lead on house floors. Wallace (2016, 336) suggests that leadworking was an everyday practice in some of the Fishamble Street houses where artefacts including weights and spindle whorls were manufactured. Only a single lead object, however, was found on the Dublin Castle site – an offcut recovered from underneath the floor of House III at the Cross Block, suggesting that specialist craft production was concentrated in particular quarters of the Hiberno-Scandinavian town.

A single crucible fragment recovered from an early tenth-century level in the Cork Tower area had been used for melting natron glass, and a fragment of natron glass, probably produced in the Levant around the fourth century, was recovered from the Cross Block. Broken glass dating back to Roman times (cullet) was widely traded in the early medieval period and was melted down for recycling into a range of items.

DOMESTIC AND MISCELLANEOUS ITEMS

A range of common everyday items used in a domestic context was also recovered. The remains of fourteen iron knives, mostly from the Cross Block houses, and several stone hones as well as a rotary whetstone were identified. Locks and barrel padlock keys are well represented, and a stone lamp was associated with House IV. A rotary quern stone associated with House V provides evidence for grinding of grain. The function of twelve small bone cylinders, the majority of which were recovered from the Cross Block, remains rather enigmatic. Similar cylinders are common finds on sites of medieval date in Ireland and over 800 were recovered from nearby Wood Quay and Fishamble Street. Their function has variously been suggested as beads, loom weights, gaming pieces or textile implements but the current consensus appears to favour their use as spacers / weights along the edges of fishing nets.

There was limited importation of pottery into Ireland until the arrival of the Anglo-Normans in 1169 after which there was a vast increase in imported wares and the setting up of local kilns. It must be presumed that vessels required for the preparation, serving and consumption of food and drink at this time were made from metal and wood. A fragment of a turned wooden plate or platter was recovered from a pit in the Cork Tower area and wooden staves of vessels ranging from tankard size to barrels together with wooden discs were also recorded. Although domestic pottery was not in use, the technology to produce ceramic vessels did exist, as evidenced by the presence of tuyères and crucibles as noted above. Further evidence for such technology is the number of ceramic curved roof tiles recovered from the Powder Tower area. Six fragments came from twelfth/thirteenth-century contexts, but four fragments can be assigned to the eleventh century. These latter tiles, the earliest type known in Ireland, were most likely made in Dublin and would have been used on large stone buildings such as the roof of nearby Christ Church Cathedral.

A number of thirteenth/fourteenth-century pottery sherds were found in intrusive contexts in the Cork Tower area in particular and these can be explained by disturbance caused by the digging of the castle moat and the overlying post-medieval structures. The earliest stratified pottery at Dublin Castle is a body sherd of Seine valley white ware, an import from northern France, that was recovered from a Phase 12 context in Powder Tower 2 (Area K) and was possibly deposited towards the end of the eleventh century. A body sherd of Ham Green A pottery imported from south-west England was found in a Phase 17 context in the same area and was possibly deposited shortly before the arrival of the Anglo-Normans in Dublin in 1170. The evidence for a local pottery industry does not appear until after the establishment of Anglo-Norman control, when two sherds of Leinster Cooking Ware and two sherds of Dublin-type glazed ware were recovered from Phase 3 levelling deposits at the Powder Tower and probably belong to the period just before the completion of the castle *c.* 1225.

Items relating to warfare were scarce. An iron spearhead was associated with House 3 and three iron arrowheads were recovered from the Cross Block area, one of which came from the same context as the remains of iron shackles. The collection of 333 pebbles found near the hearth in House III were interpreted by the excavator as possible sling stones but petrographical analysis suggests this is unlikely. Their proximity to the hearth could mean they were stockpiled for use in heating water, similar to the 'hot stone' technology commonly used in the Bronze Age. However, the absence of heat-cracked stones in any associated context (or indeed in any of the house remains) militates against such an interpretation. Pebbles were used as 'paving stones' in the corner compartment of a house (FS102) at nearby Fishamble Street (Wallace 2016, 115) and perhaps the Cross Block examples had been stockpiled for a similar purpose. An iron bridle cheek piece associated with House III and an iron horseshoe nail from the Cork Tower area are the only evidence for the presence of horses, other than a small number of horse bones in the animal bone assemblage.

The Hiberno-Scandinavian town was a thriving port where shipbuilding and ship repair must have been important local industries. A significant number of ships' timbers from vessels ranging from small boats to large ships have been recovered from sites including Wood Quay, Fishamble Street and Christchurch Place. No ships' timbers were excavated at Dublin Castle but fifteen iron nails/rivets (most with roves still attached) were recovered from among the timbers of an eleventh-century pathway at the Cross Block. Described by the excavator as having been found 'among the paving timbers of the street' (Ó hEochaidhe 1962), these are most probably ships' nails. He also described the 'street' as 'plank paving in which the split tree trunks were pegged into the ground', which does not suggest the presence of ships' timbers. It is possible that the nails were removed from ships' timbers that were reused for some construction in the immediate vicinity and were discarded onto the surface of the pathway. Evidence from Wood Quay suggests that the hulks of ships were dismembered for reuse as causeways, revetment walls and drains or jetty sides (Wallace 2016, 184).

Diet and Living Conditions

In spite of small sample sizes, the analysis of animal and fish bones, as well as the palaeobotanical evidence, have shed some light on the diet and living conditions of the inhabitants of tenth/eleventh-century Dublin. The animal bone assemblage is dominated by cattle, pigs and sheep, with cattle identified as the main food source. Veal may also have been consumed. The pigs appear to have been slaughtered relatively young and there is evidence suggesting that they were reared in the backyards of the house plots. Sheep were killed between two and five years old and would have been kept for wool production as well as a source of meat. There was no evidence recovered for the exploitation of wild animals apart from the use of shed antler for comb making. The small assemblage of bird bones is dominated by domestic fowl. Hens reared in the backyards would have been kept for the supply of eggs (eggshells were found throughout the site) as well as meat. Geese were also present and would have been valued for their down as well as their meat and eggs. Goose feathers would have been used for the fletching of arrows while the recovery of wing bones of the white-tailed eagle suggests a trade in eagle wings from Scandinavia for a similar purpose. The only evidence for the exploitation of wild birds are the few bones of wild duck recovered. Fragments of marine shell were recorded in all phases of occupation and quantities of cockle and mussel shells in particular were noted in refuse deposits, and oyster shell was identified in a Phase 6 context at the Cork Tower. Fish bones recovered indicate that hake, ling, herring, eel, whiting, salmon, ray and trout were consumed. A single whale bone could indicate the consumption of meat from a stranded whale.

The plant remains suggest a high-fibre diet and fruit species gathered from the wild include strawberries, bilberries, blackberries / raspberries, sloes and rowan berries. Crab-apples were also present and hazelnut fragments were found throughout all levels. Cultivated barley, oats and, to a lesser extent, wheat were identified and would have been used in a variety of foodstuffs including breads, pottages and stews and perhaps in the production of beer. Bran of either wheat or rye was also consumed. The seeds of flax were well represented and most likely relate to linen production, although their consumption and use for cooking oil is also a possibility. Common cereal weeds such as fat hen, oraches, black bindweed and knotgrass may have been cultivated to provide additional food resources.

The maintenance of some level of hygiene within the town is indicated by the careful disposal of cess material and domestic refuse in pits in the backyards of the Cork Tower house plots. Personal hygiene may have been difficult to maintain, as suggested by a perfectly preserved human flea recovered from one of these pits. Such fleas would also have been vectors for disease. Fly puparia commonly associated with animal dung were present in occupation deposits outside the houses, providing further evidence for the keeping of domestic animals within the town. Compacted organic deposits comprising ferns, straw, wood chips, moss, twigs, leaves and feathers were recorded in what would have been the sleeping / seating areas within the Cork Tower houses. Beetle remains normally associated with animal dung and rotting plant material as well as puparia of the common house fly and small mites were recovered from this material. Beetle remains from House 1 also indicate the presence of fowl or perhaps the nesting of birds in the roof. Cats and dogs were present within the town and coprolites, probably of canine origin, suggest the presence of a dog in House 2.

The Occupations, Relative Wealth, Ethnicity and Beliefs of the People who Lived in the Houses

The excavations have revealed evidence of contemporary settlement on two property plots throughout the tenth and early eleventh centuries. The Cork Tower plot was located on the south-east facing slope of the ridge while *c.* 125m downslope to the east, the Cross Block plot was close to the eastern defences of the Viking town and the River Poddle. The evidence suggests that ironworking, textile production, leather and antler/bone working were carried out in both locations. Non-ferrous metalworking and glass working were only recorded at the Cork Tower. The limited amount of amber waste and associated artefacts were also restricted to the Cork Tower plot. Metal artefacts predominated in the Cross Block houses, including locks and keys and a decorated child's bracelet, suggesting households of some status. This is reinforced by the presence of a stone lamp, rare in a Viking Dublin context, and, of course, the iron shackles which could suggest involvement in the slave trade or the holding of hostages. These indicators, together with the fact that a greater number of artefacts was recovered from the Cross Block plot (including the concentration of six combs in House III alone), give a general impression of more well-to-do households.

While there can be no doubt of the Scandinavian ethnicity of most of the people who lived in these houses, their material culture has also been greatly influenced by that of contemporary Ireland and Britain. First and foremost among the Scandinavian elements of their material culture are the houses, the plans of which are typical of Scandinavian settlements in Ireland and are thought to have a north-west continental / Scandinavian origin, although native building methods and materials were utilised in their construction (Wallace 2016, 12). The combs also show strong Scandinavian influence, and a few may even have been brought from Scandinavia, including one with a runic inscription found in an early/mid-tenth-century layer at the Cork Tower. Other combs are of Irish type or types that developed in an Hiberno-Scandinavian context. One type with connecting plates of trapezoidal section could even have been a Dublin innovation and one of these combs, found in an early eleventh-century context at the Cross Block, has an ogham inscription indicating that the owner was an Irishwoman called Áine ('ANE'). These two inscribed combs epitomise the mixed ethnicity of the population of Viking-age Dublin especially by the eleventh century. Most other artefacts found are of types with a broad distribution in Western Europe at the time. Ringed pins, on the other hand, were an Irish type that was adopted by the Scandinavians.

The presence of diverse ancestral and cultural identities in Viking-age Dublin is being reinforced by the results of ongoing cutting-edge DNA analysis. Recent genome sequencing of three men and a woman from Irish Viking burials (three from Dublin and one from Co. Galway) has revealed that Irish Vikings derived much of their genetic ancestry from Norway. The male buried in a Viking tradition in Ship Street Great, just south of the castle, however, had genetic ancestry probably in north-west Ireland. Their skin colour was generally pale and, although the stereotypical combination of blonde hair and blue eyes was recorded, dark brown hair and brown eyes were also noted (L. Cassidy, pers. comm.; Margaryan *et al.* 2020).

The archaeological evidence throws little or no light on the belief systems of the people and none of the artefacts could be described specifically as being either pagan or Christian. The bear tooth is likely to have been a talismanic object certainly brought from abroad and, while such use of bear teeth has a very ancient pedigree, it could not be used as an indication that the owner was not Christian. Indeed, by the year 1000 it is likely that many of the inhabitants of Dublin were at least nominally Christian and, not long thereafter, Dublin came to have its own bishop and cathedral and by about 1100 a plethora of churches. The roof tiles found may have come from the roof of one of these churches.

Conclusion

Though the excavated areas of Viking-age deposits were small and scattered over a wide area, they are informative about urban life and town defences in this part of the Hiberno-Scandinavian town. They also contribute to our overall understanding of the early development of Dublin between the late ninth and the twelfth centuries.

The deposits at the Cross Block, Cork Tower and Powder Tower, though mostly truncated by later activity, consisted of successive occupation layers containing evidence for a minimum of eight rectangular post-and-wattle houses, some evidence for property boundaries and pathways and possible evidence for a street mostly dating to the tenth and eleventh centuries. These houses and plots must have related to two north-south streets and suggest that this part of the town, at least in the tenth and eleventh centuries, was laid out with plots and houses like other contemporary areas of the town that have been excavated. The assumption of many writers that Dublin Castle was the site of a stronghold within the Viking-age town from its foundation is not borne out by the excavated evidence, though it has to be admitted that very small areas of the overall site were investigated. The construction of a stronghold, if there ever was such a feature within the Viking-age town, may have been a late development associated with the holding of Dublin by Irish provincial kings starting in the late eleventh century. The pre-1204 wall found at the Bermingham Tower could be part of such a stronghold but could also be part of the first Anglo-Norman castle at Dublin, built in the 1170s.

The earliest evidence for occupation on the site (Phase 1 at the Cork Tower) has been radiocarbon dated to the late ninth century, suggesting that the ridge between the Liffey and the Poddle was in the process of being developed as a town in the late ninth century. No evidence was found for the *longphort* (ship-camp) mentioned in 841 or associated occupation and it is likely that this was located around the former pool in the Poddle estuary immediately south of the castle.

Evidence for three successive banks were found at the Powder Tower, dating from the tenth and eleventh centuries. These were part of the eastern defences of the town. Over time they became more substantial and can be compared with banks found on other excavation sites in Dublin.

The richest and best-preserved pre-castle deposits were found at the Cross Block and they indicate that comparable deposits could survive within the footprint of the medieval castle and especially under the surface of the Upper Yard. Completion of the excavation at the Cross Block and targeted research excavation at other points within the castle have the potential to answer many of the questions that remain about the Dublin Castle site.

Appendix
List of finds by category

Category	Material	Type	CT2	PT1	PT2	CB	Total
Dress accessories	Bone/antler	Pin	7	2	1	14	24
	Iron	Loop-headed ringed pin	2	0	0	0	2
	Copper alloy	Loop-headed ringed pin	0	0	0	1	1
	Copper alloy	Stick pins	2	2	0	4	8
	Iron	Buckle	1	0	0	0	1
	Iron	Buckle pin	0	1	0	0	1
	Copper alloy	Strap-end	0	0	0	1	1
	Wood	Pins	2	0	0	0	2
	Leather	Belt/strap	4	0	0	0	4
	Leather	Lacing thong	0	0	0	1	1
			18	**5**	**1**	**21**	**45**
Clothing	Animal skin (leather)	Fur trimming	0	0	0	1	1
	Textile	Wool cloth	2	0	0	0	2
	Textile	Wool yarn	1	0	0	0	1
			3	**0**	**0**	**1**	**4**
Footwear	Leather	Shoe	2	0	0	0	2
			2	**0**	**0**	**0**	**2**

Category	Material	Type	CT2	PT1	PT2	CB	Total
Personal possessions	Antler	Comb	8	2	2	7	19
	Antler	Comb case	0	0	1	0	1
	Tooth	Bear tooth	1	0	0	0	1
	Iron	Barrel padlock bolt	0	0	0	2	2
	Iron	Barrel padlock key	1	0	0	4	5
	Iron and tin	Tweezers	1	0	0	0	1
	Stone	Lamp	0	0	0	1	1
	Wood	Stave	2	0	0	1	3
	Wood	Disc	4	0	0	0	4
	Wood	Binding hoop	1	0	0	2	3
	Wood	Plate	1	0	0	0	1
	Wood	Withy rope	1	0	0	0	1
	Ceramic (pottery)	Seine valley white ware	0	3	1	0	4
	Ceramic (pottery)	Seine valley highly decorated ware	0	4	0	0	4
	Ceramic (pottery)	Ham Green A ware	0	0	1	0	1
	Ceramic (pottery)	South-east Wiltshire	0	1	0	0	1
	Ceramic (pottery)	Leinster Cooking Ware	0	2	0	0	2
	Ceramic (pottery)	Dublin-type glazed ware	0	2	0	0	2
	Ceramic (pottery)	Saintonge	0	1	0	0	1
	Ceramic (pottery)	Portuguese red ware	0	1	0	0	1
	Glass	Linen smoother	0	0	0	1	1
			20	**16**	**5**	**18**	**59**

Category	Material	Type	CT2	PT1	PT2	CB	Total
Jewellery	Copper alloy	Bracelet	0	0	0	1	1
	Jet/jet-like material	Bangle	1	1	0	0	2
	Jet/jet-like material	Finger-ring	1	0	1	0	2
	Jet/jet-like material	Disc or bead	0	0	0	1	1
	Amber	Bead	1	0	1	0	2
	Amber	Ring	3	0	0	1	4
	Amber	Pendant	1	1	0	0	2
	Amber	Inset	1	0	0	0	1
	Amber	Unfinished proto bead	1	0	0	0	1
	Glass	Bead	1	0	0	0	1
	Glass	Inset	0	0	1	0	1
			10	**2**	**3**	**3**	**18**
Craft implements	Bone	Cylinder	0	0	2	10	12
	Bone	Clamp	0	0	0	1	1
	Bone	Motif piece	0	1	0	0	1
	Antler	Axe blade cover	1	0	0	0	1
	Antler	Bow saw	1	1	0	0	2
	Antler	Wedge/notched wedge	0	0	5	0	5
	Antler	Spacer or ferrule	0	0	0	1	1
	Iron	shears	0	0	0	1	1
	Iron	Knife (complete)	2	0	0	10	12
	Iron	Knife (tang)	0	0	0	2	2
	Iron	punch	0	0	0	1	1
	Iron	file	0	0	0	1	1
	Iron	wedge	0	0	0	1	1
	Stone	Hones	4	1	1	0	6
	Stone	Rotary whetstone	1	0	0	0	1
	Stone	Rotary quern	0	0	0	1	1
			9	**3**	**8**	**29**	**49**

Category	Material	Type	CT2	PT1	PT2	CB	Total
Textile manufacture	Bone	Spindle whorls	1	1	0	7	9
	Stone	Spindle whorls	0	0	0	2	2
	Bone	Pin-beater	3	0	1	1	5
	Bone	Needle	8	0	0	5	13
	Bone	Needle or pin	2	2	0	2	6
	Bone	Needle case	0	0	1	0	1
	Iron and tin	Needle	0	0	0	1	1
	Iron	Needle	0	0	0	1	1
	Bone	Awl	1	0	0	1	2
	Wood	Loom	1	0	0	0	1
	Wood	Ripple comb	0	0	0	1	1
	Wood	Spindle	0	0	0	1	1
			16	**3**	**2**	**22**	**43**
Leatherworking	Iron	Awl	0	0	0	4	4
	Iron	Creaser	0	0	0	1	1
			0	**0**	**0**	**5**	**5**
Glass working	Ceramic	Crucible	1	0	0	0	1
			1	**0**	**0**	**0**	**1**
Metalworking	Ceramic	Tuyère	23	2	6	0	31
	Ceramic	Crucible	1	1	0	0	2
			24	**3**	**6**	**0**	**33**
Hunting and fishing	Bone	Small pointed blade	1	0	0	0	1
	Bone	Large pointed blade	0	0	1	0	1
			1	**0**	**1**	**0**	**2**

Category	Material	Type	CT2	PT1	PT2	CB	Total
Weapons	Iron	Arrowhead	0	0	0	3	3
	Iron	Spearhead	1	0	0	0	1
			1	**0**	**0**	**3**	**4**
Slave management	Iron	Shackle	0	0	0	1	1
			0	**0**	**0**	**1**	**1**
Items of recreation	Antler	Gaming piece	1	0	0	0	1
	Antler and iron composite	Gaming piece	1	0	0	0	1
	Bone	Gaming piece	0	1	0	0	1
	Stone	Gaming piece	0	0	1	0	1
	Bone	Perforated pig metapodia	0	1	1	0	2
			2	**2**	**2**	**0**	**6**
Horse equipment	Iron	Bridal cheek piece	0	0	0	1	1
	Iron	Horseshoe nail	1	0	0	0	1
			1	**0**	**0**	**1**	**2**
Structural	Iron	Nail	8	1	0	27	36
	Iron	Rivet and rove	1	0	0	14	15
	Iron	Rivet	0	0	0	5	5
	Iron	Strap hinge	0	0	0	2	2
	Iron	Wall hook	0	0	0	1	1
	Iron	Hasp	0	0	0	1	1
	Wood	Peg	2	1	0	2	5
	Wood	Treenail	1	0	0	0	1
	Ceramic (roof tiles)	Dublin curved tile	0	7	3	0	10
	Glass	Window glass	0	0	0	1	1
			12	**9**	**3**	**53**	**77**

Category	Material	Type	CT2	PT1	PT2	CB	Total
Objects of uncertain function	Bone	Polished bird bone	1	0	0	0	1
	Copper	Casket mount	1	0	0	0	1
	Iron	bar	1	0	0	0	1
	Copper	wire	1	0	0	0	1
	Lead	offcut	0	0	0	1	1
	Stone	Unworked pebbles	0	0	0	1	1
	Wood	Miscellaneous	7	1	0	2	10
			11	**1**	**0**	**4**	**16**
Totals			**131**	**44**	**31**	**161**	**367**

Bibliography

Allason-Jones, L. and Davis, M. 2002 Investigating 'jet' and jet-like artefacts from prehistoric Scotland. *Antiquity* **76,** 812–25.

Allason-Jones, L. and Jones, J.M. 2001 Identification of 'jet' artefacts by reflected light microscopy. *European Journal of Archaeology* **4** (2), 233–51.

Allen, D. 2002 Roman window glass. In M. Aldhouse-Green and P. Webster (eds), *Artefacts and archaeology, aspects of the Celtic and Roman World*, 102–12. Cardiff.

Ambrosiani, K. 1981 *Viking-age combs, comb making and comb makers in the light of finds from Birka and Ribe.* Stockholm Studies in Archaeology **2**. Stockholm.

Andersson, E. 2003 *Tools for textile production from Birka and Hedeby: excavations in the Black Earth, 1990-1995.* Birka Studies **8.** Stockholm.

Andrefsky, W. 1998 *Lithics: Macroscopic approaches to analysis*. Cambridge.

Andrews, J.H. 1983 The oldest map of Dublin. *Proceedings of the Royal Irish Academy* **83**C, 205–37.

Armstrong, E.C.R. 1921 Two Irish finds of glass beads of the Viking period. *Man* **21,** 71–3.

Armstrong, E.C.R 1922 Some Irish antiquities of unknown use. *The Antiquaries Journal* **2** (1), 6–12.

Ashby, S. 2007 Bone and antler combs. The Finds Research Group AD 700–1700. *Datasheet* **40.** (https://eprints.whiterose.ac.uk/75225/).

Ashby, S. 2010 A typological guide for the spot-identification of medieval bone/antler combs from the British Isles and Northern Europe. Unpublished datasheet for the ICAZ Worked Bone Research Group (http://www.wbrg.net).

Atkin, M., Carter, A. and Evans, D. 1985 *Excavations at Norwich 1971–78, part II*. East Anglian Archaeology Report **26.** Norwich.

Badreshany, K. forthcoming The ICP-AES and MS analysis of medieval and post-medieval tiles from a kiln site, James's Gate Street, Dublin.

Banerjea, R.Y., Badura, M., Brown, A., Kalejs, U., Kos, K., Hamilton-Dyer, S., Maltby, M., Seetah, K., and Pluskowski, A. 2017 A multi-proxy, diachronic and spatial perspective on the urban activities within an indigenous community in medieval Riga, Latvia. *Quaternary International* **460,** 3–21.

Ballin Smith, B. 1994 *Howe: Four millennia of Orkney prehistory*. Society of Antiquaries of Scotland Monograph **9.** Edinburgh.

Barber, J. 1984 Medieval wooden bowls. In D. Breeze (ed.), *Studies in Scottish antiquity presented to Stewart Cruden*, 125–47. Edinburgh.

Barnes, M.P., Hagland, J.R. and Page, R.I. 1997 *The runic inscriptions of Viking Age Dublin*. Medieval Dublin Excavations 1962-81, Series B, vol. 5. Dublin.

Barrett, J.H., Hall, A.R., Johnstone, C., Kenward, H.K., O'Connor, T. and Ashby, S. 2007 Interpreting the plant and animal remains from Viking-age Kaupang. In D. Skre (ed.), *Kaupang in Skiringssal*. Kaupang Excavation Project Publication Series **1,** 283–319. Aarhus.

Barton, K.J. 1963 A medieval pottery kiln at Ham Green, Bristol. *Transactions of the Bristol and Gloucestershire Archaeological Society* **82,** 95–126.

Barton-Murray, R. and Riddler, I.D. 2012a Plain pins. In G. Eogan, *Excavations at Knowth 5: the archaeology of Knowth in the first and second millennia AD*, 327–9. Dublin.

Barton-Murray, R. and Riddler, I.D. 2012b Bone stick-pins. In G. Eogan, *Excavations at Knowth 5: the archaeology of Knowth in the first and second millennia AD*, 300–5. Dublin.

Barton-Murray, R., Johnson, C. and Riddler, I.D. 2012 Gaming pieces of the Viking and medieval periods. In G. Eogan, *Excavations at Knowth 5: the archaeology of Knowth in the first and second millennia AD*, 423–7. Dublin.

Batey, C.E. 2019a Worked bone. In D. Griffiths, J. Harrison and M. Athanson, *Beside the ocean. Coastal landscapes at the bay of Skaill, Marwick, and Birsay Bay, Orkney. Archaeological research 2003–2018*, 252–62. Oxford.

Batey, C.E. 2019b Glass linen smoother (with a contribution by J. Bayley). In D. Griffiths, J. Harrison and M. Athanson, *Beside the ocean. Coastal landscapes at the bay of Skaill, Marwick, and Birsay Bay, Orkney. Archaeological research 2003–2018*, 265–6. Oxford.

Bayley, J., 1992 *Anglo-Scandinavian non-ferrous metalworking from 16–22 Coppergate*. The Archaeology of York. The Small Finds **17,** (7) York.

Bayley, J. 2008 *Lincoln. Evidence for glass-working on Flaxengate and other sites in the city*. Technology report. English Heritage Research Department Report Series **68.**

Bayley J. 2009 Early medieval lead-rich glass in the British Isles–a survey of the evidence. In K. Janssens, P. Degryse, P. Cosyns, J. Caen and L. Van't dack (eds), *Annales of the 17th Congress of the International Association for the History of Glass 2006, Antwerp*, 255–60. Antwerp.

Bayley, J. and Doonan, R. 2000 Glass manufacturing evidence. In A.J. Mainman and N.S.H. Rogers, *Craft, industry, and everyday life: finds from Anglo-Scandinavian York*, 2519-28. The Archaeology of York. The Small Finds **17** (14). York.

Becker, C. 1989 Die Geweihfunde vom Spandauer Burgwall. In A. von Müller and K. von Müller-Muči (eds), *Ausgrabungen, Funde und naturwissenschaftliche Untersuchungen auf dem Burgwall in Berlin-Spandau*, 101–274. Berlin.

Becker, C. 2001 Bone points–no longer a mystery? Evidence from the Slavic Urband fortification of Berlin-Spandau. In A.M. Choyke and L. Bartosiewicz, *Crafting bone: skeletal technologies through time and space*, 129–48. British Archaeological Reports, International Series **937.** Oxford.

Behre, K.-E. 1983 *Ernährung und Umwelt der wikingerzeitlichen Siedlung Haithabu: Die Ergebnisse der Untersuchungen der Pflanzenreste*. Neumünster.

Behre, K.-E. 1999 The history of beer additives in Europe–a review. *Vegetation History and Archaeobotany* **8** (1), 35–48.

Behre, K.-E. 2008 Collected seeds and fruits from herbs as prehistoric food. *Vegetation History and Archaeobotany* **17** (1), 65–73.

Beijerinck, M.W. 1947 *Zadenatlas der Nederlandische Flora*. Wageningen.

Berggren, G. 1969 *Atlas of seeds. Part 2: Cyperaceae*. Stockholm.

Berggren, G. 1981 *Atlas of seeds. Part 3: Salicaceae–Cruciferae*. Stockholm.

Bernard, W. 1879 Exploration and restoration of the ruin of the Grianan of Aileach. *Proceedings of the Royal Irish Academy*, Series 2, **9,** 415–23.

Bersu, G. 1948 Preliminary report on the excavations at Lissue, 1947. *Ulster Journal of Archaeology* **11,** 131–3.

Bersu, G. and Wilson, D.M. 1966 *Three Viking graves in the Isle of Man*. The Society for Medieval Archaeology Monograph Series **1.** London.

Bertsch, K. 1941 *Früchte und Samen: ein Bestimmungsbuch zur Pflanzenkunde der vorgeschichtlichen Zeit*. Handbücher der praktischen Vorgeschichtsforschung **1.** Stuttgart.

Bhreathnach, E. 2020 Saints' dedications and the ecclesiastical landscape of Hiberno-Norse Dublin: Irish, Scandinavian and others. In S. Duffy (ed.), *Medieval Dublin XVIII*, 143–68. Dublin.

Biddle, M. 1990 Tweezers. In M. Biddle (ed.), *Object and economy in medieval Winchester: Artefacts from medieval Winchester*, vol. 2, 690–92. Winchester Studies **7.** Oxford.

Bigger, F.J. 1925 Ancient brain-balls or sling stones in Ireland. *The Irish Naturalists' Journal* **1** (2), 32–3.

Bill, J. 1994 Iron nails in Iron Age and medieval shipbuilding. In C. Westerdahl (ed.), *Crossroads in Ancient Shipbuilding. Proceedings of the Sixth International Symposium on Boat and Ship Archaeology Roskilde 1991*, 55-63. Oxbow Monograph **40.** Oxford.

Bill, J. 2014 Nails. In I. Russell and M.F. Hurley (eds), *Woodstown: a Viking-age settlement in Co. Waterford*, 141–50. Dublin.

Binchy, D.A. 1938 Bretha Crólige. *Ériu* **12,** 1–77.

Binchy, D.A. 1966 Bretha Déin Chécht. *Ériu* **20,** 1–66.

Blake, H. and Davey, P. (eds) 1983 *Guidelines for the processing and publication of medieval pottery from excavations*. London.

Blomquist, R. 1942 Kammar från Lunds medeltid. *Kulturen 1942*, 133–62. Lund.

Blomquist, R. and Mårtensen, A.W. 1963 *Thulegrävningen 1961*. Acta Archaeologica Lundensia **2.** Lund.

Boardman, S. and Jones, G. 1990 Experiments on the effects of charring on cereal plant components. *Journal of Archaeological Science* **17** (1), 1–11.

Bøe, J. 1940 *Viking antiquities in Great Britain and Ireland. Part III: Norse antiquities in Ireland*. Oslo.

Boessneck, J. 1969 Osteological differences between sheep and goat. In D.R. Brothwell and E. Higgs (eds), *Science in Archaeology: a survey of progress and research*, 331–58. 2nd edition. London.

Bond, J.M. 1996 Burnt offerings: Animal bone in Anglo-Saxon cremations. *World Archaeology* **28,** 76–88.

Borremans, R. and Warginaire, R. 1966 *La céramique d'Andenne: Recherches de 1956–1965*. Rotterdam.

Bourke, C. 2007 The monastery of Saint Mo-Choí of Nendrum: the early medieval finds. In T. McErlean and N. Crothers (eds), *Harnessing the tides. The early medieval tidal mills at Nendrum Monastery, Strangford Lough*, 405–22. Northern Ireland Archaeological Monographs **7.** Belfast.

Bourke, E. 1987 Glass vessels in Ireland, 100–1400 AD. MA thesis, National University of Ireland.

Bourke, E.C. 1988–9 Two eleventh-century Viking houses from Bride Street, Wexford and the layout of properties on the site. *Journal of the Old Wexford Society* **12,** 50–61.

Bourke, E. 1989 Bride St./South Main St., Townparks. In I. Bennett (ed.), *Excavations 1988*, 38–9. Dublin.

Bourke, E. 1994 Glass vessels of the first nine centuries AD in Ireland. *Journal of the Royal Society of Antiquaries of Ireland* **124,** 163–209.

Bourke, E. 1995 Life in the sunny south-east: housing and domestic economy in Viking and medieval Wexford. *Archaeology Ireland* **9** (3), 33–6.

Boyd, R. 2015 Where are the longhouses? Reviewing Ireland's Viking-age buildings. In H.B. Clarke and R. Johnson (eds), *The Vikings in Ireland and beyond: before and after the battle of Clontarf*, 325–45. Dublin.

Boyle, J.W. 2009 The production and use of bone and antler dress pins in early medieval Ireland, *c.* AD 400–800. PhD dissertation, New York University.

Bradley, J. 1991 Excavations at Moynagh Lough, County Meath. *Journal of the Royal Society of Antiquaries of Ireland* **121,** 5–26.

Bradley J. 1992 The topographical development of Scandinavian Dublin. In F.H.A. Aalen and K. Whelan (eds), *Dublin city and county from prehistory to present: studies in honour of J.H. Andrews*, 43–56. Dublin.

Brady, L. 2011 Apples on willow trees: a metaphor for grafting and spiritual succession in the early Irish saints' 'Lives' of Berach and Coemgen. *Proceedings of the Harvard Celtic Colloquium* **31,** 56–73.

Breen, T. 1980 Stray finds of early Christian and medieval date from the greater Dublin area in the National Museum of Ireland. 2 vols. MA thesis, University College Dublin.

British Museum and Amgueddfa Cymru–National Museum Wales. Portable Antiquities Scheme (http://finds.org.uk).

Britnell, W.J. 2000 Small pointed blades. In J.C. Barrett, P.W.M. Freeman and A. Woodward, *Cadbury Castle, Somerset. The later prehistoric and early historic archaeology*, 183–6. English Heritage Archaeological Report **20.** London.

Bronk Ramsey, C. 2000 Comment on 'The use of Bayesian statistics for 14C dates of chronologically ordered samples: a critical analysis'. *Radiocarbon* **42** (2), 199–202.

Bronk Ramsey, C. 2019 OxCal 4.3 Manual (http://c14.arch.ox.ac.uk/oxcalhelp/hlp_contents.html. Updated 25/11/2019).

Brown, D. 1990 Weaving tools. In M. Biddle (ed.), *Object and economy in medieval Winchester: Artefacts from Medieval Winchester*, vol. 2, 225–32. Winchester Studies **7.** Oxford.

Buck, C., Kenworthy, J., Litton, C., and Smith, A. 1991 Combining archaeological and radiocarbon information: a Bayesian approach to calibration. *Antiquity* **65** (249), 808–21.

Buckland, P., Greig, J. and Kenward, H. 1974 York: an early medieval site. *Antiquity* **48** (189), 25–33.

Buckley, L., Cross May, S., Gregory, N., Murray, C., Ó Néill, J., Roche, H. and Stevens, P. 2005 Catalogue of finds. In M. Gowen, J. Ó Néill and M. Phillips (eds), *The Lisheen Mine Archaeological Project 1996-8*, 311–28. Bray.

Byrne, F.J. 2008 The inscriptions in the main passage tomb at Knowth. In F.J Byrne, W. Jenkins, G. Kenny and C. Swift, *Excavations at Knowth 4: Historical Knowth and its hinterland*, 89–119. Dublin.

Byrne, M. 1995 20–25 Castle Street, Dublin 2. In I. Bennett (ed.), *Excavations 1994*, 21–2. Bray.

Byrne, M. 2015 Viking-Age domestic settlement at 26–29 Castle Street, Dublin: a preliminary view based on archaeological excavations. In H.B. Clarke and R. Johnson (eds.), *The Vikings in Ireland and beyond: before and after the battle of Clontarf*, 346–54. Dublin.

Callmer, J. 1977 *Trade beads and bead trade in Scandinavia, c. 800-1000 A.D.* Acta archaeologica Lundensia. Series **4** (11). Bonn.

Campbell, E. 2007 *Continental and Mediterranean imports to Atlantic Britain and Ireland, AD 400-800*. Council for British Archaeology (CBA) Research Report **157.** York.

Cappellini, E., Gilbert, M.T., Geuna, F., Fiorentino, G., Hall, A., Thomas-Oates, J., Ashton, P.D., Ashford, D.A., Arthur, P., Campos, P.F., Kool, J., Willersley, E. and Collins, M.J. 2010 A multidisciplinary study of archaeological grape seeds. *Naturwissenschaften* **97** (2), 205–17 (https://doi.org/10.1007/s00114-009-0629-3).

Cappers, R.T.J. and Bekker, R.M. 2013 *A manual for the identification of plant seeds and fruits*. Groningen.

Cappers, R.T.J. and Neef, R. 2012 *Handbook of plant palaeoecology*. Groningen.

Carey, A. 2014 Stone. In I. Russell and M.F. Hurley (eds), *Woodstown: a Viking-age settlement in Co. Waterford*, 299–320. Dublin.

Carlisle, I. 1998 Man bites leather shock in York. *Archaeological Leather Group Newsletter* **7,** 7.

Carroll, A. and Quinn, M. 2003 Ferrous and non-ferrous artefacts. In R.M. Cleary and M.F. Hurley (eds.), *Cork city excavations 1984-2000*, 257–60. Cork.

Carroll, A. and Quinn, M. 2014 Knives. In M.F. Hurley and C. Brett (eds). *Archaeological excavations at South Main Street 2003-2005*, 164–7. Cork.

Carson, R.A.G. and O'Kelly, C. 1977 A catalogue of the Roman coins from Newgrange, Co. Meath and notes on the coins and related finds. *Proceedings of the Royal Irish Academy* **77**C, 35–55.

Caulfield, S. 1969 The rotary quern in Ireland. MA thesis, University College Dublin.

Charleston, R.J. 1984 *English glass and the glass used in England circa 400–1940*. London.

Cherry, J. 2001 Leather. In J. Blair and N. Ramsey (eds), *English medieval industries: craftsmen, techniques and products*, 295–318. London.

Clapham, A.R., Tutin, T.G. and Moore, D.M. 1987 *Flora of the British Isles*. Cambridge.

Clark, J. 1986 Medieval horseshoes. *Finds Research Group AD 700–1700. Datasheet* **4,** 1–4.

Clark, J. 1995 Bits. In J. Clark (ed.), *The medieval horse and its equipment c.1150–c.1450*, 43–52. London.

Clarke, H.B. 1977 The topographical development of early medieval Dublin. *Journal of the Royal Society of Antiquaries of Ireland* **107,** 29–51.

Clarke H.B. 1990 The topographical development of early medieval Dublin. In H.B. Clarke (ed.), *Medieval Dublin: the making of a metropolis*, 52–69. Dublin.

Clarke, H.B. 2002 *Dublin, Part I, to 1610*. Irish Historic Towns Atlas No. 11. Dublin.

Clarke, H.B. 2020 Foreword. In C. Corlett and M. Potterton (eds), *The town in medieval Ireland in the light of recent archaeological excavations*, vii–viii. Dublin.

Clarke, H.B., Dooley, S. and Johnson, R. 2018 *Dublin and the Viking world*. Dublin.

Clutton-Brock, J. 1984 *Neolithic antler picks from Grimes Graves, Norfolk and Durrington Walls, Wiltshire: a biometrical analysis*. London.

Coffey, G. and Armstrong, E.C.R. 1910 Scandinavian objects found at Island-Bridge and Kilmainham. *Proceedings of the Royal Irish Academy* **28,** 107–22.

Collins, A.E.P., Proudfoot, B. and Smith, A.G. 1959 A trial excavation in Clea Lakes Crannog, Co. Down. *Ulster Journal of Archaeology* **22,** 92–101.

Collins, B. 1988 Environmental archaeological remains from Dublin Castle. *Archaeology Ireland* **2** (4), 150–2.

Comber, M. 2002 M.V. Duignan's excavations at the ringfort of Rathgureen, Co. Galway. *Proceedings of the Royal Irish Academy* **102**C, 137–97.

Comber, M. and Hull, G. 2010 Excavations at Caherconnell cashel, the Burren, Co. Clare: implications for Cashel chronology and Gaelic settlement. *Proceedings of the Royal Irish Academy* **110**C, 133–72.

Comey. M.G. 2010 *Coopers and coopering in Viking Age Dublin*. Medieval Dublin Excavations 1962–81, Series B, vol. 10. Dublin.

Connelly, C.J. 2015 A partial reading of the stones: a comparative analysis of Irish and Scottish ogham pillar stones. MSc thesis, University of Wisconsin-Milwaukee.

Connolly, M. and Coyne, F. 2005 *Underworld. Death and burial in Cloghermore cave, Co. Kerry*. Bray.

Conway, M. 1999 *Director's first findings from excavations in Cabinteely*. Margaret Gowen and Company Transactions **1.** Dublin.

Conwell, E.A. 1866 Examination of the ancient sepulchral cairns on the Loughcrew hills, Co. Meath. *Proceedings of the Royal Irish Academy*, Series 1, **9,** 355–79.

Cooke, J. 1903 *Wakeman's handbook of Irish antiquities*. 3rd edition. Dublin.

Cooney, G. and Mandal, S. 1998 *The Irish Stone Axe Project*. Monograph **1.** Dublin

Cornish, J.M. 2015 *A guide to ceramic building materials: an insight report*. York.

Cotter, C. 2013 *The Western Stone Forts Project: Excavations at Dún Aonghasa and Dún Eoghanachta*. Vol. 3. University of York Archaeology Data Service (E-publication).

Coughlan, T. 2000 The Anglo-Norman houses of Dublin: evidence from Back Lane. In S. Duffy (ed.), *Medieval Dublin I*, 203–33. Dublin.

Coulter, C. 2015 Consumers and artisans: marketing and amber and jet in the early medieval British Isles. In G. Hansen, S. Ashby and I. Baug (eds), *Everyday products in the Middle Ages: crafts, consumption and the individual in northern Europe c. AD 800–1600*, 110–24. Oxford.

Crone, A. and Barber, J. 1981 Analytical techniques for the investigation of non-artefactual wood from prehistoric and medieval sites. *Proceedings of the Society of Antiquaries of Scotland*, **111,** 510–5.

Crone, A. and Campbell, E. 2005 *A crannóg of the first millennium AD. Excavations by Jack Scott at Loch Glashan, Argyll, 1960*. Edinburgh.

Cropper, C. 2014 Glass. in I. Russell and M.F. Hurley (eds), *Woodstown: a Viking-age settlement in Co. Waterford*, 282–5. Dublin.

Crowfoot, G.M. 1945 The bone 'gouges' of Maiden Castle and other sites. *Antiquity* **19,** 157–8.

Culliton J.A. 1987 City Hall, Dublin. *Dublin Historical Record* **41** (1), 2–15.

Curle, C.L. 1982 *Pictish and Norse finds from the Brough of Birsay 1934–74*. Society of Antiquaries of Scotland Monograph **1.** Edinburgh.

Curriculum Development Unit 1978 *Viking settlement to medieval Dublin. Daily life 840–1540*. Dublin.

Davey, N. 1961 *A history of building materials*. London.

Davidson, A. 1999 *The Oxford companion to food*. Oxford.

Deforce, K., Brinkkemper, O., van Haaster, H. and Van Waijjen, M. 2018 Small things can make a big difference: a comparison of pollen and macrobotanical records of some food plants from medieval and post-medieval cesspits in the Netherlands and northern Belgium. *Vegetation History and Archaeobotany* **28** (4), 433–45.

De Neergarrd, M. 1987 The use of knives, shears scissors and scabbards. In M. Cowgill, M. de Neergarrd and N. Griffiths (eds), *Knives and scabbards. Medieval finds from excavations in London*, 51–61. London.

Dillon, F. 1997 Lithic assemblage. In G. Eogan and H. Roche (eds), *Excavations at Knowth, volume 2*, 33–7. Dublin.

Doyle, M. 2014 Dress and ornament in early medieval Ireland-exploring the evidence. In B. Kelly, N. Roycroft and M. Stanley (eds), *Fragments of lives past: archaeological objects from Irish road schemes*, 67–80. Dublin.

Duffy, P. 2014 Seagrange Road, Baldoyle, Dublin. *Excavations.ie: Database of Irish Excavation Reports* (http://www.excavations.ie/report/2014/Dublin/0024015/; accessed 27 /11/ 2017).

Duffy, P. 2016 The church of Bearach, the grange of Baldoyle and the town of the dark stranger. In S. Duffy (ed.), *Medieval Dublin XV*, 89–118. Dublin.

Duffy, S. 2022 The medieval period. In S. Duffy, J. Montague, K. Mulligan and M. O'Neill, *Dublin Castle: from fortress to palace. Volume 1: Vikings to Victorians: a history of Dublin Castle to 1850*, 3–73. Dublin.

Duffy, S. Montague, J., Mulligan, K. and O'Neill, M. 2022 *Dublin Castle: from fortress to palace. Volume 1: Vikings to Victorians: a history of Dublin Castle to 1850*. Dublin.

Dunlevy, M. 1988 A classification of early Irish combs. *Proceedings of the Royal Irish Academy* **88**C, 341–422.

Düwel, K. and Tempel, W.D. 1970 Knochenkämme mit Runeninschriften aus Friesland. *Palaeohistoria* **14,** 353–91.

Dye, T.S. 2016 Long-term rhythms in the development of Hawaiian social stratification. *Journal of Archaeological Science* **71,** 1–9.

Eames, E.S. and Fanning, T. 1988 *Irish medieval tiles*. Dublin.

Earwood, C. 1993 *Domestic wooden artefacts in Britain and Ireland from Neolithic to Viking times*. Exeter.

Edwards, C.J., Suchard, M.A., Lemey, P., Welch, J.J., Barnes, I., Fulton, T.L., Barnett, R., O'Connell, T.C., Coxon, P., Monaghan, N., Valdiosera, C.E., Lorenzen, E.D., Willerslev, E., Baryshnikov, G.F., Rambaut, A., Thomas, M.G., Bradley, D.G., Shapiro, B. 2011 Ancient hybridization and an Irish origin for the modern polar bear matriline. *Current Biology* **21,** 1251–8.

Edwards, N. 1996 *The archaeology of early medieval Ireland*. London.

Egan, G. and Pritchard, F. 2002 *Dress accessories c.1150–c.1450: medieval finds from excavations in London*. Woodbridge.

Eogan, G. 2012 *Excavations at Knowth 5: The archaeology of Knowth in the first and second millennia AD*. Dublin.

Fanning, T. 1970 The Viking grave-goods discovered near Larne, Co. Antrim, in 1840. *Journal of the Royal Society of Antiquaries of Ireland* **100,** 71–8.

Fanning, T. 1994 *The Viking Age ringed pins from Dublin*. Medieval Dublin Excavations 1962–81, Series B, vol. 4. Dublin.

Fitter, A 1987 *Collins new generation guide to the wild flowers of Britain and northern Europe*. London.

FitzGerald, M. 2000 Textile production in prehistoric and early medieval Ireland. PhD thesis, Manchester Metropolitan University.

FitzGerald, M. 2012 Textile production. In G. Eogan, *Excavations at Knowth 5: the archaeology of Knowth in the first and second millennia AD*, 552–63. Dublin.

Fitzsimmons, L. 2020 Trinity researchers sequence genomes of Irish Vikings and uncover Norwegian origins. (http://www.Trinitynews.ie/2020/09).

Forbes, R.J. 1966 *Studies in ancient technologies*. Leiden.

Ford, B. 1987 Iron objects. In P. Holdsworth (ed.), *Excavations in the medieval burgh of Perth 1979-81*, 130–40. Edinburgh.

Forsyth, K. 1995 The ogham-inscribed spindle-whorl from Buckquoy: evidence for the Irish language in pre-Viking Orkney? *Proceedings of the Society of Antiquaries of Scotland* **125,** 677–96.

Forsyth, K. 2012 Ogham-inscribed plaque. In N. Sharples (ed.), *A Late Iron Age farmstead in the Outer Hebrides. Excavations at Mound 1, Bornais, South Uist*, 271–3. Oxford.

Foster, H.E., Jackson, C.M. 2009 The composition of 'naturally coloured' late Roman vessel glass from Britain and the implications for models of glass production and supply. *Journal of Archaeoogical Science.* **36** (2), 189–204 (https://doi.org/10.1016/j.jas.2008.08.008).

Fox, C.L., Juan, J. and Albert, R.M. 1996 Phytolith analysis on dental calculus, enamel surface, and burial soil: Information about diet and paleoenvironment. *American Journal of Physical Anthropology* **101,** 101–13.

Foy, D., Picon, M., Vichy, M., Thirion-Merle, V. 2003 Caractérisation des verres de la fin de l'Antiquité en Méditerranée occidentale: l'émergence de nouveaux courants commerciaux. In *Échanges et commerce du verre dans le monde Antique. Actes du colloque de l'Association Française pour l'Archéologie du Verre, Aix-en-Provence et Marseille (7–9 juin 2001)*, 41–86. Montagnac.

Freestone, I.C. 2003 Primary glass sources in the mid-first millennium A.D. In *Annales du 15e Congres de l'Association Internationale pour l'Histoire du Verre*, 111–5. Association Internationale pour l'Histoire du Verre, Nottingham.

Freestone, I.C. 2004 The provenance of ancient glass through compositional analysis. *MRS Online Proceedings Library* **852,** 188–201 (https://doi.org/10.1557/PROC-852-OO8.1).

Freestone, I.C. 2015 The recycling and reuse of Roman glass: analytical approaches. *Journal of Glass Studies* **57,** 29–40.

Freestone, I.C., Gorin-Rosen, Y. and Hughes, M.J. 2000 Composition of primary glass from Israel and the production of glass in late antiquity and the early Islamic period. In M.D. Nenna (ed.), *La Route du Verre: Ateliers primaires et secondaires de verriers du second millénaire av. J.-C. au Moyen-Âge*, 65–88. Travaux de la Maison l'Orient Méditerranéen **33.** Lyon.

Fulford, M. Handley, M. and Clark, A. 2000 An early date for ogham: the Silchester ogham rehabilitated. *Medieval Archaeology* **44,** 1–24.

Gahan, A. and McCutcheon, C. 1997 The medieval pottery. In M.F. Hurley, O.M.B. Scully with S.W.J. McCutcheon, *Late Viking age and medieval Waterford: excavations 1986–1992*, 285–336. Waterford.

Gaskell-Brown, C. and Harper, A.E.T. 1984 Excavations on Cathedral Hill, Armagh, 1968. *Ulster Journal of Archaeology* **47**, 109–61.

Geraghty, S. 1996 *Viking Dublin: botanical evidence from Fishamble Street. Medieval Dublin Excavations 1962–81.* Series C, vol. 2. Dublin.

Gilbert J.T. 1859 *A history of the city of Dublin.* Vol. 2. Dublin.

Gilligan, N. 2015 Archaeobotanical analysis of charred plant remains. Seagrange Road, Baldoyle, Co. Dublin. Unpublished report for Grassroots Archaeology.

Godwin, H. 1975 *The history of the British flora: a factual basis for phytogeography.* 2nd edition. Cambridge.

Goodall, I.H. 1990a. Shears and scissors. In M. Biddle (ed.), *Object and economy in medieval Winchester: Artefacts from Medieval Winchester,* vol. 2, 861–3. Winchester Studies **7.** Oxford.

Goodall, I.H. 1990b Knives. In M. Biddle (ed.), *Object and economy in medieval Winchester: Artefacts from Medieval Winchester*, vol. 2, 835–60. Winchester Studies **7.** Oxford.

Goodall, I.H. 1990c Locks and keys. In M. Biddle (ed.), *Object and economy in medieval Winchester: Artefacts from Medieval Winchester*, vol. 2, 1001–36. Winchester Studies **7.** Oxford.

Goodall, I.H. 1990d Tanning, currying and leather-working tools In M. Biddle (ed.), *Object and economy in medieval Winchester: Artefacts from Medieval Winchester*, vol.2, 247–50. Winchester Studies **7.** Oxford.

Goodall, I. H. 1990e Building ironwork. In M. Biddle (ed.), *Object and economy in medieval Winchester: Artefacts from Medieval Winchester*, vol.2, 328–49. Winchester Studies **7.** Oxford.

Goodall, I.H. 2011 *Ironwork in Medieval Britain: an archaeological study.* Society for Medieval Archaeology Monograph **31.** Abington.

Goret, J.-F. 2009 Les outils en os du haut Moyen Âge. État de la question et présentation d'une expérience en cours. In F. Gentili and A. Lefèvre, *L'habitat rural du haut Moyen Âge en Île-de-France*, 79–92. Guiry-en-Vexin.

Goubitz, O. 2001 *Stepping through time: archaeological footwear from prehistoric times until 1800.* Zwolle.

Gowen, M. 1992 Excavation of two souterrain complexes at Marshes Upper, Dundalk, Co. Louth. *Proceedings of the Royal Irish Academy* **92**C, 55–121.

Gowen M. 2001 Excavations at the site of the church and tower of St Michael le Pole, Dublin. In S. Duffy (ed.), *Medieval Dublin II*, 13–53. Dublin.

Gowen, M. with Scally, G. 1996 *A summary report on excavations at Exchange Street Upper/Parliament Street, Dublin.* Temple Bar Archaeological Report no. 4. Dublin.

Gowen, M., Simpson, L., McGarry, C., Edden, L., Greene, S. and Ní Mhearáin, Ú. 2004 *Dublin city walls and defences: conservation plan.* Dublin.

Graham-Campbell, J. 1980 *Viking artefacts. A select catalogue.* London.

Graham-Campbell, J. (ed.) 1992 *Viking treasure from the north west: the Cuerdale hoard in its context.* Liverpool.

Grant, A. 1975a The animal bones. In B. Cunliffe (ed.), *Excavations at Portchester Castle, Vol. 1: Roman*, 378–408. London.

Grant, A. 1975b Appendix B: The use of tooth wear as a guide to the age of domestic animals. In B. Cunliffe (ed.), *Excavations at Portchester Castle, Vol. 1: Roman*, 437–50. London.

Gräslund, A.-S. 1973 Barn i Birka. *Tor* **15,** 161–79.

Graves, Rev. J. 1856 Proceedings and papers. *Journal of the Kilkenny and South-East of Ireland Archaeological Society.* New series **1**(1), 147–69.

Greig, J. 1982 Garderobes, cesspits, sewers and latrines. *Current Archaeology* **8,** 49–61.

Grew, F.O. 1987 Introduction. In M. Cowgill, M. de Neergarrd and N. Griffiths (eds), *Knives and scabbards. Medieval finds from excavations in London*, 51–61. London.

Griffin, L.C. and Rowlett, R.M. 1981 A 'lost' Viking cereal grain. *Journal of Ethnobiology* **1** (2), 200–7.

Griffiths, D. 2010 *Vikings of the Irish Sea. Conflict and assimilation AD 790–1050.* Dublin.

Grimm, O. 2014 Bear-skins in northern European burials and some remarks on other bear-related furnishings in the north and middle of Europe in the 1st millennium AD. In O. Grimm, U. Schmölcke (eds), *Hunting in Northern Europe until 1500 AD. Old traditions and regional developments, continental sources and continental influences*, 277–96. Neumünster.

Guido, M. 1978 *The glass beads of the prehistoric and Roman periods in Britain and Ireland.* Report of the Research Committee of the Society of Antiquaries of London **35.** London.

Gustafsson, N.B. 2009 Vikingatida blästerskydd av sten och lera från Mälardalen. (Viking period bellows shields made of stone and clay from the Lake Mälaren area.) *Fornvännen* **104** (4), 253–61.

Gutiérrez, A. 2007 Portuguese coarsewares in early modern England: reflections on an exceptional pottery assemblage from Southampton. *Post-Medieval Archaeology* **41**(1), 64–79.

Hagen, A. 1992 *A handbook of Anglo-Saxon food processing and consumption.* Pinner.

Hagen, A. 2010 *Anglo-Saxon food and drink: production, processing, distribution and consumption.* Ely, Cambridgeshire.

Hald, M. 1972 *Primitive shoes: an archaeological-ethnographical study based upon shoe finds from the Jutland Peninsula.* Copenhagen.

Hall, A.R. and Kenward, H.K. 2004 Setting people in their environment: plant and animal remains from Anglo-Scandinavian York. In R.A. Hall, D.W. Rollason, D.W.M. Blackburn, D.N. Parsons, G. Fellows-Jensen, A.R. Hall, H.K. Kenward, T.P. O'Connor, D. Tweddle, A.J. Mainman and N.S.H. Rogers, *Aspects of Anglo-Scandinavian York.* The Archaeology of York: Anglo-Scandinavian York **8** (4), 372–426. York.

Hall, A.R., Kenward, H.K., Williams, D. and Greig, J.R.A 1983 *Environment and living conditions at two Anglo-Scandinavian sites.* The Archaeology of York: the past environment of York **14** (4). York.

Hall, R. 1990 *Viking age archaeology in Britain and Ireland.* Princes Risborough.

Hall, R.A. 1996 'A dashing old blade' (old saws). *Archaeology in York* **21** (1) 20–7.

Hall, R.A. 2007 *Exploring the world of the Vikings.* London.

Hallén, Y. 1994 The use of bone and antler at Foshigarry and Bac Mhic Connain, two Iron Age sites on North Uist, Western Isles. *Proceedings of the Society of Antiquaries of Scotland* **124,** 189–232.

Halpin, A. 2000 *The port of medieval Dublin. Archaeological excavations at the Civic Offices, Winetavern Street, Dublin, 1993.* Dublin.

Halpin, A. 2005 Development phases in Hiberno-Norse Dublin: a tale of two cities. In S. Duffy (ed.), *medieval Dublin VI*, 94–113. Dublin.

Halpin. A. 2008 *Weapons and warfare in Viking and Medieval Dublin.* Medieval Dublin Excavations 1962–81. Series B, vol. 9. Dublin.

Halpin. A. 2010 Weapons and warfare in Viking-Age Ireland. In J. Sheehan and D. Ó Corráin (eds), *The Viking Age: Ireland and the west. Proceedings of the Fifteenth Viking Congress*, 124–35. Dublin.

Hamilton, J.R.C. 1956 *Excavations at Jarlshof, Shetland.* Ministry of Works Archaeological Reports **1.** London.

Hansson, A.-M. 1994 Grain-paste, porridge and bread. Ancient cereal-based food. *Laborativ Arkeologie* (Journal of Nordic Archaeological Science) **7**, 5–20.

Hansson, A.-M. 1996 Bread in Birka and on Björkö. *Laborativ Arkeologie* (Journal of Nordic Archaeological Science) **9**, 61–78.

Harde, K 1984 *A field guide in colour to beetles.* London.

Harper, A.E.T. 1973/4 The excavation of a rath in Crossnacreevy Townland, County Down. *Ulster Journal of Archaeology* **36/37,** 32–41.

Harrison, S. 2014a Discussion of the Viking burial. In I. Russell and M.F. Hurley (eds), *Woodstown: a Viking-age settlement in Co. Waterford*, 90–102. Dublin.

Harrison, S. 2014b Weapons and grave-goods. In I. Russell and M.F. Hurley (eds), *Woodstown: a Viking-age settlement in Co. Waterford*, 155–71. Dublin.

Harrison, S. and Ó Floinn, R. 2014 *Viking graves in Ireland: a catalogue of furnished Viking age burials and their content.* Medieval Dublin Excavations 1962–81. Series B, vol. 11. Dublin.

Hartnett, P.J. and and Eogan, G. 1964 Feltrim Hill, Co. Dublin: a Neolithic and Early Christian site. *Journal of the Royal Society of Antiquaries of Ireland* **94,** 1–37.

Harvey, P. 2014 Amber. In I. Russell and M.F. Hurley (eds), *Woodstown: a Viking-age settlement in Co. Waterford*, 285–7. Dublin.

Hayden, A. 2000 West side story: archaeological excavations at Cornmarket and Bridge Street Upper, Dublin–a summary account. In S. Duffy (ed.), *Medieval Dublin I*, 84–116. Dublin.

Hayden, A. 2002 The excavation of pre-Norman defences and houses at Werburgh Street, Dublin: a summary. In S. Duffy (ed.), *Medieval Dublin III*, 44–68. Dublin.

Heckett, E. 1987 Some Hiberno-Norse head coverings from Fishamble Street and St John's Lane, Dublin. *Textile History* **18** (2), 159–74.

Heege, A. 2002 *Einbeck im Mittelalter. Eine archäologisch-historische Spurensuche.* Studien zur Einbecker Geschichte, **17.** Oldenburg.

Hencken, H. O'N. 1936 Ballinderry Crannog No. 1. *Proceedings of the Royal Irish Academy* **43**C, 103–239.

Hencken, H. O'N. 1938 *Cahercommaun: a stone fort in County Clare.* Extra volume of the Royal Society of Antiquaries of Ireland. Dublin.

Hencken H.O'N. 1942 Ballinderry Crannog No.2. *Proceedings of the Royal Irish Academy* **47**C, 1–76.

Hencken, H. O'N. 1950 Lagore Crannog: an Irish royal residence of the 7th to 10th centuries AD. *Proceedings of the Royal Irish Academy* **53**C, 1–247.

Henderson, J. 1984 The glass. In R. Ivens, Movilla Abbey, Newtownards, County Down: excavations 1981. *Ulster Journal. of Archaeology* **47**, 71–108.

Henderson, J. 1988 The nature of the Early Christian glass industry in Ireland: evidence from Dunmisk Fort, Co. Tyrone. *Ulster Journal of Archaeology* **51,** 115–26.

Henderson, J. 2000 The production technology of Irish Early Christian glass with specific reference to beads and enamels. In J. Price (ed.), *Glass in Britain and Ireland AD 350-1100*. British Museum Occasional Paper **127,** 143–61. London.

Hennessy, W.M. (ed. and tr.) 1866 *Chronicum Scotorum: a chronical of Irish affairs from the earliest times to A.D. 1135, with a supplement containing the events from 1141 to 1150*. London.

Henry, P. 1999 Development and change in late Saxon textile production: an analysis of the evidence. *Durham Archaeological Journal* **14–15,** 69–76.

Herbig, C. and Maier, U. 2011 Flax for oil or fibre? Morphometric analysis of flax seeds and new aspects of flax cultivation in Late Neolithic wetland settlements in southwest Germany. *Vegetation History and Archaeobotany* **20** (6), 527–33.

Hillman, G. 1981 Crop husbandry practices from charred remains. In R. Mercer (ed.), *Farming practice in British prehistory*, 123–62. Edinburgh.

Hjelmqvist, H. 1984 Botanische analyse einiger brote. In G. Ardwidsson (ed.), *Birka II, I. Systematische Analysen der Gräberfunde*, 261–72. Stockholm.

Hobbs, CJ. 1984 Skull fracture and the diagnosis of abuse. *Archives of Disease in Childhood* **59,** 246–52.

Hodkinson, B. 1987 A reappraisal of the archaeological evidence for weaving in Ireland in the early Christian period. *Ulster Journal of Archaeology* **50,** 47–53.

Hodkinson. B. 2015 Viking Limerick and its hinterland. In H.B. Clarke and R. Johnson (eds), *The Vikings in Ireland and beyond: before and after the battle of Clontarf*, 183–8. Dublin.

Holck P. 2006 The Oseberg ship burial, Norway: new thoughts on the skeletons from the grave mound. *European Journal of Archaeology* **9** (2–3), 185–210.

Holm, P. 1986 The slave trade of Dublin, ninth to twelfth centuries. *Peritia* **5,** 313–45.

Hughes, J. Coughlan, J., O'Mahony, D. and Stevens, P. 2018 Stratigraphic report for City Square Shopping Centre, Arundel Square, Sully's Lane, Peter Street, Waterford (licence ref. 16E0601). Unpublished preliminary excavation report for Irish Archaeological Consultancy Ltd.

Hull, V. (ed. and trans.) 1938 *Aided Meidbe*: the violent death of Medb. *Speculum* **13,** 52–61.

Hunter, F. 2008 Jet and related materials in Viking Scotland. *Medieval Archaeology* **52,** 103–17.

Hunter, F. 2016 'Coal money' from Portpatrick (south-west Scotland): reconstructing an early medieval craft centre from antiquarian finds. In F. Hunter and A. Sheridan (eds), *Ancient Lives. Objects, people and place in early Scotland. Essays for David V. Clarke on his 70th Birthday*, 281–302. Leiden.

Hunter, F. and Sheridan, A. 2014 Lignite, oil shale and cannel coal artefacts. In I. Russell and M.F. Hurley (eds), *Woodstown: a Viking-age settlement in Co. Waterford*, 320–3. Dublin.

Hunter, F.J., McDonnell, J.G., Pollard, A.M., Morris, C.R. and Rowlands, C. 1993 The scientific identification of archaeological jet-like artefacts. *Archaeometry* **35,** 69–89.

Hunterian Museum, Glasgow (https://www.gla.ac.uk/hunterian accessed 30/10/ 2017).

Hurley, M.F. 1988 Recent archaeological excavations in Waterford city. *Archaeology Ireland* **2** (1), 17–21.

Hurley, M.F. 1995 The Vikings in Munster – evidence from Waterford and Cork. *Archaeology Ireland* **9** (3), 23–5.

Hurley, M.F. 1997a The defences. In M.F. Hurley, O.M.B. Scully with S.W.J. McCutcheon, *Late Viking-age and medieval Waterford: excavations 1986–1992*, 20–33. Waterford.

Hurley, M.F. 1997b Artefacts of skeletal material. In M.F. Hurley, O.M.B. Scully with S.W.J. McCutcheon, *Late Viking-age and medieval Waterford: excavations 1986–1992*, 650–99. Waterford.

Hurley, M.F. 2003 Artefacts of skeletal material. In R.M. Cleary and M.F. Hurley, *Excavations in Cork city 1984–2000*, 329–48. Cork.

Hurley, M.F. 2014a Discussion and conclusions. In I. Russell and M.F. Hurley (eds), *Woodstown: A Viking Age settlement in Co. Waterford*, 347–57. Dublin.

Hurley, M. F. 2014b Knives. In M.F. Hurley and C. Brett (eds), *Archaeological excavations at South Main Street [Cork] 2003–2005*, 372–3. Cork.

Hurley, M.F. and Brett, C. (eds) 2014 *Archaeological excavations at South Main Street [Cork] 2003-2005*. Cork.

Hurley, M.F. and McCutcheon, S.W.J. 1997 Wooden artefacts. In M.F. Hurley, O.M.B. Scully with S.W.J. McCutcheon, *Late Viking Age and medieval Waterford: excavations 1986–1992*, 553–634. Waterford.

Hurst, J.G., Neal, D.S. and van Beuningen, H.J.E. 1986 *Pottery produced and traded in North West Europe 1350–1650*. Rotterdam.

Jackson, K.H. 2011 *The oldest Irish tradition: a window on the Iron Age*. Cambridge.

Jankuhn, H. 1943 *Die Ausgrabungen in Haithabu, 1937–9*. Berlin-Dahlem.

Jensen, S., Flemming, B. and Fredsgaard Nielsen, R. 1991 *The Vikings of Ribe*. Ribe, Denmark.

Jensenius, J. 2000 Research in medieval Norwegian wooden churches. Relevance of available sources. *Nordisk arkitekturforskning* **4,** 7–23.

Johnson, C. 2014 Ferrous and non-ferrous metal. In I. Russell and M.F. Hurley (eds), *Woodstown: a Viking-age settlement in Co. Waterford*, 115–25. Dublin.

Johnson, C.E. 2019 A comparative study of portable inscribed objects from Britain and Ireland, AD 400–1100. Vol. 1: text. PhD thesis, University of Glasgow.

Johnson, R. 2004 *Viking Age Dublin*. Dublin.

Johnston, P. 2018 Analysis of Carbonised Plant Remains, City Square Shopping Centre, Arundel Square, Sully's Lane and Peter Street, Waterford (licence no.16E0601). Unpublished technical report for Irish Archaeological Consultancy.

Jones, S., Taylor, J. and Ash, F. 2004 *Seed identification handbook. Agriculture, horticulture and weeds*. 2nd edition. Cambridge.

Jonuks, T. 2017 Bronze tooth pendants from the Late Iron Age: between real and fictional zooarchaeology. *Norwegian Archaeological Review* **50,** 135–48.

Jonuks, T. and Rannamäe, E. 2018 Animals and worldviews: a diachronic approach to tooth and bone pendants from the Mesolithic to the Medieval period in Estonia. In A. Livarda, R. Madgwick, S.R. Mora (eds), *The bioarchaeology of ritual and religion*, 162–78. Oxford.

Joyce, P.W. 1906 *A smaller social history of ancient Ireland*. London. (https://www.libraryireland.com/SocialHistoryAncientIreland/I-III-4.php, accessed 3/2/ 2019).

Kaminska, J. and Nahlik, A. 1958 Wlokiennictwo Gdanskie w X-X111 wieku. *Acta Archaeologica Universitatis Lodziensia* **6.** Lodz.

Karg, S. and Robinson, D.E. 2002 Secondary food plants from medieval sites in Denmark: fruits, nuts, vegetables, herbs and spices. In K. Viklund and R. Engelmark (eds), Nordic Archaeobotany–NAG 2000 in Umeå, 133–42. *Archaeology and Environment* **15.** University of Umeå (Sweden).

Katz, N.J., Katz, S.V. and Kipiani, M.G. 1965 *Atlas and keys of fruits and seeds occurring in the Quaternary deposits of the USSR*. Moscow.

Kavanagh, J. 2007 4–8 Church Street, Finglas. In I. Bennett (ed.), *Excavations 2004*, 139–40. Dublin.

Kavanagh, R. 1988 The horse in Viking Ireland. In J. Bradley (ed.), *Settlement and society in medieval Ireland*, 89–121. Kilkenny.

Kavánová, B. 1995 Knochen- und Geweihindustrie in Mikulčice. In F. Daim and L. Poláček (eds), *Studien zum Burgwall von Mikulčice*, 113–378. Band 1. Brno (Czech Republic).

Kearns, T., Martinón-Torres, M. and Rehren, T. 2010 Metal to mould: alloy identification in experimental casting moulds using XRF. *Historical Metallurgy* **44** (1), 48–58.

Kelleher, H. 2004 Washington Street, Cork. In I. Bennett (ed.), *Excavations 2002*, 73. Dublin.

Kelleher, H. 2007 35–39 Main Street, South, Cork. In I. Bennett (ed.), *Excavations 2004*, 52–3. Dublin.

Kelly, E.P. 1986 Ringed pins of County Louth. *Journal of the County Louth Archaeological and Historical Society* **21** (2), 179–99.

Kelly, E.P. 2010 The Vikings in Connemara. In J. Sheehan and D. Ó Corráin (eds), *The Viking Age: Ireland and the west. Proceedings of the Fifteenth Viking Congress*, 174–87. Dublin.

Kelly, F. 1988 *A guide to early Irish law*. Early Irish Law series **3.** Dublin.

Kelly, F. 2000 *Early Irish farming: a study based mainly on the law-texts of the 7th and 8th centuries AD*. Early Irish Law series **4.** Dublin.

Kenward, H.K., Hall, A.R. and Carrott, J. 2000 Environment, activity and living conditions at Deer Park Farms: evidence from plant and invertebrate remains. Reports from the Environmental Archaeology Unit, York 2000/57. York.

King, H.A. 2008 An ogham-inscribed antler handle from Clonmacnoise. *Peritia* **20,** 315–22.

Kirkinen, T. 2017 'Burning pelts'–brown bear skins in the Iron Age and early medieval (1–1300 AD) burials in south-eastern Fennoscandia. *Estonian Journal of Archaeology* **21,** 3–29.

Kivisalo, N. 2008 The Late Iron Age bear-tooth pendants in Finland: symbolic mediators between women, bears and wilderness? *Temenos* **44** (2), 263–91.

Knudson, K. J., O'Donnabhain, B., Carver, C., Cleland, R. and Price, T.D. 2012 Migration and Viking Dublin: paleomobility and paleodiet through isotopic analyses. *Journal of Archaeological Science* **39** (2), 308–20.

Kontrovitz, M. and Snyder, S.W. 2008 Ostracods and foraminifera from two Viking sites in Dublin. *The Irish Naturalists' Journal* **29,** 58–9.

Kosiba, S.B., Tykot, R.H. and Carlsson, D. 2007 Stable isotopes as indicators of change in the food procurement and food preference of Viking Age and Early Christian populations on Gotland (Sweden). *Journal of Anthropological Archaeology* **26** (3), 394–411.

Kossack, G. 1954 Pferdegeschirr aus Gräbern der älteren Hallstattzeit Bayerns. *Jahrbuch der Römisch-Germanischen Zentralmuseums Mainz*, vol. 1, 111–78.

Kurisoo, T. 2018 Late Iron Age pendants (800–1250 AD) in the north-eastern Baltic Sea region: adorning, self-definition, religion. PhD thesis, University of Kiel.

Laing, L. 2006 *The archaeology of Celtic Britain and Ireland c. AD 400–1200*. Cambridge.

Lang, J.T. 1988 *Viking-age decorated wood. A study of its ornament and style*. Medieval Dublin Excavations 1962–81. Series B, vol. 1. Dublin.

Lanigan, H. 1964 Jet bracelets in Ireland: rings of fossil wood. MA thesis, National University of Ireland, Dublin.

Lecler, E and Calderoni. P. 1999 Le Moyen Age et l'époque moderne. In N. Roy (ed.), *Pots de terre, fragments d'histoire*, 50–86. Rouen.

Lehmkuhl, U. 1982 Archäozoologische und typologische Untersuchungen an durchlochten Schweinemetapodien von slawischen Fundplätzen in Mecklenburg. *Bodendenkmalpflege in Mecklenburg* **30,** 199–222.

Lindblom, K.G. 1940 *The sling, especially in Africa: additional notes to a previous paper*. Statens Etnografiska Museum. Smärre Meddelanden **17.** Lund and Stockholm.

Lindstrom, M. 1982 Medieval textile finds in Lund. In L. Bender Jørgensen and K. Tidow (eds), *Textilsymposium Neumünster, Archäologische Textilfunde*, 179–191. Neumünster.

Lionard, P. 1960–61 Early Irish grave-slabs. *Proceedings of the Royal Irish Academy* **61**C, 95–170.

Liversage, G.D. 1968 Excavations at Dalkey Island, Co. Dublin, 1956–1959. *Proceedings of the Royal Irish Academy*, **66**C, 53–233.

Locatelli, M., Coïsson, J.D., Travaglia, F., Bordiga, M. and Arlorio, M. 2015 Impact of roasting on identification of hazelnut (*Corylus avellana* L.) origin: a chemometric approach. *Journal of Agricultural and Food Chemistry* **63** (32), 294–303.

Lodwick, L.A. 2017 Agricultural innovations at a Late Iron Age oppidum: archaeobotanical evidence for flax, food and fodder from Calleva Atrebatum, UK. *Quaternary International*, **460,** 198–219.

Lorenzen, E. 1971 Textilier (vaevninger, net, snor). In H. Hellmuth Andersen, P.J. Crabb and H.J. Madsen, *Århus Søndervold, en byarkaeologisk undersøgelse*. Jysk arkaeologiske selskabs skrifter, bind IX, 247–50. Copenhagen.

Lucas, A.T. 1956 Footwear in Ireland. *Journal of the County Louth Archaeological Society* **13** (4), 309–94.

Lucas, A.T. 1973 National Museum of Ireland: archaeological acquisitions in the year 1970. *Journal of the Royal Society of Antiquaries of Ireland* **103,** 177–213.

Lynch, A. and Manning, C. 1990 Dublin Castle: the archaeological project. *Archaeology Ireland* **4** (2), 65–8.

Lynch, A. and Manning, C. 2001 Excavations at Dublin Castle, 1985–7. In S. Duffy (ed.), *Medieval Dublin II*, 169–204. Dublin.

Lynch, A., Manning, C. and Wiggins, K. forthcoming a *Dublin Castle: from fortress to palace. Volume 3, part 1: Medieval and post-medieval archaeology: the sites.*

Lynch, A., Manning, C. and Wiggins, K. forthcoming b *Dublin Castle: from fortress to palace. Volume 3, part 2: Medieval and post-medieval archaeology: the finds and specialist reports.*

Lyons, S. 2015 Food plants, fruits and foreign foodstuffs: the archaeological evidence from urban medieval Ireland. *Proceedings of the Royal Irish Academy* **115**C, 111–66.

Mac Airt, S. and Mac Niocaill, G. (eds and trans) 1983 *The Annals of Ulster, to AD 1131*. Dublin.

Macalister R.A.S. 1945 *Corpus Inscriptionum Insularum Celticarum*. vol.1. Dublin.

Macalister, R.A.S. and Praeger, R.L. 1931 The excavation of an ancient structure on the townland of Togherstown, Co. Westmeath. *Proceedings of the Royal Irish Academy* **39**C, 54–83.

MacGregor, A. 1974 The Broch of Burrian, North Ronaldsay, Orkney. *Proceedings of the Society of Antiquaries of Scotland* **105,** 63–118.

MacGregor, A. 1985 *Bone, antler, ivory and horn. The technology of skeletal materials since the Roman period*. London.

MacGregor, A., Mainman, A. and Rogers, N.S.H. 1999 *Bone, antler, ivory and horn from Anglo-Scandinavian and medieval York*. The Archaeology of York. The Small Finds **17** (12). York.

Magnus, B. 2003 The importance of amber in the Viking period in the Nordic countries. In C.W. Beck, I.B. Loze and J.M. Todd (eds), *Amber in archaeology. Proceedings of the Fourth International Conference on Amber in Archaeology, Talsi 2001*, 126–38. Riga (Latvia).

Mainman, A.J. 2000 Amber working. In A.J. Mainman and N.S.H. Rogers, *The archaeology of York. the small finds: craft, industry and everyday life: finds from Anglo-Scandinavian York*, 2500–17. The Small Finds, **17** (14). York.

Mainman, A.J. and Rogers, N.S.H. 2000 *Craft, industry and everyday life: Finds from Anglo-Scandinavian York*. The Archaeology of York. The Small Finds **17** (14). York.

Mälarstedt, H. 1984 Nadelbüchsen. In G. Arwidsson (ed.), *Birka II:1: Systematische Analysen der Gräberfund*. Stockholm.

Mandal, S. 1997 Striking the balance: the roles of petrography and geochemistry in stone axe studies in Ireland. *Archaeometry* **39** (2), 289–308.

Manning, C. 1987 Excavation at Moyne graveyard, Shrule, County Mayo. *Proceedings of the Royal Irish Academy* **87**C, 37–70.

Manning, C. 2017–18 'But you are first to build a tower'– the Bermingham Tower, Dublin Castle. *Ulster Journal of Archaeology* **74,** 145–54.

Manning, C. 2022 Where was Áth Cliath–the ford of the hurdles? *Archaeology Ireland* **36** (1), 24–9.

Marchant, R.T. and Sevastopulo, G. 1980 The calp of the Dublin district. *Journal of Earth Sciences* **3,** 195–203.

Margaryan, A., Lawson, D., Sikora, M., Racimo, F. *et al.* 2020 Population genomes of the Viking world. *Nature* **585,** 390-96 (https://doi.org/10.101038/s41586-020-2688-8).

Marshall, M. 2018 Roman small finds, glass and leather from excavations at the Broadgate ticket hall site, Liverpool Street (XSM10). Unpublished report for Museum of London Archaeology (MOLA).

McCarthy, M. 1988 Animals in the economy of medieval and post-medieval Cork. MA thesis, University College, Cork.

McCarthy, M. 1992 The animal bones from excavations at Washington Street, Cork. Unpublished report for the Office of Public Works.

McCarthy, M. 2011 The animal bones from Baronstrand Street, Waterford. Unpublished report submitted to the National Monuments Service.

McClatchie, M. 2003 The plant remains. In R.M. Cleary and M.F. Hurley (eds), *Cork city excavations 1984–2000*, 391–413. Cork.

McClatchie, M., Bogaard, A., Colledge, S. and Whitehouse, N.J. 2016 Farming and foraging in Neolithic Ireland: an archaeobotanical perspective. *Antiquity* **90** (350), 302–18.

McClatchie, M., McCormick, F., Kerr, T.R. and O'Sullivan, A. 2015 Early medieval farming and food production: a review of the archaeobotanical evidence from archaeological excavations in Ireland. *Vegetation History and Archaeobotany* **24** (1), 179–86.

McConway, C. 2003 Ninch, Laytown, Co. Meath. In I. Bennett (ed.), *Excavations 2001: summary accounts of archaeological excavations in Ireland*, 311–3. Bray.

McCormick, F. 1997 The animal bones. In M.F. Hurley, O.M.B. Scully with S.W.J. McCutcheon, *Late Viking Age and medieval Waterford: excavations 1986–1992*, 819–53. Waterford.

McCormick F. 2007 The horse in early Ireland. *Anthropozoologica* **42** (1), 85–104.

McCormick, F., Kerr, T., McClatchie and O'Sullivan, A. 2011 *The archaeology of livestock and cereal production in early medieval Ireland, AD 400–1100*. Early Medieval Archaeology Project (EMAP2). EMAP Report 5.1, submitted for Irish National Strategic Archaeological Research (INSTAR) programme.

McCormick, F. and Murphy, E.M. 1997 Mammal bones. In C. Walsh, *Archaeological excavations at Patrick, Nicholas and Winetavern Streets*, 199–218. Dingle.

McCormick, F. and Murray, E. 2007 *Excavations at Knowth 3: Knowth and the zooarchaeology of Early Christian Ireland*. Dublin.

McCutcheon, C. 2000 Medieval pottery in Dublin: new names and some dates. In S. Duffy (ed.), Medieval Dublin I, 117–25. Dublin.

McCutcheon, C. 2003 Pottery. In R.M. Cleary and M.F. Hurley (eds), *Excavations in Cork city 1984–2000*, 197–235. Cork.

McCutcheon, C. 2006 *Medieval pottery from Wood Quay, Dublin*. Medieval Dublin Excavations 1962–81. Series B, vol. 7. Dublin.

McCutcheon, S.W.J. 1997 The stone artefacts. In M.F. Hurley, O.M.B. Scully with S.W.J. McCutcheon, *Late Viking age and medieval Waterford: excavations 1986–1992*. Waterford.

McGrath, C. 2010 The apple in early Irish narrative tradition: a thoroughly Christian symbol? *Studia Celtica Fennica* **7**, 18–25.

McLaren, F., Monk, M. and Sexton, R. 2004 'Burning the biscuit': evidence from the Lisleagh excavations reveals new secrets twenty years on! *Archaeology Ireland* **18** (3), 8–20.

McMahon, M. 1990 Wintavern Street, South City Ward. In I. Bennett (ed.), *Excavations 1989*, 21. Dublin.

McMahon, M. 1991 Archaeological excavations at Bridge Street Lower, Dublin. *Proceedings of the Royal Irish Academy*, **91**C, 41–71.

McMahon, M. 2002 Early medieval settlement and burial outside the enclosed town: evidence from archaeological excavations at Bride Street, Dublin. *Proceedings of the Royal Irish Academy*, **102**C, 67–135.

McManus D. 1991 *A guide to ogam*. Maynooth.

McManus, D. 2004 *The ogam stones at University College Cork*. Cork.

Meyer, K. 1906 *The Triads of Ireland*. Royal Irish Academy Todd Lecture Series **13.** Dublin.

Mitchell, G.F. 1984 Cross-Block, Dublin Castle. DC 1/1962. Unpublished typescript. National Monuments Service.

Mitchell, G.F. 1987 *Archaeology and environment in early Dublin*. Medieval Dublin Excavations 1962–1981: Series C, vol. 1. Dublin.

Mitchell, G.F. 1990 *The Shell guide to reading the Irish landscape*. Dublin.

Moffett, L. 2009 The archaeology of medieval plant foods. In C.M. Woolgar, D. Serjeantson and T. Waldron (eds), *Food in medieval England*, 41–55. Oxford.

Monk, M.A. 1985 Evidence from macroscopic plant remains for crop husbandry in prehistoric and early historic Ireland: a review. *Journal of Irish Archaeology* **3**, 31–6.

Monk, M.A. 1991 The archaeobotanical evidence for field crop plants in early historic Ireland. In J.M. Renfrew (ed.), *New light on early farming*, 315–28. Edinburgh.

Monk, M.A. and Johnston, P. 2001 Plants, people and environment: a report on the macro-plant remains within the deposits from Troitsky Site XI in medieval Novgorod. In M. Brisbane and D. Gaimster (eds), *Novgorod: the archaeology of a Russian medieval city and its hinterland*, 113–8. British Museum Occasional Paper **141**. London.

Moore F. 1998 Munster ogham stones: siting, context and function. In M.A. Monk and J. Sheehan J. (eds), *Early medieval Munster: archaeology, history and society*, 23–32. Cork.

Moore, F. 2009 Ogham stones. In E. Byrne, U. Egan, S. Ronan, C. Murphy, D. Power with A. McQueen and R. Cronin (comps), *Archaeological inventory of County Kerry: volume I: south-west Kerry*, 175–81. Dublin.

Moore, F. 2010 The ogham stones of County Kerry. In G. Murray (ed.), *Medieval treasures of County Kerry*, 6–18. Tralee.

Moore F. 2017 The ogham inscriptions. In D. Pollock, *Barryscourt Castle, Co. Cork: archaeology, history and architecture*, 278–80. Archaeological Monograph Series **11.** Dublin.

Moore, M. J. 1977 Stone lamps and cressets in Ireland. MA thesis, University College Dublin.

Moore, M.J. 1997 The stone and pottery lamps. In M.F. Hurley and O.M.B. Scully with S.W.J. McCutcheon, *Late Viking age and medieval Waterford: excavations 1986–1992*, 432–36. Waterford.

Morfitt, C. 1852 *The arts of tanning, currying and leather dressing*. Philadelphia.

Morris, C.A. 2000 *Craft, industry and everyday life: wood and woodworking in Anglo-Scandinavian and medieval York*. The Archaeology of York. The Small Finds **17** (13). York.

Moscetti, R., Frangipane, M.T., Monarca, D., Cecchini, M. and Massantini, R. 2012 Maintaining the quality of unripe, fresh hazelnuts through storage under modified atmospheres. *Postharvest Biology and Technology* **65**, 33–8.

Mould, Q., Carlisle, I. and Cameron, E. 2003 *Craft, industry and everyday life: leather and leatherworking in Anglo-Scandinavian and medieval York*. The Archaeology of York. The Small Finds **17** (16). York.

Mullins, C. 2007 Socketed longbone points: a study of the Irish material with reference to British and continental examples. *Journal of Irish Archaeology* **16,** 35–60.

Murphy, D. 1998 Archaeological investigation of a souterrain at Farrandreg, Dundalk, County Louth. *Journal of the County Louth Archaeological and Historical Society* **24,** 261–80.

Murray, H.K. 1981 Houses and other structures from the Dublin excavations, 1962–1976: a summary. In H. Bekker-Nielsen, P.G. Foote and O. Olsen (eds), *Proceedings of the Eighth Viking Congress, Århus, 24–31 August 1977*, 57–68. Odense.

Murray, H. 1983 *Viking and early medieval buildings in Dublin. A study of the buildings excavated under the direction of A.B. Ó Ríordáin in High Street, Winetavern Street and Christchurch Place, Dublin. 1962–63, 1967–76*. British Archaeological Reports, British Series **119.** Oxford.

Murray, N. 2018 Digging into the past reveals Cork settled much earlier than thought (https://www.irishexaminer.com/breakingnews/views/analysis/digging-into-the-past-reveals-cork-settled-much-earlier-than-thought-825239.html).

Murphy, M. and Potterton, M. 2010 *The Dublin region in the Middle Ages: settlement, land-use and economy*. Discovery Programme Monograph. Dublin.

Murtagh, D. 1990 1–3 High Street, Wood Quay Ward. In I. Bennett (ed.), *Excavations 1989*, 23. Dublin.

Museum of Cultural History, Oslo. Museum No. C20168, Museum of Cultural History, Oslo. (http://www.unimus.no/foto; accessed 22/ 3/2018).

Nahlik, A. 1964 *Tkaniny welniane importowane i miejscowe, Nowogrodu Wielkiego, X–XV wieku*. Zakład Narodowy imienia Ossolińskich. Wydawnictwo Polskiej Akademii Nauk (Polish Academy of Scienes).

Nahlik, A. 1965 *Tkaniny wsi wschodnioeuropejskiej X–XIII w.* Łódzkie Tow. Nauk. Łódź, Poland.

Newton, R. and Davison, S. 1989 *Conservation of glass*. London.

Nicholl, J. 2016 The leather finds from Drumclay Crannog. Unpublished excavation report for Northern Ireland Dept. of Communities.

Nicholl, J. 2021 The leather finds from Chancery Lane. Unpublished excavation report for Archaeological Projects Ltd.

Ní Loingsigh, M. 2006 Main Street, South, Cork. In I. Bennett (ed.), *Excavations 2003*, 50–1. Dublin.

Ní Loingsigh, M. 2008 40–48 Main Street, South, Cork. In I. Bennett (ed.), *Excavations 2005*, 54. Dublin.

Ní Loingsigh, M. 2014 Houses. In M.F. Hurley and C. Brett, C. (eds), *Archaeological excavations at South Main Street (Cork) 2003-2005*, 55–83. Cork.

Nørlund, P. 1948 *Trelleborg*. Nordiske Fortidsminder **4.** Copenhagen.

O'Brien, E. 1995 A tale of two cemeteries. *Archaeology Ireland* **9** (3), 13–15.

Ó Carragáin, T. 2010 *Churches in early medieval Ireland*. New Haven and London.

O'Connor, T.P 1989 *Bones from Anglo-Scandinavian levels at 16–22 Coppergate*. The Archaeology of York **15** (3). London.

O'Connor, L. 1991 Irish Iron Age and Early Christian whetstones. *Journal of the Royal Society of Antiquaries of Ireland* **121,** 45–76.

Ó Corráin, D. 1983 Some legal references to fences and fencing in early historic Ireland. In T. Reeves-Smyth and F. Hamond (eds), *Landscape archaeology in Ireland*, 247–52. British Archaeological Reports, British Series **116.** Oxford.

OCarroll, E. 2018 Wood analysis from excavations at Dean Street, Dublin. Unpublished technical report for Aisling Collins Archaeology (ACA).

OCarroll, E. and Moore, C. 2013 Worked wood and woodland resources. In N. Jackman, C. Moore and C. Rynne (eds), *The mill at Kilbegly: An archaeological investigation on the route of the N6 Ballinasloe to Athlone national road scheme*, 45–60. Dublin.

O'Curry, E. and Sullivan, W.K. 1873 *On the manners and customs of the ancient Irish: a series of lectures*. 3 vols. London.

O'Donnabhain, B. 2011 The social lives of severed heads: skull collection and display in medieval and early modern Ireland. In M. Bonogofsky (ed.), *The bioarchaeology of the human head: decapitation, decoration and deformation*, 122–38. Gainesville, FL.

O'Donnell, L. 2004 Wood identifications from Fishamble Street II and III. Unpublished report for Margaret Gowen & Company.

O'Donnell, L. 2010 Wood identifications from Irishtown, Co. Kilkenny. Unpublished report for Margaret Gowen & Company.

O'Donovan, E. 2008 The Irish, the Vikings and the English: new archaeological evidence from excavations at Golden Lane, Dublin. In S. Duffy (ed.), *Medieval Dublin VIII*, 36–130. Dublin.

O'Donovan, J. (ed. and trans.) 1851 *Annala rioghachta Eireann: annals of the Kingdom of Ireland, by the Four Masters, from the earliest period to the year 1616*. 7 vols. Dublin.

Ó Floinn, R. 1988 Handmade medieval pottery in S E Ireland –'Leinster Cooking Ware'. In G. Mac Niocaill and P. Wallace (eds), *Keimelia: studies in medieval archaeology and history in memory of Tom Delaney*, 325–49. Galway.

Ó Floinn, R. 1998 The archaeology of the early Viking age in Ireland. In H.B. Clarke, M. Ní Mhaonaigh and R. Ó Floinn (eds), *Ireland and Scandinavia in the early Viking Age*, 131–65. Dublin.

O'Hara, R. and Scully, O. forthcoming Archaeological excavations in the Deanery Gardens, Waterford City, Co. Waterford. Ministerial Consent No: C396, National Museum Reg. No: E4188.

Ó hEochaidhe, M. 1962 An account of the archaeological investigations carried out at the Cross Block, Dublin Castle, November 1961–February 1962. Unpublished typescript, National Monuments Service.

O'Kelly, M.J. 1962 Two ring-forts at Garryduff, Co. Cork. *Proceedings of the Royal Irish Academy* **63**C, 19–124.

O'Kelly, M.J. 1955–6 An island settlement at Beginish, Co. Kerry. *Proceedings of the Royal Irish Academy* **57**C, 159–94.

Olsen, S.L. 2003 The bone and antler artefacts: their manufacture and use. In N. Field and M. Parker Pearson, *Fiskerton. An Iron Age timber causeway with Iron Age and Roman votive offerings: the 1981 excavations*, 92–110. Oxford.

Ó Neill, J. 2004 Excavations at Longford Street Little, Dublin: an archaeological approach to Dubh Linn. In S. Duffy (ed.), *Medieval Dublin V*, 73–90. Dublin.

O'Rahilly, C. (ed. and trans.) 1967 *Táin Bó Cúailnge: from the Book of Leinster*. Irish Texts Society, **49.** Dublin.

O Rahilly, C. 1998 A classification of bronze stick-pins from the Dublin excavations 1962–72. In C. Manning (ed.), *Dublin and beyond the Pale: studies in honour of Patrick Healy*, 23–33. Dublin.

O'Regan, H.J. 2018 The presence of the brown bear *Ursus arctos* in Holocene Britain: A review of the evidence. *Mammal Review*. (doi.org/10.1111/mam.12127).

Ó Ríordáin, A.B. 1970 Dublin. *Current Archaeology* **2** (22), 312–6.

Ó Riordáin, A.B. 1971 Excavations at High Street and Winetavern Street, Dublin. *Medieval Archaeology* **15** (1), 73–85.

Ó Ríordáin, A.B. 1972 Dublin: city of Dublin. *Medieval Archaeology* **16,** 168.

Ó Ríordáin, A.B. 1973 Dublin City. In T. Delaney (ed.), *Excavations 1972*, 11–12. Belfast.

Ó Ríordáin, A.B. 1976 The High Street excavations. In B. Almqvist and D. Greene (eds), *Proceedings of the Seventh Viking Congress, Dublin 15–21 August 1973*, 135–40. Dublin.

Ó Ríordáin, A.B. 1981 Aspects of Viking Dublin. In H. Bekker-Nielsen, P. Foote and O. Olsen (eds), *Proceedings of the Eighth Viking Congress*, 43–5. Odense, Denmark.

Ó Ríordáin, A.B. 1984 Excavations in old Dublin. In J. Bradley (ed.), *Viking Dublin exposed: The Wood Quay saga*, 134–43. Dublin.

Ó Ríordáin, S.P. 1940a Pole-lathe from Borrisokane, Co. Tipperary. *Journal of the Cork Archaeological and Historical Society* **45,** 28–32.

Ó Ríordáin, S.P. 1940b Excavations at Cush, Co. Limerick (1934 and 1935). *Proceedings of the Royal Irish Academy* **45**(C), 83–181.

Ó Ríordáin, S.P. 1949 Lough Gur excavations: Carraig Aille and the 'Spectacles'. *Proceedings of the Royal Irish Academy* **52**C, 39–111.

Ó Ríordáin, S.P. 1954 Lough Gur excavations: Neolithic and Bronze Age houses on Knockadoon. *Proceedings of the Royal Irish Academy* **56**C, 297–459.

O'Rourke, D. 1990 The leather finds from the Dublin Castle excavations. Unpublished report for the Office of Public Works.

O'Sullivan, A. 1994 The use of trees and woodland in early medieval Ireland. *Irish Forestry* **51,** 80–94.

O'Sullivan, A., McCormick, F., Kerr, T.R. and Harney, L. 2014 *Early medieval Ireland, AD 400–1100. The evidence from archaeological excavations*. Dublin.

O'Sullivan, J. 2014 Beads of glass, stone and amber. In S. Harrison and R. Ó Floinn, *Viking graves and grave-goods in Ireland: a catalogue of furnished Viking-age burials and their content*. Medieval Dublin Excavations 1962–81, Series B, vol.11, 141–7. Dublin.

O'Sullivan, T. 1990 The exploitation of birds in Viking Dublin (an avi-faunal analysis of a bone sample from Fishamble Street II). MA thesis, University College Dublin.

Ottaway, P. 1992 *The Anglo-Scandinavian ironwork from 16–22 Coppergate*. The Archaeology of York. The Small Finds **17** (6). York.

Owen, A. 1841 *The ancient laws and institutes of Wales*. London.

Pals, J.P. and van Dierendonck, M.C. 1988 Between flax and fabric: cultivation and processing of flax in a medieval peat reclamation settlement near Midwoud (Prov. Noord Holland). *Journal of Archaeological Science* **15,** 237–51.

Panter, I. 2000 Amber working tools and techniques. In A.J. Mainman and N.S.H. Rogers, *Craft, industry and everyday life: finds from Anglo-Scandinavian York*, 2501–3. The Archaeology of York. The Small Finds **17** (14). York.

Papazian, C. 1989 The medieval pottery from the Dublin Castle excavations. MA thesis, University College Cork.

Papazian, C. and McCutcheon, C. forthcoming Medieval pottery. In A. Lynch, C. Manning and K. Wiggins, *Dublin Castle: from fortress to palace. Volume 3, part 2: medieval and post-medieval archaeology: the finds and specialist reports*.

Paynter, S. 2008 Experiments in the reconstruction of Roman wood-fired glassworking furnaces: waste products and their formation processes. *Journal of Glass Studies* **50,** 271–92.

Pearce, J.E., Vince, A.G. and Jenner, M.A. 1985 *A dated type-series of London medieval pottery. Part 2: London-type ware*. London.

Peel, M.C., Finlayson, B.L. and McMahon, T.A. 2007 Updated world map of the Köppen-Geiger climate classification. *Hydrology and Earth System Sciences* **11** (5), 1633–44.

Penton, S. 2008 *Cumwhitton, Cumbria. Analytical investigation of jet-like objects from a Viking cemetery*. Portsmouth.

Petersen, J. 1914 Bretspillet i Norge i forhistorisk tid. *Oldtiden: tidskrift for norsk forhistorie* **4,** 75–92.

Petersen, J. 1951 *Vikingstiden Redskaper*. Oslo.

Petillon, J.-M., Plisson, H. and Cattelain, P. 2016 Thirty years of experimental research on the breakage patterns of Stone Age osseous points. Overview, methodological problems and current perspectives. In R. Iovita and K. Sanu, *Multidisciplinary approaches to the study of Stone Age weaponry*, 47–64. New York.

Phelan S. 2010 The bank, the ditch and the water: Hiberno-Norse discoveries at Church Street and Hammond Lane. In S. Duffy (ed.), *Medieval Dublin X*, 165–97. Dublin.

Phelps, M. 2011 35–39 South Main Street, Cork, Ireland: analysis of medieval glass vessels: technology report. English Heritage Research Department Report 9-2011. Portsmouth.

Phelps, M., Freestone, I.C., Gorin-Rosen, Y. and Gratuze, B. 2016 Natron glass production and supply in the late antique and early medieval Near East: the effect of the Byzantine-Islamic transition. *Journal of Archaeological Science* **75,** 57–71 (https://doi.org/10.1016/j.jas.2016.08.006).

Phillips, R. and Grant, S. 1977 *Wild flowers of Britain*. New York.

Plahter, U. 2011 Analyses of jet-like objects. In D. Skre (ed.), *Things from the town: artefacts and inhabitants in Viking-age Kaupang*, 133–41. Kaupang Excavations Project Publication Series, vol. 3. Norske Oldfunn, vol. 24. Aarhus.

Ponsford, M. 1991 Dendrochronological dates from Dundas Wharf, Bristol and the dating of Ham Green and other medieval pottery. In E. Lewis (ed.), *Custom and ceramics: essays presented to Kenneth Barton*, 81–103. Wickham, UK.

Ponsford, M. 1998 Pottery. In R. Price with M. Ponsford, *St Bartholomew's Hospital, Bristol. The excavation of a medieval hospital: 1976–8*. CBA Research Report **110,** 136–56. York.

Porter, D. 1997 Small finds. In S. Buteux, *Settlements at Skaill, Deerness,Orkney. Excavations by Peter Gellling of the prehistoric, Pictish, Viking and later periods, 1963–1981*. British Archaeological Reports, British Series **260,** 96–146. Oxford.

Power, C. 1994 A demographic study of human skeletal populations from historic Munster. *Ulster Journal of Archaeology* **57,** 95–118.

Power, P. 1906 On four (or five) 'stone chalices' from early church sites in the Decies. *Journal of the Waterford and South-East of Ireland Archaeological Society* **9,** 143–9.

Power, P. 1915 The subsoil of Irish history (papers on elementary archaeology). Part IV–The Neolithic. *Journal of the Waterford and South-East of Ireland Archaeological Society* **18,** 113–28.

Price, J. and Cottam, S. 1998 *Romano-British glass vessels: a handbook*. Practical Handbooks in Archaeology **14.** York.

Pritchard, F. 1984 Late Saxon textiles from the city of London. *Medieval Archaeology* **28,** 46–76.

Pritchard, F. 1991 Glass. In A.G. Vince (ed.), *Aspects of Saxo-Norman London: finds and environmental evidence*. Special paper, London and Middlesex Archaeological Society, vol. 2, 172–4. London.

Prummel, W. and Frisch, H.J. 1986 A guide for the distinction of species, sex and body side in the bones of sheep and goat. *Journal of Archaeological Science* **13,** 567–77.

Prummel, W., Halici, H. and Verbaas, A. 2011 The bone and antler tools from the Wijnaldum-Tjistma terp. *Journal of Archaeology in the Low Countries* **3-1/2,** 65–106.

Rackham, H. (ed. and trans.) 1952 *Pliny: Natural History, Volume IX: Books 33–35*. Loeb Classical Library **394.** Cambridge, MA.

Raftery, J. 1966 The Cuillard and other unpublished hanging bowls. *Journal of the Royal Society of Antiquaries of Ireland* **96,** 29–38.

Raftery, B. 1969 A late ogham inscription from Co. Tipperary. *Journal of the Royal Society of Antiquaries of Ireland* **99,** 161–4.

Reed, R. 1972 *Ancient skins, parchments and leathers*. London.

Rehren, T. and Freestone, I.C. 2015 Ancient glass: from kaleidoscope to crystal ball. *Journal of Archaeological Science* **56,** 233–41 (https://doi.org/10.1016/j.jas.2015.02.021).

Reichstein, H. and Tiessen, M. (eds) 1974 *Untersuchungen an Tierknochenfunden (1963–4)*. Bericht über die Ausgrabungen in Haithabus **7.** Neumünster.

Reilly, E. 2003 The contribution of insect remains to an understanding of the environment of Viking-age and medieval Dublin. In S. Duffy (ed.), *Medieval Dublin IV*, 40–63. Dublin.

Reilly, E. 2012 Fair and foul: analysis of sub-fossil insect remains from Troitsky XI-XIII, Novgorod (1996–2002). In M. Brisbane, N. Makarov and E. Nosov (eds), *The archaeology of medieval Novgorod in context: studies in centre/periphery relations*, 265–82. Oxford.

Reilly, E. 2014 From Christchurch Place to Fishamble Street: developments in archaeoentomology in Dublin, Ireland, since 1981. *Quaternary International* **341,** 143–51.

Reilly, E., Lyons, S., OCarroll, E., O'Donnell, L., Stuijts, I. and Corless, A. 2016 Building the towns: the interrelationship between woodland history and urban life in Viking Age Ireland. In B. Jervis, L.G. Broderick and I.G. Sologestoa (eds), *Objects, environment, and everyday life in medieval Europe*, 67–92. Turnhout.

Reimer, P.J., Bard, E., Bayliss, A., Beck, J.W., Blackwell, P.G., Bronk Ramsey, C., Buck, C.E., Edwards, R.L., Friedrich, M., Grootes, P.M., Guilderson, T.P., Haflidason, H., Hajdas, I., Hatté, C., Heaton, T.J., Hoffmann, D.L., Hogg, A.G., Hughen, K.A., Kaiser, K.F., Kromer, B., Manning, S.W., Niu, M., Reimer, R.W., Richards, D.A., Scott, E.M., Southon, J.R., Turney., C.S.M., Van der Plicht, J. 2013 IntCal13 and Marine13 radiocarbon age calibration curves, 0–50,000 years cal BP. *Radiocarbon* **55,** 1869–87.

Reynolds, M. 1978 Irish combs from the ninth to the thirteenth century. In H. Clarke (ed.), *Supplement to Dublin Arts Festival programme*, 15–20. Dublin.

Riddler, I.D. 2005 Bone and antler. In H. Wallis, *Excavations at Mill Lane, Thetford*. East Anglian Archaeology **108**, 58–66. Norwich.

Riddler, I.D. 2007a A composite comb. In A. Vince and Q. Mould, New thoughts on the chronology of Saddler Street, Durham: pottery, leatherwork and some implications. *Archaeologia Aeliana*, 5th series **36,** 87.

Riddler, I.D. 2007b Objects of antler and bone. In S. Mays, C. Harding and C. Heighway, *The churchyard. Wharram: a study of settlement on the Yorkshire Wolds* **11,** 313–7. York.

Riddler, I.D. 2009 Hollowed cylinder. In S. Lucy, J. Tipper and A. Dickens, *The Anglo-Saxon settlement and cemetery at Bloodmoor Hill, Carlton Colville, Suffolk*, 278. East Anglian Archaeology **131.** Cambridge.

Riddler, I.D. 2013 Bone and antler. In C. Evans, G. Appleby, S. Lucy and R. Regan, *Process and history. Romano–British communities at Colne Fen, Earith*, 415–17. CAU Landscape Archives: the archaeology of the lower Ouse Valley, vol. 2. Cambridge.

Riddler, I.D. and Trzaska-Nartowski, N.I.A. 2009a Appendix 15: worked bone. In R. O'Hara, Report on the archaeological excavation of Roestown 2, Co. Meath. Final text for the National Roads Authority, 1–29. Unpublished report by Archaeological Consultancy Services.

Riddler, I.D. and Trzaska-Nartowski, N.I.A. 2009b Appendix 13: worked bone. In L. Clarke, Report on the archaeological excavation of Ardsallagh 5, Co. Meath. Final text for the National Roads Authority, 1–2. Unpublished report by Archaeological Consultancy Services.

Riddler, I.D. and Trzaska-Nartowski, N.I.A. 2011 Chanting upon a dunghill: working skeletal materials in Anglo-Saxon England. In M. Hyer and G. Owen-Crocker, *The material culture of daily life in Anglo-Saxon England*, 116–41. Exeter.

Riddler, I.D. and Trzaska-Nartowski, N.I.A. 2012 Lundenwic and the Middle Saxon bone interlude. *Anglo-Saxon Studies in Archaeology and History* **18,** 75–96.

Riddler, I.D. and Trzaska-Nartowski, N.I.A. 2014 Antler and bone working in early medieval rural Ireland. In M. Stanley, *Fragments of lives past. Archaeological objects from Irish road schemes*, 39–52. National Roads Authority (NRA) Seminar Papers **7**. Dublin.

Riddler, I.D. and Trzaska-Nartowski, N.I.A. forthcoming a Combs and comb-making in Viking and medieval Dublin. Medieval Dublin Excavations 1962–81, Series B. Dublin.

Riddler, I.D. and Trzaska-Nartowski, N.I.A. forthcoming b Objects and waste of antler, bone and ivory. In C. Manning, Excavations at the Steeple Garden, Clonmacnoise.

Riddler, I.D. and Trzaska-Nartowski, N.I.A. forthcoming c Objects and waste of antler and bone. In J. McDowell, Excavations at Drumclay Crannóg, Enniskillen, Co. Fermanagh. Northern Ireland Archaeological Monographs. Belfast.

Riddler, I.D. and Trzaska-Nartowski, N.I.A. forthcoming d Objects and waste of antler and bone. In H. King, Excavations at the New Graveyard, Clonmacnoise.

Riddler, I.D., Trzaska-Nartowski, N.I.A. and Barton-Murray, R. 2012 The antler combs. In G. Eogan, *The archaeology of Knowth in the first and second millennia AD. Excavations at Knowth* 5, 369–89. Dublin.

Riddler, I.D., Trzaska-Nartowski, N.I.A. and Hatton, S. forthcoming *An early medieval craft. Antler and bone working from Ipswich: excavations 1974–1994*. Bury St Edmunds.

Riddler, I. D. and Walton Rogers, P. 2006 Early medieval small finds. In K. Parfitt, B. Corke and J. Cotter, *Excavations at Townwall Street, Dover, 1995–6*. The Archaeology of Canterbury, New Series III, Canterbury, 255–318.

Riehl, S. 2009 Archaeobotanical evidence for the interrelationship of agricultural decision-making and climate change in the ancient Near East. *Quaternary International* **197** (1-2), 93–114.

Ritchie, A. 1976–7 Excavations of Pictish and Viking-age farmsteads at Buckquoy, Orkney. *Proceedings of the Society of Antiquaries of Scotland* **108,** 174–227.

Robinson, D 1987 Spice and famine food? The botanical analysis of two post-Reformation pits from Elgin, Scotland. *Circaea* **5** (1), 21–7.

Robinson, D. 1991 Plant remains from the Late Iron Age/early Viking Age settlement at Gammel Lejre. *Journal of Danish Archaeology* **10** (1), 191–8.

Roes, A. 1963 *Bone and antler objects from the Frisian Terp-mounds*. Haarlem.

Rogerson, A. and Dallas, C. 1984 *Excavations in Thetford 1948–59 and 1973–80*. East Anglian Archaeology **22.** Norfolk.

Rohde Sloth, P., Lund Hansen, U. and Karg, S. 2012 Viking Age garden plants from southern Scandinavia–diversity, taphonomy and cultural aspects. *Danish Journal of Archaeology* **1** (1), 27–38.

Ronan, M. 1927 The Poddle river and its branches. *Journal of the Royal Society of Antiquaries of Ireland* **57**, 39–46.

Ronan, M. 1948 The Poddle River (1803–1829). *Journal of the Royal Society of Antiquaries of Ireland* **78,** 5–10.

Rondelez, P. 2014 Ironworking in late medieval Ireland, c. AD 1200 to 1600. PhD thesis, University College Cork.

Rondelez, P. 2016 Preliminary report on the metalworking remains from Roscrea Town Centre, Co. Tipperary (C325/E3991). Unpublished specialist report.

Russell, I. 2014 The excavation. In I. Russell and M.F. Hurley (eds), *Woodstown: a Viking-age settlement in Co. Waterford*, 28–89. Dublin.

Russell, I. and Hurley, M.F. (eds) 2014 *Woodstown: a Viking-age settlement in Co. Waterford*. Dublin.

Rynne, E. 1964 Some sites at Shannon Airport, County Clare. *Proceedings of the Royal Irish Academy* **63**C, 245–77.

Salisbury, E.J. 1961 *Weeds and aliens*. London.

Sayers, W. 1994 Diet and fantasy in eleventh-century Ireland: the vision of Mac Con Glinne. *Food and Foodways* **6** (1), 1–17.

Scally, G. 2002 The earthen banks and walled defences of Dublin's north-east corner. In S. Duffy (ed.), *Medieval Dublin III*, 11–33. Dublin.

Scannell, M.J.P and Synnott, D.M. 1987 *Census catalogue of the flora of Ireland*. Dublin.

Schibille, N. and Freestone, I.C. 2013 Composition, production and procurement of glass at San Vincenzo Al Volturno: an early medieval monastic complex in Southern Italy. *PLOS One* **8** (10), e76479 (https://doi.org/10.1371/journal.pone.0076479).

Schibille, N., Sterrett-Krause, A. and Freestone, I.C. 2016 Glass groups, glass supply and recycling in late Roman Carthage. *Archaeological and Anthropological Sciences* **9,** 1223–4. (https://doi.org/10.1007/s12520-016-0316-1).

Schietzel, K. 2014 *Spurensuche Haithabu. Archäologische Spurensuche in der frühmittelalterlichen Ansiedlung Haithabu. Dokumentation und Chronik 1963–2013*. Neumünster.

Schmölcke, U., Groß, D., Nikulina, E.A. 2017 Bears and beavers. 'The Browns' in daily life and spiritual world. In B.V. Eriksen, A. Abegg-Wigg, R. Bleile, U. Ickerodt (eds), *Interaction without borders. Exemplary archaeological research at the beginning of the 21st century*, 901–16. Schleswig.

Schwarz-Mackensen, G. 1976 *Die Knochennadeln von Haithabu*. Berichte über die Ausgrabungen in Haithabu **9.** Neumünster.

Schweingruber, F.H. 1990 *Microscopic wood anatomy*. 3rd edition. Swiss Federal Institute for Forest, Snow and Landscape Research, Birmensdorf, Switzerland.

Scully, O.M.B. 1997a Domestic architecture: introduction and discussion. In M.F. Hurley, O.M.B. Scully with S.W.J. McCutcheon (eds), *Late Viking Age and medieval Waterford: Excavations 1986–1992*, 34–9. Waterford.

Scully, O.M.B. 1997b The metal artefacts. In M.F. Hurley, O.M.B. Scully with S.W.J. McCutcheon (eds), *Late Viking Age and medieval Waterford: Excavations 1986–1992*, 438-89. Waterford.

Scully, O.M.B. 1997c Ferrous and non-ferrous metal artefacts. In R.M. Cleary, M.F. Hurley and E. Shee Twohig (eds), *Skiddy's Castle and Christ Church Cork: Excavations 1974-7 by D.C. Twohig*, 165–90. Cork.

Scully, O.M.B. 2014 Ferrous and non-ferrous metal. In I. Russell and M.F. Hurley (eds), *Woodstown. A Viking-age settlement in Co Waterford*, 125–40. Dublin.

Seager-Thomas, M. 2013 Reassessing slingstones. (https://www.researchgate.net/publication/264974746 accessed 20/2/2019.)

Sellers, O.R. 1939 Slingstones of Biblical times. *The Biblical Archaeologist* **2**, 41–4.

Sellwood, L. 1984 Objects of bone and antler. In B.W. Cunliffe, *Danebury. An Iron Age hillfort in Hampshire. Volume 2. The excavations, 1969–78: the finds*, 317–95. Council for British Archaeology (CBA) Research Report **52.** London.

Serjeantson, D. 2009 *Birds*. Cambridge Manuals in Archaeology. Cambridge.

Serjeantson, D. and Gardiner, J. 1995 Antler implements and ox scapulae shovels and animal bone. In R.M.J. Cleal, K.E. Walker and R. Montague, *Stonehenge and its landscape: twentieth-century excavations*, 414–30 and 437–5. English Heritage Archaeological Report **10.** London.

Serra, D. and Tunberg, H. 2013 *An early meal – a Viking Age cookbook and culinary odyssey*. Furulund, Sweden.

Sexton, R. 1998 Porridges, gruels and breads: the cereal foodstuffs of early medieval Ireland. In M.A. Monk and J. Sheehan (eds), *Early medieval Munster: archaeology, history and society*, 76–86. Cork.

Sheehan, J. and Ó Corráin, D. (eds) 2010 *The Viking Age: Ireland and the west. Proceedings of the Fifteenth Viking Congress*. Dublin.

Shepherd, J. and Wardle, A. 2009 *The glass workers of Roman London*. London.

Shoesmith, R. and Johnson, A. (eds) 2000 *Ludlow Castle, its history and buildings*. Little Logaston, UK.

Shortland, A., Schachner, L., Freestone, I.C. and Tite, M. 2006 Natron as a flux in the early vitreous materials industry: sources, beginnings and reasons for decline. *Journal of Archaeological Science* **33** (4) 521–30 (https://doi.org/10.1016/j.jas.2005.09.011).

Sikora, M. 2010 The Finglas burial: archaeology and ethnicity in Viking-age Dublin. In J. Sheehan and D. Ó Corráin (eds), *The Viking Age: Ireland and the west*, 402–17. Dublin.

Sikora, M. and Moore, F. 2020 A decorated and ogham-inscribed weft-beater from Leabeg, Lemanaghan bog, Co. Offaly. *Journal of the Royal Society of Antiquaries of Ireland* **150**, 63–89.

Sikora, M., Ó Donnabháin, B. and Daly, N. 2011 Preliminary report on a Viking warrior grave at War Memorial Park, Islandbridge. In S. Duffy (ed.), *Medieval Dublin XI*, 170–84. Dublin.

Silver, I.A. 1969 The ageing of domestic animals. In D.R. Brothwell and E. Higgs (eds), *Science in archaeology: a survey of progress and research*, 282–302. London.

Silvestri, A., Molin, G. and Salviulo, G. 2008 The colourless glass of Iulia Felix. *Journal of Archaeological Science* **35,** 331–41 (https://doi.org/10.1016/j.jas.2007.03.010).

Simms A. 1990 Medieval Dublin in a European context: from proto-town to chartered town. In H.B. Clarke (ed.), *Medieval Dublin: the making of a metropolis*, 37–51. Dublin.

Simonsen, P. 1953 Smedgraven fra Ytre Elgsnes. *Viking* **17,** 109–18.

Simpson, L. 1995 *Excavations at Essex Street West, Dublin*. Temple Bar Archaeological Report **2.** Dublin.

Simpson, L. 1999 *Director's findings: Temple Bar West*. Temple Bar Archaeological Report **5.** Dublin.

Simpson, L. 2000 Forty years a-digging: a preliminary synthesis of archaeological investigations in medieval Dublin. In S. Duffy (ed.), *Medieval Dublin I*, 11–68. Dublin.

Simpson, L. 2004 Excavations on the south side of the medieval town at Ship Street Little, Dublin. In S. Duffy (ed.), *Medieval Dublin V*, 9–51. Dublin.

Simpson, L. 2005 Viking warrior burials in Dublin: is this the *longphort*? In S. Duffy (ed.), *Medieval Dublin VI*, 11–62. Dublin.

Simpson, L. 2011 Fifty years a-digging: a synthesis of medieval archaeological investigations in Dublin city and suburbs. In S. Duffy (ed.), *Medieval Dublin XI*, 9–112. Dublin.

Simpson, L. 2017 The contribution of development-led archaeology to our understanding of the medieval urban archaeology of Dublin. *Archaeology Ireland* **31** (3), 33–7.

Simpson, W.G. 1972 A gaming board of Ballinderry-type from Knockanboy, Derrykeighan, Co. Antrim. *Ulster Journal of Archaeology* **35,** 63–4.

Small, A. 1973 The site: its history and excavation. In A. Small, C. Thomas and D.M. Wilson, *St Ninian's Isle and its treasure*, 1–7. Aberdeen University Studies **152.** Oxford.

Smirnova, L. 2005 *Comb-making in medieval Novgorod (950–1450). An industry in transition*. British Archaeological Reports, International Series **1369.** Oxford.

Smith, A.N. 2007 Worked bone. In J. Hunter, *Investigations at Sanday, Orkney. Vol 1: excavations at Pool, Sanday. A multi-period settlement from Neolithic to late Norse Times*, 459–514. Kirkwall, Scotland.

Smith, D.N. 2013 Defining an indicator package to allow identification of 'cesspits' in the archaeological record. *Journal of Archaeological Science* **40,** 525–3.

Smyth, W.J. 2012 Flax cultivation in Ireland: the development and demise of a regional staple. In A. Fraser (ed.), *Anniversary essays: forty years of Geography in Maynooth*, 158–78. 2 vols. Maynooth.

Spennemann, D.H.R. 1988 Bone toggles reconsidered. In H. Hickmann and D.W. Hughes (eds), *The archaeology of early music cultures*, 23–9. Orpheus-Schriftenreihe zu Grundfragen der Musik **51.** Bonn.

Stalley R. 2010 The construction of the medieval cathedral *c.* 1030–1250. In K. Milne (ed.), *Christ Church Cathedral Dublin, a history*. Dublin.

Stevens, P. 2017 Early medieval jet-like jewellery in Ireland: production, distribution and consumption. *Medieval Archaeology* **61** (2), 239–76.

Stevens, P. 2018 Doing God's work? The role of the church in the expansion of the early Irish economy. Ph.D thesis, National University of Ireland.

Stevens, P. 2019 Drumclay crannog excavations 2010-12: early medieval jet/jet-like and stone jewellery. Unpublished finds report for Historic Environment Division of the Dept. for Communities, Belfast.

Stevens, P. forthcoming a Note on the jet-like jewellery. In S. Delaney and E. Murphy, *Archaeological excavations at Ranelagh, Co. Roscommon–N61 Roscommon to Coolteige Road Scheme.*

Stevens, P. forthcoming b Jet and jet-like objects. In A. Lynch, C. Manning and K. Wiggins, *Dublin Castle: history and archaeology. Volume 4: Medieval and post-medieval archaeology: the finds and specialist reports.*

Stika, H.-P. 1996 Traces of a possible Celtic brewery in Eberdingen-Hochdorf, Kreis Ludwigsburg, southwest Germany. *Vegetation History and Archaeobotany* **5** (1), 81–8.

Stokes, P. and Rowley-Conwy, P. 2002 Iron Age cultigen? Experimental return rates for fat hen (Chenopodium album L.). *Environmental Archaeology* **7** (1), 95–9.

Stone, D. 2018 Analysis of non-wood plant macro-remains. The Coombe, Dublin. Unpublished report for Aisling Collins Archaeological Services (ACAS).

Struckmeyer, K. 2011 *Die Knochen-und Geweihgeräte der Feddersen Wierde. Gebrauchsspurenanalysen an Geräten von der Römischen Kaiserzeit bis zum Mittelalter und ethnoarchäologische Vergleiche*. Studien zur Landschafts- und Siedlungsgeschichte im südlichen Nordseegebiet **2.** Rahden, Germany.

Stuart, A.J. and Van Wijngaarden-Bakker, L.H. 1985 Quaternary vertebrates. In K.J. Edwards and W.P. Warren (eds), *Quaternary History of Ireland*, 221–50. London.

Stuijts, I. 2001 Wood identifications from Temple Bar West. Unpublished report for Margaret Gowen & Company.

Taylor, G.W. 1989 Detection and identification of dyes. In P. Walton, *Textiles, cordage and raw fibre from 16-22 Coppergate*. The Archaeology of York. The Small Finds, **17** (5), 398–404. York.

Tempel, W.-D. 1969 Die Dreilagenkämme aus Haithabu. Studien zu den Kämmen der Wikingerzeit im Nordseeküstengebiet und Skandinavien. Unpublished dissertation, University of Göttingen.

Thiagarajan, B. 2013 Fracture frontal bone and its management. *Otolaryngology Online Journal* **3**, 1–5.

Thomas, G. 2001 Strap-ends and the identification of regional patterns in the production and circulation of ornamental metalwork in Late Anglo-Saxon and Viking-age Britain. In M. Redknap, N. Edwards, S. Youngs, A. Lane and J. Knight (eds), *Pattern and Purpose in Insular Art*, 39–48. Oxford.

Thomas, G. 2003 Late Anglo-Saxon and Viking-age strap-ends 750–1100: Part 1. *The Finds Research Group AD 700–1700. Datasheet* **32,** 1–8.

Thomas, G. 2004 Late Anglo-Saxon and Viking-age strap-ends 750–1100: Part 2. *The Finds Research Group AD 700–1700. Datasheet* **33**, 1–7.

Thrane, H. 1963 De første broncebidsler i Mellem-og Nordeuropa. *Aarbøger Nordisk Oldkyndighed og Historie*, 50–99.

Tierney, J. and Hannon, M. 1997 Plant remains. In M.F. Hurley, O.M.B. Scully with S.W.J. McCutcheon, *Late Viking Age and medieval Waterford: excavations 1986–1992*, 854–93. Waterford.

Ulbricht, I. 1978 *Die Geweihverarbeitung in Haithabu*. Berichte über die Ausgrabungen in Haithabu **7.** Neumünster.

Ulbricht, I. 1984 *Die Verarbeitung von Knochen, Geweih und Horn im mittelalterlichen Schleswig*, Ausgrabungen in Schleswig. Berichte und Studien **3.** Neumünster.

Unité Archaéologie de la ville de Saint-Denis (UASD). *Les Antéfixes* (http://www2.culture.gouv.fr/culture/arcnat/saint-denis/en/1_2a4_ville.htm; accessed 4/ 6/ 2019).

Vigors, P.D. 1888 Slings and sling-stones. *Journal of the Royal Historical and Archaeological Association of Ireland*. Fourth Series. **8** (75), 357–66.

Vince, A.G. 1988 Early medieval English pottery in Viking Dublin. In G. Mac Niocaill and P. Wallace (eds), *Keimelia: studies in medieval archaeology and history in memory of Tom Delaney*, 254–70. Galway.

Wallace, P.F. 1981 Dublin's waterfront at Wood Quay. In G. Milne and B. Hobley (eds), *Waterfront archaeology in Britain and northern Europe*, 109–18. Council for British Archaeology (CBA) Research Report **41.** London.

Wallace, P.F. 1984 A reappraisal of the archaeological significance of Wood Quay. In J. Bradley (ed.), *Viking Dublin exposed: the Wood Quay saga*, 112–33. Dublin.

Wallace, P.F. 1987a Wood Quay now: the Dublin excavations project. *Archaeology Ireland* **1** (1), 26–9.

Wallace, P.F. 1987b The economy and commerce of Viking-age Dublin. In K. Düwel, H. Jankuhn, H. Siems and D. Timpe (eds) *Untersuchungen zu Handel und Verkehr der vor- und frühgeschichtlichen Zeit in Mittel- und Nordeuropa, 4, der Handel der Karolinger–und Wikingerzeit*, 200–45. Abhandlungen der Akademie der Wissenschaften in Göttingen, Philologisch-Historische Klasse, 3rd series, 156. Göttingen.

Wallace, P.F. 1988 A Viking Dublin perspective on Irish vernacular architecture studies. In G. Mac Niocaill and P.F. Wallace (eds), *Keimelia: studies in medieval archaeology in memory of Tom Delaney*, 573–96. Galway.

Wallace, P.F. 1992 *The Viking-age buildings of Dublin*. Two parts. Medieval Dublin Excavations 1962–81, Series A, vol. 1. Dublin.

Wallace, P.F. 2016 *Viking Dublin: The Wood Quay excavations*. Dublin.

Wallace, P.F. and R. Ó Floinn 1988 *Dublin 1000 – discovery & excavation in Dublin, 1842-1981*. Dublin.

Walsh, C. 1988 High St./Peter St., Custom House B Ward. In I. Bennett (ed.), *Excavations 1987*, 27–8.

Walsh, C. 1989 Peter St./Olaf St./Custom House B Ward. In I. Bennett (ed.), *Excavations 1988*, 36–7.

Walsh, C. (ed.) 1997 *Archaeological excavations at Patrick, Nicholas and Winetavern Streets, Dublin*. Dingle.

Walsh, C. 2001 Dublin's southern town defences, tenth to fourteenth centuries: the evidence from Ross Road. In S. Duffy (ed.), *Medieval Dublin II*, 88–127. Dublin.

Walsh, C. 2012 The excavation of an early roadway and Hiberno-Norse houses at the Coombe. In S. Duffy (ed.), *Medieval Dublin XII*, 113–37. Dublin.

Walters A. 1985 The reconstruction of the Abbey Church at St-Denis (1231–81): the interplay of music and ceremony with architecture and politics. *Early Music History* **5**, 187–238.

Walton, P. 1988 Dyes of the Viking age: a summary of recent work. *Dyes in History and Archaeology* **7**, 14-20.

Walton, P. 1989a Tests for dye in textile samples from Dublin Castle yard, Waterford city, Deerpark Farm and Loch Tay. Reports from The Anglo-Saxon Laboratory (ASLab REP 890120 on behalf of Elizabeth Wincott Heckett).

Walton, P. 1989b *Textiles, cordage and raw fibre from 16-22 Coppergate*. The Archaeology of York. The Small Finds **17** (5). York.

Walton, P. and Taylor, G. 1991 The characterisation of dyes in textiles from archaeological excavations. *Chromatography and Analysis*, June, 5-7.

Walton Rogers, P. 1997 *Textile Production at 16–22 Coppergate*. The Archaeology of York. The Small Finds **17** (11). York.

Walton Rogers, P. 2005 Dyestuff analysis of E ware pottery, in A. Crone and E. Campbell, *A crannog of the first millennium AD. Excavations by Jack Scott at Loch Glashan, Argyll, 1960*, 61-2. Edinburgh.

Walton Rogers, P. 2007 *Cloth and clothing in early Anglo-Saxon England, AD 450–700*. Council for British Archaeology Research Report **145**. London.

Wamers, E. 2009 Von Bären und Männern: Berserker, Bärenkämpfer und Bärenführer im frühen Mittelalter. *Zeitschrift für Archäologie des Mittelalters* **37**, 1–46.

Ward Perkins, J.B. 1940 *London Museum medieval catalogue*. London.

Warner, R.B. 1990 A proposed adjustment for the 'old-wood' effect. In W. Mook and H. Waterbolk (eds), *Proceedings of the Second International Symposium of 14C and Archaeology, Groningen 1987*, 159–72. Pact 29. Strasbourg.

Waterman, D.M. 1959 Late Saxon, Viking and early medieval finds from York. *Archaeologia* **97**, 59–105.

Watkins, A.E. n.d. Aelfric's Colloquy: translated from the Latin. Paper No. 16. Kent Archaeology Society (http://www.kentarchaeology.ac/authors/016).

Watson, J., Graham, K., Karsten, A., Skinner, L., Schaeder, U., Penton, S., Gao, J., Fell, V. and Jones, J. 2011 Townfoot Farm, Cumwhitton, Cumbria: investigative conservation of material from the Viking cemetery. English Heritage Research Department Report 72–2011. Portsmouth.

Watts, S. and Pollard, A.M. 1998 Identifying archaeological jet and jet-like artifacts using FTIR. *Postprints: IRUG2 at the V&A*, 37–52. London.

Westphal, F. 2006 *Die Holzfunde von Haithabu*. Berichte über die Ausgrabungen in Haithabu **11**. Neumünster.

Westphalen, P. 1989 *Die Eisenschlacken von Haithabu: Ein Beitrag zur Geschichte des Schmiedehandwerks in Nordeuropa*. Berichte über die Ausgrabungen in Haithabu **26**. Neumünster.

Westphalen, P. 1999 Die Kleinfunde aus der frühgeschichtlichen Wurt Elisenhof. *Offa-Bücher* **80**, 1–232.

Wheeler, R.E.M. 1943 *Maiden Castle, Dorset*. Reports of the Research Committee of the Society of Antiquaries of London **12**. London.

White, A.J. 1981 Lincoln: Hawhill, Swanpool. *Lincolnshire History and Archaeology* **16**, 74.

White, A.J. 1984 Finds from the Anglican monastery at Whitby. *Yorkshire Archaeological Journal* **56**, 33–40.

White Marshall, J. and Walsh, C. 2005 *Illaunloughan Island. An early medieval monastery in County Kerry*. Bray.

Whitfield, N. 1997 The Waterford kite-brooch and its place in Irish metalwork. In M.F. Hurley, O.M.B. Scully with S.W.J. McCutcheon, *Late Viking age and medieval Waterford: excavations 1986–1992*, 490–517. Waterford.

Whyte, E. 2016 Medieval pottery. In K. Wiggins, *A place of great consequence: archaeological excavations at King John's Castle, Limerick, 1990–98*, 335–54. Dublin.

Wiggins, K. 2016 *A place of great consequence: archaeological excavations at King John's Castle, Limerick, 1990–98*. Dublin.

Wilde, W.R. 1866–69 On the Scandinavian antiquities lately discovered at Islandbridge, near Dublin. *Proceedings of the Royal Irish Academy* **10**, 13–22.

Williams, B.B. 1984 Excavations at Ballyutoag, County Antrim. *Ulster Journal of Archaeology* **47**, 37-49.

Willmot, H. and Welham, K. 2013 Late seventeenth-century glassmaking at Glastonbury Abbey. *Journal of Glass Studies* **55**, 71–83.

Wilson, D.M. 2008 *The Vikings in the Isle of Man*. Aarhus.

Wincott Heckett, E. 1997 Textiles, cordage, basketry and raw fibre. In M.F. Hurley, O.M.B. Scully with S.W.J. McCutcheon, *Late Viking Age and medieval Waterford: excavations 1986–1992*, 743–61. Waterford.

Wincott Heckett, E. 2003 *Viking-age head coverings from Dublin*. Medieval Dublin Excavations, 1962-81; Series B, vol. 6. Dublin.

Wincott Heckett, E. 2010 Textiles that work for their living: a late eleventh-century cloth from Cork, Ireland. In J. Sheehan and D. Ó Corráin (eds), *The Viking Age: Ireland and the west*, 555–64. Dublin.

Wincott Heckett, E. and Janaway, R.W. 1997 Textiles, animal hair and fibres. In R.M. Cleary, M.F. Hurley and E. Shee Twohig (eds), *Skiddy's Castle and Christ Church, Cork: excavations 1974–77 by D. C. Twohig*, 340–8. Cork.

Woodland, M. 1990 Spindle whorls. In M. Biddle (ed.), *Object and economy in medieval Winchester: Artefacts from medieval Winchester*, vol. 2, 216–25. Winchester Studies **7**. Oxford.

Woodman, P., Finlay, N. and Anderson, L. 2006 *The archaeology of a collection: The Keiller-Knowles Collection of the National Museum of Ireland*. Dublin.

Wood-Martin, W.G. 1886 *The lake dwellings of Ireland: or ancient lacustrine habitations of Erin, commonly called crannogs*. Dublin.

Woods, A. 2015 Prelude to the Hiberno-Norse coinage: the Castle Street and Werburgh Street Hoards. In H.B. Clarke and R. Johnson (eds), *The Vikings in Ireland and beyond: before and after the battle of Clontarf*, 355–72. Dublin.

Wren J. 2002 Roof tiles. In M. McMahon, Early medieval settlement and burial outside the enclosed town: evidence from archaeological excavations at Bride Street, Dublin. *Proceedings of the Royal Irish Academy* **102**C, 97–8.

Wren J. 2006 Medieval and post-medieval roof tiles. In C. McCutcheon, *Medieval Pottery from Wood Quay, Dublin*, 177–95. Medieval Dublin Excavations 1962-81, Series B, vol. 7.

Wren, J. 2010 Roof tiles. In A. Lynch, *Tintern Abbey, Co. Wexford: Cistercians and Colcloughs. Excavations 1982–2007*, 138–44. Dublin.

Wren J. forthcoming a Clay building materials. In S. Phelan, Excavations at Hammond Lane, Dublin.

Wren J. forthcoming b Clay building materials. In J. Ó Neill, Excavations at Longford Street Little, Dublin.

York, R. and York, G. 2011 *Slings and slingstones: the forgotten weapons of Oceania and the Americas*. Kent, Ohio.

Young, T. 2009 Ferrous archaeometallurgical residues from Woodstown 6. (GeoArch Report 2009-22.) Unpublished specialist report, GeoArch Ltd.

Young, T. 2014 Discussion of metalworking evidence. In I. Russell and M.F. Hurley (eds), *Woodstown: a Viking-age settlement in Co. Waterford*, 103–13. Dublin.

Youngken, H.W. 1947 Ergot: a blessing and a scourge. *Economic Botany* **1** (4), 372–80.

Zeipiņa, S., Alsiņa, I., Lepse, L. and Dūma, M. 2015 Antioxidant activity in nettle (*Urtica dioica* L.) and garden orache (*Atriplex hortensis* L.) leaves during vegetation period. *Chemical Technology* **66** (1), 29–33.

Zori, D. 2007 Nails, rivets, and clench bolts: a case for typological clarity. *Archaeologislandica* **6**, 32–47.